# Monetary economics and financial markets

The Irwin Series in Economics
*Consulting Editor* Lloyd G. Reynolds *Yale University*

# PAUL A. MEYER
Department of Economics
University of Maryland

# Monetary Economics
# and
# Financial Markets

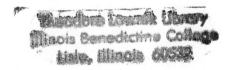
1982  **RICHARD D. IRWIN, INC.**
Homewood, Illinois 60430

ISBN 0-256-02615-7

Library of Congress Catalog Card No. 81–84892

*Printed in the United States of America*

1 2 3 4 5 6 7 8 9 0 MP 9 8 7 6 5 4 3 2

*For Chip and Carl*

# Preface

The title of this book, *Monetary Economics and Financial Markets,* suggests its economic emphasis and broad perspective to the junior-senior level course traditionally called money and banking. "Monetary economics" places the book squarely in the economics area. The economic approach is perfectly consistent with the presentation of substantial historical and institutional material, which is thoroughly integrated into a theoretical structure. It is not enough to know facts; they must be understood. Particularly in view of the Depository Institutions Deregulation and Monetary Control Act of 1980, which has made financial institutions more homogeneous, we must broaden our horizon from the narrow "banking" to "financial markets." Depository institutions other than banks now produce money (transactions) balances.

In order to analyze the effects of money and finance on goal variables such as output, prices, and economic growth, we discuss the short-run Keynesian model, the long-run neoclassical model, and labor market-aggregate supply models. While the book does mention the numerous differences which divide modern economists, it stresses the *complementarity* of Keynesian, neoclassical, and labor market models as a means of understanding economic adjustments over time. In other words, the three static models are viewed as jointly approximating a complex dynamic theory of economic fluctuations which is beyond the scope of a textbook. The response of interest rates to monetary expansion is only one of many examples where not simply the magnitude, but also the direction, of a policy's effects depend on the time period of the analysis. A higher rate of monetary expansion initially lowers but ultimately raises the rate of interest.

Although some may applaud the emphasis on the complementarity of monetarism and Keynesianism, I suspect they still want to know my position when the two theories are competitive. The book adopts an eclectic stand. It generally takes a moderate monetarist position, insofar as it states unequivocally that (1) the Federal Reserve can control the quantity of money and (2) money does affect aggregate demand, which in turn affects output in the short run and prices in the long run. At the same time, however, I recognize that situations may arise where the Fed can but should not control money and that other factors besides money matter. Our approach should annoy only extreme Keynesians who believe that money has little, if any, effect on output and prices.

My ultimate interest in monetary policy has forced me to write a book which, I believe, is completely up-to-date, at least in mid–1981. The book fully describes the new (1980) money measures, the new reserve requirements and other important features of the Monetary Control Act (1980), and the new (October 1979) open-market operating procedures. I have even anticipated the adoption of some proposed institutional changes, for example, the imposition of service charges by the Fed. Of course, policy specialists need to know much more than the latest rules and regulations. Policy is conducted to achieve some goal. In order to evaluate monetary policy, we need theories of the interrelationship among money, other financial variables, real variables, and prices. I believe my evaluation also is completely up-to-date, as it utilizes the most recent theories. The book goes beyond others in presenting a rigorous analysis of aggregate supply and discussing the topical supply side economics. The inclusion of aggregate supply along with aggregate demand reflects the modern approach to monetary/macroeconomics and contrasts sharply with the almost complete emphasis on aggregate demand in 1960s-oriented texts. The very important inflation-unemployment issue is discussed in depth. The book presents the neo-Keynesian Phillips curve, the monetarist natural rate hypothesis, and the rational expectations approach.

The book is designed to accommodate a wide range of students and teaching styles. I assume the student has taken but not thoroughly mastered (or has by now forgotten) the principles course. Given this assumption and the inconvenience of having to thumb through a principles text, most topics are developed pretty much from scratch. For example, Chapters 14 and 17 on national income accounting and the basic Keynesian C + I + G = y model, respectively, clearly are review chapters. While we may begin at a low level, we systematically reach material which will challenge the more advanced students. More than one third of the chapters have an appendix.

Adopters of the book should first assign Chapters 1 through 3, and I suspect virtually everyone will want to proceed to Chapter 4. Chapter 1 begins by discussing the goals of monetary policy, the scientific method, and the reasons for economic disagreements, and it concludes with a chapter-by-chapter summary of the book. Contrary to some monetary texts, which define money and analyze its determinants only after a 250-page or so excursion into a variety of financial topics, Chapter 2 immediately considers exchange systems and the rationale for the various money measures. Those aspects of banking essential for a preliminary analysis of the money supply are presented in Chapter 3. Chapter 4 takes a closer look at the determinants of the money supply, in particular its multiplier. After completing Chapter 4, instructors can readily adapt the order of the text or delete some chapters to best suit their approaches and students' abilities. From the viewpoint of a logical development of the money supply, Chapter 10 clearly follows Chapter 4. However, I have found that after Chapter 4 most students are anxious for a break from money-supply analysis and balance sheets. Chapters 13, 22, and, to a lesser extent, 16 should only be assigned to one's best, most highly motivated classes. Theoretically oriented courses should first skip Chapters 6–8 and return only if time permits. In addition, such courses will cover the IS–LM Chapters 19 and 20 and should altogether omit portions of Chapter 18. Institutional courses should omit Chapter 19 and 20, as well as the previously mentioned Chapters 16 and 22.

## TO THE STUDENT

Some chapters (such as Chapters 6 and 14) may be read while sunning oneself, but most should definitely not be read in that manner. If I may toot my own horn, the difficult chapters arise from my persistent refusal to select topics which underestimate college students' intelligence and not because the topics are underdeveloped or analyzed haphazardly. The complexity of some arguments necessitates careful reading and active learning. What was mumbo jumbo in a cursory reading becomes "perfectly clear," as a former president used to say, when read carefully with pen and paper on hand. Active learning is much more than underlining 25 or 75 percent of the book. Underlining does help pinpoint the topics which should be reviewed, although it contributes little toward understanding arguments in the first place. Active learning requires writing a few key phrases, linking the phrases graphically in a manner best suited to convey the logic of the particular argument, drawing diagrams, and so on. After you have read a section or two, close the book, outline what you just read, and repeat the main arguments in *your* own words. To help you in the learning process, every chapter ends with a set of questions which basically asks *you* to summarize the fundamental issues developed. The questions rarely extend the material in the chapter. The "Summary" section preceding the questions is not comprehensive but often contains food for further thought.

I strongly believe that analytical rigor does not necessarily require mathematical sophistication. There is no mathematical prerequisite beyond high school algebra, and even that is used sparingly. We use equations to *supplement* verbal and graphical analysis; equations never are an indispensable part of the exposition. Equations should rarely be memorized. A question such as, "What are the four factors which influence the income/money multiplier?" should never, never be answered with b, e, j, and k'. What do these symbols represent? Like it or not, however, economics is making increasing use of mathematics and statistics, so much so that the reader who persistently skips the mathematical appendixes may not acquire the flavor of modern economics.

## ACKNOWLEDGMENTS

I am deeply indebted to a large number of people for their comments and suggestions, which range from the thought-provoking one liner to a detailed review of the entire manuscript and from the sometimes critical review to the often laudatory evaluation. I especially want to thank my colleague Robert Bennett, who promptly read each chapter as it rolled off the typewriter and offered many valuable suggestions and encouragement. I also wish to express my gratitude to James Barth (George Washington University), Phillip Caruso (Western Michigan University), Daniel Fairchild (College of St. Thomas), Milton Friedman (The Hoover Institution, Stanford), Richard Friedman (California State University, Northridge), William Harrison (Virginia Commonwealth University), Lionel Kalish (California State University, Fullerton), Richard Lang (Federal Reserve Bank of Philadelphia), Morgan Lynge, Jr. (University of Illinois, Champaign-Urbana), John Marcis (Kansas State University), Robert Premus (Joint Economic Committee), Dennis Starleaf (Iowa State University), and Paul Wonnacott (University of Maryland). To Louise Jones, Matt McCroddan, and my other students at Maryland who have contributed to this book by their comments, I offer my thanks.

Finally, and most important, I unabashedly acknowledge my joy in Chip, Carl, and my part-time typist and editor and full-time wife, Brigitte, whose constant encouragement made this book a reality.

*Paul A. Meyer*

# Contents

## PART 3  CENTRAL BANKING

# Introduction

The contents of this book reflect the answer to a fundamental question: Why study monetary economics and financial markets? There are many other specialties in economics and many disciplines besides economics. Why has monetary economics long been the most popular upper-level economics course? These questions have a double-barreled answer.

a. Money, banks, and, particularly since the passage of the Depository Institutions Deregulation and Monetary Control Act (MCA) of 1980, other financial variables and institutions significantly influence the achievement of economic goals.

b. Money, banks, and, particularly since the passage of MCA, other financial variables and institutions can be controlled by the monetary authorities.

Both parts must be shown to be true to justify an entire book on money and finance. Indeed, nothing deserves prolonged discussion unless it "matters" and can be controlled. Why do we not have books on the economics of straight and safety pins? The topic is not sufficiently important. Years ago the sun spot theory of the business cycle was thought to be correct. The theory alleged that sun spots strongly influence the weather, which in turn strongly influences output. While the importance of the weather as a determinant of booms and busts surely has declined with the transformation from agrarian to industrial economies, in its heyday the sun spot theory was trumpeted in reverential tones but quickly dismissed. Why? Although sun spots were important, no one could control them. The first part of this book largely concerns monetary control, and the second part demonstrates the important effect of money on achieving major economic goals.

Our claim that money matters is not all encompassing in at least two respects. First, money matters, but so do other things. The importance of money does not imply the uselessness of everything else. True: money matters. False: only money matters. Second, money matters but only in certain areas. The importance of money in achieving certain highly desirable goals does not imply money can cure all our ills. While it is wrong to believe that money is the root of all evil, still money cannot eliminate pollution, discrimination, and other evils. True: money matters. False: only money matters.

## GOALS OF MONETARY POLICY

We primarily shall analyze the effect of money and finance on three major economic goals. First and foremost, society wants the output of newly produced goods and services to equal productive capacity. In other words, *actual GNP should equal potential GNP.* Goods and services are not produced out of thin air. Labor, capital, and land must be acquired by that mysterious person, the entrepreneur, who transforms the factors of production into goods and services. Labor is by far the most important factor of production as measured by its share of total income. Thus, the high GNP goal more or less has a mirror image—high employment or, equivalently, low unemployment. The goal of high GNP and low unemployment is so obvious that it needs no justification.

*The second goal is stable prices or at least a constant and predictable rate of inflation.* It is axiomatic that any unpredicted event will lead to a misallocation of resources. For example, Chrysler and other automakers misallocated resources after OPEC dramatically increased oil prices and reduced the desirability of large cars. Furthermore, if the exact path of a tornado were certain, tornadoes would cause virtually no damage. No one knowingly builds in the path of a tornado. Unable to predict tornadoes, we observe after the event that construction occurred at the wrong sites and resources were misallocated. From the viewpoint of resource allocation, unexpected inflation is more devastating than tornadoes. Unexpected inflation also redistributes income because the degree of unexpectedness varies. An event may be predictable to person A, mildly surprising to B, and totally unexpected to C. Those creditors who did not forecast double-digit inflation and lent at a "high" 6 percent rate of interest effectively subsidized debtors. Those who confidently expected double-digit inflation may have purchased durable goods instead of lending at a "low" 6 percent rate of interest. Even if inflation suddenly is forecast correctly by everyone, variations in an economic unit's reaction time misallocate resources and redistribute income. For example, retired people and those bound by long-term contracts must resign themselves to impoverishment while the wages of young, uncommitted workers are escalated for inflation.

The growth of actual output can mechanically be attributed to the closure of any gap between current and potential output and to the change of potential output over time. The failure by many journalists and politicians to distinguish between the two sources of growth often causes full employment and growth to be confounded. A high growth rate often is synonymous with getting to full employment, which we already acknowledged is a goal. We make a sharp distinction between the two sources of growth. *The third goal is a high rate of growth of output achieved through the efficient expansion of productive capacity.* A key word in the last sentence is *efficient.* Generally, efficient expansion occurs when saving increases and investors earn a high rate of return. Higher saving and lower consumption free resources for firms' investment. The resources should flow to those particular investors who earn the highest rate of return. Note that higher saving does not use *more* resources. Gone are the days when any rapid growth rate, however achieved, is justified. We do not need more commodities if their production denudes the earth. Conservation and pollution control regulations, which are relatively recent phenomena, attest to our increasing concern for the environment and our willingness to sacrifice quantity for quality. Perhaps we went overboard in the late 1970s and underestimated the cost and overestimated the benefit of conservation and pollution control, or so the early Reagan administration said.

There are other goals which are strongly influenced by money and the financial system. For example, balance of payments equilibrium in a fixed exchange rate system or exchange rate stability in a floating rate system is traditionally listed as another goal of policy. Low interest rates are an independent goal of many citizens and the Treasury. Indeed, for 10 years the Federal Reserve succumbed to the Treasury and pegged interest rates at extremely low levels, thereby largely sacrificing price stability. While we will not ignore these other goals altogether, we emphasize the relationship between money, output, prices, and growth.

As indicated earlier, the first part of this book analyzes the Federal Reserve's tools and monetary control. Of course, such an analysis requires knowledge of the behavior and structure of financial institutions and markets. We must have at least a rough idea how banks operate before evaluating Federal Reserve control. Knowledge of financial institutions serves a second purpose. *The financial system facilitates the efficient use of resources and "good" economic growth.* For example, the economies of large-scale production are realized because investment bankers sell common stocks to thousands of people nationwide. The genius of Thomas Edison and Alexander Graham Bell would have been wasted had they had to rely exclusively on their own resources to build electric and telephone companies. Channeling of funds and resources from savers to investors occurs in financial markets and institutions, of which commercial banks are the largest. The financial system enables savers, who would have earned low rates of return if forced to invest and manage businesses, to transfer resources to investors who can earn high returns by producing goods society values highly. Encouraged by the higher return they can earn by lending, savers save more. The financial system enhances both the amount of saving and investment and the return earned. While the effects of the financial system on the efficient allocation of resources and "good" growth will be analyzed explicitly quite briefly, the relatively long description of banks and other financial institutions is implicit recognition of the importance of the growth goal.

Incorporating the growth goal with monetary control issues in the first part of the book frees the second part to concentrate on the money, output, and prices nexus. The effects of money on one goal, assuming the other goal remains constant, are analyzed first. This simplifying assumption is dropped toward the end where we simultaneously determine output and prices. The high output (low unemployment) goal will receive greater attention. While the desirability of price stability should not be played down, this goal gets second billing because the precise effects of inflation on the allocation of resources and distribution of income are not constant over time but depend on tax laws, the source of the inflation, and other factors. For example, indexing social security payments certainly has reduced, but not eliminated, the hardship of inflation on the elderly. Oil producers were hurt by the inflation of the late 1960s but benefited handsomely from the late 1970s inflation, for which they were partially to blame. In short, the effects of inflation are not easily generalized.

## REASONS FOR DISAGREEMENT ABOUT THE MONEY-OUTPUT RELATIONSHIP

Why will it take so long—the major portion of the latter half of the book—to discuss the relationship between money and output? Isn't it intuitively clear that everyone responds to additional money balances by spending more, and higher demand increases output or prices? What is intuitively clear to some is extremely doubtful to others. At one time many economists seriously thought that money had no effect on spending and output. These so-called extreme Keynesians or fiscalists are a dying breed, which is fortunate because they are incorrect. If their error appears self-evident, however, perhaps one is confused about the economist's definition of money. To the layperson, *money* often is a synonym for income and earnings. Thus, the statement "They make a lot of money" means, "They have high incomes." Spending and output indeed do depend on income. However, to an economist money is those green dollar bills in your wallet and selected other items. It is less evident that, other things being equal, money so defined affects spending and output. Will someone with more money and less common stock, so that wealth remains equal, necessarily spend more? There is no mechanical link between green paper bills and the production of shoes, stereos, and other items. Money does have an indirect effect on spending and output which, however, is not known with certainty. An important difference between this book and some other books, particularly principles books, is our greater willingness to expose this uncertainty and the lack of agreement among economists. The reader looking for *the* answer must look elsewhere. Our willingness to hang economists' dirty laundry in public is one reason for the length of our money-income discussion.

Why do economists disagree about the relationship between money and output? Economics is said to have been born in 1776 with the publication of Adam Smith's *The Wealth of Nations*. One would think that a discipline which celebrated its bicentennial would have a final and conclusive answer to such a fundamental issue as the relationship between money and output. That is not the case, however. We do have many theories about money.

Before going further, what are theories? Theories are explanations of past phenomena and predictions of the future derived by inference from a set of assumptions. Theories postulate cause and effect; given this, then that. How does one evaluate a theory? What distinguishes good theory from bad theory? Many criteria have been proposed, and competing theories, that is, different explanations of the same phenomena, should be evaluated by multiple criteria. Nevertheless, one criterion is paramount from the very definition of theories. *Theories are explanations of the past and predictions of the future, and the value of a theory depends on its accuracy.* At the risk of some simplicity, all theories that yield inaccurate explanations are poor theories regardless of their other features. *Due to a lack of output data, the first 160 years of economics was unable to judge competing theories of the relationship between money and output.* It was only in the 1930s that Simon Kuznets constructed GNP estimates, a pathfinding endeavor which subsequently earned him a Nobel prize. While for many purposes Adam Smith should retain his title to paternity of economics, empirical economics in general and the evaluation of money-income theories in particular might better be dated from the 1930s work of the relatively obscure Simon Kuznets. Empirical economics is a modern science which has had less than 50 years to evaluate complex issues.

Early empirical work was extremely crude by modern standards. Economists themselves were dissatisfied with their work. *The money-income relationship is complex, and economists realized they lacked the statistical techniques and computational tools necessary to analyze large masses of data.* For all intents and purposes, *the* computational tool—the Almighty Computer—was not born until approximately 1960. While the anthropomorphism of the computer has reached disgusting proportions, current computers, like adults, completely overpower their young. A large 1960 computer was little more powerful than a sophisticated modern electronic hand calculator! Bred in an environment where theories could not be evaluated until the 1930s, and then only simplistically until 1960, positions hardened and biases developed. No one could be proven wrong, and everyone had an equal chance of being right.

Economists now have the data and computational tools. As a result, disagreement has narrowed considerably. Many extreme positions have been proved conclusively wrong. Nevertheless, definitive answers to difficult questions are not learned in a brief 20-year span. Some mathematical and scientific puzzles remain unsolved more than a century, and *unlocking economic secrets is more difficult because (1) economists unlike natural scientists cannot perform controlled experiments and (2) expectation effects are pervasive in economics.*

Chemists and other natural scientists can perform controlled experiments quite readily. In one experiment a chemist may raise temperature 25° or add 2 grams of sulfur while holding everything else constant. In this manner the effect of heat or sulfur is learned quite precisely. The monetary authority cannot hold everything else constant while changing the quantity of money. While the money supply is changing, OPEC is raising oil prices, a drought is reducing farm output by 5 percent, defense expenditures are increasing, and so on. Suppose output also changes during the period. Did money or the defense expenditures or something else cause the output variation? Economists attempt to answer such questions with statistics. However, statistical tests capable of discriminating among competing theories are difficult to construct. For example, suppose the theory says variable y depends positively on variable x. To test the theory, data for y and x are collected and plotted in Figure 1–1. Variable x and y indeed are related. Whenever x changes, y changes, so all the (x,y) points are on a straight line. Does this prove the hypothesis that y depends positively on x? No. The reverse causation, that is, x depends on y, would

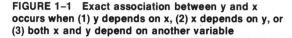

FIGURE 1–1  Exact association between y and x occurs when (1) y depends on x, (2) x depends on y, or (3) both x and y depend on another variable

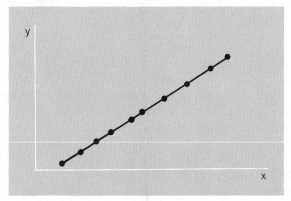

generate the same observations. Moreover, x and y may not be causally related at all. Both x and y may be responding to a third factor which cannot be controlled.[1]

The existence of expectation effects is the second reason for the delay in unearthing the money-income relationship now that the data and computational tools are available. An example best illustrates what expectation effects are and their importance.

Current and future earnings and dividend payments are the most important determinants of common stock prices. Yet one often observes a stock going down following the announcement of a large, say, 30 percent, earnings gain, while the price of another stock jumps upwards following announcement that its earnings were flat. Can such action be reconciled with the belief that stock prices are positively related to current and future earnings? Yes, if one recognizes expectations. At any one time future earnings are uncertain and must be forecast. Stock prices reflect these forecasts of expected future earnings. In our example, individuals may have been anticipating an earning gain even larger than 30 percent. The current earnings announcement caused a downward revision of future earnings, and the stock's price fell. The firm which announced constant earnings pleasantly surprised those who were expecting an earnings decline, and the stock was bid up. The current *level* of stock prices depends on current expectations, and stock price *changes* depend on the prediction error and the revision of expectations instead of past and current earnings changes.

Economic conditions similarly may reflect expectations about money instead of lagged and current realized values of money. For example, suppose firms expect the Federal Reserve (Fed) to adopt a tight money policy and in anticipation curtail output. Suppose further that firms forecast incorrectly; the Fed adopted an easy policy. One then observes a recession and easy money although tight money, which had been expected, causes recessions. Forecasts will not be systematically wrong in the same direction. Sometimes expected monetary policy will be even more expansionary than realized. The importance of money will appear exaggerated in this case. Firms greatly increase production in anticipation of the very expansionary monetary policy but realized policy is only modestly expansionary. Expectations may be unbiased; forecasts may be correct on average, sometimes overestimating and other times underestimating.[2] In this case systematic relationships can be detected, but the existence of forecast errors makes it difficult. Fortunately for chemists,

---

[1] The social scientist's statistical tests and the natural scientist's controlled experiments differ in degree rather than totality. The natural scientist controls only what is known to influence the experiment. Not controlling a significant but unknown variable could produce misleading conclusions.

[2] Unbiased expectations are also called rational expectations.

molecules do not form expectations about electric charges and jump on the basis of the discrepancy between the expected and actual charge.[3]

*Finally, and perhaps most important, economists disagree about the effects of monetary policy because different time periods are emphasized.* Theorizing draws logical inferences from a set of assumptions in order to explain phenomena. One of the most important assumptions rarely made explicit by most economists until quite recently is the time period of the analysis. A major feature of this book is the emphasis on the unfolding and variability of economic relationships over time. This is in sharp contrast to the macroeconomic section of the typical principles book and many advanced books which hardly mention the time period of the analysis. In your microeconomic principles class you discussed the demand for and supply of coffee, tea, sugar, and so on. In your macroeconomic principles class you ignored the multiplicity of commodities and assumed a single commodity, perhaps called a gizmo, schmoo, or widget. Gizmos are a universally desirable product. Consumers purchase them to satisfy hunger pangs, entrepreneurs purchase them to produce more little gizmos, and government purchases them to deter foreign aggressors. You were warned that aggression introduced some errors, but the cost of the aggregation errors were alleged to be small compared to the cost of working with an unwieldy, highly detailed model. If you took a typical macroeconomic principles course, you probably were not warned that time would also be aggregate. What happens to the short-and long-run demand and supply curves of microeconomics when one gets to macroeconomics? Typically, they just vanish along with the multiplicity of commodities. Time periods are aggregated into one.

Aggregation over time or commodities is justified only when aggregation leads to small errors. Suppose the effect over time of some government policy on GNP is shown by the solid line in Figure 1–2. Time, measured on the horizontal axis, begins when the policy is initiated. Looking at Figure 1–2, the policy in this example has an unambiguously positive effect on GNP. Moreover, the magnitude of the GNP increase is not very sensitive to one's time horizon. In this case we can dispense with the complexity of short runs and long runs and consider the GNP effect of the policy at any arbitrary time. Now assume the dashed line portrays the effect of government policy on GNP. Is the policy contractionary or expansionary? Clearly, the answer depends on the time period considered. The policy is contractionary in the short run but expansionary in the long run. Concentration on a single time period is unwarranted in this example. The book's emphasis on the adjustments of the economic system over time is justified by a sufficiently large number of cases where even qualitative effects depend on the time period.

---

[3] Heisenberg's uncertainty principle and Bohr's complementarity principle of quantum mechanics do suggest, however, a fundamental randomness in microscopic systems.

FIGURE 1-2   Effect over time of some government
policy on GNP

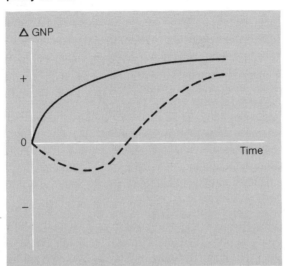

Consider a concrete problem close to home. Should you remain in college or immediately enter the labor market? Assume for simplicity that "culture" and other intangibles acquired at college are unimportant. The sole objective in going to college is to learn skills valued in the market and, thereby, increase one's lifetime earnings. Do the additional earnings of graduates justify the investment in a college education? What is the rate of return on a college education? Answers to these questions depend on the time horizon. Although data on earnings due to a college education are not completely reliable, there is general agreement on the overall shape of the rate of return curve graphed in Figure 1-3. The policy tool in this example is a college education, and time begins at graduation and entrance into the labor market. A college education is a poor investment for those who spend only a few years in the labor market. It takes about 15 years to recover all costs, the out-of-pocket cost for tuition and other items and the opportunity cost of earnings foregone while in college. The rate of return on a college education becomes positive beyond 15 years and exceeds the average rate of return on other investments when one remains in the labor market at least 30 years. The remain-in-college or enter-the-labor-market question is only one of many economic issues dependent on the time horizon.

## TOWARD A CONSENSUS

Economics is not in a state of total disarray. While fundamental disagreements still exist, a consensus is developing. The price and quantity

FIGURE 1–3   Relationship between the rate of return on
a college education and years in the labor force

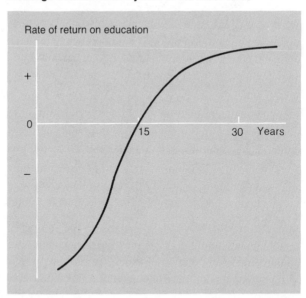

of a single commodity and of commodities in general depend on supply
and demand. There is wide agreement that the *quantity* of money does not
affect supply. In terms of Figure 1–4, a consensus exists that monetary
expansion does not shift whichever of the two supply curves may be
relevant. To be sure, the *existence* of money, banks, and other financial
instruments and institutions certainly does affect supply and its growth
over time. Without banks the vertical supply curve would be far inward.
Nearly everyone now recognizes that money does influence the demand
for commodities. Economists are often labeled by their estimate of the
strength and reliability of the effect of money on aggregate demand.
*Keynesians* and *monetarists* form the two main schools of economists.
Monetarists interpret the data as indicating that money has an important
and predictable effect on aggregate demand. Keynesians generally come
to the opposite conclusion. In terms of Figure 1–4, monetarists believe
that the demand curve shifts out far in response to monetary expansion
*and* that the extent of the shift always is more or less the same.

While we shall see that there are other important differences between
Keynesians and monetarists, the difference stated in the last paragraph
may also be expressed in terms of velocity, which is the ratio of nominal
output to money. (Nominal output is the dollar value of output, that is, the
product of price and quantity or real output.) Monetarists claim that velocity does not decline significantly as a consequence of monetary expan-

FIGURE 1-4   **Aggregate demand and supply**

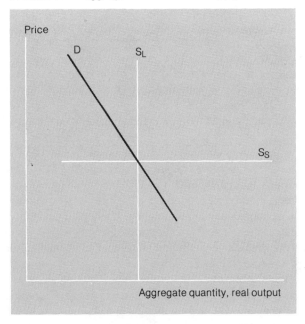

sion, so that money continues to have a large impact on nominal output. Monetarists also claim that any change in velocity for whatever reason is predictable, which from the definition of velocity means that the nominal output/money ratio is predictable.

The effect on real output and prices of aggregate demand variations produced by monetary policy or other sources depends on the shape of the aggregate supply curve. Look at Figure 1–4 again. If the aggregate supply curve is flat, aggregate demand variations are transmitted fully to quantity with price remaining constant. The opposite extreme is a vertical supply curve, where only prices respond to demand. A consensus now exists that the steepness of the aggregate supply curve is positively related to the length of the time interval. The aggregate supply is perfectly flat, or virtually so, in the short run and becomes vertical in the long run. A systematic relationship between money and nominal output is consistent with a variable relationship over time between money and real output and between money and prices. In the short run money affects real output, but in the long run it affects price.

## PREVIEW OF THE BOOK

At this point readers should want to know in some detail what is coming up. Later they will want to reflect on where they have gone. The following chapter-by-chapter summary satisfies both needs. Readers should review the preview frequently.

Chapters 2 through 13 are basically concerned with the measurement of money and rates of interest; the role of the private sector on the money supply; the behavior of financial markets and institutions, with emphasis on their effects on the allocation of resources and economic growth; the tools of monetary control; and the monetary policy operating strategy of the Federal Reserve System.

Everyone right now has a rough idea what money is. Rough ideas are sufficient for most people but not for those with any serious aspirations at being monetary experts. Chapter 2 spells out the four new (as of 1980) money measures, M–1A, M–1B, M–2, and M–3. The new money measures are compared with the pre-1980 measures, and the reasons for redefining money are explained. The functional and empirical approaches to defining money are examined. Basically, the functional approach says that money is the particular collection of assets which yield a specified service. The empirical approach lets statistical relationships determine the appropriate money measure. The chapter ends with an evaluation of the different types of money.

Having learned in Chapter 2 what money is, we begin an analysis of the money supply process in Chapter 3. Balance sheets, check collection, and the rudiments of the policy tools,—for example, open-market operations—are reviewed. A nontechnical, commonsense view of the money supply introduces its numerous determinants and shows the direction of their effect.

Chapter 4 is for the budding monetary specialist in that it digs one level deeper in the money supply process. For example, Chapter 3 says that the money supply depends on banks' desired excess reserves. Chapter 4 states precisely how money depends on excess reserves, and it states the factors which determine the excess reserves banks want.

Because Chapters 2 through 4 focus on money, they look solely at the liability side of depository institutions. Chapters 5 through 8 offer a complete overview of the financial system. Chapter 5 describes the gains from the existence of financial markets. The major characteristics of financial claims are explored, with special emphasis on interest rates. There are many interest rates which reflect peculiar computational techniques and other debt characteristics, such as the term to maturity. The important distinction between real and nominal interest rates concludes the chapter.

Chapter 6 links the major characteristics of financial claims discussed in Chapter 5 with specific financial instruments and their issuers. For example, the chapter states the similarities and differences among certificates of deposit, bankers acceptances, commercial paper, and Eurodollars. Contrary to the views of Keynes and many other economists, we think the stock market is important and, consequently, analyze its performance.

Chapter 7 explains the rationale for the existence of financial inter-mediaries, including commercial banks. Trends in the major items on both sides of banks' balance sheets and trends in bank profitability are pre-sented. Special problems of bank management are also explored. The behavior of other depository institutions, such as savings and loans, and nondepository institutions, such as life insurance companies, are analyzed in less detail since they are smaller than commercial banks. The chapter ends with a thorough analysis of disintermediation and the recent financial deregulation designed precisely to reduce disintermediation, that is, de-posit losses when market interest rates rise.

Chapter 8 looks at the regulation, structure, and performance of the banking industry. The main objective of regulation is a safe banking sys-tem. In spite of a general lack of regulatory concern for competition, the banking system is quite competitive, although not perfectly so. Empirical evidence on the relationship between banking structure and monopoly loan rates to small borrowers is presented.

Chapters 9 through 13 look at central banking. Chapter 9 presents a concise history. A central theme is that major structural reform occurs in response to a crisis, which often is produced by prior reforms which have long outlived their usefulness. Unfortunate though such a situation may be, it makes the study of history all the more important. The chapter shows that prior to the creation of the Federal Reserve in 1913 the United States did not have the institutional structure to control money. If we progressed structurally, we regressed economically in certain areas. Economists are rediscovering what Benjamin Franklin knew: money is an important source of government revenue because the inflation it produces acts as a tax.

Chapter 10 states how currency and bank reserves and, therefore, the money supply can change without any action by the Fed. It indicates that the Federal Reserve must take an active role in order to control money.

Chapter 11 discusses in much greater detail than Chapter 3 the tools or instruments of monetary policy. For example, it describes the lagged reserve requirements, which are later shown to cause wide interest rate swings and reduce monetary control. The chapter demonstrates how the mere existence of unchanging reserve requirements aids monetary con-trol. Such a demonstration is imperative because reserve requirements rarely do change. The chapter ends on a somewhat downbeat measure when it states that until quite recently the Fed did not even attempt to control money in the short run.

Chapter 12 discusses the need for a short-run operating target, and compares the pros and cons of such alternative targets as free reserves, interest rates, and the money supply. There is now fairly wide agreement among Keynesians and monetarists that the money supply generally, but not always, is the best operating target.

If Chapter 11 ends on a downbeat tone, Chapter 13 is strictly upbeat. Yes, we show the Fed undoubtedly can control the money supply nowadays if it wants to. The possibility of monetary control today does not imply control was always possible. Indeed, we just stated control was impossible prior to the existence of the Federal Reserve. The chapter stresses the importance of organizational structure. The Federal Reserve may have been ill equipped to control money during the Great Depression and late 1930s.

A sharp break occurs between Chapters 13 and 14. From Chapter 14 onward the book is concerned with the relationship between money, prices, and output. To simplify the analysis, the diversity of the financial system is ignored. We generally assume that currency is the only form of money and that homogeneous long-term bond yields "the" interest rate. Since previous sections of this chapter already discussed the money, prices, and output nexus, those chapters from 14 on are summarized more briefly.

Chapter 14 offers precise descriptions of GNP, its components, and their growth over time.

Chapter 15 first discusses the scientific method and economic theory in general. It then examines the validity of the basic classical propositions that supply creates its own demand and that money has a predictable effect on prices in the long run. The determinants of supply are analyzed carefully since they distinguish a monetarist splinter group, the so-called supply siders, a group whose stock was greatly boosted by the election of President Ronald Reagan.

Chapter 16 is quite technical. It extends the analysis of the quantity theory of money begun in the previous chapter. Adjustment processes, that is, the changes that occur as the economy reaches equilibrium, are emphasized.

Chapter 17 is the first of four chapters on Keynesian economics, which in some respect competes with neoclassical economics but more often complements it. The basic Keynesian proposition is: demand creates its own supply. This complements rather than contradicts the basic neoclassical proposition because the Keynesian proposition concerns the short run while the neoclassical proposition concerns the long run. After stating other fundamental assumptions of Keynesian economics, we review the basic $C + I + G = y$ Keynesian model.

Review of the basic model facilitates understanding the advanced Keynesian model, which introduces the demand and supply of money and interest rate effects. Chapter 18 discusses Keynes's money demand and modern extensions by William Baumol (inventory theoretic approach) and James Tobin (portfolio approach). The effect of the interest rate sensitivity of investment and money demand on the government spending and money multipliers is explored without introducing the IS–LM machinery.

Chapter 19 derives the IS–LM curves, a compact way of representing the advanced Keynesian model. Although their compactness makes understanding the IS–LM curves somewhat difficult, they are absolutely indispensable for analyzing more complex issues. The tools must be up to the job. All the determinants of the government spending and money multipliers appear in Chapter 19. Relationships among the size of the multipliers, slopes of the curves, and the magnitude of shifts are analyzed.

Chapter 20 uses the IS–LM machinery. With it we can rigorously demonstrate such complex issues as the desirability of controlling money instead of interest rates when aggregate demand is more volatile than money demand.

Chapter 21 discusses various monetary policy issues. It states the rationale for the fundamental monetarist proposition that the Fed should increase the money supply at a constant rate and not attempt discretionary countercyclical policy. Perhaps most interesting is the demonstration that monetary and fiscal policy generally should be used simultaneously in order to maximize the likelihood of attaining the goals.

Several economists have constructed empirical models of the U.S. economy in order to estimate the impact of monetary and fiscal policy and other variables. The estimates and performance of several models are reviewed in Chapter 22. The upshot of the review is that empirical economics is still in its infancy. Every model contains an implausible element. As to the strength and reliability of monetary and fiscal policy, the jury is still out.

The inflation-unemployment tradeoff is alluded to numerous times and becomes the central issue of Chapter 23. We show that our theoretical analysis to that point implies a relationship between inflation and unemployment dependent on the time elapsed since a demand shock. This viewpoint is in sharp contrast to the Phillips curve, which claims there exists a permanent tradeoff between inflation and unemployment. The errors in the Phillips curve led Milton Friedman and Edmund Phelps to introduce inflationary expectations as the source of a shifting Phillips curve. The Friedman-Phelps explanation of the inflation-unemployment relationship is derived differently than ours but confirms our viewpoint: there is a short-run but no long-run tradeoff between inflation and unemployment. The rational expectations school, another monetarist splinter group, denies the existence of even a temporary tradeoff. Rational expectations stresses that, on average, the public correctly anticipates economic policy and adjusts its behavior to its expectations.

## QUESTIONS

1. What two conditions must any policy satisfy in order to merit detailed study?
2. State the main goals of monetary policy. Does society have any goals that monetary policy does not influence?

3. What were the two main reasons for the paucity of studies prior to 1960 on the relationship between income and money?

4. Why are economic theories generally more difficult to test than relationships in the biological and physical sciences?

5. Do aggregate demand shifts always have the same effect on price and quantity? Is at least the qualitative effect, that is, positive or negative effect, of a policy independent of the time period elapsed? If not, give *three* illustrations.

# PART 1

# The measurement and determinants of money

# Functions and definitions of money  2

If you ask someone what money is, a civil person will stare while thinking, "What a dunce!" and an obnoxious soul will bluntly voice it. Doesn't everyone know that the nickels, dimes, and dollar bills in your pocket are money? True enough, currency is pocket money, but there may be something else. Having taken principles of economics you are aware that all economists additionally consider demand deposits or checking accounts to be money. Agreement ends here, however. Although some economists draw the line at currency and demand deposits, many would add other checkable deposits such as negotiable order of withdrawal (NOW) accounts, and a few highly respected economists include as part of the money stock time and savings deposits at commercial banks and deposits (technically speaking, shares) at savings and loan associations.[1]

At bottom, the precise items which should be classified as money are arbitrary. Money is not unusual in this respect; the definition of all goods is fundamentally arbitrary. No fundamental truth says that a $5 Federal Reserve note is to be called money and not dinero or Xanadu, and no fundamental truth says that the word *money* is to be reserved exclusively for $5 Federal Reserve notes and some other specified assets. While other courses may simply point out the arbitrariness of defining money and quickly proceed to pick a favorite, a serious course in monetary economics cannot be so cavalier.

The next section examines different exchange systems since everyone agrees that money is an asset related to exchanges. We discuss some of

---

[1] The basic difference between a time and savings deposit is that the former, as the name suggests, has a fixed maturity, which may be automatically renewable, while savings deposits have an indefinite term. Savings deposits usually are evidenced by a small passbook.

the difficulties of trading and indicate how societies have reduced transactions costs. This provides a justification for the alternative specific definitions of money since one approach to defining money includes as money those assets which solve, or at least substantially reduce, a particular problem buyers and sellers face. This functional approach to defining money does not yield a unique definition because traders face many problems, and economists cannot agree which problem is the most important. We then present another approach to defining money, the empirical or statistical approach. While this approach again does not yield a single preferred money measure, effective communication does require our choosing a specific definition. The concluding section discusses the advantages of different types of money.

## THE IMPORTANCE OF THE EXISTENCE OF MONEY

Does money matter? This fundamental question of monetary economics normally is understood to refer to the possible effects of changes in the quantity of money on certain policy goals. The question is somewhat ambiguous, however. Someone unfamiliar with the economic debate might reasonably think the question centers on the importance of the existence of money. Regardless of the outcome of the debate on the effects of changes in the quantity of money, everyone agrees that the existence of money is a prerequisite for the attainment of a high standard of living. The usefulness of money is not limited to capitalist economies. Despite the hostility toward money displayed by Marx, Lenin, and other communist leaders, the attempt in the Soviet Union to abolish money and restore a "natural" economy was short-lived. Faced with a chaotic situation, the New Economic Policy adopted in 1921 retreated from many favored communist dogmas, including the abolition of money.

Before we show how money facilitates the exchange of commodities, first consider why exchanges are essential in all but the most primitive societies. Individuals soon discover a fundamental principle of economics: the division of labor and machines in the production process allows the output of the sum of workers and machines to be far greater than the sum of the outputs of these same workers and machines were they to work individually. Even the aborigines of Papua-New Guinea, who supposedly are living in the Stone Age, have recognized the advantages of a division of labor, the men hunting and fishing and the women farming and preparing food. The division of labor perhaps has reached its apex in an assembly line, where each worker performs a relatively simple and minor task in the process of producing a complex product. Undoubtedly, the output of the sum of General Motors workers is much greater than the output produced were each individual worker to build an entire car. Specialization, however, brings its problems as well as its advantages. How is the larger potential output from specialization to be distributed? Individuals do not derive satisfaction from the production of goods but from current and future consumption. Each individual may specialize as a producer but as a consumer still wants a variety of goods and services. Some system must be derived whereby each individual can enjoy the fruits of the specialization of others.

Even if specialization did not exist because no one enjoyed a comparative advantage in the production of any commodity, trading would occur because of a lack of synchronization between desired consumption and work patterns. Someone anticipating retirement may accumulate a bundle of durable goods for later use. For example, just prior to retirement you may produce a car and house, assuming you are efficient at producing both these goods. However, nondurables and services, by definition, cannot be stored for your retirement. If you want your hair neatly trimmed, you cannot get 120 haircuts now to last you 10 years. During the next decade, when you are not working, you trade something to get haircuts. While there are other reasons for an exchange and distribution system, these two reasons are paramount: (1) specialization in production but not consumption and (2) desired consumption and work patterns are unsynchronized. The particular system devised reflects the degree of specialization, technical change, foreign trade, and social cohesiveness. *As economic development progressed, societies successively adopted institutionalized exchange, barter, generalized indirect exchange, and a (common) medium of exchange.*

Social cohesiveness, often achieved by kinship and marriage and sometimes maintained by brute force, is sufficiently strong among many primitive groups that production and consumption of goods and services is determined by some universally accepted schedule. Indian villages of the 19th century, and to some extent up until quite recently, had a moderately extensive division of labor. Every needed person—farmer, laborer, servant, blacksmith, barber, Brahmin priest—could be found in the Indian village, and his role and duties were known to all. "Each carried out his duties, providing a portion of the goods and services used by the villagers, and receiving an assortment of goods and services from others. Each was assured his share because each carried out his duties and each had its understood, customary rights to a part of the whole."[2] Nowadays one finds a similar situation within families, "liberated" or not. The mother repairs the family car, the father cooks for the entire family, and the child polishes the family's shoes. There is no need for formal trades. They follow the motto of the Three Musketeers: all for one and one for all.

Other than the family, the number of tradition-bound groups has declined significantly over time. Technological advances reduced the cost of transportation and increased contact with strangers. As a result, institu-

---

[2] Walter C. Neale, *Monies in Societies* (San Francisco: Chandler and Sharp, 1976), p. 26.

tional exchange became less prevalent. Not having previously encountered a foreign trader, no customary exchange for your cache of furs has been established. Would you give the furs to the trader today and trust him with bringing you beads and whiskey next week? Customary exchanges were largely replaced by barter, a higgle-haggle exchange of services or goods *which the parties intend to consume directly.* Each party to a barter exchange believes that the use value of the commodity purchased is greater than the value of the commodity sold.

Barter has two major disadvantages. First, it requires a "double coincidence of wants," that is, someone has to have what you want and also want what you have. For example, suppose Farmer Brown has milk and wants a pair of shoes. To barter, Farmer Brown must find a thirsty shoemaker. The probability of achieving a double coincidence of wants depends on the extent of specialization and economic change. In a highly specialized economy with millions of products, the probability of a double coincidence of wants between two people chosen at random is extremely small. If you search long enough and contact enough people, you might discover a double coincidence of wants. Having done so once, identical transactions can subsequently be made quite easily but new transactions require another long search. While it is impossible to state precisely at what stage in the development process different exchange systems are introduced, as economies become technologically more sophisticated and economic change more frequent, direct barter of goods and services becomes increasingly inconvenient and wasteful of time and effort.

Having acquired some information about his trading partner's preferences while searching for a double coincidence of wants, the typical individual abandoned barter and adopted a system of indirect exchange. That is, undesired commodities are accepted in payment when it is believed that they can be traded for the optimal consumption bundle. Indirect exchange significantly reduces the time spent shopping, allowing more leisure time or greater production and consumption. One can even construct examples where the optimal consumption package cannot be attained under barter.

Table 2–1 shows Tom, Dick, and Harry's preference ordering of food, shoes, and whiskey. For example, Tom is a gourmand teetotaler, preferring food to shoes and abhorring whiskey. Each person owns the item

**TABLE 2–1**

|  | Individuals | | |
|---|---|---|---|
|  | **Tom** | **Dick** | **Harry** |
| Preference ordering ......... | Food | Whiskey | Shoes |
|  | Shoes | Food | Whiskey |
|  | Whiskey | Shoes | Food |

circled in Table 2–1. For example, Tom has shoes, his second choice. How can the commodities be redistributed so that each person has his first choice? The table illustrates a lack of a double coincidence of wants. Given the preference ordering, barter is impossible. Dick has the food that Tom wants but does not want Tom's shoes. Harry wants Tom's shoes but does not have food to trade. No two individuals would exchange commodities if each had to consume the good acquired. Each would consume what he considers a less desirable commodity. The arrows in Table 2–1 show a pattern of indirect exchange which enables all three individuals to consume their preferred goods. Although Dick prefers food to shoes, he accepts shoes from Tom in order to acquire whiskey from Harry.

To be sure, indirect exchange is not costless. Returning to an earlier example, Farmer Brown exchanges milk for food, whiskey, and other commodities and temporarily postpones consumption in order to acquire a diverse inventory of tradable commodities. This inventory is a temporary abode of purchasing power; it will be exchanged shortly for the shoes Farmer Brown actually intends to consume. Individuals typically prefer current to future consumption, and maintaining a bundle of commodities for general indirect exchange necessitates storage and other costs. Nevertheless, the reduced time spent shopping when one has a temporary abode of purchasing power far outweighs the cost of acquiring and maintaining it. The temporary abode of purchasing power also allows Farmer Brown to bridge the time gap between his desired consumption and work patterns. He lives comfortably through the winter and spring by selling the temporary abode of purchasing power he acquired in the summer and fall. A simple word for the temporary abode of purchasing power surely would be helpful; let's call it money.

In spite of widely different tastes within a society, the circle of people who accept a commodity for exchange purposes gradually—often over centuries—but inevitably widens. One is hard pressed to explain why a specific commodity becomes generally acceptable. Some generally accepted commodities have religious significance while others are purely ornamental. The important point is that everyone will maintain an inventory of the generally accepted commodity and virtually all exchanges are made with this commodity. We then have a medium of exchange or means of payment. Note well that trading with a medium (singular) of exchange is only a special case of the more general indirect exchange system with various media (plural). Sellers under either system obtain a commodity which they do not intend to consume but plan to trade for other commodities. Some call the medium of exchange money.

Two views of money—temporary abode of purchasing power and medium of exchange—stem from different perspectives on the benefits derived from exchange systems designed to lower the high costs of barter due to a lack of double coincidence of wants. Just as everyone agrees that barter is more costly in terms of time and effort than generalized indirect exchange with a temporary abode of purchasing power, so everyone agrees that a medium of exchange is more efficient than generalized exchange. The medium of exchange inventory one needs for transactions is smaller than a multicommodity inventory, and the likelihood of purchases and sales at a moment's notice obviously increases with one's holdings of the medium of exchange. Some believe that the reduction of transaction costs in going from generalized indirect exchange to a medium of exchange is small *relative* to the cost reduction achieved when people stop bartering and adopt indirect exchange. These individuals emphasize the temporary abode of purchasing power and play down the medium of exchange. Others believe that transaction costs are significantly reduced only when an economy has a medium of exchange, which is called money.

The second major shortcoming of barter is the lack of any common unit to measure and state the values of goods and services. By the value or worth of a good or service is meant its exchange ratio, the quantity of other commodities that it commands in the market. In a barter system where every commodity is exchanged directly for every other good, the value of each commodity would not be stated simply as one quantity but would be stated in as many quantities as there were other commodities. For example, if 1 million commodities existed, the value of *each* would be stated in terms of 999,999 others. One apple is worth two bananas, one half clove of garlic, one onion, and so on. Few individuals or firms could readily keep track of values expressed in so many different ways. Comparison shopping would require such skill and patience that many potentially desirable trading opportunities are ignored.

Since values quite naturally are expressed in terms of the commodities being exchanged, acceptance of a medium of exchange goes a long way toward solving the second main problem of barter, lack of a common unit to measure and state values. If gold were the circulating medium, the value of an apple is stated exclusively as so much gold, and not in terms of bananas, garlic, onions, and so forth. Agreement on the commodity which is to serve as the standard of value is not sufficient, however, if the attractiveness of possible exchanges is to be determined quickly. We cannot think of any commodity which naturally comes in a standard quantity and quality. As an example, many primitive tribes expressed values in terms of cattle. The going price for a bride, who typically could be purchased in primitive societies, might be 10 cows. A young man will soon find that he cannot pick any fair maiden because fathers disagree on what cows are. Are a sickly calf and a prized bull "cows"? The father of the fairest maiden will have much higher standards for cows.

Societies which attained even moderate economic development used a medium of exchange which, perhaps coincidentally at first, could be graded quite precisely. Copper, silver, and especially gold are good examples. Metals can be graded precisely but are not naturally found in uniform quantity and quality. Supposing gold were the circulating medium, how much gold does a certain sample contain? The need for a well-defined standard of value not subject to different interpretations fortunately was met. A monetary unit such as a dollar, peso, franc, or pengo was created by stipulating, usually in terms of gold, the content of the unit. To save the public the inconvenience of continually weighing and measuring the fineness of gold dust, the monarch or some highly respected person produced coins, which originally were nothing more than metal slugs with a good-housekeeping seal indirectly certifying metallic content. Rather than stating their metallic content explicitly, coins were denominated in monetary units. For example, prior to 1933 the United States defined the dollar as 23.22 grains of fine (pure) gold, and coins containing 232.20 grains of gold were clearly and simply marked $10. A monetary unit such as the dollar replaced a physical commodity as the standard of value. Merely defining a monetary unit would not have resulted in its use. Prices were quoted in dollars instead of gold only *after* some commodities such as coins were clearly identified as being worth a fixed number of dollars. Indeed, one can hardly conceive of a society expressing values in terms of dollars if nothing were always worth a dollar.[3] The same principles apply to standards of measurement. The metric standard popular throughout the world would not be used if a certain distance were not always a meter.

With the passage of time the relationship between the monetary unit and a specific physical commodity typically has become more tenuous. This certainly is true in the United States. Although for some purposes the United States government continues to define a dollar in terms of gold, the "official" gold value of the dollar is pure fiction.[4] Nevertheless, the United States has remained on the dollar standard. Why? Because items as diverse as metal slugs, small pieces of paper, and entries on ledger sheets or computer memory banks say that they are worth a fixed number of dollars. Some of the fixed dollar claims are means of payments while others, like savings and loan deposits, are not. Pass a law banning the existence of fixed dollar claims and Americans would abandon the dollar standard. Who would continue to express values in terms of dollar when nothing is always worth a dollar? The unit of account must be anchored by the existence of commodities worth a fixed number of units.

---

[3] The British guinea/pound system, which has received more attention than it deserves as it is practiced by only a few West End shops and auction houses, does not contradict the text. Some stores do continue to express prices in terms of guineas although no coin or bill has the word *guinea* printed on its face. However, pound notes circulate, and the guinea was fixed at 1.05 pounds since 1717. Were the guinea to be 1.05 pounds today, 1.23 pounds tomorrow, and 1.15 pounds the day after, the limited practice of quoting prices in guineas would have ended long ago.

[4] Chapter 10 contains a short history of gold policy.

## CURRENT DEFINITIONS OF MONEY

The Federal Reserve recognized there is no single definition of money correct for all time. In February 1980 it revised its definitions of money and since then regularly publishes four money supply measures, conveniently called M–1A, M–1B, M–2, and M–3.[5] More comprehensive definitions of money have higher numbers.

M–1A = C + DD + TC
> = The public's *currency* plus net *demand deposits* at commercial banks + *traveler's checks*

M–1B = C + DD + TC + OCD
> = M–1A + OCD
> = M–1A plus *other checkable deposits* at banks and nonbank depository institutions

M–2  = C + DD + TC + OCD + (ST & SD) + ORP + ED + MMMF
> = M–1B + (ST & SD) + ORP & ED + MMMF
> = M–1B plus *small* denomination *time and saving deposits* plus *overnight repurchase* agreements plus *"Eurodollars"* at Caribbean branches of U.S. banks plus *money market mutual funds*

M–3  = M–2 + (LT & SD) + TRP
> = M–2 plus *large time and saving deposits* plus *term repurchase* agreements

Nonbank depository institutions are savings and loan associations, mutual savings banks, and credit unions.

Before justifying the four definitions of money, a more complete description of the components of money, however defined, is appropriate. The narrow definitions of money, M–1A and M–1B, include currency, both coins and paper bills, and demand deposits. Who issues currency in the United States? The Treasury issues all coins and a small amount of paper bills; the overwhelming proportion of paper money is issued by the Federal Reserve. Demand deposits are the liabilities of commercial banks. A typical commercial bank has plenty of cash in the till and also maintains deposits at several banks. The Treasury has accounts at thousands of banks. The money measures do *not* include the substantial quantity of currency and demand deposits held by the Fed, Treasury, and commercial banks. A money issuer's holdings of currency and demand deposits are excluded because its holdings serve an entirely different purpose than the holdings of the general public. In this respect money is no

---

[5] In addition, the Fed publishes a liquidity measure called L. We shall ignore this measure because the Fed views it more as a proxy for credit outstanding instead of money. The Fed announced in July 1981 that it may stop calculating and publishing M–1A in 1982, in which case M–1B would become simply M–1.

different than bread: a baker's inventory of bread and the loaf in my pantry serve different purposes. Besides consolidating and excluding the currency and deposits of the government and commercial banks, the M–1 definitions also exclude the domestic demand deposits of foreign commercial and central banks because these deposits are also viewed as being held for "peculiar" reasons. For example, M–1B excludes any deposits of London's Barclay Bank or the Bank of England at Chase Manhattan's New York office. The "public" whose currency and demand deposits are being measured is every economic unit *except* the Treasury, Fed, domestic commercial banks, and foreign commercial and central banks. In addition, traveler's checks are a component of M–1A. To avoid double counting, checks deposited but not yet cleared are subtracted from total demand deposits to get net demand deposits.[6]

The other checkable deposits added to M–1A to get M–1B are NOW (negotiable orders of withdrawal) and ATS (automatic transfer from saving) accounts and credit union share draft balances. All three stem basically from profit maximizers' attempts to circumvent *Regulation Q, broadly defined as ceilings on savings deposit rate and the prohibition of interest payment on demand deposits.* That is, Regulation Q, which the MCA of 1980 scheduled to be phased out, sets maximum interest rates depository institutions can pay on their deposits. The maximum is zero on demand deposits. NOW accounts, the oldest type of other checkable deposit, were first offered by Massachusetts mutual savings banks in 1972. Mutual savings banks are almost exclusively located along the eastern seaboard from Massachusetts to Maryland. If you live in California and have never entered a mutual savings bank, you will not be too far wrong if you think of it as an eastern savings and loan. In 1972 the return which savings banks were earning on their mortgages and other assets was substantially greater than their deposit rate. Profit-maximizing firms would have raised their deposit rate, thereby attracting more funds to be lent at the high interest rate. However, the Regulation Q ceiling was effective. Mutual savings banks were already paying the maximum permissible deposit rate. Demand deposits then were the exclusive prerogative of commercial banks. Frustrated but undaunted, enterprising mutual savings banks began offering saving accounts against which the depositor could write a negotiable order of withdrawal, which everyone except theologians, congressmen, and Federal Reserve officials trained to make the finest distinction agrees are equivalent to checks. For all practical

---

[6] For example, when I deposit your $100 check, my demand deposit account is credited (increases), but it may take several days until your account is debited (decreases), particularly if our banks are a substantial distance apart. The amount of checks deposited but not cleared is equal to cash in the process of collection at commercial banks plus Federal Reserve Float. These terms will be discussed more fully in Chapters 3 and 4. For a more complete discussion of the items included in the money measures see Thomas Simpson, "The Redefined Monetary Aggregates." *Federal Reserve Bulletin,* February 1980, pp. 97–114.

purposes, NOW accounts are interest-paying demand deposits. This new account was profitable and gave Massachusetts mutual savings banks a competitive edge for a short time. Authority to offer NOW accounts was quickly extended to savings and loan associations and commercial banks in New England and New York. Banks and other depository institutions in all areas were able to offer NOW accounts beginning January 1, 1981. Banks in areas where NOW accounts were prohibited before 1981 offered ATS accounts, where one maintains a zero checking balance and funds are automatically transferred from a savings to a checking account to cover any checks written. The NOW-like accounts offered by credit unions are called share draft balances. NOW, ATS, and credit union share draft balances are strictly personal, nonbusiness accounts.

In financial circles, small means less than $100,000. That is, in M–2 the small denomination time and saving deposits at banks and nonbank depository institutions include all such deposits under $100,000. Overnight repurchase (RP) agreements and Eurodollars at Caribbean branches of U.S. banks essentially are one-day loans to banks. These accounts are testimony to firms' and banks' ingenuity in circumventing Regulation Q and the prohibition on firms having other checkable deposits.

Here is how RPs arise. A firm with temporarily excessive demand deposits could write a check and purchase government securities in the open market. If a firm did this, the gross earnings of the bank holding the firm's deposits would decline since deposits provide banks the wherewithal to make loans and earn interest. Firms found the direct purchase of government securities somewhat inconvenient and around 1975 conceived RPs. The bank debits (reduces) its customers' demand deposits and credits (increases) the RP account, so called because the bank pledges to buy back at a predetermined price government securities which serve as collateral. If the bank were unable to repurchase the securities, they would become the property of the firm. So far, banks have always met their repurchase obligations. Firms earn "interest" because tomorrow's predetermined repurchase price and credit to the firm's demand account is greater than today's debit. Since deposits are loans to banks—the bank owes you the amount deposited—the shift from noninterest-paying demand deposits to interest-paying repurchase agreements simply is a change in the type of loan to banks. Bank interest costs do rise, but what is the alternative? Recall that banks created RPs to discourage firms from withdrawing their accounts altogether and thereby reducing the amount of banks' earnings assets. Bankers do have sharp pencils and attempt to maximize earnings. The higher interest cost is less than the interest income foregone without RPs.

Instead of a collateralized loan to a domestic bank, some depositors, particularly multinational firms, prefer to extend unsecured credit to the bank's Caribbean branch, a different legal entity. The Caribbean branch of a U.S. bank may be no more than a post-office box. There may be no white marble edifice or red brick building or even a hut with friendly tellers to take your currency. Nevertheless, such branches have accounts because their parents in New York or elsewhere book for them. For example, a bank in New York will debit your local account and credit your dollar account in a leather-bound ledger marked "Caribbean Branch Accounts." The entries are reversed the next day. *All dollar-denominated accounts outside the United States are called Eurodollars.* The lack of physical branches and the large amount of such overnight Eurodollars relative to trade in the Caribbean suggest that smart lawyers and bankers seeking to avoid taxes and other legal restrictions have joined forces. The Caribbean area is hardly unique. Indeed, it is a "Johnny come lately" in the Eurodollar field. Cold-war politics, tax factors, and interest rate restrictions led European banks and branches of U.S. banks in Europe in the late 1950s to offer dollar denominated deposits, hence Eurodollars.[7] The term *Eurodollar* has stuck, being used to describe dollar-denominated deposits in Europe and anywhere else outside the United States.

Money market mutual funds are the last item included in M–2. Purchasers of mutual funds receive pro-rata shares to the asset and income of the fund. Unlike depositors, the income of mutual fund holders is not predetermined but depends on the performance of the fund. In this case, the assets are exclusively very short term, readily saleable securities such as Treasury bills and commercial paper. These types of securities are called money market securities, hence the funds' name. The funds' income, while not perfectly certain, is highly predictable. Most funds allow their holders to write checks against their accounts, though typically there is a $500 minimum check requirement.

The items added to M–2 to construct M–3 need little explanation. Large time deposits are time deposits over $100,000 and term RPs are longer than overnight RPs. Both of these accounts are held almost exclusively by firms.

Table 2–2 presents the December 1980 values and prior four years' annualized rates of growth of the money measures and their major components. Figure 2–1 offers the reader a somewhat longer run perspective by graphing the annual growth rate of the money measures from 1965 to 1980. In recent years currency has been growing somewhat faster than demand deposits, reversing a long trend of lagging currency growth. Figure 2–1 and Table 2–2 illustrate that other checkable deposits are a recent phenomenon—the growth rates of M–1A and M–1B were identical through 1974—that grew dramatically in the late 1970s. Consequently the growth of M–1B outstripped M–1A, and the growth-rate gap between the two money measures seems to be widening. M–2 is always greater than the M–1 measures, by construction, and the absolute and relative difference is also widening as M–2 has consistently grown faster than either

---

[7] Chapter 6 elaborates on the factors which led to the creation of Eurodollars.

**TABLE 2–2  Money stock measures and components**

|  | December 1980 ($ billions) | Annual percentage growth, December 1976—December 1980 |
|---|---|---|
| Currency | 118.5 | 9.6 |
| Demand deposits | 276.2 | 4.7 |
| M–1A | 384.8 | 6.0 |
| Other checkable deposits | 27.1 | 58.5 |
| M–1B | 411.9 | 7.5 |
| Overnight RPs and Eurodollars | 32.2 | 24.3 |
| Money market mutual funds | 75.8 | 119.0 |
| Savings deposits | 390.9 | −3.1 |
| Small time deposits | 757.4 | 17.6 |
| M–2 | 1,673.4 | 9.4 |
| Large time deposits | 251.5 | 20.3 |
| Term RPs | 33.0 | 22.3 |
| M–3 | 1,957.9 | 10.7 |

Note: M–2 is not the sum of its components because of a consolidation adjustment. Terms RPs were estimated residually.
**SOURCE:** *Federal Reserve Bulletin,* various issues.

**FIGURE 2–1  Growth rates of money measures**

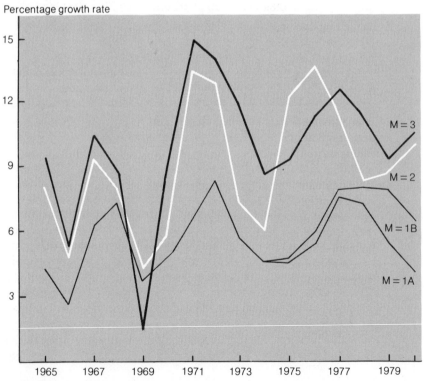

**SOURCE:** *Federal Reserve Bulletin,* various issues.

M–1 measure. In the 1950s and early 1960s saving deposits grew faster than the M–1 measures. Since then savings growth has decelerated and even turned negative in the late 1970s as depository institutions offered new and more attractive small time deposits such as $10,000 certificates with deposit rates tied to six-month Treasury bills. Individuals are not just switching from saving accounts to small time deposits, however; the sum of saving and small time deposits is growing faster than demand deposits. The explosive, if unsustainable, growth of money market mutual funds has also kept M–2 growth comfortably above either M–1 in spite of the negative savings deposit growth. Between December 1976 and December 1980, money market mutual funds grew from $3.4 to $75.8 billion! M–3 has grown faster than M–2 on balance, but not consistently so. The variability of M–3 growth was reduced in 1970 as Regulation Q deposit rate ceilings on large time deposits, which are particularly sensitive to the deposit rate, were repealed. Regulation Q ceilings currently are applicable only to small time deposits and will be dismantled altogether in the near future, much to the benefit of small savers.

## PREVIOUS DEFINITIONS OF MONEY

For many years prior to February 1980 money was defined more simply, reflecting the simpler financial structure. Because of their relative simplicity and longevity, the old definitions were widely known and, for awhile at least, took the aura of immutability. By the early 1970s, however, the shortcomings of the old definitions became apparent. The Fed responded in the traditional bureaucratic manner—it established the Advisory Committee on Monetary Statistics. The committee issued a scholarly report in June 1976. While the report was being dissected with great care, the innovations which were sweeping financial markets made the old definitions more obsolete and even rendered the report largely academic. Some change in definitions had to be made immediately, and less time and thought than usual was given to the new ones. The Fed recognized that the new definitions may have to be revised to some minor degree. Knowledge of the old definitions enables us to appreciate the advantages of the new definitions while simultaneously offering a glimpse at their shortcomings and possible directions for modification. Moreover, since economic books are not burned as soon as one page becomes dated, knowing how the old measures were constructed facilitates understanding the economic literature. Three definitions of money were widely accepted prior to 1980.

Old M–1 = C + DD + FDD
        = New M–1A + FDD – TC
        = The public's *currency* plus net *demand deposits* at commercial banks plus *foreign* commercial and central banks *demand deposits*

Old M–2 = Old M–1 + (BT & SD) − CDs

      = Old M–1 plus *bank time and saving deposits* minus *certificates of deposits*

Old M–3 = Old M–2 + NBD

      = M–2 + deposits at *nonbank depositories*

CDs are large, *negotiable* time deposits issued by large banks. There is a ready market where CDs are bought and sold. Not all large time deposits are CDs; some large time deposits cannot be sold.

Old M–1 and new M–1A are quite similar, the difference being that M–1 included the deposits of foreign commercial and central banks and excluded traveler's checks. In other words, in the past foreign commercial and central banks were considered part of the public, and their currency and demand deposits were included with yours and mine. CDs were considered distinct from other bank time and saving deposits, and for this reason were excluded from M–2. Commercial banks and nonbank depository institutions were considered sufficiently different that their deposits were not aggregated immediately. We first had only commercial bank deposits, M–2, and then the deposits of savings and loans, mutual savings banks, and credit unions were added to construct M–3. The time and saving deposits of banks and nonbanks are treated similarly today. That is, to get new M–2 one adds to M–1B the savings and small time deposits of banks and nonbanks, among other things. Overnight RPs, Eurodollars, and money market mutual funds—the other things—did not exist when the old, simpler definitions were first devised.

## JUSTIFICATIONS FOR ALTERNATIVE DEFINITIONS OF MONEY: FUNCTIONAL APPROACH

How have the four definitions of money been justified? There are two basic approaches to defining money: (1) the functional or services approach and (2) the empirical or statistical approach. The functional approach views money as those assets which were created to reduce the exchange difficulties of a barter economy. Money is the commodity unavailable in a barter economy which performs a valuable exchange function or yields some exchange service. The functional approach is conveniently summarized by the adage "Money is what money does." According to the functional approach, alternative characteristics such as the physical properties of the commodity, the identity of the issuer, and so on are not important in determining whether or not some commodity is money. This is not to deny that the physical characteristics of money are important. Many people drink water from paper cups but a few multimillionaires use gold goblets. Surely, no one would be indifferent between paper and gold cups. Similarly, gold money may be preferable to paper money on some counts but certainly not all. Note carefully we said gold *money* and paper *money.* The money-is-what-money-does approach says the services performed by commodities are of primary significance; physical characteristics are secondary.

Commodities fulfilling what specific functions are money? Lack of a double coincidence of wants and unit of account are the two main impediments to transactions in a barter economy. To overcome these impediments society created a (1) generally accepted *medium of exchange,* also called the means of payment, (2) *temporary abode of purchasing power* or store of value, *and* (3) *unit of account* or measuring rod of value.[8] Some commodities serve all three functions and, according to tradition, only these commodities would be called money. However, it is now realized that some commodities perform one or two of the stated functions of money but not all three. Should such commodities be called money? If one is a traditionalist, the answer is no. But a millenium ago conventional wisdom said the sun revolved around the earth, an idea discarded several centuries ago. Most economists who accept the money-is-what-money-does approach no longer insist that the commodity called money perform all three functions. Which function of money should be emphasized? An earlier section showed that no advanced economy can operate efficiently without a medium of exchange, temporary abode of purchasing power, or unit of account. Economists cannot agree, however, on the monetary function which should be given pride of place. We have different definitions of money according to the function thought most important.

The medium of exchange or means of payment include those items which can be and *are* used in all, or nearly all, transactions and which extinguish obligations between two parties. What is the medium of exchange in the United States? Virtually any commodity can be purchased with currency, demand deposits, or other checkable deposits. To be sure, the three means of payment are not equally desirable for all types of transactions. Distrusting the postal service or their own employees, some firms discourage the use of currency by customers who mail payments for bills. Payments with demand deposits are made by writing checks, which may not be acceptable without adequate identification. Considering such cases as anomalies, the medium of exchange function of money seemingly leads to the M–1B definition. A minority, however, claims that M–1A better measures the medium of exchange. For an item to be counted as part of the medium of exchange, you must be able to purchase virtually any commodity with the item, *and* you hold the item to purchase commodities. For example, the cash holdings and demand deposits of domestic and foreign banks are similar to ours, in that they can be used to purchase virtually anything. Yet everyone agrees that banks' cash holdings should

---

[8] Some economists choose to list money's role as a standard of deferred payment as a separate function. This, however, seems to me to be merely an extension of its role as the medium of exchange.

*not* be counted as money because banks hold cash primarily to pay-off depositors rather than to buy goods. The minority who favor M–1A point to the lower turnover rate of other checkable deposits as evidence that consumers do not hold them primarily for purchasing purposes. A deposit's turnover rate is defined as the total value of withdrawals during some period relative to the average outstanding balance. Which has a higher turnover rate, demand or saving deposits? If you said demand deposits, you understood how turnover was defined. Withdrawals are considerably more frequent from demand than savings deposit accounts. Demand deposits turnover frequently because consumers do use them to meet their daily transactions. The turnover rate of other checkable deposits is intermediate between demand and savings deposits. The minority excludes them and prefers M–1A. Having an intermediate turnover rate, other checkable deposits could just as correctly be included as excluded in the medium of exchange. Until there is better evidence that other checkable deposits are held for nontransactions purposes, the majority prefers M–1B to M–1A because other checkable deposits unquestionably can be used to purchase virtually anything. M–1A is also favored by "dinosaurs" who recall that the old money definitions made a sharp distinction between deposits of different institutions. The controversy between M–1A and M–1B will become moot when the Fed stops calculating M–1A, as it threatened in July 1981, and M–1B becomes simply M–1.

Two qualifying comments are appropriate. First, credit cards have become increasingly popular in recent years and many purchases are made with credit cards. The phrase "extinguish obligations between two parties" used above was not added accidentally. Unless you have a special credit card, which would be news to me, when you hand a merchant a credit card and walk out of the store with a package you have not extinguished all obligations. Approximately a month later you will get a notice (bill) that an obligation is due. And how do you pay this bill or debt? With a check, NOW, or currency. It may be convenient to think of credit card transactions as the simultaneous purchase of a good or service and a loan for an equal amount of money which is immediately used to pay for the good or service. A month or so later one repays the loan. Second, nonbank (American Express Company, for example) traveler's checks are means of payment, but until July 1981 were not considered money for pragmatic reasons. (Bank traveler's checks were not isolated but were included for many years in the demand deposit component of the money supply.) Nonbank issuers of traveler's checks did not publicly publish the volume of their traveler's checks outstanding on a regular (daily or even monthly) basis. The Fed proposed that all companies confidentially report their traveler's checks outstanding so that an even better measure of the medium of exchange would be available. While the nonbank issuers knew the amount of their traveler's checks outstanding on a daily basis, they opposed the Fed's proposal on the grounds that it was costly and the first step towards unnecessary reporting requirements and regulation. The Fed won this battle. The fight between the Fed and the nonbanks is just one example where government regulators tend to understate and private firms tend to overstate information acquisition costs. The acquisition of information is costly and is justified only if the benefits exceed the cost. The need to be pragmatic and settle for the second best if the ideal measure is too costly to acquire extends beyond the narrow definitions of money. Why does M–2 include overnight Eurodollars only in Caribbean branches? Why not include overnight Eurodollars in London? Data on Eurodollar outside the Caribbean is not currently available and the benefits of acquiring it may exceed the costs.

Some view money as that asset which people hold between sales and purchases, that is, the temporary abode of purchasing power. Money is the item which enables individuals to bridge the gap between the desired time patterns of income and consumption. Sales and purchases of commodities are inexorably tied together in a barter economy. A monetary economy separates the purchases and sales of commodities. Clearly, the medium of exchange is a temporary abode of purchasing power. No one would accept some commodity in exchange for a good or service if the commodity were to evaporate before one's eyes. Individuals will accept an item, which may have no use value, provided they are reasonably certain of being able to pass the item off on someone else. But this implies that the item is held during the interim. It does not follow, however, that the medium of exchange is the only temporary abode of purchasing power. What commodity is a temporary abode of purchasing power but not a medium of exchange? Such a commodity must be extremely liquid, that is, its price in the near future is highly predictable and it can be bought and sold relatively quickly. The sales price of liquid assets is hardly affected by the amount of time one spends finding a buyer: "forced" and "leisurely" sales of liquid assets realize virtually the same price. A house and common stock are assets but not temporary abodes of purchasing power. Stock prices are quite volatile. Try to sell a house overnight and you will get much less than if you advertise and sit patiently. No one would buy a house or common stock to bridge the gap between income and desired (nonhousing) consumption.

Identifying items which are *not* temporary abodes of purchasing power is easier than identifying the items held between receipts and planned expenditures. The M–2 definition of money might be justified on the grounds that it is the temporary abode of purchasing power. Supporting this view is the fact that over long periods of time the rate of return on at least the "old-time" components of M–2, that is, currency, demand deposits, and saving and small time deposits, has been lower than the returns on other assets. Liquidity is a desirable characteristic, and the most liquid assets should yield relatively low returns. In the United States today, where the temporary abode of purchasing power is composed of financial assets rather than physical assets, the lower interest income and interest opportunity cost on M–2 is the analogue of the storage costs of maintaining for exchange purposes an inventory of physical commodities, as implicitly assumed in the section on distribution systems. While overnight Eurodollars and RPs and money market funds have often yielded extremely high returns, there is little reason to believe that their high yield is permanent. These recently created assets were spawned during a period when all interest rates were far above the historical average.

Finally, money is also viewed as the unit of account or standard of value. The United States uses the dollar standard. Accountants' entries are recorded in dollars and storekeepers quote values, commonly called prices, in terms of dollars. What does it mean to say, "The price of a pair of shoes is $20?" A pair of shoes is 20 times more valuable than a dollar because it takes $20 to acquire shoes. The prices of most commodities are not constant, as many of us have sadly learned. The price, or value expressed in terms of dollars, of shoes has risen substantially. Bond prices tumbled in the early 1970s. Some commodities, however, have fixed (dollar) prices, that is, the dollar value of some items is certain. Such commodities are necessary for the existence of a dollar or any other monetary standard, as we argued earlier. No one would use the dollar standard if nothing is always worth a dollar.

The standard-of-value approach to defining money includes those items whose values are always fixed *in terms of dollars*. What items are worth a fixed number of dollars? Currency and demand deposits are fixed dollar assets, but M–1A is not as comprehensive as M–3. Time and saving deposits also are fixed dollar assets. The interest return on savings deposits can change but the principal is fixed, ignoring the possibility of default or assuming 100 percent insurance. A $1 deposit guarantees the depositor $1, plus any interest. While M–3 once was considered excessively broad, some want to widen the definition of money even further to a measure called L, as stated in a previous footnote. If you think money is all that stuff which is always worth a fixed number of dollars, select M–3 from the popular definitions of money.[9]

We are *not* saying that money consists of fixed purchasing power assets; money has a fixed *dollar* value. The real value or purchasing power of a dollar is 1/P, where P is an index of (nonmoney) commodity prices. Inflations occur when the dollar value or price, P, of commodities in-

---

[9] M–2 like M–3 contains money market mutual funds, where you participate in any capital gain or loss and, therefore, are not guaranteed the value of your initial contribution. Nevertheless, the price variability of the very short-term assets held by money market funds is sufficiently small that as a good first approximation these funds may be considered fixed dollar assets.

creases. Precisely because money is worth a fixed number of dollars, the purchasing power of money declines during inflations.[10]

## JUSTIFICATIONS FOR ALTERNATIVE DEFINITIONS OF MONEY: THE EMPIRICAL APPROACH

The second approach to the definition of money relies on empirical tests. Collect data and estimate statistically the relationship between money defined in alternative ways and other economic variables. The appropriate definition of money is the money measure which yields the strongest statistical relationship. We face a dilemma: the reader is not expected to be familiar with statistics, but he or she must be made aware of the empirical approach because most modern economists think it is far superior to the functional approach. With Caesar's remark on Gaul as our model, the empirical approach is divided into three parts. This chapter briefly summarizes the results of various tests of relationships between money, alternatively defined, and other variables. The two appendixes are for readers who want a deeper understanding of statistics in general and the empirical approach to money in particular. Appendix A presents an intuitive, graphical explanation of regression or least squares analysis, the statistical technique used most often by economists. That is, Appendix A discusses *how* relationships between variables, whatever they may be, are typically measured. Appendix B then uses the concepts developed in Appendix A toward the problem of defining money. Appendix B also extends the text by discussing empirical estimates of the elasticity of substitution among the monetary component. We do not, however, present tables full of regressions. Even there, results are summarized.

As stated, the empirical approach selects that particular money measure that is most closely associated with other variables. Unfortunately, this approach also does not lead to a unique definition of money because several empirical tests are reasonable, that is, several relationships involving money could reasonably be measured. Even for the same type of test, the best definition depends on the time period considered. What tests have been proposed? Two tests follow from the basic reason, boldly stated, for studying monetary economics: the monetary authorities can control the

---

[10] Knowledge of the three services performed by money will be used for the moment only to determine the appropriate definition of money. However, we shall see later that the great British economist, Lord Keynes, utilized these services of money in explaining how much money people want to hold. Keynes thought of total money demand as the sum of three components—transactions, precautionary, and speculative demands. Each component of money demand stressed one of the services performed by money. The transactions demand views money as a medium of exchange; the precautionary demand views money as a temporary abode of purchasing power; and the speculative demand strongly emphasizes the fixed dollar price of the unit of the account, which is held because of the risk of changes in the dollar price of bonds.

quantity of money, and money affects the total value of currently produced goods and services, GNP. The last statement needs qualification. No monetary measure is perfectly controlled by the monetary authorities in the sense that money changes when and only when the monetary authorities take some deliberate action. If nothing else, even the narrowest definition of money includes the liabilities of commercial banks, and the monetary authorities do not have guards at each bank to prevent banks from making loans and crediting the borrower's checking account. Lack of perfect control does not imply the total absence of control. All four monetary measures vary in large part because of actions taken by the monetary authorities. Exactly how the authorities influence money is the subject of several chapters and can be ignored for the moment. (For those who remember the money and banking section of their principles course, an open-market purchase or sale is an example of a policy action.) The first type of empirical test defines as money that measure whose variation is best explained by policy actions. In other words, pick that definition of money which responds most closely to actions of the Fed and, consequently, is least affected by non-Fed actions. If money is not closely related to the Fed's actions, then the Fed will be unable to achieve its goals even if the goals always respond to money.

Several examples of this type of test are available, differing in details and the period covered by the data. The overall empirical conclusion is that M–2 and M–3 are decidedly less well explained by policy variables than M–1A and M–1B. More of the variation in M–2 and M–3 is uncontrolled by the Fed. The empirical results are not surprising. M–2 and M–3 include a hodgepodge of items which are regulated differently. Currently, M–1A is somewhat better controlled than M–1B, but this is likely to change in the future. The degree of control depends on (1) the specific variable the Fed is attempting to control—some variables are "naturally" more difficult to control—and (2) the policy control tools. If the policy control tool were shouting, "Change, change," while holding hands around a Ouija board, control would be minimal indeed. In the past the Fed chose to exercise little control over other checkable deposits, but this policy of benign neglect is changing. The Fed is phasing out its pre-1980 policy which treats demand and other checkable deposits differently for regulatory purposes. In the future both types of deposits will be subject to the same regulatory reserve requirement ratios, in which case M–1B should be as well controlled as M–1A. This test then is neutral between M–1A and M–1B and casts serious doubt on the M–2 and M–3 definitions. Money is a tool to achieve the desired level of income. However important money may be, one cannot attain the desired level of income unless one first can manipulate money.

The second type of empirical test measures the relationship between GNP, the main policy goal, and alternative definitions of money. You select that definition of money which has the strongest and most consistent relationship with GNP. By doing so, you maximize your chances of achieving any desired GNP. This type of test was the brainchild of Professors Milton Friedman and David Meiselman and was refined in 1968 by Leonall Andersen and Jerry Jordan of the Federal Reserve Bank of St. Louis.[11] Since that year it appears as if everyone with "free" computer time, which includes most economists, has made one minor modification after another and estimated and reestimated the equations.[12] A thorough evaluation of all these studies would be a book by itself. The evidence is not conclusive but it appears that between 1960 and 1979 the sweepstakes winner was M–2 followed, in order, by M–1B, M–1A, and M–3.[13] The broader temporary abode of purchasing power concept of money explains a larger proportion of the variation of income.

In summary, the empirical approach to the definition of money tends to rule out M–3. The monetary authorities can control M–1A and M–1B better than M–3, and M–2 and M–1B better explain changes in GNP. The empirical approach eliminates one definition but has not presented us with a clear-cut winner, although M–1B seems to have the edge. One is forced to choose among M–1A, M–1B, and M–2 on the basis of some preconceived notion of the services performed by money. But the services or money-is-what-money-does approach fails to yield a unique definition of money. Therefore, if we are to proceed, we must make an arbitrary decision. Henceforth, money is defined as M–1B. In our defense, which is not very strong, M–1B is the most popular definition of money because it ranks no worse than second in any empirical test and most people believe that the medium of exchange function is paramount. Recognizing that our definition of money is arbitrary, the dependence of any fundamental analytical conclusions on a specific definition of money will be stated explicitly and highlighted. As you will see, this rarely happens. Usually the magnitude but not the direction of some monetary action will depend on the definition of money used. For example, a larger M–1A or M–1B increases the demand for goods and services, although not by the same amount. Small differentials due to a particular definition of money will be ignored.

Table 2–3 briefly summarizes this and the previous sections.

---

[11] Milton Friedman and David Meiselman, "The Relative Stability of Monetary Velocity and the Investment Multiplier in the United States," in Commission on Money and Credit, *Stabilization Policies* (Englewood Cliffs, N.J.: Prentice-Hall, 1963); and Leonall C. Andersen and Jerry Jordan, "Monetary and Fiscal Policy: A Test of their Relative Importance in Economic Stabilization," Federal Reserve Bank of St. Louis, *Review,* November 1968. The St. Louis model, a major source of controversy between monetarists and Keynesians, is analyzed in detail in Chapter 22.

[12] Discretion suggests a lack of citations.

[13] David J. Bennett et al., "Econometric Properties of the Redefined Monetary Aggregates," processed, Federal Reserve Board, February 1980.

**TABLE 2–3   Justifications for alternative definitions of money**

| Criteria for defining money | Appropriate money definition |
| --- | --- |
| Functional approach: | |
| 1.   Medium of exchange ............................. | M–1B, M–1A |
| 2.   Temporary abode of purchasing power ............. | M–2 |
| 3.   Unit of account ................................. | M–3 |
| Empirical approach: | |
| 1.   Controlled best by monetary authorities ............. | M–1A, M–1B |
| 2.   Best explains income (GNP) ...................... | M–2, M–1B |
| Preferred money definition ............................. | M–1B |

## TYPES OF MONEY: FIAT VERSUS FULL-BODIED

The status of money is conferred on things by their social acceptability. An individual accepts an item as money because other people so regard it. Table 2–4 illustrates that money is a social institution. Even an incomplete list of items that have served as money must be long because the number

**TABLE 2–4   Incomplete list of items that have served as money**

| | | |
| --- | --- | --- |
| salt | cattle | bronze |
| cowry shells | goats | copper |
| fish hooks | pigs | gold |
| porpoise teeth | sheep | iron |
| woodpecker scalps | nonbank liabilities | nickel |
| tobacco | bank liabilities | silver |
| wool | paper notes | boulders |

of societies is large and social institutions change over time. In the United States alone, tobacco, gold and silver coins, bank liabilities, and paper notes have served as money at various times. There must be consistency between the money a society uses and its institutions, ideas, and methods of production. Just as a currency of sheep and cattle would be inappropriate for a modern industrial state, so efforts suddenly to use bank deposits would be badly out of place in the interior of Haiti, which lacks the required framework of law and custom. Thus, while there are limits to the items which can be used as money, the limits are fairly broad. Surely gold and silver coins, if minted anew by the Treasury, would be generally acceptable today just as they were a few decades ago.

Are there any advantages in shifting from one form of money to another? Nearly everyone who writes about money has a list showing the desirable physical characteristics of money. It should be portable, divisible, durable, and easily recognizable, among other things. Portability is desirable in a medium of exchange; who wants to drag around hippopotamus carcasses? Since the prices of different goods vary considerably, divisibility without loss of value is clearly desirable. The advantages of the other characteristics are equally obvious. However, any list of items which have served as money shows many types of money not possessing all these desirable properties. Conventional wisdom says that diamonds were not used as money because they lose value on division. A two-carat diamond is worth more than two one-carat diamonds. Although the same is true about fish hooks, that is, an unbroken fish hook is worth more than the sum of all the pieces, Eskimos have used fish hooks as money. Physical characteristics are not of overwhelming importance in determining whether some specified commodity becomes money.

From the viewpoint of economic analysis and history, the different kinds of money are most effectively classified by their cost of production. *Full-bodied money* is money whose cost of production is as great as its value as money. The traditional example of full-bodied money in modern monetary systems is coins of the metal which a country uses as a standard. Prior to 1933 the United States was on the gold standard. The Treasury minted gold coins which contained bullion equal to the full value of the coins. The amount of gold in a $20 gold piece was purchased from metal dealers for $20. *Fiat money* is produced and maintained in circulation at zero cost. Paper money is approximately fiat money, the cost of production being exceedingly low. The nearest example of fiat money, however, is the Susan B. Anthony dollar coin. While coins cost more to produce than paper bills, the former last so much longer that coins cost less per year in circulation. The average life of a dollar bill is approximately one year while a coin lasts twelve years. Indeed, the main justification for minting dollar coins was the saving to the Treasury, which obviously underestimated the public's unwillingness to accept new types of money.[14] With cash register drawers and vending machines designed for

---

[14] Some economists express the difference between full-bodied and fiat money in terms of their nonmonetary value instead of cost of production. They say that the nonmonetary value of full-bodied money equals its monetary value while fiat money has no nonmonetary value. In many cases both approaches are obviously identical. For example, the cost of producing a $20 gold coin was $20, and jewelers and dentists paid $20 for the gold in melted coins. Nevertheless, we prefer the cost approach because the nonmonetary value approach sometimes misleads people into believing that the intrinsic, nonmonetary value of gold establishes the value of coins when it is the reverse, the monetary value setting the nonmonetary value, assuming the coins circulate. That is, in the 1920s the Treasury was able to acquire gold for coins only because it set such a high price for gold that gold supply exceeded private non-monetary demand. Since the Treasury was willing to buy any amount of gold at the high price, gold producers, who are not fools, did not sell to jewelers and others at a lower price. We also favor the cost approach because supporters of the nonmonetary approach invariably misclassify demand deposits as fiat money. Demand deposits barely have a physical existence, being entries in old-fashioned ledgers or a blip in a tape stored in a computer's memory. What is the nonmonetary value of something that barely exists? One's immediate reaction to classify such items as fiat money is wrong. While demand deposits may have no

the old types of money, the new money is quickly returned to the Treasury for the old.

Pennies are the best current example of monies which clearly are neither full-bodied nor fiat. The cost of producing a copper penny obviously depends heavily on the price of copper. The price of copper originally was sufficiently low that pennies were almost fiat money. When the price of copper rose significantly in the early 1970s and the metallic value of a penny approached a penny, the Bureau of the Mint produced several proofs of aluminum pennies for a congressional committee investigating the feasibility of switching from copper to aluminum. More than full-bodied money does not remain in circulation long. This is the fundamental fact underlying *Gresham's Law,* which is typically expressed as, "Bad money drives out good money." If the value of the copper in a penny were greater than one cent so that it cost more to produce a penny than its monetary value, private entrepreneurs would melt pennies for nonmonetary uses such as electric wires. The price of copper receded, and Americans had partially bodied copper pennies throughout the 1970s. However, in July 1981, when the cost of producing a copper penny rose to 0.8 cents, the Treasury announced that the copper penny was going the way of the dodo bird. Beginning in 1982, pennies are 98 percent zinc slugs with a copper coating. (A few of the aluminum penny proofs made in the early 1970s are lodged in coin collections. Although the congressional committee was supposed to return all the proofs to the Bureau of the Mint, a few proofs were "lost." The scarcity of the lost proofs makes them extremely valuable numismatically.)

The difference between full-bodied and fiat money may alternatively be expressed in terms of *seigniorage,* the profits earned by money producers. Of course, the difference between the amount of money produced and the cost of production equals profits or seigniorage. Producers of full-bodied money earn no seigniorage while fiat money producers, typically the government, earn seigniorage equal to the amount of money produced. What happens to the seigniorage? Regardless of type, fiat or full-bodied, money is placed in circulation by purchasing a physical commodity or financial asset, or as a gift from the money producer to other members of society. Much of advanced, pure monetary theory assumes fiat money enters the economic system as a handsome gift from the government; individuals gamboling through the woods pick up paper money dropped from helicopters. This assumption is convenient but unrealistic.[15] If the government

---

direct nonmonetary use at any moment in time, the maintenance of deposits over time requires resources which could produce nonmonetary goods, and the present value of these foregone nonmonetary goods equal the value of the deposits. A more detailed justification for classifying demand deposits as full-bodied money is presented shortly, and U.S. gold policy is reviewed in a subsequent chapter.

[15] This case is convenient because it holds constant the distribution of income, which usually has some effect on the equilibrium values of variables.

gives away fiat money and the seigniorage earned, it normally is distributed through the mails to some deserving group, for example, the poor
(welfare payments), elderly (social security payments), and so on. Governments that give away the seigniorage enable individuals to acquire
commodities. Governments usually are not so magnanimous, using the
seigniorage instead to purchase some item. Fiat money producers can
acquire commodities equal to the value of money created. Full-bodied
money creation does not enhance the producer; the cost of producing
money just equals the value of the commodities acquired when the money
is spent.

What are the advantages of fiat versus full-bodied money? Any commodity should be produced as cheaply as possible. Production costs measure the value of resources used. Inexpensively produced commodities
use few resources, leaving a large quantity of resources available for the
production of other commodities. Generally there is no such thing as a
free lunch; more guns means less butter. Money is the only commodity
offering society the possibility of a free lunch. Why not take advantage of
this possibility and use fiat money! Worthless—from the viewpoint of
production costs—money is good money because society as a whole can
have money without any sacrifice. By switching from full-bodied money
like gold coins to fiat paper money, the government can now hire miners
and mining equipment and offer us an excellent subway system. Society
would still have its medium of exchange, temporary abode of purchasing
value, and unit of account and, in addition, a subway. A second advantage
of fiat money is the ease with which the amount can be varied. Paper
money can be quickly increased or decreased in order to smooth the
business cycle or achieve other goals. Many, but not all, types of full-
bodied money cannot be expanded rapidly. The value of gold mined each
year is a small fraction of the current gold stock.

As just stated, *fiat money enables the government to acquire resources
and provide society with services equal to the real value of money created.*
Therein lies both the great advantage and disadvantage of fiat money.
Abuse of the resource acquisition power of fiat money has occurred all too
often. Many governments have preferred the impersonal printing press to
the tax system because the latter makes the government's voracious appe-
tite for resources more obvious.

Precisely because fiat money is costless to produce and the government
acquires resources equal to the value of money created, some governments have viewed money as an easy way to get whatever they need. The
real value or purchasing power of a unit of money is inversely related to
the price level of commodities. If prices double, the real value of money is
cut in half, by definition. The value of money created during some period
and the commodities that a fiat money producer acquires then equals the
amount of money printed divided by the price level. The most dramatic
examples of inflation are due to the seeming inability to understand that

the acquisition of goods and services through monetary expansion is limited. In other words, some governments have acted as if the price level does not depend on the amount printed. *Given some price level,* the amount of goods and services the government can purchase is directly related to the amount of fiat money printed. To get additional goods and services does the government simply print more money? Not necessarily. The price level probably will not remain fixed. Just as society will not use all its resources to produce full-bodied money, individuals will not sell unlimited quantities of goods and services to the government and simply hold the newly produced fiat money. The additional money balances will be spent, driving up prices. The government cannot simultaneously control the nominal quantity of money and its real value. By accepting fiat money society grants its government control of resources equal to the value of fiat money created but retains the power to determine the value of money through the price mechanism.

The scenario of a typical hyperinflation goes something as follows. During a war or other time of crisis the government suddenly needs a large quantity of resources. Minting full-bodied money will not do the trick since the resources that can be purchased with additional full-bodied money only equal the resources used to produce the money. The tax system is inadequate to meet the enlarged government demand. The government cranks the printing press to pay soldiers, acquire guns, and so forth. To some extent the government is successful because prices will rise only after the money supply has increased. But the higher price level means that soldiers and munition makers must be paid more. To maintain its expenditures, the government prints even more money; prices rise at a faster rate; yet more money is printed; all prices, including paper, escalate upward faster; a one-unit bill approaches full-bodied money so the minimum denomination bill becomes 1 million units. How does the story end? The economy collapses, a large proportion of the population is at least temporarily impoverished, the rascals are thrown out, and the new government solemnly promises that new currency issues will be kept in check.

The ghost of the inflation after World War I still frightens many Germans today. Germany set the printing press at full speed and flooded the country with currency. The inflation rate hit a peak of 32,400 percent per month! Prices in 1923 were 34 billion times what they had been in 1921![16] A bottle of German vintage wine cost less at night than the empty bottle the following morning.

But this was nothing compared with Hungary after World War II. From August 1945 to July 1946, the number of Hungarian pengos in circulation increased by a factor of 11.9 septillion

---

[16] Philip Cagan, ''The Monetary Dynamics of Hyperinflation,'' in *Studies in the Quantity Theory of Money,* ed. Milton Friedman (Chicago: University of Chicago Press, 1956).

(11,900,000,000,000,000,000,000,000). Over the same period, prices rose and the purchasing power of the pengo fell 3.81 octillion (3,810,000,000,000,000,000,000,000,000.) Fairly boggles the mind. Most of us unfortunately can only guess what a million dollars looks like and hope that we never will become billionaires, given the likely circumstance which would make such an outcome possible. A German billionaire in 1923 could not afford a cup of coffee. Some appreciation for these large numbers may be gained by noting that a million (1,000,000) seconds is equivalent to 12 days while a billion (1,000,000,000) seconds is equivalent to 32 years. Our earth did not exist 3.81 octillion seconds ago.

We said currency is fiat money but are demand deposits, the main form of money in the United States today, fiat or bull-bodied money? Before

*Historical Pictures Service, Chicago*

Papering a wall with inflated one-mark German notes.

answering this question, let us review the economic meaning of cost and profit.

An important cost often ignored by non-economists is the opportunity cost of capital, that is, the return capital could earn in any competitive industry. Economic profit, the relevant profit concept determining whether money is fiat or full-bodied, is the difference between reported (accounting) profit and the opportunity cost of capital. Competitive firms do earn a normal return on their capital but do not earn any economic profit, by definition. The Federal Reserve earns substantial profits on its monetary operations, its currency virtually being fiat money. It is a monopoly. Indeed, fiat money *must* be produced by a monopolist. Congress has granted the Fed an exclusive license to manufacture costless money. If free entry existed in any industry with zero production cost, the capitalist spirit would induce firms to enter the industry until the commodity becomes worthless. Grant everyone the right to produce currency which is legal tender and the veritable outpouring of currency would make even the Hungarian inflation look mild. Of course, Congress realizes that everyone wants a money machine and spends a not inconsequential amount punishing those who cannot resist the temptation. Counterfeiting is a crime!

What type of money is a demand deposit? While a demand deposit may seem like fiat money, it is much closer to full-bodied money. The cost of producing any type of money includes both the cost of creating money and the cost of maintaining it in existence. The cost of creating demand deposits typically is quite small. For example, if you come to a bank with currency and open a demand deposit account, recording the deposit in a ledger sheet or computer is not costly. However, the implicit demand deposit contract obliges the bank to send monthly statements, collect checks you deposit, pay checks you write, and so on. Including as a cost the normal return on invested capital, the cost of serving demand deposits approximately equals the earnings on assets made possible by demand deposits. Banking is a relatively competitive industry; banks earn approximately zero economic profit.

## SUMMARY

All but the most primitive groups have assets which serve as a medium of exchange, temporary abode of purchasing power, and unit of account. Associating such assets with a bourgeois mentality which they hoped to eradicate, Lenin and other communist leaders attempted to ban their existence and establish a "natural" economy. The resulting chaos convinced Lenin that all countries, capitalist as well as communist, need these assets, which are called money. Some assets perform one or two but not all three functions. For example, savings deposits at commercial banks are a temporary abode of purchasing power but not a medium of exchange. Defining money by the asset's function or service leads to three measures of money corresponding to the service emphasized. If one places paramount importance on the medium of exchange, currency and demand deposits definitely are money, and most probably so are other checkable deposits. Other measures of money correspond with the temporary abode of purchasing power and unit of account functions.

Lack of a unique money measure led some economists to abandon the functional approach and adopt an empirical approach. Collect data and estimate the relationship between money defined in alternative ways and other economic variables. The money measure selected yields the strongest statistical relationship. Unfortunately, the empirical approach also gives an ambiguous answer because economists cannot agree on the relationship to be estimated. Should we estimate the relationship between money and Federal Reserve policy actions or some other relationship?

Disagreement on the definition of money is a source of constant amusement to nonmonetary economists. "If those monetary economists are uncertain what money is, they must be uncertain about everything else. Should we believe anything they say?" To monetary specialists the choice among money measures is similar to deciding among caviar, pâté, and shrimp cocktail—all are extremely good, and all are better than anything else. Selection of M–1B and emphasis on the medium of exchange does not deny that a temporary abode of purchasing power and unit of account are essential in every civilized society. Except for the weaker relationships among M–3, Federal Reserve policy action, and GNP, the empirical tests are not that conclusive. The general conclusions of economic analysis rarely depend on the specific money measure. For example, what is the effect, positive or negative, on interest rates of increasing the quantity of money? Though possibly not to the same extent, more money, however defined, causes lower interest rates, at least initially. The specific money measure chosen is less important than a knowledge of the alternative measures and their justification. *The Wall Street Journal* and other newspapers report weekly the behavior of the money supply. Suppose one reads that the annual growth rates of M–1B and M–2 were 4 and 8 percent respectively. How does one understand economic policy unless one knows what M–1B and M–2 are and why these measures have been constructed?

## QUESTIONS

1. What are the two basic reasons for exchanges?
2. List various exchange systems. What are their distinguishing characteristics?
3. The four current measures of money are M–1A, M–1B, M–2, and M–3. State precisely what items are included in each money measure.
4. What are the three main functions or services performed by money, and what current money measures best perform these functions?
5. Are credit cards a means of payment?

6. What were the old (pre-1980) measures of money? What developments made them obsolete and led to the new measures?

7. The empirical approach to the definition of money has employed what empirical tests? What are the results of these tests?

8. Distinguish between full-bodied and fiat money. What are the main advantages and disadvantages of these two types of money?

9. Why are inflations common occurrences during wars and other times when the government's demand for resources increases significantly?

## appendix A · Regression analysis

The purpose of this appendix is to convey a *commonsense* feel for the appropriateness of the empirical tests presented in the next section and in a few other chapters. This is not a statistics book; computational methods and the underlying mathematics are ignored here. The usefulness of knowing some basic statistical techniques and the meaning of a few statistical measures extends beyond money and banking to economics in general. Like it or not, economics is becoming more empirically oriented. As stated in the first chapter, what is the main criteria for evaluating a theory? A theory is largely judged on the basis of its explanatory and predictive powers. Theories postulate relationships between economic variables, and the theories are good if the postulated relationships are in fact observed. Given this, it is hardly surprising that economists are spending more and more time spewing forth statistical tests that confirm or deny their theories. This book would not give you an accurate flavor of modern monetary economies if it totally ignored statistical techniques and tests. However, only limited space is given to empirical results because they are still inconclusive, partly because statistics is such an arcane science—there are lies, damn lies, and statistics, as Mark Twain said.

Suppose our theory says two variables, X and Y, are related. We purposely use general notation—the variables are called X and Y—because the principles to be discussed can be applied to virtually any problem. How does one test the theory? Are X and Y, in fact, related and, if so, precisely how?

The first step is data collection. The data for X and Y may be either time series or cross-section. As their names suggest, time-series data are for the same economic unit at different time periods while cross-section data are for different economic units at the same time period. For example, United States GNP from 1929 to 1981 is a time series, and 1981 GNP of United Nations member countries is a cross section. Hypothetical time series data for variables X and Y are presented in Table 2A–1. A preliminary notion of the relationship between the variables may be gained by a

**TABLE 2A–1   Variables X and Y, 1975–1979**

| Year | Variable Y | Variable X |
|------|------------|------------|
| 1975................. | 2 | 1.5 |
| 1976................. | 3 | 3.0 |
| 1977................. | 4 | 3.0 |
| 1978................. | 5 | 5.2 |
| 1979................. | 6 | 3.8 |

protracted examination of the table or by a quick glance at a graph. Each point in Figure 2A–1 graphs the annual values of X on the horizontal axis and Y on the vertical axis. Clearly, variables X and Y are positively related. Equally clearly, however, the relationship is not exact, that is, all the data points do not fall along a straight line such as LL′. The general equation for a straight line is

$$Y = a + bX \qquad (2A-1)$$

**FIGURE 2A–1   Graph of data in Table 2A–1 and regression line, LL′**

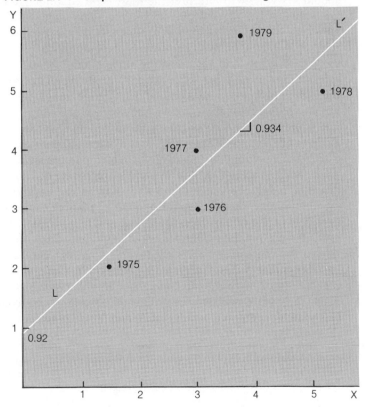

where a and b are parameters (unspecified numbers). Tables and graphs are inconvenient and imprecise means of conveying information and showing inexact relationships. *Regression or least squares analysis is the statistical technique used most often by economists to describe an inexact relationship between two or more variables. The regression equation specifies the line* (that is, estimates the parameters a and b in equation 2A–1) *which best describes the relationship between two variables. The regression line is closest to the data points and states the average value of the dependent variable Y for every value of the independent variable, X. In addition, regression analysis provides an R² (R squared or correlation coefficient squared), which measures how well the line describes the relationship between the two variables.*

Using the data shown in Table 2A–1, the regression or least squares estimate of equation (2A–1), which is graphed in Figure 2A–1 as LL′, is

$$Y = 0.92 + 0.934X \qquad R^2 = 0.64$$
$$\phantom{Y = }(0.46) \quad (0.30) \qquad\qquad\qquad (2A–1')$$

Temporarily ignore the numbers in parentheses and the term $R^2 = 0.64$. How this equation is computed is beyond the scope of this book.[1] One should know how to interpret the regression equation. It states the average value of the dependent variable for every value of the independent variable. In our example, when X equals 4, the average value of Y is $4.656 = 0.92 + 0.934(4)$. The intercept coefficient, 0.92, is the average value of Y when X is zero, and the slope coefficient, 0.934, measures the average change in Y per unit change in X. Being an average line, some of the points lie above and some below the line. Averages are informative but also hide a great deal. 0.934 is the average of 0 and 1.868 and also 0.924 and 0.944, yet the former pair is more widely dispersed than the latter. Each coefficient (average value) has a standard deviation, a measure of dispersion or variability usually written in parentheses under the coefficient. See equation (2A–1′). Instead of reporting the standard deviation directly, many economists prefer to show in the parentheses the coefficient's t-value, which is the ratio of the coefficient to the standard deviation. The t-ratio of our slope coefficient is $3.11 = 0.934/0.30$. A high t-ratio indicates predictability; the standard deviation (dispersion) is small relative to the regression coefficient (average value). The t-ratio reflects the likelihood that X has a systematic effect on Y. Generally, if the t-ratio is greater than 2, then the likelihood that an observed relationship between X and Y is systematic is greater than 95 percent or, equivalently, there is less than a 5 percent chance that X and Y are unrelated.

---

[1] To learn how to calculate the regression equation, standard deviations, and $R^2$, see any economic statistics book. The regression line is also called the least squares line because it is closest to the data points in the sense that the line is constructed to minimize the sum of the squared differences between the points and the line.

As just stated, each coefficient has its own standard deviation and t-ratio. It would be desirable to have a measure of overall "fit," the tightness of the total relationship between the variables. The correlation coefficient squared, $R^2$, is such a measure. It states how well the regression line describes the data or, equivalently, how close the line is to the data points. In statistical jargon, the $R^2$ measures how much of the variation in the dependent variable Y is explained by the independent variable X. The $R^2$ must take values between 0 and 1. When there is an exact relationship between X and Y so any variation in Y is due to X, all the data points lie along a line. In this case, the $R^2$ of the equation is 1. In virtually every case the relationship will be inexact and the $R^2$ will be less than 1. For example, the $R^2$ of the regression equation drawn in Figure 2A–1 is 0.64. We may think of the variation in Y as being explained by two forces: (1) X changes causing a movement along the line and (2) other factors causing deviations from the line. The farther the data points are from the line and, therefore, the more important are the other factors, the smaller is the $R^2$. A low $R^2$ signifies a weak relationship as other factors besides the independent variable are influencing the dependent variable. If the scatter of data points is completely random so that there is no association between X and Y, then $R^2 = 0$. In this case none of the variation in Y is due to X. The $R^2$ is often used to judge the validity of theories. $R^2 = 0$ says there is no relationship between the variables, and the theory is incorrect. $R^2 = 1$ says the relationship is perfect or exact; the dependent variable always responds in the same manner to movements in the independent variable. Intermediate values imply some association between the variables, but the dependent variable is also related to other variables.

Many theories are more complicated than the one considered. We often believe that more than one factor causes variations in another factor. Hypotheses often include two or more independent, explanatory variables. For example, we may allege that the quantity of peanuts supplied, Y, depends on the peanut price, $X_1$, the price of fertilizer, $X_2$, the wage rate of farm labor, $X_3$, and so on. Regression analysis can be used to test these more complicated hypotheses and the interpretation of the results is similar to the simpler case. The regression coefficient of the peanut price shows the average effect on the quantity supplied of a unit change in the peanut price *assuming all other factors* such as the price of fertilizer and so on *are constant*. The $R^2$ measures how well *all* the independent variables explain movements in the quantity supplied. If the theory specified every factor which causes changes in the quantity supplied, then the $R^2 = 1$. Why don't we include every factor which causes changes in the quantity supplied and therefore, make the $R^2 = 1$? We simply do not know what factors to include. Indeed, a statistical analysis of the data would be unnecessary if we knew everything beforehand. Lack of knowledge forces us to estimate the parameters a and b and produces an $R^2$ less than unity.

## appendix B · The empirical approach to defining money

The text stated, "The first type of empirical test defines as money that measure whose variation is best explained by Fed policy actions. In other words, pick that definition of money which responds most closely to actions of the Fed and, consequently, is least affected by non-Fed actions." How does one measure the closeness of the relationship between money and Fed actions? Estimate by regression analysis the equation

$$M_i = a + b(B) \qquad (2B-1)$$

where $M_i$ is some measure of money and B is a Fed policy action variable. (We shall see shortly that the base, hence B, summarizes Fed policy.) Regression analysis yields estimates of a and b, standard deviations and, more important, the equation's $R^2$, which measures the closeness of the relationship between money and Fed policy actions. Select that money measure with the highest $R^2$ because a larger proportion of the change in that money measure is due to Fed policy and, therefore, a smaller proportion is due to non-Fed factors.

**FIGURE 2B–1   Relationships betweem $M_i$ and the base, a measure of Federal Reserve policy, and between $M_j$ and the base**

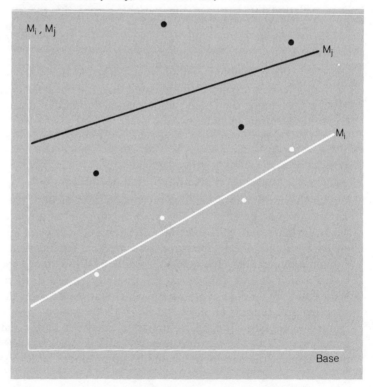

In terms of the graphical approach, different money measures, called $M_i$ and $M_j$, are measured on the vertical axis, and some composite Fed policy action variable, Base, is measured on the horizontal axis. The small dots in Figure 2B–1 represent $M_i$, and $M_j$ is represented by large dots. The first type of test toward defining money calculates the regression for both $M_i$ and $M_j$. Looking at Figure 2B–1, which money measure would you select? The preferred money definition is $M_i$. Because $M_i$ and $M_j$ respond to non-Fed action, the points for neither $M_i$ nor $M_j$ lie along a straight line. Compared to the description of the relationship between $M_j$ and Fed policy action given by the line for $M_j$, the straight line for $M_i$ better describes the relationship between $M_i$ and Fed policy. The $M_i$ points are closer to its line, indicating the Fed policy actions account for a larger proportion of its variation, and other factors are less important. As stated in the text, the Fed controls M–1A best, with M–1B a close second. M–2 and M–3 are less well explained by Fed policy.

The second type of test estimates

$$\Delta GNP = a + b\Delta M \qquad (2B-2)$$

where $\Delta GNP$ and $\Delta M$ are the changes in GNP and money, respectively, and b is the response of GNP to money. (Most equations also include lagged values of money and/or measures of fiscal policy.) For various technical reasons, the relationship is best estimated in terms of changes, $\Delta$s, instead of levels. Substituting different definitions of money in (2B–2) and reestimating the equation, one selects that definition of money which has the strongest and most consistent relationship with GNP, as measured by the $R^2$ of the regression equation.[1] In other words, money cannot explain every movement of GNP; other things affect GNP. Choose that monetary measure which explains the largest proportion of the variation in GNP. The broader temporary abode of purchasing power concept of money, M–2, explains a larger proportion of the variation of income.

The third and final empirical test follows from the economic principle that the items to be classified as money, and the appropriate degree of aggregation in general, depend on the degree of substitutability between items. The narrowest definition of money, M–1A, contains two items, currency and demand deposits, which are not exactly alike. This fact has not been lost to the American Express Company, which has tried to

---

[1] A backhand version of this test has become quite popular and may be appreciated by those with a *strong* statistical background. Those who have not mastered the forehand version can conveniently ignore what follows. Some economists estimate money demand functions by regressing alternative definition of money on GNP, interest rates, and possibly other variables and then select that money definition which has the highest $R^2$. It is alleged that the monetary authorities' ability to hit an income target is directly related to the stability of the function as measured by the $R^2$. While the allegation may be true, the direct approach mentioned in the text avoids the difficulty of comparing $R^2$s when the dependent variables are different. The monetary measure best explained (highest $R^2$) may have a low partial correlation with income and a high partial correlation with interest rates.

incorporate the best features of currency and demand deposits in its traveler's checks. Nevertheless, why does everyone include at least currency and demand deposits in their definitions of money? In other words, on what basis should we aggregate two assets, currency and demand deposits, and consider them as one, money? Assets sufficiently similar that they can readily be substituted for each other should be aggregated. How does one measure similarity or substitutability? Other disciplines may consider explicitly the physical properties of the assets, when or how the assets are used and so on. Economists eschew such approaches and rely on the price mechanism to reveal how society appraises commodities. When society regards two assets as substitutes, a higher rate of return on one asset lowers the demand for the other. The cross rate of return elasticity, the percentage change in the quantity of asset J per percentage change in the rate of return of K, is the economic measure for the degree of substitutability between any financial asset J and K. If the cross elasticity between two assets is highly negative, they are good substitutes, by definition, and can be effectively classified as one asset.[2] For example, time deposits and saving and loan deposits are good substitutes when a slightly higher time deposit rate of interest induces significant withdrawals from saving and loan associations, and vice versa. Currency and demand deposits are included in every definition of money because it is generally believed that the cross elasticity between these two assets is high. Of course, this cannot be proved because currency bears no rate of return. Should one also include other checkable deposits? The amount of M–1A people want to hold depends on other factors besides the interest rate on other checkable deposits. The empirical approach says that you should estimate the parameters a, b, and c in the following equation:

$$\text{M--1A} = a - bi_{oc} + cx \qquad\qquad (2B\text{--}3)$$

where $i_{oc}$ is the rate of interest on other checkable deposits and x represents all other variables affecting M–1A.[3] If b were large so that M–1A is highly responsive to the interest paid on other checkables, and if the t-ratio of the b coefficient is large so that one can be confident that the effect of the other checkable deposit rate on M–1A is systematic, then add other checkable deposits to M–1A and use M–1B. You will not be disappointing your second grade math teacher: you are *not* adding apples and oranges. If b is large enough, you are adding golden delicious and red delicious apples to get just plain apples. Proceeding in a similar manner one can estimate the degree of substitutability between M–1B and time and savings deposits and so on.

---

[2] Traditional micro theory usually discusses cross *price* elasticities, which are positive for substitutes. Coffee and tea are substitutes because higher coffee prices *increase* the demand for tea. We are using rates of return, not prices. Bonds and money are substitutes when higher bond rates of return *reduce* the demand for money.

[3] Actually, the logarithms of the variables are used in (2B–3).

Estimates of (2B–3) and similar equations yield inconclusive results. Some studies find that b is zero and others find b is large. One reason for different results is that the world is not an ideal laboratory in which one can hold everything else constant and see how M–1A varies with $i_{oc}$. What we observe over time are different values of M–1A, $i_{oc}$, and a whole host of other variables. Not knowing all the variables which affect M–1A and, therefore, necessarily ignoring them, we may incorrectly attribute to $i_{oc}$ the effect of the unknown variables. In terms of equation (2B–3), the inclusion of different x variables can affect the estimates of b. Tests of the degree of substitutability among assets are so mixed that they do little to pinpoint the appropriate money measures.

# Elements of money supply analysis

**3**

Measuring the quantity of money is relatively easy, even though tedious. For example, using the M–1B definition of money, the quantity of money can be measured by asking people to report their currency, demand deposits, and other checkable deposits. Because the number of money issuers is much smaller than the number of money holders, a more convenient approach becomes apparent: ask the issuers of money to report the amount of their monetary liabilities outstanding. Only the Federal Reserve and Treasury issue currency, and approximately 25,000 commercial banks and nonbank depositories issue demand and other checkable deposits. Even in these days of hand calculators and sophisticated computers, adding a column of 25,000 numbers is tedious but, in principle, a simple matter. Measurement requires patience but little skill.

The money supply problem considered in this and the following chapter is more interesting and does require some skill to solve. What are the determinants of the quantity of money? Why was the quantity of money in December 1980 $412 billion and not, say, $454 billion? Why did the quantity of money increase by approximately $155 billion in the 1970s? What must be done to increase the money supply by another $155 billion in the 1980s? We shall see that the Federal Reserve, Treasury, banks, nonbank depositories, and the public—you and I—jointly determine the quantity of money. These chapters emphasize the role of banks and the public in the money supply process. We do not ignore the Federal Reserve altogether but subsequent chapters contain a much more detailed analysis of the Fed's actions. Since we are analyzing the money supply, we emphasize depositories' liabilities, which includes demand and other checkable deposits, and largely ignore their loans and other noncash assets. Thus, a somewhat one-sided view of banks is presented in these two chapters.

## THE BALANCE SHEET

Familiarity with rudimentary bookkeeping is all but indispensible in the study of commercial banking.[1] The balance sheet identity discovered long ago says:

$$\text{Assets} = \text{Liabilities} + \text{Net worth}$$

The identity states compactly that all your valuable possessions (assets) are acquired by borrowing (liabilities) or with your own resources (net worth). A simplified balance sheet for bank A is shown below.

**Bank A**

| Assets | | Liabilities and Net Worth | |
|---|---|---|---|
| Cash | 75 | Demand deposits | 200 |
| Loans | 275 | Time deposits | 250 |
| Securities | 150 | Net worth | 50 |

Traditionally, assets are listed on the left-hand side and liabilities and net worth are on the right. From the viewpoint of a bank, demand and time deposits are liabilities; it owes you the amount deposited. You can view demand deposits as borrowings by banks at a zero interest rate but payable on demand. Does the "loans" account indicate bank A lent $275, or did bank A borrow $275? Being on the asset side of the balance sheet, loans represent bank A's claim against people who were lent $275. Throughout much of the book we will ignore net worth and present partial balance sheets called T-accounts to record the effect of a single transaction. Suppose a checking account customer deposits $10 cash. The effect of this transaction is:

**Bank A**

| Cash | +10 | Demand deposits | +10 |
|---|---|---|---|

To provide the reader some practice before getting to more important problems, the following additional examples may be helpful. Person X deposits a $10 check issued by person Y, another depositor of Bank A.

**Bank A**

| | | Demand deposits X | +10 |
|---|---|---|---|
| | | Demand deposits Y | −10 |

Assets are unchanged in this case. A larger liability to X is matched by a smaller liability to Y.

---

[1] Bookkeeping is simply the recording of transactions; accounting is much more complex. Do not for one moment think that accountants spend their entire day working on problems similar to those illustrated in this book.

A borrower pays back a $50 loan from the bank by writing a check on his account there.

| Bank A | | | |
|---|---|---|---|
| Loans | −50 | Demand deposits | −50 |

## A COMMONSENSE VIEW OF THE MONEY SUPPLY

Before getting to some simple algebra, which should not scare anyone but often does, let us see what old-fashioned common sense tells us about the determinants of the quantity of money. We narrate with the aid of balance sheets a short history of banking designed to introduce the determinants of the money supply and show their general effect.

This narrative does not pinpoint the precise effects of the determinants; it does not show the magnitude of money changes in response to some factor. Algebraic equations are necessary to determine precise effects. But the narrative gives a "good feel" for the factors that influence the money supply. Without a good feel for a problem one can get too wrapped up in algebra and believe that algebraic manipulations are *the* objective. Nothing could be further from the truth; algebra can be a useful tool in achieving greater precision but it never is the objective. To check if algebra has indeed added greater precision, see if your algebraic answer is in general accord with your commonsense answer. If the two answers are not consistent, trust your common sense as you probably made a technical error in the algebraic manipulations.

The historical narrative keeps in the forefront banks' ultimate objective, something often obscured by the algebra. Although we are interested in banks mainly because they are money producers and the amount of money affects GNP, banks are not directly interested in the amount of money they produce, as we defined money. Instead, they are mainly interested in making money as defined in the street. That is, expansion and contraction of demand deposits, which we count as money, is not banks' ultimate objective but is only incidental in their quest for profits, which in street talk is referred to as making money.

This narrative should not be read too literally. We want a general money supply framework which can be applied irrespective of the specific money definition selected. To accomplish this we introduce some general terms whose precise measure depends on the money definition. In this and the next chapters, *check deposits are those deposits included as money*. If the money measure were M–1A, only demand deposits at commercial banks are check deposits; under the M–1B measure, NOW accounts are also check deposits. *Banks are those private financial institutions which issue check deposits.* Banks could include savings and loan associations.

Government-issued coins were the first type of money. Prior to the existence of banks, the money supply problem was extremely easy: the quantity of money depended simply on the government's decision to mint coins. Throughout this section we assume coins in circulation equal $200, a figure chosen for convenience. Assuming for simplicity the public has no nonmoney assets or liabilities, its balance sheet is shown below.

**Public**

| | | | |
|---|---|---|---|
| Cash | 200 | Net Worth | 200 |

Mints do not produce individualized coins. Millions of quarters identical to the one in my pocket are in circulation. Consequently, it is virtually impossible to identify coins that are lost or stolen. The likelihood of recovering a stolen denarius is higher nowadays because denarii are unusual items. Crime is not a recent phenomenon. Our forefathers spent substantial amounts on locks, window grills, and other devices to protect their coins from burglars. Some enterprising chaps saw this and said, ''We can do a better job for less.'' These chaps were goldsmiths. Since goldsmiths already were weighing and assaying gold, had large secure vaults, and were trusted, they capitalized on their comparative advantage and became bankers. Just as banks currently rent safety deposit boxes, bankers levied a relatively large service charge on deposits. Individuals paid the service charge because their coins generally were safer in a bank than at home. Of course, some learned otherwise; a few bankers promptly absconded after accepting coins. Assuming honest bankers, depositors were given receipts and promised the coins were repayable on demand. Suppose individuals deposit $100. Figure 3-1 presents balance sheets for the consolidated banking system and public after the deposit.

**FIGURE 3-1**

| **Consolidated Banking System** | | | |
|---|---|---|---|
| Cash | 100 | Check deposits | 100 |

| **Public** | | | |
|---|---|---|---|
| Cash | 100 | Net worth | 200 |
| Check deposits | 100 | | |

Depositing coins has no *immediate* impact on the money supply. One component, currency in the hands of the public, decreases while another component, check deposits, increases an equal amount. Remember that cash held by banks is not part of the money supply.

### Check collection and reserves: A digression

Initially, deposits were not transferable. People withdrew their deposits at banks and acquired coins prior to purchases. One could not write checks, which are orders to banks to pay a designated person. Since banks earned income on their deposits outstanding, they attempted to make deposits more attractive in order to encourage their use by the public. Transferable deposits expended by writing checks greatly enhanced deposit growth and increased bank earnings. Assume person X writes a $10 check on his bank A account to pay person Y who has an account at bank B. The effect of this transaction on the balance sheets of banks A and B is shown below.

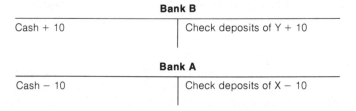

| **Bank B** | |
| --- | --- |
| Cash + 10 | Check deposits of Y + 10 |

| **Bank A** | |
| --- | --- |
| Cash − 10 | Check deposits of X − 10 |

On behalf of its depositor, bank B collects $10 from bank A and credits person Y's deposit account. After paying bank B, bank A debits the account of person X. Balance sheets cannot show the extra convenience to depositors from the ability to write checks. They do show that issuing checks is identical to a cash withdrawal and subsequent cash deposit. The convenience to the public was not without additional cost and risk to banks, which now had to transfer cash among themselves. Wells Fargo was the leading "armored stagecoach" company in 19th-century America. Presumably, the additional income and deposits generated by making them more attractive justified the cost.

Ingenious and earnings-conscious bankers asked the currency issuer to accept their deposits and thereby reduce transfer costs. Of course, bankers do not want the currency issuer to compete with them and accept deposits from the public. The Federal Reserve complied. It issues currency and accepts deposits from banks but not from private citizens and corporations. Bank A will retain some cash—appropriately called vault cash—since some depositors may want to switch back from deposits to cash, and any request for cash must be met on demand. However, bank A will ship the overwhelming proportion of its cash holdings to the Fed and have its account credited.

| **Bank A** | | |
| --- | --- | --- |
| Cash | −10 | |
| Deposits at Fed | +10 | |

**Fed**

| | | |
|---|---|---|
| | Cash | −10 |
| | Deposits of bank A | +10 |

The Fed issued the cash outstanding so its return to the Fed reduces its liability.[2] As depositors write checks to other parties, a far more important way of expending deposits than depositor requests for cash, banks transfer deposits at the Fed instead of transporting cash. Assuming the transaction described earlier involving banks A and B, bank B sends the check deposited by person Y to the Fed, which credits bank B's account and debits bank A's account.

**Fed**

| | | |
|---|---|---|
| | Deposits of bank A | −10 |
| | Deposits of bank B | +10 |

Of course, banks also record the transaction on their balance sheets, adjusting private check deposits and bank deposits at the Fed.

**Bank deposits at the Fed are equivalent to vault cash.** Suppose bank B wants currency instead of a credit at the Fed. How do we know the Fed can provide bank B with currency? Simple, it costs virtually nothing to print currency. It is no more difficult for the Fed to crank the press than write on a ledger sheet. Commercial banks do not print currency and may be unable to pay depositors. Withdrawals from commercial banks reduce a bank asset, vault cash, but deposit withdrawals at the Fed only change the composition of Fed liabilities. From a legal as well as economic viewpoint, bank regulators treat vault cash and bank deposits at the Fed as equivalent.[3] It is convenient to give these two assets one name—*reserves*. Introduction of this term saves qualifying adjectives. Just plain currency henceforth means currency held by the public because currency held by banks is called reserves. The majority of bank reserves, in fact, are kept as deposits at the Fed. Assuming that all reserves are held as deposits at the Fed simplifies the exposition without affecting any of the conclusions. But do not be awed by such terms as reserves and deposits at the Fed. If you think of reserves as currency held by banks you cannot go wrong.

---

[2] Receipt by the Fed of Treasury-issued currency would require different account entries but not change the essence of the argument.

[3] This was not true prior to 1959, when the Fed began allowing banks to count their vault cash in meeting legally required minimum cash ratios. Thus one has the paradoxical situation where until 1959 bank deposits at the Fed were in some respects more like cash than cash itself.

## DETERMINANTS OF THE MONEY SUPPLY

Total currency, whether held by the public or banks, provides the foundation for the money supply. The public's currency is a component of the money supply and banks must attract some currency, that is, acquire reserves, in order to issue check deposits. No one would accept check deposits if banks held no reserves and deposits were inconvertible into currency. Because they provide the foundation for the money supply, *currency and reserves are called the monetary base.*[4]

$$\text{Monetary base} \equiv \text{Currency} + \text{Reserves}$$
$$\text{B} \equiv \text{C} + \text{R} \qquad (3\text{--}1)$$

The identity symbol indicates that the above is true by definition. Since reserves are banks' currency holdings, whether in the green paper variety familiar to all or the equivalent deposits at the Fed, the monetary base identity in effect says that total currency is held by either the public or banks. The base in this example equals $200, the value of coins initially minted. Looking back at Figure 3–1, currency and reserves each equal $100. (As shown, writing checks redistributes reserves among banks but has no final effect on total reserves of the banking system.)

Provided bank reserves equal deposits, as has been implicitly assumed so far, the base also equals the money supply. Additional currency is either held by the public or deposited in banks, which do nothing but accept currency. Banks which support their deposits dollar-for-dollar with reserves do not reduce the monetary authority's perfect control of money. In such cases, the money supply equals the base provided by the authorities, and classifying the base as currency and reserves is of little practical importance. But banks no longer are currency warehouses holding 100 percent reserves, that is, reserves equal to deposits. Bankers quickly learned that not everyone simultaneously demands currency or writes checks. *Reserves equal to a fraction of check deposits are adequate.* Bankers perhaps surreptitiously at first and then openly lent the funds deposited and earned interest. Bank loans increase depositors' risk as some loans may become uncollectible. No banker has an incentive to fail, however, and most bankers correctly appraise the credit worthiness of borrowers. To placate depositors disgruntled by risk exposure, banks reduced service charges but still increased earnings from the interest on loans. Fractional reserves introduce additional determinants to the money supply which eliminate the monetary authority's perfect control. Besides the base, the money supply now depends on (1) the division of the base between currency and reserves, and (2) the fraction of reserves held

---

[4] The term *monetary base* is not altogether standard. The St. Louis Federal Reserve Bank adjusts our definition for changes in legally required minimum cash ratios to get what it calls the monetary base. In your outside readings you may encounter the term *high-powered money,* which is the name some give to the monetary base.

against check deposits. The public's relative preference for currency and check deposits determines the composition of the base. The bills in my wallet are counted dollar-for-dollar in the money supply. Reserves are not part of the money supply but check deposits are. Saying that reserves are a fraction of check deposits is equivalent to saying that check deposits are a multiple of reserves. As individuals reduce their currency holdings, banks acquire reserves which support multiple check deposits.

Two balance sheets for the consolidated banking system illustrate these ideas more concretely. We ignore the public's balance sheet, where currency and check deposits appear as assets. The currency component of the money supply is readily calculated by subtracting bank reserves from the base ($200 in this example). The banking system's balance sheet prior to loans and security purchases is shown on line 1. Loans and security purchases are recorded on line 2, which differs in the two balance sheets due to different assumptions about the proceeds of the loan. Figure 3–2 assumes the public prefers currency while Figure 3–3 assumes a preference for deposits.

**FIGURE 3–2**

| Loan Expansion—Public Prefers Currency | | | |
|---|---|---|---|
| (1) | Deposits at Fed | 100 | Check deposits | 100 |
| (2) | Deposits at Fed<br>Loans and securities | −75<br>+75 | | |

**FIGURE 3–3**

| Loan Expansion—Public Prefers Check Deposits | | | |
|---|---|---|---|
| (1) | Deposits at Fed | 100 | Check deposits | 100 |
| (2) | Loans and securities | +300 | Check deposits | +300 |

The $75 reduction in deposits at the Fed reflects an equal currency increase. (Summing lines 1 and 2 of Figure 3–2, reserves equal $25. With a fixed $200 base, currency after the loans equals $175.) *Bank loans and security purchases increase the money supply irrespective of the manner in which the proceeds are held.* The magnitude of the money increase depends on the public's assessment of the relative desirability of currency and check deposits.

Figure 3–2 assumes the proceeds of the loan are held in cash. Of course, the borrower probably does not hold the cash; few people borrow and pay interest simply to hold cash. The borrower pays others, who hold cash. Clearly, if the public requested cash equal to the amount lent, the maximum loan expansion and money supply increase is $100. Banks cannot lend more currency than they have. According to Figure 3–2, banks lent $75. The money supply is $275, $100 in deposits and $175 in currency. To fulfill the instant repayment in cash promise, banks need to hold some reserves. In this case banks believe a 25 percent ratio of reserves to check deposits is adequate.

Provided individuals are willing to hold check deposits, the banking system can lend and expand the money supply by $300, as Figure 3–3 assumes. Indeed, the monetary expansion could be even larger. At this point many may think bankers have suddenly been granted godly or at least magical powers of creating something from nothing. Far from it. Look at the transaction again. The banking system acquires pieces of paper saying people will pay it $300 in exchange for banks' promises to pay $300, in cash and on demand. Loans and deposit expansion are nothing more than exchanges of one type of debt for another. Individuals pay banks interest for the privilege of exchanging their debt, called loans and securities, for bank debt, called check deposits, because other people find bank debt more attractive. Banks attempt to minimize the risk of holding their debt, send monthly statements to lenders (depositors), allow transfer of their debt, promise to repay the debt on demand, and in other ways make bank debt attractive. Provided individuals continue to find bank debt attractive and, therefore, hold check deposits, banks can acquire earning assets. Indeed, if individuals found bank debt so attractive that they never wanted additional cash, banks could expand loans and deposits without limit. You too could purchase anything you wanted provided people were willing to accept your IOUs and never requested repayment.

Figures 3–2 and 3–3 illustrate *the negative relationship between the currency/check deposit ratio and the money supply.* As just stated, the currency ratio is 7/4 ($175/$100) in Figure 3–2, and the money supply is $275. In Figure 3–3, the lower currency ratio of 1/4 ($100/$400) leads to a $500 money supply. While $1 in currency uses up $1 of the base, $1 in check deposits uses up less than $1 of the base. Any given base provided by the Fed can support a larger money supply when the public prefers check deposits to currency.

Since Figures 3–2 and 3–3 were designed to show the importance of the cash ratio, the ratio of reserves to check deposits was purposely the same (25 percent) in both cases. *Banks' desired reserve fraction against check deposits is an additional determinant of the money supply. The desired reserve fraction is negatively related to the money supply.* As banks believe that lower reserves are adequate, they make additional loans and the money supply increases. What determines the reserve fraction or, equivalently, what determines the check deposit multiple? Four factors influence the amount of check deposits that can be supported by some given quantity of reserves. First, the Fed sets legal minimum reserve ratios, constraining the maximum quantity of check deposits. Banks do not take the legal reserve ratio lightly; punishment for repeatedly violating reserve requirements is fairly severe. Second, the maximum multiple need not prevail, however, because banks may well choose to hold reserves in excess of legal minimum requirements. As was indicated, banks hold reserves to meet deposit withdrawals. This is true whether or not banks are legally required to do so. If banks expect large deposit withdrawals, their reserves will exceed legal requirements. Looking at the other side of the coin (no pun intended), a given amount of reserves can support less check deposits when banks demand large excess reserves in anticipation of withdrawals.

Third, bankers realize that the demand for check deposits is limited. Like most other producers, bankers offer a diversified product line in order to maximize size and profits. The other bank liabilities subject to reserve requirements shall be given the generic name *time deposit*. That is, check deposits are the money liabilities and time deposits are the non-money liabilities subject to reserve requirements. We choose this name because the Fed has traditionally set required reserves on at least some of what are legally time deposits. However, on occasion the Fed has set required reserves on bank Eurodollar borrowings, RPs, and federal funds borrowings, so time deposits have taken an expanded meaning. Some reserves must be used to support time deposits, by definition, making less reserves available to support check deposits. Therefore, any given *total* amount of reserves can support a smaller quantity of check deposits when banks issue time deposits. Check deposits are a smaller multiple of reserves, or the fraction of reserves to check deposits rises. This is true even if the reserve ratio on time deposits is less than the check deposit reserve ratio. So long as any reserves are necessary to support time deposits, which are not money, the base available for currency and check deposits must be reduced. The reserves necessary for nonmoney purposes depend positively and, therefore, check deposits and money depend negatively on (a) the public's relative preference for time and check deposits and (b) the required reserve ratio on time deposits. Factors (a) and (b) are the third and fourth determinants of the total reserve fraction.

Let us summarize what the commonsense approach to the quantity of money tells us. The monetary base, defined as currency held by the public plus reserves, may be viewed as total currency since bank reserve deposits at the Fed are equivalent to currency. If the Fed or Treasury increases the base, then the quantity of money increases, other things being equal. The extent of the money supply increase depends on who ends up with the base. If all the additional base is held by the public, then the currency component of the money supply increases by the same amount. This extreme situation is most unlikely; some of the currency will find its way into the hand of bankers who use currency (reserves) to support a multiple quantity of check deposits. Legal requirements against check deposits, banks desired excess reserves due to anticipated withdrawals and other factors, the public's relative preference for time and check deposits, and the required reserve ratio against time deposits determine the quantity of check deposit supported by bank reserves.

The monetary base is a dollar magnitude while all other determinants of the money supply are pure numbers. We shall see that all the nonbase determinants can be incorporated in a term called the *multiplier,* a pure number greater than one. The money supply, M, can be expressed as the product of the multiplier, m, and the base, B.

$$M = m \cdot B$$

Thus, the money supply multiplier depends on (1) the division of the base between the public and banks, which reflects the public's relative preference for currency and check deposits, (2) banks' legal reserve requirements against check deposits, (3) desired excess reserves, (4) the public's relative preference for time and check deposits, and (5) the required reserve ratio against time deposits.

## OPEN-MARKET OPERATIONS AND DISCOUNTS

This and the next chapter emphasize the money supply multiplier. We assume the monetary base is exogenously determined by Fed policy. How does the Fed vary the base? Although we cannot simultaneously analyze the multiplier and base in detail, some knowledge about base changes is desirable before further discussion of the multiplier. We limit ourselves here to two Fed policy tools; a more complete analysis of other sources of the monetary base is postponed until Chapter 10.

You may have received the impression that the Fed increases the base by cranking a money machine. While the Fed does not act quite so crudely, the impression is basically correct. Changes in the monetary base are accomplished largely through open-market operations, which is a fancy name for Fed purchases and sales of securities, typically Treasury bills or other short-term Treasury securities. The side of the transaction from the Fed's viewpoint determines whether there is an open-market sale or purchase. That is, if the Fed buys a security, and a bank or individual sells the security, an open-market purchase has occurred. Conversely, sales of securities by the Fed are called open-market sales. Payment for open-market purchases is made by a check *issued by the Fed on itself.* The Fed does not need to own anything *before* buying securities or any other item. That is the beauty of being the money producer. The security seller may well accept larger deposits at the Fed, which are equivalent to currency. If this is unacceptable, the Fed will cash the check by printing money.

Open-market purchases increase the monetary base while sales decrease the base. Figure 3–4 illustrates the effect of an open-market purchase on the balance sheets of the Fed and banking system. Suppose the Fed buys $20 worth of Treasury securities (through a dealer) from banks.

**FIGURE 3–4  Open-Market Purchase from (1) Banks and (2) the Public**

| | Banking System | | | |
|---|---|---|---|---|
| (1) | Deposits at Fed | +20 | | |
| | Treasury securities | −20 | | |
| (2) | Deposits at Fed | +20 | Check deposits | +20 |

| | Federal Reserve | | | |
|---|---|---|---|---|
| (1) | Treasury securities | +20 | Deposits of banks | +20 |
| (2) | Treasury securities | +20 | Deposits of banks | +20 |

This transaction is shown on line 1.[5] Payment for open-market purchases is made by a check issued by the Fed on itself which banks deposit. The open-market purchases increase the reserve component of the base. The Fed need not own anything before buying securities or any other item. This fact is somewhat obscured because banks usually collect from the Fed—the bankers' bank—by having their accounts credited. Were preferences to change because, say, the security was stolen and a trip to Brazil was anticipated, the Fed will cash its check by cranking a money machine, clearly revealing to all that it is a fiat money producer.

Suppose the Fed purchased the securities from individuals instead of banks. Individuals deposit the Fed's check at banks, which credit check deposits and collect the proceeds of the check by maintaining larger deposits at the Fed. See the transactions entered on line 2 of Figure 3–4. If the Fed sells rather than buys securities, the entries are the same except that signs are reversed, that is, substitute − for + and vice versa.

The effect of an open-market purchase on the Fed's balance sheet is independent of the seller. The same is not true for the banking system, at least initially. In either case reserves increase, but purchases from banks reduce their securities while purchases from the public immediately increase deposits. The reader is warned not to make much of this initial difference. Ultimately, after the banks and the public have had a chance to react to the increase in reserves, the money supply increase is independent of the identity of the seller. This is not surprising. Since the Fed does not know who sells securities, its control over the money supply would be

---

[5] One can think of securities dealers forwarding the Fed's check to the selling banks.

poor indeed if the particular seller mattered. The money supply depends on the monetary base; how or why the base was created has no ultimate effect.

The discount mechanism is a second source of the monetary base. Banks can borrow from the Federal Reserve. To make this sound more esoteric, the Fed says it has accommodated a bank with a discount.[6] The Fed is not altogether accommodating; it does not make interest-free loans. The Fed states that its loans to banks should be called discounts and, for consistency, refers to the interest rate on these loans as the discount rate. The Fed sets the discount rate and accommodates banks' demand, within limits to be discussed later. Thus, discounting is at the discretion of banks. Banks determine the volume of borrowing from the Fed at the given discount rate. Figure 3–5 illustrates a $20 increase in discounts.

**FIGURE 3–5  Discounts**

| Banking System | | | |
|---|---|---|---|
| Deposits at Fed | +20 | Discounts at Fed | +20 |

| Federal Reserve | | | |
|---|---|---|---|
| Discounts to banks | +20 | Deposits of banks | +20 |

The Fed credits a bank's deposit account by the amount of the discount. Discounting like open-market purchases from banks has no immediate impact on the money supply. Neither check deposits nor currency increases directly. Discounts clearly are negatively related to the discount rate. Banks borrow less when the discount rate is high. Any further discussion of the determinants of discounting and the relative advantages of open-market operations versus the discount mechanism must be postponed. We simply needed to show how the monetary base can be changed.

### SUMMARY

Stripped to essentials, open-market operations illustrate a fiat money producer's power to purchase whatever it may wish by cranking the press. The Fed purchases only government-issued securities, unlike some fiat money producers whose tastes are more catholic. While payment for

---

[6] In fairness to the Fed it must be stated that even before the Fed's existence the term *discount* was, and still is, widely used in banking circles to designate a type of loan where interest is prepaid. The public cannot borrow at the Fed except in extreme situations.

the security is made by check, Fed checks drawn against itself are equivalent to currency. Security sellers often prefer a credit (deposit) to Fed currency, obscuring the power of the Fed. Were preferences to change, the Fed would pay its creditors (depositors) by cranking the big green machine. Bank deposits at the Fed, called reserves, plus currency are the monetary base.

The marketing skill of bankers often is unrecognized. No one must hold check deposits any more than savings and loan deposits or Fly-by-Night Company stock. If individuals believed that check deposits were completely inferior, the money supply would equal the currency base provided by the Fed. Bankers must sell their products like any other producer. At rock concerts you slip a $10 bill to someone in a cage and receive an admission ticket. You do something similar in a bank. You receive a deposit slip instead of an admission ticket. People purchase check deposits because they are safe and convenient. The composition of the monetary base and the diversity of bank products reflects the marketing skill of banks. Greater preferences for checks reduce currency and provide banks with reserves.[7] This has a powerful effect on the money supply. Banks no longer are secured vaults with reserves equal to their deposits. Bankers learned long ago that fractional reserves are adequate. In other words, check deposits are a multiple of reserves. Check deposits and the money supply are positively related to the reserves banks attract and negatively related to the reserve-check deposit fraction deemed adequate. Bankers' need to hold reserves against a diverse product line of nonmoney items reduces the money supply.

**QUESTIONS**

1.  Assume the First National Bank (FNB) sells $25,000 of securities to:
    a.  A depositor of FNB who pays by check.
    b.  A depositor of FNB who pays in cash (currency).
    c.  A nonbank corporation.
    d.  Another bank.
    e.  The Federal Reserve.
    What is the effect of each of the five transactions above on the reserves of (1) FNB and (2) the entire banking system? If not enough information is given for the answer to be certain, state what additional information is necessary.
2.  Define the monetary base.
3.  When did the money supply equal the monetary base? Is the money supply greater than, equal to, or less than the monetary base today?
4.  What is the (1) immediate and (2) ultimate impact on the money supply of the deposit of currency?

---

[7] The next chapter initially assumes banks are so skillful that no one wants currency. Of course, the assumption is unrealistic but a convenient starting point.

5. Under what conditions can the new loans extended by the banking system exceed its cash holdings?

6. What factors besides the monetary base and the public's preference for currency determine the money supply?

7. Define open-market operations. Show the effect on the balance sheets of the Fed and commercial banks of a $100 open-market sale to an individual who pays for the security by writing a check.

8. What is the immediate impact of discounts at the Fed on (1) reserves and (2) the money supply?

# Determinants of the money supply: The multiplier

4

To get more precise estimates of the effect of various factors, let us now formalize the commonsense approach to the quantity of money presented in Chapter 3. Begin by writing the definition of money in algebraic form.

$$M \equiv C + DC \qquad (4\text{--}1)$$

The money supply equals currency, C, plus adjusted check deposits, DC instead of the seemingly more natural CD because CD is the well known abbreviation for certificates of deposit. The identity symbol (three parallel lines) shows the equation holds at all times by definition. Temporarily ignore the adjustments made to total check deposits, such as subtracting Treasury deposits at commercial banks, since the adjustments are relatively minor. The most important relationship in determining the quantity of money is the equilibrium condition for the monetary base.

$$B^s = R^d + C^d \qquad (4\text{--}2)$$

To emphasize that equation (4–2) is an *equilibrium* condition, the equality notation and superscripts s and d are used. The base was defined in Chapter 3 as reserves plus currency. We are not repeating ourselves; equation (4–2) does not state a definition true at all times. Just as the peanut market is in equilibrium when the demand and supply for peanuts are equal, the market for the monetary base is in equilibrium when the supply of the base, $B^s$, provided by the Fed and Treasury, equals the demand for the base by banks, (reserves, $R^d$) and the public (currency, $C^d$). The importance of this equilibrium condition in the money supply process stems from the fact that if supply and demand for the base are not equal, then balance sheet adjustments by banks cause monetary changes. *The actual quantity of money equals the (equilibrium) money supply only when the monetary base market is in equilibrium.*[1] The validity of the last two sentences cannot be proven rigorously at this point but is supported by the subsequent analysis of adjustment processes and empirical observation.

At times we may wish to focus on the equilibrium change rather than the level of the money supply. Similar equations hold,

$$\Delta M \equiv \Delta C + \Delta DC \qquad (4-1')$$

$$\Delta B^s = \Delta R^d + \Delta C^d \qquad (4-2')$$

where $\Delta$ is the symbol for change or, technically speaking, the first difference. The equilibrium money supply change, which is the sum of the currency and check deposit change, occurs only when the change in the base provided by the Fed and Treasury equals the change in the demand for reserves and currency.

Equations (4–1) and (4–2), or the corresponding equations for change, are the two central equations of money supply theory. One always begins with these two equations. Throughout this chapter the supply of the base is exogenously determined by the authorities. The basic problem is determining the demand for the base, which is set equal to the given supply of the base. The demand for the base incorporates the various determinants of the money supply discussed in Chapter 3. For example, the demand depends on legal reserve ratios. To highlight the effect of each determinant, we begin with a simple model and introduce one determinant at a time.

## MONEY SUPPLY MODEL I

$$DER = 0, C = 0, \text{ and } TD = 0$$

As just stated, this and all subsequent models begin with the money supply definition and the equilibrium condition in the market for the base, i.e., equations (4–1) and (4–2). Albeit unrealistic, let us assume that individuals do not hold any currency—banks are master marketers—and check deposits are the only liabilities of banks. There are no time deposits, $TD = 0$, or other bank liabilities. Ignoring superscripts, with $C = 0$ the two basic equations become

$$M \equiv DC \qquad (4-1.1)$$

$$B = R \qquad (4-2.1)$$

The money supply and check deposits coincide, given our assumptions. Deleting the superscripts makes the equation look less cluttered but the

---

[1] To emphasize that the actual *quantity* of money need not equal the money *supply* and that the money supply is the outcome of an optimization process involving banks and the public instead of being mechanically determined, we often refer to the "equilibrium" money supply.

reader should not forget that B stands for the exogenous supply of the base and R represents the demand for reserves. The two are equal only at equilibrium. The Fed imposes required reserve ratios, or minimum ratios of reserves to check deposits. For simplicity, assume a uniform reserve ratio for all banks. In this model banks hold reserves only to meet the legal requirements. Desired excess reserves are zero, DER = 0. Thus the demand for reserves is a fraction of the check deposits supplied by the banks; the fraction equals the required reserve ratio, $r_c$, set by the Fed.

$$R = r_c DC \qquad (4\text{--}3.1)$$

Set the demand for reserves expressed by equation (4–3.1) equal to a given base supply, B.

$$B = r_c DC, \text{ or } DC = B/r_c \qquad (4\text{--}4.1)$$

Given the assumptions that individuals do not hold currency, time deposits do not exist, and banks demand reserves simply to satisfy legal requirements, equation (4–4.1) is a specific example of the general equation (4–2).

Substituting in equation (4–1.1) gives the equilibrium money supply.[2]

$$M = DC = \frac{1}{r_c} \cdot B \qquad (4\text{--}5.1)$$

Since $r_c$ is less than one, $1/r_c$ is a multiple, that is, a number greater than one. The money supply always is the product of a multiplier times the base. Given the assumptions of this model, the multiplier is $1/r_c$. Please take note, however, that the money supply multiplier does *not* always equal $1/r_c$ but depends on the assumptions made.

Equation (4–5.1) is the naive money supply relationship of your typical principles course, where it is assumed the Fed and Treasury can peg the money supply at whatever amount they wish. Looking at the equation shows that the money supply is negatively related to the required reserve ratio. If the Fed cuts the reserve ratio in half, the money supply doubles.[3] The reserve ratio is easily changed; the Fed simply announces that henceforth the reserve ratio is, say, two percentage points higher. Nevertheless, the Fed rarely changes reserve ratios. Changes in the base largely explain money stock changes. The change or first difference form of the last equation is

$$\Delta M = \frac{1}{r_c} \Delta B \qquad (4\text{--}5.1')$$

---

[2] The reader may wonder why at this point we use the equality notation in the money supply equation. The reason is simple: we made use of the equilibrium condition $B = r_c DC$. Assuming individuals do not hold currency, the money supply always equals check deposits. Only at equilibrium does it equal $B/r_c$.

[3] Since we always will consider one change at a time, the qualifying phrase "other things being equal" is unnecessary. Throughout this chapter we assume that a change in one variable on the right-hand side of the equation will not cause another variable on the same side to change.

If the reserve ratio is 20 percent (.20), according to equation (4–5.1) the money stock is five times the base, and from equation (4–5.1′) the same relationship holds for changes in the base.

The naive model is a convenient starting point, but only that. Our main quarrel is its false implication of precision. Even if currency and time deposits do not exist and banks do not want any excess reserves, the Fed cannot control the money supply exactly because the required reserve ratio is not uniform. Prior to 1980 the Fed regulated the reserves of its members alone. Nonmember banks were regulated by state banking commissions, which set reserve ratios much lower than the Fed did. One of the main purposes of the Monetary Control Act (MCA) of 1980 was to eliminate the diversity of reserve ratios. MCA made all issuers of check deposits, including nonbanks such as savings and loans, subject to the Fed's reserve requirement policies. However, the new universal provision is being adopted gradually. Depositories brought under the Fed's regulations by MCA have until 1987 before their requirements will equal member bank requirements. Even then, reserve ratios will *not* be uniform. The reserve ratio will continue to be higher for large banks than for small banks.[4]

When many reserve ratios exist, "the" reserve ratio can only be an average reserve ratio. Assuming n classes of required reserve ratios, the total dollar demand for reserves is the sum of the demands by the n classes. Algebraically

$$R = \sum_{1=1}^{n} r_{ci} DC_i = \sum_{i=1}^{n} r_{ci} \frac{DC_i}{DC} DC$$

where the second equality clearly follows since $DC/DC = 1$. Comparing the last equation with equation (4–3.1), "the" reserve ratio $r_c$ is a weighted average of the n reserve ratios, where the weights for the ith class is its share of total check deposits, $DC_i/DC$. Individuals decide where to bank. When individuals currently transfer their deposits from member to nonmember banks with low reserve requirements, or when individuals currently or after 1987 transfer deposits from large to small banks with low reserve ratio, then the average required reserve ratio falls and the money supply expands. The Fed and the public jointly determine the average reserve ratio.

The numerical examples that follow will assume reserve requirements are uniform and thereby ignore aggregation effects.

## MONEY SUPPLY ADJUSTMENTS: AN AGGREGATE VIEW

A specific example illustrates best the money supply adjustment process. The initial balance sheets of all banks are consolidated and shown on

---

[4] The cut-off point between small and large banks and technical aspects of reserve requirement policy are discussed in Chapter 11.

**FIGURE 4-1  Consolidated banking system**

(1) Initial equilibrium, (2) Open-market purchase,
(3) Loan and deposit expansion, and (4) Final equilibrium,
sum of lines (1)–(3).

| | | | | |
|---|---|---|---|---|
| (1) | Deposits at Fed | 100 | Check deposits | 500 |
| | Loans and securities | 400 | | |
| (2) | Deposits at Fed | +20 | | |
| | Loans and securities | −20 | | |
| (3) | Loans and securities | +100 | Check deposits | +100 |
| (4) | Deposits at Fed | 120 | Check deposits | 600 |
| | Loans and securities | 480 | | |

Figure 4–1, line 1. Temporarily ignore lines 2 and 3. The assumptions of the last section still hold. Assuming a 20 percent required reserve ratio, the demand for required reserves, $100, equals the amount available, and the banking system is in equilibrium. Line 2 records a $20 open-market purchase from commercial banks which increases reserves to $120. According to our formula the new equilibrium money supply is $600, or, equivalently, the money supply increases by $100. Let us see why this is so and how the equilibrium is reached.

Total reserves, R, can be divided into required reserves, RR, and reserves not required by law, which are conventionally called excess reserves, ER.

$$R \equiv RR + ER \qquad (4\text{--}6)$$

This identity will be used often. We might even dignify it and call it the third basic relationship of the money supply process. Because of its importance, and because one usually solves the equation for excess reserves, rewrite it as follows:

$$ER \equiv R - RR \qquad (4\text{--}6')$$

Immediately after the open-market purchase total reserves in this example are $120, required reserves are $100 (.2 × $500), and excess reserves equal $20. But by assumption banks demand reserves only to meet the legal requirements. Therefore, the $20 of excess reserves is undesired and banks cannot be at equilibrium. Banks will adjust their balance sheets to eliminate the $20 of unwanted excess reserves. It might appear the adjustment entails either a decrease in total reserves or an increase in required reserves totaling $20. However, our assumption precludes a decrease in total reserves. Remember that bank reserves, whether held as vault cash or deposits at the Fed, are equivalent to currency. If the public does not want to hold any currency, banks cannot lose any reserves. The entire adjustment process involves an increase in required reserves. How does this come about? Banks make loans or purchase securities worth

$100 and credit the check deposits of the public by an equivalent amount. These transactions are shown on line 3 of Figure 4–1. With check deposits now equal to $600, banks want reserves of $120. An equilibrium has been reached; unwanted excess reserves of the banking system have been eliminated. The equilibrium money supply change is $100 ($600 − $500). This is precisely what our formulas (4–5.1) and (4–5.1′) say. In this example, $r_c$ = .2, B = 120, and ΔB = 20. Therefore, M = 600 and ΔM = 100.

The following sketch without balance sheets shows that the same conclusion holds when the Fed purchases securities from the public. Recall that the immediate impact of a $20 open-market purchase from the public is an equal increase in reserves and check deposits. Required reserves on the deposits are $4 in our example. Excess reserves are $16. How are these unwanted excess reserves eliminated? Banks make loans and credit checking accounts by $80. The total money supply changes by $100 ($20 + $80).

## INDIVIDUAL BANK ADJUSTMENTS

Approximately 14,700 banks make up the banking system. What role does an individual bank play in the adjustment process? Assume all banks except one are in equilibrium. The $20 of excess reserves is concentrated in bank A, from which the Fed bought a Treasury security.

**Bank A:**

(1) Initial equilibrium, (2) Open-market purchase, (3) Loan expansion, and (4) Induced deposit withdrawals

| | | | | |
|---|---|---|---|---|
| (1) | Deposits at Fed | 8 | Check deposits | 40 |
| | Loans and securities | 32 | | |
| (2) | Deposits at Fed | +20 | | |
| | Loans and securities | −20 | | |
| (3) | Loans and securities | +100 | Check deposits | +100 |
| (4) | Deposits at Fed | −100 | Check deposits | −100 |

The initial position of bank A and the open-market purchase are shown by the top two lines of its balance sheet. Continue to assume the required reserve ratio is 20 percent. Total reserves are $28 and required reserves are $8, so excess reserves are $20. Can bank A loan $100 and credit the check deposit accounts of its customer? (Remember we are assuming individuals do not hold currency so the proceeds of bank loans must result in increased check deposits.) Bank A could make such a loan, as shown on the third line of the balance sheet, and *temporarily* at least it would still meet the legal requirement. Check deposits now are $140 and reserves are $28, which is 20 percent of deposits and just what the Fed requires. However, an important word in the penultimate sentence is "temporarily.'' In the very near future bank A will be drastically short of reserves. Do individuals borrow and pay interest on their loans in order to keep check deposits sitting in the bank? Of course not. An individual borrows in order to buy something. When the individual writes a check to purchase something, the seller of the item will deposit the check in a bank. But which bank? With 14,700 banks the probability is virtually nil that the check will be deposited in bank A. The person who receives the check almost certainly has an account in another bank, called bank B. The final effect on the balance sheet of a $100 check drawn on bank A and deposited at bank B is shown on the fourth line. *Bank reserve losses due to payment of depositors' checks are called clearing-house drains.*

Bank A would be deeply embarrassed if it made a $100 loan. After borrowers spend the proceeds, the Fed would quickly note that payment of the check would overdraw bank A's account by $72. (Bank A's deposits at the Fed are $28, but it is supposed to pay bank B $100 on behalf of its customer.) Failure to meet reserve requirements is bad enough but overdrawing an account is grounds for closure. The Fed does not extend overdrafts! Asking customers to repay recently made loans may be impossible and, in any case, will hardly enhance good will. While bank A may once have considered only the temporary effect of its loans and ignored the final effect, by now it has learned not to loan $100 when its excess reserves are $20. An increase in bank loans or security holdings is almost immediately followed by an equal decrease in reserves. Therefore, deposit expansion by a single bank is limited by its excess reserves.[5] Erase lines 3 and 4 in the previous balance sheet. Bank A will loan only $20 in this example. The effect of this transaction on the balance sheets of banks A and B after the loan proceeds have been spent and checks have cleared is shown below.

**Bank A**

| | | | | |
|---|---|---|---|---|
| (3) | Loans and securities | +20 | Check deposits | +20 |
| (4) | Deposits at Fed | −20 | Check deposits | −20 |

**Bank B**

| | | | | |
|---|---|---|---|---|
| (4) | Deposits at Fed | +20 | Check deposits | +20 |

This is not the end of the story, however. While bank A is now in equilibrium, bank B is not. Bank B with $20 in new deposits requires $4 in additional reserves. Since it has acquired $20 in reserves, $16 represents

---

[5] This conclusion generally is independent of the type of asset acquired with the excess reserves. Suppose bank A placed an order to buy government securities instead of making loans. The people who sold securities most likely have accounts at other banks. When the sellers deposit bank A's check (called a cashier's check) at their bank and the check clears, we get the previous balance sheet.

unwanted excess reserves which can be lent to customers. The loan and subsequent payment by the borrower to a depositor at another bank, called bank C, is recorded next.

**Bank B**

| | | | |
|---|---|---|---|
| Loans and securities | +16 | Check deposits | +16 |
| Deposits at Fed | −16 | Check deposits | −16 |

**Bank C**

| | | | |
|---|---|---|---|
| Deposits at Fed | +16 | Check deposits | +16 |

Bank C now is in a disequilibrium position, and the adjustment process continues, affecting, in turn, banks D, E, F, and so on. The role played by each bank in the expansion process is shown in Table 4–1. In general, the

TABLE 4–1 Summary of deposit expansion process by individual banks, no cash or time deposits*

| Banks | New deposits created by | New loans made by | New deposits retained by | Reserves retained as required reserves by |
|---|---|---|---|---|
| A | 20.00 | 20.00 | — | — |
| B | 16.00 | 16.00 | 20.00 | 4.00 |
| C | 12.80 | 12.80 | 16.00 | 3.20 |
| D | 10.24 | 10.24 | 12.80 | 2.56 |
| E | 8.19 | 8.19 | 10.24 | 2.05 |
| F | 6.55 | 6.55 | 8.19 | 1.64 |
| G | 5.24 | 5.24 | 6.55 | 1.31 |
| H | 4.19 | 4.19 | 5.24 | 1.05 |
| I | 3.35 | 3.35 | 4.19 | 0.84 |
| J | 2.68 | 2.68 | 3.35 | 0.67 |
| All other | 10.76 | 10.76 | 13.44 | 2.68 |
| Total by entire banking system | 100.00 | 100.00 | 100.00 | 20.00 |

* Numbers have been rounded.

expansion at the first step in this sequence is $\Delta B$, and the expansion at each step equals the expansion in the previous step times the constant $(1 - r_c)$. The cumulative process may be represented by a geometric series.

$$
\begin{aligned}
\Delta M &= \Delta B + \Delta B(1 - r_c) + \Delta B(1 - r_c)^2 + \cdots + \Delta B(1 - r_c)^n \\
&= \Delta B[1 + (1 - r_c) + (1 - r_c)^2 + \cdots + (1 - r_c)^n] \\
&= 20[1 + .8 + .64 + \cdots + (.8)^n]
\end{aligned}
$$

But as n, the number of rounds in the expansion process, becomes sufficiently large, the value of such a series which decreases proportionally at each round approaches:[6]

$$\Delta M = \frac{\Delta B}{1 - (1 - r_c)} = \frac{\Delta B}{r_c} = \frac{\$20}{.2} = \$100$$

An optimist prefers an expansionary situation. A pessimist explaining a contraction would arrive at the same general result. Suppose bank Z's total reserves are $20 less than required. This bank almost certainly would cover the reserve shortage by selling only $20 of securities. The purchaser of the securities quite probably has an account at another bank, bank Y, and bank Z collects by having its account at the Fed credited by $20. Of course, at the same time the Fed credits the account of bank Z it debits the account of bank Y, which now is short $16 in required reserves, or has excess reserves of $−16. Reserves at bank Y decreased by $20, but the check deposits of its customers also fell by the same amount, reducing required reserves by $4. The public reduces its checking balances by another $16 to buy the securities sold by bank Y. The story continues but you can anticipate the punch line. Many banks are involved before equilibrium is reached. Equilibrium often will be reached quite rapidly but at other times the lags are quite long.

Why can a single bank create check deposits only equal to its excess reserves while the banking system expands by a multiple of the excess reserves? The public wants to hold check deposits—indeed in this example it holds nothing else—but it it does not want all its deposits at a single bank. From the viewpoint of a single bank, the clearing-house drain equals the increase in loans and newly created deposits, but the entire banking system faces no clearing-house drain, by assumption. The reserves lost by one bank become the reserves of another bank. With banking system reserves fixed, multiple deposit expansion is necessary to transform the initial excess reserves into required reserves.

In subsequent sections the adjustment made by each bank in the expansion process generally is ignored because we are mainly interested in aggregate changes. The surveyor uses his chain to measure your property. To check the accuracy of his chain, the surveyor measures each link with a ruler and adds the measurements. Having done this once, he discards the ruler. We follow the same principle.

---

[6] Let $A = \Delta B[1 + (1 - r_c) + (1 - r_c)^2 + \cdots (1 - r_c)^n]$.
Then, $(1 - r_c)A = \Delta B[(1 - r_c) + (1 - r_c)^2 + \cdots + (1 - r_c)^n + (1 - r_c)^{n+1}]$.
Subtracting, $A - (1 - r_c)A = \Delta B[1 - (1 - r_c)^{n+1}]$.
Dividing by $r_c$, $A = \Delta B[1 - (1 - r_c)^{n+1}]/r_c$
As $n + 1$ becomes very large, $(1 - r_c)^{n+1}$ approaches zero since $(1 - r_c) < 1$.

$$\lim_{n \to \infty} \Delta B[1 - (1 - r_c)^{n+1}]/r_c = \Delta B/r_c$$

## MONEY SUPPLY MODEL II

$$C = 0 \text{ and } TD = 0$$

Bank depositors are fickle. They are continually writing checks and making deposits. As we saw in the last section, the change in check deposits *and* reserves at any one bank equals the difference between checks drawn on and payable to other banks.[7] Assuming a bank's depositors are writing more checks than they are depositing so that there is a negative net clearing balance, required reserves fall by only a fraction of the decrease in deposits and reserves. Since total reserves decrease more than required reserves, a bank without excess reserves would no longer meet the legal requirements and would have to sell liquid assets or gain reserves in some other way. A bank with sufficient excess reserve would avoid the bother and cost of selling assets. What is sufficient? Suppose the required reserve ratio is 20 percent and a bank suffers net check deposit withdrawals of $1. The deposit loss reduces reserves by an equal amount, and required reserves fall by 20¢. How much excess reserves does a bank need in order to avoid selling liquid assets? Continue if you said 80¢; otherwise, reread this paragraph. A bank cannot anticipate its deposit losses with certainty. Indeed, it may not even be sure that it will lose deposits as the bank's depositors could receive more checks than they issue. Nevertheless, there always exists some possibility of a deposit loss and the possible deposit losses are positively related to bank size. During the next week depositors might withdraw $100,000 from the First National Bank of Podunk. The Third National Bank of New York would not be altogether surprised if deposits fell $10 million tomorrow. As a first approximation then assume the amount of desired excess reserve, DER, is some fraction, $r_{ec}$, of check deposits.

$$DER = r_{ec} \cdot DC \qquad (4-7)$$

The fraction $r_{ec}$ is the desired excess reserve ratio, as dividing both sides of equation (4–7) by DC confirms. While the discussion has been phrased in terms of a single bank, summing over banks yields a similar relationship between aggregate desired excess reserves and deposits.

How does the introduction of a demand for excess reserves alter the money supply equations? Continuing to assume that the public does not want any currency, the two basic equations are:

$$M = DC \qquad (4-1.2)$$

$$B = R \qquad (4-2.2)$$

Similar to the preceeding case so far. The difference lies in the demand for reserves, which is now made up of two components: (1) the demand for

---

[7] If the issuer of a check and the depositor have accounts at the same banks, total check deposits and reserves are unchanged. One account is debited, and the other credited.

required reserves to meet the law, and (2) the demand for excess reserves to meet possible deposit outflows without having to sell securities or borrow.

$$R = r_c DC + r_{ec} DC \qquad (4\text{--}3.2)$$

Perform the substitutions shown in Case I. That is, set the demand for reserves expressed by equation (4–3.2) equal to a given base supply B. One gets

$$B = r_c DC + r_{ec} DC, \qquad (4\text{--}4.2)$$

$$M = DC = \frac{1}{r_c + r_{ec}} \cdot B \qquad (4\text{--}5.2)$$

Case I could be viewed as a specific example of Case II where $r_{ec} = 0$. In this slightly more general case the money supply multiplier is $1/(r_c + r_{ec})$, which clearly is smaller than $1/r_c$. Suppose $r_c = .20$ and $r_{ec} = .05$. If the monetary authorities increase the base by $20, by how much does the money supply change?

$$\Delta M = \frac{1}{r_c + r_{ec}} \cdot \Delta B = \frac{1}{.2 + .05} \cdot \$20 = \$80$$

The money supply would have increased $100 if banks had not wanted any excess reserves. Since the required reserve ratio and the desired excess reserve ratio appear additively in the denominator, a reduction in either is expansionary, and vice versa. Note that the reason why banks hold reserves has no effect whatever on the money supply; what matters is the total proportion of reserves to deposits that banks demand. Let the Federal Reserve increase reserves by 5 percentage points while, *by chance,* banks' desired excess reserve ratio falls by 5 percentage points.[8] What happens to the money supply? Nothing. Why? Required reserves plus desired excess reserves are unchanged.

**Commercial Banking System**

| | | | |
|---|---|---|---|
| Deposits at Fed | | 125 | Deposits | 500 |
| Required reserves | 100 | | | |
| Excess reserves | 25 | | | |
| Desired excess | ? | | | |
| Undesired excess | ? | | | |
| Loans and securities | | 375 | | |

---

[8] Do not for a moment think that an increase in required reserve *causes* desired excess reserves to fall by an equal amount. The Federal Reserve once made this mistake, and the nation suffered greatly, as we shall see shortly.

Recognition of banks' demand for excess reserves is extremely important for monetary policy because it implies that the monetary authorities are unable to control the money supply at all times. Even if the Fed controlled the monetary base exactly and the required reserve ratio were uniform, the money supply would vary in response to the *bank-determined* desired excess reserve ratio. Banks file financial statements. From the statements the Fed can readily make *legal* distinctions between reserves. If the required reserve ratio is 20 percent, required reserves are $100 and excess reserves are $25. *The seemingly mechanical separation of total reserves into required and excess reserves had economic significance when we assumed all excess reserves were undesired.* In such a situation the existence of excess reserves implies that the money supply would increase. Once we admit that banks demand excess reserves, can we state for sure what, if anything, will be happening to the money supply? We now must separate excess reserves, ER, into desired, DER, and undesired excess reserves, UER.

$$ER = DER + UER \qquad (4\text{--}8)$$

With this separation of excess reserves, total reserves may be written as

$$R = RR + DER + UER \qquad (4\text{--}9)$$

It is difficult but essential for economic policy to make the *economic* distinction between required and desired excess reserves on the one hand and undesired excess reserves on the other. If banks demand excess reserves equal to 5 percent of deposits, will the money supply change, given the last balance sheet? No.[9] Reserves are just at the right level. Any adjustment by the system causes the reserve ratio to deviate from the desired value. Now suppose banks' demand changes and they do not want to hold excess reserves. The balance sheet no longer represents an equilibrium. Undesired excess reserves are zero at equilibrium by definition, so deposits and loans expand by $125. At the new equilibrium money supply of $625, banks want $125 in reserves. Deposits increase when the actual reserve ratio is greater than the total desired ratio, which is the sum of the required and desired excess ratios. Of course, if the Fed had realized that the desired excess reserve ratio had fallen, a $25 open-market sale reducing the base or an increase in required reserves to 25 percent would have kept the money supply on course.[10] And if the Fed had given me $1 million, I would be skiing in Davos. The important point is: The Fed's inability to discriminate perfectly between desired and undesired excess reserves causes unintentional, and sometimes disasterous, money changes.

---

[9] Substituting the values of this example in equation (4–5.2), what does the equilibrium money supply equal? 500.

[10] Since $M = DC = 1/(r_c + r_{ec})B$, $M = 500$ when $r_c = .2$, $r_{ec} = .05$, and $B = 125$. If $r_{ec} = 0$, $M = 625$, an increase of 125. To keep $M = 500$, make either $B = 100$ or $r_c = .25$.

## DETERMINANTS OF THE DESIRED EXCESS RESERVE RATIO

What determines the desired excess reserve ratio? Why did banks last year want excess reserves to equal, say, 1 percent of deposits while today they want 2 percent? Banks are uncertain about the behavior of their depositors and, therefore, whether they will be gaining or losing reserves. Many outcomes with different probabilities are possible. The desired excess reserve ratio depends on the distribution of deposit and reserve percentage changes.[11] Figure 4–2 graphs a simple distribution. The percent-

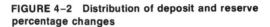

**FIGURE 4–2   Distribution of deposit and reserve percentage changes**

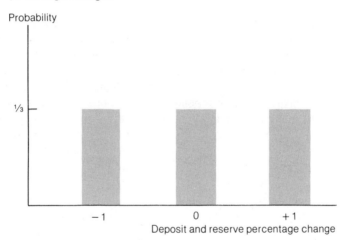

age change in deposits and reserves is plotted on the x-axis, and the y-axis shows the probability of the event. According to Figure 4–2, the three possible outcomes are a one percent loss, no change, and a one percent gain in reserves. Each outcome is equally likely; the probability attached to any one outcome is one third. An important characteristic of the distribution is its expected or average value. The expected value, which is computed by summing the products of the probability times the outcome, is zero in this example. (Expected value = $1/3(-1) + 1/3(0) + 1/3(+1) =$ 0.) Deposits sometimes rise and fall by one percent but remain unchanged on average. *The greater the expected percentage change in deposits, the smaller is the desired excess reserve ratio.* You demand less excess reserves today when you expect reserves and deposits to increase in the near future. Particularly at seashore resorts and other recreational areas, the expected deposit and reserve change varies considerably during the year.

---

[11] The excess reserve *ratio* depends on the *percentage* change in reserves while the amount of excess reserves demanded depends on the dollar change in reserves.

Suppose you were a banker in Ocean City, Maryland. Would you demand less or more excess reserves at the beginning of the summer, before the influx of tourists and temporary workers, than toward the end of the summer? If you said "less" you might just have a future in banking. At the beginning of the summer the expected reserve and deposit percentage change is positive. Tourists bring their money to Ocean City and spend it on services provided by temporary workers who open bank accounts. Banks' demand for excess reserves is extremely low. There simply is no need for excess reserves now as they expect to gain reserves. By late August, however, the expected deposit change is negative, that is, banks expect withdrawals, and banks want large excess reserves. The money leaves Ocean City when the temporary workers close their accounts and go home.

The variability of deposits and reserves, as measured by the range or standard deviation, is an important additional factor. Suppose the three equally likely outcomes are a 5 percent loss, no change, and a 5 percent gain in reserves and deposits. Compared to the situation illustrated by Figure 4–2, the expected or average change still is zero, but deposits are more variable. Wider deposit swings are possible. Again, see whether you would make a good banker. How is the desired excess reserve ratio related to the variability or dispersion of deposits and reserves? A positive relationship exists. Following a series of runs on banks and failures, vague rumors concerning the stability of one bank and then another are much more likely to induce individuals to shift their deposits among banks in hopes of finding a safe bank.[12] At such times banks in general will view their deposits as highly variable, and the aggregate desired excess ratio is high.

The careful reader probably noticed that the justification for desired excess reserves in terms of possible deposit losses was not sufficient. Even if a bank knows with certainty that it will lose reserves tomorrow, why should it hold excess reserves today? A bank could buy liquid assets with the excess reserves today and regain reserves by selling tomorrow. Such a strategy would yield a bank interest income. There is a hitch, however. In buying and selling liquid assets the bank incurs brokerage costs. These costs include the commission paid to security dealers as well as the cost of bank executives' time spent arranging the transaction, which may be substantially more than commission charges. Clearly, brokerage costs must be balanced against the extra income earned by maintaining zero excess reserves and buying and selling liquid assets. Excess reserves are positively related to brokerage cost. It becomes profitable to hold more excess reserves and less liquid assets when brokerage costs are high. At the extreme situation where brokerage costs

---

[12] This was particularly true before deposit insurance. Even now, deposit insurance coverage is limited to $100,000. While relatively few individuals or firms have accounts over $100,000, large uninsured accounts are a substantial proportion of total deposits.

are zero, banks would demand no excess reserves. At another extreme, banks would hold only excess reserves if the rate of interest were zero. As interest rates rise, banks demand less excess reserves because the interest income from liquid assets surpasses brokerage costs. Excess reserves and interest rates are negatively related.

For those who like mathematical expressions, the discussion can be conveniently summarized.

$$r_{ec} = f(\underset{-}{\mu},\ \underset{+}{\sigma},\ \underset{-}{i_m},\ \underset{+}{b})$$

where

$\mu$ = expected or average percentage change in check deposits
$\sigma$ = variability of check deposits
$i_m$ = interest rate on marketable securities
$b$ = brokerage costs

The equation says the excess reserve ratio is a function of or depends on (that's what the letter "f" means) the variables in parentheses. The signs under the variables indicate the direction of the relationship between a variable and the excess reserve ratio. For example, larger expected deposits reduce desired excess reserves.

## DESIRED EXCESS RESERVES IN THE 1930s

Don't think that economists know everything about the desired excess reserve ratio. We know quite a bit, as the last few paragraphs demonstrated, but brokerage costs, interest rates, expected deposit changes, and the variability of deposits do not explain everything. Other factors which still have not been isolated cause the desired excess ratio to change over time. However, the Fed has come a long way since the 1930s when it thought Case I existed—banks demand no excess reserves. Between 1933 and 1936 the unemployment rate fell from 24.9 to 16.9 percent, and the consumer price index (1929 = 100) rose from 75.4 to 80.9. The economy definitely was improving, but by any absolute standard it hardly was a period of prosperity. Nevertheless, the Fed feared that inflation would soon raise its ugly head. Banks were flush with excess reserves, which almost equalled required reserves. If all the excess reserves were undesired, as the Fed thought, the money supply would expand greatly and aggravate the "inflationary" potential of the economy. In a series of bold strokes the Fed doubled reserve requirements between August 16, 1936 and May 1, 1937. Naturally, excess reserves fell. The Fed sadly learned that banks did want large excess reserves. Bank loans and deposits fell because excess reserves, which were still substantial after the reserve requirement increase, were less than the desired amount.

The Fed relented nearly a year later, cutting required reserve ratios somewhat. Largely due to random factors which the Fed chose not to counteract, reserves increased steadily and dramatically. The reserve increase and moderation in requirements placed the money supply back on track by December 1938. Look at Table 4-2. Can you explain the behavior of the excess reserve ratio?

**TABLE 4-2   Check deposits, reserves, and interest rates, 1936-1938**

| Date | 6/30/36 | 12/31/36 | 6/30/37 | 12/31/37 | 6/30/38 | 12/31/38 |
|---|---|---|---|---|---|---|
| Check deposits* ............ | 23,780 | 25,483 | 25,198 | 23,959 | 24,313 | 25,986 |
| Required reserve ratio† ...... | .10 | .15 | .20 | .20 | .175 | .175 |
| Total reserves* .............. | 5,633 | 6,606 | 6,900 | 7,027 | 8,024 | 8,724 |
| Required reserves‡ ......... | 2,916 | 4,622 | 6,035 | 5,815 | 5,149 | 5,519 |
| Excess reserves ............ | 2,717 | 1,984 | 865 | 1,212 | 2,875 | 3,205 |
| Treasury bill rate (percent per year) ......... | 0.226 | 0.209 | 0.561 | .104 | .023 | .007 |
| Excess reserve ratio ......... | .114 | .078 | .034 | .051 | .118 | .123 |

* Deposits and reserves, in $ millions, are for member banks only.
† The second row gives the check deposit required reserve ratio for reserve city banks.
‡ Required reserves include those on both check and time deposits. Therefore, required reserves are greater than the product of check deposits and the check deposit required reserve ratio.
**SOURCE:** Board of Governors of the Federal Reserve System, *Banking and Monetary Statistics* (Washington, D.C., 1943).

Could banks have demanded large amounts of excess reserves in June 1936? Individuals and bankers recalled the 1929–33 debacle. Demand deposits had fallen approximately one third. Expansionary policies by the Fed and Treasury during 1933–36 succeeded in restoring the 1929 level of demand deposits. Could the expansionary policies be temporary? Banks might have been expecting a policy reversal and reserve losses. In any case, confidence in the banking system was hardly at its high point, and banks viewed their deposits as highly variable. The second to last row in Table 4–2 contains no typographical mistake. If you had invested $1,000 in Treasury bills on June 30, 1936 your grant total three months later would have been $1,000.54.[13] Hardly worth the bother. All these factors suggest that desired excess reserves were large, and undesired excess might have been zero. The excess ratio was .114, seemingly just what banks demanded.

The reserve requirement increase between June and December 1936 naturally reduced excess reserves. Perhaps because banks had made prior loan commitments they were unable to reduce check deposits. Compare the first two columns, June 30, 1936, and December 31, 1936. By early 1937 banks started to reduce their check deposits and loans to restore the desired excess reserve ratio. Adjustments take time, however. Banks' attempts to increase excess reserves were counterbalanced by even

---

[13] The interest rates in Table 4–2 are annualized. 0.226 percent per year is equivalent to 0.054 per quarter.

higher required reserve ratios between January and June 1937. The excess reserve ratio continued to decline. Compare columns 2 and 3. Undesired excess reserves were negative or, equivalently, the desired excess ratio was greater than the actual ratio. In the fall of 1937 the Fed maintained high required reserve ratios but did not raise them further. Banks continued to contract and succeeded in raising the actual excess reserve ratio from .034 to .051, still far below earlier desired excess reserve ratios. Check deposits fell by nearly 6 percent between December 1936 and December 1937. Not altogether unrelated, the unemployment rate rose from 14.3 to 19.0 percent between 1937 and 1938. It appears the Fed recognized its folly. The increase in total reserves and the reserve requirement cut in spring 1938 were so substantial that banks simultaneously were able to restore the desired excess reserve ratio and expand deposits. Compare columns 4 and 5. Total reserves continued to increase in fall 1938 and, with the required reserve ratio constant, so did check deposits, in spite of a higher actual and presumably desired excess reserve ratio. It hardly seems possible that in December 1938 the annualized interest rate on 90-day Treasury bills was less than one one hundredth of one percent! Millionaires had to dip into their capital; their interest income was a paltry $70 per year.

## EXCESS RESERVES IN THE 1970s

Actual and presumably desired excess reserve ratios have been very low for many years. Knowledge of the determinants of the ratio suggests why this is so. Market interest rates and, therefore, the opportunity cost of excess reserves, have been high. Moreover, the development of new financial markets has reduced brokerage costs, making frequent purchases and sales profitable. For example, prior to 1930 the government typically balanced its budget and few government bonds were outstanding. Although the government issued bonds to finance moderate deficits during the 1930s, dealers failed to react immediately and did not create a wide market by standing ready to buy and sell large amounts of government bonds. Government bonds became highly marketable during World War II, when the deficit and bond issues soared. Readily salable assets like government bonds greatly reduced the need for excess reserves. Development of the federal funds market around 1960 further reduced the desired excess reserve ratio. Federal funds are bank deposits at the Federal Reserve.[14] In a typical federal funds transaction, a bank with excess reserves sells some of its deposits at the Fed to a bank with deficient reserves, on an overnight basis and at an agreed-upon interest rate. Thus, banks lend excess reserves directly to other banks instead of purchasing government securities or other assets.

---

[14] Do not ask embarrassing questions: Why introduce a new term, federal funds, when bank deposits at the Fed are also known as reserves? Inconvenient office hours and its own vocabulary are essential to sustaining the banking mystique.

## MONEY SUPPLY MODEL III

Look in your wallet. You probably are holding some currency. In addition, many individuals have "legal" time deposits and bank nonmoney liabilities subject to reserve requirements. It is time we drop the assumption that individuals do not hold currency or time deposits broadly defined to be any nonmoney liability subject to reserve requirements. This broad definition of time deposits leads to a single money supply formula irrespective of the preferred money definition, as we shall see shortly. Currency held by the public reduces bank reserves, and time deposits reduce the reserves available to support check deposits. Both tend to decrease check deposits and the money supply.

As a first approximation, *individuals always hold their desired proportions of check deposits, currency, and time deposits, which we call the preferred asset ratio.* The Fed and Treasury cannot force you to hold currency. Banks will gladly accept your currency and credit your check or time deposit account. While banks initially credit check deposit accounts when they purchase securities or make loans, individuals can readily convert the proceeds to currency or time deposits according to their preferences. It is true that banks have the legal prerogative of requiring 30-days notice before savings accounts may be closed. However, banks rarely exercise this prerogative. Loss of interest (or even a negative interest) is the worst penalty for closing small time deposit accounts before maturity. CDs are one class of time deposits not payable before maturity. However, since CDs are negotiable, the rate of return adjusts rapidly to satisfy the preferred asset ratio. On balance, banks' liabilities are readily convertible into each other and into cash.[15] The current preferred asset ratio in the United States is approximately $1 check deposits to $0.35 currency to $1.8 time and savings deposits. That is, currency is 35 percent of check deposits, and time deposits equal 180 percent of check deposits. Using general notation to express currency and time deposits as a proportion of check deposits,

$$C = kDC = 0.35DC$$
$$TD = tDC = 1.80DC$$

where k is the factor of proportionality between currency and check deposits or, equivalently, the ratio of currency to check deposits. The interpretation of t should be clear.

Note carefully what is and is not being said. Satisfaction at all times of the public's preferred asset *ratio* implies nothing about dollar amounts. Proportions can be correct even if the total is not. Consider an example

---

[15] For short periods of time during the 19th century and the "bank holiday" of 1933, banks suspended payments, that is, banks refused to exchange currency for check deposits. Currency sold at a premium over check deposits. These periods where the actual currency/ check deposit ratio was less than the desired ratio were quite short and can be ignored. We foresee no likelihood of such events reoccurring.

which ignores time deposits for simplicity. Given income and other factors, suppose the desired money balances of a typical person are $1,350, composed of $350 in currency and the balance in check deposits. Might the individual be holding more or less money for a significant period of time? Definitely yes. An individual may not be holding the desired amount of money for some time because the costs of acquiring money are quite high. Whatever amount of money the individual may be holding, transferring funds from one account to another is sufficiently simple that the currency/check deposit ratio equals the preferred 35 percent except for fleeting moments. The currency/check deposit ratio, $k$, and the time/check deposit ratio, $t$, are not immutable numbers. Nevertheless, following the procedure of the last section, we first consider the effects of currency and time deposits on the money supply and then analyze the determinants of the ratios.

The fundamental money supply equations are:

$$M \equiv DC + C \equiv DC + kDC \equiv (1 + k)DC \qquad (4\text{--}1.3)$$

$$
\begin{aligned}
B &= R + C = R + kDC \\
&= r_cDC + r_{ec}DC + r_ttDC + kDC \qquad (4\text{--}2.3) \\
&= (r_c + r_{ec} + r_tt + k)DC
\end{aligned}
$$

Equation (4–1.3) uses the preferred asset ratio, expressing currency as a fraction of check deposits. The monetary base equilibrium equation (4–2.3) contains two new terms on the demand side. Besides the previously discussed required and desired excess reserves against check deposits, $r_cDC + r_{ec}DC$, the demand for reserves now includes required reserves against time deposits, which equals the time deposit required reserve ratio, $r_t$, multiplied by time deposits, $TD = tDC$. The required reserve ratio is substantially smaller on time than check deposits, that is, $r_t$ approximately $.33r_c$.[16] Currency, again expressed as a fraction of check deposits, is the nonbank demand for the base. The total demand for the base per dollar of check deposits is $r_c + r_{ec} + r_tt + k$, *given the public's preferences of t and k for time deposits and currency, respectively.* The base equilibrium equation yields the quantity of check deposits. Rearranging (4–2.3) and solving for check deposits,

$$DC = \frac{1}{r_c + r_{ec} + r_tt + k} \cdot B \qquad (4\text{--}4.3)$$

The equilibrium values of the other variables follow readily. Substituting the last equation in (4–1.3) gives the equilibrium money stock.

$$M = \frac{1 + k}{r_c + r_{ec} + r_tt + k} \cdot B \qquad (4\text{--}5.3)$$

---

[16] Banks may want excess reserves against time deposits as well as check deposits. We leave it to the reader to develop a money supply equation for such a case.

From the proportionality assumptions, equilibrium currency and time deposits are[17]

$$C = \frac{k}{r_c + r_{ec} + r_t t + k} \cdot B = kDC \qquad (4\text{–}10.3)$$

$$T = \frac{t}{r_c + r_{ec} + r_t t + k} \cdot B = tDC \qquad (4\text{–}11.3)$$

Similar equations hold for changes in the base and the items on the left-hand side. For example,

$$\Delta T = \frac{t}{r_c + r_{ec} + r_t t + k} \Delta B = t\Delta DC \qquad (4\text{–}11.3')$$

Don't worry, these are our most complex equations. The money supply, equation (4–5.3) still is expressed as the product of a multiplier times the base. However, recognition of time deposits and currency complicates the multiplier. Three new variables, $r_t$, t, and k, have been introduced. How is this final money supply equation related to these three variables? From a purely mechanical viewpoint, we see that $r_t$ and t appear in the denominator of the money supply multiplier, so the money supply varies inversely with the required reserve ratio against time deposits, $r_t$, and the public's preferred time/check deposit ratio, t. Economically speaking, as the time deposit reserve ratio or the quantity of time deposits rises, less reserves are available to support check deposits and the money supply. The currency/check deposit ratio appears in both the numerator and denominator of the money supply multiplier. Nevertheless, a larger ratio reduces the money supply. With a fixed base, reserves decrease when individuals hold more currency. Since check deposits are a multiple of reserves, check deposits ultimately fall by more than the increase in currency. Therefore, the money supply falls when the currency/check deposit ratio rises.[18]

Compared to the simplest model, this realistic model gives a substantially smaller money supply multiplier. Look at equations (4–5.1), (4–5.2) and (4–5.3) and see how the multiplier becomes smaller as one introduces excess reserves, currency, and time deposits. While the final money supply equation (4–5.3) may seem complex, the equation simply formalizes the common-sense approach presented in Chapter 3. The equation shows more precisely how the Fed, bank, and public jointly determine the money supply.

---

[17] Those who like algebra should solve for the equilibrium quantity of reserves and loans and securities. Hint: balance sheets do balance. Ignoring net worth, check deposits + time deposits − loans and securities = reserves.

[18] For those who are familiar with the calculus, $\partial M/\partial k = B(D - N)/D^2$, where D and N are the denominator and numerator, respectively, of the money supply multiplier. As $D < N$, then $\partial M/\partial k < 0$.

Let us give some economic flesh to these mathematical bones. A specific example illustrates the adjustment process.

**FIGURE 4–3**   **(1) Initial equilibrium, (2) Open-market purchase from banks, (3) First-round bank expansion, and (4) the Public's adjustment to the preferred asset ratio**

| | **Banking System** | | | |
|---|---|---|---|---|
| (1) | Deposits at Fed | 30 | Check deposits | 100 |
| | Loans and securities | 270 | Time deposits | 200 |
| (2) | Deposits at Fed | +16 | | |
| | Loans and securities | −16 | | |
| (3) | Loans and securities | +80 | Check deposits | +80 |
| (4) | Deposits at Fed | −5 | Check deposits | −55 |
| | | | Time deposits | +50 |

| | **Fed** | | | |
|---|---|---|---|---|
| (1) | Treasury securities | 50 | Deposits of banks | 30 |
| | | | Currency in circulation | 20 |
| (2) | Treasury securities | +16 | Deposits of banks | +16 |
| (3) | | | | |
| (4) | | | Deposits of banks | −5 |
| | | | Currency in circulation | +5 |

| | **Public** | | | |
|---|---|---|---|---|
| (1) | Check deposits | 100 | Loans from banks | 100 |
| | Time deposits | 200 | Net worth | 500 |
| | Currency | 20 | | |
| | Treasury securities | 80 | | |
| | Other assets | 200 | | |
| (2) | | | | |
| (3) | Check deposits | +80 | Loans from banks | +80 |
| (4) | Check deposits | −55 | | |
| | Time deposits | +50 | | |
| | Currency | +5 | | |

The initial equilibrium balance sheets of the banking system, Fed and the public are represented by the first line of Figure 4–3. The required reserve ratios against check and time deposits are 0.18 and 0.05, respectively, and banks' desired excess reserve ratio equals 0.02. Suppose the public's preferred asset ratio, which is satisfied at all times, is $1 check deposits to $0.20 currency to $2.00 time deposits. Since check deposits are $100, the public holds $20 in currency. The initial money supply equals $120.

Look at line 1 of Figure 4–3 more carefully. Does it satisfy our equa-

tions and, thereby, represent an equilibrium? Given our assumptions, total (required and excess) desired reserves against check deposits are $20,
(.18 + .02)$100. Required reserves against time deposits are $10,
0.05 × $200. Therefore, bank reserves are at the desired level, $30, and
banks will not be adjusting their assets and liabilities, that is, banks are in
equilibrium. According to the Fed's balance sheet, the monetary base is
$50. The Fed's balance sheet is convenient but unnecessary; the banking
system's balance sheet is sufficient to determine the base. Since the
currency/check deposit ratio is 20 percent, the $100 check deposit liability
on the banking system's balance sheet implies currency is $20. Adding
currency and reserves gives the $50 base. The first three assets are the
important accounts in the public's balance sheet; the other accounts are
listed for balance. The public's preferred asset ratio is satisfied, and the
public is in equilibrium for purposes of money supply analysis. Money
equals $120. Does our formula give this number? Rewriting the money
supply equation (4–5.3) and using the values in this example,

$$M = \frac{1 + k}{r_c + r_{ec} + r_t t + k} \cdot B \qquad (4\text{–}5.3)$$

$$M = \frac{1 + .2}{.18 + .02 + (.05)2 + .2} \cdot 50 = 120$$

Line 2 of Figure 4–3 shows a $16 open-market purchase. How do banks
and the public react?[19] Concentrate first on the banking system's balance
sheet. Reserves now are $46 while the demand for reserves is $30 ($18
required against check deposits plus $2 desired excess against check de-
posits plus $10 required against time deposits). The recent $16 open-
market purchase explains undesired excess reserves. Banks attempt to
eliminate the undesired excess reserves by expanding loans and check
deposits. Required plus desired excess reserves equal 20 percent in this
example. Therefore, the banking system expands loans and check deposits by $80, thereby eliminating undesired excess reserves, that is,
$80 = $16/.2. The expansion shown on line 3, Figure 4–3, brings banks to
a new equilibrium. (Sum lines 1–3. The demand for reserves, $46, equals
the amount available.) If the public did not want currency or time deposits, as was assumed in Case II, the adjustment process would end here.
The public would hold the additional check deposits, and the monetary
increase is $80.[20] Assuming a preferred asset ratio is more realistic, how-
ever, and causes further adjustments, this time by the public. Banks
create check deposits but the ultimate recipients, presumably someone
other than the borrower, do not have to hold them. Given the public's

---

[19] Most readers will find the adjustment process quite difficult. Do not spend an inordinate
amount of time on this paragraph as subsequent material is more important.

[20] The Case II money supply equation (4–4.2) is $\Delta M = (1/r_c + r_{ec})\Delta B$. In this example,
$\Delta M = (1/.18 + .02)\$16 = \$80$.

preferred asset ratio, they immediately withdraw $55 from their checking account, request $5 in cash, and place the balance in time deposit accounts, as shown on line 4, Figure 4–3.[21] Summing lines 3 and 4 of the public's balance sheets shows the preferred asset ratio of $1 check deposits to $0.20 currency and $2.00 time deposits is restored. Banks reduce their deposits at the Fed to provide the public with currency. Satisfaction of the public's preferred asset ratio throws the banking system out of equilibrium. Combining lines 1 through 4 of the banking system's balance sheet shows that undesired excess reserves are $3.5, so banks would again adjust loans and check deposits.[22] We refrain from showing the next and subsequent step. There are many rounds of bank loan and check deposit expansion followed by the public's adjustment to restore the preferred asset ratio. The individual bank round-by-round adjustment shown earlier illustrates how the banking system reaches equilibrium. The sequential interaction presented here illustrates how the banking system and public reach equilibrium.

Many may wish to ignore the adjustment sequence, which is a pity but permissible. You cannot ignore the final effect of the open-market purchase. The first two lines of the previous set of balance sheets are reproduced in Figure 4–4. How did we get the line 3, which shows the changes induced by the $16 open-market purchase when the public demands additional currency and time deposits? Use the formulas. First, calculate the supply of the base after the $16 open-market purchase. The base is $66, $46 in reserves and $20 in currency. Rewriting the last five equations in level and first difference form and using the numbers given in this example we get:

$$B = R + C$$
$$= (r_c + r_{ec} + r_t t + k)DC \qquad (4\text{–}2.3)$$
$$66 = (.18 + .02 + (.05)(2) + .2)DC = .5DC$$

$$\Delta B = \Delta R + \Delta C$$
$$= (r_c + r_{ec} + r_t t + k)\Delta DC$$
$$16 = (.18 + .02 + (.05)(2) + .2)\Delta DC = .5\Delta DC$$

---

[21] How did we get these numbers? The ratio of check deposits to check deposits equals one, of course. Therefore, the ratio of check deposits to total assets (check deposits, currency, and time deposits) is 1/3.2, where 3.2 is the sum of the three ratios: the check deposit ratio, 1; the currency ratio, 0.2; and the time deposit ratio, 2. Whenever banks create $1 in check deposits, the public retains only 1/3.2 and immediately uses 0.2/3.2 and 2/3.2 to acquire currency and time deposits, respectively. The three fractions sum to unity as the public must do something with the deposits banks create. Banks initially created $80 in check deposits, so the public retains $25 ≡ $80(1/3.2). The public withdraws $55 (the difference between the amount created, $80, and retained $25) and gets currency $5 ≡ $80(0.2/3.2), and time deposits, $50 ≡ $80(2/3.2).

[22] Combining lines 1 through 4, reserves are $41. Legal (.18) and desired excess (.02) reserves against check deposits ($125) are $25. Legal reserves (.05) against time deposits ($250) are $12.5. Therefore, total desired reserves are $25 + $12.5 = $37.5. Undesired excess reserves are $41 − $37.5 = $3.5.

**FIGURE 4–4**   **(1) Initial equilibrium, (2) Open-market purchase from banks, (3) Equilibrium adjustments, and (4) New equilibrium values, sum of (1)–(3)**

### Banking System

| (1) | Deposits at Fed | 30 | Check deposits | 100 |
|-----|------------------|------|-----------------|-----|
|     | Loans and securities | 270 | Time deposits | 200 |
| (2) | Deposits at Fed | +16 | | |
|     | Loans and securities | −16 | | |
| (3) | Deposits at Fed | −6.4 | Check deposits | +32 |
|     | Loans and securities | +102.4 | Time deposits | +64 |
| (4) | Deposits at Fed | 39.6 | Check deposits | 132 |
|     | Loans and securities | 356.4 | Time deposits | 264 |

### Fed

| (1) | Treasury securities | 50 | Deposits of banks | 30 |
|-----|---------------------|------|----------------------|-----|
|     | | | Currency in circulation | 20 |
| (2) | Treasury securities | +16 | Deposits of banks | +16 |
| (3) | | | Deposits of banks | −6.4 |
|     | | | Currency in circulation | +6.4 |
| (4) | Treasury securities | 66 | Deposits of banks | 39.6 |
|     | | | Currency in circulation | 26.4 |

### Public

| (1) | Check deposits | 100 | Loans from bank | 100 |
|-----|----------------|-------|------------------|-----|
|     | Time deposits | 200 | Net worth | 500 |
|     | Currency | 20 | | |
|     | Treasury securities | 80 | | |
|     | Other assets | 200 | | |
| (2) | | | | |
| (3) | Check deposits | +32.0 | Loans from banks | +102.4 |
|     | Time deposits | +64.0 | | |
|     | Currency | +6.4 | | |
| (4) | Check deposits | 132.0 | Loans from banks | 202.4 |
|     | Time deposits | 264.0 | Net worth | 500.0 |
|     | Currency | 26.4 | | |
|     | Treasury securities | 80.0 | | |
|     | Other assets | 200.0 | | |

$$\text{DC} = \frac{1}{r_c + r_{ec} + r_t t + k}\, B = \frac{1}{.5}\, B = 2.0(66) = 132$$

$$\Delta \text{DC} = \frac{1}{.5}\, \Delta B = 32 \tag{4–4.3}$$

$$\text{M} = \text{DC} + \text{C} = (1 + k)\text{DC} = \frac{(1 + k)}{r_c + r_{ec} + r_t t + k}\, B$$

$$= \frac{(1 + .2)}{.5}\, 66 = 2.4(66) = 158.4 \tag{4–5.3}$$

$$\Delta \text{M} = 2.4\Delta B = 38.4$$

$$C = kDC = (.2)132 = 26.4$$
$$\Delta C = k\Delta DC = (.2)32 = 6.4 \qquad (4-10.3)$$

$$TD = tDC = (2)132 = 264$$
$$\Delta TD = t\Delta DC = (2)32 = 64 \qquad (4-11.3)$$

As stated, line 3, Figure 4–4, shows the changes due to the open-market purchase, and line 4, which sums lines 1–3, is the new equilibrium level. We checked the initial equilibrium and the reader should verify the new numbers in a similar manner. The difference between line 3 in Figures 4–3 and 4–4 arises from different assumptions about currency and time deposits. Comparing line 3 illustrates that when the public's preferred asset ratio is satisfied (1) the growth of the money supply is smaller, (2) the growth of bank credit and a more broadly defined money supply are larger, and (3) the ultimate increase of reserves is less than the amount of the open-market purchase.

## THE EFFECT OF THE MONEY DEFINITION ON THE PREFERRED ASSET RATIO

The left-hand side of the money supply equation (4–5.3) is simply M without a number (1, 2, or 3) or letter (A or B) because the equation is valid irrespective of the preferred money definition, provided the terms in the equation are analyzed conformably. The term *currency* offers no special difficulty, it *always* is coins plus paper money. However, recall that *check deposits* represents all bank liabilities counted in the money measure. We chose this name because given our preference for M–1B, which includes demand and other checkable deposits, the generic term is literally correct. If the preferred measure were M–2, check deposits would include a hodgepodge of items and would not be literally correct. Similarly, *time deposits* is all bank *nonmoney* liabilities subject to reserve requirements, where nonmoney liabilities clearly depend on the money definition. Since check and time deposits depend on the money definition, the corresponding reserve ratios and the preferred asset ratio also depend on the money definition.

To clarify the previous paragraph and simultaneously fulfill our promise in Chapter 2 to highlight any factor which affects alternative definitions of money in different directions, consider the effect of a shift from demand deposits to NOW accounts. Line 1 of Figure 4–5 illustrates the initial balance sheet. For simplicity, assume the public holds no currency and banks want no excess reserves. Let the legal reserve ratio on demand deposits be 20 percent, while the reserve ratio on regular time deposits and NOW accounts is 10 percent. Given these assumptions, the initial equilibrium money supply equation (4–5.3) for M–1A, M–1B, and M–2 becomes

$$M\text{-}1A = \frac{1}{r_c + r_t t}\ B = \frac{1}{.2 + .1(1.0)}\ 150 = 500$$

$$M\text{-}1B = \frac{1}{r_c + r_t t}\ B = \frac{1}{(1.1)/6 + .1(4/6)}\ 150 = 600$$

$$M\text{-}2 = \frac{1}{r_c + r_t t}\ B = \frac{1}{.15}\ 150 = 1{,}000$$

**FIGURE 4-5**  **(1) Initial equilibrium (2) Shift from regular time deposits to NOW**

| Banking System | | | |
|---|---:|---|---:|
| (1) Deposits at Fed | 150 | Demand deposits | 500 |
| Loans and securities | 850 | NOW | 100 |
| | | Regular time deposits | 400 |
| (2) | | NOW | +100 |
| | | Regular time deposits | −100 |

From the viewpoint of M–1A, only demand deposits are check deposits, so $r_c = .2$. NOW accounts and regular time deposits are "time deposits," so $t = 1 = (100 + 400)/500$ and $r_t = 0.1$. When analyzing M–1B the weighted average reserve ratio on check deposits is $1.1/6 = 0.2(5/6) + 0.1(1/6)$. The reader should be able to explain the rationale for the value of the other terms above. (When money is defined as M–2, $r_t$ and t equal zero.) Line 2 of Figure 4–5 shows a $100 shift from regular time deposits to NOW. Since the reserve requirements on regular time and NOW accounts are assumed equal, this shift in the public's preferences does not induce further adjustments by the banking system. The shift increased M–1B by $100—M–1B now equals $700—but had no effect on the values of either M–1A or M–2. Supporters of the M–1A (M–2) measure would claim that the shift only altered the composition of nonmoney (money). The new numerical example of the money supply formula for M–1B is

$$M\text{-}1B = \frac{1}{r_c + r_t t}\ B = \frac{1}{(1.2)/7 + 0.1(3/7)}\ 150 = 700$$

The parameters $r_c$ and t change from the viewpoint of M–1B only. Making different assumptions about reserve ratios, for example, let the required reserve ratio on demand and NOW accounts be equal, and considering different shifts generate other examples where alternative money measures change in opposite directions.

Since the specific items composing check and time deposits in the equations depend on the preferred money definition, the value and determinants of ratios involving these terms also depend on the money definition. Consistent with our preference for M–1B, the implicit denominator in our discussion of the determinants of the excess reserve ratio was demand and other checkable deposits. Since other checkable deposits are a relatively recent phenomena and are still quite small compared to demand deposits, our discussion of the excess reserve ratio is essentially correct even if one prefers M–1A, and the denominator of the excess reserve ratio is simply demand deposits. Similarly, the immediately following analysis of the currency ratio is essentially correct whether the money definition is M–1A or M–1B. M–2 and M–3 are sufficiently different from M–1B that the sections on the determinants of excess reserves and currency are unreliable when the broader money measures are preferred. Required reserve ratios traditionally were set on demand and time deposits exclusively. Reserves still are required on at least some time deposits, but in recent years an ever widening collection of accounts are subject to sporadic reserve requirements. For example, reserve requirements were imposed temporarily on consumer credit. This recent behavior makes it virtually impossible to state with great precision the determinants of the generic time/check deposit ratio, whatever the definition of money. In the next section the determinants of the *literal* time/demand deposit are analyzed and thereby offer a *partial* understanding of the generic time/check deposit term in the money supply equation.

## DETERMINANTS OF THE PREFERRED ASSET RATIO

The currency/check deposit ratio during an 80-year span is depicted in Figure 4–6. A quick glance reveals that the ratio has been far from constant. Looking at the broad outlines of Figure 4–6, the period up to approximately 1960 is characterized by almost uniformly declining currency ratios temporarily interrupted by two sharp rises. More specifically, the currency ratio fell more or less continually until 1930; rose sharply between 1930 and 1933; continued to decline between 1933 and 1941, albeit while at a higher level than 1930; rose dramatically between 1941 and 1946, surpassing all previous ratios; and reverted between 1946 and 1960 to a declining trend quite similar to the 1920s. Since approximately 1960 the currency ratio has risen slowly but steadily. Why has the currency ratio behaved in this manner? A short review of the major characteristics of currency and check deposits preceeds enumeration of the determinations of the currency ratio. The review provides the rationale for the determinants.

### Major characteristics of currency and check deposits

Currency is public money while deposits are private money. This is the cause of the main differences between the two types of money. Abstracting from forgeries and numismatic differences, one unit of currency is identical to another of the same denomination, and different denomina-

FIGURE 4-6   Currency ratio

Currency/check deposits

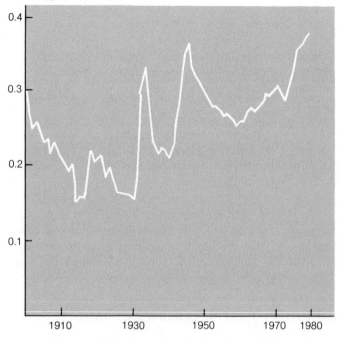

tions are freely interchangeable. The issuer of currency is of no consequence today and throughout the period during which the currency ratio is to be explained.[23] You can exchange at will Federal Reserve currency for Treasury currency. Moreover, the value of currency in no way depends on the particular person holding it. If a store accepts my currency, it surely will accept yours, which is identical to mine. Currency is so convenient in transactions between strangers where the buyer takes immediate possession of a commodity that such transactions are often called cash-and-carry. Currency also predominates in transactions which best are unrecorded. You have no idea how an individual acquired currency, and once all the currency is in the till you cannot identify the specific bill received. Being identical and so readily acceptable is a mixed blessing. Currency is not easily recovered if lost or stolen, as Chapter 3 emphasized.

Check deposits are expended by orders to a bank to make payment to specified individuals. Check deposits offer a convenient method of making

---

[23] During the "wildcat" state banking period prior to the Civil War, notes issued by banks circulated at varying exchange rates, depending on the public's estimate of the liquidity and solvency of the issuing bank. Following the Civil War gold coins sold at a premium over government paper money—greenbacks. By 1879 all currency normally was interchangeable at par. We are abstracting from temporary "penny shortages" and the like, which often are over by the time newspapers mention them.

payment when the parties to a transaction are geographically distant. There is no risk of loss in transit. If someone other than the drawee (the person to whom the check is made payable) cashes the checks, neither the drawee nor the drawer of the check bears the loss. Whoever accepts a fraudulently endorsed check pays the penalty. In addition, check deposits provide a receipt for debts paid. Lest forgetful depositors think that their account has been incorrectly debited, banks return cancelled checks and statements. Because checks are orders for payments, they are only as good as the authority of the drawer to issue orders. Banks refuse to follow orders when a check is greater than the deposit account. The more information the drawee has about the drawer, the greater is the likelihood that checks will be accepted for immediate payment.

The last two paragraphs have emphasized the advantages and disadvantages of currency and check deposits in flight. The main difference between these two assets at rest is their expected net return, which equals interest payments minus expected losses due to bank failures. Service charges are negative interest payments. Currency yields no interest, and we can assume expected losses due to theft and misplacements were constant throughout the period. Therefore, the net return on currency was constant. Both components of the net return on check deposits have varied considerably over time. U.S. banks paid interest on check deposits until 1934 and resumed the practice nationwide on at least some check deposits in 1981. Throughout much of U.S. history, bank failures were a common occurrence, both in good times and bad. Many banks failed in the prosperous 1920s. Of course, bank failures peaked during the Great Depression, making the net return on deposits highly negative.

### Determinants of the currency ratio

We are now ready to tackle the currency ratio. Income, the net return on check deposits, tax rates, and the crime rate are the main determinants of the currency ratio. While we do not know in detail the causes of income growth, it is associated with lower information costs and an increase in the relative volume of transactions where checks are specially advantageous. Consequently, the currency ratio is *negatively* related to income. For example, higher incomes are associated with increased specialization. More people are engaged in the production of intermediate goods and fewer people produce and sell final goods and services. Check deposit transactions between firms who are familiar with each other increase relative to cash sales of final goods to strangers. Moreover, markets are narrow when incomes are low. Trades occur among neighbors. The technical progress which accompanies income growth reduces transportation costs and expands markets. California strawberries are shipped to Maryland supermarkets. Geographically distant payments are made by check to reduce the risk of loss. Technical progress also lowers information costs.

Improved communication systems enable sellers to acquire information on your credit record quite inexpensively. Checks become more readily accepted, enhancing their use. We resist the temptation to give additional theoretical justification for the observed negative relationship between income and the currency ratio. Indeed, the growth of income by itself explains nearly all of the currency ratio's decline between 1900–29 and 1946–60. Even many of the wiggle-waggles of the currency ratio, particularly during 1900–29, are the result of the business cycle.

Why did the ratio rise sharply between 1930 and 1933? The United States and the rest of the world was in the Great Depression. Income fell dramatically, and the currency ratio rose as expected. However, there is a more important reason for the 1930–33 rise in the currency ratio. Bank failures and deposit losses were an everyday occurrence. In response to the falling net expected return of demand deposits, individuals stood in long lines to withdraw their deposits. Since bank reserves are only a fraction of deposits, the fear of deposit losses is self-fulfilling.[24]

By 1934 bank failures were largely something of the past and income started to rebound. The currency ratio continued its decline from a high level because income was low but increasing, and the net return of check deposits was still negative but rising. The creation of the FDIC (Federal Deposit Insurance Corporation) restored some confidence in banks, but the experience of 1930–33 was too fresh to be ignored altogether. Moreover, in the late 1800s and early 1900s several states had deposit insurance schemes that were quite successful provided hardly any banks failed. As soon as several banks failed, state deposit insurance corporations folded right along with the banks. Of course, states cannot print money like the federal government can, which should make federal insurance much more reliable. However, will the federal government exercise its powers? The answer was far from clear in the late 1930s, particularly since the federal government had let the money supply fall by approximately a third between 1929 and 1933.

In 1940 the average personal tax rate was 3.3 percent. To finance World War II the tax rate rose to 12.1 percent in a five-year period and stayed more or less at this level until 1960. High tax rates encourage some people to hold check deposits rather than currency in order to have better records for the tax collectors. A cancelled check is a good receipt for a deductible expense. On the other hand, some people may be willing to forego some deductions provided they are able to understate income even more. Many are unable to understate income because taxes are withheld on wages and salaries. Dividends and interest payments are reported to the IRS, making it somewhat risky to ignore such receipts. Public corporations that face independent auditors usually need accurate records. However, many independent professionals, skilled workers, and unincorpo-

---

[24] Since depositors are wiped out by bank failures, the *actual* currency ratio mechanically rises with failures. However, failures increase the *desired* currency ratio even more.

rated businesses have good opportunities to cheat. It is a disheartening fact that tax chisellers predominate. As stated earlier, currency is ideal for no-questions-asked-and-no-records-please transactions. The higher are tax rates, the greater is the incentive to conceal income and make cash payments.[25] Because tax rates were high but approximately constant between 1945–60, the currency ratio was high but declined during this prosperous period.

Beginning around 1960 we embarked on what seems like a determined effort to make the United States the crime nation of the world. Some crimes are one-shot affairs, for example, a lover's quarrel becomes a homicide. However, some crime is a continuous business—for example, gambling, prostitution, and drugs. Although statistics on this "underground economy" are inevitably imprecise, I am told it is growing and that it is conducted on a strictly cash-and-carry basis. During the 1960s and 1970s personal tax rates increased steadily and, allegedly, so did the underground economy. The higher tax rate and crime effect swamped the income growth effect, producing a higher currency ratio.[26] Moreover, the proclivity to cheat at any *given* tax rate may be greater since 1960. Crime statistics do not include tax evasion and bribes. Nevertheless, do certain basic forces cause parallel movements in blue- and white-collar crimes? Proclivities to steal at gun point and from governments at tax collection dates should run together.

A final point regarding the currency ratio. Do you think the currency ratio exhibits a seasonal pattern? Check your answer by looking at a Federal Reserve *Bulletin,* which is full of interesting statistics. What explains the seasonal pattern?

### Determinants of the time/demand deposit ratio

The time/demand deposit ratio depends on income, the time deposit rate, and market interest rates. During this century the time deposit ratio has risen more or less continuously. For example, between 1941 and 1980 the ratio climbed from approximately .35 to 1.8. Demand deposits are a

---

[25] Ideally we should be using the marginal rather than average personal tax rate. However, the former is difficult to compute and most likely both tax rates move together.

[26] The classic study of tax effects on the currency ratio is Phillip Cagan's, *Determinants and Effects of Changes in the Stock of Money, 1875–1960* (New York: Columbia University Press, 1965). Congress was sufficiently disturbed in 1947 by the possibility of tax evasion and black marketeering during World War II to introduce a bill creating a new currency. Individuals would receive new (blue) currency in exchange for the old demonetized green currency. Had the bill passed, the tax chiseler would have faced the dilemma of either abandoning his ill-gotten gain or swapping currency and attracting IRS attention. It may be best to accept the loss quietly in such situations. Several years ago the wife of a Dallas dentist, not knowing about her husband's financial affairs, threw out an old coffee can stuffed with $20,000 in currency. On discovering that the can had been collected with the other trash, the dentist rented a bulldozer for $5,000 to sift the Dallas dump. The whole town was talking about it. The IRS was not far behind, much to the dentist's chagrin. He was sentenced to prison for tax evasion.

neutral good or perhaps even a necessity. That is, demand deposits increase proportionally, or slightly less than proportionally, with income. Time deposits clearly are a luxury good having risen proportionally more than income. Consequently, the time deposit ratio and income move together. The reason for this empirical phenomenon is not clear. Financial assets rise relative to income during the development process because saving increasingly takes the form of accumulating financial assets rather than physical capital. As the degree of specialization and incomes expand, there is less overlap between savers and investors, that is, those individuals who decide to build factories and buy machines. People use the difference between income and the amount spent on consumption goods to acquire such financial assets as time deposits, saving and loan shares, common stocks, and bonds. While check deposits also are financial assets, it appears plausible that financial wealth better explains time deposits rather than an asset associated with transactions, such as check deposits. Putting the matter somewhat differently, income instead of financial wealth is more closely related to transactions and should explain demand deposits better than time deposits.[27] This explanation for the time/demand deposit ratio is consistent with the approximately 80 percent increase in the ratio of financial wealth to income between 1870 and 1952.[28] Since we foresee no substantial differences in the development and income growth process, the time deposit ratio should continue to rise, assuming interest rates are constant.

A positive relationship between the rate of interest paid on time deposits and the time deposit ratio needs no explanation. Since time deposits are held mainly for their interest return, one might expect that time deposits are more sensitive than demand deposits to the return than can be earned on other assets. This indeed is the case. The time deposit ratio is negatively related to market interest rates. When the interest rate on Treasury bills or some other market instrument rises, the public desires a lower time/demand deposit ratio. High market rates mean that the opportunity cost of holding either deposit type is high, but the opportunity cost weighs more heavily on time deposits, causing a decline in the time deposit ratio.

## SUMMARY

Money, M, may be expressed as the product of a multiplier, m, and the base, B.

$$M = m \cdot B$$

---

[27] Note well that the text does *not* make the debatable statement: Demand deposits are better explained by income than financial wealth.

[28] John G. Gurley and Edward S. Shaw, "The Growth of Debt and Money in the United States, 1800–1950: A Suggested Interpretation," *Review of Economics and Statistics,* August 1957.

The Fed controls money mainly by changing the base. For this reason, we additionally write the change or first difference form of the money equation with a given multiplier.

$$\Delta M = m \cdot \Delta B$$

The money supply multiplier depends on the assumptions of the model. Most principles courses begin and end with our Case I, where the public holds only check deposits and banks hold reserves simply to meet legal requirements. In this case, the base corresponds with bank reserves and the multiplier is the inverse of the check deposit required reserve ratio. Money supply analysis becomes very mechanical. The Fed pulls some strings and a predictable outcome follows. Banks are the puppets of a monetary authority which always hits the target money supply by changing reserve requirements or the amount of reserves. However pedagogically useful the simple model may be as a starting point, realism requires going beyond it. Banks' desired excess reserve ratio and the public's preferred asset ratio for currency, time deposits, and check deposits enter the multiplier and can thwart monetary policy. In fact, control of reserves and reserve requirements does not guarantee monetary control. Banks and the public play an important role in the money supply process. The money supply equation of our realistic Case III is

$$M = \frac{\overset{- \; - \; + \; +}{1 + k\,(y,\,i_c,\,p,\,x)}}{\underset{+\; -\; -\; +}{r_c + r_{ec}\,(b,\,i_m,\,\mu,\,\sigma)} + \underset{-\; -\; +\; +}{k\,(y,\,i_c,\,p,\,x)} + \underset{+\; +\; -}{t\,(y,\,i_t,\,i_m)\,r_t}} \cdot B \qquad (4\text{--}5.3)$$

This is the same equation we have used several times before. It may not look familiar because the determinants of the ratios are shown explicitly in order to emphasize that they are determined by banks and the public and are not immutable constants. The determinants are

$y$ = income
$i_c$ = net return (or net cost if negative) on check deposits
$i_t$ = interest rate paid on time deposits
$i_m$ = interest rate on marketable securities
$b$ = brokerage cost of buying or selling securities
$p$ = tax rate (for painful, since "t" has already been used for the time deposit ratio)
$x$ = crime rate
$\mu$ = expected (percentage) change in check deposits
$\sigma$ = variability of check deposits

The sign above or below a variable indicates the relationship between a variable and ratio. For example, the currency ratio, $k$, is negatively related to income and positively related to tax rates. The determinants of the time deposit ratio are known with the least accuracy because time deposits here mean the wide assortment of nonmoney accounts subject to reserve requirements. As written, the equation ignores the effect of the public on the required reserve ratio due to lack of uniformity.

Answer two controversial questions to demonstrate mastery of the chapter. Does the money supply depend on market interest rates and, if so, why? Will the money supply vary over the business cycle even if the Fed sits on its hands? The answer is made easier by equation (4–5.3), which shows explicitly the determinants of the money supply.

## QUESTIONS

1. What conditions must exist in order for the Fed to control perfectly the money supply multiplier?

2. As various assumptions are relaxed and we move from Case I to Case II to Case III, does the size of the multiplier change? When is the multiplier largest?

3. Look at the balance sheet of any bank. Reserves always are a small fraction of check deposits. Therefore, any single bank can expand the money supply by a multiple of its excess reserves. True or False. Explain.

4. Go back to question 1 of Chapter 3. How do those transactions affect the *excess* reserves of (1) FNB and (2) the entire banking system?

5. If banks have excess reserves, must the money supply be increasing?

6. Predicting is hazardous. Nevertheless, predict the behavior of the excess reserve ratio during the next five years. Carefully state the assumptions underlying your predictions.

7. If the required and desired excess reserve ratios on check and time deposits are identical, what is the effect of a shift from check to time deposits on (1) the money supply and (2) bank credit?

8. The *algebraic expression* of the money supply multiplier for M–1B and M–2 are identical. Are the *numerical values* of the money supply multipliers for M–1B and M–2 also identical? Does the measurement and interpretation of the parameters in the algebraic expression depend on the money definition?

9. What are the determinants of the currency and time deposit ratios?

10. Does the money supply depend on market interest rates and, if so, why? Will the money supply vary over the business cycle even if the Fed sits on its hands?

11. The following information is necessary to answer parts a–d below.

### Commercial Banking System

| | | | |
|---|---|---|---|
| Vault cash | 5,500 | Check deposits | 100,000 |
| Deposits at Fed | 24,500 | Time deposits | 180,000 |
| Loans and securities | 250,000 | | |

Assume the public's preferred asset ratio, which is satisfied at all times, is $2 currency to $18 time deposits to $10 check deposits. The reserve ratios are: $r_c = 0.19$, $r_{ec} = 0.02$, and $r_t = 0.05$.

a. Is the banking system in equilibrium? How much currency is in the hands of the public? What does the base equal? What does the quantity of money equal? Substitute the numbers in this example in the general formula (Case III). Does the quantity of money equal the equilibrium money supply given by the formula?

b. Assume an open-market purchase of $10,000 from banks. What is the (equilibrium) change of the following items: (1) check deposits, (2) currency, (3) money supply, (4) time deposits, (5) reserves, and (6) bank loans and securities?

c. Assume the Fed cuts the required reserve ratio to 0.09. What is the new equilibrium values of the six items in part b? (In answering this part, assume the initial balance sheet, i.e., ignore the $10,000 open-market purchase.)

d. Suppose that, by coincidence, desired excess reserve ratio rose to 0.12 when the Fed cut the required ratio to 0.09. What is the equilibrium values of the six items in part *b*?

# PART 2

## Financial markets and instruments

# Financial markets, debt, and interest rates

# 5

The first part of this book focused on the liability side of banks' balance sheets; loan expansion was an incidental part of monetary expansion. The initial emphasis on bank liabilities was justified because the nature of their liabilities distinguish banks from other financial institutions and private lenders. (Other checkable deposits still are a small proportion of nonbank deposits.) Virtually anyone can extend credit and lend money, but only banks can simultaneously lend and *create* money. The credit markets in which banks participate with other institutions are extremely important, however. This part examines the behavior of credit markets and, more generally, the process of transferring purchasing power among economic units. We look at the numerous institutions engaged in the transfer process and the numerous financial instruments which evidence the transfer. Even when the focus is on credit instead of money, more attention must be given to commercial banks because they are the largest member of the financial system.

This chapter first discusses the advantages stemming from credit markets and a financial system. The major types of financial instruments and markets are then described. The main characteristic or attribute of a financial instrument is its rate of interest or yield to maturity. We show how one computes the rate of interest and other measures of return. The existence of truth-in-lending laws confirms, however, that the computation of rates of return can be neither easy nor uniform. Other characteristics of securities and their relationship to a security's return are then explored. An analysis of the effect of inflation on interest rates concludes the chapter.

## THE BENEFITS OF FINANCE

Money and purchasing power are transferred from surplus to deficit units in financial markets. Surplus units are those economic units whose income from current production exceeds expenditures on currently produced goods and services, while deficit units spend more than their income. Although deficit household units are not uncommon, households on balance are surplus units. Their income exceeds consumption, that is, household expenditures on currently produced goods and services. Households are net savers. Firms are deficit units; their net investment spending exceeds retained earnings. In recent years the consolidated government sector, that is, federal, state, and local, has invariably been a deficit unit. As fast as taxes have risen, they have failed to keep pace with government expenditures. While deficit sectors sometimes are denounced as profligates and surplus sectors are extolled as candidates for sainthood, the two types of economic units complement each other. Without deficit units there would be no surplus units. Total deficits must equal total surpluses because your expenditures are the receipts of another economic unit, and your earnings are someone else's expenditures. While surplus units are unlikely to want to keep accumulating money as their surpluses persist, they at least have the luxury of this option. Deficit units are not so fortunate. Lacking unlimited money balances, deficit units unable to issue financial claims against themselves eventually must continually balance their budgets. (Deficit units that sell common stocks or borrow issue financial claims against themselves.) Since total deficits equal total surpluses, lack of finance eventually forces every economic unit to continually balance its budget. *Whatever the advantages of a balanced budget by government, we will show that other sectors' relatively long-run deficits and surpluses made possible by finance enhance income and welfare.*

Most people enter this world with nothing and leave behind little, so over their entire lifetimes most households are quite modest surplus units, almost approaching balanced-budget units. However, the typical household does not enjoy a modest surplus throughout its lifetime. During its early years following entrance into the labor market, the typical household incurs a deficit as it acquires durable goods. A mortgage finances a home, and the household purchases its first automobile, TV, and washing machine on credit. With the stock of durable goods on hand and the repayment requirements, the typical household switches from a deficit to a small surplus unit. The surplus becomes larger as households anticipate the expenses of college for their children. Household incomes increase but the surplus shrinks as children do enter college and parents correctly decide they need one fling before the inevitable. The long postponed Caribbean cruise, luxury car, and remodeled kitchen become reality. Having enjoyed the good life, the household runs its largest surpluses in anticipation of retirement and, if it anticipates correctly, ends its existence as a deficit unit with little to spare. This scenario clearly is preferable to living one's early adult years in parents' basements or a shack without TV, washing machine, and so on, which would be the likely result if one could not borrow. *Financial claims allow consumption and income patterns to differ.*

While the typical household switches from a deficit to a surplus and back to a deficit, a successful firm may well remain a deficit unit throughout the lifespan of a household. Most entrepreneurs claim they have a better mousetrap but lack the resources to launch a new enterprise. The public is rightly skeptical; many have tried but failed to build a better mousetrap. Because of this, the terms for borrowing and issuing common stock typically are quite onerous. The Ford Motor Company case is unusual. Unlike Henry Ford, few struggling inventors and entrepreneurs retain complete ownership of a corporation. The founder of a company typically becomes a minority, though often controlling, stockholder while venture capitalists and other risktakers become the majority owners at relatively modest cost. *The ability of entrepreneurs to issue financial claims, even at onerous terms due to risk, is one of the most important characteristics of a dynamic, progressive society.* As the track record of the successful firm becomes well-known and the cost of finance becomes more favorable, previously unexploitable ideas and products become reality. Even private firms like the Ford Motor Company eventually go public and sell stock in order to expand and remain competitive in industries subject to economies of scale. A successful, growing firm like AT&T repays its maturing debt by borrowing more and widening its deficit. The debt outstanding is not built on a house of cards. The additional telephones made possible by AT&T's debt generates the revenue to pay the debt and yield stockholders a return on their investment.

Surplus units benefit equally with deficit units from the existence of financial claims. Consider the plight of the typical household during its surplus phase. If financial claims were lacking, households could accumulate cash or invest directly by starting their own firms. Neither alternative is appealing. Cash yields no return and the average firm's return exceeds the return on direct investments by households which, by definition, lack management skills. Firms gladly offer and households gladly accept financial claims with interest and dividend payments above the household rate of return and below firms' rate. The separation of household/savers from firm/investors increases the rate of return on any given amount of saving and investment.

Besides increasing the return earned on any surplus and rearranging consumption patterns so that they are not tied to current income, the availability of financial claims usually produces larger surpluses. The household deciding whether to consume or save must consider what to do with the saving. Households that can purchase financial claims have an additional opportunity for their saving and tend to save more. If households are overly myopic and underestimate the satisfaction they will derive from future consumption, the encouragement of additional savings due to the existence of financial claims is particularly beneficial. To be sure, financial claims and the transfer of purchasing power and command over resources among economic units is not universally beneficial. Everyone has heard of the small saver who purchased the common stock of Pie-in-the-Sky Corporation, much to his dismay later. Nevertheless, such losses are far outweighed by the benefits of financial claims.

## MAIN TYPES OF FINANCIAL INSTRUMENTS AND MARKETS

Financial instruments evidence the transfer of funds and specify the rights and obligations of the parties. For example, they spell out the repayment terms. Perhaps the sharpest classification scheme based on the most important difference among financial claims lists them as debt or equity. *Debt instruments are contractual obligations to repay specified amounts in the future.* Debt instruments differ in the number of future specified payments, the certainty individuals attach to the fulfillment of the obligation, and in many other ways which will be discussed shortly. The essential aspect of debt, however, is the obligatory specified payments. Failure to make the payments forces the debtor to declare bankruptcy. Examples of debt are tuition loans, AT&T bonds, and Treasury bills. *Equity instruments are ownership claims.* Holders of equities participate in the management of the issuing firm, usually indirectly by voting for members of the board of directors. *Common stocks* are the most common type of equity, so common that the qualifying adjective is often ignored. Common stocks allow one to participate pro-rata in a firm's earnings and losses and in its assets if dissolution occurs. Some earnings typically are reinvested and some are distributed as dividends. Common stock is the residual claim; everyone from the firm's employees to its creditors is paid before stockholders. *Preferred stock,* the second major type of equity claim, stipulates the amount of future payments out of earnings, current or retained. Although debt instruments also stipulate the amount of future payments, preferred stock *dividends* are nonobligatory payments from earnings, while debt interest payments are an obligatory *expense.*[1] Preferred dividends must be made in full before paying common stock dividends. Preferred stock are purchased by those who want relatively certain

---

[1] Interest payments are treated like any other expense. They are deducted from revenue before paying taxes. Preferred stock dividends on the other hand are paid with after-tax dollars. For example, suppose a corporation's net *operating* income (income before interest, taxes, and dividends) is $100, and the tax rate is 50 percent. If the interest payment on the debt is $20, the corporation's net (after tax) income is $40 = ($100 − $20) × 0.5. If the preferred stock dividend were the same $20, net income would be $30 = ($100 × 0.5) − $20. This tax aspect currently favors the issuance of debt instead of preferred stock. At the turn of the century, when there were no income taxes, the difference between expenses and dividends was irrelevant, and preferred stock was issued more frequently.

and constant dividends while common stock, being the residual claim, appeals to those willing to bear risk in hopes of making a "killing."

The markets in which financial instruments are created and traded can be effectively divided into two types: (1) *the direct financial market* serviced by brokers, dealers, and investment bankers and (2) *the intermediary market* where banks, savings and loans, and other intermediaries participate. Surplus units purchase in direct financial markets the claims issued by ultimate deficit units, often with the aid of brokers, dealers or investment bankers. As just indicated, debt or equity is the major, but hardly the sole, difference among claims. The differences reflect the particular needs of the issuing deficit units. Brokers and investment bankers are effective matchmakers. They reduce the search and information cost of finding surplus units who want the type of security being offered by deficit units. *In the intermediary market, as the name suggests, a financial institution such as a savings and loan stands between the surplus and ultimate deficit unit.* A surplus unit purchases claims issued by the intermediary, which then purchases claims issued by an ultimate deficit unit. For example, when a mother decides to no longer lend her son money and tells him to borrow at the bank where she just opened an account, finance switched from the direct to the intermediary market. The distinction between direct and intermediary finance is sufficiently important that a single name, *primary securities,* is given to all claims, whether equity or debt, issued by ultimate deficit units.

## DIRECT FINANCE, INVESTMENT BANKERS, AND BROKERS

Since money is produced mainly by banks, monetary economics books traditionally have emphasized intermediary finance. While we shall not break tradition, the direct finance market cannot be ignored altogether. We content ourselves with describing *how* purchases and sales are made and offer no advice on *what.*

Assume a firm is planning a new issue of primary securities. The firm may be able to sell the new issue directly to one or more institutional buyers such as pension funds, in which case a *private* or *direct placement* has occurred. Normally, however, the firm will contact an investment banker who finds buyers for the issue. Some leading investment banking firms are Morgan Stanley, Merrill Lynch, Paine Webber-Blyth Eastman, Salomon Brothers, and Bache. Note that investment bankers are neither investors—they are marketers who do not hold securities for any significant length of time—nor bankers—at least commercial bankers like Bank of America and Chase Manhattan. Indeed, (commercial) bankers are prohibited from being investment bankers, except for general obligation issues of governmental units. The investment firm may be fortunate and contact one or more buyers who purchase the entire issue, in which case again a direct placement is said to occur. The new issue usually is too large for one buyer and even one investment banker. When this occurs, the contacted or lead investment banker forms a temporary partnership with other investment bankers to jointly market the new issue. Such a temporary association is called a *syndicate*. The syndicate usually *underwrites* the new issue, that is, it purchases all the new issue, either in a competitive (auction) sale or through direct negotiation, and then resells the securities in smaller units to the public. Of course, the underwriters' anticipated sales price is greater than the purchase price. Underwriters do assume the risk of general security price declines in the time interval following the purchase. Sometimes the risk is realized as the securities fail to fetch the anticipated sale price. Since the risk of loss depends directly on the length of the time interval between purchase and resale, and since the public's general lack of good information about small firms lengthens the time needed to resell their new issues, the new issues of small, less-well-known firms often are not underwritten but sold on a commission or "best-effort" basis.

The new issues or primary market functions so effectively in large part because of the existence of a secondary market where outstanding securities are traded. The prime example of a secondary market is the New York Stock Exchange where, in spite of its name, some bonds are also traded. Few individuals would buy new securities if they could not be resold. Participants in the secondary market are brokers and dealers. *A broker is a middleman* who finds buyers (sellers) for sellers (buyers) and is rewarded for his or her effort by a commission. Brokers do not own securities even for short time periods. So-called discount brokers are strict middlemen who simply execute buy and sell orders, while Merrill Lynch and other large, well-known financial brokers, like their cousins the marriage brokers, also offer advice, at a price. A dealer is a "used" investment banker. That is, *dealers purchase previously issued securities* hoping to sell them later at a higher price. Like the investment banker, the dealer bears the risk of a decline in the market value of his or her securities' inventory. Years ago a firm concentrated on either the primary or secondary market; it was either an investment banker or a broker/dealer. Nowadays nearly all large investment bankers are also brokers and dealers, and vice versa.

The precise form of middleman service, broker or dealer, that a firm offers in the secondary market depends on the type of market and security traded. The word "market" conjurs up a cavernous place filled with people. Financial markets of this type are called exchanges, for example, the New York and American Stock Exchanges. Firms act as brokers when executing buy or sell orders for securities traded on exchanges. Orders received at branch offices of brokerage firms such as Merrill Lynch are transmitted to the firm's floor representative, who physically meets another representative at the exchange floor and executes the order. The stock of most smaller companies and nearly all debt instruments are traded in the over-the-counter market. Although the stock of some large, established firms is unlisted and trades in the over-the-counter market, being listed on one of the exchanges often is interpreted as "having arrived." Unlike exchanges, the over-the-counter market is not located in a specific place but is the network of individual broker and dealer offices located throughout the country and connected by telephone and telex. Firms behave as dealers and make the over-the-counter market by standing ready to buy and sell on their own behalf the securities in which they specialize. The number of dealers specializing in a specific security varies with the value of the security outstanding. For example, a local brokerage house may be the only dealer for the securities of a small company while there are more than thirty dealers in government securities. No firm, however large, can be a dealer in every security. This does not prevent your being able to purchase virtually any unlisted security because the nonspecialist brokerage firm knows who the dealers are. This suggests, however, that you can avoid one middleman and get a better price by trading directly with the specialist. The next chapter takes a closer look at the operating procedures and rules of the New York Exchange.

## INTEREST RATES AND MARKET VALUES OF BONDS

Debt has many different characteristics, the most important clearly being the rate of interest or yield to maturity. The rate of interest measures the annual percentage return on a debt instrument. There is universal agreement on this. Moreover, at the general level everyone agrees on a more precise concept of the rate of interest: it measures the percentage rate at which the current value of the debt grows over time to equal the future payments. When one tries to apply the concept and calculate the rate of interest on a specific debt instrument, disagreement becomes rampant. For example, suppose someone promises you $109 next year (365 days from today) in exchange for $100 today. What is the rate of interest on such a loan? Nine percent is one correct answer. After all, $100 grows by 9 percent in order to equal $109 next year. Or does it? The instantaneous growth rate, or rate of interest compounded continuously, is less than 9 percent, approximately 8.6 percent. The simple, annual rate of interest is 9 percent; the $109 next year is 9 percent more than $100 today. Even assuming simple annual interest is appropriate, some would claim the rate of interest on this loan is less than 9 percent because they assume (obviously incorrectly) that a year has 360 days. In our example the loan promises 9 percent in a "year" and 5 days, so the annual interest rate is less than 9 percent. While the assumption is bizarre in some respects, it is convenient to have a "standard" year instead of years with 365 or 366 days. We just scratched the surface on the difficulties of measuring the rate of interest on a particular security. Reams of paper were necessary to write truth-in-lending laws. If there are many ways to skin a cat, there are more ways to compute the rate of interest. We largely ignore technical issues in the remainder of this section and present a measure of the rate of interest and other popular measures of return.

Debt was defined as contractual obligations to repay specified amounts in the future. When the original term to maturity, that is, the time interval between the dates of issue and final payment, is more than one year, virtually all debt instruments promise periodic payments, typically every six months, and a final larger payment. The periodic payments are called the coupon payments, and the final payment is the principal, par, or face value of the debt. Figure 5–1 pictures a bond, the name given to a debt instrument with a maturity greater than 10 years. Years ago nearly all bonds were coupon or bearer bonds like the one pictured in Figure 5–1. To receive payment the bondholder presents to the issuer the clipped coupon—the reason for scissors in most safety deposit booths. The issuer maintains no record of ownership, and the bearer of the bond is always presumed to be the rightful owner. Because of the risk of total loss due to theft or fire, many bondholders now prefer registered bonds, where the issuer maintains ownership records and automatically sends the periodic payments, which are still called coupon payments although no coupons are sent.[2] Coupon payments typically are not made on government and business debt when the original term to maturity is one year or less. In this case the only payment is the principal or face value.

The (annual) *coupon or nominal yield* is the ratio of the (annual) coupon payment to the principal. The coupon rate remains fixed throughout the life of the bond. The rate of interest or yield to maturity is not fixed, however. The rate of interest is derived by computing the present value of the stream of future payments. The relationship between any present value (PV), annual interest rate written as a decimal (i), and future value one year hence ($FV_1$) is given below.

$$PV (1 + i) = FV_1 \qquad\qquad (5–1)$$

For example, what will $100 today (PV = $100) equal next year if the rate of interest is 10 percent (i = 0.1)? $110, according to equation (5–1). Continuing on, what will the $100 equal 2 years from now assuming interest is compounded annually? $121 (the interest earned in the second year is $11, ten percent of $110). In general,

$$PV(1 + i)^2 = FV_2 \qquad\qquad (5–2)$$

where $FV_2$ is a value two years hence. For any number n,

$$PV(1 + i)^n = FV_n \qquad\qquad (5–3)$$

where $FV_n$ is the value n years hence.

---

[2] Coupon bonds are resurging largely because they are a convenient way to evade taxes. Since firms are unaware of the ownership of coupon bonds, they cannot comply with the IRS requirement of reporting interest payments.

**FIGURE 5–1  Coupon bond**

Most people can readily compute the future value of a current sum. The reverse process for some reason is more troublesome, perhaps indicating that division is more difficult than multiplication. What does $110 next year ($FV_1 = \$110$) equal today if the rate of interest is 10 percent ($i = 0.1$)? In other words, how much do I need today in order to have $110 next year when the rate of interest is 10 percent? $100. We can use equation (5–1) although in this case it is more conveniently written as (5–1′) so the variable to be solved, PV, stands by itself.

$$PV = FV_1/(1 + i)$$
$$100 = 110/(1.1)$$
(5–1′)

Similarly,

$$PV = FV_n/(1 + i)^n$$
(5–3′)

The process of computing present value is also called discounting.

The price of a bond ($P_B$) is simply the present value of all coupons (C) and the face (F). Assuming an n period bond with a coupon each period, the price of the bond is given by

$$P_B = \frac{C_1}{(1 + i)} + \frac{C_2}{(1 + i)^2} + \cdots + \frac{C_n}{(1 + i)^n} + \frac{F}{(1 + i)^n}$$
(5–4)

Buyers and sellers of bonds like any other commodity quote the price. Since the bond contract specifies the coupon and face, the interest rate can be calculated when the price is given, although it is no easy task. For example, assume a 3 period bond (n = 3) where C = 6, F = 100, and $P_B$ = 94.80 so

$$P_B = 94.80 = \frac{6}{(1 + i)} + \frac{6}{(1 + i)^2} + \frac{6}{(1 + i)^3} + \frac{100}{(1 + i)^3}$$
(5–4′)

What is the rate of interest on this bond? The *coupon yield* is 6 percent but the *rate of interest* or yield to maturity is approximately 8 percent. The difficulty of solving an equation like (5–4) increases exponentially with n. Fortunately, bond tables which contain the answer to these equations are available.

Two important relationships follow from equations (5–1) and (5–4). First, bond prices and interest rates are negatively related. When bond prices rise, the rate of interest falls, and vice versa. Even if one did not see equation (5–4), the negative relationship should have been clear provided one recalled that the rate of interest is the growth measure linking the current value and future payments. If the current price falls, then it must grow at a faster rate to equal the given future payments. Alternatively, if the growth rate falls, the current price must rise for it to equal the given future payments. Second, the rate of interest is greater than, equals, or is less than the coupon rate according to whether the current bond price is less than, equals, or is greater than the face value. In our example, the 8 percent rate of interest exceeds the 6 percent coupon because a capital gain will be realized, that is, the current price ($94.80) is less than the face value ($100).

Perpetuities or consols are one case where the negative relationship between bond prices and the rate of interest is especially straightforward. Perpetuities have perpetual coupons (infinite maturity) but no repayment of the principal. Suppose the perpetuity offered $1 per year until the end of time. How much would you pay for such an obligation? You and your heirs will receive an infinite sum, assuming the payments in fact will be made, yet you should pay only a very modest sum. If the rate of interest were 10 percent, the price of this bond would be $10. For any perpetuity,

$$P_B = C/i \qquad (5-5)$$

where the terms are as previously defined. The validity of equation (5–5) may be appreciated by asking how much money earning 10 percent annually is necessary in order to receive $1 per year? $10. The price of perpetuities and their yield are inversely related; if the price of a perpetuity doubles, the yield is cut in half.

Because the yield to maturity is difficult to calculate, other measures of return are popular. The *current yield* for a bond is the ratio of the coupon to the price. For common stocks the current yield is measured analogously: the ratio of the dividend to the price. Besides reporting prices and trading volume for each stock listed on the New York and American Exchanges, *The Wall Street Journal* reports the current yield under a column simply called "yield." The current yield ignores the fact that stock and bond prices can change, giving rise to capital gains and losses. If the current or running yield is 10 percent but the bond falls 2 percent in value, the total return is only 8 percent. The *average total return to maturity* (ATRT), which is a good approximation to the rate of interest, is the sum of the coupon, C, plus the average annualized capital change to maturity $(F - P_B)/n$, all relative to the "average" price during the maturity of the security, $(P_B + F)/2$.

$$\text{ATRT} = \frac{C + (F - P_B)/n}{(P_B + F)/2} \qquad (5-6)$$

Using the numbers in our previous example where the rate of interest was 8 percent, the ATRT is 0.0793 or 7.93 percent.[3]

$$\text{ATRT} = \frac{6 + (100 - 94.80)/3}{(94.80 + 100)/2} = 0.0793 \qquad (5-6)$$

---

[3] The ATRT cannot be computed for perpetuities or common stock because neither has a finite maturity. However, for any prior time period one can calculate a similar measure by substituting the realized percentage capital change for the capital change to maturity.

Equation (5–6) demonstrates an important relationship between return, security prices, and term to maturity; *the security price change necessary to induce any given change in the total return varies directly with the term to maturity.* This tends to make long-term bond prices more volatile.[4] For example, assume two securities, a 1-year and a 20-year bond; both have 8 percent coupon rates and sell at their $100 face or par value. Assume further that the price of the 1-year bond falls to $97 so its total return to maturity rises to approximately 11 percent, the sum of the approximately 8 percent current yield and the 3 percent capital gain at maturity. If the price on the 20-year bond fell the same amount, its return would rise to only approximately 8.15 percent because the $3 capital gain must be spread over 20 years. A 20-year, 8-percent coupon bond yields approximately 11 percent when its price falls to $71.43, as substitution in equation (5–6) shows.

$$\text{ATRT} = \frac{8 + (100 - 71.43)/20}{(71.43 + 100)/2} = .11 \text{ or } 11 \text{ percent} \qquad (5\text{–}6'')$$

The yield on Treasury bills and other securities with an original maturity less than a year is conventionally computed in a peculiar manner. When the original maturity is less than a year, coupon payments are not made. These types of securities are called *discount securities* because they always sell below face, the difference between the current price and face being the interest. "The" rate of interest on these securities, which we shall call the *discount yield,* $i_d$, for reasons which will become clear immediately, is computed as follows,

$$i_d = \frac{F - P}{F} \times \frac{360}{\text{days to maturity}} \qquad (5\text{–}7)$$

where F is the face value and P is the price of the Treasury bill. The term $(F - P)/F$ is the percentage gain on the *face,* and (360/days to maturity) annualizes this gain, assuming 360 days is a year. For example, assume the price of a $10,000 Treasury bill maturing in three months (days to maturity = 90) is $9,760. What is the interest rate or discount yield on this instrument? Using equation (5–7), 0.096 or 9.6 percent.

$$i_d = \frac{10,000 - 9,760}{10,000} \times \frac{360}{90} = 0.096 \text{ or } 9.6 \text{ percent} \qquad (5\text{–}7')$$

Since the buyer of a discount security does not pay and the issuer does not receive the face value, the discount yield according to equation (5–7), which measures the percentage gain on the face value, is misleading. Use equation (5–8) to compute the rate of interest defined as the rate of return

---

[4] This is true even though the rates of return are more stable on long-term than on short-term securities.

on the current value, that is, the rate at which the present value grows in order to equal the future value.

$$i = \frac{F - P}{P} \times \frac{360}{\text{days to maturity}} \tag{5-8}$$

In our example the discount yield is 9.6 percent but the true rate of interest is 9.84 percent.

$$i = \frac{10,000 - 9,760}{9,760} \times \frac{360}{90} = 0.0984 \text{ or } 9.84 \text{ percent} \tag{5-8'}$$

Equations (5–7) and (5–8) show that *a security's discount yield is always less than its effective rate of interest* since the face value always is greater than the current price. Given this, lenders should prefer to quote the discount yield because it appears they are offering lower interest rate loans. This is indeed the case. Years ago banks almost exclusively lent short term to firms, which made one payment at maturity. A $100 loan contract may have specified a 6 percent rate of interest but, being a discount loan, interest was taken off the top, that is, the borrower received $94, and the effective interest rate was more than 6 percent, specifically 6.38 percent.

When quoting discount yields became standard practice, lenders dominated the market in the sense that the average lender could easily accommodate many average borrowers and the average borrower borrowed relatively infrequently. These conditions no longer hold. In particular, Treasury debt is widely held; the assets of the largest financial institution do not begin to approach the value of Treasury debt outstanding. Moreover, the Treasury issues bills weekly. Nevertheless, the Treasury has been unable to change the way bankers and other major lenders quote the yield on its debt. The return on Treasury bills continues to be quoted on a discount basis although the Treasury and any other borrower prefer that the return on their debt be quoted on an effective interest rate basis. In our previous example the discount yield was 9.6 percent while the effective interest rate was 9.84 percent. Would you be more willing to buy a Treasury bill when you are told "the" interest rate is 9.6 or 9.84? Quoting the 9.84 percent effective interest rate instead of the 9.6 percent discount yield would facilitate the sale of Treasury bills.

While it is true that the financially sophisticated realize that a 9.6 discount yield equals a 9.84 effective interest rate, many are not financially sophisticated, and the side-by-side use of the two ways of measuring return may induce many to accept a lower return. The small money-market certificates are a good illustration. Banks and savings and loan associations issue 6-month certificates with rates tied to the Treasury bill rate at the previous weekly auction. The formula tying the certificate and Treasury bill rates is complicated; depending on the type of financial institutions and other factors the certificate rate may equal or marginally exceed the Treasury bill rate. Assume for simplicity the certificate rate equals the Treasury bill rate. The minimum denomination on this type of certificate and Treasury bills is the same, $10,000. The advertised returns may be equal but should an individual be indifferent about the security purchased? Ignoring transactions costs, taxes, and other factors, an individual would be better off by purchasing a Treasury bill because the advertised return on the bill is its discount yield while the return on the certificate is an effective rate of interest. Consider another example. Suppose a 6-month (days to maturity = 180), $10,000 Treasury bill sells for $9,500. Using equation (5–7), the discount yield is 10 percent.

$$i_d = \frac{10,000 - 9,500}{10,000} \times \frac{360}{180} = 0.1 = 10 \text{ percent} \qquad (5\text{–}7'')$$

Banks then announce they will pay the same rate, 10 percent annually, and they do. Ignoring the minimum denomination requirement for simplicity, the same $9,500 deposited in a bank would be worth $9,975 six months later. (The interest income on $9,500 at 10 percent annually is $475 (= $950/2) for six months, which when added to $9,500 gives $9,975.) An individual is better off purchasing the Treasury bill because a 10 percent discount yield is a greater return than a 10 percent interest rate. In other words, the effective interest rate on the Treasury bill is more than the 10 percent discount yield.

## ATTRIBUTES OR CHARACTERISTICS OF DEBT

The rate of interest is only one, albeit the most important, attribute or characteristic of any debt instrument. Other characteristics are sufficiently important that debt instruments differing in these characteristics often are given different names. For example, government securities with an original maturity of a year or less are Treasury *bills* while similar securities maturing within 1 to 10 years are Treasury *notes,* and those maturing beyond 10 years are Treasury *bonds.* A perpetuity or consol is the ultimate long-term bond issued by some governments other than the United States. The classic example is the 2½ percent English perpetuity. Private securities in particular are classified into two categories by their term to maturity. *Money market instruments* are securities maturing within a year, and *capital market instruments* are securities maturing beyond a year.

Risk is another important characteristic of debt. We should distinguish between two types of risk: (1) *default risk* and (2) *market risk.* Default risk is the probability that the contractual payments will not be made, or at best significantly delayed. Market risk is the current uncertainty of a security's value at the time one intends to convert it to cash. Bonds which one intends to hold to maturity are free of market risk. Bond price fluctuations are irrelevant if a sale is not anticipated. Long-term bonds do carry substantial market risk if the planned holding period is short, as is traditionally assumed. Long-term bond prices can fluctuate significantly over short periods of time. The possible market risk of short-term bonds often is not appreciated. If one's planned holding period is 30 years, 1-year bonds bear market risk.[5] Future interest rates are unknown. An individual with $1,000 to invest is uncertain about the value of this investment, including interest, 30 years hence if 1-year securities are purchased each year. In contrast, the value 30 years hence of a currently 30-year-to-maturity, $1,000 bond is a guaranteed $1,000 plus the coupons, abstracting from default risk. The two types of risk typically are positively related but examples to the contrary exist. Treasury bonds are default risk free—the government can always crank the big green money machine—but are *not* free of market risk. Conversely, check deposits over $100,000 (the current FDIC insurance maximum) are market-risk free—banks offer fixed dollar-denominated deposits—but are *not* free of default risk.

Default risk is so important to investors, yet so difficult for them to estimate directly, that debtors pay public bond-rating firms, such as Moody's Investors Service and Standard & Poor, to evaluate their debt. Although a firm may be quite confident its debt will receive a relatively low quality rating (high default risk rating), it gladly pays bond-rating firms because the sale of unrated bonds is virtually impossible. Investors first have to know the risk of default before deciding what compensation is necessary. Table 5–1 summarizes the Standard & Poor rating system. Bonds rated CC are not as risky as they may seem. The "outright speculations" which Standard & Poor classifies as CC often have met their obligations on a timely basis. This is not surprising if one recalls that only relatively strong firms can issue bonds in the first place. The Standard & Poor ratings accurately reflect relative default risk. That is, compared to AAA bonds which almost never default, CC bonds default much more frequently, even though the absolute number of CC defaults is not large.

Market risk may be measured by the dispersion of the security's return over time. If the return was highly variable, predictions should be highly uncertain. *A security's beta, β, is a relative measure of market risk* which has become increasingly popular. Many investment advisory firms report the beta for each stock, and betas have been calculated for some bonds. A stock's beta is the slope coefficient of the regression of a stock's return (dependent variable) on the return of a broad market index such as Standard & Poor's 500 stock index (independent variable). More simply, beta shows the average change in the return of a stock per unit change in the return of the market index. Over a short period of time, the return on a stock may move contrary to the market and its beta will be negative. Over longer periods of time, the prices of most stocks move in the same direc-

---

[5] Henceforth we shall follow conventional practice and let "bonds" represent any debt instrument regardless of term to maturity.

**TABLE 5-1  Standard & Poor's bond ratings**

| Rating | Description |
| --- | --- |
| AAA | The highest grade obligations. They possess the ultimate degree of protection as to principal and coupons. |
| AA | High grade obligation. In the majority of cases differ from AAA issues only in small degree. |
| A | Upper medium grade obligations. Coupons and principal ultimately are safe but severe economic condition might cause some delay. |
| BBB | Medium grade category which is borderline between definitely sound and those where the speculative element begins to predominate. Their susceptibility to depressions necessitates constant watching. *This group is the lowest which qualifies for commercial bank investment.* |
| BB | Lower medium grade. |
| B | Speculative bonds whose coupon payments cannot be assured under difficult economic conditions. |
| CCC—CC | Outright speculations, particularly the lower rated. Interest is paid but continuation is uncertain. Income bonds, i.e., bonds which pay interest only if the firm is profitable, typically are rated CC. |
| C | Income bonds on which no interest is being paid. |
| DDD—DD—D | All bonds rated DDD, DD, or D are in default with the rating indicating the relative salvage value. |

tion and nearly all betas are positive. The common price pattern in the long run occurs because major economic events like booms, depressions, and inflations ultimately affect firms in a similar manner. Beta equals one when a security is as volatile as the market and beta rises (falls) as its volatility rises (falls) relative to the market.

The *taxability* of coupon payments effectively distinguishes many bonds. The interest payments of state and local governments currently are exempt from federal income taxes, and interest on Treasury securities is exempt from state and local income taxes.

*Marketability* measures the ease and cost of being "in and out," that is, buying an item and selling it shortly thereafter. An item must satisfy two conditions to be readily marketable: (1) the brokerage and other transactions cost associated with it must be low, and (2) the purchase and sales price should be relatively independent of the time spent searching for sellers and buyers. One should think before purchasing nonmarketable instruments because mistaken purchases are costly. Nonmarketable instruments are suitable only for these with long holding-period horizons. Houses and other real estate are not readily marketable assets. Houses which must be sold within a week typically fetch a price much lower than one would get by standing pat and keeping the house on the market for six months. Moreover, the usual realty commission is 6 percent of the sales price, making a buy and sell strategy costly. Treasury bills in contrast are readily marketable. Treasury bills worth billions of dollars are sold daily and the commission rate is quite small, especially on large denomination bills. Standardized items which are widely held often are marketable. Investors coined words to express compactly a debt instrument's degree of marketability. What is the main difference between a loan and a security? Loans are nonmarketable while securities are readily marketable debt instruments.

Most loan service costs do not increase proportionally with *loan size,* making size a major debt characteristic. Some loan service costs are fixed, that is, independent of the size of the loans. It costs no more to record a $1 million loan than a $1,000 loan. Spreading these fixed costs over a large number of dollars reduces the loan service cost per dollar lent. Some service costs even decline absolutely as well as relatively with loan size, at least up to a point. The information about small firms that a lender believes is necessary to evaluate a loan request often is costly to acquire, while similar information about large firms is readily available virtually free. Loan size often is not independent of the other debt characteristics. For example, consumer credit and other small loans often carry substantial default risk, which further increases loan costs even if one recovers the full amount lent. Continuously monitoring high-risk loans and immediately notifying the borrower of any payment delay is costly but does tend to encourage prompt repayment in the future and reduce default losses. Moreover, as will be discussed more fully in the next section, loan size, borrower size, and the number and type of potential lenders are all positively related.

Liquidity was saved for last because everyone recognizes its importance while simultaneously disagreeing on its precise qualities. Generally, *liquid securities are said to encompass two characteristics already mentioned: (1) ready marketability and (2) little short-term market risk.* That is, a liquid security can be sold on short notice easily and at little cost, and the near future sales or redemption price is known with a high degree of certainty. Treasury bills, commercial paper, certificates of deposit, and U.S. savings bonds, which will be described fully later, are examples of liquid securities. Most liquid assets are short-term which, by definition, mature in the near future and are free of short-term market risk. U.S. savings bonds are a conspicuous exception. The Treasury stands ready to redeem savings bonds at predetermined prices, which effectively makes them riskless and marketable even if they cannot be sold to other individuals.[6] Many securities possess one but not both qualities of liquid securities. For example, the common stock of large companies listed on the New York Stock Exchange and long-term government bonds are readily marketable but possess significant short-term market risk. Stock and bond prices sometimes change more than 10 percent in a quarter. Short-term consumer-oriented money market certificates like the 6-month certificates tied to the Treasury bill rate are virtually free from market risk but lack marketability. A substantial interest penalty is incurred in cashing these certificates before maturity.

### DETERMINANTS OF THE RATE OF INTEREST: A CROSS-SECTION ANALYSIS

Throughout the latter part of this book we will assume a standard bond which offers "the" rate of interest. This is a useful simplification. In point of fact, at any moment one observes a multitude of interest rates. What explains the different rates of interest on alternative debt instruments? Why is it that some securities yield higher rates of return than others? The various characteristics of debt instruments are not altogether independent. In particular, the rate of interest on any security, relative to the yields on other securities at the same time, largely reflects the other important attributes listed in the last section. For example, the taxability of a security influences its rate of interest. Largely because people are in different tax brackets, the quoted rate of interest always is computed on a pre-tax basis. However, individuals are interested in the after-tax return instead of the pre-tax return. To equalize the after-tax return on securities, the (quoted) rate of interest is low on securities which are lightly taxed. In particular, *the taxability effect lowers the rate of interest on (1) state and local securities (2) U.S. Treasury securities, and (3) low-coupon bonds*. As indicated in the last section, state and local securities are exempt from federal income tax. Other things being equal, someone in the 40 percent tax bracket is indifferent between a 10 percent fully taxable bond and a 6 percent tax-exempt bond.[7] State and local bonds typically yield 30 to 40 percent less than comparable fully taxed securities. Thus, state and locals are not purchased by those in the lowest tax brackets but are tax "loopholes" for those in the highest tax brackets. States do not tax the interest on Treasury securities so the interest rate on these securities is low, *ceteris paribus*. Since the federal income tax rates are much higher than state and local tax rates, Treasury securities yield substantially more than state and locals on a pretax basis.

Taxability reduces the quoted rate of interest on low-coupon bonds. The total yield on any bond is generated by the coupon payments and any

---

[6] From the viewpoint of the savings bond holder, Treasury redemption is equivalent to purchase by someone else.

[7] Calling state and local securities "tax-exempts" can be a misnomer because states tax each other's securities.

capital gain, which is taxed at a lower rate than coupon (interest) income. Consequently, individuals prefer capital gains to coupon payments, which reduces the yield on low-coupon, high-capital-gain securities, just as the lightly taxed state and local offer a low return. An example may be helpful. Assume a recently issued 12 percent coupon security is selling at par so its total return is also 12 percent. Also assume a comparable 6 percent coupon security issued sometime ago when interest rates were lower. The latter security clearly cannot sell at par and yield only 6 percent when a comparable security is offering 12 percent. The price of the low-coupon security will fall in order to realize a capital gain at maturity. The price decline will not be enough to cause an annualized 6 percent capital gain and equalize the (quoted) rate of interest because the gain is taxed at a lower rate. Assuming interest and capital gains are taxed at 50 and 25 percent respectively, the high coupon, 12 percent, bond yields 6 percent after taxes. To equalize after-tax returns, the low coupon bond would have to yield only 10 percent, the 6 percent coupon plus a 4 percent capital gain. In summary, buyers are willing to pay a higher price for any lightly taxed security and, consequently, lower its pretax return.

After taxability, loan size is the most important determinant of cross-sectional interest rates for three reasons. First, just as taxability influences the rate of interest on loans because lenders are interested in their *net* after-tax returns, *the cost of making and administering loans influences the rate of interest.* As mentioned earlier, small loans are especially costly to make and administer, per dollar lent. Consistent with this, interest rates on consumer and other small loans are among the highest. Second, *small loans generally are riskier,* which further increases administration costs, such as the collection services of Badger and Browbeat (a firm that fell on hard times when aggravated assault was raised from a misdemeanor to a felony). Besides its effect on interest rates through administration costs, default risk clearly affects interest rates directly. The direct effect is discussed shortly.

Loan and firm size are positively related. A small firm which gets a large loan will no longer remain a small firm. In addition to high administration costs, *interest rates on small loans are high because lenders often exercise monopoly powers against small borrowers.* Unlike other industries where the degree of monopoly power depends almost exclusively on the type of firms in the industry, monopoly power in banking depends more on the customer than the bank. For example, the Bank of America is the largest bank in the United States, yet it exercises virtually no monopoly power when dealing with IBM, AT&T, GM, GE, and other large companies. These large companies can borrow anywhere throughout the United States, indeed throughout the world. The thousands of potential lenders to large firms are disorganized and cannot form a cartel like the relatively few OPEC countries. Moreover, large firms maintain deposit accounts at many banks. If any one bank attempted to exercise monopoly power, the large firm would quickly find another bank only too willing to accept its deposits and make a loan.

Contrast the above with the opportunities available to small borrowers. Where can the owner of Joe's Diner borrow? Banks outside the immediate geographical area will not even consider the loan requests of small borrowers. Banks in New York lack information about small firms in San Francisco, and information costs increase with the distance between small borrowers and lenders. If a small California firm were audacious enough to inquire about a loan at a New York bank, it would be told politely but firmly that it should maintain its banking ties in California. Given the existence of only a handful of banks in most geographical areas, banks do organize against small borrowers. Both large and small banks exercise monopoly power against small firms. The Bank of America with numerous competitors in San Francisco probably is less of a monopolist than the First National Bank of Podunk, a one-bank town. While small firms are discriminated against, discrimination is less important than administration costs in explaining the differential between interest rates to large and small borrowers. Empirical estimates are presented in Chapter 8.

Lenders demand an interest premium on high default-risk bonds. The rate of interest is higher on bonds rated CCC than AAA. The size of the default-risk premium depends on (1) the probability of default and (2) the public's attitude towards risk taking. From the viewpoint of the lender, *collateral,* which increases recoveries during defaults, is equivalent to lower default probabilities. Consequently, borrowers offer collateral and thereby lower borrowing cost. The specific property being financed almost always serves as collateral for real estate loans. In some cases the same property is collateral for several loans. In case of default and sale of the real estate, the first mortgage is paid in full before any payment on the second mortgage. Some debt has prior claim on all assets instead of being secured by specifically identified assets. Secured bonds of manufacturing firms generally are of this type. Bonds without collateral are called *debentures*.

Bond ratings accurately measure relative default risk at all phases of the business cycle, but it appears the ratings overestimate default risk in the boom and underestimate default risk in the trough. Interest rates reflect this. The BBB interest rate is always greater than the AAA interest, but the spread narrows during a boom and widens during a trough. During a boom virtually any fool can make a profit. The default risk of marginal firms will appear quite low, and the BBB–AAA interest rate differential will narrow. Default risk rises across the board during a trough, the more so for marginal firms. Earnings of blue-chip firms decline, often significantly, during recessions but the likelihood of default remains virtually nil. Marginally profitable firms on the other hand do not have the resources to weather a recession. A recession is an economic pneumonia: it temporarily debilitates the strong but kills the old and weak. Interest differentials widen during a recession.

Figure 5–2, which graphs several long-term bond yields, confirms the major assertions of this section. State and local government bonds have

**FIGURE 5–2   Long-term bond yields**

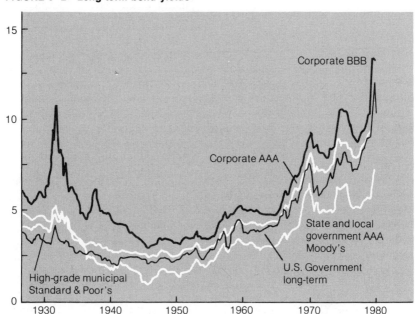

SOURCE: Federal Reserve, *Historical Chart Book, 1980.*

offered the lowest yields since 1940 because federal income tax rates have been high. Prior to 1940, however, a combination of very low tax rates and high default risk drove the yield on state and local government bonds above the yield on riskless U.S. Treasury bonds. Note the width of the BBB–AAA interest rate differential throughout the entire 1930s and particularly during the depth of the Great Depression of 1929–33. The differential again widened during the 1974–75 recession.

The remainder of this section examines attitudes towards risk taking, the second determinant of the default-risk premium. However, the remainder is geared more toward understanding term structure theories presented in the following section than default risk. What may be overkill for default risk alone is essential for the term structure. We proceed by analyzing several risky events. Suppose completely risk-free bonds offer a 10 percent yield. What is the interest rate on similar bonds with a two percent probability of (total) default? Clearly, the interest rate on risky bonds must be greater than 10 percent since more is preferred to less. A 10 percent risky bond never offers more, and sometimes (2 percent of the time in our example) offers less, than a 10 percent safe bond. Before indicating the size of this example's risk premium, consider another example which, we hope, conveys the applicability of the principles discussed here to any risky event, and not simply to default risk. Suppose you are given the opportunity to flip an unbiased coin. Heads earns you $1 million while tails pays nothing. What value do you place on this risky event? The *expected value* or average payout is $500,000. However, what is the *certainty equivalent* of the risky event, that is, what guaranteed, certain amount makes you indifferent to the gamble? Persons are said to be *risk-neutral* when their certainty equivalent equals the expected value. Risk-neutral people are indifferent to risk, by definition, and decide solely on the basis of the expected return. In our example, a risk-neutral person prefers the risky event ($500,000 expected value) to, say, a guaranteed $490,000. On balance, most people in most circumstances are *risk averters*. Their certainty equivalent is less than the expected value. In lieu of the gamble, the risk averter may accept a guaranteed $490,000, or possibly much less. The *risk premium,* which is the difference between the expected value and certainty equivalent, measures attitudes towards risk. The risk premium is positive for risk-averters. Some quite risk-averse person will forego our gamble for a small guaranteed amount, say, $150,000. Risk aversion is the foundation for the insurance industry while *risk-lovers* gamble. Risk lovers pay to gamble; their certainty equivalent exceeds the expected value. The risk "premium" is negative for risk lovers. Claiming that "baby needs a new pair of shoes," a real risk lover might forego a guaranteed $750,000 in our example and flip a coin. Oh yes, we had an earlier example about a 2 percent default-risk bond. Can you state how the interest rate on such a bond depends on the public's attitude toward risk? When will its interest rate be approximately 12.25 percent?

## TERM STRUCTURE OF INTEREST RATES

Economists have analyzed most extensively the effect of term to maturity on the rate of interest. *The term structure of interest rates curve or yield curve shows the relationship at any one instant between the yield to maturity and term to maturity on otherwise comparable securities.* Several yield curves are plotted in Figure 5–3. The interest rate or yield to maturity is on the vertical axis and term to maturity is on the horizontal axis. Traditionally, the yield curve of marketable Treasury securities is computed because no other unit has issued as many securities spanning a wide maturity range. Comparability except for maturity is most likely satisfied by securities of the same issuer. To repeat, the yield curve utilizes cross-section data; it shows interest rates at any one instant. The four yield curve patterns most often encountered are illustrated in Figure 5–3. The

**FIGURE 5–3  Term structure of interest rates or yield curves**

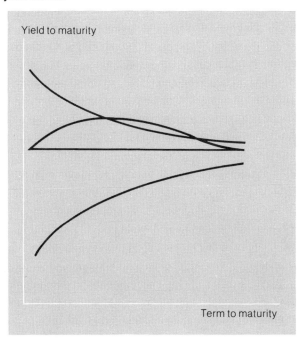

yield curve typically is (1) upward sloping, (2) flat, (3) downward sloping, or (4) humped, rising at first and then declining.

What determines the term structure of interest? Why does the term structure curve have a particular shape this year and a different shape next year? *There are three main theories of the term structure of interest rates: (1) the market segmentation or hedging or supply and demand hypothesis, (2) the expectations hypothesis, and (3) the risk premium hypothesis.*[8]

*Extreme risk aversion and institutional restrictions are the fundamental assumptions underlying the market segmentation hypothesis of the term structure of interest rates.* As indicated earlier, market risk depends on the relation between the bond's term to maturity and the holder's planned holding period. The extremely risk-averse bondholder will match the planned holding period and term to maturity. Five-year and 30-year bonds are risky to an individual who plans to hold securities for 20 years. The

---

[8] The risk premium hypothesis is more often called the liquidity preference hypothesis. We believe the former name is less confusing. "Liquidity preference" often is equated with Keynes' speculative demand for money, which assumes that risk-neutral individuals maximize expected return. This is the assumption of the expectations hypothesis, as we shall see shortly. The risk premium or liquidity preference hypothesis *of the term structure* assumes partial risk aversion.

proceeds of the 5-year bond will have to be reinvested for 15 years at an uncertain rate of interest, while the current 30-year bond will still have a 10-year term to maturity when it is sold 20 years hence, and the sales price of every item 20 years hence is uncertain. Similarly, borrowers incur risk when the maturity of the bond issued differs from the life of the asset being financed. For example, assume the life of a steel mill is 40 years; over that period the steel company expects to recover the cost of the mill and earn a normal return. The steel mill will not generate sufficient revenues in one year to cover its construction cost. The steel company which issues 1-year bonds to finance the mill runs the risk of not being able to "roll over" the bonds next year. On the other hand, a firm which issues 30-year bonds in order to purchase inventories which are liquidated in three months incurs the risk of finding a suitable investment for the funds thrown off by the inventory liquidation. Such a firm could buy its outstanding bonds but the purchase price would be uncertain. The risk premium demanded by extreme risk averters are economically unfeasible and, consequently, they match holding periods and term to maturity.

Supporters of the market segmentation hypothesis recognize that not everyone is extremely risk averse. Indeed, some are not risk averse at all; Las Vegas was built for risk lovers. Nevertheless, they feel the loan market is dominated by naturally extremely risk-averse individuals and individuals who act extremely risk averse due to institutional and legal factors. For example, suppose someone is willing to bear the risk of financing a house with successive one-year loans. Such an individual almost certainly will not be accommodated. Savings and loans traditionally make long-term mortgages, and restrictions on savings and loans and other financial institutions close whatever avenues tradition left open.

Assuming for simplicity two types of loans, short- and long-term, extreme risk aversion implies that the short-term (long-term) interest rate is totally irrelevant to bondholders with long (short) holding periods. The short- and long-term interest rates can be analyzed with ordinary supply and demand curves. Figures 5–4a and 5–4b graph on the horizontal axis the quantity of short- and long-term loanable funds, respectively, and the corresponding interest rate is graphed on the vertical axis. (Loans and loanable funds are identical; borrowers demand loans or loanable funds. While brevity would suggest a preference for loans, economists are contrary minded in this respect.) The demand for short-term loanable funds is downward sloping because at lower short-term interest rates borrowers are encouraged to undertake more *short-term* projects. The demand for short-term loanable funds is *not* downward sloping because borrowers temporarily finance long-term projects with short-term credit. A change in the short-term interest rate has no effect on the long-term supply and demand for loanable funds. The markets are segmented, at least the *private* part of the market. The term structure of interest rates simply reflects

**FIGURE 5–4  Segmented markets approach to the term structure of interest rates**

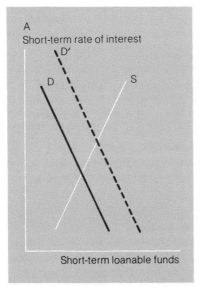
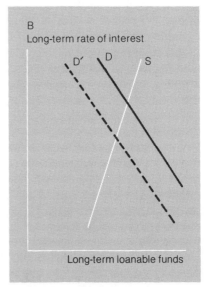

the strength of the demand and supply for loanable funds by term to maturity.

The market segmentation hypothesis suggests that the Treasury can significantly influence the term structure of interest rates by changing the composition of its debt. When the Treasury borrows short-term, it supplies short-term bills or, equivalently, *demands* short-term loanable funds. If the Treasury borrows short term instead of long term, the short-term demand for loanable funds and its rate of interest increase, and the long-term demand and its rate of interest fall, as illustrated by the dashed curves in Figures 5–4a and 5–4b, respectively.

The expectations hypothesis is the second major theory of the term structure of interest rates. *The expectations hypothesis assumes individuals (1) form expectations about future interest rates and (2) are risk neutral, deciding solely on the basis of the highest expected rate of return.* For the moment, assume everyone forms identical expectations. In terms of our previous example, this theory assumes an individual would be indifferent between a certain $500,000 and a 50-50 chance of nothing or $1 million. *Given these two assumptions, it follows that (1) long-term interest rates are an average of current and expected future short-term interest rates, and (2) the expected holding period yield is independent of the security held.* An example best demonstrates that the two conclusions do follow from the assumptions. Assume for simplicity only two time periods, t and t + 1, called "years." Let the rate of interest on one-year loans at time t be 8 percent, and the expected, as time t, interest rate on one-year loans in period t + 1 is 12 percent. Algebraically,

$$i_{1,t} = 8 \qquad \text{and} \qquad _{t+1}i^e_{1,t} = 12 \qquad (5\text{--}9)$$

where i is the rate of interest, the first subscript following i is the length of the loan, the second subscript following i is the time period, the subscript preceding i is the future time period for which the expectation is formed, and e is expected. Given (5–9), what is the interest rate on a two-year loan in period t?

$$i_{2,t} = ? \qquad (5\text{--}10)$$

A two-year loan may be viewed as a one-year loan today and a one-year loan a year hence. Viewed in this manner, the interest rate on two-year loans is an average of the current one-year interest rate and the expected interest rate a year hence, assuming risk-neutral individuals. Ignoring compounding, in our example[9]

$$i_{2,t} = (i_{1,t} + _{t+1}i^e_{1,t})/2 = (8 + 12)/2 = 10 \qquad (5\text{--}10')$$

Arbitrage drives the two-year rate of interest to 10 percent. Suppose the interest rate were above 10 percent, say, 11 percent. A two-year loan would bring the lender a total of 22 percent over the two years while a succession of two one-year loans would bring only a 20 percent expected return, again ignoring compound. Such a situation cannot persist. Lenders intent on maximizing their expected return will shift to the two-year loan market and drive the interest rate down to 10 percent. Similar reasoning indicates that arbitrage prevents the rate of interest from being below 10 percent. Generalizing equation (5–10')

$$i_{n,t} = (i_{1,t} + _{t+j}\sum_{j=1}^{n-1} i^e_{1,t})/n \qquad (5\text{--}11)$$

The n-period interest rate is an average of the expected 1-year interest rates during the period. *The yield curve is upward sloping when interest rates are expected to rise in the future, flat when interest rates are expected to remain constant, and downward sloping when interest rates are expected to fall.*

The expected return earned by those who lend for two years is independent of the type of loan, that is, a two-year loan or two one-year loans. Is the same true for one-year lenders? That is, will the bondholder earn the same expected return in period t whether he or she owns a one-year or

---

[9] The long-term interest rate is not a simple *arithmetic* average of the current and expected future short-term interest rates when compounding is taken into account. Nevertheless, the long-term rate is *an* average of the short-term rates, the precise type of average depending on the pattern of payments. Assuming discount loans with the only payment at maturity, the long-term rate is a geometric average of the short-term rates.

two-year bond? Yes. In our example, the holder of a one-year bond earns 8 percent in period t, and the holder of a two-year bond expects to earn the same 8 percent in period t, *not* the 10 percent equation (5–10') might suggest. The annual interest rate for the two years t *and* t + 1 is 10 percent, that is, the two-year interest rate is 10 percent, but the rate of return on two-year bonds in period t alone is only 8 percent. Let us see why this is so. The two-year bond at period t becomes a one-year bond at period t + 1. If expectations are correct so one-year bonds are offering 12 percent in period t + 1, what must happen to the capital value of the 10 percent coupon ("old" two-year) bonds during year t? The capital value falls from 100 to approximately 98. In this manner the bondholder earns 8 percent in period t and 12 percent in period t + 1, a 10 percent coupon in both years minus a 2 percent capital loss in t and plus a 2 percent capital gain in t + 1.[10] Figure 5–5 illustrates the expected price of the two-year

**FIGURE 5–5   Bond prices over time**

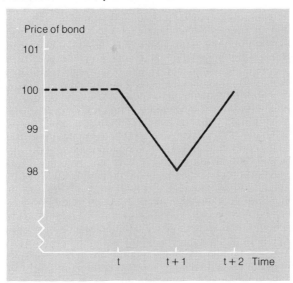

bond between periods t and t + 2. Since newly issued one-year bonds in period t + 1 are offering a 12 percent coupon, the old two-year bond will be purchased only if it offers a 2 percent capital gain. *The return is a function of the holding period; it does not depend on the maturity of the bond purchased.*

The expectations hypothesis denies that changes in the composition of

---

[10] We are ignoring taxes and other complications. Repayment of the principal in period t + 1 generates the capital gain.

Treasury debt *directly* affect the yield curve.[11] If long-term Treasury borrowing tended to drive the long-term rate up, arbitrage by profit maximizers would occur until the long-term rate equalled an average of current and expected future short-term rates. Changes in the composition of Treasury debt may *indirectly* affect the yield curve by changing expectations. For example, if long-term Treasury borrowing is interpreted as indicating that a more restrictive policy of higher future rates will be adopted, the yield curve should become steeper.

Of course, everyone's expectations are not identical as we have been assuming so far. Differences of opinion make horse races and financial markets, causing one person to sell and another to buy. Recognizing differences of opinion simply means that the two major implications of the expectations hypothesis should be expressed only for the representative or marginal individual. That is, (1) long-term interest rates are an average of the current and expected future short-term interest rates of the representative person and (2) the expected holding yield for the representative person is independent of the security held. Suppose you are not the representative person, where your expectations of future interest rates are much *higher* than the expectations of others. In this case you will *not* be indifferent between short- and long-term bonds. In your mind long-term interest rates are too low; they incorporate the low expected future rates of the representative person. You believe short-term securities will offer a higher yield than long-term securities. Conversely, suppose your expectations of future interest rates are much *lower* than the expectations of others. In this case you will prefer long-term over short- term securities. Assuming you do not have any better basis for forming accurate forecasts of future interest rates than the other market participants, which security should you purchase? In this case you should consider yourself the representative person, and according to the expectations hypothesis, the term to maturity selected does not influence the expected holding period yield. You may ponder at length over the choice of maturities but a decision based on the flip of a coin will be as profitable on average.[12]

The risk-premium hypothesis of the term structure is an intermediate hypothesis incorporating elements of the other two hypotheses. The risk premium hypothesis assumes (1) *individuals are moderately risk averse and (2) long-term bonds are risky to bondholders because, on balance, their planned holding period is short.* According to this hypothesis, the rate of interest on two-year bonds is *greater than* an average of the current and future interest rates on one-year bonds in order to compensate bond-

---

[11] We are assuming expectations are approximately homogeneous.

[12] The reader familiar with the investment literature will note the similarity between the expectations hypothesis of the term structure and the random walk hypothesis of common stock prices.

holders for the riskiness of two-year bonds. The hypothesis says that equation (5–10′) should be

$$i_{2,t} = (i_{1,t+t+1} \, i^e_{1,t} + \alpha)/2 = (8 + 12 + \alpha)/2 > 10 \qquad (5–10'')$$

where $\alpha$ is the positive risk premium. Equation (5–10″) replaces the final equality in equation (5–10′) with an inequality. *In this case, the expected yield for any holding period is less for liquid, short-term bonds than long-term bonds which earn a risk premium.*[13] Equations (5–9) and (5–10″) clearly show the implications of the risk premium hypothesis for a two-year holding period: the two-year bond yields more than a succession of two one-year bonds. The somewhat more difficult one-year holding period case is made easier by letting the risk premium $\alpha$ take a specific value, say, two. The interest rate on two-year bonds then is 11 percent. In our example, a one-year bond yields 8 percent while a two-year bond held for the first year yields 10 percent, assuming correct interest rate expectations. The capital value of a two-year, 11 percent coupon bond must fall 1 percent this year—making the total return 10 percent—in order to raise its total yield to 12 percent next year. The 8 percent return on a one-year bond is two percent ($\alpha = 2$) less than the 10 percent *expected* return on two-year bonds held for a year because the expected rate of interest next year is uncertain and may not materialize. If interest rates rise markedly next year, causing bond values to fall dramatically this year, the *realized* yield on a two-year bond held for a year could be less than 8 percent. Bondholders must be compensated for this risk.

Why do borrowers (bond issuers) willingly pay long-term rates which are higher than the average expected return on one-year bonds? The risk premium theory implicitly assumes borrowers in general are financing long-term projects. Given this, short-term credit is risky from the viewpoint of the borrower. Long-term bonds avoid the risk of not being able to borrow at some point in the future. Risk-averse borrowers willingly pay a premium to *avoid* this risk. The risk premium of the lender is a safety premium to the borrower.

## OPERATION TWIST, RECESSION, AND THE BALANCE OF PAYMENTS

The term structure of interest rates has been analyzed most extensively by economists because major economic goals are alleged to be influenced by the rate of interest on specific term to maturity bonds. In particular, GNP and employment are supposed to be influenced mainly by the long-term rate of interest while the balance of payments is supposed to be

---

[13] Note that the sentence mentions holding period yields, not yields to maturity. The risk-premium hypothesis does *not* state that the yield to maturity is always less on short-term bonds, that is, it does *not* state that the yield curve is always upward sloping.

influenced mainly by the short-term rate of interest. In subsequent theoretical chapters, where we abstract from the myriad of interest rates, we shall learn that "the " rate of interest effect on investment spending is a major link between money on the one hand and GNP and employment on the other. Investment spending here means the (1) acquisition of new plant and equipment by firms; (2) construction of homes, apartment buildings, and other structures; and (3) additions to firms' inventories. The value of new plant and equipment and structures overwhelms additions to inventories. The former types of investments are long-lived, while inventories typically are held for a short period of time and then sold. This suggested to many economists, particularly those who adhered to the market-segmentation theory of the term structure of interest rates, that the long-term interest rate was "the" interest rate influencing investment spending. In order to increase GNP and employment, monetary policy had to induce more investment spending by lowering long-term interest rates.

Throughout much of the 1950s the United States incurred a balance-of-payments deficit. At first, the deficit was viewed as a temporary phenomenon without cause for alarm. By 1960, however, Fed and other officials became concerned and decided the deficit had to end before the United States lost its entire gold stock or the dollar depreciated. In order to prevent a balance of payments deficit from becoming even larger and simultaneously maintain the exchange rate, the Treasury must induce foreigners to hold and not sell their dollar-denominated assets. What will induce foreigners to hold more dollar assets and reduce the balance of payments deficit? Higher interest rates in the United States than abroad. In particular, it was thought that foreign holdings of short-term dollar assets were sensitive to short-term rates in the United States.

The United States seemingly faced a dilemma. 1960 also was a recession year. To stimulate the economy, long-term interest rates should fall, but short-term interest rates should rise for balance of payments purposes. In order to simultaneously achieve both balance of payments equilibrium and full employment the yield curve had to be twisted clockwise, raising short-term interest rates and lowering long-term rates. The Federal Reserve and Treasury thought the task was relatively simple. They, like many bond dealers and financial analysts at the time, adhered to the market-segmentation hypothesis of the term structure, which suggested that the yield curve can be twisted by changing the composition of Treasury debt in private hands. The Fed and Treasury engaged in Operation Twist or, as some prefer to call it, Operation Nudge. Up until 1960, Federal Reserve open-market operations were executed almost exclusively by buying and selling short-term Treasury bills. On February 20, 1961, the Fed abandoned this policy, announcing, "The System Open-Market Account is purchasing in the open market U.S. Government bonds and notes of varying maturities, some of which will exceed five years." For its part, the Treasury could accommodate the natural shortening over time of the average term to maturity by concentrating new issues in the short-term area. In addition, both the Treasury and Federal Reserve could engage in outright swaps of Treasury bills for outstanding long-term bonds.

Operation Twist was only modestly successful, if not a total failure. Some blame the lack of success on insufficient effort. Federal Reserve swaps of shorts for longs as well as its net purchases of longer maturities were limited in scale. Moreover, the Treasury offset these operations to some extent by redeeming some of its maturing securities, which are necessarily short term, with long-term securities. Nevertheless, statistical studies indicate that anything short of a massive change in the composition of Treasury debt outstanding would have an insignificant impact on the term structure.[14]

## TERM STRUCTURE EVIDENCE

While the statistical studies generally do not support the market-segmentation hypothesis, the behavior of certain financial institutions suggests that the hypothesis has an element of truth. Consider life insurance companies. The premiums of a growing life insurance company will outstrip its current payments and both its assets and contingent liabilities will increase. Since the time of death of its policyholders is staggered but primarily in the distant future, the market segmentation hypothesis suggests that insurance companies will be holding mainly long-term assets. The prediction is verified repeatedly: all insurance companies throughout history have held mainly long-term bonds. This fact is consistent with the expectations hypothesis only if all insurance companies' expectations of future interest rates always were less than the expectations of others, which is unlikely.

If the behavior of insurance companies contradicts the expectations hypothesis, changes in the shape of the yield curve over the business cycle strongly support the expectations hypothesis. Figure 5–6 shows that short-term rates are much more variable than long-term rates because the yield curve typically is upward sloping during a recession and downward sloping during a boom. This is precisely what the expectations hypothesis predicts. Interest rates in general are low during a recession because firms are not borrowing due to poor sales. Interest rates are lowest on short-term securities. Recessions are temporary phenomena, by definition; re-

---

[14] Franco Modigliani and Richard Sutch, "Debt Management and the Term Structure of Interest Rates: An Empirical Analysis of Recent Experience," *Journal of Political Economy*, August 1967, supplement, pp. 569–89.

**FIGURE 5–6  Yield curves during booms and recessions**

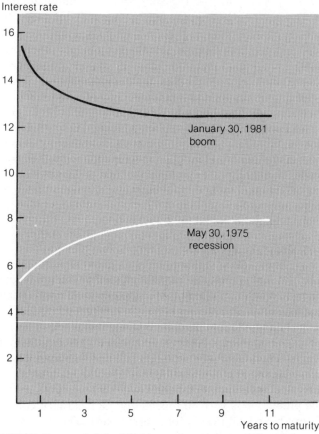

SOURCE: *Treasury Bulletin.* (Fitted by eye to produce a smooth curve.)

cessions occur when output falls and then rebounds. During a recession people should be expecting higher future interest rates as the economy and borrowing rebound. Therefore, according to the expectations hypothesis, the yield curve should be upward sloping. Conversely, during a boom people should be expecting a return to normal times and lower future interest rates, making the yield curve downward sloping. Stated somewhat differently, people realize that current (short-term) interest rates, like income, fluctuate up and down. Given this, (average) expected future rates (plural) of interest should be (1) relatively stable and (2) above (below) the current short-term rate when the latter is low (high). If long-term interest rates are an average of current and future expected rates (plural) of interest, then long-term rates should be more stable than short-term rates and the yield curve should shift from upward sloping to downward sloping as the economy moves from recession to boom.[15]

The general pattern of yield curves over the business cycle is also consistent with the risk-premium theory, which is basically a modification of the expectations theory. One may distinguish between the two theories by constructing a yield curve averaged over many years, say 50 to 75 years. *The expectations hypothesis predicts the long-run average yield curve will be flat.* Sometimes the current short-term rate will exceed expected future rates and vice versa. Averaged over many years the current and expected future rates should be approximately equal, giving a flat yield curve. Advocates of the risk premium theory agree that current and expected future rates averaged over many years should be approximately equal. Given this, however, *the risk premium theory concludes that the yield curve should be upward-sloping because long-term rates include a risk premium. The recent evidence supports the risk premium hypothesis. The average yield curve for 1930–80 is upward sloping,* even ignoring the period when the Fed pegged interest rate. However, during other relatively long periods, for example, 1900–30 in this country and throughout much of the 19th century in England, yield curves were flat.

In summary, each theory has some empirical support. Risk premiums do seem to exist, at least recently, but they are not large. Short-term liquid securities do offer a somewhat lower rate of return on average. However, the simpler expectations hypothesis is a good approximation for the more complex risk premium hypothesis. Although the behavior of insurance companies is consistent with the market segmentation approach, the failure of Operation Twist casts serious doubt on this approach.

## NOMINAL RATES, REAL RATES, AND INFLATION

"The" rate of interest, or yield to maturity, as defined earlier and as published in *The Wall Street Journal* and other financial publications, is the *nominal* rate of interest. That is, we defined the rate of interest as the growth rate linking a current *dollar* sum and a future *dollar* sum. When prices are constant, the nominal rate also equals the *real rate of interest, that is, the additional goods a lender can purchase in the future by sacrificing consumption today.* Inflation creates a wedge between nominal and real rates of interest. As a first approximation for inflation rates that are not too high, the realized nominal rate of interest equals the real rate of interest plus the rate of inflation. Algebraically,

$$i_{nominal} = i_{real} + \pi$$
$$i_{real} = i_{nominal} - \pi \qquad (5-13)$$

---

[15] Undoubtedly, the upward shift in the 1975 and 1981 yield curves illustrated in Figure 5–6 is partially explained by inflationary expectations, which are discussed in the next section.

where $\pi$ is the rate of inflation.[16] For example, someone who lends \$100 and receives \$110 at the end of the year earns a 10 percent nominal return. If goods cost 6 percent more at the end of the year ($\pi = 6$ percent), then the lender can purchase only 4 percent more goods a year hence ($i_{real} = 4$ percent). Lenders clearly are concerned about the real rate of interest; people ultimately are interested in acquiring goods rather than dollars. Although the analysis has been cross-sectional, that is, why rates of return at one moment in time vary across securities, and inflation is a time-series phenomenon of rising prices over time, now that inflation is relatively high no discussion of interest rates can ignore the question: Does inflation reduce the real rate of interest, raise the nominal rate, or produce some combination of the two? When the rate of inflation changes, which term adjusts to satisfy equation (5–13)? In answering this question, we abstract from cross-sectional differences and assume a standard loan and rate of interest. The answer depends on whether inflation is unanticipated or anticipated. Unanticipated inflation, by definition, catches people by surprise; behavior is not adjusted for any unanticipated event. *When inflation is unanticipated, loans continue to be made at the old nominal rate of interest, and the real rate of interest falls.* Unanticipated inflation benefits borrowers at the expense of lenders. Inflation is likely to be unanticipated when it starts or, more accurately, whenever the rate of inflation changes sharply.

Matters are quite different when inflation is anticipated. Although loan contracts continue to specify nominal interest rates, the nominal rate is adjusted upward for inflation precisely because borrowers and lenders ultimately are concerned about goods and services rather than dollars. *As a first approximation, the nominal rate of interest rises upward by the rate of anticipated inflation, and the real rate of interest remains constant.* Look at Figure 5–7, which plots real (adjusted for the price level) loanable funds on the horizontal axis and the nominal rate of interest on the vertical axis. Let the solid curves represent behavior prior to inflation. Now assume a 6 percent rate of inflation is anticipated. *As a first approximation,* the loan-supply curve shifts upward by 6 percent as lenders are interested in their

---

[16] The precise formula is:

$$1 + i_{real} = (1 + i_{nominal})/(1 + \pi)$$

where the interest and inflation rates are expressed in *decimal* form. The equation says that the goods one can buy in the future per dollar lent (left-hand side) equal the number of dollars one has in the future per dollar lent today (numerator of right-hand side) divided by the future price of goods (denominator of right-hand side). Expanding the equation,

$$i_{nominal} = i_{real} + \pi i_{real} + \pi$$

equation (5–13) ignores the interaction term, which is small when the rate of inflation or real rate is small. For example, if the real interest rate and rate of inflation are both 10 percent (written as 0.1 in the equation), then the interaction term is 0.01. The correct nominal rate is 0.21 while equation (5–13)'s approximation is 0.20.

**FIGURE 5-7   The demand and supply of loanable funds shift upward by the rate of anticipated inflation**

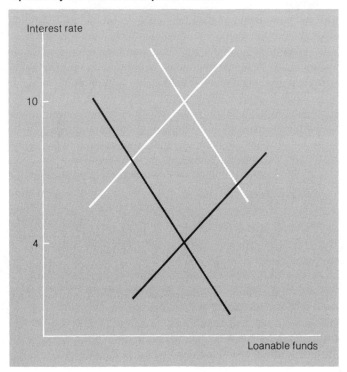

ability to purchase goods and services. Will the loan-demand curve also shift upward by 6 percent as a first approximation? Yes. Borrowers can afford to pay 6 percent more dollars because each dollar purchases 6 percent less. When inflation persists and becomes anticipated, the nominal rate of interest rises and neither borrowers nor lenders gain in real terms.

This section is admittedly incomplete. The second part of the book analyzes how other factors besides inflation affect the real rate of interest. Moreover, we have stressed that the one-for-one relationship between anticipated inflation and nominal interest rates is only a first approximation, as Figure 5-8 confirms. The gap between the corporate AAA bond rate of interest and the rate of inflation lines is not constant. Chapter 23, on inflation and its consequences, takes a closer look at the relationship and introduces such "real world" complications as taxes, which make the relationship inexact. Nevertheless, Figure 5-8 shows there is a very strong, if inexact, positive relationship between nominal interest rates and inflation. The inflation rate seemingly is predicted relatively accurately.

FIGURE 5–8    Long term bond yields and the rate of inflation

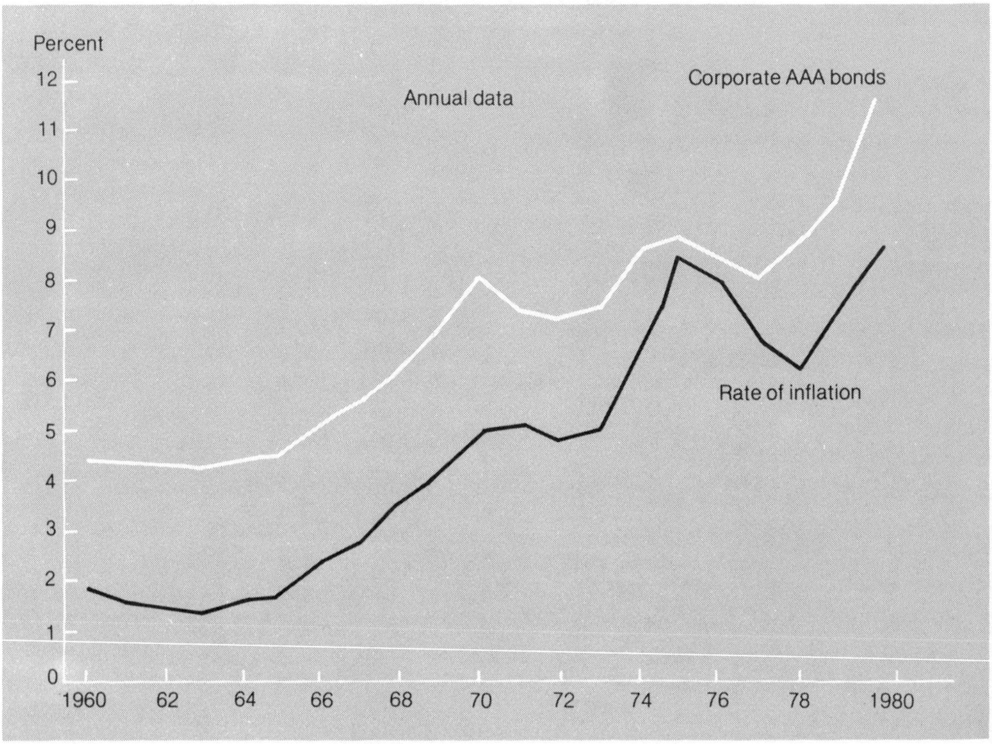

**SOURCE:** Federal Reserve Bank of St. Louis *Review*, August/September 1980, p. 19.

## SUMMARY

Any issue of *The Wall Street Journal* confirms the diversity of rates of interest, and truth-in-lending laws confirm that many people encounter measurement and conceptual difficulties with interest rates. We discussed one peculiar way of measuring interest, the discount yield. Perhaps the best-known interest rate, the prime rate, is easily measured but its relevance is becoming increasingly unclear. Until about 1975, the prime rate was the rate of interest on short-term bank loans to the highest quality borrowers. Some consumer organizations and small firms claim that by the late 1970s banks' best customers were paying less than the prime rate, which simply became a base for scaling other interest rates upward. Perhaps the bank critics are correct. One large New York bank adopted a new definition: the prime rate is the rate that the main office says is the prime rate!

Rates of interest on alternative securities move together over time. During a business cycle peak, for example, interest rates in general are high. However, all interest rates do not change equally, which causes the spread between them to vary and sometimes produces what appear to be "really good deals." Were three-month Treasury bills yielding 16 percent in 1980 really good deals when the rate of interest on long-term government bonds was only 12 percent? Was either one a good deal when one considers the rate of inflation? The very practical orientation of this chapter helps answer such questions. If short-term interest rates in the following months fall much more than the average investor expects, then the person who locked-in a 12 percent return is a savvy investor. And if interest rates fell because actual and anticipated inflation moderated, then holders on long-term bonds are veritable financial wizards.

## QUESTIONS

1. What are the major benefits stemming from the existence of a financial system? Give some examples.

2. What are the main differences between (a) common stock, preferred stock, and debt; (b) direct and intermediary finance; (c) investment bankers, dealers, and brokers; (d) bearer and registered bonds? Consider each part (a)–(d) separately.

3. Assume that a 10-year to maturity, $100 par value bond with a $7 annual coupon currently sells for $80. What is this bond's (a) nominal or coupon yield, (b) current yield, and (c) average total return to maturity, ATRT, which is a good approximation of its yield to maturity or rate of interest? If bond tables are available, compute the exact rate of interest.

4. What is the relationship between a bond's price and its rate of interest? How is the magnitude of the change in bond prices necessary to produce any *given* interest rate change related to the term to maturity of the bond?

5. Assume the price of a six-month (180 days), $10,000 par value Treasury bill is $9,400. What is the bill's (a) discount yield, and (b) effective rate of interest?

6. List the major characteristics of debt instruments.

7. State how taxability and loan size affect an instrument's rate of interest. Give examples.

8. State the relationship between the expected value, certainty equivalent, and risk premium for a (a) risk averter, (b) risk-neutral person, and (c) risk lover.

9. Define and draw the term structure of interest rates or yield curve. Explain the three main theories of the term structure, paying particular attention to the fundamental assumptions of each theory.

10. Suppose the current one-year interest rate is 12 percent and the expected one-year rate next year is 14 percent. Ignoring compounding, what does the expectations hypothesis say the current two-year interest rate equals? According to the expectations hypothesis, what rate of return is earned by the average investor in year 1 assuming he or she held a two-year bond? For the next two questions answer: greater, less, equal, or uncertain. Compared to the expectations hypothesis, the risk premium hypothesis says the two-year rate is _____. Compared to the expectations hypothesis, the hedging or market segmentation hypothesis says the two-year rate is _____.

11. Define Operation Twist. What factors led the Treasury and the Fed to attempt Operation Twist?

12. Present some evidence in favor of each of the three theories of the term structure of interest rate.

13. What is the relationship between the nominal rate of interest, real rate of interest, and rate of inflation? How, if at all, does (*a*) unanticipated and (*b*) anticipated inflation influence the real and nominal interest rate?

# A closer look at financial instruments

**6**

The last chapter listed the major characteristics or attributes of financial claims and the interrelationships between other characteristics and yield to maturity. We did not, however, strongly link the major characteristics with specific financial instruments. That is, we offered only few examples of securities containing any given characteristic. This chapter focuses on the major types of securities and their issuers. We state the main characteristics of each major security and explain how its creation filled a void in the financial system. U.S. Treasury securities are classified first because the value outstanding and the value traded in any period dwarf other securities. Moreover, U.S. Treasury securities play a crucial role in the conduct of monetary policy. Other securities classified by maturity, that is, money or capital market securities, are then described.

## U.S. TREASURY SECURITIES

Table 6–1 lists the gross public debt of the United States Treasury by type and holder. Both dollar amounts and percentages of the total are shown for December 1979. A comparison of the percentage figures for December 1954 and December 1979 shows the trend in the relative importance of each component during the 25 years. As mentioned earlier, *Treasury bills,* nicknamed T-bills, are Treasury securities with an initial maturity under a year which are sold at a discount. The minimum denomination is $10,000. The Treasury *auctions* 91-day and 182-day bills every week, and nine-month and one-year bills are auctioned monthly. The submitted bid prices determine the discount yield earned. The Treasury does *not*

**TABLE 6–1  Gross public debt of the U.S. Treasury: Type and ownership**

| Type and holder | Billions of dollars, December 1979 | Percent of total, December 1979 | Percent of total, December 1954 |
|---|---|---|---|
| Marketable: | | | |
| Bills* | 172.6 | 20.4 | 17.2 |
| Notes | 283.4 | 33.5 | 10.0 |
| Bonds | 74.7 | 8.8 | 29.3 |
| Nonmarketable: | 314.3 | 37.2 | 43.4 |
| Savings bonds | 79.9 | 9.5 | 20.7 |
| Government accounts series | 177.5 | 21.0 | 15.3 |
| Foreign issues | 28.8 | 3.4 | 0.0 |
| Miscellaneous | 28.0 | 3.3 | 7.4 |
| Total† | 845.1 | 100.0 | 100.0 |
| By holder: | | | |
| U.S. agencies and trust funds | 187.1 | 22.1 | 17.8 |
| Federal Reserve banks | 117.5 | 13.9 | 8.9 |
| Private investors: | 540.5 | 63.9 | 73.3 |
| Commercial banks | 97.0 | 11.4 | 24.8 |
| Insurance companies | 14.4 | 1.7 | 5.4 |
| Mutual savings banks | 4.2 | 0.5 | 3.2 |
| Other corporations | 23.9 | 2.8 | 6.9 |
| State and local governments | 68.2 | 8.1 | 5.2 |
| Individuals: | 114.1 | 13.5 | 22.8 |
| Savings bonds | 79.9 | 9.5 | 17.9 |
| Other securities | 34.2 | 4.0 | 4.9 |
| Foreign and international units | 123.8 | 14.6 | n.a. |
| Other miscellaneous investors | 94.8 | 11.2 | 5.0 |
| Total | 845.1 | 100.0 | 100.0 |

* Certificates of indebtedness, which had an original maturity of less than a year, are included in bills in 1954.
† May not add due to rounding.
n.a. = not available.
**SOURCE:** *Federal Reserve Bulletin.*

follow the fixed price, take-it-or-leave-it sales method. Since many feel uncertain about the price they should bid, the number of competitive bidders is small relative to the amount auctioned, about $8 billion weekly nowadays, composed almost equally of 91- and 182-day bills. The 30 or so government security dealers are the active bidders. Many middle-size banks and nonfinancial corporations prefer to buy from the dealers who are successful in the primary auction market. Most "small" individuals enter *noncompetitive* bids and pay that week's average bid price. In addition to the "regular" Treasury bills, the Treasury sporadically offers so-called tax anticipation bills (TABs). These are similar to Treasury bills except that they always mature one week after corporate income taxes are due. Although TABs are discount securities and sell below par prior to maturity, the Treasury accepts them at full face value on the tax date.[1]

Even the huge amount outstanding, more than $170 billion, underestimates the importance of Treasury bills. These securities are the major money market trading instrument. The average *daily* value of Treasury bills bought and sold by *private nonbank* investors was over $4 billion in December 1979, or approximately half the value of the weekly new issues.[2] Although T-bills are short term, they often are sold before maturity. To reduce the transaction and safekeeping costs of transferring beautifully engraved negotiable certificates, nearly all bills are sold in book-entry form on computer at the Treasury's Bureau of Public Debt or at Federal Reserve banks. Purchasers receive nonnegotiable receipts, and ownership changes are recorded on the computer. The New York Stock Exchange has been pondering the adoption of such a system but continues with its cumbersome system because the volume on the stock exchange does not begin to approach the volume of the government securities market.

### Treasury notes and bonds

Treasury notes, the most common type of government debt currently have initial maturities of between one and 10 years, and bonds mature beyond 10 years. Notes and bonds are virtually identical except for original maturity. The change in the relative importance of notes and bonds between 1954 and 1979, as shown in Table 6–1, is in part illusory. The Treasury has been raising the arbitrary maturity demarcation line between notes and bonds. In 1954 the maximum maturity of a note was five years. It subsequently was raised to seven years and now is 10 years. Although these securities are default-free and quite marketable, they differ in many respects from T-bills. For example, notes and bonds are coupon instruments, the denominations of which are in multiples of $1,000. With the exception of two-year notes which are issued every month, notes and bonds are sold irregularly and in relatively large chunks. The Treasury attempts to "tailor" bonds to the needs of pension funds or some other financial unit. Perhaps because bonds are tailored, the ratio of transactions to value outstanding is much smaller for these instruments than for T-bills. The value of notes and bonds outstanding is about twice T-bills outstanding, but average daily transactions are only about one half.

---

[1] This special feature of TABs is not altogether without precedent. The Treasury accepts in payment of estate taxes a limited number of long-term bonds at full face even though they are selling below face. These are called flower bonds; the taxes saved can be spent on nicer flowers at the funeral.

[2] Most of the new issues are for refinancing or "rolling over" maturing issues instead of for raising new money. The trading value was estimated from the *Federal Reserve Bulletin* by eliminating dealer and bank transactions, which amount to approximately $8 billion.

The Treasury sells notes and bonds in order to refinance maturing issues or raise new funds. New issues are sold either by a cash offering to the public or by a refunding available only to holders of selected issues. In a cash offering anyone may buy the bonds. After setting the coupon on its notes and bonds, the Treasury makes cash offerings either at fixed prices or at auction. Years ago the Treasury almost exclusively offered bonds on a fixed price, take-it-or-leave-it basis. Sometimes the price was set too high, given the coupon, and the yield to maturity was too low. In this case the Treasury issue "failed", that is, only a small proportion of the issue was sold. Because new issues are marketed just a few days before the Treasury needs the funds, a market failure is a great embarrassment and inconvenience as the Treasury must scurry for other sources of funds. As a result, the price often was set sufficiently low to minimize failures. Once in the early 1970s the Treasury mistakenly set a truly bargain basement price, and it was flooded with buy orders. Hundreds of thousands of people with small orders inundated a market formerly patronized by a few hundred people ordering bonds worth millions. The Treasury offered for sale $3 billion and received buy orders for $29 billion! The excess demand was met by limiting each buyer to $200,000. Those who did notice the Treasury's mistake were handsomely rewarded. Within a day after issue the price of the bonds rose 1.5 percent. If one could find such bonds every day, the annual return would be over 500 percent! Since that fiasco, Treasury cash offerings generally are made at auction, which guarantees the issue will not fail without the Treasury having to estimate the market clearing price.[3]

If a refunding is made, the new issue is offered only to the holders of a maturing bond. The Treasury also engages in so-called advance refunding, that is, offers to exchange a new issue for a bond maturing several years hence. Typically, the term to maturity of the bond being advance refunded has been shortened substantially. For example, the Treasury may offer to advance refund an original 25-year term to maturity bond with a current 5-year term. The purpose of such advance refunding is to prevent market "churning." As stated earlier, insurance companies have a distinct preference for long-term investments. By making a direct offer to swap, the insurance companies avoid having to buy in the open market longer-term issues to replace their current holdings, which necessarily become shorter term with the passage of time.

The secondary market for Treasury securities is so broad that *The Wall Street Journal* and leading nonfinancial newspapers such as the *Washington Post* publish daily quotations for all Treasury issues. Table 6–2 is a sample of quotations from the October 6, 1980, *Wall Street Journal*. For

---

[3] Although bills had been sold at auction for many years, the Treasury resisted the auction approach for longer-term issues because it feared auctions discourage small participants, who purchase most other goods on a fixed-price basis. The Treasury wants a broad market where bonds are widely held.

**TABLE 6-2   Treasury issues: Bonds, notes, and bills**

| Rate | Mat. | Date | Bid | Asked | Bid Chg. | Yld. |
|------|------|------|-----|-------|----------|------|
| 7 1/8s | 1980 | Nov. n .............. | 99.12 | 99.16 | +.1 | 11.57 |
| 9 1/8s | 1981 | Jun. n ............. | 98 | 98.4 | +.3 | 11.86 |
| 6 3/8s | 1982 | Feb. ............... | 93.8 | 93.24 | +.12 | 11.47 |
| 11 7/8s | 1982 | Sep. n ............. | 100.20 | 100.24 | +.30 | 11.44 |
| 10 1/2s | 1983 | Dec. n ............. | 97.16 | 97.27 | +1.11 | 11.35 |
| 11 3/4s | 1985 | Nov. ............... | 101.14 | 101.18 | +1.26 | 11.34 |
| 10 3/4s | 1989 | Nov. n ............. | 96.7 | 96.15 | +2.13 | 11.38 |
| 10 3/8s | 1995 | May ............... | 92.6 | 92.14 | +2.30 | 11.45 |

| Mat. | Bid | Asked | Yield | Mat. | Bid | Asked | Yield |
|------|-----|-------|-------|------|-----|-------|-------|
|  | Discount |  |  |  | Discount |  |  |
| 1980 |  |  |  | 1981 |  |  |  |
| 10–9 | 11.21 | 10.67 | 10.83 | 2–5 | 11.39 | 11.21 | 11.81 |
| 10–30 | 10.71 | 10.51 | 10.73 | 2–26 | 11.38 | 11.20 | 11.88 |
| 12–4 | 11.19 | 11.03 | 11.41 | 4–18 | 11.19 | 11.09 | 11.82 |
| 12–11 | 11.23 | 11.03 | 11.41 | 6–18 | 11.19 | 11.03 | 11.93 |
| 12–26 | 11.19 | 11.05 | 11.44 | 9–10 | 10.87 | 10.79 | 11.85 |

**SOURCE:** *The Wall Street Journal,* October 6, 1980. Quotations are for October 3, 1980.

bonds and notes, the rate column shows the issue's coupon or nominal yield. The next two columns are the maturity year and month. The letter $n$ following the month designates a note; otherwise the issue is a bond. The fourth and fifth columns give the dealers' bid and asked price expressed in that quaint financial "decimal" system. That is, the figures to the right of the decimal point are in 32ds instead of 100ths. Thus the 99.16 asked price in the first row indicates that dealers are selling the note at $99.50 or $99^{16}/_{32}$ per $100 par value.[4] The asked or selling price is always greater than the bid or buying price, the difference between the two being the dealers' profit. The next-to-last column shows that bid prices rose sharply from the previous day. The final column is the interest rate or yield to maturity based on the asked price. For Treasury bills, rates alone are quoted explicitly, and the prices are implicit. Following the maturity date is the bid and asked *discount yield.* Since the bid price always is less than the asked price, the bid yield is greater than the asked yield. The last column shows the effective, coupon equivalent yield to maturity based on the asked price. Note that the asked discount yield is always less than the effective yield to maturity. (Recall that the discount asked yield computes the return on the par value while the effective yield computes the return on the current asking price.)

---

[4] $^{1}/_{32}$d equals 3.125 basis points, another quaint financial measurement unit. One percent equals 100 basis points, or 1 basis point equals 0.01 percent.

### Nonmarketable debt

About 35 percent of the current federal debt is nonmarketable according to the traditional classification scheme whereby marketability depends on the existence of a broad secondary market. This way of measuring marketability can be misleading, however. *U.S. savings bonds* are the best known "nonmarketable" debt. While these cannot be traded to others in a financial market, they are extremely marketable and liquid because the Treasury redeems them prior to maturity at stipulated prices through commercial banks and other financial institutions. There are two types of savings bonds, Series EE and HH, which were introduced in the days of double-digit inflation (January 1980) to replace the single-letter series. The EE bonds are purchased at a discount like Treasury bills and upon maturity pay face value, which may be a small sum. These are one of grandparents' favorite graduation gifts, perhaps because they prominently display the face value instead of the lower purchase price. The HH bonds are bought at face value, pay interest semiannually, and typically are a larger denomination than EE bonds.

In general, savings bonds have proven to be quite popular. The value of savings bonds outstanding jumped from $6.1 billion in December 1941 to $48.2 billion in December 1945 as the flag was wrapped around them during World War II. While their patriotic appeal has diminished, they continued to be popular with small savers. Nearly $80 billion worth of savings bonds are currently outstanding. Provided one had the ability to save money one received and did not need payroll deductions, savings bonds were not particularly attractive investments for many years. The administratively determined interest rates often were below market-determined interest rates. Many claimed the Treasury was "ripping off" the small saver, particularly when inflation hit double digits. The relative importance of savings bonds dropped sharply between 1954 and 1979, as Table 6–1 shows. Congress realized that there was some validity to the criticism and tried to stem the decline in the importance of savings bonds by passing legislation giving the Treasury authority to raise savings bond rates as much as one percentage point every six months if market conditions warrant. Effective May 1, 1981, the Series EEs are nine-year bonds offering 9 percent, and the HH's are 10-year bonds offering 8.5 percent.

The government account series, the largest nonmarketable component of the federal debt, is held almost entirely by U.S. government agencies and trust funds such as the FDIC and the Federal Old Age and Survivors Insurance Trust Fund (social security). These trust funds are the captive pawns of the Treasury; they are legally required to hold only U.S. government securities. In some respects the very issuance of the series and interest payments are a purely internal, bookkeeping matter of robbing Peter to pay Paul. Nevertheless, the Treasury plays the game honestly, paying interest at a rate equivalent to the rate on marketable securities.

Finally, the foreign issues, some of which are denominated in foreign currencies, are held by foreign governments and central banks. The Treasury issued these securities to help sop up the huge foreign accumulation of dollars from the persistent U.S. balance of payments deficits.

The *gross* debt in December 1979 was approximately $845 billion. The *net* debt held by the public was "only" about $540 billion because the Federal Reserve banks and U.S. government agencies and trust funds held $305 billion, or 36 percent of the debt. The increased share of the debt held by U.S. agencies and trust funds reflects the larger role of government spending and transfer programs. Similarly, the increased share of the Fed reflects the excessive money supply created through open-market purchases, which consequently generated inflation. Private ownership of U.S. Treasury securities declined but remains widespread. Let us abstract from the hodgepodge which makes up the "other miscellaneous investor" class. *Foreign and international organizations are the most important private holders of marketable Treasury securities.* Although U.S. citizens' holdings of Treasury securities are not far behind those of foreigners, the majority of individuals own nonmarketable savings bonds. Matters were quite different in 1954. Foreign holdings were so small that the Fed did not list them separately. Foreigners' share has been increasing steadily for the last 25 years as a result of the persistent U.S. balance of payments deficit. The turmoil in the international monetary system and the quadrupling of OPEC oil prices in 1973–74 accelerated the upward trend.

*Commercial banks are the next most important private holders of Treasury securities.* A comparison of the second and third columns of Table 6–1 indicates, however, that their importance is declining. During World War II the private loan market was at a virtual standstill as the war effort totally dominated the economy. Without a demand for private loans and severely limited in their choice of earning assets, commercial banks, insurance companies, and mutual savings banks turned to Treasury securities. The war's end saw the banking system and other financial institutions swollen with Treasury securities. As the private sector expanded, commercial banks accommodated the private demand by dumping large quantities of Treasury securities or not subscribing to refunding issues. One still observes this pattern of holding long-term Treasury securities only when nothing better is available. Banks sell Treasury securities during business upswings when the private demand for credit is strong, and they buy Treasury securities during recessions when private demands for credit have dried up. The insurance companies' and mutual savings banks' downward pattern of Treasury security holdings has paralleled the commercial bank pattern, even if their absolute holdings have always been much smaller. Separate listing of mutual savings banks today is an anachronism reflecting their earlier importance.

*State and local government units have been expanding their holdings of*

*Treasury securities,* holding approximately $62.2 billion in December 1979. Some portion of these holdings are long-term bonds held for retirement programs for local government employees. The remainder are temporary investments held between tax receipts and expenditures. For many years state and local governments were notoriously poor money managers. A combination of high interest rates and pressure from various organizations when state and local taxes fell behind expenditures led local officials to manage their funds more efficiently, switching from cash to U.S. Treasury bills and other short-term securities.

## MONEY MARKET INSTRUMENTS

*Money market instruments are short-term* (less than a year), *large denomination, readily marketable debt instruments.* These instruments are used to make adjustments in one's money balances. The participants in the money market can be virtually any individual, firm, or government unit with temporarily excessive or deficient money balances. All suppliers of funds to the money market have one underlying motive: the desire to earn interest on money not needed immediately. While demanders of funds, like buyers of goods and services, have no desire to pay, competition forces them to do so. Ranked by the amount outstanding and trading volume, Treasury bills are the most important money market instrument. Negotiable certificates of deposit (CDs) perhaps are the second most important money market instrument. *CDs are large*—the minimum denomination is at least $100,000 and generally $1 million—*negotiable time deposits.* They are evidenced by a certificate issued to the depositor, hence their name. The amount outstanding on December 31, 1979, at large (weekly reporting) commercial banks equalled approximately $100 billion, and other banks probably issued an additional $40 billion. These numbers are particularly impressive when one considers that CDs were developed only in 1961. Besides the CDs, there are more than $75 billion worth of time deposits over $100,000 that are nonnegotiable.

The negotiability factor led to the explosion of CDs. In 1961 banks lacked an instrument to compete effectively for the temporarily excess money balances of large companies. Interest was not paid on demand deposits, and corporations were reluctant to hold nonnegotiable time deposits, which would tie up their funds unconditionally until maturity or be subject to a significant penalty if withdrawn. Ever sharp bankers developed a secondary market for CDs, which enables investors to sell their CDs and acquire cash from someone other than bankers.

The growth path of CDs has been strongly upward but quite variable until recently because Regulation Q ceilings fixed maximum interest rates banks could pay. When the rate of interest on similar negotiable instruments rose above the Regulation Q ceiling rate, banks were unable to roll over their maturing CDs, which shrank precipitously. Between 1970 and

1973 the Fed phased out the rate restrictions on CDs, and their growth path has become much more stable.

Nearly all CDs are coupon instruments and trade on a 360-day basis. The minimum initial maturity is 30 days. Because the denomination of most CDs exceeds the FDIC insurance maximum, the financial condition and reputation of the issuing bank influence the rate of interest. CDs of larger, prime quality banks generally carry a lower interest rate than those of smaller, regional banks.

Table 6–3 shows the dollar amounts of the main money market instru-

**TABLE 6–3  Money market instruments, January 1970 and December 1979 ($ billions)**

|  | January 1, 1970 | December 31, 1979 | Percent change |
|---|---|---|---|
| Treasury bills | 80.6 | 172.6 | 114.1 |
| Certificates of deposit* | 10.9 | 97.8 | 797.2 |
| Commercial paper | 32.6 | 106.5 | 226.7 |
| Bankers acceptances | 5.5 | 49.9 | 807.3 |
| Eurodollars† | 24.7 | 273.8 | 1,008.5 |

* At large (weekly reporting) banks only.
† At foreign branches of U.S. banks only.
**SOURCE:** Federal Reserve *Bulletin* and *Flow of Funds Accounts: Assets and Liabilities Outstanding, 1969–79.*

ments at the beginning and end of the 1970s and the percentage change during the decade.

*Commercial paper is the unsecured promissory note of a nationally known, prime quality corporation* with an initial maturity of less than 270 days, generally between one and six months.[5] Minimum denominations are $5,000. Commercial paper is a substitute for short-term bank loans. It is an old money market instrument in England and the continent that has staged a strong resurgence in the United States. Firms had to find new sources of funds as banks abandoned the tradition of concentrating on short-term business loans and entered the consumer loan and mortgage markets. The amount of commercial paper outstanding rose markedly during the 1960s, remained about constant during the early 1970s, and more than doubled between December 1976 and December 1979 alone when it equalled $106 billion. Similar to their long-term cousin the corporate bond, large issues of commercial paper are evaluated by credit rating firms.

The name *commercial paper* stems from the fact that the original issuers of this instrument were predominantly commercial firms financing inven-

---

[5] The term to maturity is less than 270 days in order to avoid the expense and delay of registering the issue with the Securities and Exchange Commission.

tories or accounts receivable from customers. The paper or IOUs might more correctly be called finance paper today. Approximately 75 percent of commercial paper is issued by financial companies, for example, finance companies, mortgage bankers, and commercial bank holding companies. Sales finance companies, which extend credit for the installment purchase of such major consumer items as cars and which may be a subsidiary of a manufacturing corporation, are the largest issuers of commercial paper. General Motors Acceptance Corporation (GMAC) is such a company. The method of primary sale largely depends on the degree of the issuer's activity in the market. By participating in the market on a virtually continuous basis, sales finance companies know the large, ready buyers of commercial paper and place their issues directly. The occasional issuer places its commercial paper with one of six regular commercial paper dealers, who sells it to others.

Commercial paper is a substitute for bank loans from the viewpoint of the issuer and, perhaps surprisingly, from the viewpoint of banks. That is, banks were the major purchasers of commercial paper until the 1960s and still continue to purchase significant amounts. The market has broadened considerably, however. Nonfinancial firms now are the major purchasers of commercial paper, but many other types of institutions participate in the commercial paper market.

*Bankers acceptances are short-term time drafts on a bank issued by less well-known corporations and guaranteed by the bank.* The guarantee of the bank raises the credit quality of the draft and makes it negotiable. Let us look at the function of these instruments and the mechanics of their creation. Assume a relatively small American firm cannot pay cash and needs credit in order to import goods. To sell its wares, the foreign producer generally is willing to extend credit but is reluctant in this case due to its inability to assess the credit worthiness of the importer. If the importer can guarantee repayment, the foreign producer would extend credit for, say, 90 days. The importer gets such a guarantee from its banker. It issues a draft on the bank ordering it to pay the foreign producer the amount due in 90 days. At this point the draft is simply a postdated check, and on the future date, the bank will not honor it unless the importer has the funds on deposit. However, the importer then takes the draft to its bank, which stamps "accepted" across its face. By accepting the note, the bank has obligated itself to pay the draft when it comes due, whether or not the importer has sufficient funds on deposit. The bank charges the importer for guaranteeing repayment. Moreover, the bank may require collateral. Acceptance by the bank has made the draft a negotiable, marketable instrument. The foreign producer may hold the acceptance until the due date or sell it at a discount. On the due date, whoever is holding the acceptance presents it for payment. If all went well, the importer deposited funds by the due date, and the bank simply transfers the funds from the account of the importer to the holder of the acceptance.

For many years bankers acceptances were primarily associated with foreign trade (hence our example of the importer) because information and contract enforcement costs are high when firms are located in different countries. In recent days, however, less than half of the bankers acceptances arise from foreign trade. Domestic firms in growing numbers are unwilling to rely on another firm's word and require banker acceptances. The acceptance market is small—about 50 percent—compared to the commercial paper market, but both are growing rapidly.

*Federal funds,* or fed funds for short, *are commercial bank deposits at the Federal Reserve system.* As mentioned in Chapters 2 and 3, cash and these deposits (fed funds) are the bank reserves which the Fed requires. Banks which do not meet the reserve requirement are penalized by the Fed, and banks with unwanted excess reserves forego income by holding cash and fed funds instead of earning assets. Fed funds are a means of adjusting reserves to satisfy the Fed requirement. That is, banks which would have failed to meet the reserve requirement borrow or, as the participants prefer to say, "purchase" fed funds from banks which would have had excess reserves. For example, bank A may agree to lend or "sell" bank B $1 million in fed funds for a day at a 10 percent annual rate. Since the two banks typically are aware that each is in excellent financial condition, the loan (sale) usually is unsecured. There are degrees of excellence, however. The fed funds rate at any moment depends somewhat on the reputation of the purchaser, with prime quality banks such as Morgan Guaranty paying slightly lower rates. After reaching agreement, bank A simply instructs the Fed by telephone or telex to transfer $1 million from its reserve balances to bank B. The Fed does so immediately through its electronic transfer system. The next day bank B repays bank A the $1 million plus interest. Yes, $1 million is the typical minimum denomination in the fed funds market, and one day is the typical maturity of the loans (sales), though the loan may be extended from day to day if the seller and buyer agree.[6]

---

[6] A careful reading of footnotes is becoming more important in understanding the fed funds account on banks' balance sheets as published in various Federal Reserve tables. Often the fed funds account will include the type of transaction described in the text as well as repurchase agreements to nonbank bond dealers and banks. For example, suppose a nonbank dealer has excess deposits for a few days which it would rather *not* use at the moment to increase its bond inventory. A search for short-term investments begins. The dealer approaches its banker, who is mindful that the dealer has excess deposits which will be withdrawn if the dealer is not accommodated. The dealer and banker come to a repurchase agreement. That is, the dealer relinquishes the excess demand deposits to purchase some of the bank's government securities, which the bank guarantees to repurchase at a higher price on some specified date. The transaction *should* be recorded by decreasing demand deposits and increasing the liability "securities sold under repurchase agreements." However, in many Federal Reserve tables this transaction would reduce demand deposits and increase "fed funds purchased," which footnotes state also includes securities sold under repurchase agreement. Fed funds are not shown in Table 6–3 precisely because the data are unreliable.

Strictly speaking, fed funds are not money market instruments because they are not negotiable. However, their maturity is so short, typically one day, that they are always classified as money market instruments.

Although an incipient fed funds market existed in the 1920s it became significant only in the 1950s as the excess reserves of the banking system were reduced. In the 1950s fed funds were used most exclusively by the largest banks as a means of adjusting reserves to satisfy Fed requirements. While the fed funds market still serves this function, it now is also a permanent source of funds for the largest banks, and small banks participate indirectly. That is, the largest banks are net purchasers of Fed funds almost continuously. Demand deposit fluctuations and consequent reserves fluctuations determine the extent to which the largest banks are net purchasers. By increasing the liability "fed funds purchased," the largest banks can make even more loans or acquire other assets. While the size of the minimum denomination precludes smaller banks from participating directly in the market, the large banks readily buy outside the organized fed funds market any amount, however small, from their respondents, that is, small banks which maintain deposits at large banks as a means of implicit payment for check collection and other services. The largest banks retain what they need for their own purposes and sell the remainder, if any, to each other.

The Eurodollar market is the largest international money market. *Eurodollars are dollar-denominated deposits of banks outside the United States, including foreign branches of U.S. banks.* The deposits sometimes are demand deposits but usually are time deposits, with maturities from 14 to 90 days being most common. Most foreign countries do not prohibit interest payments on demand deposits, and both Eurodollar demand and time deposits earn interest. As stated in Chapter 2, Eurodollars are somewhat of a misnomer. European banks, particularly London banks, were the first to offer dollar-denominated accounts, hence Eurodollars. Banks in the Caribbean, Hong Kong, Singapore, Tokyo, and Canada now offer dollar-denominated accounts, which are also considered Eurodollars. This market is strictly for big spenders. The minimum denomination is at least $1 million and sometimes $10 million.

Statistics about the size of worldwide Eurodollar market are relatively unreliable, but it probably equaled about $400 billion in 1979. Table 2–3 shows that the Eurodollar deposits of foreign branches of U.S. banks were $274 billion. Approximately 80 percent of this amount, however, was owed to banks, including the parent bank and sister branches. Private firms and citizens of every country do participate actively in this market, but less so than in the Treasury bills market.

There are several reasons why someone prefers a Eurodollar to an Americodollar, that is, a dollar account in a bank located in the United States. (There are no Americomarks or Americopounds; U.S.-based banks do not offer mark or pound-denominated accounts.) We have to thank the Russians for Eurodollars, which were created because of their fear at the height of the cold war in the early 1950s that their bank deposits in the United States might be expropriated. The Russians needed dollar accounts since the dollar was the universally accepted currency in international trade and finance. The fear that their U.S. deposit balances would be expropriated was not entirely irrational; German assets had been expropriated just a decade earlier. The Russians convinced London banks to accept dollar-denominated deposits and transferred their deposits from New York to London. The London banks now owned the deposits of the Russians in New York. The fear by Russians and others that their deposits will be expropriated by the United States continues to play a minor role in explaining the existence of Eurodollars. The Ayatollah undoubtedly was sorry Iran had any U.S. deposits, which were blocked though not expropriated.

Although the dollar depreciated considerably in the 1970s, it remains the currency of international trade. Because of this, a foreign exporter who receives dollars and expects to need dollars in the near future may prefer to hold dollars in the interim rather than convert the dollars to his or her local currency and then reverse the process when dollars are needed. The foreign exporter who follows the latter strategy incurs either the risk that local currency may depreciate relative to the dollar or the cost of foreign exchange future contracts, in addition to the transactions cost of exchanging currencies. Why do firms and individuals who want dollar accounts prefer Eurodollars to Americodollars? (1) Interest rates are unregulated and typically higher on Eurodollars than U.S.-based money market instruments; (2) Eurodollars are more convenient than Americodollars for anyone located abroad; and (3) Eurodollars offer tax and legal advantages compared to Americodollars. The small Russian-created Eurodollar market received a big boost from interest rate regulations in the United States. Prior to 1973 the Fed imposed maximum interest rate ceilings on CDs, which are comparable to Eurodollars in terms of denomination and maturity. The interest rate ceiling became particularly binding several times, and banks suffered severe runoffs in their CDs as money market interest rates rose above the CD ceiling rate. To stem the tide, large New York banks encouraged their depositors to acquire Eurodollars in their branches abroad instead of commercial paper or some other money-market instrument.

Figure 6–1 shows the balance sheet effects of maturing CDs and the creation of Eurodollars. Line 1 records the *initial* effect of a maturing CD which is not renewed. Assuming Mammoth Bank was at equilibrium and reserves equaled the desired value, the bank subsequently would have to sell earning assets. To prevent this, Mammoth Bank induces firm X, the depositor, to transfer its maturing CD to its foreign branch, as recorded in lines 2 and 3. The parent and subsidiary are supposed to be operated as independent, profit-maximizing firms. A noncaptive foreign bank would not pay interest on its Eurodollar while simultaneously holding an *equal* amount of sterile demand deposits in the United States. The branch may want to retain a small amount of the U.S. deposits as (unrequired) reserves, just as a U.S. bank not subject to any reserve requirement would hold some cash. Ignoring any demand for reserves, the branch can lend the $100 to anyone—U.S. or foreign consumers, firms, or banks. Suppose the subsidiary lends the funds to its parent, as recorded on line 4. Everyone benefits, as they must in any arms length transactions. Firm X accepts Eurodollars because the return on Eurodollars, including an allowance for risk, convenience, and other loan terms, is greater than the return on alternative money market instruments. Consolidating the bank and its foreign branch, interest is paid to firm X, but presumably the interest paid is less than the interest earned on the bank's assets.[7] While the transaction illustrated in Figure 6–1 is not unusual, note well that most Eurodollars are borrowed by someone other than the parent of a foreign branch.

**FIGURE 6–1**   **(1) Maturing CDs which are not renewed, (2) and (3) Maturing CDs are used to acquire Eurodollars, (4) Branch makes loan to its parent**

| Mammoth Bank | | | |
|---|---|---|---|
| (1) | Reserves | −100 | CDs                                           −100 |
| (2) | | | CDs                                           −100 |
| | | | Demand deposits, firm X                        +100 |
| (3) | | | Demand deposits, firm X                        −100 |
| | | | Demand deposits, foreign branch +100 |
| (4) | | | Demand deposits, foreign branch −100 |
| | | | Eurodollar borrowing                           +100 |

| Mammoth Bank, Foreign Branch | | |
|---|---|---|
| (1) | | |
| (2) | | |
| (3) | Dollar deposits, home office  +100 | Dollar deposits, firm X                  +100 |
| (4) | Dollar deposits, home office  −100 | |
| | Loans to home office              +100 | |

Just as consumers do not realize how much they "need" a product until they have become accustomed to it, foreign firms and especially foreign subsidiaries of U.S. multinational companies now find Eurodollars extremely convenient. A firm based in Brussels, for example, prefers having its dollar account in a Brussel's bank where the firm does all its other business. You and I find nearby banks more convenient, *ceteris paribus,* and foreign companies feel likewise. While an interest rate differential in favor of Eurodollars may have been necessary at first, the mundane con-

---

[7] Another advantage of these transactions in the early 1970s was the reduction in required reserves because Eurodollar borrowings were not subject to ordinary reserve requirements. The MCA of 1980 set the same reserve ratio on Eurodollar borrowings and nonpersonal time deposits so that the transactions in Figure 6–1 do not reduce required reserves today.

venience factor is perhaps the most important explanation of its continued growth in an era when Eurodollar interest rates have occasionally fallen below U.S. money market rates.

The complicated accounting and legal system is another important explanation for the Eurodollar market, particularly in "offshore" branches located on some remote island. As was mentioned in Chapter 2, billion-dollar post office box branches cannot be explained by local economic needs.

## CAPITAL MARKETS AND STOCK EXCHANGES

> It is usually agreed that casinos should, in the public interest, be inaccessible and expensive. And perhaps the same is true of stock exchanges.
>
> John Maynard Keynes, 1936

Capital markets are the markets for long-term, relatively marketable financial instruments. Bonds are one type of capital instrument. Bonds have many different characteristics or attributes, as discussed in Chapter 5, and are issued by many groups, mainly commercial firms, the Treasury, federal agencies, and state and local governments. Nevertheless, to paraphrase the inimitable Gertrude Stein, "A bond is a bond is a bond." *All bonds are long-term marketable debt instruments issued by economic units other than households.* The paraphrase of Gertrude Stein suggests that we can be brief at this point, in view of our earlier discussion on bond attributes, the direct finance market, and government securities. The suggestion indeed is correct. We should mention, however, that the type of underwriter and secondary market varies by issuer. The new issues of commercial firms and *some* state and local governments are marketed by investment bankers. Commercial banks are prohibited from underwriting private bonds, but they are the main underwriters of general obligation and certain special state and local government bonds. General obligation bonds, also called full faith and credit bonds, technically have up to a 100 percent tax lien on all property within the issuer's jurisdiction. The term also means that the issuer will exert every effort to collect taxes in order to repay the debt. Commercial banks routinely underwrote all types of new issues until the 1930s, when the restrictions were set in order to reduce abuses. The commercial banking division often was forced to buy at par the unsold bonds which the investment banking division had mistakenly overpriced. This trick inflated the balance sheet and income statement because losses went unrecorded. Worse yet, banks sometimes violated their fiduciary responsibilities by placing their overpriced bonds with their trust departments. The prohibition of investment banking activities by commercial banks was not complete because municipal bonds were not that prevalent in the 1930s—state and local governments still believed in a balanced budget—and because many local issuers were believed to satisfy the little person, widows, and orphans argument for aid. While virtually every locality has a bank, most do not have investment bankers/dealers. The commercial bank is considered to perform a public service when it underwrites issues for small local government units, which borrow infrequently and are unfamiliar with the intricacies of investment banking.

Banks have agitated in recent years for the restoration of full investment banking powers. They claim it is only just since investment bankers have invaded their turf by sponsoring money market funds. Support for the bankers' position has increased significantly.

Treasury and federal agency new issues nearly always are sold directly, with the Fed accepting bids for auction sales or selling fixed-price securities on a "best effort" basis for the Treasury. On rare occasions investment bankers officially underwrite Treasury issues. The 1950s and 1960s Fed policy of "even-keel," which will be discussed more fully later, stabilized interest rates during major Treasury financing. The stabilization of interest rates, and particularly the prevention of upward movements after the Treasury announced the terms on its new issues, facilitated their sale and was an indirect and informal means of underwriting Treasury issues.

The secondary market for private bonds is quite thin. Many private bonds are held to maturity, so the ratio of sales of bonds outstanding to new bond issues is quite low. A small fraction of private bonds outstanding are listed on the New York Exchange. However, the secondary market for even listed private bonds typically is the communications network among dealers called the over-the-counter (OTC) market. That is, all nonlisted and most listed private bonds, as well as all federal, state, and local government bonds, are sold in the OTC market. *The Wall Street Journal* publishes transaction data daily for Treasury securities, federal agency securities, and bonds listed on the exchanges. Price and other information about other bonds is not readily available to small investors.

### Common stock and the New York Stock Exchange (NYSE)

The primary market for stocks, which was described in Chapter 5, attracts great attention when a high-flying genetic engineering or personal computer firm offers a new issue. However, the primary stock market is rather small. The $12 billion raised in the new-issues equity market in 1971 broke all records, far surpassing the average $6 billion raised annually during the decade. Far more was raised in the corporate bond market. The stock market is predominantly a secondary market where outstanding securities are traded. In late 1980 the volume of trading on the stock exchanges was approximately $1.5 billion daily. If the trading on the OTC market were included, the total is nearly $2 billion *daily*. Contrast this with the $6 billion *annual* average volume in the primary market. Large as the secondary equities market is, it is paled by the secondary market for government securities. As stated earlier, the average *daily* transactions in Treasury bills alone by private, nonbank investors exceed $4 billion, and trades among dealers and banks approximates $8 billion daily.

All statistics on trades not withstanding, the stock market has captured the public's interest. We should take a closer look at the secondary market for stocks because many think economics *is* the stock market. Admit you are an economist to a layperson and the immediate response is a request for investment advice, particularly about stocks. Yet many economists have dismissed the stock market in a line or paragraph, as if it were simply a national casino where one's gambling instincts can be satisfied without traveling to Las Vegas or Atlantic City. Being ownership claims, stocks are risky; owners get the residual, if any, after everyone else is paid. But the stock market is much more than a national casino. While many firms do not issue bonds, every firm *must* have equity funds. Family and friends are the source of equity funds for most small firms. However, in order to take advantage of economies of scale, the equity funds of thousands nationwide must be gathered by investment bankers, and a secondary stock market must be maintained. A secondary market where "old" stocks can be bought and sold is especially important since these instruments are infinitely lived securities without maturity date. We thoroughly disagree with this section's lead quotation.

There are 10 stock exchanges or organized, continuous auction markets for stock. The New York Stock Exchange is the largest with the American Stock Exchange a far distant second. The stocks of approximately 2,000 of the largest corporations are traded on the New York Exchange, and the stock of the giants in this select group are sometimes also listed in the small "regional" exchanges, particularly when the regional exchange and head office of the firm are located in the same city. An exchange will list or admit for trading a stock if the company meets certain requirements, such as being larger than a specified size, publishing financial information, guaranteeing stock holders certain rights, and so on. Besides cross-listing stocks, the regional exchanges—for example, the Pacific Stock Exchange—also list the stock of small firms on an exclusive basis. The typical size of firms listed on the American Exchange falls between the size of firms on the New York and regional exchanges. Since the American Exchange is also located in New York, it does not duplicate the list of its bigger brother across the street. The approximate percentages of total dollar volume of stock transactions on exchanges is (1) New York Exchange, 80 percent, (2) American Exchange, 10 percent, and (3) regional exchanges, 10 percent.

*The primary purposes of the exchanges are to provide various types of trading facilities and to regulate trading practices.* The former include a building which houses the trading floor where brokers effect transactions for their customers, a ticker tape which reports trades and prices, and facilities for clearing and settling transactions. Concentrating on the dominant New York Exchange, the orders from customers of thousands of broker-dealers nationwide flow to the floor of the Exchange. The trading floor is as hectic as shown in the movies. In order to prevent total pandemonium, each stock is assigned a trading post where brokers with buy and sell orders congregate. There are two types of orders, *market and limit orders*. A market order instructs the broker to act in the customer's best interests immediately, buying at the lowest price or selling at the highest price, whichever it may be. Limit orders stress price instead of immediacy. They specify a maximum buying price below the current price or a minimum selling price above the current price so that the order cannot be executed immediately. Limit orders may be either good 'til canceled (GTC), or they may specify some time period.

Many transactions are effected smoothly by brokers representing their clients without any outside aid. Large market orders, however, are likely to cause unnecessarily large, short-run price fluctuations. Moreover, each of the hundreds of exchange member firms cannot conveniently have representatives at each trading post waiting for the price to rise or fall to limit prices. To minimize these problems the exchange has assigned a specialist to each stock. The specialist "makes the market" by acting as a dealer, buying (selling) for his or her own account when there is a temporary imbalance of market sale (buy) orders. Thus, the specialist is supposed to stabilize the market. The specialist also "maintains the book" listing all limit orders. When the market price reaches the limit price, the specialist buys or sells for the brokers who gave the limit order to the specialist.

Winds of change similar to those which are sweeping the commercial banking industry started earlier in the New York Exchange. *For many years the exchange was a cartel.* Until the 1970s trading on the exchange was limited to members. Nonmember broker-dealers had access to the trading facilities of the exchange only through members, which were required to charge the nonmember broker-dealer the same commission paid by the general public. Since nonmembers are not eleemosynary institutions and must tack on their commission, the higher commission rates nonmembers charged their customers tended to restrict their participation in the exchange. Moreover, the exchange rules tended to prohibit member firms from trading listed securities outside the exchange. The impact of these rules produced two markets for listed stocks, the exchange for members and the so-called Third Market, an informal, OTC market for listed securities among nonmembers. The rules which created two markets with different participants also prevented arbitrage, which eliminates price differences on identical commodities.

The Third Market grew as the New York Exchange, like other cartels, fixed relatively high prices. The commission structure guaranteed that even the most inefficient brokers could make a profit. The commission rates were outrageously high on large transactions, which did not receive any discount. The commission on 10,000 shares (the minimum size "large block" as defined by the NYSE) was 100 times the commission on 100 shares, the typical "round lot," although resources costs increase only fractionally with transaction size. Unable to compete by price, the large brokerage houses in particular offered free research advice and financial publications, plush offices which pampered their customers, and other services designed to attract business. Pressure from large institutional buyers and from exchange members themselves who were losing sales to the Third Market led between 1971 and 1975 to the abolition of fixed commission rates and the introduction of negotiable rates, much as deposit rate ceilings are being eliminated in the banking market. Lower commission rates were accompanied with NYSE Rule 390 changes, which reduced market segmentation and facilitated arbitrage between the Third Market and the New York Exchange, just as portfolio regulation changes are reducing market segmentation among intermediaries.

The lower commission rates also were associated with an unbundling of services. Discount brokerage firms which simply execute your buy and sell orders were established. Full-service brokerage houses throw in some "free" market research with their higher commission structure. However, even the full-service houses now charge for newsletters and other services which formerly were free. This benefits the consumer, who now can buy only those services he or she wants. Moreover, even consumers who want the same bundle of services are better off because they can buy the various pieces from different firms. For example, the consumer previously had to purchase transactions *and* research services from a full-service brokerage while now he or she can purchase transactions services from a discount brokerage and research services from an investment advisory firm. Specialization of services should promote efficiency.

The extent to which a specialist should stabilize short-run price fluctuations and the restriction of information on limit orders to specialists are other controversial issues. Many claim that specialists lack sufficient capital to prevent unnecessary short-run price fluctuations, and the restriction of limit order information to specialists prevents others from speculating and stabilizing the market. These criticisms are partially valid, or at least Congress thought so. In 1975 Congress ordered the Securities and Exchange Commission (SEC) and the New York Exchange to develop as soon as possible a national market system, a computer-based information system which is supposed to (1) report the price and size of all transactions as they occur and (2) record all limit orders and construct a composite limit-order book which, after a person pressed a few buttons, would flash on a screen the limit-order information now available only to the New York specialist. The second objective of the national market system remains unfulfilled although a similar information system for OTC stocks has been developed.[8] In 1971, NASDAQ, an acronym for National Association of Security Dealers Automated Quotations, started displaying on TV screens in the offices of thousands of dealer-brokers the prices each dealer was bidding and asking for many nonlisted issues. This significantly improved the efficiency of the OTC market. Buyers can quickly call those selling at the lowest price, and sellers can put their shares on those buying at the highest price. Prices became more uniform, and the bid-asked spread narrowed. Moreover, the availability of a complete list of buyer and seller prices reduces the impact of large blocks on short-run prices as the owners of the blocks know whom to contact.

The riskiness of stocks due to their residual nature cannot be reduced. However, the riskiness of stocks due to lack of information or even misinformation can be. Such a reduction was the basic objective of the Securities Act of 1933 and Securities Exchange Act of 1934. Potential buyers of goods can examine quality directly, but stock purchasers must rely almost completely on others for information about the future earnings and dividend stream to which stock ownership entitles one. The securities acts prohibited some of the unwise practices which in part enabled the stock market to climb to dizzying heights in the 1920s and to drop precipitously between 1929 and 1933. In particular, these acts outlawed the distribution of false reports, manipulative practices to move the stock price either up or down, exaggerated trading designed to suggest extraordinary interest, transactions based on insider information, and so on. To attain compliance, issuers of securities with few exemptions are required to register the issue with the SEC prior to sale to the general public. The registration process is designed to elicit fair and full information, rather than pass on the price and terms of the security. In other words, the SEC will not block the sale of extremely risky stock at very high prices provided potential buyers are made aware of the risk. Caveat emptor still reigns, and rightly so.

For day-to-day compliance with security laws by firms, the SEC relies on "self-regulation" by the exchange or dealer association under the SEC's watchful eye. That is, the exchange and the National Association of Securities Dealers (NASD) are supposed to make and enforce rules consistent with SEC laws and regulations. Self-regulation of any industry is controversial. Self-regulators find it in their self-interest to penalize gross abuses; unpenalized gross abuses eventually lead to the termination of self-regulation. It is only natural, however, that at times self-regulators overemphasize the interests of their members and discount the harm to the general public. Many of the New York Exchange's cartel practices of the 1960s (for example, the restriction of trading to a limited number of members) were justified as necessary for self-regulation. Five and a half

---

[8] The reason for the delay is explored later when we discuss self-regulation. The logical third step of the system is automated trading. The computer is programmed for continuous searches, and a trade is automatically executed when it finds an identical bid and offer.

years after Congress mandated the national market system, Wall Street continues foot-dragging. It still has not developed a computerized trading system which would allow investors to shop around for the best price nationwide.[9]

## THE MORTGAGE MARKET AND HOUSING AGENCIES

*Mortgages are long-term, relatively illiquid debt instruments issued to purchase real estate, which serves as collateral for the loan.* Mortgages are the largest debt market. Financial intermediaries, particularly savings and loans, are the main holders of mortgages. Nearly everyone issues a mortgage in order to acquire a home; few have the cash to buy a home without one. The term to maturity of mortgages is between 20 and 40 years, usually 30 years, but the average life of a mortgage is substantially less, about 10 years. Two factors explain the difference between maturity and average life. First, mortgages are amortized. That is, the monthly mortgage payment includes the interest expense and a sum credited towards repayment of the principal. (Note that mortgage payments are made monthly while bond coupons are paid semiannually.) Second, most mortgagors may prepay with little or no penalty, and mortgagees may require prepayment when a house is sold, that is, the mortgagee may not allow the new homeowner to assume the mortgage.

Until the 1970s the interest rate and monthly payment were fixed throughout the life of the mortgage. Variable rate mortgages (VRMs) and graduated payment mortgages (GPMs) are now becoming popular although the fixed-rate, fixed-payment mortgages still are most prevalent. VRMs adjust the mortgage rate up and down periodically to reflect the current level of interest rates. Some home buyers want VRMs in order to avoid being saddled with a 16 percent mortgage for 30 years—interest rates some day may fall back to 6 percent. But buyers with VRMs also run the risk that rising rates will push their loan payments still higher.[10] GPMs allow lower monthly payments in the early years of the mortgage and

---

[9] The SEC has hardly applied great pressure on Wall Street. In October 1979, four and a half years after the congressional mandate, the SEC chairman told the annual meeting of the National Security Traders Association to avoid "precipitous" development of NSM. At the same meeting a year later the chairman did criticize the industry for foot-dragging. Interestingly, prior to the latter meeting, "the House Commerce Committee on Oversight and Investigations likened the SEC's go-slow approach to the pace of an 'arthritic gastropod on a drizzly day.' The SEC says there is no connection between the subcommittee's blast and its sudden tougher stance." (*Business Week,* October 27, 1980, p. 56.)

[10] The advantages of VRMs to intermediaries will be discussed in the following chapter. Shared appreciation mortgages are a still newer and not yet common type of mortgage. In this case the mortgagor receives a mortgage rate that is one-third lower than the prevailing rate but gives the mortgagee one third of the profits from the eventual sale of the house. If the real mortgage rate were zero, that is, the nominal interest rate equals the inflation rate, the mortgagee would be indifferent between standard and shared appreciation mortgages, ignoring taxes. Tax considerations may lead the mortgagee to prefer shared appreciation mortgages even when the real rate of interest is positive.

higher monthly payments later. For example, the monthly payment on a $100,000, 13 percent mortgage at its inception might be $792, or $236 lower than the fixed payment, but by the sixth year the monthly payment would be $1,136, or $108 higher. GPMs were developed in order to facilitate home ownership, or better housing, in an inflationary environment. Recalling our earlier discussion about inflation and interest rates, anticipated inflation raises the mortgage rate and monthly payment. A 5 percent higher interest rate on a $100,000 loan increases the monthly payment by approximately $400. Inflation raises monthly mortgage payments relative to current income and makes home ownership more difficult. However, in an inflationary environment with rising incomes, any fixed payment declines relative to income. Thus GPMs are a means of keeping housing expenditures as a percent of income approximately constant instead of declining sharply from a high initial level.

Residential mortgages, more than mortgages for apartment buildings and other large structures, were quite illiquid, at least until the 1970s. Lack of knowledge of the credit worthiness of the typical household greatly reduces the marketability of individual outstanding mortgages. Moreover, mortgages do not have standard denominations, which help develop a broad market. The relative illiquidity of mortgages also stems from their substantial servicing requirement, which many lenders are incapable or unwilling to perform. For example, the higher delinquency rates on mortgages may require the wise counsel of the legal firm of Dewey, Cheatem, and Howe and the collection services of Badger and Browbeat. More accountants are needed to record the more frequent payments, maintain escrow accounts for property tax payments, and so on.

While the federal government after World War II increased the marketability of mortgages somewhat, new federal agencies and tools were developed in the 1970s to increase significantly, if indirectly, the marketability of mortgages, largely by attempting to divorce the "pure finance" and service aspects of a mortgage. As part of the package to encourage home ownership after World War II, the Veterans Administration (VA) and Federal Housing Administration (FHA) guaranteed mortgage payments, the former at no fee for qualified veterans and the latter for a premium. With the guarantee, mortgagees lent to potential homeowners who otherwise would not qualify for a mortgage. While the programs were designed to increase the origination of mortgages, they had the side benefit of making outstanding mortgages more marketable. A California mortgage banker could more easily sell a VA or FHA insured mortgage to, say, a Chicago insurance company because the guarantee reduced the insurance company's uneasiness about its inability to appraise the credit worthiness of the California mortgage.[11] Most mortgages, however, con-

---

[11] Since payments from an insurer inevitably must be delayed, any lender prefers timely payments from the borrower.

tinued to be "conventional" or uninsured, and insured mortgages never became readily marketable nationwide.

In the face of several housing crunches in the late 1960s and 1970s, the "old-line" Federal National Mortgage Association (FNMA or Fannie Mae) greatly expanded its scope of operations.[12] Fannie Mae issued larger quantities of bonds and used the proceeds to acquire mortgages from banks and savings and loans, which now had the funds to originate mortgages or meet deposit outflows. Fannie Mae was joined by the Federal Home Loan Bank System (FHLB), the regulatory agency for federally chartered savings and loan associations. It lent more to its member associations. Contrary to the Fed, which also lends to its members, the FHLB cannot create money; it first must sell its bonds in the capital market and then lend to savings and loans. Fannie Mae and the FHLB could not do the job alone, so in 1968 and 1970 Congress created the Federal Home Loan Mortgage Corporation and the Government National Mortgage Association, dubbed Freddie Mac and Ginnie Mae, respectively, by the wags on the Street. While Freddie Mac and Ginnie Mae differ in many respects, our interest centers on their common feature: both guarantee and sell pass-through mortgage certificates which the originators of the mortgage continue to service. That is, mortgage makers form a mortgage pool, and Freddie Mac and Ginnie Mae guarantee the payment of interest and principal on pass-through mortgage certificates based on the pool. As payments are made on the mortgages in the pool, the proceeds (interest plus principal), less a service charge, are passed through to the certificate holders. Certificates with standardized terms are traded on the secondary market, which is somewhat reduced by the $25,000 minimum denomination. Ginnie Mae pass throughs have proven very popular because amortization of the principal makes annual receipts larger than bond coupons. Moreover, those who live off their interest receipts prefer the monthly payments of pass-throughs to semiannual bond coupons.

## SUMMARY

At any moment the overwhelming majority of economic units are simultaneously debtors and creditors, often with the same economic unit. For example, most homeowners have issued a mortgage (debt) and own demand and time deposits (credit to commercial banks), and often the bank holds the mortgage. The simultaneous debtor-creditor relationship occurs because within broad limits economic units can tailor debt to their needs. The tailoring of debt to particular needs has accelerated, concomitantly widening the menu of assets available to economic units in

---

[12] Fannie Mae was established by Congress in 1938. It was an agency within the Department of Urban and Housing Development when it was spun off and became a quasi-independent firm. Its shares are listed on the New York Stock Exchange.

their role as creditors. For example, prior to World War II banks passively waited for demand and time deposits to come their way. When the demand for bank loans increased following the war and demand and time deposits failed to keep pace, banks introduced CDs, and nonbanks now had available a new money market instrument. Money and capital market instruments often offer the consumer a higher return than time and saving deposits but are dismissed as too complicated. That simply is not the case. We hope this chapter will aid the reader in the very practical quest for the best asset.

## QUESTIONS

1. What are the main differences between Treasury bills, notes, and bonds? Do *not* limit your answer to their term to maturity.
2. Are U.S. savings bonds marketable? What are the two main differences between Series EE and HH savings bonds?
3. State the major trends in the relative importance of different classes of holders of U.S. Treasury securities.
4. Compare the main money market instruments. In particular, state how they differ from each other by (1) issuer, (2) minimum denomination, and (3) overall market size.
5. How are various types of bonds marketed, and what organizations market them?
6. What are the primary purposes of stock exchanges? What operating rules and practices has the NYSE adopted in order to meet its goals?
7. State the two main functions of the NYSE specialist.
8. What rules enabled the NYSE to act as a cartel for years? State the recent changes which have made the NYSE much more competitive.
9. VRM and GPM are acronyms for what? Compare VRMs and GPMs with the traditional fixed-rate, fixed-payment mortgages.
10. Describe various government programs and agencies which have increased the marketability of mortgages.

# Banks and other financial intermediaries

**7**

Financial intermediaries are firms with mainly financial assets—for example, stocks, bonds, and mortgages. Intermediaries stand between surplus units (lenders) and deficit units (borrowers). They purchase primary securities issued by deficit units (borrowers) with funds acquired from surplus units (lenders), who prefer the claims issued by intermediaries to primary securities. Most financial intermediaries are profit-oriented firms. The return on their financial assets exceeds the interest they pay on their liabilities. Since surplus units could purchase primary securities directly and earn higher returns than intermediaries pay, intermediaries must transform unwanted primary securities into desirable claims in order to exist. How can they do this?

The first part of this chapter discusses the fundamental reasons for the existence of financial intermediaries. We then describe the major types of financial intermediaries, beginning with commercial banks. We examine the banking system's balance sheet and income statement. Banks' goals are then reviewed. Although banks are profit-oriented institutions, attempts to maximize short-run profits may lead to insolvency, particularly when banks are illiquid. How do banks reconcile their multiple objectives of profitability, solvency, and liquidity? After answering this question, we take a closer and more narrowly focused look at "banking theories." These theories of bank management are, in fact, little more than monuments of rationalizations concerning bank liquidity. Descriptions of *actual* banking behavior became theories purportedly indicating *optimal* behavior.

The next part examines nonbank depository and nondepository financial intermediaries. We emphasize their main differences and the void in

**171**

the financial system which existed prior to their creation. Compared to commercial banks, the other intermediaries are specialized institutions which normally encounter no problem purchasing illiquid assets and issuing liquid claims against themselves. Occasionally, however, they run into difficulties. Some of the difficulties are inherent to their very existence, but they were compounded by unchanging regulations in a changing financial system. Congress finally realized that many regulations were outdated. The Depository Institutions Deregulation and Monetary Control Act of 1980 phased out many of the regulations which inhibited smoothly functioning intermediaries. The final section of the chapter analyzes the occasional inherent weaknesses of intermediaries and financial deregulation designed to reduce disintermediation.

## THE RATIONALE FOR FINANCIAL INTERMEDIARIES

Chapter 5 discussed how the issuance of financial claims, which permit long-period deficits and surpluses, greatly increases income and welfare. Financial claims provide firms with investment funds and enable households to attain the time pattern of consumption which corresponds with their preferences instead of being dictated by current income. These same benefits flow from financial intermediaries because *without intermediaries many deficit units could not issue financial claims.* For example, intermediaries and federal housing agencies hold over 90 percent of mortgages outstanding. Even usurious interest rates probably would fail to induce surplus units to hold 50 percent of the mortgages outstanding. We shall not repeat ourselves by stating the advantages of finance. This should not be interpreted as an implicit denial of the important role that financial intermediaries play by transferring purchasing power and, subsequently, reallocating resources among economic units and over time.

Why can intermediaries exist? Why do surplus units acquire intermediaries' securities instead of purchasing primary issues directly? *Financial intermediaries exist because by pooling funds they are able to take advantage of (1) the law of large numbers and (2) economies of scale.* The law of large numbers states that as the number of independent random (uncertain) events increases, risk is reduced relative to the expected outcome. As the number of uncertain events becomes infinitely large, the average or expected outcome becomes highly predictable. In other words, the law of large numbers states that although the outcome of any one event may be highly uncertain, the average outcome of many events is predictable. While the law is important to every intermediary, it is absolutely essential to the life insurance industry, so much so that the law of large numbers is sometimes called the *insurance principle.* How can insurees be extremely confident that insurance companies will meet their obligations when premiums equal, say, 2 percent of the insurance in force and the likelihood of death is only somewhat less than 2 percent? If the company insures only one person, it either earns the 2 percent premium—the person lives—or it loses the amount insured—the person dies—which may bankrupt the company. When the company insures many people, it can be quite confident that somewhat less than 2 percent of its policyholders will die. Increases in the number of policyholders aid the company in predicting the percentage of deaths but not the specific people who will die.

The law of large numbers affects both sides of the balance sheet and income statement. The last paragraph considered large numbers and the liability/expense side of insurance companies. The analog for commercial banks and other depository intermediaries is *relative* certainty of the percentage outflows and inflows of total deposits, compared to the uncertainty about the behavior of any one depositor. Of course, the expected percentage flows and their predictability vary over time, as the analysis of desired excess reserves in Chapter 4 indicated. During any particular time period, however, *the reduction in the uncertainty of expected deposit flows due to the law of large numbers enables depository institutions to issue highly liquid liabilities although the overwhelming proportion of their assets are illiquid.* For example, suppose a bank or savings and loan estimates that 10 percent of its many depositors will withdraw their funds. Knowing full well that deviations from the 10 percent expected value will be small and the likelihood of a 20 percent outflow is virtually nil, the institution can effectively, if not legally, make its deposits payable on demand even though 80 percent of its assets are illiquid mortgages. *On the asset side, the law of large numbers reduces the risk of default on the portfolio although each asset is risky.* That is, the law of large numbers turns the *risk of default on one asset* into a more *certain portfolio default rate.* Ignoring capital gains and losses, a depository intermediary can guarantee the rate on its liabilities even though the return on any one asset may be quite unpredictable due to default risk. In summary, large numbers (diversification) of depositors and assets let the intermediary purchase illiquid, uncertain return assets while simultaneously issuing liquid, guaranteed return liabilities.

The existence of economies of scale is the second reason why surplus units prefer intermediary claims to those issued by ultimate deficit units. While economies of scale are important to all intermediaries, they provide the almost complete rationale for mutual funds or open-end investment companies, where one acquires pro rata shares of the assets and earnings of a fund of financial instruments. The relatively new money market mutual funds, a component of M–2, were discussed in Chapter 2. They were predated by stock, bond, and balanced (stocks and bonds) mutual funds, all of which charge an annual management fee. Unlike depository intermediaries, the assets and liabilities of which have different characteristics, the asset portfolio and claims issued by mutual funds are, of necessity, virtually identical since the latter are pro rata shares on the former. For example, higher interest rates and lower bond values have no effect on savings deposit rates, at least in the short run. However, bond market behavior is directly and immediately passed through to bond mutual fund owners. Since the products that mutual funds offer are identical to the products they own, individuals willingly pay the mutual fund a management fee because the fund either (1) acquires information on financial instruments relatively inexpensively or (2) administers the portfolio more inexpensively than individuals can. By pooling funds, intermediaries realize economies of scale of information and administration. To repeat, however, all intermediaries, and not just mutual funds, participate in these economies to some extent. The cost of *The Wall Street Journal,* the literally thousands of stock market newsletters, and other sources of information is independent of the size of one's portfolio while their value is proportional to the portfolio. The prince and the pauper pay the same amount for *The Wall Street Journal,* but the former gains more by reading it. Those with small sums to invest should not spend the time and money trying to ferret out the best investment, considering the size of the possible benefits. Their time would be better spent on other pursuits. Managers of large sums, however, find the acquisition of information profitable. Administration costs are broadly interpreted here to include the transaction costs of buying and selling, bookkeeping costs, safekeeping costs, and so on. Specialization and the frequent repetition of the same operation produce economies of administration. Moreover, now that brokerage costs on the New York Exchange are negotiated, administration costs relative to assets should decline further.

## THE BANKING SYSTEM'S BALANCE SHEET AND INCOME STATEMENT

Commercial banks are the oldest form of intermediary. The first bank in this country of a modern type was the Bank of North America, which was established in 1781 in Philadelphia. Perhaps because they had a head start on other intermediaries, banks were by far the largest intermediary as measured by total assets in 1945. This section reviews in graphic form some salient features of banks' balance sheets and income statements. Look at the asset side first. The left-hand panel of Figure 7–1 shows the dramatic decrease in the relative importance of cash and securities and the increase in total loans during the postwar period. Using the late 1940s as a starting point can be misleading since it immediately followed a most abnormal period, World War II. Shifting the starting point to the late 1950s, by which time the effects of World War II and the less important Korean War should have vanished, the trend in the total loans and securities ratios is still visible. However, the later starting point eliminates the upward trend in the commercial and industrial loan ratio. Relatively speaking, over the past 20 years banks have been substituting other loans

**FIGURE 7-1   Commercial banks' balance sheet ratios**

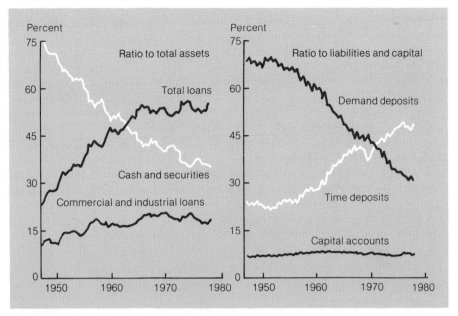

**SOURCE:** Federal Reserve, *Historical Chart Book, 1979.*

for securities while keeping commercial loans relatively constant. Consequently, the ratio of commercial to total loans has fallen.

Figure 7-2 shows the principal classes of loans and securities. Banks are department stores of finance; their asset portfolio is well diversified. The vertical axis in Figure 7-2 is a logarithmic scale, so the slopes of the lines measure growth rates. Real estate and other loans to individuals have been growing faster than commercial and industrial loans, causing the just mentioned decline in the ratio of commercial to total loans. The annual growth rates of loans to nonbank financial institutions and for real estate have been the most variable and stable, respectively. The latter fact may be surprising, in view of the well-publicized sensitivity of the real estate industry to monetary policy. The instability in the supply of real estate loans is due mainly to nonbanks, particularly savings and loans, while banks are a reliable source of real estate loans, at least relative to other loan classes. The decline in the total securities ratio hides significant differences among principal security classes. The total ratio fell because U.S. Treasury securities remained relatively constant while total assets grew. However, state and local government securities and, since 1960, other (principally federal agency) securities have grown faster than loans.

Turning to the sources side of the balance sheet, pronounced changes in

**FIGURE 7-2   Principal classes of commercial bank loans and securities**

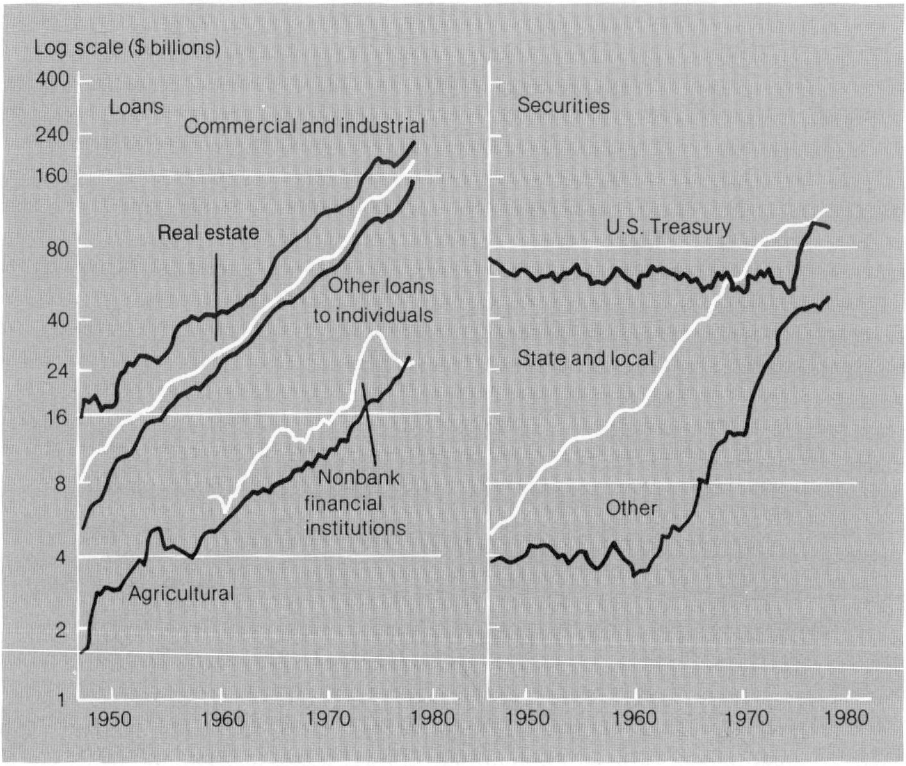

**SOURCE:** Federal Reserve, *Historical Chart Book, 1979.*

the relative importance of demand and time (and saving) deposits began in the late 1950s and have continued more or less unabated to the present. (See Figure 7-1.) The spectacular growth of consumer certificates and CDs explains why time deposits have surpassed demand deposits. The capital account ratio increased slightly from the end of World War II until 1960 and then decreased slightly. The average capital ratio is approximately 7 percent of total liabilities and capital or, equivalently, total assets. Other sources of funds such as RPs and discounts at the Fed explain why the three items do not sum to 100 percent.

Figure 7-3 shows total operating revenue and expenses as well as two expense components, salaries and interest paid, from 1920. Operating income (operating revenue less expenses) and net income (operating income minus taxes, loan losses, and charge-offs) expressed as a percent of capital are also plotted in Figure 7-3. Operating income has been positive even during the Great Depression when large loan losses did produce a negative net income. Bank interest paid exceeded salaries during the

**FIGURE 7–3  Member bank operating revenue and expenses, dollar amounts, and percentage of capital**

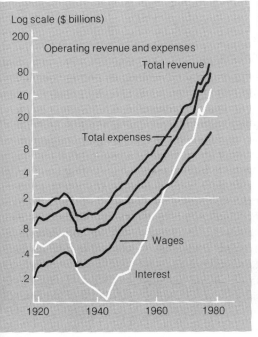
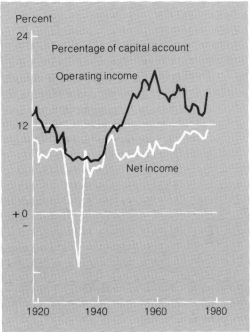

**SOURCE:** Federal Reserve, *Historical Chart Book, 1979.*

1920s but fell below salaries during the 1930s as interest rates in general and the time/demand deposit ratio fell. These two factors were reversed after the war, and by 1965 interest paid again exceeded salaries.

Banking is not a particularly profitable industry. Banks did earn nearly $100 billion in 1979, but expenses ate up an overwhelming proportion of this sum. Between 1945 and 1965, net income as a percent of bank capital averaged about 9 percent, a rate of return exceeded by many other industries. The (nominal) rate of return in banking, as in other industries, has risen in this inflationary age but is still less than 12 percent, a return many market instruments offer. Net income as a percent of total assets is much less. Since the capital/asset ratio is approximately 7 percent, even a 12 percent net income/capital ratio translates into a 0.84 percent net rate of return on assets.

## MULTIPLE GOALS: PROFITABILITY, SOLVENCY, AND LIQUIDITY

Why do banks or anyone else hold a diversified asset portfolio? If banks were unregulated profit maximizers, and only profit maximizers, with a homogeneous pool of funds to invest, then their portfolio would consist of that single asset which yields the highest net rate of return. Regulation explains some bank diversification. For example, banks hold zero-earning cash and deposits at the Fed in order to meet reserve requirements. Regulation, however, accounts for only a small part of bank diversification. Two factors are paramount in explaining bank diversification.

1. Banks have other goals besides profit maximization. In particular, banks maximize profits subject to liquidity and solvency constraints.
2. Specific asset and liability accounts are interrelated so there is not a general pool of funds to be invested. Depositors will close their accounts and bank elsewhere if their loan requests are continually denied.

Defining terms, (economic) *insolvency or bankruptcy occurs when liabilities exceed assets valued at the prices they would fetch given a reasonable selling time (say, a month) rather than at immediate, distress sale prices.*[1] When banks are insolvent and closed, depositors or the Federal Deposit Insurance Corporation suffer some loss, and the bank's stockholders lose their investment. *Illiquidity occurs when banks are unable to meet cash and legitimate loan requests immediately without incurring sizable costs and losses.* Legitimate loan requests admittedly is a somewhat nebulous concept. Nonmafia types can make illegitimate loan requests. Legitimate loan requests are those which, if denied, generate a high probability of future withdrawals.

The three bank objectives of profitability, solvency, and liquidity are interrelated. A bank which is invariably unprofitable eventually becomes insolvent. A profitable bank may be thrown into insolvency if it is highly illiquid. For example, a bank which has to sell its consumer loans in order to raise cash for its (former) depositors' withdrawals may easily become insolvent.[2] The need for liquidity stems from an inability to predict depositor and borrower demands. While nonfinancial firms also cannot always predict accurately the demand for their products, the banking products make prediction errors more serious. When General Motors overestimates its sales and produces too many cars, its inventories rise. General Motor's inventories would fluctuate much more if it also gave current

---

[1] In the last chapter we implicitly assumed assets were perfectly marketable so "distress" and "leisurely" sale market prices coincide. Economic and accounting insolvency then differed because the former valued assets at market and the latter at cost. We are now introducing two market prices, a distress price and a leisurely price.

[2] There often is safety in numbers. When many banks are simultaneously illiquid but solvent, they stop or limit convertibility of deposits to cash, creating a so-called bank holiday. Convertibility resumes when the demand for cash returns to normal levels or after the passage of sufficient time for an orderly liquidation of assets. The last nationwide bank holiday occurred in 1933. All banks were temporarily closed but most subsequently reopened. Localized holidays occur nowadays after a natural disaster which disrupts the flow of cash from the Fed to banks. For example, banks in Mississippi's Gulf Coast region suspended convertibility following Hurricane Frederick in 1979.

owners the option of returning existing cars on demand. The owners of most bank products do enjoy an instant return privilege. Demand deposits are de jure and savings deposits are de facto convertible on demand into cash.

Assets are such that a trade-off usually exists in their contribution to the three banking goals. When is a bank most liquid? A bank is most liquid and can clearly meet any cash or loan request when it is holding only cash. However, cash yields no income, and a bank without revenues but with expenses eventually will fail. Liquidity may also be attained by owning readily marketable short-term securities such as Treasury bills. The risk-premium hypothesis of the term structure of interest rates states that the holding period yield is less on short-term Treasury bills than on long-term bonds, and marketable Treasury bills generally yield less than nonmarketable short-term assets such as consumer loans, even after adjustment for default risk. A trade-off also exists between income and solvency. Since forecasts are much more accurate for the near than for the distant future, and since banks expect loans to be repaid while recognizing the risk to the contrary, risky loans tend to increase current income as banks charge higher interest on risky loans yet few defaults occur immediately. Defaults are prediction errors, and these are less likely in the near future. As time passes, the bank's mistakes will manifest themselves, and some borrowers will default. Particularly if the default risk is underestimated, the initial additional income will be less than the subsequent losses, which could cause bankcruptcy.

The profitability, liquidity, and solvency objectives, the depositor-borrower interrelationship, and legal constraints suggest the following priority of bank asset management.[3]

1. Maintain the required or primary reserves. Cash and deposits at the Fed yield no income, but bankers must make some sacrifice if they want to remain in business.
2. Acquire open-market, short-term securities, that is, secondary reserves. The interest earned usually will compensate for the reduction in liquidity compared to holding cash.
3. Make customer, both consumer and business, loans. These assets tend to be most profitable, and while they decrease liquidity, they also reduce the need for liquidity by tying depositors more closely to the bank. Generally, customer loans are more risky than open-market securities and increase the likelihood of insolvency.
4. Invest the remainder, if any, in open-market, long-term securities, such as government bonds.

---

[3] To aid the reader with any subsequent banking studies, we have acceded to the banking practice of stating that the objectives are profitability, liquidity, and solvency. Given our emphasis on time and the dependence of future demand on current behavior, the banking objectives might better be expressed as the maximization of the expected present value of the entire earnings stream, where various variables, particularly deposits, are stochastic with probability distributions at any moment dependent on the history of past decisions.

The asset management sequence is made more concrete by considering the adjustment pattern in response to an exogenous deposit increase. The immediate impact of the deposit increase is an equal cash increase. After setting aside any required amount, the banker will invest the remainder in the shortest money market instrument. For example, the bank may sell overnight Federal funds, that is, lend the cash to another bank for a day. The deposit inflow today may be an outflow tomorrow, so the bank cannot afford to make illiquid, if profitable, customer loans immediately. As time passes and the deposit inflow seems more permanent, the banker shifts the funds to the longer end of the money market and then makes customer loans or, lacking customer demand, enters the capital market.

## LIQUIDITY AND BANKING THEORIES

Let us look at the liquidity goal more carefully. How can an *individual* bank best provide for its liquidity? The answer, which has changed significantly over time, is elevated to the status of a "banking theory." The theory most widely accepted at any moment corresponds with actual banking practice. This suggests that to some extent banking theories are rationalizations. Yet it is unclear that during any period something other than actual banking practice would have *greatly* increased the average bank's liquidity. Banking theories changed largely because the entire financial system and range of alternatives available to banks has changed and only in small part because of a fundamental change in the bank's objectives.

From the time of its initial exposition by Adam Smith in *The Wealth of Nations* until approximately 1910, the *real bills or commercial loan theory* reigned supreme. The real bills doctrine encompasses elements of bank management and monetary policy, but discussion of the latter aspect is postponed until the section on the discount rate. Regarding individual bank management, *the real bills theory states that banks should make short-term, self-liquidating loans to finance the current production, transportation, or storage of physical goods, either manufactured or agricultural.* Short-term inventory loans to a toy retailer in early fall and agricultural loans for the purchase of seed and other variable factors of productions are examples of ideal loans according to the theory. These loans are self-liquidating in the sense that they finance goods which the borrower does not intend to consume personally and which, therefore, will be sold directly (toys in our example) oɪ indirectly after further processing (seed). What types of loans were verboten according to the real bills theory, a name we prefer to the commercial loan theory because agricultural loans were not precluded? *Any* long-term loans, consumer loans, and loans to purchase stocks or other financial assets were no-no's.

Yesterday's bankers, like today's merchandisers, were guilty of hyperbole in claiming that real bills *guarantee* bank liquidity. Real bills need not be monetarily self-liquidating in the sense that such loans definitely will be repaid and, thereby, yield a large, predictable cash flow. True, physical goods always can be *quantitatively* self-liquidating—anything can be sold at some sufficiently low price—but no loan is *monetarily* self-liquidating because the monetary value of the (nonmoney) goods being financed may fall. Nevertheless, if bankers had more frequently practiced what they preached, they would have been illiquid less frequently. Prior to the early 1900s, there was no well-organized securities market where banks could readily sell large quantities of securities when they needed cash. Banks had to look to their loan portfolio for liquidity. During any given short-time period, a portfolio consisting of long-term loans generates little cash flow, by definition. But all short-term loans are not equally desirable. Particularly in an era when financial markets were relatively undeveloped and workers could be readily fired, short-term financial loans and consumer loans were more risky and generated less certain cash flows than real bills.

Bankers sometimes violated the spirit while maintaining the letter of the real bills doctrine. Officially short-term loans often were effectively long-term loans. Firms counting on their short-term loans continually being renewed purchased long-lived assets, which even in the best of circumstances did not generate sufficient cash to repay the loan in the short run. Even when firms are less daring and, in fact, use the loans to finance short-term assets, banks may be forced to continually renew loans.[4] Our toy retailer must maintain some inventory at all times. This perpetual need for short-term assets may create a perpetual need for short-term loans which banks must satisfy.

By the beginning of this century a national market for various types of assets had developed to the point that ''shiftability'' became possible. *The shiftability hypothesis states that a bank's portfolio of marketable assets is its main source of liquidity.* This hypothesis received big boosts from the U.S. entry into World War I and the long bull market of the roaring 1920s. In order to finance the war effort the Treasury issued large—by previous standards—quantities of bonds, which the Fed encouraged banks to purchase by allowing banks to offer government bonds along with real bills as collateral for Fed discounts. Throughout the 19th and early 20th centuries banks made some stock market loans, contrary to the real bills doctrine. Stock market loans soared during the 1920s when the public's enhanced participation in the market made stocks more liquid. A broad and deep stock market makes exercise of the demand or call provision typical on such loans less likely to trigger a financial panic. While the Fed opposed stock market loans, it did not have the tools to prohibit or even discourage banks from making such loans. The Fed could hardly base its objections

---

[4] Ascertaining the specific asset financed by a loan is an extremely difficult task, as we shall show later.

on the real bills doctrine when it had encouraged similar violations so banks would buy government bonds.

The hypothesis is aptly named because satisfaction of one bank's liquidity needs by selling liquid assets shifts the problem to another bank. For example, a bank with a large stock of Treasury bills can readily meet its depositors' requests for cash by liquidating part of its portfolio. Provided payment for the bills is made by check, as is most likely, the reserves of another bank will fall, requiring it to adjust. Liquid assets do not prevent *multiple* contractions and expansions. The money creator is the only economic agent to which the entire banking *system* can shift depositors requests for cash. More simply, the Fed currently is the main source of liquidity for the banking system. Chapter 4's analysis of excess reserves in 1936–38 is one of several illustrations of the Fed's failure to meet its duties.

As the composition of bank assets paralleled the shift of resources from the government to the private sectors following cessation of World War II, the anticipated income hypothesis gained popularity. This hypothesis formulated in the late 1940s repudiates the real bill doctrine while simultaneously and implicitly accepting the shiftability hypothesis that liquid assets are a single bank's best source of liquidity. *The anticipated income hypothesis states that the likelihood of loan repayments, which generates a cash flow that supplements bank liquidity, depends on the anticipated income of the borrower instead of the type of borrower or the use made of the funds.* To some extent this was well known; banks which lent to the W. T. Grant's and Penn Central's of the 19th century were less liquid than banks with consumer loans to Horatio Alger. While everyone recognizes the possibility of exceptions to any rule, like the real bills theory, the anticipated income hypothesis is a statement about the average or typical borrower and loan in the late 1940s. It states that no particular large class of borrowers or loans is much more likely to produce a stable and predictable cash flow. Thus, the hypothesis suggests that banks should evaluate loan requests on an individual basis because rough-and-ready rules of thumb are not very accurate.

Real estate loans in particular the term loans generally are good examples of the validity of the anticipated income hypothesis.[5] Structural changes since 1900 have increased the liquidity of mortgages. The typical mortgage in 1900 was not amortized, that is, the borrower paid the loan principal in full at maturity instead of making periodic payments. Moreover, the typical interest payment was made less frequently than monthly. Amortization and monthly interest payment have increased the short-term cash flow from mortgages and made them more liquid. Greater use of variable rate mortgages, which in many ways transforms a long-term loan

---

[5] The anticipated income hypothesis is associated with Herbert Prochnow, *Term Loans and Theories of Bank Liquidity* (Englewood Cliffs, N.J.: Prentice-Hall, 1949).

into a short-term loan, will enhance the liquidity of mortgages even further. Besides changes in the contract terms, the creation of housing insurance and intermediaries, such as FHA and Ginnie Mae, which we mentioned earlier, have increased the liquidity of mortgages to the point that they are not categorically unsuitable investments.

Prior to 1960 the liability side of banks' balance sheets provided little liquidity. Demand and passbook savings deposits made up the overwhelming proportion of bank liabilities; few time deposits were outstanding. In response to withdrawals by one group of depositors, banks could change the terms of its deposits and attract another group. Many deposit terms (for example, the number of tellers and the length of the banking day) cannot be readily adjusted in the short run although they strongly influence the amount of bank deposits. Regulation Q often precluded use of the deposit rate, the term most easily adjusted in the short run. Even if Reg Q were not binding or banks could quickly lower service charges, net deposit rate changes would have been very costly because demand and savings deposits are not very responsive to the deposit rate, and the higher deposit rates would be earned by *all* demand and savings deposits, new as well as existing deposits. Beginning around 1960, with the development of the CD and Fed funds markets, and continuing with the Eurodollar and RP markets, large banks created money market liabilities which *normally* could be adjusted readily without increasing the cost of already existing deposits. This led to the liability management theory of banking. *In its infancy the extreme form of the liability management theory stated that banks could satisfy any liquidity need by issuing money market liabilities such as CDs.* In other words, liability management stated that banks in need of cash should borrow instead of selling assets (shiftability hypothesis) or planning an orderly cash flow (anticipated income hypothesis). Although Reg Q generally was less binding on bank money market instruments than savings deposits, it became binding during the so-called credit crunches of the 1960s and at other times when banks needed to borrow most. With the dismantlement of Reg Q, institutional impediments to liability management will diminish but not vanish altogether. The *moderate* version of the liability management theory recognizes these impediments and states that money market bank liabilities should be used along with bank assets to satisfy liquidity needs.

The four banking theories presented so far are rules of thumb relative to what has recently been classified as the latest banking theory: the computer or statistical model of banking. A banking model here means a set of mathematical equations describing the interrelationship among bank assets, liabilities, and income over time. The equations are estimated with a computer programmed to perform regressions or some other type of statistical analysis. The models are large scale, complex, quantitative versions of back-of-the-envelope models bankers and economists guesstimated before the computer. For example, we mentioned that assets and liabilities are not independent as depositors expect their loan requests to be honored. A computer model's estimate of the income effects of selling a short-term, open-market instrument in order to make a relatively long-term consumer loan will incorporate measurement of the deposit flows associated with different assets, forecasts of future interest rates, and other factors besides the obviously important current interest rate differential between the two assets. The computer model differs from the four earlier banking models in two important respects: (1) the computer model forecasts liquidity needs in addition to indicating how the needs should be met, and (2) computer models are flexible and do not indicate that some course of action is always best, irrespective of the characteristics of the individual bank, local economy, and the financial system.

## DEPOSITORY INTERMEDIARIES

Table 7-1 shows the asset size and growth during the post-World War II period of the four depository intermediaries and summarizes their current balance sheet. In view of the earlier graphical presentation of banks' balance sheets and income statements, we now emphasize the relative position of banks. Although banks continue to outrank other financial intermediaries by a wide margin, their postwar growth rate has lagged, particularly in comparison to savings and loans and credit unions. Consequently, the share of commercial banks in the depository market has fallen significantly. The proportion of bank assets to total depository assets was 86 percent in 1945 but only 62 percent in 1980. Banks' slide was particularly pronounced during the early postwar period but has been arrested. Their annualized growth rate was only 3.2 percent between 1945 and 1960 and rose to 8.7 percent between 1960 and 1979. The different subperiod growth rates are largely explained by the introduction around 1960 of new types of time deposits and money market instruments, such as CDs and Eurodollars. The growth rate in the latter period would have been even higher except the interest rate prohibition and other restrictions on demand deposits prevented banks from making them competitive in an era when market interest rates rose to historical heights. The ability of banks nationwide to offer NOW accounts beginning in January 1981 should enhance their growth rate.

Compared to other intermediaries which are specialty boutiques concentrating on one type of asset and liability, commercial banks are department stores of finance. Banks long ago stopped emphasizing short-term business loans, although they still are the dominant force in this market. The percentages of total assets by major classes do correctly indicate the importance of the asset classes to an intermediary's operations, but the percentages are a misleading measure of the importance of an intermediary in the various asset markets unless one considers the intermediary's size. For example, consumer installment loans amounted

**TABLE 7-1  Size, growth, and summary balance sheet of depositories**

| Intermediary | Total assets, December 1945 ($ billions) | Total assets, March 1980 ($ billions) | Percent change | Median size, December 1979 ($ millions) |
|---|---|---|---|---|
| Commercial banks | 160.3 | 1,362.7 | 750 | 24 |
| Savings and loans | 8.7 | 589.5 | 6,676 | 39 |
| Mutual savings banks | 17.0 | 165.1 | 871 | 125 |
| Credit unions | 0.37 | 65.7 | 17,656 | 1 |

**Commerical banks (percent of total)**

| | | | |
|---|---|---|---|
| Cash items | 13.2 | Demand deposits | 30.8 |
| U.S. government securities | 11.3 | Time and saving deposits | 49.4 |
| State and local securities | 10.1 | Funds purchase and | |
| Real estate loans | 17.0 | other debt | 8.4 |
| Commercial loans | 17.8 | Other liabilities | 4.3 |
| Consumer loans | 13.5 | Net worth | 7.1 |
| Other assets | 17.1 | | |

**Savings and loans (percent of total)**

| | | | |
|---|---|---|---|
| Mortgages | 86.0 | Savings deposits | 26.3 |
| Cash and securities | 7.5 | Time deposits | 56.0 |
| Other assets | 6.5 | FHLB advances and other | |
| | | borrowings | 8.2 |
| | | Capital and other liabilities | 9.5 |

**Mutual savings banks (percent of total)**

| | | | |
|---|---|---|---|
| Mortgage assets | 67.8 | Savings deposits | 37.4 |
| Bonds | 19.0 | Time deposits | 50.7 |
| Cash assets | 3.8 | Other liabilities | 4.8 |
| Consumer loans | 3.8 | General reserves | 7.1 |
| Other assets | 5.6 | | |

**Credit unions (percent of total)**

| | | | |
|---|---|---|---|
| Consumer credit | 77.4 | Savings deposits | 90.2 |
| Cash assets | 9.0 | Reserves and others | 9.8 |
| Other assets | 13.6 | | |

**SOURCES:** National Association of Mutual Savings Banks, *Fact Book;* U.S. League of Savings Associations, *Fact Book;* Credit Union National Association, *Yearbook;* FDIC, *Annual Report; Federal Reserve Bulletin* and *Flow of Funds,* various issues.

to only 10.1 percent of bank assets in December 1979 but were 73.2 percent of credit union assets.[6] However, because banks are much larger than credit unions, installment consumer credit outstanding by banks and credit unions was $149 and $48 billion, respectively. Banks are the dominant force in the municipal bond market, holding approximately 45 percent of the outstanding issues. Differences in the tax brackets of other depositories and banks explain why the former do not and the latter do purchase tax-exempt municipal securities. Most other depository inter-

---

[6] Consumer loans in Table 7-1 include installment and single-payment loans.

mediaries are mutuals or cooperatives which do not issue common stock. They can accumulate an equity cushion only by retaining earnings. Tax laws allow nonbank intermediaries to classify a larger proportion of their earnings as nontaxable "reserves for losses" so that they can accumulate an adequate equity cushion while paying competitive deposit rates. Banks, however, are stock companies subject to federal corporate income tax regulations.

### Mutual savings banks

Mutual savings banks (MSBs) are the next oldest intermediary. In 1804 the Farmers Bank of Annapolis, Maryland, became the first commercial bank to pay interest on its deposits. While Annapolis was a much more important city in those days than it is now, its banks had to offer special inducements since they were overshadowed by Baltimore and Philadelphia banks. The practice of paying interest on deposits, at least on small local deposits, did not become widespread immediately. *MSBs were organized by wealthy individuals or social groups in order to encourage saving among the poorer classes by providing convenient facilities and paying interest on their deposits.* The first MSB and currently the largest, Philadelphia Savings Fund Society, was established in 1816. The names of many MSBs still reflect their origin as depositories for small amounts by working classes. New York City still has the Emigrant Savings Bank, Dime Savings Bank, and Dollar Savings Bank, and Boston has the Five Cent Savings. The Dollar is larger than the Five Cent but smaller than the Dime.

MSBs have not expanded much geographically. They are concentrated in New England and the Middle Atlantic states with approximately 75 percent of the 463 MSBs in the three states of Massachusetts, New York, and Connecticut. Thirty three states do not have a MSB. There are several reasons for their failure to expand geographically. First, until very recently a MSB had to receive a charter from a state authority before commencing operations; it could not just hang out a shingle and start raking in the money. Being mutual or cooperative institutions with a semieleemosynary outlook and lacking stockholders, charters were denied MSBs but given to stock-issuing commercial banks, which had more to gain and offer state authorities. In an example of Gresham's Law, MSBs also lost out to savings and loan associations, which were granted broader branching powers and had smaller net worth requirements. The Financial Institutions Regulatory and Interest Rate Control Act of 1978 grants MSBs the option of converting to federally chartered organizations, and the less restrictive federal regulations have encouraged some to do so. Second, banks did meet the competition. Interest-bearing time and saving deposits at commercial banks became standard and eliminated the need for MSBs. Even in those areas where MSBs became established, the industry atrophied numerically. The average age of MSBs exceeds the average age of other intermediaries, including banks, as few new MSBs were founded. Less than 10 percent of MSBs were organized after 1900. For these reasons and because MSBs are located along the eastern seaboard, which has grown less rapidly than other areas in the postwar period, they have been eclipsed by their kissing kin, savings and loan associations. MSBs should not be dismissed lightly, however. Their geographic concentration and age make them much more important collectively and individually than the aggregates may suggest. In several eastern states and metropolitan areas, such as Boston and New York, the MSB industry in general and many individual MSBs are powerhouses. As is often the case, old firms are large firms. The median size of MSBs is approximately $125 million, which is about five times the median size of commercial banks.

Mortgages and government and corporate bonds comprise approximately 68 and 20 percent, respectively, of MSBs total assets. Thus, compared to banks, the assets of MSBs are much longer lived. The maturity structure of liabilities is also somewhat longer for MSBs than banks. Although Massachusetts MSBs have been offering NOW accounts for more than 10 years, these accounts only equal about 1 percent of total liabilities. Regular time and saving deposits equal about 88 percent of total liabilities and capital in 1980. The saving deposits of both intermediaries are effectively payable on demand, but MSBs have a larger proportion of time deposits, which are more stable due to the interest penalty on withdrawals prior to maturity. There still remains a substantial imbalance in the maturity structure of the long-term assets and relatively short-term liabilities.

### Savings and loan associations (S&Ls)

The first S&L, Oxford Provident Building Association, was organized—guess where?—in Philadelphia in 1831 to *finance residential housing,* something shunned by the major intermediaries of the day except MSBs.[7] Mortgages were only incidental to MSBs, which had to own some earning asset in order to pay interest on their deposits, but mortgages were the *raison d'être* for S&Ls. The first S&Ls were mutuals patterned after British building societies. Each member of some affinity group contributed the same specified amount per period. When the savings pool reached a certain amount, it was lent to the member willing to pay the highest interest rate, with the proviso that it be used to finance a house. The first house financed by Oxford Provident still stands at 4276 Orchard Street, Philadelphia. It is a small—500 square feet—2½-story frame house, but it was a steal at $375. With the proceeds from members'

---

[7] Actually, Oxford Provident originally was located in Frankford, Pennsylvania, a suburb which officially became a part of Philadelphia 23 years later in 1854.

additional contributions and the repayment of mortgages, the association continued making mortgages until each member became a homeowner, at which time the association was dissolved with each member receiving an equal share.

S&Ls did not spread rapidly. Six years passed before the second S&L was established, and another six years passed before there was a third. Following the Civil War, however, S&Ls changed their method of operations and took off. Membership and the equal "deposit" requirements were eliminated; now anyone could walk in and "deposit" any amount. In view of their earlier method of operations, S&Ls technically issue shares, although these shares have the same characteristics as time and saving deposits at banks. The new, open-to-all S&Ls often were sponsored directly or indirectly by builders, who naturally continued to emphasize mortgages to the virtual exclusion of other assets. However, the strong link between the two sides of the balance sheet was broken. Depositors were no longer guaranteed mortgages. Operations became more profit oriented. This greater profit orientation became most obvious when some new S&Ls chose to be stock firms instead of mutuals. About 14 percent of S&Ls are private stock companies, and they hold about 20 percent of the industry's assets, being somewhat larger than the average S&L.

The attempt by S&Ls to appeal to a deeper market was not altogether successful prior to 1950. Although concentrated in a few states, in 1930 MSBs were about as large as S&Ls, which were located throughout the country. Thus, S&Ls had a very small share in virtually every geographic market, while MSBs either had a large share or did not participate. The reasons for the nationwide weakness of S&Ls are not well known. The assets and liabilities of MSBs and S&Ls are quite similar. Why were S&Ls weak competitors in the markets where MSBs did not participate? While there is no definitive answer, their inability to shake the popular view—misconception?—that they were not altogether safe and reputable certainly did not help them attract deposits. A few S&Ls did sacrifice deposit safety by making risky mortgages in order to help builders sell houses, and guilt by association is more prevalent in an era without deposit insurance. The Great Depression hit S&Ls particularly hard in spite of governmental efforts to shore them up. Their relatively poor reputation induced larger withdrawals than usual, and the small net worth of many households caused them to default shortly after becoming unemployed. By 1935 real estate acquired through foreclosures equaled 20 percent of S&Ls assets. S&Ls became landlords as well as lenders. Various federal housing credit agencies were established to help S&Ls by lending them funds at below market rates, purchasing S&L mortgages above market prices, and by aiding mortgagors meet their payments to S&Ls. The Federal Savings and Loan Insurance Corporation (FSLIC) was established but was unable to instill confidence in S&Ls. On the other hand, MSBs were regarded as pillars of strength. From parity with MSBs in 1930, S&Ls fell to half the size in 1945.

Increased insurance coverage of S&L accounts to $10,000, more rapid FSLIC payoffs in the event of default, the strengthening of the FSLIC itself in 1950, and the postwar boom were the catalysts which launched S&Ls into orbit. Besides the direct benefit of the higher coverage, the expanded insurance was interpreted by many as a government imprimatur. Would the government consent to lend the FSLIC more and increase the insurance on S&L accounts if the likelihood of bankruptcies were high? Is it not true that only the healthy can buy life insurance and the rich borrow? The greater strength of S&Ls in California and other Sun Belt states is a second fortuitous reason for their postwar takeoff. Finally, S&Ls grew more rapidly than other intermediaries because they were relatively unregulated. S&Ls, free until 1966 from the maximum interest rate ceilings which shackled commercial banks, consistently offered higher deposit rates and attracted funds away from local and distant intermediaries. New Englanders became an important source of funds for California S&Ls.

The severe restrictions on both sides of S&Ls balance sheet are being relaxed. We already mentioned in the last chapter that the standard fixed-rate, fixed-payment mortgage is gradually being replaced by VRMs and GPMs. The former makes the current yield on mortgages depend on market conditions and effectively transforms long-term mortgages into short-term loans, at least with regard to their yield. In recent years these indirect means of shortening the maturity of S&Ls assets have been supplemented by direct regulatory changes enabling S&Ls to extend short-term loans, particularly consumer credit. These changes began in April 1975 and culminated with the Monetary Control Act of (MCA) of 1980, which allows S&Ls to issue credit cards and extend more consumer credit. In time S&Ls may be an important source of consumer credit, but today they still are almost exclusively mortgage lenders which hold a little cash and marketable securities for liquidity purposes. On the liability side, FHLB advances remain small but are an important source of funds during periods of credit tightness. Advances let S&Ls maintain their portfolio when they experience deposit outflows. The most important development on the liability side was the ability of all S&Ls to offer NOW accounts since January 1981. Off the balance sheet altogether, MCA gave S&Ls trust powers and, thereby, another source of income totally free of interest rates. (S&Ls also service mortgages sold to Fannie Mae and others.)

### Credit unions

Credit unions are consumer/employee-oriented saving and lending institutions. The asset side of the balance sheet is paramount in understanding credit unions. The general lack of consumer credit prompted Monsignor Pierre Hevey and Mr. Alphonse Desjardins to organize Saint Mary's Cooperative Credit Association in Manchester, New Hampshire, in 1908. All credit unions are mutuals which accept deposits from and primarily make loans to their members. Common employment is the membership characteristic of approximately 85 percent of credit unions. In other words, the vast majority of credit unions are sponsored by firms and government agencies on behalf of their employees. The remaining 15 percent are operated by social and fraternal organizations. Credit union "deposits," technically shares since credit unions are mutuals, may be insured by the National Credit Union Share Insurance Fund for the same $100,000 coverage as other depositories' accounts.

Credit unions are the newest and smallest yet fastest growing depository. Several factors explain their extraordinary growth. First, the deposit rate ceilings were higher for credit unions than other depositories. Of course, the ceiling rate need not be paid. In practice, the ceiling becomes a floor. This is particularly true for credit unions because employers often regard them as a fringe benefit. Employers usually provide the facilities and release employees from their other duties to work "free" for the credit union. With their lower expenses, credit unions are able to pay higher deposit rates, *ceteris paribus*. Other things often are not equal, however. In this case, the differences work in the same direction. Besides low expenses, a high interest income lets credit unions pay high deposit rates. Although credit unions typically charge lower rates than consumer finance companies, their earnings are high because of their relatively low default rate. Credit unions pride themselves on being able to assess correctly the credit worthiness of borrowers. It is doubtful, however, if credit unions are any better than other intermediaries at assessing risk. Their default rate is low probably because the personal and employment ties between credit unions and borrowers induce the latter to pay the former first, before other creditors. Delays and defaults are embarrassing. When one can meet some but not all his or her obligations, one selects to default on those loans which minimize the damage to one's reputation. Defaults are not selected at random. One deliberately chooses to pay the furniture store instead of the doctor, knowing full well that the former can repossess the sofa while the latter cannot repossess your gall bladder. Moreover, credit unions can pay high deposit rates because they are the only financial intermediaries which are not subject to any income taxes.[8] Finally, the rapid growth rate of credit unions is explained by the convenience factor. They typically are located where the depositor works.

Credit unions are much smaller than other intermediaries. Their median size is about $1 million. Membership restrictions severely limit the growth of any one institution. Regulatory changes reducing specialization and homogenizing depositories have touched credit unions. In April 1977 credit unions were empowered to make 30–year mortgages. Until then they only had made relatively short-term home improvement loans. On

---

[8] Another peculiar feature of credit unions is the voting scheme at general meetings. Each depositor (shareholder) has one vote irrespective of the amount deposited.

the liability side, in August 1974 the National Credit Union Administration permitted credit unions to offer interest paying checkable deposits called share drafts.

## NONDEPOSITORY INTERMEDIARIES

Insurance companies do fall within our definition of intermediaries, that is, firms with mainly financial *assets*. Yet the liabilities of insurance companies are quite different from the liabilities of commercial banks and other depositories, so much so that perhaps the definition of intermediaries should also consider its liabilities. At first blush an insurance company appears to be a negative lottery, that is, tickets are sold for "prizes" one does *not* want to win. The prize may be $100,000 for dying. Further reflection, however, indicates that insurance policies differ from common stocks in degree rather than substance, and everyone agrees common stocks are financial claims. Consider what happens when one purchases common stocks. One pays a *given* amount for a claim to a firm's *uncertain* stream of earnings and dividend. The value of the claim a year, or any other time period, hence is unknown now and depends on the actual and expected earnings during the interim, expected future earnings, society's willingness to bear risk, and so on. It is sad, but some firm's earnings and stock prices would be enhanced by the death of current management, just as death of the insured increases the value of an insurance policy. Now consider what purchases of insurance policies entail. One pays a *given* amount for a claim to an *uncertain* amount depending on whether one dies, a house burns, and so forth. Should we extend Keynes and add insurance policies to stocks as examples of disguised lotteries?

### Life insurance companies

Life insurance companies provide two major, diametrically different types of insurance: (1) life insurance, or financial protection against "dying too soon," and (2) annuities, or financial protection against "living too long." The first type of insurance, however, distinguishes life insurance companies; many firms offer annuities. The insured and annuitants contribute over a period of time. The beneficiary collects when the insured dies, while annuitants receive monthly payments as long as they live. Issuance of both types of policies insures the insurance company. If its policyholders die sooner than expected, the company "loses" on life insurance but "wins" on annuities. Two basic types of life insurance are offered, (1) term and (2) ordinary or whole life. A term policy grants protection for a limited period and contains no savings fund accumulation. The company pays, say, $1,000 in the event of death during the term, nothing being paid in case of survival. The premiums each term equal the expected mortality costs (death benefits) plus operational expenses and a normal return. Since expected mortality costs increase with age, the insured's term premiums increase over time. The whole life premiums on the contrary are fixed. Such a policy requires the company to charge premiums higher than term insurance during the early years of the policy. The difference between the whole life and term premiums is the insured's savings fund, called the insurance "reserve" or the policy's cash and surrender value. This reserve will be drawn down in later years when, due to the increased hazard associated with aging, the uniform annual premiums become insufficient to meet current cost. If the policy is surrendered, the insured receives the reserve. Whole life contracts let the insured borrow the reserve at a specified interest rate, usually quite low. Consequently, insurance policy loans rise during periods of tight money.

Philadelphia is the mother of the financial system, having given birth to the first bank, MSB, and S&L. She also gave birth to the first life insurance company in 1759, more than 20 years before she bore the first bank. Years ago a company's name was supposed to convey information instead of being short and catchy. The first insurance company was The Corporation for Relief of Poor and Distressed Presbyterian Ministers and of the Poor and Distressed Widows and Children of Presbyterian Ministers. The company now is simply the Presbyterian Minister's Fund. Insurance companies grew quite rapidly until 1945, at which time they were the second largest intermediary, more than three times larger than S&Ls. In spite of the Great Depression, the assets of life insurance companies increased from $18 to $30 billion between 1930 and 1940. Since 1945, however, the life insurance industry has grown quite slowly compared to other intermediaries. Table 7–2 presents data similar to Table 7–1 for nondepository intermediaries. Why have life insurance companies grown more slowly than other intermediaries? With the breakdown of the extended family there is a greater need for annuities or insurance against living too long. Can you trust your children to provide for you in your old age? Although the need for annuities has grown, it increasingly has been provided by noninsurance sources such as social security (technically, Old Age and Survivors Insurance Fund) and private noninsured pension funds. Individuals previously purchased annuities singly, but similar coverage now is compulsory (social security) or provided for a group, most often by noninsurance companies. Insurance companies now manage one third of pension fund assets, down significantly from 1945.

Term insurance generates substantial revenues but almost equal expenses, so that it is not a significant source of assets. Ordinary insurance and annuities with their savings funds are the main source of insurance company *assets*. Since young households purchase insurance and tend to collect when they are old, insurance companies match their long-term liabilities with long-term assets, as the segmented markets theory of the term structure suggests. Table 7–2 indicates that bonds and mortgages equal approximately 45 and 30 percent, respectively, of life insurance companies. Insurance companies are the major holders of corporate

**TABLE 7–2   Size, growth, and summary balance sheet of other intermediaries**

| Intermediary | Total assets, December 1945 ($ billions) | Total assets, December 1979 ($ billions) | Percent change |
|---|---|---|---|
| Life insurance companies . . . . . . . . . . . . . . . . . | 43.9 | 420.5 | 857.9 |
| Other insurance companies . . . . . . . . . . . . . . | 6.3 | 156.7 | 2,387.3 |
| Private pension funds . . . . . . . . . . . . . . . . . . . . . | 2.8 | 236.8 | 8,357.1 |
| State and local retirement funds . . . . . . . . . . . | 2.6 | 178.9 | 6,780.8 |
| Mutual funds . . . . . . . . . . . . . . . . . . . . . . . . . . . . | 1.3 | 46.2 | 3,453.8 |
| Finance companies . . . . . . . . . . . . . . . . . . . . . | 4.3 | 168.9 | 3,827.9 |

**Life insurance companies (percent of total)**

| | | | |
|---|---|---|---|
| Bonds . . . . . . . . . . . . . . . . . . . . . | 45.9 | Life insurance reserves . . . . . | 47.9 |
| Mortgages . . . . . . . . . . . . . . . . . . | 28.3 | Pension fund reserves . . . . . . . | 33.0 |
| Stocks . . . . . . . . . . . . . . . . . . . . . | 9.5 | Capital and other | |
| Policy loans . . . . . . . . . . . . . . . . | 8.2 | liabilities . . . . . . . . . . . . . . . . | 19.1 |
| Other assets . . . . . . . . . . . . . . . . | 8.1 | | |

**Other insurance companies (percent to total)**

| | | | |
|---|---|---|---|
| State and local bonds . . . . . . . . | 47.6 | Policy payables . . . . . . . . . . . . | 71.2 |
| Corporate and | | Capital . . . . . . . . . . . . . . . . . . . . | 28.8 |
| treasury bonds . . . . . . . . . . . . . | 26.1 | | |
| Stocks . . . . . . . . . . . . . . . . . . . . . | 16.3 | | |
| Other assets . . . . . . . . . . . . . . . . | 9.9 | | |

**Private pension funds (percent of total)**

| | | | |
|---|---|---|---|
| Stocks . . . . . . . . . . . . . . . . . . . . . | 57.6 | Pension reserves . . . . . . . . . . . . | 100.0 |
| Bonds . . . . . . . . . . . . . . . . . . . . . | 34.0 | | |
| Other assets . . . . . . . . . . . . . . . . | 8.4 | | |

**State and local retirement funds (percent of total)**

| | | | |
|---|---|---|---|
| Bonds . . . . . . . . . . . . . . . . . . . . . | 68.3 | Retirement reserves . . . . . . . . . | 100.0 |
| Stocks . . . . . . . . . . . . . . . . . . . . . | 24.4 | | |
| Other assets . . . . . . . . . . . . . . . . | 7.3 | | |

**Mutual funds (percent of total)**

| | | | |
|---|---|---|---|
| Stocks . . . . . . . . . . . . . . . . . . . . . | 72.9 | Shares outstanding . . . . . . . . . | 100.0 |
| Bonds . . . . . . . . . . . . . . . . . . . . . | 17.1 | | |
| Other assets . . . . . . . . . . . . . . . . | 10.0 | | |

**Finance companies (percent of total)**

| | | | |
|---|---|---|---|
| Consumer credit . . . . . . . . . . . . | 48.9 | Commercial paper . . . . . . . . . . | 36.2 |
| Business loans . . . . . . . . . . . . . . | 41.6 | Bonds . . . . . . . . . . . . . . . . . . . . . | 33.7 |
| Other assets . . . . . . . . . . . . . . . . | 9.5 | Bank loans . . . . . . . . . . . . . . . . | 12.3 |
| | | Capital and other | |
| | | liabilities . . . . . . . . . . . . . . . . | 17.8 |

**SOURCES:** Federal Reserve, *Flow of Funds and Assets and Liabilities Outstanding, 1945–1972, and 1969–1979.*

bonds with one half of corporate bonds outstanding. Stocks, equal to nearly 10 percent of assets, are held mainly because some companies prefer variable rate annuities dependent on the stock market. High interest rates induced policyholders to borrow from their insurers and explains the final major asset.

### Other insurance companies

Other insurance includes that against damage to property by fire, floods, earthquakes, and other natural catastrophies; auto, ship, and plane accidents; burglary and embezzlement; personal liability for injury to others; and defective titles to property. There is still substantial specialization in the provision of life and other insurance, though less so than several decades ago.

Table 7–2 indicates that the other insurance industry is smaller than the life insurance industry but has grown faster in the postwar period, perhaps because individuals feel that they need greater protection against the higher crime rate and an increasingly litigious society. Most now feel that burglary and personal liability insurance is absolutely essential. The proportions of mortgages and state and local bonds in the portfolios of life and other insurance companies are quite different. Other insurance companies have acquired virtually no mortgages but hold state and local bonds equal to nearly a half of their assets. Two factors explain the portfolio differences. First, most other insurance companies are stock corporations, the earnings of which are subject to federal corporate income tax. This makes tax-exempt state and locals very attractive. Much of the earnings of life insurance companies on the other hand is regarded by the federal tax code as nontaxable reserves to be paid to policyholders instead of taxable income. State and locals are poor investments for life insurance companies or anyone else in low tax brackets. Second, the risks, such as floods and earthquakes, that other insurance companies insure are less predictable than deaths. Given this, other insurance companies avoid mortgages, which are the least liquid capital market instrument.

### Private noninsured pension funds, state and local government retirement funds, and investment companies or mutual funds

As just stated, private noninsured pension funds and state and local government retirement funds are similar to the annuities and pension funds managed by insurance companies except for the fund manager, which is not an insurance company, by definition, and the type of contributor to the funds. The extremely rapid growth of *contributions* to pension and retirement funds has partially come at the expense of life insurance companies, but part of the growth is due to the greater need for pensions, whoever the manager may be.[9] We already mentioned that the breakdown of the traditional family unit has contributed to the growth of pensions. Even if the percentage contribution per capita remained constant, an increasing labor force and pay scale enlarges the aggregate pension fund. But employer and employee contributions have also in-

[9] Contributions have increased much more rapidly than asset values in recent years because of the dismal performance of the stock and bond markets.

creased, both absolutely and relatively. The deferred taxability of employer contributions and the earnings on the fund increase the desirability of fringe benefits, such as pensions, relative to salary.

The amount of the pension/retirement payment may either be stipulated in the contract (defined benefit) or depend on the contributions and earnings of the fund (defined contribution). Most state and local government retirement funds and a significant portion of private noninsured pension funds are defined benefit funds, where the benefit is generally related to the participant's final years' income and the number of years employed. Contributions typically are made by both the employer and employee. Perhaps because more state and local government funds than private funds define benefits, the state and local government funds hold a larger proportion of fixed income assets such as bonds. (See Table 7–2.)

Defined contribution pension funds are quite similar to mutual funds (open-end investment companies) insofar as the payoff depends on the funds' performance. The main difference between pension and mutual funds is that the former place restrictions on the assets being cashed while the latter redeem their shares on demand at the current pro rata net asset value of their portfolio. The assets of most mutual funds are relatively homogeneous; they tend to specialize in a particular segment of the financial market. Most are equity funds, that is, hold common stock, but some are bond and balanced (stocks and bonds) funds. Within equity funds there is further specialization by industry—for example, utility stocks, by stocks' growth or risk class, and by dividend ratios. The bond funds also specialize in short-term or long-term, taxable or nontaxable municipals, and corporate or federal government bonds. The data in Table 7–2 exclude money market funds, which are a component of M–2.

The overall postwar growth rate of mutual funds has been relatively high because mutual funds grew extremely rapidly in the first 25 years. Since 1970, nonmoney market mutual funds have actually declined slightly. The annualized growth rate was 11.4 percent between 1950 and 1970 but −0.1 percent between 1970 and 1979. The difference in the two subperiods' growth rate largely reflects the difference in the stock market's behavior. The portfolio of equity funds naturally increased during the long bull market of 1950–70. Moreover, during that period an increasing number of people regarded stocks as *the* investment and inflation hedge. This was reflected by higher direct participation rates in the stock market and higher indirect participation rates through mutual fund purchases. Since 1970, however, the stock market and the value of funds' portfolios have gone nowhere, and redemptions of funds' shares have exceeded gross sales as individuals have become disillusioned with common stocks. The image of mutual fund managers as sages of Wall Street has been tarnished by their inability to outperform the market. High interest rates have encouraged the growth of bond funds, but these funds have been unable to compensate for the decline in equity funds. Similar problems have beset the portfolio of pension funds, which have managed to grow only because contributions have greatly exceeded benefits paid.

### Finance companies

These intermediaries directly or indirectly finance consumer purchases. We should distinguish between consumer and sales finance companies. Consumer finance companies, often called small loan companies, lend directly to consumers for the purchase of specific items or for "debt consolidation." Small loan companies often are the last resort; they accept risks that banks, credit unions, and other intermediaries turn down. Given this and the small size of the typical loan, consumer loan rates are quite high. Household Finance and Beneficial Finance are the two largest small loan companies with offices throughout the United States. Although often unbeknownst to the consumer, sales finance companies sometimes directly finance the purchase of durable goods at lower rates than small loan companies. All the largest sales finance companies are "captive" firms owned by manufacturers of consumer goods or by retailers; for example, General Motor's GMAC, Ford Motor Credit, General Electric Credit, and Sears Roebuck Acceptance. You may not realize that your friendly Cadillac dealer is simply acting on behalf of GMAC when those E–Z payments are extended. The subsidiary, Sears Roebuck Acceptance Corporation, rather than the store itself, finances all consumer purchases at Sears's stores. Sales finance companies also lend indirectly to consumers by financing the inventories of and leasing equipment to consumer-oriented firms such as auto dealers and apparel manufacturers.

As indicated in the last chapter and shown in Table 7–2, commercial paper is an important source of funds for finance companies. These intermediaries also sell bonds and borrow at banks. Finance companies more than other intermediaries "denominate downward," that is, the amount of the average liability greatly exceeds the average asset. Mutual funds on the other hand denominate upwards; the average size of the assets in their portfolio exceeds the average stockholder's position.

Table 7–3 summarizes some of the discussion in the two sections by showing the relative importance of all intermediaries over time.

## DISINTERMEDIATION AND FINANCIAL DEREGULATION

Depository intermediaries normally function quite smoothly. Sometimes, however, this is not the case. Disintermediation is the problem which has attracted the most attention in recent years because it was significantly exacerbated by regulations appropriate for a depression era. *Disintermediation is the withdrawal of funds from depository intermediaries in order to purchase primary securities when primary yields rise substantially above deposit rates.* Much of the current financial deregulation and indus-

**TABLE 7–3  Relative importance of intermediaries over time (percent of assets to total intermediary assets)**

| Intermediary | Year | | | |
|---|---|---|---|---|
| | 1950 | 1960 | 1970 | 1979 |
| Commercial banks | 51.9 | 38.9 | 38.5 | 38.3 |
| Savings and loans | 5.9 | 12.0 | 13.4 | 17.7 |
| Mutual savings banks | 7.6 | 6.9 | 6.1 | 5.1 |
| Credit unions | 0.3 | 0.8 | 1.4 | 1.9 |
| Life insurance companies | 21.8 | 19.6 | 15.3 | 12.9 |
| Other insurance companies | 4.2 | 4.4 | 3.8 | 4.8 |
| Private pension funds | 2.4 | 6.4 | 8.4 | 7.3 |
| State and local retirement funds | 1.7 | 3.4 | 4.6 | 5.5 |
| Mutual funds | 1.0 | 2.9 | 3.7 | 1.4 |
| Finance companies | 3.1 | 4.6 | 4.9 | 5.2 |

**SOURCE:** Federal Reserve, *Flow of Funds and Assets and Liabilities Outstanding, 1945–1972*, and *1969–1979*. Columns may not add to 100 due to rounding.

try innovation can be understood only as attempts to undo the past and reduce disintermediation.

Why do depository intermediaries allow the spread between the yield on primary securities and their deposit rates to widen at times and result in disintermediation? In other words, why don't depositories maintain a constant differential between the yield on primary securities and the interest paid on deposits so disintermediation does not occur? Government policies, particularly Regulation Q and asset and liability restrictions, unintentionally encouraged disintermediation. However, the very nature of depository intermediaries is such that disintermediation is occasionally inevitable, even in a totally free market. The law of large numbers or insurance principle, which is one of the main reasons why intermediaries like savings and loans can exist in the first place, sometimes precludes sufficient interest rate changes by intermediaries. The law of large numbers allows intermediaries to purchase long-term, illiquid primary assets such as mortgages and offer short-term, highly liquid deposits, thereby inducing individuals to hold deposits instead of primary securities. The long-term assets of depositories have substantial short-term market risk. That is, the price of mortgages, if marketable, and other long-term securities can change substantially in the short run. Upward movement in the interest rate or yield to maturity of primary securities places depositories with long-term assets and short-term liabilities between the proverbial rock and hard place. This is best illustrated with a balance sheet and income statement (see Figure 7–4).

To sharpen the illustration, assume the depository's single earning asset is a perpetuity paying $1 per period so its price, $P_B$, is $1/r$, where r is the yield to maturity. Assume the interest rate had been constant at 5 percent

# FIGURE 7-4 Effect of rising interest rates and disintermediation on balance sheet and income statement of depository institutions

Initial *accounting and economic* statements, (2) *economic* statements after interest rate rises, (3) *accounting* statements after interest rate rises, (4) *accounting* statements after interest rate rises with $50 withdrawals and bond sales at end of period, (4) *accounting* statements after deposit rate is increased, (5) *accounting* statements after interest rate rises with $50 withdrawals and borrowing

## Depository balance sheet

| | Assets | | Liabilities and net worth | | Income statement | |
|---|---|---|---|---|---|---|
| **(1)** | Cash | $ 75 | Deposits | $1,025 | Interest income | $50,000 |
| | Perpetuities | 1,000 | Net worth | 50 | Deposit expense | 46.125 |
| | (50 bonds) | | | | Dividends | 3,875 |
| | Total | $1,075 | Total | $1,075 | Retained earnings | 0 |
| **(2)** | Cash | $ 75 | Deposits | $1,025 | Interest income | $ 50.000 |
| | Perpetuities | 500 | Net worth | −450 | Deposit expense | 46.125 |
| | (50 bonds) | | | | Dividends | 3.875 |
| | | | | | Capital loss | 500.000 |
| | Total | $575 | Total | $ 575 | Retained earnings | −500.000 |
| **(3)** | Cash | $ 75 | Deposits | $975 | Interest income | $50.000 |
| | Perpetuities | 900 | Net worth | 0 | Deposit expense | 46.125 |
| | (45 bonds) | | | | Dividends | 3.875 |
| | | | | | Capital loss | 50.000 |
| | Total | $975 | Total | $975 | Retained earnings | −50.000 |
| **(4)** | Cash | $ 32.75 | Deposits | $1,025.00 | Interest income | $50.00 |
| | Perpetuities | 1,000.00 | Net worth | 7.75 | Deposit expense | 92.25 |
| | (50 bonds) | | | | | |
| | Total | $1,032.75 | Total | $1,032.75 | Retained earnings | −42.25 |
| **(5)** | Cash | $ 75 | Deposits | $ 975 | Interest income | $50.000 |
| | Perpetuities | 1,000 | Borrowings | 50 | Interest (deposit and | |
| | (50 bonds) | | Net worth | 50 | borrowing) expense | 46.125 |
| | | | | | Dividends | 3.875 |
| | Total | $1,075 | Total | $1,075 | Retained earnings | 0 |

so the cost and market price of each bond was $20. According to line 1 of Figure 7–4, the deposit rate was 4.5 percent ($46.125/$1025) so depositors sacrifice a modest return, 0.5 percent, in order to hold more desirable deposits instead of perpetuities. So long as the interest rate remains constant, the depository earns a 7.5 percent return on its net worth—quite tidy considering the return on perpetuities is only 5 percent.

Now assume the interest rate doubles to 10 percent with the value of each bond cut in half to $10. An *economic* balance sheet which values assets at market prices would record a capital loss of $500 at the end of the period. From an economic viewpoint, the depository is bankrupt; its assets equal $575 while its liabilities are $1,025. The depository has a negative net worth of $450, which equals the initial $50 net worth and the negative retained earning of $500. (See line 2 of Figure 7–4.) Except for a very few bonds held in so-called trading accounts, however, the regulatory authorities allow depositories to mark at cost. From a legal and accounting viewpoint, capital losses are recorded only when they are realized. Provided depositors continue to hold 4.5 percent deposits in spite of the current availability of 10 percent perpetuities, the depository could operate exactly as before. (See line 1 again.) The higher yield does *not* increase the depository's interest income because the coupon is fixed. The higher yield simply means one has to pay less (the bond price fell) for the given stream of coupons. The depository surely will incur withdrawals if it does not raise deposit rates. Line 2, the economic balance sheet, would be realized if deposit withdrawals were complete. That is, the withdrawal of the $1,025 in deposits bankrupts the depository, and the depositors receive $575. This too is unrealistic. Something between no withdrawals and complete withdrawals will occur. Line 3 of Figure 7–4 assumes withdrawals equal $50 or approximately 5 percent of assets, which also equals net worth. Even from a legal and accounting viewpoint, the depository is brought to the verge of bankruptcy as its net worth plummets to zero. Assuming the depository wishes to maintain $75 cash, no amount of creative accounting can hide the fact that five bonds valued at $100 must be sold in order to raise $50, causing a $50 capital loss.[10] We shall ignore for now the possibility that the perpetuities may not be readily marketable.

If maintaining deposit rates and realizing capital losses is not appealing, the alternative of raising deposit rates and incurring operating losses is not much better. Line 4 assumes the depository doubles its rate so that relative rates of return remain constant. This should stem any deposit outflow, but it causes an operating loss of $42.25 and reduces net worth to

---

[10] While the depository may well draw on its cash balances to meet some withdrawals, the fundamental principle being illustrated here remains valid: relatively small deposit withdrawals can bankrupt a depository when its assets are overvalued. Even if a depository could operate without any cash, 12.5 percent withdrawals would bring the depository to the edge of bankruptcy in our example.

$7.75. The depository could be saved from the Scylla of capital losses and the Charybdis of operating losses by tapping a new source of funds to counterbalance the deposit outflow, as line 5 assumes. If the depository could borrow at the deposit rate or create new deposits which people find more desirable and are willing to hold at the existing low deposit rate, then it can continue its operation. Lines 1 and 5 are effectively identical.

Which depositories face the greatest difficulty when market interest rates rise? S&Ls and MSBs, because their assets are longer lived, and their deposits are more sensitive to market interest rates. The average maturity of commercial bank and credit union assets is shorter, so their income responds sooner to interest rates and the capital loss is smaller. Whichever strategy is adopted, either maintenance of deposit rates while incurring capital losses or higher deposit rates while incurring lower operating earnings, the losses are less when assets are short term. Demand deposits, an important liability of commercial banks, are less responsive than time and saving deposits to market interest rates. Therefore, when market interest rates rise, commercial banks experience smaller withdrawals and capital losses or smaller deposit rate increases and operating losses. Between S&Ls and MSBs, higher market rates probably impose a greater hardship on S&Ls because they hold a larger proportion of less marketable mortgages.

The problems that intermediaries in general face when market rates rise often are exacerbated by asset restrictions to improve housing and Regulation Q. Good housing is a long-established policy goal. This goal is reflected in many ways: (1) public housing and other forms of housing subsidies to the poor, (2) mortgage interest and property tax deductions for homeowners and landlords, and (3) accelerated depreciation and other tax benefits for landlords. In terms of financial intermediaries, this good housing goal is reflected in restrictions on the nonmortgage assets that S&Ls and MSBs can acquire. Restricting nonmortgage assets increases the availability of mortgages and lowers mortgage rates. However, it also has the effect of lengthening the average maturity of intermediary assets and intensifying disintermediation.

Reg Q, which prohibits interest payments on demand deposits and sets positive ceilings on time and saving deposit rates, also aggravates matters. The regulation initially applied only to commercial banks. The reasons for both the initial enactment and subsequent extension of Reg Q illustrate that poor policy occurs when government officials and politicians fail to analyze events and examine the data before acting. We elaborate on the last sentence before linking Reg Q and disintermediation. Reg Q, initially enacted in 1933, was part of the panoply of regulations designed to subvert the free market system, which was alleged to have fostered the Great Depression. So-called fair trade laws set floors on product prices, and Reg Q set ceilings on bank costs. The advocates of Reg Q claimed that banks were too competitive. Left to their own devices in the 1920s, banks supposedly paid excessively high deposit rates, and profit margins tumbled. Hemorrhaged by a protracted period of below normal earnings, a larger than normal number of banks succumbed to the Great Depression. This theory could be correct. However, it has one basic flaw: it is wrong. The data do not show a significant decline in profit margins during the 1920s. Without the benefit of hindsight, no one in 1929 would have claimed banks were weaker than in 1925.[11] The sound loans of 1929 were the defaults of 1933 through no fault of the banks. The justification for Reg Q implies that bankers have been misjudged. Instead of bespectacled, pin-striped pillars of society, bankers are reckless go-go financiers. Lack of empirical support for the theory should have been anticipated since it attributes schizophrenia to bankers. When managing their liabilities, bankers allow their competitive instincts to rival the self-destructive tendencies of lemmings, yet the collusive, fraternal attitude of bankers is so strong when they extend credit that society must be protected by usury laws.

Deposit rate ceilings were extended to S&Ls in 1966 in an effort to support the housing industry. Although low by the standards of the late 1970s, interest rates rose rapidly and sharply during 1965 and 1966. The higher interest rates had a strong impact on the housing industry, which is especially sensitive to the rate of interest. In view of the good housing policy, the government attempted to insulate the housing industry by (1) lowering the Reg Q ceiling on bank deposits and (2) installing somewhat higher (0.75 percent originally) ceilings on S&L deposits. These two acts were supposed to increase the flow of credit to the housing industry by giving S&Ls, which are specialists in the mortgage market, a competitive edge over the generalist commercial banks. Moreover, the two acts supposedly would reduce the overall (bank and S&L) mortgage rate because intermediary deposit costs were lower, assuming the ceilings were effective. Granting S&Ls a competitive edge over banks did ameliorate the perverse impact of the Reg Q extension on the housing industry. In other words, *given* that ceilings were placed on S&L deposit rates, the good housing policy was served by a positive differential in favor of S&L's. However, the good housing policy would have been better served by not imposing any ceiling on S&L deposits.

Consider why the financial authorities incorrectly thought that a deposit rate ceiling and lower intermediary costs would reduce mortgage rates and stimulate housing. Everyone knows that when the wage rate or fertilizer costs fall, the cost curves for peanuts shift downward, and the peanut price falls. Shouldn't intermediary prices, that is, the mortgage rate, also follow costs, or are banks and S&Ls that different from peanut farmers? No, S&Ls and peanut farmers indeed are similarly motivated, but S&Ls will not reduce the mortgage rate in this case. There is an

---

[11] George Benston, "Interest Payment on Demand Deposits and Bank Investment Behavior," *Journal of Political Economy,* October 1964, pp. 431–49.

important difference between the *ability to buy* inputs at low prices and the *necessity of paying* lower prices for inputs. In the former case the farmer can buy more inputs and produce more, which lowers price. In the latter case, however, the ceiling reduces the amount of input (deposits) that can be purchased, reduces output (mortgages), and *raises* the product price (mortgage rate.) Lines 3 and 4 of Figure 7–4 confirm the last sentence, particularly when the assumption of an exogenous loan rate is dropped. Line 3 illustrates that when intermediaries do not raise deposit rates or cannot because of Reg Q, their costs are lower but so are their holdings of perpetuities. Mortgages are the S&Ls earning asset equivalent of the perpetuities in Figure 7–4. Therefore, Reg Q *reduces* the mortgages S&Ls can make. Moreover, the bond sales (lower mortgages) due to Reg Q will *raise* interest rates further. Some intermediaries in an unregulated economy would respond to higher market rates by raising their deposit rates, as illustrated by line 4 of Figure 7–4. When intermediaries act in this manner, they can make more loans. Reg Q prevents any banks from responding and intensifies disintermediation.

How can disintermediation be reduced? This was one of the questions addressed by the Hunt Commission Report in 1971 and the FINE (an acronym for Financial Institutions and the National Economy) Report of 1976, and their recommendations finally were incorporated in the Depository Institutions Deregulation and Monetary Control Act (MCA) of 1980. Depositories did not wait for the regulators; in the 1960s and 1970s they created new financial instruments to reduce disintermediation. However, as mentioned earlier, nothing can totally prevent disintermediation since depositories must differentiate their deposits from their assets.

Consolidate material presented in this and the previous chapter by listing various *financial innovations designed to reduce disintermediation.* Complete your list before continuing to read.

1. Abolish Reg Q. This is occurring gradually. Congress instructed the financial authorities to eliminate Reg Q ceilings no later than 1986.
2. Allow intermediaries to acquire a broader range of assets, particularly short-term assets. As of January 1981, MCA let S&Ls place up to 20 percent of their assets in credit card loans, other consumer credit, commercial paper, and other corporate debt. Prior to that date S&Ls held less than 2 percent in such assets.
3. Let each intermediary offer demand deposits or other checkable deposits since these are a new source of less interest-sensitive funds. MCA let nonbanks offer NOW accounts.
4. Let each intermediary offer a wide variety of time accounts, so that it can tap new sources of longer-term funds, and stiffen the penalty for early withdrawals. In the 1970s, intermediaries began to issue a wide variety of time deposits, six-month and two-and-a-half-year money

market certificates tied to the comparable government security rate being the most popular. Time deposits have supplanted passbook deposits as the major source of depository funds. By segmenting the market and offering a maturity matching each person's preferences, intermediaries lower their interest cost. When market interest rates rise, they are able to raise the rate on the interest-sensitive types of deposits while keeping the rate constant on less sensitive deposits. In 1980 the penalty on the early withdrawal of six-month certificates was raised to three months' interest. One received less than the amount deposited when the funds were withdrawn before three months had elapsed.

5.  At least in terms of the rate of interest, transform legally long-term assets into economically short-term assets. Variable rate mortgages are the prime example.
6.  Strengthen government housing agencies which lend to intermediaries, for example, the Fed and FHLB, and make a secondary mortgage market by purchasing and pooling mortgages, for example, Freddie Mac, Ginnie Mae, and old Fannie Mae.

## SUMMARY

The majority of individuals do not have any contact with the direct financial market, but virtually everyone deals with intermediaries on a regular basis. That is, only a small percentage of people own stocks and bonds directly, but many own them indirectly through a mutual fund account, the savings provision of an ordinary life insurance policy, and a pension or retirement fund. This is not to say that the direct finance market is unimportant. Small numbers in some direct finance markets are more than compensated by the large size of each member. The value of stocks owned directly still exceeds the value of stock owned by intermediaries.

One market, however, is thoroughly dominated by intermediaries. This is the mortgage market. S&Ls are far and away the largest intermediary in the mortgage market. This market is also distinguished by its much closer tie to the commodities market. If consumer credit suddenly were unavailable for whatever reason, the demand for automobiles, other durables, and even services would fall significantly. However, the percentage decline in the demand for consumer goods would be small compared to the percentage decline suffered by the construction industry were mortgages no longer available. Congress and the Carter and Reagan administrations feared in the late 1970s and early 1980s that sharply higher market rates would lead to the collapse of depositories and the construction industry. A depository would incur large operating losses if it adjusted its deposit rate upward or would realize large capital losses if it kept its rate constant and permitted disintermediation.[12] Prospects were not bright under either case. S&Ls were thought to be the most vulnerable, largely because regulations make their assets so long term and specialized.

Deregulation proposals of the 1961 Commission on Money and Credit, the 1971 Hunt Report, and the 1976 FINE Report largely went unheeded because the "need" was not urgent enough. Although the next chapter criticizes regulatory authorities for their overconcern about the failure of *individual* institutions, the failure of an entire *industry*, such as the S&L industry, would be good cause for concern. Housing and the construction industry, which depend so heavily on S&Ls, simply are too important. The Monetary Control Act (MCA) of 1980 ratified many of the earlier and some new proposals. In general, MCA is an excellent act. At this writing (mid-1981), however, concern about the safety of depositories has reached such a fevered pitch that new proposals to bail them out surface virtually daily. Some of the proposals seem worthwhile, but others are pure boon-doggles. Which, if any, of these proposals will be adopted is uncertain at this time without a crystal ball. We can, however, state one of the main reasons for the sweeping financial deregulation of the late 1970s and early 1980s: higher market interest rates threatened massive disintermediation, which would have led to the failure of highly regulated and specialized depositories.

## QUESTIONS

1. What are the main reasons financial intermediaries can exist even though the interest rates they pay are less than the rates on primary securities?
2. What are the major items on banks' balance sheets, and how have they changed over time?
3. What are the three main goals of the typical bank? How do the goals influence the allocation of a bank's assets?
4. While balance sheets balance, that is, total assets equal total liabilities plus net worth, the individual accounts are unrelated. True, false, or uncertain. Explain your answer.
5. Describe the major banking theories, and explain their relationship to the structure of the economy.
6. For each of the three nonbank depositories, state (1) the circumstances which led to their creation, (2) their main assets and liabilities, and (3) any distinguishing characteristics.
7. Explain how the sale of annuities reduces risk for life insurance companies.
8. State the main assets and liabilities and any distinguishing characteristics of nondepository intermediaries.

---

[12] Note carefully that higher (upward change), and not high, interest rates produce problems for depositories. If the return on their assets has been high for some time, they can afford to pay high deposit rates.

9. Which intermediary is most closely associated with the following terms: (*a*) department store of finance, (*b*) mortgages, (*c*) consumer credit, (*d*) economies of scale, (*e*) denominate downward, (*f*) law of large numbers, (*g*) interest on deposits, and (*h*) denominate upward.

10. Illustrate with the aid of balance sheets and income statements that a depository with long-term assets and short-term liabilities must incur capital and/or income losses when market interest rates rise. What action avoids capital losses? What action avoids income losses?

11. Define disintermediation. List several innovations and regulatory changes designed to reduce disintermediation.

# Regulation, structure, and performance of the banking industry

**8**

> The dual banking system: The banking practice
> of paying high wages to loan officers, usually
> males, and low wages to tellers, usually females.
>
> Anonymous student who
> failed Money and Banking

We are not sure that the student who gave the above definition of the dual banking system deserved to fail a money and banking course. There certainly is much truth to that observation of bank hiring practices, but the dual banking system refers to something altogether different.

It is time to learn more about the banking industry. It would be wrong to conclude that only one chapter is being devoted to banking. The beginnings of banking with goldsmiths was described in Chapter 3, and every subsequent chapter has analyzed some aspect of the banking business. Moreover, this chapter will not conclude our discussion of banking. What distinguishes this chapter, then, is the set of specialized topics instead of the units under observation—banks. The chapter has a strong industrial organization focus.

The banking industry is more regulated than most other industries. There are some advantages to our seemingly backward process of learning first who regulates what and to whom and then stating why regulation may be necessary. Basically, regulation should attempt to achieve that industry structure which leads to cost and loan rate minimization. The empirical literature on economies of scale and monopoly power in banking are reviewed with an eye toward ascertaining how regulation may achieve its objectives. What regulation *should* and *does* accomplish are two different things. Regulation is almost exclusively designed to prevent bank failures. The capital adequacy controversy reflects the tug of war between profit-oriented bankers and regulators overly concerned about failures.

## THE BANK REGULATORS

Banking has long been one of the most highly regulated industries. The dual banking system refers to one aspect of bank regulation. More specifically, *the dual banking system is a banking system chartered, regulated, and supervised by federal and state agencies*. The historical circumstances which led to the dual banking system in 1863 are presented in the next chapter. For our purposes it is sufficient at this point to note that initially dual banking might better have been called the dichotomous banking system because for all practical purposes the regulatory powers of the federal and state banking authorities did not overlap. A bank was either a state bank regulated by a state bank commissioner exclusively or a national bank regulated solely by the Comptroller of the Currency.[1] Although the specific regulatory functions performed by state bank commissioners have changed over time, each state has managed with a single bank regulator. Not so for the federal government. When a major, new banking function was necessary, the federal government created a new banking agency. *The three federal banking agencies, with the date of their establishment shown in parenthesis, are: the Comptroller of the Currency (1863), Federal Reserve System (1913), and the Federal Deposit Insurance Corporation, FDIC (1933).* Congress gave each new agency an immediate constituency by requiring all banks already subject to federal regulations to join the new agency. Moreover, it gave state banks an opportunity to join too. The availability of discounts and deposit insurance encouraged many state banks to become members of the Federal Reserve System and FDIC, respectively. While banks joined these agencies for special reasons, as members they were subjected to the full regulatory and supervisory power of the federal agency.[2] For example, state banks joining the FDIC in order to purchase deposit insurance were subject to Reg Q limiting deposit rates and other regulations. Not wanting to "rock the boat" as the federal regulatory base expanded, the new agencies assumed *primary* responsibility for the banks brought under federal control for the first time and let existing federal agencies continue to regulate their banks.

---

[1] When the Office of the Comptroller of the Currency, an agency within the Treasury Department, was established by the National Bank Act of 1863, its name was appropriate. The comptroller did control, or at least significantly affect, the amount of currency. As we shall see in the following chapter on commercial and central banking history, the Office of the Comptroller was created to charter a class of banks which would issue a safe, uniform type of currency called national bank notes. With the creation of the Federal Reserve System, national bank notes were supplanted by Federal Reserve notes. Thus, the charter and supervision of national banks no longer is a means of controlling currency.

[2] Discounting no longer is the main reason for Fed membership.

**FIGURE 8–1   Bank regulatory authorities and bank classes, December 1979***

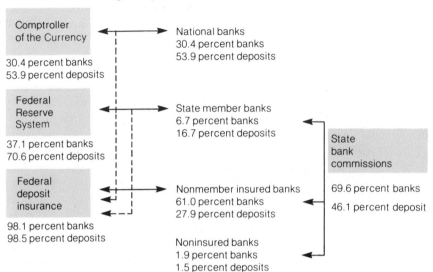

* Solid arrows connect bank class and effective supervisor. Broken arrows connect existing bank class and new nominal supervisor as bank class was automatically brought under control of federal agency.
**SOURCE:** FDIC, *Annual Report, 1979.*

Figure 8–1 shows this layering of regulators and the relative importance of bank classes as measured by the percent of all banks and
deposits. For example, Figure 8–1 shows that all national banks must be
members of the Federal Reserve System and the FDIC, and the old-line
Office of the Comptroller has been allowed to continue supervising national banks largely without the interference from the "new" federal
agencies. Federal and state authorities have failed to achieve effective
cooperation. Insured state banks, which are virtually all state banks, are
supervised by a state authority and either the Fed of FDIC. Thus, the dual
banking system has moved from a state or federal supervisory system to a
state and/or federal system.

Besides the information presented directly, Figure 8–1 indirectly shows
the relative size of banks in each class by comparing the percent of banks
and percent of deposits. For example, national banks tend to be large
since they make up approximately 30 percent of all banks yet hold over
half of total deposits. Summarizing the more important features of Figure
8–1:

1.  The Comptroller of the Currency is the most important banking
    agency as measured by the percent of deposit subject to its *primary*
    supervision.

2. The Federal Reserve regulates a largely captive group of banks; only a few large state banks have voluntarily joined the system. In 1979 approximately 70 percent of total deposits were held by Fed member banks.
3. Membership in the FDIC is largely voluntary but virtually complete.
4. Nonmember insured state banks tend to be small.
5. Noninsured banks are the only class of banks nominally and effectively regulated by a single agency.

There is a common set of tasks performed by all banking agencies. For example, each is responsible for annually examining its banks and evaluating merger proposals. While the precise way this common set of tasks is performed varies somewhat across agencies, the bank regulators share similar objectives and criteria, which reduces the importance of the choice of regulator in these areas. Similarity goes only so far. Some banking tasks are performed by one regulator exclusively. The bank regulations which are laid down by one regulator alone and which significantly distinguish the regulators in terms of bank profitability, the structure of the bank industry—that is, the number and size distribution of banks— and bank performance are:

*Comptroller of the Currency:* Charters national banks.

*Federal Reserve System:* Sets reserve requirements and regulates all bank holding companies.

*FDIC:* Insures deposits, and, thereby, has effective veto power over state banking commissions' charter decisions.

*State Bank Commission:* Charters banks and determines the extent of branching within the state.

Note that the Fed and the FDIC do *not* charter banks. When the comptroller grants a charter, the FDIC more or less automatically insures its deposits. However, the FDIC is not so accommodating to the state banking commissions, the other issuers of bank charters. The FDIC seriously evaluates state bank applications for insurance. Since most new banks believe that deposit insurance is essential for their operation, the FDIC has effective veto power over state banking commissions' chartering decisions. The Federal Reserve exercises several important powers not shown above because they have little effect on banking structure and relative bank profitability; for example, open-market operations and discounting. One regulation did make the Fed member/nonmember distinction meaningful. Until recently the zero-earning reserve requirements imposed by the Fed were significantly higher than the cash requirements set by the typical state bank commission for nonmember banks, so Fed membership tended to reduce profits, *ceteris paribus*. However, November 1980 was the beginning of an eight-year period during which Fed reserve requirements will gradually be applied to nonmember Fed banks as well.[3] Thus by 1988 the member/nonmember classification will be economically meaningless, at least with regard to reserve requirements.

## BRANCHING AND BANK HOLDING COMPANIES

Each state determines the extent of branching within its borders, whether by state or national banks. Federal law prohibits interstate branching. Branching laws traditionally divide states in three classes: (1) unit banking, (2) limited branch banking, and (3) statewide branch banking. Unit-banking states prohibit branching altogether; a unit bank is located in one spot.[4] Statewide branch-banking states, as the name implies, allow banks to operate a branch anywhere within the state. Between these two extremes are limited branch-banking states. The limitation concerns geographical dispersion rather than number of branches or some other factor. Limited-branching states typically let banks operate branches within the county of the main office and contiguous counties. Figure 8–2

FIGURE 8–2 State branching laws

Statewide branching
Limited branching
Unit banking

[3] Current and future reserve requirements are described more fully in Chapter 11.

[4] The "one spot" rule is often interpreted broadly. Illinois permits two *drive-in* facilities within two miles of the main bank office, yet Illinois is traditionally classified a unit-banking state.

shows the type of branching permitted in 1981 by the 50 states. A pattern to this crazy quilt of state branching statutes emerges: (1) the Atlantic coast states generally permit statewide branching, (2) the remainder of the states in the eastern half permit limited branching, (3) the Great Plains states are unit-banking states, and (4) statewide branching prevails in the Far West.

Years ago the pattern of state branching statutes was quite simple: unit banking virtually blanketed the country. The liberalization of branching laws and the banking system's response is one of the more dramatic banking developments of this century. Figure 8–3 shows that in 1920 the

**FIGURE 8–3   Banks and branches, 1917–1979**

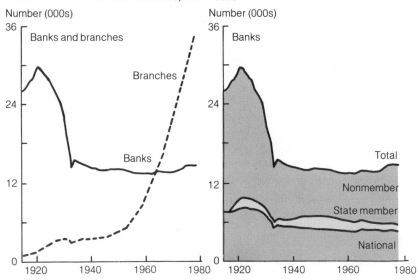

**SOURCE:** Federal Reserve *Historical Chart Book, 1979.*

United States was a nation of unit banks, which even more than today were *nonmembers* of the Federal Reserve System. Throughout the 1920s the number of small nonmember banks decreased significantly, largely due to bank failures, while branches increased moderately. The shakeout of the banking industry during the Great Depression had a more or less permanent effect on the number of banks; the number of banks has remained approximately constant since 1934. In contrast, the depression slowed the growth of branching temporarily, but by the mid-1950s a strong upward trend emerged. The typical bank now operates three branches.

While the expansion of branching has been occurring throughout the century, the formation of holding companies is a more recent (since 1960) phenomenon. Virtually every nationally known bank now is affiliated with a *bank holding company* (*BHC*), *a corporation which controls one or more banks and possibly a nonbank business*. More simply, a BHC is a specialized conglomerate which has at least one subsidiary bank. To explain the growth and importance of BHCs, one should distinguish between two types of holding companies, one-bank and multibank. While the names should be sufficient to explain the difference between the two types, lack of definitions occasionally causes misunderstanding. A one-bank holding company (OBHC) owns only one bank subsidiary, which may be a unit, limited branch, or statewide branch. A multibank holding company (MBHC) owns more than one bank subsidiary. Thus, an OBHC may have more banking *offices* than a MBHC. Both OBHCs and MBHCs may own one or more nonbank firms.

Table 8–1 presents absolute and relative measures of BHCs. The extent of the BHC movement often is underestimated by the public because the

**TABLE 8–1  Bank holding companies and subsidiary banks, December 31, 1977**

|  | Bank Holding Company | | |
|  | One-bank | Multibank | Total |
|---|---|---|---|
| Number or dollars: |  |  |  |
| Holding companies | 1,620 | 305 | 1,925 |
| Subsidiary banks | 1,620 | 2,345 | 3,965 |
| Deposits ($ billions) | 403 | 411 | 814 |
| Percent of insured banks: |  |  |  |
| Holding companies | 11.2 | 2.1 | 13.3 |
| Subsidiary banks | 11.2 | 16.3 | 27.5 |
| Deposits | 38.6 | 39.4 | 78.0 |

**SOURCE:** Bernand Shull, "Federal and State Supervision of Bank Holding Companies: Some Proposals for Change," in Federal Reserve Bank of Chicago, *Proceedings of a Conference on Bank Structure and Competition, 1979*, and FDIC, *Annual Report, 1979*.

subsidiaries of multibank companies are legal entities with separate names, and the nonbank subsidiaries generally keep a low profile. More than one quarter of the banks with more than three quarters of total deposits are controlled by BHCs. Large banks in particular have found the holding company structure advantageous. Should this cause concern? The BHC movement is widespread, and is it also economically important? While the BHC movement definitely is economically significant, its significance has been exaggerated, particularly in the popular press. Consider first the importance of OBHCs. While a few OBHCs existed for many years, prior to 1960 the bank typically was the junior subsidiary. For example, a large manufacturing firm in a relatively small town may have owned a bank largely for the convenience of its employees. The company bank has not been glorified in song but it did exist. The relative importance of the bank and nonbank subsidiaries changed as the BHC movement got underway around 1965. Large banks formed holding companies in order to acquire nonbank firms, some quite large and in industries totally unrelated to banking. Many feared that this was the beginning of *zaibatsus,* Japan's vast bank-industrial combines. Would these vast combines engage in cutthroat practices until they had driven out the competition and then exercise monopoly power? While attempts to monopolize the economy do explain a few OBHCs, much more mundane factors explain the creation of most of them. First, Reg Q restrictions in the late 1960s often made CDs an unreliable source of funds. Banks formed holding companies to acquire reliable sources of funds and circumvent Reg Q. In particular, the holding company could float its commercial paper not subject to these ceilings, using the proceeds to acquire loans from the bank subsidiary. Second, *de novo* entry in "closely related" industries let OBHC improve banking services and simultaneously take advantage of complementarity in production. For example, a bank may not have sufficient business to justify purchase of a computer. However, the establishment of a bookkeeping and data processing subsidiary may justify the computer and lead to better service for the bank's customers.

The apparition of potential *zaibatsus* was put to rest by the 1970 amendments to the Bank Holding Company Act of 1956, which stated that BHCs could engage only in those businesses "so closely related to banking as to be proper incident thereto." All BHCs are regulated by the Fed, although the subsidiary banks still are supervised by their primary regulator as shown in Figure 8–1. For example, the comptroller examines national banks owned by a BHC. Fed regulation of BHCs means that the Fed (1) specifies the "closely related" nonbank businesses which a BHC may enter and (2) determines whether a BHC may purchase a specific nonbank or bank, which then would become a subsidiary. The Fed's list of permissible activities includes finance companies, mortgage banking, credit life insurance, financial advising, leasing, and data processing. Of course, a bank/closely related nonbank combine may decrease competition, though perhaps not to the extent of *zaibatsus.* Any decrease in competition is supposed to be outweighed by increased convenience and efficiency.

MBHCs were established mainly to surmount state branching restrictions and the prohibition on interstate banking. Many thought the bank subsidiaries of MBHCs effectively were branches although legally distinct, independent banks. Thus it seemed incongruous that some unit and limited-branching states would permit statewide MBHCs, and the federal government would ban interstate banking while permitting holding companies to operate across state lines. In recent years, however, it has become clear that circumvention of branching laws is not the sole purpose of MBHCs, some of which now operate entirely within a single statewide branching state. In some cases complicated tax laws favor the MBHC route to branch banking. Second, banks in relatively small towns in particular are alleged to lose substantial goodwill when they merge with a large city bank, so these banks retain their "independent" status. To be sure, banks under the holding company umbrella are not totally independent; management does set some guidelines for subsidiary banks. MBHCs exist in statewide-branching states because management believes the limited autonomy of subsidiaries enhances performance. The optimal degree of decentralization varies from firm to firm and, consequently, so does the position of subsidiary banks in the spectrum of decision making from independent bank to branch. Perhaps because of this diversity, the effect of affiliation within a MBHC is inconclusive.[5]

## BANK REGULATION, LACK OF INFORMATION, AND EXTERNAL EFFECTS

Why has banking long been one of the most highly regulated industries? Is this justified? Why should *any* industry be regulated? Under most circumstances an unfettered industry which produces a homogeneous product will achieve maximum internal or productive efficiency, at least in the long run. That is, industry production costs normally are minimized in the absence of any regulation. Cost minimization simply is in the producer's self-interest. In an age when too many believe in conspiracies and zero-sum games, that is, what benefits one person harms another, we must emphasize the validity in this case of Adam Smith's dictum: the pursuit of one's self-interest benefits society. Cost minimization benefits society because it increases the availability of resources for other uses. *Considering an industry's internal or productive efficiency alone, there exists a strong presumption against regulation.* In order to reduce costs, firms call consultants and not their well-meaning regulator, who typically is not a better manager and technician than the average existing business person. Although regulations typically increase average costs, they may be justified on four grounds:

1. Lack of information about the product.
2. External effects.
3. Economies of scale, also called natural monopolies.
4. Monopolies not explained by economies of scale.

We consider the first two reasons for regulation and the type of regulation adopted before discussing economies of scale and monopoly.

When economies were largely agrarian, lack of product information was particularly acute in the financial industry alone. Consumers could more easily evaluate the relative merits of tangible commodities such as varieties of wheat than the relative merits of intangible deposits at the

---

[5] See Robert J. Lawrence and Samuel H. Talley, "An Assessment of Bank Holding Companies," *Federal Reserve Bulletin,* January 1976, pp. 15–21.

First or Second National Bank. Increasing sophistication in production has produced more basic as well as more sophisticated products. The consumer protection movement generally and bank regulation in particular is partially explained by the increasing awareness and importance of lack of product information. Lack of information misallocates resources. Products the value and quality of which are underestimated are produced and consumed suboptimally.

Lack of information in banking has more serious consequences than selecting a bank with higher than average service costs. Lack of information exacerbates the external effects of bank failures, which sometimes are sufficiently widespread to produce a depression. External effects occur when the *private* cost and benefit do not equal *social* cost and benefit because someone other than the producer or consumer of the product incurs a cost or benefit. A classic example of external effects in environmental economics is the air pollution generated by the production of steel. In this case the social cost of steel exceeds the private cost by the cost of dirty air, and an external *dis*economy occurs. Financial economics also has a classic example of external diseconomies: bank failures. Any bankruptcy may generate some external effects as the full costs of the bankruptcy are not borne by the owners. The bankrupt firm's employees and suppliers may be temporarily unemployed, and its customers may lack alternative sources of the product. The external effects of failures are positively related to the size of the bankrupt firm. For example, the Detroit job market cannot quickly place thousands of auto workers, while the disruptions in the labor and products markets are short lived when a small pencil producer fails. Thus the Chryslers and Lockheeds in the economy are aided while ma and pa operations are left to fend for themselves.

For any size firm, the rippling effect of *bank* failures is wider and produces greater external diseconomies, at least prior to the FDIC. Depositors rarely lose everything when a bank fails; they simply do not recover the full value of their deposits. Typically, however, the partial recovery was significantly delayed, and during the interim depositors were greatly inconvenienced and forced to reduce their spending, which in turn had negative effects on the suppliers to the depositors. Moreover, the sight of one failure generates widespread suspicion in everyone's mind. When one bank fails, is it not likely that some other banks are suffering from the same ailments? True, some negative factors are industrywide, but some are particular to a bank, for example, theft or poor management. Lacking information about the quality of the loan portfolio and other aspects of banks, depositors unable to distinguish between industrywide and particular factors run and test all banks. The outcome often was a banking panic which induced a recession.

Lack of information and external effects have invoked what types of regulation? At least with regard to large banks, the bank regulatory agencies have largely—not entirely—abdicated to the SEC their responsibility of providing investment information. The SEC defines and enforces "full disclosure" by large firms, including banks, to current and potential creditors and stockholders. (The extent of the additional information forthcoming because of the SEC's full disclosure laws is debatable.) Bank borrowers and other debtors have fared somewhat better in gaining information due to the bank agencies. The Federal Reserve administers the truth-in-lending laws, which have provided more and better interest rate information.[6] While SEC full disclosure and Fed truth-in-lending laws are designed to provide bank stockholders and borrowers with more information, regulations quite properly have *not* been designed to provide depositors with an important piece of information—the likelihood of bank failures. From the viewpoint of depositors, regulations mainly reduce (1) the need for information by making banks more homogeneous and (2) the consequences of misinformation. Restrictive chartering and bank examinations are the main means of producing more homogeneous banks, and deposit insurance reduces the consequences of misinformation. We shall return to charter and examination policy shortly.

### Deposit insurance

The banking authorities have attacked external effects in two ways. First, and most important, a deposit insurance program was adopted. Insurance frees deposits at failed banks; depositors are paid off virtually immediately. Insured depositors of failed banks can continue spending, and the insured depositors of existing banks do not have to test their banks' solvency. Deposit insurance is incomplete, however. Deposit insurance covers virtually all accounts—Figure 8–1 shows that 98.1 percent of all banks are insured, and these banks hold 98.5 of total deposits—but insurance covers less than 70 percent of total deposits because coverage of each account at insured banks is limited to $100,000.[7] In other words, the uninsured large deposits at insured banks greatly exceed the deposits of uninsured banks. Consequently, large firms and wealthy individuals are still concerned about bank failures, just as nearly everyone was prior to the creation of the FDIC. In the five months between publication of the precarious financial condition of the Franklin National Bank and its official failure, the Fed lent the Franklin $1.7 billion at the discount window in an effort to keep the bank afloat as large depositors were closing their accounts.

Why isn't deposit insurance complete in order to reduce more fully the

---

[6] The greater information gain from Fed truth-in-lending than SEC full disclosure may simply reflect the small initial demand for information by unsophisticated borrowers rather than better administration by the Fed.

[7] Stanley Silverberg, "Implications of Changes in the Effective Level of Deposit Insurance Coverage," in Federal Reserve Bank of Chicago, *Proceedings of a Conference on Bank Structure and Competition, 1980.*

external effects of bank failure? While reducing the external effects of bank failures is the major justification for deposit insurance, it also was adopted to protect deserving groups. This is the widows and orphans—long a popular political group—argument for insurance. That is, small depositors cannot be expected to have good information and should be protected against misinformation. Large depositors on the other hand should be able to evaluate the solvency of banks and need no protection, or at least no more than widows and orphans. The second argument against 100 percent deposit insurance is that uninsured depositors limit risk taking by bankers. Risktakers normally earn a higher average return although, of course, it will vary significantly from period to period. *If* banks were able to pass forward to depositors the reward of risk, at least risk lovers who want a high expected return would be attracted to risktaking banks. However, Reg Q deposit ceilings and other institutional and operational factors greatly hamper banks' ability to pass forward to depositors the rewards of risk. With little to gain and much to lose from risktaking bankers, the uninsured depositor selects the conservative banker with a gray pin-stripe suit. In order to maintain their uninsured deposits and grow, bankers limit their risktaking and, *ceteris paribus,* bank failures are less likely.

The *ceteris paribus* condition in the last sentence is extremely important. Because the condition often will not be satisfied, limited deposit insurance does *not* necessarily reduce bank failures. Anything less than 100 percent deposit insurance does not altogether stop withdrawals when a bank's condition is thought to be precarious. Particularly when banks are illiquid, massive withdrawals and the forced sale of assets enhances the likelihood of failure. Compared to 100 percent insurance, limited deposit insurance increases the likelihood of bank failures due to bank runs and illiquidity while reducing bank failures due to risktaking by bankers. Which of these factors dominate? While adoption of the current limited deposit insurance system clearly has reduced bank failures, it is unclear that extention to 100 percent insurance will further decrease failures. One can get too much of a good thing.[8]

Because of the way failed banks have been handled in recent years, data on the proportion of deposits insured and the distinction between limited and 100 percent insurance are important *ex-ante* but not *ex-post*. The just stated experience of the Franklin National Bank after its problems became known indicates that many large depositors expect the $100,000 insurance ceiling will be effective, so that deposits above $100,000 will incur some loss. However, no depositor or general creditor, however large, incurred any loss. The FDIC has handled the majority of bank failures and all large bank (over $100 million deposits) failures

---

[8] Technically speaking, the relationship between bank failures and the insurance limit may not be monotonic.

through purchase and assumption (P&A). In the P&A method another bank bids to purchase some or all of the assets and assumes *all* the deposit liabilities of the failed bank. Since the bank failed because its liabilities exceeded assets, the FDIC makes a cash payment to the low bidder. In P&A cases every depositor in a failed bank one day holds equal deposits in a solvent bank the next day. The alternative method of handling failures is the payout, where the FDIC immediately pays off the *insured* deposits, acquires but eventually liquidates the assets, and shares the loss with uninsured depositors to the extent the liquidated assets exceeded insured deposits. The method of disposal, P&A or payout, supposedly is selected to minimize FDIC cost, but the exclusive use of the P&A method for large banks suggests that external effects are considered. Because large depositors do suffer losses when the payout method is adopted, the payout method has been applied only to small banks, which have few large depositors—if there were many, the bank would not be small. So far, then, there effectively has been 100 percent deposit insurance, although the Franklin National case illustrates the public has not expected it, and rightly so. Past policy is not a perfect predictor of future policy, particularly since the tenure of policymakers typically is quite short.

## BANK FAILURES: DESIRABLE OR UNDESIRABLE?

If the external effects of bank failures could not be eliminated, then it would be worthwhile to attempt to reduce failures themselves. Is a policy of reducing failures desirable now that the external effects have largely been eliminated? Bankruptcies often are the termination of a long string of losses. During relatively prosperous times losses are signs that resources are being misallocated, since the value of goods produced is less than the cost of resources used. Viewed in this manner, bankruptcies are worthwhile, signaling that "no more good money is being thrown after bad." To be sure, it would have been best not to have created the firm in the first place, thereby avoiding the losses and ultimate death. Can bank regulations prevent the formation of banks which ultimately become insolvent? Generally, what is the best safeguard against insolvency? Recall that solvency is one of the bank's objectives. *Honest bankers' desire to succeed, rather than any regulation, is the most effective safeguard against failure*. If bankers wanted to fail, it is doubtful that regulations could be devised to prevent them from doing so. Honest bankers and other managers suffer significant hardships when a firm is bankrupt. Besides the immediate loss of jobs, the future prospects of the insolvent bankers are dim. Visualize the following résumé: Previous employment: President, U.S. Prestige Bank, (now bankrupt). Hardly a résumé likely to gain one job offers. Besides the loss of jobs, the insolvent bank's stockholders lose their investment.

We mentioned at several points that *honest* bankers have no incentive to fail, but the *dishonest* banker is successful if the bank does fail. Bankruptcy may occur precisely because the dishonest banker stole too much and made too many loans to the wrong people. Blatant dishonesty is a major reason for bank failures nowadays, and less obvious dishonesty enters in many failures officially diagnosed as mismanagement. For example, are delinquent loans to one's friends and relatives examples of dishonesty or mismanagement? Banking history shows that the industry has attracted some crooks. The portability of the product and the difficulty in ascertaining quality made banking a nightmare in the 1850s, as we shall show later. Merely passing laws barring crooks from the banking industry would be as successful in achieving its objective as legislation against foreign aggression prevents wars. *The bank charter and annual examination gather information that depositors often cannot acquire. The charter and examination process should and does check the honesty and reputation of management. This has made banks more homogeneous and reduced failures.*

To be sure, honest bankers like other people do make mistakes, and some fail. Regulators should be quite blasé about honest failures which do not produce external effect. What should be and what is do not always coincide. *While bank regulators do have multiple goals, bank solvency is their premier goal.* The multitude of government regulations and examinations can be understood only against this backdrop of regulators' overwhelming desire to prevent bank failures. Regulations severely restricting risktaking and protecting the banking industry have indeed reduced bank failures, but at the cost of more commercial firm failures and a more monopolistic, uninnovating banking sector. Banks are intermediaries and a major source of funds for small firms. *For every conservative bank there are dozens of small firms which failed for lack of financing.*

A liberal charter policy would foster a dynamic environment. In fact, charter policy is geared more to the creation and maintenance of monopolies than to their elimination. A 1980 report prepared by the Democratic staff of the Senate Banking Committee is the latest of many studies claiming that recent Comptrollers of the Currency were "more interested in protecting existing banks during this period (1970–77) than in promoting and meeting the banking needs of the public."[9] In order for a new bank to acquire a charter, regulators must be convinced that it will be profitable and not significantly harm existing banks. Many charter applications are denied on the grounds of alleged unprofitability. Who is the best judge of future success, the detached regulator or the (honest) entrant willing to commit funds? Charters are rarely, if ever, granted when some banks in an area are unprofitable, on the grounds that losses are prima facie evidence of overbanking. While this may be the case, this policy ignores the

---

[9] The classic study to arrive at this conclusion is Sam Peltzman, "Bank Entry Regulation: Its Impact and Purpose," *National Bank Review*, December 1965, pp. 163–77. The Banking Committee report is summarized in the *Washington Post*, October 27, 1980, p. D3.

real possibility that the existing banks are unprofitable because they are poorly managed. The (honest) entrant who has every hope of succeeding should not be denied the opportunity. Sheltering the market from the rigors of competition is undesirable when external effects are absent.

### Bank examinations

The annual bank examination in general and the "capital adequacy" aspect of the exam are integral elements of this policy of preventing failures. Bank examiners spring unannounced at a bank generally once a year. The examination has some elements of a financial audit. Cash, securities, and other assets which may become attached to sticky fingers are audited to verify that they are on hand. They typically are.[10] While attempting to ferret out dishonest bankers by its financial audit aspects, *the bank examination primarily is designed to verify compliance with banking regulation and, more important, be an early warning system*. For example, the examiner will check compliance with size of loan and interest rate limitations. Above all, the examination is supposed to identify potential problems while still minor and correctable.[11] An appraisal of the quality and collectibility of the loan portfolio has traditionally been one of the key elements of the exam as an early warning system. Loans are classified as good, substandard, doubtful, and loss. The usual rule of thumb used in interpreting these categories is that virtually all loans categorized "good" will be collected; losses will be incurred on 20 percent of the substandard loans, 50 percent of the doubtful loans, and virtually 100 percent of the loss loans.

While there always was some diversity among regulators in the loan evaluation process, congressional hearings following the Franklin National Bank debacle in 1974 uncovered significant diversity in the other factors analyzed and in the bank rating system. This made evaluation of the condition of the overall banking system difficult. Uniformity was achieved in 1978 with the new Uniform Interagency Bank Rating System which assigns ratings from 1 to 5, with 1 indicating "strength" and 5 "unsatisfactory and in need of immediate remedial attention," to five aspects of a bank's operation and condition: (1) Capital adequacy, (2)

---

[10] The movies may have the bank vice president packing a suitcase full of cash and securities and flying to Rio, but this is rarely how defalcations actually occur. The suitcase approach can be tried only once. An essentially similar scheme can be used repeatedly and will likely net one more than a suitcase full. Even in crime, bankers adhere to double-entry bookkeeping. The dishonest banker takes the cash and books a loan to the ABC company. When the examiners arrive there is no cash, which is just what the records indicate because ABC got a loan. The problem is: ABC is a fictitious company or a company headed by the banker's relative, who has no intention of paying off the loan. By the time this is discovered the banker has gone through the alphabet and lent to XYZ.

[11] Because examinations occur only annually, the quarterly financial statements banks submit to regulators are incorporated in the early warning system.

*A*sset quality, (3) *M*anagement and administration, (4) *E*arnings quantity and quality, and (5) *L*iquidity level.[12] While the five performance dimensions are somewhat interdependent, each is rated separately. An acronym: examiners want a Number 1 CAMEL. In addition, examiners offer a composite judgment incorporating these five aspects and other factors, such as local economic conditions and affiliation with a bank holding company, where the composite rating also is scaled from 1 to 5. A composite 1-rated bank receives little attention between examinations while a composite 5 bank is subject to constant monitoring. Examiners usually "suggest" a corrective action program for 5 banks. Banks are not legally required to adopt the corrective program, but they usually find it advantageous to do so. One does not fool with bank examiners. They can get a bank's deposit insurance canceled (often a kiss of death) or ultimately a cease and desist order.

At this point the reader should have a general impression of the factors examiners consider in evaluating the five performance dimensions except possibly the quality of earnings and capital adequacy. The main factor in the quality of earnings is the amount of the bank's additions to valuation or loss reserves so that at each moment in time the balance sheet shows reasonably accurate valuations, and realized losses do not cause a "surprise."

### Bank failures and capital adequacy

*Capital adequacy was the performance dimension mentioned first because it is the heart of the bank examination process.* Capital is the owners' contribution and measures the magnitude of mistakes honest bank managers can make before bankruptcy occurs. The capital adequacy problem entails estimating the capital/asset ratio consistent with a "small" likelihood of insolvency. Capital adequacy is especially controversial within banking circles because the capital/asset ratio has important but opposite effects on bankers' profitability and solvency. Bankers estimate the trade-off while regulators, interested only in bank solvency, ignore the opportunity cost of a high capital/asset ratio. The rate of return on the stockholders' capital may be written as

$$\text{Rate of return} = \frac{\text{Profits}}{\text{Assets}} \frac{\text{Assets}}{\text{Capital}}.$$

A low capital/asset ratio (high asset/capital) ratio may decrease the likelihood of remaining solvent but the equation shows that, *ceteris paribus,* it increases owners' rate of return. However, regulators do not participate in the bank's profit. Regulators are praised when bank failures are low not when bank profits are high.

---

[12] George G. Juncker, "A New Supervisory System for Rating Banks," Federal Reserve Bank of New York *Quarterly Review,* Summer 1978, pp. 47–50.

The capital adequacy tug-of-war between bankers and bank regulators has continued for so long because, besides disagreeing on what constitutes a "low" probability of failure, the relationship between failure and capital is imprecise. Figure 8–4 graphs the bank capital/asset ratio from 1920

**FIGURE 8–4   Banks' capital/asset percentage, 1920–1979**

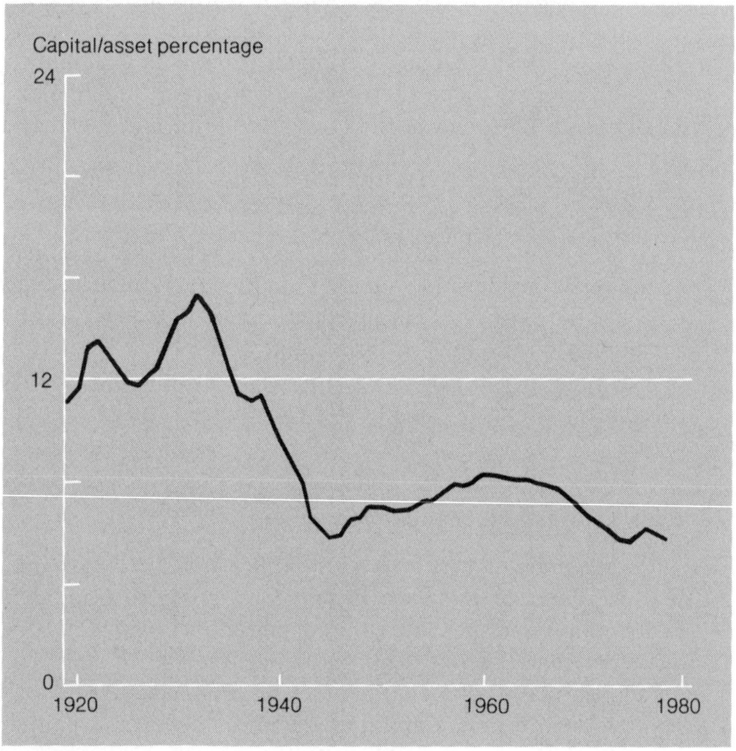

**SOURCE:** Federal Reserve, *Historical Chart Book, 1979.*

forward, and Table 8–2 shows the average annual number and percentage of bank failures for selected years since 1920. Clearly, a high capital/asset ratio is no guarantee against failure. In the prosperous 1920s about 700, or 2.5 percent, of the banks failed annually, and the capital/asset ratio averaged 13 percent. In the 1960s and 1970s about 6 banks, or 0.05 percent, failed annually, and the capital/asset ratio was only 7 percent. However, one should not conclude from the figure and table that the capital/asset ratio does not influence the failure rate. During the Great Depression years of 1930–33, failures were a common occurrence, but the capital/asset ratio was *increasing* because the banks with a low capital/asset ratio were failing.

Why are banks able to operate with less capital nowadays? What factors influence how much capital is "adequate," that is, the capital consis-

**TABLE 8–2  Average annual number and percentage of bank failures**

| Time period | Failures, number | Failures, percent |
|---|---|---|
| 1920–22 | 346.0 | 1.17 |
| 1923–29 | 692.0 | 2.57 |
| 1930 | 1350.0 | 5.81 |
| 1931 | 2293.0 | 10.76 |
| 1932 | 1453.0 | 7.88 |
| 1933 | 4000.0 | 28.68 |
| 1934–39 | 48.0 | 0.32 |
| 1960–74 | 5.6 | 0.04 |
| 1975–79 | 10.8 | 0.07 |

**SOURCE:** Federal Reserve, *Banking and Monetary Statistics* (Washington: National Capital Press, 1943) for data up to 1939, and FDIC, *Annual Report, 1979,* for data since 1940.

tent with a given small probability of failure? Answers to these questions are presented in tabular form in Table 8–3. According to Table 8–3, the decline of the *actual* capital/asset ratio should not be a source of great concern. Except for the greater importance of risky foreign loans, all the factors which *reduce* the adequate amount of capital have *increased*. Consequently, the *adequate* capital/asset ratio has also fallen.

Which factors listed in Table 8–3 are most important in explaining the

**TABLE 8–3  Factors reducing the adequate capital/asset ratio and their change over time**

| Factors | Change over time |
|---|---|
| (1) Adaptability to demand and population changes. | Increase as (1) banking markets expanded due to greater branching, (2) management techniques improved, and (3) banks became less specialized lenders. |
| (2) Economic stability | Increase, perhaps because government is committed to full employment. |
| (3) Bank liquidity | Increase due to (1) the development of organized, national financial markets, and (2) greater commitment by the Federal Reserve to aid banks at the discount window, e.g., Franklin National Bank. |
| (4) Asset quality | (a) Increase with government commitment to aid firms, e.g., Lockheed. (b) Decrease as banks make more foreign loans and government intervention for business purposes, e.g., the Dominican Republic during the Johnson Administration, is less likely. |
| (5) Deposit stability | Increase due to (1) deposit insurance and (2) a higher time deposit ratio. |

inadequacy of the high capital/asset ratio in the 1920s and 1930s? Why were bank failures so much more common in the 1920s and 1930s in spite of high capital/asset ratios? The 1920s generally were prosperous years for most Americans except small-town bankers, particularly those in farming areas. The growing use of automobiles and greater mobility generally reduced the monopoly power of small-town banks as individuals now had access to larger, more distant banks. Besides losing depositors to other banks, the continuing relative decline of agriculture and farm income led to out-migration, reduced the average size of deposits, and lowered the quality of assets of banks in farm areas. Inability to adapt to these changes in demand and population is the main explanation for the failures of the 1920s. *Unit banking laws are artificial constraints severely hampering adaptability to demand shifts.*

The high concentration of the 1920s bank failures in the Plain States from Texas to North Dakota supports this demand shift explanation. Moreover, Figure 8–3, which shows that branching was rare in the 1920s, is consistent with the hypothesis that unit banking magnifies the consequences of any given shock, hampers adaptability, and increases failures. Branching is a means of diversification; branch banks draw on a wider geographical area, which reduces the consequence of many shocks. The decline of one branch due to, say, a new highway bypass is not catastrophic when it is one of 10 branches. In fact, the decline of one branch may aid another branch, leaving the total system relatively unaffected. Mergers are a possible response to demand shift. Large banks could purchase failing small banks and convert them to branches. A branch office may be a profitable branch although it will fail as an independent bank because branching facilitates the transfer of funds and loans. In order for a unit bank to succeed, it must encounter both a source of funds and a demand for loans. Branch banks on the other hand may have some branches which effectively act as collectors of deposits, which are lent by other branches where loan demand is high. In unit-banking states, however, mergers typically are not a viable response because the banking office must be closed.

Economic and deposit instability clearly are the primary reasons for the failures in the early 1930s. During the Great Depression many otherwise safe loans became uncollectible. The collapse of the real sector dragged down the financial sector.[13] Failure by these banks produced external effects ranging from mild deposit instability to severe runs on banks.

## BANK REGULATION, ECONOMIES OF SCALE, AND MONOPOLY

The existence of economies of scale and monopolies are two other reasons for regulation. We mentioned earlier that cost minimization is in a

---

[13] The feedback effect which made the Depression great can be ignored here.

banker's self-interest. This entrepreneurial quest to minimize cost naturally leads to a monopoly when there are pervasive economies of scale,
that is, total costs increase less than proportionally with output or, equivalently, average unit costs decline with output. When economies of scale
exist, cost minimizing firms merge and eventually become a monopoly,
which maintains itself by blocking entry through its ability to produce at
lower unit costs than new, small firms.

A monopoly is no more profit oriented than any other firm; it simply is
in a better position to achieve its goal. Lacking rivals and restricted only
by the demand for the product, the monopolistic firm raises price, reduces
output, and earns excessive profits. *Monopoly creates external or allocative
inefficiency*. Compared to other products, too little of the monopoly product is produced, precisely because the monopolist charges and earns too
much. *In a free market system with economies of scale, attainment of internal or operating efficiency causes external or allocative inefficiency*. Regulation must strike a balance between the low cost-low price objectives.

Economies of scale are not a necessary condition for monopoly. Since a
monopoly, however achieved, can earn supernormal profits, self-interest
creates a tendency toward collusion and monopolistic industries whenever
possible. Monopolies not explained by economies of scale generate all the
evils of monopolies without yielding any benefits. Regulations which prevent or terminate monopolies are justified, although in some cases they
may be unnecessary because monopolization may not be feasible. For
example, an unregulated wheat industry is unlikely to act monopolistic
because entry is easy and collusion among large numbers is difficult.

Are there economies of scale in banking? Is banking monopolistic?
Before looking at the empirical results, the only way to answer these
questions, consider the types of regulation possible. Economies of scale
are generally believed to be present in the communication, transportation,
water, and power industries. In order to attain large-scale, low-cost production, regulation typically bars entry and *grants* a monopoly—this prevents the blood-letting which invariably occurs in the process of selecting
the monopolist with a knockout free market system—while simultaneously imposing a price schedule such that the monopolist earns only a
normal rate of return and the benefits of the low production cost are
passed forward to consumers. Regulations of this type, common in the
utilities industry, attempt to eliminate the trade-off between productive
and allocative efficiency that exists in a free market system subject to
economies of scale. Other objectives and the nature of banking products
make utility-type price regulation of the banking industry neither feasible
nor desirable, even if scale economies exist.

First, bureaucratic considerations reduce the speed of adjustment of
regulated prices in other industries, and we may expect the same in banking. Direct regulation of bank loan rates and the prices of other bank
products would make them sluggish while banks' role in the overall eco-

nomic stabilization process often necessitates large and frequent interest rate/bank price changes. Second, unlike electricity and other utilities, banking products such as loans depend very much on the specific purchaser. Loans to AT&T and Chrysler are hardly identical. This diversity of "products" is reflected in the significant cross-sectional interest rate variation mentioned in Chapter 5. Even if frequent interest rate changes were unnecessary, the need to establish many interest rate classes, coupled with the fact that banks would decide in which class any particular borrower falls, makes direct interest rate/bank price regulation unfeasible.

*Charter, merger, and branching policies are the main regulatory policies available to banking authorities in order to create an efficient and competitive banking industry.* These policies work indirectly; they create the industry structure most compatible with the regulatory goals.[14] *Bank structure henceforth refers to the number and size distribution of banks and branches.* Bank regulators have exercised charter and branching powers for many years, although often *not* to promote a competitive environment, as we just indicated. However, antitrust policy generally and merger restrictions in particular are relatively new for banking, even though these tools are the traditional remedies for monopoly. Actual bank merger policy is briefly summarized in the appendix.[15]

---

[14] While charter, merger, and branching policy can strongly influence the operating performance of banks, other general policies beyond the control of bank regulators can have equally powerful effects but often go unrecognized. For example, the "double taxation of dividends"—that is, profits are taxed first at the corporate level and then taxed again at the personal level (aside from a small exclusion) when distributed as dividends—coupled with the lower tax rate on capital gains than on dividend income, has probably increased the size of banks and other firms more than antitrust policy could reduce it. An example is helpful. Assume a corporation's pretax earnings are $100, the corporate and personal tax rates are 50 percent, and the capital gains tax rate is 25 percent, where the tax rates are representative for the well-to-do. As matters now stand, the corporation's posttax earnings in our example are $50 whether it pays dividends or retains earnings. If the corporation distributes the $50 earnings as dividends, the stockholder will have $25 after personal taxes. On the other hand, suppose the corporation retains the $50 and expands. Assuming for simplicity that this strategy raises the value of its stock by the same $50 it invested, the stockholder will be $37.50 richer when the stock is sold and the capital gains tax is paid. Thus the stockholder wants the corporation to retain earnings and grow instead of paying dividends. If dividends were taxed only once, that is, the corporation does not pay taxes on earnings distributed as dividends, then a dividend policy would net the stockholder $50, which is more than the retained earnings-growth policy yields. In the 19th century prior to income taxes one bought "a cow for her milk, a hen for her eggs, and a stock by heck, for her dividends." Now stocks are for retained earnings and growth. While the double taxation of dividends may be justified on the basis of its progressivity or some other grounds, its effects on the structure of the banking or any other industry should not be ignored.

[15] For a more detailed summary, see Douglas V. Austin, "The Line of Commerce and the Relevant Geographic Market in Banking: What Fifteen Years of Trials and Tribulations Has Taught Us and Not Taught Us About the Measure of Banking Structure," in Federal Reserve Bank of Chicago, *Proceedings of a Conference on Bank Structure and Competition, 1977.*

## BANKING STRUCTURE AND ECONOMIES OF SCALE

This and the following sections are empirically oriented. After presenting some measures of the structure of the banking industry, the data on economies of scale in banking and the relationship between industry structure and bank loan rates are reviewed. From these empirical results we draw implications concerning the specific charter, merger, and branching policies which can best create a structure consistent with low cost, efficient production and low interest rate, competitive credit allocation.

Banks are hardly homogeneous. Perhaps the most important difference among banks is size, as measured by total assets. Table 8–4 presents

**TABLE 8–4  Number, assets, and percent of commercial banks grouped by asset size, December 31, 1979**

| Banks assets | Number | Number as percent of total | Total assets ($ billions) | Total assets as percent of total |
|---|---|---|---|---|
| Less than $5 million | 1,104 | 7.5 | 3.3 | 0.2 |
| $5.0–$9.9 million | 2,147 | 14.6 | 16.3 | 0.9 |
| $10.0–$24.9 million | 4,745 | 32.2 | 79.2 | 4.6 |
| $25.0–$49.9 million | 3,378 | 22.9 | 119.5 | 6.9 |
| $50.0–$99.9 million | 1,772 | 12.0 | 122.7 | 7.1 |
| $100.0–$299.9 million | 1,071 | 7.3 | 171.6 | 10.0 |
| $300.0–$499.9 million | 178 | 1.2 | 69.9 | 4.1 |
| $500.0–$999.9 million | 157 | 1.1 | 105.6 | 6.1 |
| $1.0–$4.9 billion | 153 | 1.0 | 311.9 | 18.1 |
| $5.0 billion or more | 33 | 0.2 | 724.1 | 42.0 |
| Total | 14,738 | 100.0 | 1724.1 | 100.0 |

**SOURCE:** FDIC, *Annual Report, 1979*, p. 154.

absolute and relative measures of the importance of different size banks. The table shows that the United States is a country of pigmy banks and several giants. The total assets of the 8,000 smallest banks, or approximately 55 percent of all banks, are approximately 5.5 percent of total industry assets. Moreover, the total assets of these 8,000 banks are less than the assets of the single largest bank, the Bank of America! This structure is in sharp contrast to that found in most developed countries, where the industry comprises a dozen or so banks and most are fairly large. If the United States has many small banks, it also has many large banks. Given the size of the U.S. economy, it hardly is surprising that U.S. banks rank among the largest in the world. What is surprising is the result of the more valid comparison of U.S. banks and firms in other industries. No other industry comes close to having 33 firms with assets over $5.0 billion. Banking is a big business! Table 8–5 lists the behemoths.

**TABLE 8-5  Assets of ten largest U.S. banks ($ billions)**

| | | | | |
|---|---|---|---|---|
| 1. | Bank of America (California) ..... | $103.6 | 6. Continental Illinois .............. | $41.1 |
| 2. | Citibank (New York) ............. | 98.9 | 7. Chemical (New York) ............ | 39.5 |
| 3. | Chase Manhattan (New York) ..... | 72.3 | 8. Bankers Trust (New York) ........ | 30.0 |
| 4. | Morgan Guaranty (New York) ..... | 50.4 | 9. First National, Chicago .......... | 28.0 |
| 5. | Manufacturers Hanover (New York) | 46.8 | 10. Security Pacific (California) ...... | 24.2 |

**SOURCE:** *Polk World Bank Directory,* Midyear 1980.

Some are household names, but others maintain a low profile. Unmask the industry and learn the name of a bank a day.

Tables 8–4 and 8–5 present static, single-period measures of the structure of the national banking industry. Has the structure changed over time? Are banks becoming more homogeneous? Tables similar to 8–4 and 8–5 for different dates would shed little light on these questions. Such tables would show that banks are becoming larger, but so are other firms, particularly in this inflationary environment. (Of course, the assets and income of other firms may be increasing *because* bank assets and deposits—money—expand.) Instead of dollar benchmarks we need relative measures. Such measures show that first, the banking industry is not growing faster than the economy as a whole. The ratio of total bank *assets* to GNP has remained roughly constant during the past 20 years.[16] Second, the structure of the entire banking industry has remained relatively stable. Small banks are growing at approximately the same rate as large banks, so the share of total assets held by bank classes has remained relatively constant. One of the empirical regularities of the past 20 years is the approximate 50/50 split of the industry between the top 100 and the remainder. That is, *the 100 largest banks have consistently controlled approximately 50 percent of the industry's assets.*[17] Banks are marching in step with each other and the rest of the country.

Are there economies of scale? Would an industry structure resembling that found in most other developed countries reduce operating costs and promote efficiency? Are there too many small banks? Recall that economies of scale exist when total costs increase less than proportionally with output, so average unit cost declines with output. A problem immediately arises: what is bank output? We have repeatedly referred to banks as department stores of finance because their diversified asset portfolio makes them similar to multiproduct firms. Small consumer loans, which

---

[16] The ratio of demand deposits to GNP has fallen, but time deposits and the newer bank liabilities have made up the difference.

[17] Benjamin F. Kleboner, "Recent Changes in the Structure of Banking," in Federal Reserve Bank of Chicago, *Bank Structure and Competition, 1970;* and Bernard Shull, "Multiple Office Banking and Competition: A Review of the Literature," in United States Senate Committee on Banking, Housing, and Urban Affairs, *Compendium of Issues Relating to Branching by Financial Institutions.* Notice that our Table 8–4 also supports this empirical regularity.

are costly to service per dollar lent, may be viewed as a different product than large industrial loans to prime companies. The diversity on the liability side is almost as great. If the banking products were produced in fixed proportions, then total output would still be well defined, and product diversity would not be troublesome. But such is clearly not the case. A typical large bank is *not* simply a magnified small bank. Borrowers at large banks include the Fortune 500 giants, stock brokers, and wealthy individuals financing tax shelters, while farmers and consumers purchasing used cars are the customers of small banks. Care must be exercised to distinguish true economies of scale from cost differences due to product mix.

One of the earliest and best studies was by Lyle Gramley, who collected data for *unit* banks.[18] After standardizing for product mix by including such variables as the ratio of consumer to total loans, regression or least squares analysis was used to analyze the relationship between average cost and size, as measured by total assets.[19] The curve UU' in Figure 8–5 graphs the estimated relationship for unit banks. The graph indicates the existence of economies of scale: average costs decrease with bank size. The magnitude of economies of scale are not uniform, however. Economies of scale are significant when banks are small but rapidly diminish as bank size increases. Economies of scale are virtually exhausted when the bank attains assets of $100 million. Diseconomies do not set in, that is, the curve does not turn upward.

Another study by Schweiger and McGee arrived at essentially the same conclusion about economies for *branch* banks.[20] However, for any given size bank the average cost is greater for a branch bank. This is as expected. For example, the costs of operating a $100 million asset branch bank with, say, 10 branches should be greater than the cost of operating the same size unit bank. The curve BB' graphs the economies of scale relationship for branch banks.

Given the efficiency objective, the implications of Figure 8–5 for

---

[18] Lyle Gramley, *A Study of Scale Economies in Banking,* Federal Reserve Bank of Kansas City, 1962. The appendix presents the regression equation which the text illustrates graphically.

[19] Two approaches to the measurement of output have been followed. First, the approach mentioned in the text, where a *dollar* measure of total output, typically total assets or sometimes deposits, is standardized for product mix. The second approach rejects the concept of "total output" altogether. Numerous *physical* measures of output are constructed, such as the *number* of demand deposit accounts, and cost accounting data allocate costs to each output measure. While the second approach is methodologically preferable, the diversity of results makes it difficult to summarize. Fortunately, the conclusion of the more rigorous second approach confirms the simpler total assets/product mix approach. The pioneering studies using physical measures of output and cost accounting data are George Benston, "Economics of Scale and Marginal Costs in Banking Operations," *National Banking Review,* June 1965, pp. 507–49; and Frederick Bell and Neil Murphy, *Costs in Commercial Banking: A Quantitative Analysis of Bank Behavior and Its Relation to Bank Regulation,* Research Report No. 41, Federal Reserve of Boston, April 1968.

[20] Irving Schweiger and John McGee, "Chicago Banking," *Journal of Business,* July 1961, pp. 320ff.

FIGURE 8-5  Relationship between average cost and bank size

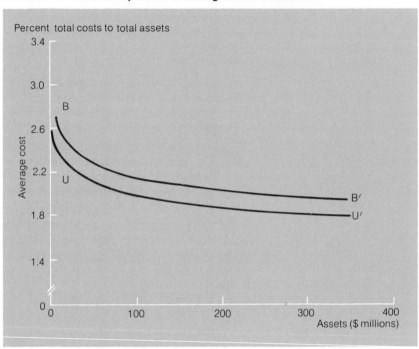

merger policy are clear, assuming mergers are not associated with changes in the type of bank organization. Mergers between small banks should be encouraged. There are many to encourage. According to Table 8–4 the assets of approximately 90 percent of all banks are less than $100 million, the point at which economies become less pronounced. The cost savings through mergers of large banks are minimal, but diseconomies of scale do not set in. The implications for charter policy are somewhat less clear. A liberal charter policy increases the number of banks and reduces average size since the new small banks take some business away from the established large banks. Therefore, a presumption against chartering banks is appropriate, assuming operating efficiency is the sole objective. The presumption must be tempered, however, by the realization that the regression equations which the graph illustrates give average or mean relationship for all banks. The costs for some banks will be less than the graph suggests, and it may be that the banks attempting to enter are precisely the efficient ones.

Contrary to the first impression one may get from Figure 8–5, branching does not increase average cost and reduce operating efficiency. If bank size were independent of the type of banking organization, or, equivalently, if branch banking did not facilitate the existence of larger banks than would otherwise exist under unit banking, then the operating efficiency criterion would indicate that branching should not be permitted. However, branching increases average bank size. Branch banks could not attain their large size without also incurring the extra costs of branches. While it is true that the costs of, say, a $60-million branch bank are greater than the costs of a $60-million unit bank, if the alternative to a $60-million branch bank is two $30-million unit banks, then economies of scale may make the two $30-million unit banks less efficient. In terms of Figure 8–5 the alternative is many banks up the low UU' curve or one bank down the high BB' curve. Are the average costs of a branch bank less than the costs which the branches would incur as unit banks? A priori, the answer is yes. In some ways branch banks are an assemblage of unit banks. The recording of checks by individual branches and the duplication of other functions inhibit the specialization possible in a similar size unit bank. However, like in a unit bank, the management of the investment portfolio of a branch bank is centralized, and specialists on various industries approve large loans. Empirically, the answer is a *qualified* yes. For example, using Schweiger and McGee's regression, average costs per $100,000 assets of a $240-million branch bank are $154 lower than the average costs of an assemblage of two $60-million and six $20-million unit banks. While it is possible to find a combination of unit banks with lower costs than an equal size branch bank, branching reduces costs *somewhat* for many bank size combinations. The efficiency gains from branching typically are *not* that large, however.

## BANKING STRUCTURE, MONOPOLY, AND LOAN RATES

With respect to large firms, bank loans are part of a larger credit market. The geographic boundaries of the close substitutes for bank credit, such as commercial paper and bonds, are national and even international. Like the close substitutes, bank loans to larger firms are made in a national market. A large firm is well-known throughout the United States. Its financial position can be ascertained by all potential lenders at minimum costs. The cost of acquiring information which a bank feels is necessary in order to evaluate risk is small and independent of the distance between potential lender and large borrower. Similarly, convenience does not dictate that the large borrower select a nearby bank. The large firm usually maintains deposits in several banks within a city, banks in different cities, and banks in different regions. Moreover, the large firm's officers are aware of the "going" rate on bank credit substitutes.

Although the number of effective banks to large firms is substantially smaller than the approximately 15,000 banks—small banks cannot service the needs of large firms—there are a sufficient number of large banks to assure competitive credit allocation to large firms. Look at Table 8–4 again. The assets of nearly 200 banks exceed $1 billion! The 100 largest banks control only 50 percent of the industry's assets. Such a statement could be made about few other industries. The national market for large loans is extremely competitive. Anything less than interstate banking coupled with the approval of all mergers is unlikely to change the competitive structure of the large-loan market. Mergers between medium size banks will make *them* more competitive in the market but will not increase competition. It is immaterial if the assets of 200 or 201 banks exceed $1 billion.

For consumers and small firms the geographic boundary of the bank-loan market is not national. Indeed, many bank-loan markets exist. Small firms generally are known only by the banks in the immediate location. Banks lending to small firms outside their immediate area encounter additional information costs, and their risk evaluation will probably be greater. As the extra costs and higher risk evaluation of lending interregionally would have to be passed forward in terms of higher loan rates, interregional loans become poor substitutes for local loans. Thus, the market for loans to consumers and small firms is fragmented. These fragmented markets explain why small banks can exist in spite of economies of scale. Some small banks have the entire market.

The banking market in most small towns and SMSAs (standard metropolitan statistical areas) is not a monopoly in the strictest sense of the term. There typically are several banks. However, observation of the structure of local banking markets indicates that monopolistic elements could be present. Three structural measures of local markets influence loan rates paid by *consumers* and *small firms*.[21]

1. Number of banks in the area.
2. Concentration ratio, defined here as the percentage of the area's banking deposits held by the three largest banks.
3. Average deposit size of bank in the area.

Consider first the effect of banking structure in towns and small cities. In such areas, the concentration ratio typically is 100 percent: few towns have more than three banks. *The number of banks is the best means of distinguishing structure in towns.* Scheiger and McGee used data gathered by comparison shoppers for standard automobile loans in the towns of six counties surrounding Chicago.[22] Illinois is a unit banking state, so each banking office sets its loan rate. For each county the "shopped" banks' rates were averaged on the basis of the number of banks in the town. They found that in each county *the average rate on identical loans was negatively correlated with the number of banks in a town.* For example, the average rates on automobile loans in one-, two-, and three-and-more-bank towns in Lake County, Illinois, were 11.7, 11.0, and 10.7 percent, respectively. Note that the most dramatic reduction in consumer loan rates occurs when the number of banks increases from 1 to 2. Further

---

[21] Because the banking market for large firms is the national or even international market, the structure of the local market has no effect on loan rates paid by large firms. The use of assets instead of deposits in the concentration and size variables does not affect any of the conclusions.

[22] Ibid., p. 261.

bank expansion does not bring as significant rate reductions. A second bank reduces loan rates by 0.70 percentage points or approximately 7 percent. This is substantial considering that Lake County is quite densely populated; cities are nearby; and Lake and Cook counties, Illinois, are contiguous. In more sparsely populated areas where cities are farther apart, the interest rate differential should be larger.

What are the implications of this study for policy, assuming competitive credit allocation is the sole objective? In rural areas charters should be freely granted and mergers *between banks already in the market* should be prohibited, particularly when there are only two banks. Mergers between unit banks in small towns and branch banks that did *not* previously operate in the market will *not* reduce competition as the number of banks is unchanged. Indeed, it may even increase competition and lower loan rates. Although the small loan market typically is more monopolistic in small towns than large cities, the branch bank can exercise only the smaller degree of monopoly power because administrative reasons dictate a common rate schedule at all branches. A second reason for statewide branching is the increase in the number of banks in *small* areas. As our discussion on failures indicated, branches can operate profitably in areas where a unit bank cannot. Branching encourages charter applications.

The results for small towns, showing that loan rates fall more sharply in going from one to two banks than from two to three banks, suggest there is some critical number of banks beyond which additional banks do not reduce loan rates. The analysis for SMSAs confirms this suspicion. Unlike rural areas, the number of banks in metropolitan areas is not significant because it exceeds the critical number. *In SMSAs, the (three-bank) concentration ratio and average size of banks are the structure variables which influence loan rates to small firms.*[23] Bankers in highly concentrated markets are aware that their decisions and rivals' response determine loan rates, and the large market share of a few banks facilitates collusion and the exercise of market power. Loan rates indeed are higher in the more concentrated local markets. Concentration in local markets does not influence the loan rate to large firms, which borrow in the national market. Consequently, concentration increases the difference between small and large borrower loan rates. On average for all local markets, concentration explains about 25 percent of the difference in the loan rate to small and large borrowers.

Average bank size is the second market structure determinant of loan rates in SMSAs. As bank size and loan portfolios increase, so do the profits from restricting competition. The prospect of large profits to each bank encourages tacit agreement to limit competition. Banks are more likely to use their market power and restrict competition when average bank size is large. The relationship between average bank size and

---

[23] Paul A. Meyer, "Price Discrimination, Regional Loan Rates, and the Structure of the Banking Industry," *Journal of Finance,* March 1967, pp. 37–48. The appendix shows the regression equation of loan rates on the concentration ratio and average bank size.

**FIGURE 8–6  Small borrower loan rates and average bank size in SMSAs**

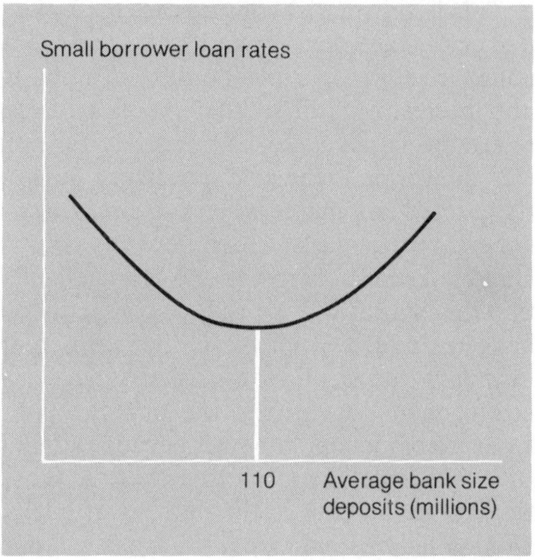

loan rates is parabolic, as illustrated in Figure 8–6. Increasing average bank size first lowers and then raises loan rates. Loan rates are minimized with respect to bank size when the latter equals approximately $110 million. *Economies of scale and gains from market power explain the parabolic relation between bank size and loan rates.* When the average bank is small, expansion places a large downward pressure on rates as economies of scale are substantial, and there is little incentive to curtail competition. Economies of scale become less pronounced as bank size increases. Past a certain size the net effect on interest rates of larger banks is positive because the small downward pressure on rates due to economies is more than offset by the upward pressure of a decrease in competition that enhances bank profits.

What are the implications of these results for charter, merger, and branching policy in metropolitan areas, assuming competitive credit allocation is the sole objective? Unqualified answers are impossible because of the parabolic relationship between loan rates and average bank size. For example, entry reduces, or at least does not increase, concentration so charters should be granted freely, *ceteris paribus*. However, entry also reduces average bank size, the effect of which depends on whether the market is on the downward or upward-sloping portion of the curve. If the average bank is larger than the size minimizing loan rates so that the upward-sloping portion of the curve is applicable, then entry should be encouraged. However, a too liberal charter policy could create an over-banked city with too many small banks. Mergers have the opposite effect on size; they increase it. Just as in the case of entry, the desirability of the size effect is ambiguous, depending on the size of existing banks. Mergers in areas with a preponderance of small banks are desirable, *ceteris paribus*. Mergers involving one of the three largest banks or mergers between relatively large banks which leapfrog into the top three are undesirable because concentration is increased.

In small areas such as towns, branching increases the number of banks, decreases average bank size, and reduces concentration as distant banks establish branches which would be unprofitable independent banks. In large areas such as an entire country, the converse is true. While branching produces more banks in a small area, the same branch banks are in the many small areas which compose the total. Nationwide branching is the major force explaining the previously stated difference between the banking structure in the United States on the one hand and Western Europe, Canada, and Japan on the other. From the viewpoint of the effect of branching on structure, are SMSAs small or large areas? Branching produces "large area" effects in SMSAs. Table 8–6 shows the concentration ratio in SMSAs entirely within a state, classified by branching laws. (SMSAs which straddle state lines are excluded from Table 8–6. Deposits were allocated among branches so SMSA concentration ratios in branching states are *not* inflated by deposits outside the SMSA.) The cumulative percent SMSAs column shows that the highest deposit concentration is found in SMSAs in statewide branching states and the lowest in unit banking SMSAs. For example, the concentration ratio is 70 percent or more in approximately 65 percent of the SMSAs in statewide branching states, 50 percent of the SMSAs in limited branching states, and 30 percent of the SMSAs in unit banking states. Other measures show much less difference between SMSAs in statewide and limited branching states. For example, the median concentration ratios differ by 5 percent, and the concentration ratio is greater than 80 percent for a somewhat larger percentage (34.3 versus 30.3) of limited branch SMSAs. Considering that deposits have been allocated among branches and limited branching typically allows banks to operate within the entire SMSA, only slight differences in concentration between SMSAs in statewide and limited branching states was expected. *Branching is associated with higher banking concentration in SMSAs and leads to high loan rates for small borrowers. The extent of branching, limited area or statewide, has little influence on concentration in SMSAs.*

Consistent with its "large area" effect on concentration, *branching is associated with larger banks in SMSAs,* counting only deposits within the SMSA.[24] The desirability of such an effect again is ambiguous, depending

---

[24] Average bank size and the three-bank concentration ratio are not necessarily related. For example, suppose an area has three $100-million deposit banks and five $20-million deposit banks. Average bank size is $50 million ($400 million/8), and the three-bank concentration ratio is 75 ($300/$400). If all five small banks merged, average bank size would increase to $100 million, but concentration remains constant.

TABLE 8–6  Percent of deposits held by three largest banks or bank groups in standard metropolitan areas located in only one state, June 30, 1975

| Percentage of deposits held by three largest banks | Statewide branching | | | Limited area branching | | | Unit banking | | |
|---|---|---|---|---|---|---|---|---|---|
| | Number of SMSAs | Percent of SMSAs | Cumulative percent SMSAs | Number | Percent | Cumulative percent | Number | Percent | Cumulative percent |
| 90–100.0 | 5 | 6.6 | 6.6 | 13 | 11.7 | 11.7 | 3 | 3.6 | 3.6 |
| 80–89.9 | 18 | 23.7 | 30.3 | 25 | 22.5 | 34.3 | 10 | 11.9 | 11.5 |
| 70–79.9 | 26 | 34.2 | 64.5 | 19 | 17.1 | 51.3 | 12 | 14.3 | 29.8 |
| 60–69.9 | 19 | 25.0 | 89.5 | 24 | 21.6 | 72.9 | 19 | 22.6 | 52.4 |
| 50–59.9 | 5 | 6.6 | 96.1 | 19 | 12.1 | 90.0 | 19 | 22.6 | 75.0 |
| 40–49.9 | 1 | 1.3 | 97.4 | 9 | 8.1 | 98.1 | 13 | 15.5 | 90.5 |
| 30–39.9 | 2 | 2.6 | 100.0 | 2 | 1.8 | 99.9 | 7 | 8.3 | 98.8 |
| 20–29.9 | 0 | 0 | 0 | 0 | 0 | 0 | 1 | 1.2 | 100.0 |
| Total | 76 | 100 | 100 | 111 | 100 | 100 | 84 | 100 | 100 |

SOURCE: Alan E. Grunewald, "Economic Necessity for Interstate Banking," in Federal Reserve Bank of Chicago, *Proceedings of a Conference on Bank Structure and Competition, 1979,* p. 241.

on the size of the average unit bank in the SMSA relative to the size minimizing loan rates. *Greater convenience is a definite plus for branching*. The factors which produce more *banks* in towns located in branching states produce more *banking offices* in SMSAs located in branching states, where either a branch or unit bank is one banking office. For example, in New York City and Chicago there are 9,000 and 34,000 people, respectively, per banking office.[25] New York permits branching while Illinois does not.

If SMSAs are the markets for small firms and the nation is the market for large firms, are states the market for medium-size firms? Since statewide branch banking certainly does increase statewide concentration ratios, should it be prohibited? The answer to both questions is no. There certainly are firms that can borrow outside the city in which they are located but not throughout the entire country. However, states with boundaries often determined by the whim of a monarch 200 years ago are the banking markets for few such firms. Because states are not banking markets, statewide concentration ratios are meaningless. Moreover, the theory of linked oligopoly—which alleges that performance is enhanced by different oligopolists in each market, as occurs in unit and limited branch banking states, instead of a common set of oligopolists in all markets, as occurs in statewide branching states—is untested. In *United States* v. *Marine Bancorporation* the Supreme Court rejected statewide banking markets and linked oligopoly theory.

> Apart from the fact that the Government's statewide approach is not supported by the precedents, it is simple to speculate on this record. There has been no persuasive showing that the effect of the merger on a statewide basis may be substantially to lessen competition within the meaning of Section 7 [of the Clayton Act]. The Government's underlying concern for a linkage or network of statewide oligopolistic banking markets is, on the record at least, considerably closer to "emphemeral possibilities" than to "probabilities." To assume, on the basis of essentially no evidence, that the challenged merger will tend to produce a statewide linkage of oligopolies is to espouse a per se rule against geographic market extension mergers like the one at issue here. No Section 7 case from this Court has gone that far, and we do not do so today.[26]

## SUMMARY

The previous two sections really are a unit. They provide the information necessary to evaluate the structure of the banking industry. One should consider the effect of charter, merger, and branching policy on *both* operating efficiency and the allocation of credit. Some policies are

---

[25] Alan E. Grunewald, "Economic Necessity for Interstate Banking," in Federal Reserve Bank of Chicago, *Proceedings of a Conference on Bank Structure and Competition, 1979*, p. 234.

[26] 418 U.S. 602 (1974) as quoted in ibid., pp. 236–37.

desirable on both counts. For example, branch banking in *rural* areas generally lowers operating costs and allocates credit more competitively because (1) branch banking increases bank size and *tends* to reduce cost somewhat, compared to smaller unit banks, and (2) branching increases the number of banks in small towns and rural areas. Some policies, however, produce a trade-off. Mergers by the larger banks in an SMSA save resources, but the higher concentration increases discrimination against small borrowers. In such cases detailed information on bank size and other factors is necessary to ascertain the precise shape of the trade-off and evaluate the desirability of the proposal. Knowledge of these sections alone is sufficient to state pros and cons without arriving at a definitive conclusion in some cases.

To be sure, banking authorities implicitly disagree with our measure of performance. Actual bank regulation is primarily designed to produce a sound default-free banking system, with low cost, operating efficiency, and low interest rate, competitive credit allocation being secondary objectives. Thus regulators' performance measure would give heavy weight to a bank failure probability. Now that deposit insurance has largely eliminated the external effects of failures, we and most economists believe the authorities should reverse their priorities.

The courts have implicitly criticized the regulatory authorities' objectives as well as ours. The courts now are simply interested in the competitive effects of mergers. If banks exercised market power over all the assets in their portfolio, then the policy of ignoring operating efficiency may be understandable. While consumer and small business loans are absolutely important, they are only a small fraction of banks' immense assets. Lower operating costs affect 100 percent of the bank portfolio while greater monopoly power affects, say, 25 percent of the portfolio. Precisely because consumer and small business loans are *absolutely* important but a *relatively* unimportant part of banks' portfolio, our two positions are perfectly consistent:

1. Regulation should attempt to reduce monopolies in local banking markets.
2. The banking industry is basically competitive. Banks earn near normal profits, and checkable deposits are approximately full-bodied money.

## QUESTIONS

1. List the four bank regulators and state the relative number and size of the banks for which each regulator is primarily responsible.
2. What are the main responsibilities which distinguish the banking regulators?
3. What are OBHCs and MBHCs? Why were they formed?
4. When may the regulation of any industry be justified?

5.  Precisely what regulations can be explained by lack of information and external effects of banking?

6.  Discuss the pros and cons of limited versus 100 percent deposit insurance.

7.  Explain the difference between the purchase and assumption (P&A) and payout methods of handling bank failures.

8.  Assuming external effects do not exist, what types of policies which reduce bank failures are justified? What are the disadvantages of policies which attempt to reduce bank failures by limiting risktaking by banks?

9.  What are the main purposes of bank examinations? What factors are considered when banks are evaluated?

10.  Why is there a capital adequacy controversy, and what factors influence the "adequate" amount of capital?

11.  Describe the current structure of the overall U.S. banking industry with respect to (1) the number and size distribution of banks and (2) the extent of branching and holding company formation. How has the structure changed over time? How does the structure at any one time depend on the size of the borrower?

12.  Do economies of scale exist? What charter, merger, and branching policies promote economies of scale and operating efficiency?

13.  What measures of local banking structure influence loan rates paid by consumers and small firms in ($a$) small towns, and ($b$) SMSAs? What charter, merger, and branching policies promote competitive credit allocation in local markets?

14.  What is the dual banking system?

---

## appendix · Regression equations and antitrust policy

Lyle Gramley collected cross-section and time-series data for unit banks. Regression or least squares analysis was used to test the economies of scale hypothesis. Gramley's estimated regression equation is[1]

$$\text{Average cost} = 1.37 - .39 \log \text{total assets} + .016x_2$$
$$+ .022x_3 - .013x_4 + .016x_5 \qquad (8A-1)$$
$$+ .008x_6, \qquad R^2 = 0.78,$$

where average cost = total cost divided by total assets (output)

$x_2$ = Ratio of time to total deposits,
$x_3$ = Ratio of total loans to total assets,
$x_4$ = Ratio of non-Treasury securities to total assets,
$x_5$ = Ratio of consumer to total loans,
$x_6$ = Percent growth of assets.

---

[1] Lyle Gramley, *A Study of Scale Economies in Banking,* Federal Reserve Bank of Kansas City, 1962, p. 18.

Assets were measured in millions and all ratios are expressed as percentages. While the equation is written to highlight the relationship being tested, in the estimation process the log of total assets and the variables standardizing for product mix, $x_2 - x_6$, are treated identically. The reader is encouraged to be aware of the specific standardizing variables and justify the sign of their regression coefficients.[2] *The equation indicates economies of scale do exist:* the coefficient of log total assets is negative. Keeping product mix constant, average cost on balance changes by $-0.39$ when the log of total assets increases by one unit. The author did not report the t statistics but stated that all were greater than 2. Thus there is at least a 95 percent chance that one may rely on the relationship. Asset size and the standardizing variables explain 78 percent of the variation in average cost, that is, $R^2 = .78$.

The relationship between average cost and *log* total assets is linear so that the relationship between average cost and total assets is the nonlinear curve graphed in Figure 8–6. This means economies are not uniform. Economies of scale are significant when banks are small but rapidly diminish as bank size increases. For example, when assets, measured in millions, increase from 1 to 10 so the *log* increases by one unit—from 0 to 1—then average costs decrease 0.39, which is the coefficient of log total assets in equation (8–A1). For average costs to decrease another 0.39, size would have to increase to 100 (million).

**Loan rates and local bank structure.** In 1955 the Federal Reserve conducted a relatively detailed nationwide survey of loans to small firms (assets under \$1 million) in large cities (technically, SMSAs). The data were averaged by SMSA. We want to test the relationship between loan rates and banking structure. Using a cross-section of SMSAs, the following regression equation was estimated.[3]

$$
\begin{aligned}
\text{Loan rate} = 7.032 + &\underset{(2.41)}{.007} \text{ Concentration} - \underset{(-1.91)}{.006} \text{ Bank size} \\
&+ \underset{(2.27)}{2.7(10^{-5})} \text{ Bank size squared} \\
&- \underset{(-13.28)}{.56X_4} + \underset{(3.55)}{.009X_5} + \underset{(2.20)}{.009X_6}, \quad R^2 = 0.73
\end{aligned}
\tag{8A-2}
$$

---

[2] Total cost includes interest payments, hence the time to total deposits variable. For purposes of testing the operating efficiency hypothesis, the best measure of cost would exclude interest payments, but such a measure was not constructed by Gramley. However, the relationship between average wages and salaries and log total assets is very similar to that shown. Wages and salaries are too narrow a measure of cost; it ignores capital costs. Since the too broad and the too narrow measures give similar results, the lack of a proper measure probably is unimportant.

[3] Paul A. Meyer, "Price Discrimination," Regional Loan Rates, and the Structure of the Banking Industry," *Journal of Finance,* March 1967, pp. 37–48.

where

$X_4$ = Log of average loan size (in \$1,000s),
$X_5$ = Percentage of loans with maturities greater than one year,
$X_6$ = Percentage change in nonagricultural wage and salary employment, 1950–55.

The regression equation again is written to highlight the relationship of particular interest. The numbers in parenthesis are t statistics. Variable $X_6$ is a proxy for loan demand and loan size and maturity are "standardizing" variables. Lack of data or constancy across SMSAs explains the omission of other determinants of cross-sectional interest rates listed in Chapter 5.

The regression coefficient of concentration is positive, as expected. The t statistic greater than 2 strongly suggests the relationship is systematic. The *absolute* value of the concentration coefficient is small (.007) because the survey data were collected years ago when interest rates were low. However, market power explained a significant portion of the *difference* in loan rates to small and large borrowers in 1955, and we may expect the same today. We indicated that large borrowers deal in a virtually competitive national market. Average concentration was 73 percent in the SMSAs whose small borrower rates were analyzed. Therefore, rate discrimination against small borrowers due to the different types of markets in which small and large firms deal was approximately 0.50 percentage points (.007 × 73). The difference between loan rates to small and large borrowers was 1.80 percent in 1955. Consequently, bank monopoly power explains more than one fourth (0.50/1.80) of the difference in rates to small and large firms.

Average bank size, measured by millions of deposits, is the second market structure determinant of loan rates in SMSAs. The coefficient of bank size is negative, while the coefficient for size squared is positive. This implies a parabola that opens upward, as drawn in Figure 8–6. Familiarity with calculus is essential to determine the average bank size which minimizes small borrower loan rates. Set the derivative of the loan rate with respect to bank size equal to zero and solve for bank size. That is, d(loan rate)/d(bank size) = $-.006 + 5.4 \, (10^{-5})$ bank size = 0, or bank size = $6/5.4(10^{-2}) \cong 110$. The t statistics are just significant at conventional levels, which suggests that the relationship is systematic.

**Bank merger policy.** The results of the last section are not altogether surprising; many industries have monopolistic elements. What is surprising is that for many years antitrust laws, the traditional remedy against monopolies, were applicable to nonbanks alone. Until 1961 the Department of Justice alleged that commercial banks were exempt from the major antitrust laws, the Sherman and Clayton Acts. This is not to say that every proposed merger was consummated. Some bank regulatory agency always has had to approve any merger, which necessarily reduces the number of banks and increases average bank size. While approval of the most blatantly anticompetitive mergers was not forthcoming, the legal immunity of banking from the Clayton Act tended to encourage regulatory laxity. If the Department of Justice did not take action against monopoly in banking, why should the regulatory agencies take a tough stance? Congress provided an answer. The Bank Merger Act of 1960 forced regulators to adopt a more restrictive merger policy. The truly rude shock occurred the following year when the Department of Justice reversed its earlier position and filed a civil antitrust action against the approved merger of the Philadelphia National Bank and Girard Corn Exchange Bank, two large banks in Philadelphia. In 1963 the Supreme Court upheld the Justice Department's position that banks were subject to the Sherman and Clayton Acts, which were more restrictive than the Merger Act of 1960. In 1966 Congress joined the Court in implicitly criticizing bank regulators by strengthening the Bank Merger Act of 1960. A detailed analysis of recent antitrust banking law and court cases is beyond the scope of this book. The important point is: there no longer is any doubt that the Justice Department working within the legal system and bank regulatory agencies by administrative determination may block any proposed merger which would result in a monopoly or substantially lessen competition in any section of the country.

# PART 3

## Central banking

# Central banking history and the Federal Reserve System

**9**

Money does not manage itself. About President Woodrow Wilson's signing into law with three gold pens the Federal Reserve Act at 6:02 P.M. on Tuesday, December 23, 1913, Wilson's biographer Arthur Link said, "Thus ended the long struggle for the greatest single piece of constructive legislation of the Wilson era and one of the most important domestic acts in the nation's history."[1] While Link may be guilty of some literary license, the banking situation often was chaotic in the 19th and early 20th century. This chapter should give us an appreciation of our central banking accomplishments since the birth of this country. But study of banking history fulfills more than our collective need to stroke our egos. Knowledge of the past gives order to the present. For example, the seemingly bizarre system of 12 Federal Reserve Banks, each of which may be charging a different discount rate, can be better understood if one is aware of the rural idealism versus urban reality and states' rights versus federal power conflicts, two conflicts ever present in American history but fortunately less virulent nowadays. Past social and political controversies shape present economic institutions. Dispensing with further justifications, we proceed directly to a history of banking and the structure of the Federal Reserve System.

## COLONIAL AMERICA AND THE FIRST BANKS

The financial sector sometimes leads and sometimes lags behind the real sector, but most often the two sectors mirror each other. The real

---

[1] Arthur Link, *Wilson: The New Freedom* (Princeton, N.J.: Princeton University Press, 1956), p. 238.

sector in colonial America is easily characterized: it was agrarian. Benjamin Franklin conjectured that for one artisan or merchant there were at least a hundred farmers. The enormous expanse of empty and fertile land and a poor transportation system made the colonial farmers much more self-reliant than their English cousins. Consistent with an economy largely composed of self-sufficient farms, the financial sector in colonial America was quite primitive. The English pound was the unit of account but not the medium of exchange. That is, prices were quoted and records were kept in terms of pounds, shillings, and pence, but this money did not circulate. Spanish, French, and Portugese coins and paper money issued by some of the colonies were the means of payment. The notes of most colonies were issued to finance specific projects. They remained in circulation for a short period of time and then were withdrawn. English currency did not circulate because there was a perennial trade deficit with England. As soon as a merchant acquired an English pound, it was used to finance imports from England. Moreover, European coins were quite scarce. To supplement the supply of specie, wealthy and respectable individuals or temporary partnerships operating in a side office issued notes which did circulate as money. However, *colonial America had no banks in the modern sense.* That is, there were *no incorporated firms with a permanent and specialized staff and separate office which issued notes, accepted deposits, and made loans.*

The American Revolution radically changed this monetary scene. With few exceptions, Rhode Island being the most notable, the notes (paper currency) of the prerevolutionary colonies did *not* depreciate relative to specie. A Pennsylvania 10-pound note could be exchanged for 10 pounds sterling, when available, or the equivalent in European coins. The notes issued by the Continental Congress during the Revolution did depreciate. Continental notes are an excellent example of Chapter 2's analysis of fiat money. "Regular" tax systems typically are inadequate whenever there is a dramatic increase in the government's need for resources, such as during wars. The alternatives the patriots faced were quite simple: issue fiat money to finance the Revolution or give up the struggle. The war effort did demand significant resources and the country was flooded with continental notes. The outcome was inevitable: prices in terms of continentals skyrocketed to the point that anything valueless was said not to be worth a continental. Inflation was the price the country had to pay to win the war.

The patriots well recognized the power of fiat money. David Ramsay, a member of the Continental Congress and author of *History of the United States,* first published in 1789, said,

> America, having never been much taxed in any direct way, and being without established government, and especially as she was contending against what was lately lawful authority, could not immediately proceed to taxation. Besides, as the contest was on the subject of taxation, the laying of taxes adequate to the exigencies of war, even though it had been practicable,

would have been impolitic. The only plausible expedient, in their power to adopt, was the emission of bills of credit.

\* \* \* \* \*

[These paper notes] circulated for several months, without any depreciation, and commanded the resources of the country for public service, equally with the same sum of gold or silver. The United States derived for a considerable time as much benefit from this paper creation of their own, though without any established funds for its support or redemption, as would have resulted from a free gift of as many Mexican dollars. While the ministry of England were puzzling themselves for new taxes, and funds, on which to raise their supplies, congress raised theirs by resolutions directing paper of no intrinsic value to be struck off, in form of promissory notes. But there was a point, both in time and quantity, beyond which this congressional alchymy ceased to operate. The time was about eighteen months from the date of their first emission, and that quantity about twenty million of dollars.[2]

Benjamin Franklin recognized that Congress acquired resources because it indeed was taxing its citizens by printing money and inflating. *Inflation is a tax. An inflation which reduces the purchasing power of money by, say, 50 percent is identical to a 50 percent tax on money balances.* This point is sufficiently important to risk prolixity. Suppose the price of widgets goes from 50 cents to $1 so that the purchasing power of money falls 50 percent. A dollar formerly purchased two widgets but now purchases one. Instead of that scenario, suppose a dollar is taxed 50 percent but prices remain constant, so after taxes the moneyholder can purchase one widget. The moneyholder is indifferent between inflation and taxation. Both policies reduce one's command over goods and services equally. Franklin said,[3]

> The general effect of the depreciation [inflation] has operated as a *gradual tax*. . . . Every man has paid his share of the tax according to the time he retained any of the money in his hands, and to the depreciation within that time. Thus it has proved a tax on money.

Were we fighting for or against taxation without representation?

Although the English continued to occupy selected areas and a peace treaty was two years away, fighting in the Revolutionary War ceased with the Battle of Yorktown on October 18, 1781. The government's need for resources was much reduced but not totally eliminated. Considering that continentals had become worthless and the tax system remained inadequate, another revenue source was necessary. On December 31, 1781, the Continental Congress meeting in Philadelphia chartered the Bank of North

---

[2] David Ramsay, *History of the United States* (Philadelphia: M. Carey, 1817), vol. 3, appendix 4, pp. xvii, xviii.

[3] Benjamin Franklin, *The Writings of Benjamin Franklin,* ed. Albert H. Smyth (New York: Macmillan, 1907), vol. 9, p. 234. Franklin goes on to say that he favors the inflation tax. Italics in original.

America, the first modern bank in America. The powers of Congress being uncertain, for safety's sake the Pennsylvania legislature also chartered the bank a month later. Private citizens and the Congress subscribed to the bank's capital. Consistent with the ownership distribution, the bank was supposed to lend to the private and government sectors, generally by creating its own notes (paper currency). *There is no essential difference between note and deposit expansion.* In one case the borrower's account is credited, and in the other case the borrower is given fresh notes (paper currency). In neither case did the bank have these items beforehand. Banks usually created notes because borrowers and the public in general preferred them to deposits. Recall that the currency/deposit ratio is negatively related to income. When incomes are low and transportation and communication systems are poor, currency is preferable to deposits. The reserves of the Bank of North America were specie. Just as its modern counterparts, the bank operated with fractional reserves because not everyone demanded specie for notes and deposits. At the same time, some people always want specie for their notes. This meant that the bank could not expand without limit, and it held some specie although it was not required to do so. The bank was cautious. It did not expand its loans and notes beyond the amount its reserves could support. The bank's notes circulated at par with specie. The conservatism which allowed its notes to circulate at par meant that the bank largely failed in its objectives of being an important source of loanable funds for the government, which sold its bank stock shortly after the bank began operations. The Bank of North America's success inspired the formation of other banks in major cities. The respective state legislatures chartered the Bank of New York in 1784, the Bank of Massachusetts (Boston) also in 1784, and the Bank of Maryland (Baltimore) in 1790. Thus in 1790 the United States had four banks— not many but the same number as in England.[4]

## THE FIRST BANK OF THE UNITED STATES, 1791–1811

The Revolutionary War ended in 1783, but the Republic as we know it was not created until 1789. The six-year interregnum was marked by a struggle between states' rightists (Jeffersonian Republicans) and Federalists over the appropriate form of government. The political struggle reflected a more fundamental and enduring social conflict which we shall call rural idealism versus urban reality. The expression of these two social forces has varied over time. Rural idealism initially elevated the farmer to mystical superiority. Benjamin Franklin, a successful businessman, espoused the rural position as if he were a farmer. He said, "There seem to be but three ways for a nation to acquire wealth. The first is *war. . . .* This is *robbery.* The second by *commerce* which is generally

---

[4] Banks here mean incorporated firms. Numerous partnerships extended credit in England.

*cheating*. The third by *agriculture,* the only *honest way,* wherein man receives a real increase . . . as a reward for his innocent life and his virtuous industry."[5] With the shift away from agriculture, rural idealism embraced any occupation, provided it entailed hard work and self-reliance, and any small business.

> His brow is wet with honest sweat,
> He earns whate'er he can,
> And looks the whole world in the face
> For he owes not any man.
> "The Village Blacksmith," by Henry Wadsworth Longfellow

Rural idealism extolls the free, simple, and unregulated life, the little person, and the competitor who slays the monopolist. Urban reality stresses industrialization and large-scale production as a means of material progress. While urban reality does not advocate monopolies and oppression, it tolerates such conditions if they aid growth. Urban reality never captured the imagination of the masses; large corporations, advanced technology, and profit maximization are not inspirational. The pastoral poetry of rural idealism contrasts sharply with the matter-of-fact aphorisms of urban reality: the business of America is business.[6] Although not logically related, urban reality in its early years strongly supported federal power. Presumably, a strong central government and national economic market are more profitable than the small protected markets under states' rights. Conflicts between conservationists and international oil companies and between service-oriented local stores and chain discounters are modern examples of the rural idealism versus urban reality conflict. In the monetary area, the conflict years ago between hard specie and soft currency has shifted to one between visible checks and invisible automatic transfers.

The interests of the small urban class coincided with those of patriots like George Washington, Alexander Hamilton, and James Madison, who argued that the confederated government was too weak. After much debate, which we do not even begin to summarize, the Constitution finally was adopted, and urban realists and Federalists came to power. The monetary clauses of the Constitution give Congress the power "to coin Money, regulate the Value thereof." A mint which produced gold and silver coins was established in 1791. The unit of account was a dollar patterned after the Spanish dollar, that is, the silver content of the U.S. and Spanish dollars both equalled 371.25 grains. Gold was to be coined at a ratio of 1 gold to 15 silver, the prevailing market ratio at the time. The relative price of gold increased shortly thereafter, and the United States

---

[5] Benjamin Franklin, *The Papers of Benjamin Franklin,* ed. William B. Wilcox (New Haven: Yale University Press, 1972), vol. 16, p. 109. Italics in original.

[6] Calvin Coolidge, in a speech before the Society of American Newspaper Editors, January 17, 1915.

was on a de facto silver standard until 1834, illustrating Gresham's Law: bad (overvalued silver) coins drove good (undervalued gold) coins out of circulation. Most believed the Constitution barred the federal government from issuing paper money. Hamilton and a few others disagreed, but the sorry record of the continentals was too fresh in people's minds to permit the issue of *government* paper money.

The rural idealism versus urban reality conflict resurfaced in the debate about the [First] Bank of the United States, the major political controversy following ratification of the Constitution.[7] The main protagonists were Secretary of the Treasury Alexander Hamilton and Secretary of State Thomas Jefferson. Hamilton urged Congress to charter a national bank. Jefferson argued against the bank. Hamilton won the debate.

In 1791 Congress chartered the First Bank of the United States for 20 years. The bank garnered a congressional majority for various reasons. *First, and most important, it became a symbol of federal power.* Confederation had just been defeated, but the principle of a strong central government was still not firmly established. Hamilton needed a major issue. He finally selected banking, which was totally abhorrent to the agrarians. Hamilton argued that Congress could charter a national bank under the constitutional clause giving it all the powers "necessary and proper" to perform its responsibilities. Congress lacked only those powers *specifically denied* in the Constitution. Jefferson responded that the federal government had only those powers *specifically granted* it by the Constitution, with the states retaining all power not specifically relinquished. Since the Constitution was silent about congressional incorporation of banks or other types of firms, Jefferson said the First Bank was unconstitutional. While the states' rightists may have opposed the establishment of other national institutions, the opposition to an incorporated national bank verged on the irrational. Any corporation was an "unnatural" organization, and an incorporated bank was additionally immoral. President John Adams said that "banks have done more injury to the religion, morality, tranquility, prosperity, and even wealth of the nation than they can have done or ever will do good."[8] The bank violated the agrarian principles of a natural and moral life.

Second, political and philosophical principles aside, Hamilton argued for the bank on the grounds of convenience. The new federal government levied taxes and spent. It needed a fiscal agent, that is, an organization which would collect the taxes, hold the government's funds, transfer funds among regions and offices, and make authorized payments. While the existing state banks could have performed these services, a single nationwide bank could do them more efficiently.

Third, any bank tended to foster commerce and industry. The real bills

---

[7] The bank became the First only after it ceased to exist and the Second was chartered.

[8] John Adams, *The Works of John Adams,* ed. Charles Francis Adams (Boston: Little, Brown, 1856), vol. 10, p. 375.

doctrine never precluded agricultural loans, but particularly in the early days, commercial loans were banks' first priority.

Fourth, debtors and others favoring higher prices supported the bank on the grounds that any fractional reserve bank expands the money supply and is inflationary. Each dollar that a bank acquires supports multiple notes and deposits.

Finally, Secretary Hamilton was anxious to have some unit more or less committed to extending credit to the Treasury whenever necessary. He hoped the First Bank of the United States would fulfill for the federal government the same role the Bank of North America was supposed to play for the confederation.

The capital stock of the First Bank was $10 million, five times more than the next largest banks, the Bank of North America and Manhattan Company, the forerunner of the Chase Manhattan Bank. The bank was an early example of joint private and public enterprise. The federal government subscribed for stock worth $2 million, and the remainder was over-subscribed by private individuals. Government and private directors were allocated on the same one-fifth/four-fifth basis. The stock was a good buy. Within three months of its issue the bank's stock rose from $25 to $300 per share! Fully one third of Congress owned bank stock, creating the suspicion that Congress chartered the bank to enrich itself. The bank was headquartered in Philadelphia and eventually had eight branches from Boston to New Orleans. It was extremely large relative to other banks and commercial firms.

In most respects the First Bank acted like a private bank. It made loans, accepted deposits, and issued notes. It considered itself the exemplar of a well-managed conservative bank, and justly so. It had a high capital ratio, made sound loans, and always maintained adequate reserves (specie). Its notes circulated at par throughout the country. Besides its private functions, the First Bank performed two functions normally associated with a central bank. First, as already mentioned, it was the fiscal agent for the Treasury. Second, it adopted policies to create a sound, default-free banking system. The tools on hand in order to accomplish its second objective were quite primitive. It could not set required reserve ratios, examine banks, or specify a capital ratio.[9] Much like any large firm or wealthy person, the First Bank maintained large credit balances with the state banks. *The First Bank created a sound banking system mainly by frequent unannounced large calls on its credit balances.* Aware that the First Bank might be testing their liquidity and solvency by withdrawing its deposits, the state banks maintained large (excess) reserves, held a more liquid loan portfolio, and reduced their note and deposit expansion. As

---

[9] The banks did report their condition to the states; Massachusetts set reserve requirements in 1792, and other states followed; and bank charters typically specified a capital ratio. However, these requirements imposed by the *states,* and not the First Bank, were often ignored.

Chapter 4 indicated, the demand for excess reserves is negatively related to the expected change in deposits (and in those days, bank notes) and positively related to deposit (and note) variability. The First Bank with its branches throughout the country was sufficiently large that its customers were continually bringing in notes and depositing checks drawn on every state bank. With the liabilities of state banks always on hand, it could continually test them by demanding payment in specie. If a bank repeatedly passed the test, the First Bank would maintain the bank's notes in circulation instead of redeeming them. Thus, the state bank had a strong incentive to be especially prudent.

The 20-year charter of the First Bank of the United States expired in 1811 and was not renewed. The debate on recharter largely echoed the debate 20 years earlier, with the same constitutional issues paramount. Two new issues did surface. First, a significant portion of the bank's stock had been purchased by foreigners. Some feared that foreigners would gain control of the First Bank, the largest corporation of its day, and thereby dominate the economy. Second, state bankers who resented the First Bank's control formed a coalition with debtors and others favoring higher prices, who came to realize that the First Bank over its short life time had shifted from being an inflationary to a deflationary force because the banking system had grown rapidly. Only four state banks existed when the First Bank was chartered in 1791. By 1811 there were 90 banks. When few banks exist, the creation of a new bank, often in bankless areas, reduces the demand for specie as individuals find bank notes and deposits more convenient. Given a fractional reserve banking system, the new bank expands the money supply. When there are many banks, however, an entrant has little effect on the money supply, *ceteris paribus,* because it acquires deposits at the expense of existing banks instead of specie. In other words, the effect of a new bank on the currency/deposit ratio depends on the number of existing banks. When few banks exist, a new bank significantly increases convenience, reduces the currency ratio, and increases money and prices. By 1811 the slight positive effect of the First Bank on the money supply due to the convenience factor was outweighed by its control tactics which forced state banks to hold larger reserves. *Unreconstructed states' rightists, rural idealists, xenophobes, expansionary-minded bankers, and debtors defeated recharter by one vote in each house of Congress.*[10] The First Bank was dissolved in 1811.

## THE SECOND BANK OF THE UNITED STATES, 1816–1836

The demise of the First Bank made banking more profitable as banks could operate with less specie and more earning assets. As expected, the

---

[10] James Madison, president in 1811, and other Jeffersonian Republicans, but not Mr. Jefferson himself, put principle aside and favored recharter in 1811 on the grounds of economic convenience. Conservative banks like the Bank of New York also supported recharter.

number of state banks increased dramatically, from 90 in 1811 to approximately 250 five years later. From the viewpoint of the Treasury, dissolution of the First Bank could hardly have come at a more inopportune time. A year later the United States was embroiled in the War of 1812. As in other wars, government expenditures increased, and greater regional transfers of funds were necessary. The loss of a fiscal agent with branches throughout the country hampered smooth money management. The government maintained accounts in many state banks. Transfer of the funds among banks and regions was difficult. The War of 1812 was financed mainly through the sale of bonds. Here again the First Bank, partially owned by the government, would have been preferable to private banks. To be sure, the state banks did issue some notes to buy government bonds.

The quest for victory overrides constitutional principles during wartime. The government discovered that it did have the authority to issue paper money. Between 1812 and 1815 the Treasury issued $36 million, which had limited circulation because its denomination was quite large. The Treasury notes were promptly redeemed after the war. The monetary expansion by the Treasury and banks reduced the currency ratio to dangerously low levels in the best of times, and times were not the best. The English attack on Washington and Baltimore induced runs on banks for specie. Except in New England, a general suspension occurred, that is, banks stopped converting their notes and deposits into specie. Bank notes sold at varying discounts.

The peace treaty with England in December 1814 did not restore convertibility or a smoothly functioning banking system. By early 1816 President Madison, Speaker of the House Henry Clay, and Congressman John C. Calhoun led the fight for a second Bank of the United States. The arguments pro and con remained essentially unchanged since 1791, but the emphasis shifted. The fiscal agent, reliable credit source, and bank regulatory functions were highlighted instead of constitutional principles. The bill chartering the Second Bank of the United States passed in 1816. The Second Bank was quite similar to its predecessor—it was headquartered in Philadelphia, had a 20-year charter, and one fifth of its capital was subscribed by the government. It was much larger, however. The Second Bank's capital was $35 million, and it eventually had 25 branches.

The Second Bank embarked on stormy seas. Baltimore tried but failed in its bid to be headquarters of the Second Bank. Determined to surpass Philadelphia, James Buchanan, president of the Baltimore branch, lent large amounts to local firms in an early effort at "regional development." Buchanan's honest mistakes were compounded by James McCulloch, cashier of the same Baltimore branch, who embezzled a significant sum. McCulloch and Buchanan were replaced in 1819, and the Second Bank began competently performing the functions of a private and central bank. It lent and issued notes prudently. It was the government's fiscal agent, and it tested the state banks' solvency and liquidity by frequently presenting notes for redemption.

By 1828 artisans and merchants were welcomed within the agrarian fold provided they opposed big government, monopolies, and the urban elite. Members of the expanded rural movement grew tired of being governed politically by squires from Virginia, Pennsylvania, and Massachusetts, and of being economically subservient to the urban elite. They elected Andrew Jackson, who interpreted his election as a mandate to humble the economic power structure and eradicate monopolies. Labeled as a menace to American democracy, the large and powerful Second Bank became Jackson's prime target. Personality clashes exacerbated economic and political differences. The president of the Second Bank was Nicholas Biddle, the patrician scion of a Philadelphia family. General Jackson, a self-made man of humble origin, was a soldier, planter, slaveowner, lawyer and, ultimately, president of the United States. He belonged to the aristocracy of the frontier. The birth and breeding of the Philadelphia gentry clashed with the cock-fighting, horse-racing, whisky-drinking frontier aristocracy. Clearly aware of Jackson's opposition, the Second Bank's supporters thought its only salvation lay at the polls. Since its charter expired in April 1836, the November 1836 election was too late. The bank began its defense early. Henry Clay, President Jackson's opponent in the 1832 election, pushed through Congress a bill extending the Second Bank's life. Jackson promptly vetoed the bill. Inconsistency, disingenuousness, and outright sham riddled the veto message. The battle lines were drawn. The Second Bank became the major issue in the 1832 presidential campaign. Jackson put together a coalition which, incongruities and strange bedfellows notwithstanding, proved most effective. He won resoundingly. We met many elements of the Jacksonian coalition at the execution of the First bank. The coalition deserves enumeration again because the influence of many elements extended beyond banking to 19th century political and economic history in general. The Second Bank was killed by:

1. States' rightists, who said the federally chartered bank violated the Constitution.[11]
2. State bankers, who were restrained by the central banking functions of the federal bank. They were joined by speculators and other advocates of inflation.
3. Moderate rural idealists, who claimed that all banks aided urban enterprise at the expense of farmers and artisans.
4. Extreme rural idealists, for whom all corporations were unnatural and all banks were immoral. The Second Bank was a monopoly monster

---

[11] The Baltimore branch of the Second Bank refused to pay a tax levied by the state of Maryland and was sued in the name of James McCulloch, the dishonest cashier. The Supreme Court clearly affirmed in the famous *McCulloch* v. *Maryland* case of 1819 that Congress had the power to incorporate a bank and that states could not interfere with its operation. Thus the constitutional issue was raised over a decade later merely to stir passions.

which oppressed the little person. The Equal Rights Party, or Loco Focos as they came to be called, held this position.
5. Xenophobes, who saw foreign control everywhere. The American Party, or Know Nothings, exemplify this viewpoint.

The previously mentioned personality clash between Jackson and Biddle rates first place in the special factors category. Second, nations have political and financial capitals. Philadelphia was both when the republic was born. Washington soon replaced Philadelphia as the political capital. Baltimore had sought financial leadership. By 1832 upstart Wall Street challenged staid Chestnut Street. While Baltimore suffered from a flight of fancy, New York delivered the coup de grace to Philadelphia.

The election sealed the bank's fate, and Jackson did not wait for its official death in 1836 before dismembering it. In 1833 President Jackson withdrew the U.S. government deposits from the Second Bank and distributed them among several private banks. Roger Taney, a Maryland gentleman who subsequently was appointed chief justice of the Supreme Court, was the secretary of the Treasury at the time. Mr. Taney was a stockholder of Baltimore's Union Bank, which just happened to receive government deposits. The other banks were equally well-connected politically and came to be called "pet banks."

## FREE BANKING, 1837–1863

The death of the Second Bank, effectively in 1833, ushered in a period of profitable bank expansion. Between 1834 and 1837, 194 new banks were organized, increasing the banking system by approximately one third. The normal increase in the demand for specie associated with the banking expansion—recall our friend of Chapter 4, the currency ratio—was fictitiously augmented by the July 1836 specie circular forbidding anything but specie in payment of public lands. The inevitable occurred. Banks could not meet the demand for specie and in concert suspended convertibility. Inconvertibility remained widespread for three years.

The odoriferous pet banks scheme and the general suspension of convertibility convinced many that state banks were inappropriate fiscal agents. The government needed unbiased and safe depositories. Lacking a federal bank, the Independent Treasury system was adopted in 1840, only to be repealed the following year. But in 1846 the system was adopted again and, with some modification in 1867, remained in effect until the creation of the Federal Reserve System in 1913. *In order to divorce government finances from the banking system, the Independent Treasury system stipulated that (1) all payments to the government were to be made in specie or government notes, and (2) all, later revised to most, government funds would be held in "safety deposit boxes" constructed throughout the country.* The goldsmiths of old would have been proud!

What was the effect of the Independent Treasury? It hampered monetary stability. Specie and government notes were the reserves of the banking system. An excess of government receipts over expenditures filled the strongboxes but drained reserves from the banking system. This produced a multiple money contraction in a fractional reserve system. Government deficits had the opposite effect. Lack of synchronization of government receipts and expenditures, particularly during relatively short time periods such as quarters, made the money supply quite volatile. If banks had continued to function as fiscal agents, tax payment simply would have reduced private deposits and increased Treasury deposits at the banks. As time passed and the effect of deficits and surpluses on the money supply became clearer, several secretaries of the Treasury diligently attempted to synchronize receipts and expenditures. A few even became nascent central bankers practicing open-market operations. That is, any surplus was expended on the few government bonds outstanding. Moreover, the spirit of the law sometimes was ignored with impunity. The Independent Treasury system eventually did let the Treasury maintain small deposit balances for special reasons. A few secretaries interpreted "small" and "special" quite liberally.

The rural idealism, antielitism, and antimonopoly spirit which contributed to the demise of the Second Bank next challenged the state banks, and with good reason. Every state bank had been chartered by a special act of the legislature. Most incorporation acts stipulated that stockholders pay the state a significant "license" fee, the bank lend the state certain amounts on demand, meritorious organizations (often colleges) be allowed to purchase bank stock at favorable prices, and so on. The incorporation act did not stipulate, but it was clear to all, that bribes, or at least good political connections, were often essential. While not universally true, banks were means to reward political friends and punish political enemies. The charter of most banks purposely was quite short. Political meddling on the wrong side was grounds for denial of charter extensions. To correct these abuses, Michigan in 1837 and New York in 1838 passed so-called *free banking laws, which automatically granted bank charters upon satisfaction of specified requirements.* A key word is *automatically.* A special act of the legislature was no longer required to establish a bank. Anyone who qualified could become a banker. Virtually all the states soon followed the example of Michigan and New York.

If Michigan and New York were the leaders of the democratic spirit in banking, they were at opposite ends of the spectrum in terms of the quality of their banks. The banking laws of the two states were quite similar. In terms of regulations and the CAMEL of modern bank examination, free banking laws typically did specify *c*apital ratios, *a*sset quality, and *l*iquidity ratios.[12] However, enforcement in Michigan and many other

---

[12] See the previous chapter's section on bank examinations.

states was almost nonexistent. Taking the free banking and equal rights spirit to its *reductio ad absurdum,* Michigan did not check the honesty and capability of management and the bank's earnings potential—the M and E of CAMEL. New York banks generally were pillars of integrity, while *bank* in Michigan was a four letter word. Any crook could become a Michigan banker. We shall return to the diversity of bank operations shortly.

Banks developed several cooperative practices which made the banking system more efficient and profitable and simultaneously lowered bank failures. Many of these practices began during the era of the Second Bank but flourished after it ceased to exist. The Suffolk Bank of Boston pioneered a regional deposit and note redemption and collection system. Country banks around Boston opened accounts at the Suffolk Bank. Instead of sending checks and notes directly to each other, it was much cheaper and faster for each bank to send them to a central location. The Suffolk Bank debited and credited the appropriate bank's account. The country banks did hold some specie for over-the-counter redemptions. However, the deposits at the Suffolk Bank and similar banks in other areas became the principal reserves of the country banks. Thus began the *pyramiding of reserves, where deposits at a city bank are the reserves of a country bank.* The Suffolk Bank treated bank and other deposits similarly. It maintained the same specie (reserve) ratio against all deposits. Consequently, pyramiding reduced the ratio of banking system cash holdings to deposits and notes outstanding and increased the vulnerability of the banking system to shifts in the public's currency ratio. In time, the Suffolk Bank extended the variety of services it offered the country banks. We still have a *correspondent banking system whereby small banks maintain deposits at large banks in exchange for collection and other services.* Since most checks and notes that a bank receives are drawn on nearby banks, it would be silly for, say, a Georgia bank to have a Massachusetts collection agent. Lacking a nationwide bank, banks in each region produced their versions of the Suffolk system. Nationwide check collection remained difficult.

Bank insurance schemes are the second major example of industry cooperation. In response to bank depositors' and note holders' pleas for a liquid and solvent banking system, the New York legislature passed the Safety-Fund Act of 1829. Basically the act established the first precursor to the FDIC. The banks contributed to a fund administered by the New York bank commissioner, who made payments to failed banks' noteholders and depositors. Bank diversity made the safety fund controversial within the banking fraternity. The insurance premiums reduced profitability. However, insurance enhanced bank solvency and liquidity from the viewpoint of depositors and reduced deposit instability. Banks were able to hold more relatively illiquid, high-return assets. The New York City banks already enjoyed the public's confidence. In their minds, the premiums exceeded the value of the insurance, in terms of their ability to operate with less zero-earning cash due to greater public confidence. The smaller upstate banks, which deservedly were somewhat less well-regarded, did favor insurance from its inception. With the passage of several crises, even the city banks came to favor the safety fund, which was dissolved with the establishment of the national banking system in 1863. The New York safety fund remained solvent, although barely so at times, because other New York bank regulations emphasized safety, and in the chaotic national market the New York banks chose to project a conservative image. Most other state bank insurance schemes failed within a few years.

To appreciate the diversity and problems under the free banking system, let us examine the process of putting a bank into operation in Michigan and New York. A Michigan bank promoter would proceed to a distant and inaccessible county and request a certificate of incorporation from the secretary of state. The free banking laws specified that at least 30 percent of the capital stock had to be paid in specie, while the remaining 70 percent could be subscribed by a personal bond (IOU). In other words, loans to stockholders could finance up to 70 percent of a bank's capital or net worth. Line 1 of the balance sheet illustrates the establishment of New Bank. Bank commissioners then verified the New Bank had specie, took possession of the bonds of stockholders, and countersigned $700 in notes beautifully engraved by the New Bank. Each bank issued personalized notes (paper currency). The signature of the bank commissioner verified the possession of collateral equal to the notes outstanding. Line 2 illustrates that notes are placed in circulation by the acquisition of bonds, mortgages, or something else.

**New Bank of Michigan**

| | | | | |
|---|---|---|---|---|
| (1) | Specie (cash reserves) | 300 | Net worth | 1,000 |
| | Bonds of (loans to) stockholders | 700 | | |
| (2) | Assets acquired with notes | 700 | Notes in circulation | 700 |

(1) Establishment of the bank, and (2) notes are placed in circulation.

Were the New Bank's notes safe? Could they be converted dollar-for-dollar into specie or other assets? At first glance the answer seems yes. The capital (net worth) ratio was extremely high. Assets were $1,700 while notes equalled only $700. The bank commissioner held $700 in bonds of stockholders which could be sold to pay off note holders. The similar regulations in Michigan and New York were strict enough if administered and enforced. True, the law requiring only a 30 percent cash payment was somewhat lax, but "payment" of a bank's capital stock by a loan from the bank itself is not necessarily any more reprehensible than bank credit for purchases of other companies stock. The difference between Michigan and New York was that New York bank operators were persons of means who were required to offer sufficient collateral *other than the bank stock,* while Michigan bank operators were deadbeats without collateral except the stock being financed. The IOUs backing Michigan bank notes were worthless. The Michigan authorities should have known something was amiss: why would any *honest* person establish a bank in an inaccessible place? There is only one conclusion: the banker was dishonest. When the ordeal of examination had been safely passed, specie was promptly withdrawn. "The specie found by them [examiners] in one bank was sent by hurried journey ahead of them to be counted at the next. Gold and silver flew about the country with the celerity of magic."[13] Conservative New York banks purchased canal or railroad bonds with their notes. The *wildcat banks,* so called because of their location in areas more heavily populated by wildcats than humans, placed the notes in circulation by satisfying their whims for high living. Very simply, wildcat bankers were given a license to steal. "Perjury and direct robbery of associates seem to have been frequent in the history of these associations, and no legal penalties appear to have been inflicted."[14] Holders of wildcat notes found the bank's cupboard bare or at least less than full.

Similar swindles would be discovered sooner today because bank liabilities are deposits, which do not circulate. That is, checks are cashed or deposited but rarely endorsed payable to someone else. Currency circulates, passing through various hands before finally reaching a bank. Given the poor communications system of the 19th century and the location of wildcat banks, worthless and partially valuable notes stayed in circulation for a long time.[15] Speculators purchased wildcat notes from the knowledgeable at deep discounts and, like holders of the Old Maid card, passed them off on the unsuspecting. Personalized notes compounded the chaotic currency situation. Counterfeit notes of safe banks easily duped a citizenry unfamiliar with the notes of all 1,600 banks existing in 1860. In any economic environment, however gloomy, enterprising people see a need and make a buck. Thompson saw a need. His *Bank Notes Reporter and Counterfeit Detector* became required reading. Still, the marvel is how long some wildcat notes circulated, particularly at the beginning of the free banking era. Thompson's *Reporter* and public outcries for a safe currency eliminated the worst abuses by 1860, but outcries for further reform justifiably continued.

Table 9–1 shows the variability of state bank notes and deposits between the effective demise of the Second Bank in late 1833 and 1860. A

---

[13] John J. Knox, *A History of Banking in the United States* (New York: Bradford Rhodes & Company, 1903), pp. 733–34.

[14] Ibid., p. 734.

[15] Most crook/bankers found that they could embezzle a larger amount by making some legitimate loans, which gave their notes some value. Use of all notes for strictly nonbanking purposes attracts attention and reduces the time period of circulation.

TABLE 9-1    Percent change of state bank notes and deposits, 1834–1861

| Period | Bank notes | Deposits | Total notes and deposits |
|--------|-----------|----------|--------------------------|
| 1834–37 ............... | +56 | +68 | +61 |
| 1837–43 ............... | −60 | −56 | −58 |
| 1843–48 ............... | +120 | +84 | +102 |
| 1848–49 ............... | −11 | −12 | −11 |
| 1849–54 ............... | +110 | +107 | +109 |
| 1854–55 ............... | −29 | +2 | −12 |
| 1855–57 ............... | +13 | +21 | +18 |
| 1857–58 ............... | −28 | −20 | −23 |
| 1858–61 ............... | +30 | +38 | +35 |

**SOURCE:** John J. Knox, *A History of Banking in the United States* (New York: Bradford Rhodes & Company, 1903), p. 312.

rapid expansion following termination of the Second Bank's restraining influence started the period on its roller-coaster path.

## THE NATIONAL BANKING SYSTEM, 1863–1913

Many of the controversies which engulfed the First and Second Bank of the United States came to a head in 1861. The Civil War erupted. It was financed through taxes and bond sales at first. The Continental Congress's experiment with paper money was such a disaster that it deterred the federal government until there was no alternative. In 1862 the federal government issued *greenbacks,* the popular name given to the *first government-issued paper money of any real consequence* (*large amount*). Greenbacks were more successful than continentals; they always had some value. Nevertheless, the detrimental side effects of large greenback issues were predictable. Within a few months prices rose, and the United States went off the gold standard. No government can maintain a fixed-price for gold, as required by the gold standard, during inflation. When the prices for commodities in general rise, gold at a fixed-dollar price appears cheap, and the public attempts to convert its dollars into gold. The government eventually runs out of gold. Just as overexpansion by banks ultimately made their deposits inconvertible into currency, so over-issued paper money became inconvertible into gold at a fixed-exchange rate. Between 1862 and 1879 the United States was on an inconvertible paper standard, much as it is today. Gold was like any other commodity. Its dollar price rose and fell instead of remaining constant, as the gold standard requires.

Important as greenbacks were, the so-called National Banking Act of 1863, amended in 1864 and 1865—Congress was determined to get it right—influenced currency and banking more strongly.[16] This act was designed to (1) reduce bank abuses and create a safe banking system, (2) correct the chaotic state bank note situation, and (3) aid the federal government's financing of the Civil War. In order to fulfill these objectives, the act provided for the creation of a national banking system while simultaneously attempting to extirpate the state banking system.

The National Banking Act accepted the principle of free banking. It established the Office of the Comptroller of the Currency, which would charter any bank meeting certain minimum standards. The act created a sounder banking system by setting minimum standards higher than those of most states and by enforcing the standards vigorously. The act also encouraged the free flow of information. The more prominent regulations were:

1. Organizers of all national banks had to pay cash for the bank's stock. This prevented assetless deadbeats from gaining control of banks by having the bank itself finance its capital stock. Moreover, the capital requirement was high.
2. Reserve requirements against deposits were high, and bank notes were fully backed by government bonds at all times, which made them convertible into specie. We shall return to these requirements later.
3. Assets were restricted in order to improve quality and encourage diversification. In particular, real estate loans, which often were quite speculative, and loans exceeding 10 percent of the bank's net worth were prohibited.
4. National banks were required to file reports of condition with the comptroller and publish the reports in newspapers accessible to their stockholders and depositors.
5. Banks were examined to verify compliance with the law. Penalties for regulatory violations ranged from harassment to closure, and the legal authorities were promptly advised of defalcations and other crimes.

Establishment of higher standards accomplishes nothing per se unless a mechanism is devised whereby banks join the system and become subject to the standards. What inducement did the National Banking Act provide for the state banks to become national banks? A national bank could issue notes, appropriately called national bank notes, equal to 90 percent of the par or market value of special government bonds, whichever was lower. The bank's bonds were deposited with the comptroller, who would sell the bonds and pay noteholders if the bank could not redeem its notes. Possession by the comptroller of pledged bonds always exceeding by at

---

[16] The act is officially the National Currency Act but is now called the National Banking Act because it had a more lasting effect on banking than currency.

least 10 percent the amount of bank notes outstanding guaranteed the notes' convertibility. Aside from affixing the name of the issuing bank, the notes were uniform and well designed, which made detection of counterfeits easier. Since banks earned the interest on the bonds, which the comptroller held merely for safekeeping, the government thought banks would find the note-issue privilege extremely profitable. The interest-earning bonds provided the basis for notes, which could be lent out again to earn more interest. The notes issued could equal a bank's net worth (capital). *The carrot to join the banking system would have produced a safe currency and helped finance the war by increasing banks' demand for government bonds.* A minor problem arose: the carrot was insufficiently sweet. Banks also kept the interest on the assets pledged for their state bank notes. While most states limited bank notes to a fraction of a bank's capital, the ability of national banks to issue notes equal to their capital was insufficient compensation for the onerous federal regulations.

In 1865 the stick was applied. State bank notes were taxed 10 percent annually. The comptroller thought this surely would extirpate the state banks. Since the assets the notes were financing earned less than 10 percent, state bank notes became unprofitable and were quickly retired. Many banks immediately changed status from state to national in order to issue the untaxed national notes. Tax avoidance created a uniform, safe currency and increased the demand for government bonds. Within two years, however, the rush to join the national banking system ended. Many banks decided that the lower reserve requirements and generally less exacting regulations of the states outweighed their need to issue notes. Deposit banking was on the rise. Look at Table 9–1. In most subperiods deposits rose more or decreased less than notes. By 1867 a dual banking system was firmly rooted.

The National Banking Act did correct the main monetary problem of its time, an unsafe currency system. *It had a major fault: the quantity of currency was inelastic.*[17] *This fault was compounded by two flaws of the free banking period which were uncorrected by the act, namely, the pyramiding of reserves and an inefficient check-collection process.* Consider the pyramiding of reserves first. For purposes of reserve requirements, the National Banking System established three bank classes determined by location. The information is presented in Table 9–2. Although the *quoted* reserve ratios were quite high, effective reserve ratios, that is, bank currency/ deposit ratios, were relatively low because banks did pyramid reserves, as allowed by the law. Banks held reserves in the form of deposits at larger banks instead of currency because (1) larger banks paid interest on deposits, and (2) deposits at larger banks facilitated check clearance and collection.

Three types of currency circulated: (1) gold and silver coins, (2) gov-

---

[17] The fault often is inaccurately labeled an inelastic money supply.

**TABLE 9-2  Reserves under the National Banking System, 1863-1913**

| Type of bank | Required reserve ratio | Composition of reserves |
| --- | --- | --- |
| Central reserve city (New York, Chicago, and St. Louis) . . . . . . . . . . . . . . . . . . . . . . . . | 25 | All cash in vault |
| Reserve city (47 other large cities). . . . . . . . . . . . . . . | 25 | Up to one half of reserves (12.5 percent of deposits) as deposits at central reserve city banks and remainder as vault cash |
| Country . . . . . . . . . . . . . . . . . . . . . . . . . . . . . . | 15 | Up to three fifths of reserves as deposits at central reserve or reserve city banks and remainder as vault cash. |

ernment paper money (greenbacks), and (3) national bank notes. *All three types of currency were inelastically supplied, that is, currency was virtually fixed in the short run and did not respond to seasonal and cyclical needs.* Little gold and silver can be mined or imported in the short run. An 1878 statute placed a ceiling of $347 million on greenbacks outstanding. Greenbacks are reissued periodically to satisfy demands for a crisp currency, but the amount outstanding remains fixed at this amount. National bank notes were secured by special (circulation privilege) government bonds. These bonds were relatively fixed, and any change was dictated by the government's surplus or deficit instead of seasonal or cyclical needs for currency. The inelastic currency supply was particularly troublesome because the agrarian economy and lack of deposit insurance produced large seasonal and erratic variations in the desired currency/deposit ratio. Because currency was inelastic, the public's greater demand for currency could be met only through decreases in bank currency reserves and a multiple deposit contraction. The pyramiding of reserves meant that banks held little currency, and any pressure within the system was quickly transmitted and magnified at the apex, particularly the New York City banks. These banks typically called their stock market loans when country banks withdrew their deposits. Of course, borrowers for stock market purposes did not have sufficient idle money and were forced to sell their stock. If enough calls were made, stock prices fell precipitously, producing a so-called panic or crisis. Even this could be insufficient. The seller of stock typically was paid by check, which was deposited to pay off the loan. Banks needed currency, however. Banks sometimes halted the multiple contraction process by universally agreeing on suspension and inconvertibility. So long as the public demanded large amounts of currency, banks in unison agreed not to provide it. They simply could not. Convertibility resumed when the public no longer wanted to convert deposits into cash. Major panics and suspensions of currency payments occurred in 1873, 1884, 1893, and 1907. The panic of 1907 was the last straw. The country needed an elastic currency. The National Monetary Commission established in 1908 undertook a broad and exhaustive study of America's financial needs.

## STRUCTURE OF THE FEDERAL RESERVE SYSTEM

While a concensus on the need for a central bank existed, disagreement on the structure of the Federal Reserve System was so intense as to almost block its creation. Five years elapsed between creation of the National Monetary Commission and passage of the Federal Reserve Act. Congress and bankers recognized that the structure of any organization, which sometimes is dismissed as a mere mechanical detail, has great practical importance. For example, who should select Federal Reserve officials, bankers or the president? The answer to this question clearly would influence the objectives and operational methods of the system. Rural idealists favored a decentralized organization managed by officials who were appointed by the president and confirmed by the Senate and whose primary allegiance was to the public. They were convinced that control of America's banking and financial system rested in the hands of a small Wall Street cadre, the so-called Money Trust. A decentralized, geographically dispersed Federal Reserve System would be less likely to come under the Money Trust's control. The agrarians wanted a public-oriented Federal Reserve to regulate the Money Trust out of existence. Urban realists on the other hand denied the existence of a money trust. They favored a centralized, banker-dominated organization free from government interference and guided by the nation's laissez-faire economic policy. The structure of the Federal Reserve System reflects the carefully crafted compromise between rural idealists and urban realists.

### Federal Reserve Banks

The full title of the Federal Reserve Act is, "An Act to provide for the establishment of Federal reserve banks, to furnish an elastic currency, to afford means of rediscounting commercial paper, to establish a more effective supervision of banking in the United States, and for other purposes."

The Federal Reserve Act (and amendments in 1914) divided the country into 12 districts, with each district having a Federal Reserve Bank and typically some branches. Figure 9–1 shows district boundaries, bank cities, and branch cities. (In what district do you live? Districts are identified by number or by the bank city.) The boundaries of the Federal

**FIGURE 9–1   The Federal Reserve System: Boundaries of Federal Reserve districts and their branch territories**

Reserve districts were drawn "with due regard to the convenience and customary course of business and shall not necessarily be coterminous with any State or States."

Each of the Federal Reserve Banks is a corporation. Member banks subscribed to the capital stock of their district Federal Reserve Bank an amount equal to 6 (subsequently 3) percent of their own net worth. With this net worth the Fed Banks were able to operate from their inception without congressional appropriations. The rural/urban compromise granted sole ownership to the member banks but effectively made the Fed Banks' stock preferred stock paying a 6 percent dividend. The member banks do not have the proprietory rights, powers, and privileges that belong to stockholders of private corporations. After payment of the required dividend, virtually all profits are distributed to the Treasury.

The management selection process also reflects the private and public nature of the Fed Banks. Each Fed Bank has nine directors divided into three classes, A, B, and C. The three class A directors are bankers, and the three class B directors are merchants, industrialists, or farmers who are not directors or controlling stockholders of banks. The class A and B directors are elected by member banks, one director of each class being elected by small banks, one of each class by medium-size banks, and one of each class by large banks. The three class C directors, who must be nonbankers, are designated by the Washington-based Board of Governors, whose members are selected by the president and confirmed by the Senate. One of the class C directors is designated as chairman of the Reserve Bank's board. The directors are responsible for the conduct of the affairs of the Reserve Bank. They appoint the Reserve Banks' operating officers, but the law requires approval of the president and first vice president by the Washington-based board.

Although the Fed's precise goals, instruments, and operating procedures have varied significantly over time, the act's full title alludes to its two constant and general goals: (1) management of currency, money, credit, and/or interest rates; and (2) creation of an efficient and smoothly functioning banking and financial system. The Fed's main "housekeeping" chores which maintain a smoothly functioning financial system and, thereby, economy are (1) the supervision and regulation of the banking system, (2) the clearance and collection of checks, and (3) the fiscal agent function for the Treasury. The last chapter discussed the first housekeeping chore, which the Fed shares with other banking authorities, and the next chapter describes how the other two chores are performed. The Fed has performed the second goal so efficiently that it now is unappreciated and taken for granted. The early banking history was presented in part to dispel the all too common view that the unglamorous second goal matters little. The important point here is: what Fed unit performs these two housekeeping functions? Banks, and not some board or committee, must perform these functions. The act specified the creation of Federal Reserve Banks.

Besides performing the important housekeeping functions, the Reserve Banks participate in monetary and interest rate policy decisions. Indeed, *the Federal Reserve Act specified that the Banks should be the main, or at least an equal, partner in the monetary policy decision-making process.* The full title of the act indicates that an elastic currency and, therefore, monetary base was to be provided by the rediscounting of commercial paper or real bills. That is, commercial banks could borrow or discount at the Reserve Banks and acquire currency or a deposit credit by offering real bills as collateral.[18] (The balance sheet effects of discounting were illus-

---

[18] Because the real bills which served as collateral typically were discounted, that is, interest was prepaid so the borrower received less than the face value of the loan from the commercial bank, the Fed was said to "rediscount" the bills.

trated in Chapter 3.) *The discount rate for each district is jointly determined by the district Bank and the Washington-based board. The district Bank proposes discount changes, which must be approved by the board.* Thus, in (agrarian) principle, one could simultaneously have 12 different discount rates. Principle has never corresponded with reality. Discount rates have not always been uniform, but differences typically have been short-lived.

In the early years of the Federal Reserve System, the board routinely acquiesced to the banks, which were led by the New York Bank. Although the organization chart has remained constant, officials change, and by force of personalities the board gradually seized power over discounting. By the late 1920s, the board did not immediately approve banks' proposed discount rate changes. The board now dominates discount policy. The board tells the banks what it believes the appropriate discount rate is, and most banks are sufficiently compliant to "request" the board's desired rate. The remainder then quickly fall in line for the sake of unity within the system. The banks' diminished role in the discount process understates their decline in monetary policy decision making. The framers of the Federal Reserve Act envisaged that discount policy would be the main monetary policy tool. However, discounting has long been eclipsed by reserve requirement policy and open-market operations, particularly the latter.

### Board of Governors of the Federal Reserve System

The Board is composed of seven members appointed by the President and confirmed by the Senate. The term of office is 14 years, and members who have served a full term may not be reappointed. The members must come from different Federal Reserve districts, and in making appointments the president is to "have due regard to a fair representation of the financial, agricultural, industrial, and commercial interest and geographical divisions of the country." It is incongruous that an economic policy board existed for nearly 50 years before a practicing economist was first appointed a member in the early 1960s! Economists have been represented ever since, often by several members. The president designates one of the members as chairperson. Arthur Burns was the first economist to assume the chair.

The Board of Governors, and particularly its chairperson, is the central controlling authority within the Federal Reserve System. While the Board's power grab over the discounting mechanism began in the 1920s and was based solely on the force of personalities, the general activism of Franklin D. Roosevelt's presidency in 1933 and "the need to do something" to lift the economy from the depression doldrums officially centralized control within the board. The Banking Act of 1935 gave the Board (1) *sole* authority to set reserve requirements, within broad ranges specified by Congress; and (2) a majority on the Federal Open Market

Committee.[19] Until 1935 reserve requirements were set by Congress and could *not* be changed by any unit within the Fed. Reserve requirements were phased in, becoming fully effective in 1917, and remained constant until 1936, when the board raised reserve requirements to reduce excess reserves and eliminate the "inflationary potential" of an economy suffering more than 15 percent unemployment. (See Chapter 13.) Fortunately, subsequent reserve requirement policy has been more judicious. Requirement changes still occur relatively infrequently. Open-market operations are the main monetary policy tool.

### Federal Open Market Committee (FOMC)

The Federal Reserve Act gave the system the power to buy and sell government securities and a few other types of marketable financial instruments. This power was granted almost as an afterthought of little consequence. The act was passed during calm times when belief in the automaticity of the gold standard ruled supreme. The banks themselves thought that active intervention in financial markets generally was inappropriate and would occur only on special occasions. However, within a year the world became embroiled in a war, and many countries were forced off the gold standard, making intervention much more feasible. By the time the United States entered the war in 1917, the Reserve Banks were conducting modest open-market operations in order to support the government bond market and for the very practical reason that they needed some income.[20] Bank discounts, the other Fed earning asset, were insufficient. Surprisingly enough, the Fed in its early years did not realize that open-market purchases have the same effect on currency and re-

---

[19] Broadly defined perks of office and other auxiliary information, which often are better indicators of power than job descriptions, confirm the shift of power from the banks to the board. For example, in banking circles governor is a more prestigious title than president. Prior to the 1930s, the head of each Fed Bank was a governor, while only the head of the five-member, Washington-based Federal Reserve Board was a governor. The Banking Act expanded the Federal Reserve Board to seven members (the two ex-officio members were dropped) and rechristened it the Board of Governors of the Federal Reserve System. Each member of the board was elevated to governor status, and the head officer of the banks was demoted to president. In addition, the governors received a significant salary increase, and their term of office was lengthened from 10 to 14 years. However, even after the increase, Board of Governor salaries were only about one third the salaries of bank presidents because the banks officially are private firms which are not bound by civil service regulations. By 1980 bank salaries were only somewhat higher than board salaries. Significant salary differentials between government employees and employees of government-sponsored agencies still exist today. For example, the heads of Fannie Mae and the Synthetic Fuel Corporation earn much more than cabinet secretaries.

[20] Support of the government bond market came mainly through relaxation of the real bills requirement and allowance of discounts secured by government bonds. The Fed preferred the lesser visibility of this indirect means of supporting the bond market to direct purchases.

serves as discounts. The effect of discounts is clear because the Fed immediately credits the commercial bank's deposit account. However, the effect of open-market purchases on currency or reserves appears only after the seller deposits the Fed's check. Although the time interval between open-market purchases and check collection is very short, several years passed before the Fed clearly recognized that purchases increase reserves.

The Banks in 1923 formed a committee of five eastern Fed Bank presidents, expanded in 1930 to all 12 bank presidents, which coordinated system open-market operations. Prior to that date individual banks engaged in independent open-market operations, some banks selling while others were simultaneously buying. The Banking Act of 1935 sealed the transfer of monetary powers from the banks to the board by creating a Federal Open Market Committee (FOMC). Like its predecessor committee, the FOMC has 12 voting members, but the 7 bank presidents added in 1930 were replaced by the entire Board of Governors. The president of the New York Bank retained a permanent seat on the FOMC. The remaining four slots on the FOMC are rotated annually among the other 11 bank presidents. The seven nonvoting bank presidents attend the FOMC meetings and participate in the debate. Consistent with the FOMC's makeup, the committee's staff, who also attend the meetings and advise the members, is drawn from the entire system. Although the FOMC officially determines only open-market operations, discount and reserve requirement policy are discussed at the meetings in order to coordinate all three monetary policy tools.

**Advisory committees**

The Federal Reserve System has two formal, legislated advisory groups, the Federal Advisory Council and the Consumer Advisory Council. The creation of a Federal Advisory Council was inserted into the Federal Reserve Act to appease the American Bankers Association, which had denounced a "public" board as communistic, confiscatory, un-American, and generally a snake in the grass. The Federal Advisory Council consists of 12 bankers, one from each Federal Reserve district, who meet quarterly in Washington and serve as a liaison between the Reserve Banks and the board. The Consumer Advisory Council, which is composed of approximately 30 creditors, consumers, and others, was established in 1976 pursuant to the Equal Credit Opportunity Act to advise the board on consumer matters. Besides these legislated advisory groups, the Fed has created several informal committees. While not a committee, no mention of advice received by the Fed would be complete without mention of its staff. As far as government staffs go, the Fed staff clearly is one of the best.

## Monetary power beyond organization charts

Who shapes monetary policy? Open-market operations have totally eclipsed discounting as a source of currency and reserves, and reserve requirements are changed quite infrequently. Thus the shapers of open-market policy largely set monetary policy. The seven to five majority on the FOMC enjoyed by the board suggests that it sets monetary policy. Voting strength does facilitate the exercise of power. However, numbers of potential voters do *not* always equal power, as political analysts or anyone who has served on a committee knows. Limitations on campaign contributions are attempts to transform "one person, one vote" into "each person equal." Power does not necessarily require a vote, as the phrase "power behind the throne" implies. Given this, who actually sets monetary policy? The best answer was given by someone intimately involved. Sherman J. Maisel, professor of economics at the University of California at Berkeley and a governor of the Federal Reserve from 1965 to 1972, estimated that during his tenure monetary power within the Federal Reserve System was shared in the following proportions: (1) the chairman, 45 percent; (2) the staff of the board and FOMC, 25 percent; (3) the other governors, 20 percent; and (4) Federal Reserve Banks, 10 percent.[21] According to Maisel, the paid staff of advisers advise, while the legislated advisory committees scurry the corridors of power unable to find an attentive ear.

We caution the reader that these percentages are not immutable. Power depends partially on personalities. William McChesney Martin and Arthur Burns were the chairmen between 1965 and 1972 while Paul Volcker is the current chairman. Nevertheless, the percentage estimates remain reasonably accurate today. Why is the chair so powerful? First, outside the system the Federal Reserve is the chair and a group of faceless people. As titular head and spokesperson of the Fed, the chair testifies before Congress and participates in many decisions which never come before the board. For example, overall economic policy often is coordinated by the Quadriad, who are the secretary of the Treasury, chair of the Council of Economic Advisers, director of the Office of Management and Budget, and the Federal Reserve Board chair. The chair's power outside the system attracts votes and reinforces its power within the system. Second, the chair in any committee system is strengthened by its ability to select the agenda and shape the debate.

## SUMMARY

The Federal Reserve Act established a central bank the goals and structure of which have changed considerably over time. The framers of the act

---

[21] Sherman J. Maisel, *Managing the Dollar* (New York: W. W. Norton, 1973), p. 110.

primarily wanted an elastic currency so that an increase in the demand for currency did not lead to a decrease in reserves and a multiple money contraction. In terms of the analysis of Chapters 3 and 4, a higher currency ratio reduces the money multiplier and money supply, *ceteris paribus*. The framers of the act wanted to break the *ceteris paribus* condition. They wanted a higher currency ratio to be countered by a monetary base augmented by discounting, thereby keeping the money supply constant. Over longer periods they wanted the money supply to follow the dictates of the gold standard and passively adjust to economic activity. The Fed continues to neutralize the effect of shifts in the currency ratio. However, such offsetting policy is now considered a technicality, albeit important. Monetary policy now actively manages the money supply with a view to full employment and price stability.

The change in goals affected and was affected by the structure of the Fed. A passive monetary policy was consistent with decentralized decision making and discounting, which is at the discretion of commercial banks. Although the board and the 12 Fed Banks legally continue to share power over the discounting mechanism, the Fed Banks now effectively are very junior partners. The Banking Act of 1935 legitimatized the centralization of power and the activist orientation of the Fed. Creation of a board-dominated FOMC officially recognized the importance of open-market operations. Moreover, the board alone was granted the power to change reserve requirements. The Fed has lost its rural idealist roots.

## QUESTIONS

1. Describe the colonial monetary system. What was the unit of account? What was the medium of exchange? Did the Revolutionary War significantly change the financial structure?

2. Explain how inflation is a tax.

3. What are the essential elements of the rural idealism versus urban reality controversy? How has its precise expression changed over time?

4. State the arguments for and against the First Bank of the United States which resurfaced when the Second Bank's charter was considered. The charter of each bank was not renewed largely because the political strength of their advocates declined during the interim. However, in each case some new issues arose which contributed to its demise. For both the First and Second Bank, state some issues discussed during the charter renewal period but not during the original charter period.

5. What two functions normally associated with central banks did both the First and Second Bank of the United States perform?

6. Define the Independent Treasury system. How did it affect the stability of the monetary system?

7. Define free banking. When did it exist? What are the pros and cons of free banking?

8. What were the two main cooperative practices developed by banks during the free banking period?

9. What were the main reasons for the establishment of the National Banking System? Did it meet its goals?

10. What were the major faults of the National Banking System which the creation of the Federal Reserve System was supposed to rectify?

11. How does the organizational structure of the Federal Reserve reflect the rural idealism versus urban reality controversy?

12. Precisely what group within the Federal Reserve System determines (1) open-market operations, (2) the discount rate, and (3) reserve requirement ratios? Describe the decision-making groups in terms of appointment procedures, term of office, and so on.

13. State the changes in the decision making responsibilities within the Fed that occurred during 1933–35?

# Determinants of the money supply: The monetary base

# 10

This chapter explains the final link in the money supply, the monetary base. Thus in some respects it should have immediately followed Chapter 4, where we analyzed the money supply multiplier. In other respects, though, this chapter is an extension of the preceding one. We describe with the aid of balance sheets two major Federal Reserve housekeeping chores, check collection and the fiscal agent function. Important as these housekeeping chores are, the Fed was created primarily to provide an elastic currency, as the last chapter stated. Creators of the Fed stressed the need for elasticity because changes in the demand for currency and the composition of a *fixed* base produce monetary instability in a fractional reserve system through money multiplier variations. The Fed was supposed to neutralize currency demand shifts by varying the supply of currency and the base. The chapter shows how the Fed neutralizes the effect of currency shifts, but it goes further. The overwhelming proportion of *the chapter analyzes the variables uncontrolled by the Fed which influence the monetary base.* Contrary to the assumption of Chapter 4, the base is not perfectly controlled by the Fed. Indeed, we learned in Chapter 3 that discounts increase reserves and the base, and discounts are initiated by commercial banks themselves. In some ways the base is too elastic; discounting is only one of several uncontrolled sources producing variations in the base. The final section explains how the Fed manipulates the base in order to (1) offset the effect of uncontrolled influences such as discounting, and (2) neutralize the effect of currency shifts.

## BALANCE SHEETS AND THE MONETARY BASE EQUATION

Currency is issued by and is a liability of the Federal Reserve or the Treasury, and reserves are vault cash and bank deposits at the Fed. *Therefore, the monetary base is the liability of either the Fed or the Treasury and is included within Tables 10–1 and 10–2, which present the Fed and Treasury monetary account balance sheets, respectively. In particular, lines K and L in Table 10–1 show the Fed's contribution toward the base, and line Q in Table 10–2 shows the Treasury's contribution.* Our explanation of the monetary base relies heavily on the fundamental principle of double-entry bookkeeping that every transaction must affect at least two accounts. Any

**TABLE 10–1   Federal Reserve System balance sheet, December 31, 1979 ($ millions)**

| | Assets | | |
|---|---|---|---|
| (A) | U.S. government securities | | $126,167 |
| (B) | Discounts to banks | | 2,158 |
| (C) | Float | | 6,767 |
| | Cash in process of collection | 13,571 | |
| | Deferred availability item | 6,804 | |
| (D) | Miscellaneous assets | | 5,613 |
| (E) | Gold certificates | | 11,112 |
| (F) | Special drawing rights certificates | | 1,800 |
| (G) | Treasury currency | | 403 |
| | Total assets | | $154,020 |

| | Liabilities and Net Worth | |
|---|---|---|
| (H) | Treasury deposits | $   4,075 |
| (I) | Foreign and other deposits | 1,841 |
| (J) | Miscellaneous liabilities and net worth | 4,957 |
| (K) | Federal Reserve notes in circulation | 113,355 |
| (L) | Bank reserve deposits | 29,792 |
| | Total liabilities and net worth | $154,020 |

**TABLE 10–2   Treasury monetary account balance sheet, December 31, 1979 ($ millions)**

| | Assets | |
|---|---|---|
| (M) | Gold | $11,112 |
| (N) | Treasury currency outstanding | 12,947 |
| (O) | Federal Reserve notes | 275 |
| | Total assets | $24,334 |

| | Liabilities and Net Worth | |
|---|---|---|
| (P) | Gold certificates | $11,112 |
| (Q) | Treasury currency in circulation | 12,796 |
| (R) | Treasury cash | 426 |
| | Total liabilities and net worth | $24,334 |

change in the base must be accompanied by a change in some other item on the monetary authorities' balance sheets. Stated somewhat differently, a change in any other item on the balance sheets *might* change the base. To show more compactly all the accounts that could possibly affect the base, the two balance sheets are consolidated and rearranged in Table 10–3 to express the base as the difference between Fed and Treasury

**TABLE 10–3  Consolidated Treasury and Federal Reserve balance sheet; monetary base equation, December 31, 1979\* ($ millions)**

| Sources (Assets) | |
|---|---|
| U.S. government securities (A) | $126,167 |
| Discounts to banks (B) | 2,158 |
| Float (C) | 6,767 |
| Miscellaneous Fed assets (D) | 5,613 |
| Gold (M) | 11,112 |
| Special drawing rights certificates (F) | 1,800 |
| Treasury currency outstanding (N) | 12,947 |
| Total sources (assets) | $166,564 |
| | |
| Uses (Other Liabilities) | |
| Treasury deposits (H) | $  4,075 |
| Foreign and other deposits (I) | 1,841 |
| Miscellaneous Fed liabilities and net worth | 4,957 |
| Treasury cash (R) | 426 |
| Total uses (other liabilities) | $11,299 |
| | |
| Monetary base = Sources-uses | $155,265 |
| Monetary base composition from Fed and Treasury balance sheets | |
| Bank reserve deposits (L) | $ 29,792 |
| Currency held by public *and* banks (K + Q − G − O) | $125,473 |

\* Letter in parentheses following account indicates similar account in Table 10–1 or 10–2.

assets and "other liabilities" (net worth plus all liabilities except currency in circulation and reserves). In other words, the balance sheet identity says that

$$\text{Assets} = \text{Liabilities} + \text{Net worth}$$

In the case at hand, some of the liabilities are the monetary base. Calling the remaining liabilities and net worth "other liabilities," the balance sheet identity for the monetary authorities may be expressed as

$$\text{Assets} = \text{Other liabilities} + \text{Base}$$
$$\text{Assets} - \text{Other liabilities} = \text{Base}$$

The consolidated balance sheet does not show gold certificates since this account cancels, being an asset of the Fed and a liability of the Treasury. According to the balance sheets of the Fed and Treasury, currency in circulation is $113,355 and $12,796 million, respectively. However, the

Fed and Treasury hold $678 million of each others currency. (Lines G and O in Tables 10–1 and 10–2, respectively.) From the viewpoint of the Fed *and* Treasury, currency in circulation is $125,473 ($113,355 million plus $12,796 million, minus $678 million). The reader is encouraged to examine carefully Tables 10–1 through 10–3 before continuing reading.

Table 10–3 is often called the monetary base equation instead of the consolidated Treasury and Federal Reserve balance sheet. The table's new name is appropriate since it is constructed to highlight the items which can cause the base to change. Those who favor the name *monetary base equation,* and most economists do, express the balance sheet identity differently. If Fed or Treasury assets increase *and* other liabilities are constant, then the base increases. An increase in other liabilities with assets constant implies that the base falls. The last two sentences suggest calling Fed and Treasury assets sources of the base, and other liabilities uses.[1] The new nomenclature expresses the balance sheet identity as

$$\text{Sources} - \text{Uses} = \text{Base}$$

Of course, an increase in a source does not necessarily increase the base; the compensating double-entry bookkeeping account could be a decrease in another source or an increase in a use. For example, if a transaction causes an increase in the gold and Treasury cash accounts, the base remains constant as a source and use increase. The numerous items on the Fed and Treasury balance sheets suggest, however, that the base could change for many reasons. The compensating balance sheet entry associated with changes in many sources and uses is a change in the base. Do not let the nomenclature for the table and balance sheet identity obfuscate the identity of the individual items. What items, albeit somewhat rearranged and consolidated, appear in the monetary base equation? Only Federal Reserve and Treasury assets, which are called sources, and Fed and Treasury other liabilities, which are called uses.

The opening sentence stated that the monetary base would be explained. However, this chapter does not "explain" the base in any profound sense. Explaining the base simply means showing *how* the base changes. *We illustrate the series of balance sheet entries associated with a change in a source or use, paying particular attention whether the compensating change on the balance sheet is the base or some other account.* Giving the word *explain* this meaning involves a simplification. To a substantial extent we are deliberately avoiding a difficult question (why?) and substituting an easy question (how?). Don't be disappointed; the easy question is not that easy and it is enough for one chapter. In addition, illustrating how all the accounts in Tables 10–1 and 10–2 change is time consuming. At this point our only concession to the difficult (why?) question is

---

[1] Some call other Fed and Treasury liabilities *"negative sources"* and retain the term *uses* for the composition of the base, such as currency and reserves.

answering the following: Is the specific source or use being discussed directly and immediately under the control of the monetary authorities, or does it change due to random events or forces only indirectly affected by the authorities? We also consider whether any change is somewhat long lasting or is likely to be reversed immediately. If a source is not directly controlled by the monetary authorities we attempt no elaborate explanation of the factors causing the source to vary. Our concession to the difficult question is necessary for the extremely important discussion of monetary control in subsequent chapters. Can the Fed counteract the effect of all other factors and control the base and the money supply? The message of this and previous chapters is: Monetary control is not easy and requires some agility.

In some respects this is the book's most technical chapter up to this point. To breathe some life to what can be a series of sterile bookkeeping entries, we present substantial historical and institutional material. This blend of technical and institutional matter may obscure the primary objective of this chapter. Therefore, the objectives deserve special emphasis. The reader should learn (1) what items are included in the monetary base equation and for each item learn (2) the typical compensating entry required by double-entry bookkeeping, (3) whether the item is controlled directly by the Fed or changes for various reasons, and (4) the relative size and importance of each item as a contributor to short-run variations of the base.

## GENERAL COMMENTS ON THE FEDERAL RESERVE AND TREASURY BALANCE SHEETS

Before considering specific accounts, a general overview of the balance sheets is appropriate. The sizes of the two balance sheets, Tables 10–1 and 10–2, suggest that the Treasury is decidedly the junior monetary authority. This is indeed the case. The Treasury's monetary prerogatives are quite limited. Moreover, no convincing argument can be made today for granting the Treasury the two monetary powers, issuance of coins and ownership of gold, reflected in the Treasury monetary account.[2] The Treasury's role in the money supply process is a vestige of the past, stemming from the early uncertainty about the private banking or public orientation of the Fed. The relatively recently created Federal Reserve was not granted exclusive rights over all the functions a central bank normally performs. The Treasury retained its earlier authority to issue

---

[2] We are not saying that the Treasury should play a minor role in monetary policy *decisions*. Good arguments, both pro and con, can be made for an "independent" Federal Reserve. The statement in the text simply means that monetary policy should not be *executed* by the Treasury. This is perfectly compatible with a situation where the Treasury determines policy and has the Fed do its bidding, as was true during the 1940s. Two authorities with the ability to change the money supply, perhaps at cross purposes, makes little sense.

coins and currency. The Treasury plays an additional monetary role because of a 1934 law (now rescinded) prohibiting private, including Federal Reserve, ownership of gold. The accounting entries necessary to explain variations in the base would be simplified if the Treasury were to stop issuing coins and transfer ownership of the gold stock to the Fed.

The Treasury also is the fiscal authority. It collects billions in taxes each year, and the federal government often expends even more. A key to understanding Table 10–2 is the realization that the balance sheet shows only the Treasury *monetary account*. As such, the Treasury's balance sheet is incomplete, not showing the asssets and liabilities acquired by the Treasury in its role as fiscal authority. For example, 1600 Pennsylvania Avenue, Yellowstone National Park, and F–111 airplanes do not appear in the asset column, and billions of Treasury bonds are glaringly absent from the liability side. Treasury deposits at the Fed is a liability of the Fed but does not appear as a Treasury asset because it is assumed that all Treasury deposits at the Fed arise from the Treasury's taxing authority and bond sales. The assumption may not be altogether accurate; any division of receipts by functions is bound to be somewhat arbitrary. Nevertheless, from the viewpoint of the money supply, the Treasury monetary account as shown is precisely what we want.

Understanding the sources and uses of the base would be easier if the account traditionally called *Treasury cash,* which appears on the liability side of the Treasury's balance sheet, were called Treasury net worth on monetary account. Treasury cash includes but in general is not limited to cash held by the Treasury. Treasury cash is a balancing account; it makes the balance sheet balance. Treasury cash represents the additional amount the Treasury could spend without collecting taxes or selling bonds. Alternatively stated, Treasury cash is the additional spending power of the Treasury due to its monetary responsibilities.

While generally indicating first how the accounts on the Fed's balance sheet change, we postpone discussion of gold certificates and international assets until we analyze the Treasury's balance sheet. Since all transactions are symmetric, we discuss only the plus side, that is, increases in sources or uses. Substituting words like *sell* for *buy* changes the sign of the entries.

## U.S. GOVERNMENT SECURITIES AND DISCOUNTS

The first account in Tables 10–1 and 10–3, U.S. government securities held by the Fed, is easy to analyze and can well illustrate our approach to the monetary base. What is the typical compensating balance sheet entry when the Fed's holdings of U.S. government securities change? Do changes in the U.S. government securities account reflect policy decisions, or does the account change because of random forces and actions by others? The U.S. government securities account on the Fed's balance sheet equals the cumulative net open-market purchases. Although the mechanics of open-market purchases were presented earlier, they are repeated here. U.S. securities may be purchased from banks or the public, as illustrated in lines 1 and 2, respectively, of Figure 10–1. In either

**FIGURE 10–1  Open-market purchases from (1) banks and (2) the public**

| Banking System | | | |
|---|---|---|---|
| (1) U.S. securities | − 100 | | |
| Deposits at Fed | + 100 | | |
| (2) Deposits at Fed | + 100 | Check deposits | + 100 |

| Fed | | | |
|---|---|---|---|
| (1) U.S. securities | + 100 | Deposits of banks | + 100 |
| (2) U.S. securities | + 100 | Deposits of banks | + 100 |

case, the deposit of banks at the Fed component of the base increases. The U.S. government securities account is directly controlled by the Fed; It does not change unless the Fed makes a deliberate decision to buy or sell.[3]

As stated earlier, the Fed has purchased on the open market a minor amount of securities issued by such U.S. agencies as the Federal Home Loan Bank and Federal National Mortgage Association (Fanny Mae). Strictly speaking then, the U.S. government securities account is somewhat of a misnomer. From the view point of the money supply, however, the specific item purchased is irrelevant. The Fed could just as well purchase IBM shares or mosquito nets. When the private sector (banks or the public) receive checks issued by the Fed, the base increases irrespective of the Fed's motive for issuing the check.

Like open-market operations, discounting needs no long explanation at this stage. Figure 10–2 shows that discounts increase the base.

**FIGURE 10–2  Discounting**

| Banking System | | | | Fed | | | |
|---|---|---|---|---|---|---|---|
| Deposits at Fed | + 100 | Discounts at Fed | + 100 | Discounts to banks | + 100 | Deposits of banks | + 100 |

---

[3] The existence of repurchase clauses for some securities does not contradict the text since the Fed must agree to the repurchase clause.

The Fed does not directly control discounts. The Fed sets the discount rate but banks decide how much to borrow at the Fed, and their response to the discount rate is not always the same.

Discounting is a relatively minor source of the base. During the past several years discounts have averaged less than 1 percent of the base. During relatively short periods of time, however, changes in the volume of discounts are substantial, both absolutely and relative to the base. For example, in early August 1977 market interest rates started rising quite sharply. In the week ending August 24, 1977 discounts averaged $1.7 billion. Four weeks earlier, when market interest rates were substantially lower, bank discounts averaged only $295 million. The volume of discounts is small relative to the base but sometimes discounts are a major source of short-run monetary instability.[4]

## FLOAT: CASH IN THE PROCESS OF COLLECTION MINUS DEFERRED AVAILABILITY ITEMS

Float, which is the difference between cash in the process of collection and deferred availability items, stems from time lags in clearing checks. As stated in the last chapter, check collection was no simple matter before the existence of the Federal Reserve because all banks did not directly or indirectly maintain accounts at one bank, which would clear checks by debiting one bank's account and crediting another bank. It could involve the Wells Fargo Company shipping coins and currency around the country.[5] Indeed, check collection was sufficiently expensive and time consuming that many checks were not paid at par. That is, the bank against which a check was drawn paid a small (say, 50 cents) amount less than the stated amount of the check although it debited the check issuer's account by the full face value of the check, the difference between the amount debited and paid being a service charge. A few (about 10 and decreasing) small banks in Louisiana have refused to give up their check collection service charges. These banks are called nonpar banks. Therefore, do not be altogether surprised if your bank credits your account by less than the amount of the check you deposited; the check may have been drawn on a nonpar bank, and your bank received less than the face amount of the check. Complaints should be directed to the person who gave you the check. That individual knew that the check was drawn on a nonpar bank and should have issued a check larger than the amount due.

---

[4] The sentence in the text may sound incorrect because the important distinction between current values and changes is often confused. Suppose that discounts increase from 1 to 2 during some time period, and the base changes from 100 to 101. Discounts are always small compared to the base—1 percent at the beginning and about 2 percent at the end of the period—but the change in discounts is a substantial proportion (100 percent in this case) of the change in the base.

[5] More often, however, check collection involved an elaborate system of correspondent banks.

The Federal Reserve Act provided for an efficient and rapid system of check collection through Federal Reserve Banks and branches scattered throughout the country. The Fed's check collection system, which is available to all par banks, is one of the least glamourous housekeeping operations performed by the Fed that, nonetheless, is vital to the proper functioning of the financial sector. Ignoring nonpar banks, suppose you deposit at the Union Trust Company of Maryland a $100 check drawn on the Bank of Winnemucca (an exciting little town in northern Nevada). Union Trust forwards the check to the Baltimore branch of the Federal Reserve for collection.[6]

**FIGURE 10–3  Check collection**

| Union Trust | | Fed | |
|---|---|---|---|
| Cash in the process of collection  +100 | Check deposits  +100 | Cash in the process of collection  +100 | Deferred availability items  +100 |

Note that the Fed does not immediately increase the reserves of Union Trust and decrease the reserves of the Bank of Winnemucca. Because of this some banks do not allow you to write checks against very recent deposits. The Fed debits cash in the process of collection, funds it is attempting to collect from the bank of Winnemucca, and credits deferred availability items, a temporary account showing the amount to be credited to Union Trust in the near future.

Why doesn't the Fed immediately credit the account of one bank and debit the account of the other? The answer is simple but not obvious. It has nothing to do with rubber checks. The Fed does not immediately decrease the deposits of the Bank of Winnemucca because *reserve management is complicated by debits unbeknown to a bank*. Banks are required to hold reserves at least equal to a specified fraction of deposits. A bank unaware of debits to its reserve account would have substantial difficulty meeting the reserve requirement. You surely would have a difficult time balancing your checkbook if you were unaware of debits to your account. Therefore, the Fed does not debit the Bank of Winnemucca's account until the bank receives its depositor's check. But when will this check be

---

[6] Some banks clear directly with the Fed but many others clear indirectly by means of a correspondent. That is, many banks, including small member banks which have accounts at the Fed, send checks received to larger banks where they maintain accounts for check collection and other purposes. From our viewpoint of the effect on check collection on the base, direct or indirect collection is equivalent. The actions of the Union Trust in our example are independent of the type of depositor. We ignore the interdistrict settlement accounts among Federal Reserve Banks as these are bookkeeping accounts of no consequence whatsoever to the money supply or any other economic variable.

presented to the Bank of Winnemucca? It has to be processed, flown across the country, and then delivered to the Bank of Winnemucca. If all goes well, the Bank of Winnemucca receives the check within two days. However, a check processing staff inadequate to handle the peak volume of checks, bad weather delaying the transportation process, mechanical failures, and other unexpected events could delay the check for several days.

Just as reserve management is complicated by debits unbeknown to a bank, lack of knowledge when one's account will be credited complicates reserve management. To eliminate this uncertainty the Fed has established a deferred availability schedule indicating when payment will be made. The schedule is based on the location of the bank against which the check is drawn and the location of the bank receiving the check. Union Trust will have its account credited the same day, one, or at most, two days following delivery of the check to the Fed. The deferred availability schedule is relatively optimistic. It often takes longer than the scheduled time for checks to reach banks. This is immaterial to the Union Trust as on the second day, in this case where the banks are very distant, the following entries are recorded.

**FIGURE 10–4   Check collection (continued)**

| Union Trust | | Fed | |
|---|---|---|---|
| Cash in process of collection   −100 | | Deferred availability items   −100 | |
| Deposits at Fed      +100 | | Deposits of Union Trust      +100 | |

At this point float has increased $100. Combining Figures 10–3 and 10–4, the Fed shows that cash in process of collection still is $100 but there is no deferred availability item. On the Fed's balance sheet, Table 10–1, deferred availability items, shown as a negative item on the asset side, is subtracted from cash in the process of collection to give float. The base varies directly with float. In this example, Union Trust has larger reserves while reserves of the Bank of Winnemucca are unchanged. Float is no inconsequential amount, averaging around $6 billion in recent years. More important, random factors such as bad weather cause float to vary by literally hundreds of millions of dollars from day to day.

Float is a short-run phenomenon. Continuing this illustration, the entries shown in Figure 10–5 are recorded when the Bank of Winnemucca finally receives the check.

FIGURE 10–5 Check collection (concluded)

| Bank of Winnemucca | | | Fed | | |
|---|---|---|---|---|---|
| Deposits at Fed | −100 | Check deposits −100 | Cash in process of collection −100 | Deposits of Bank of Winne-mucca | −100 |

Consolidation of the last three balance sheets confirms that in the final analysis checks simply shuffle reserves between banks. During the process of collection, checks may (not must) give rise to float and increase the base. Not every check generates Fed float. However, the number of checks written is sufficiently large that float always is positive if variable due to bad weather, and so on.

Large payments formerly made by check are now made through Fed wire transfers, which may be viewed as an instantaneous check collection system through computers linked nationwide. For example, suppose a Houston oillionaire in search of a tax shelter purchases a Vermont ski lodge. The Houston bank, following the oillionaire's instructions, tells the Fed's Houston branch to reduce its account and credit the account of Green Mountain National, the bank of the former owner of the ski lodge. Through a computer system linking all the Fed units, the appropriate transactions and notifications are effected virtually instantaneously, so that float does not arise.

In principle, float could be negative if the deferred availability schedule were lengthened. The check would reach the Bank of Winnemucca before the account of Union Trust is credited. The Fed has retained an optimistic deferred availability schedule but attempts to minimize the impact of its optimism on its earnings. Soon after commercial airlines started bumping bags of checks in favor of other cargo, the Fed contracted a cargo airliner to transport checks more expeditiously. There was reason to this apparent madness. Float, like discounts, is a short-term extension of credit by the Fed to a commercial bank. Until 1981 there was an important difference, however. Float was an interest-free credit to the banking system. In our example Union Trust Bank did not pay interest on the reserves it acquired due to the Fed's optimistic deferred availability schedule. The Fed is primarily a macroeconomic policy and bank regulatory authority; its actions generally are not motivated by a desire to maximize profits. However, the Fed objected to extensions of interest-free credits and contracted for the airplanes in order to reduce float. To provide the same amount of the base with a lower level of float, the Fed could own a larger quantity of interest-bearing securities and earn greater profits. The Fed now is more blatantly opposed to letting float reduce its profits. It recently started charging banks for float much as it charges banks which discount.

Is the Fed's more profit-oriented attitude desirable? In recent years the Fed's interest receipts have been about $8 billion annually. Since the Fed's expenses are less than 10 percent of its receipts, the Fed like all fiat money producers makes a substantial profit. What happens to these profits? They are transferred back to the Treasury, about $7.5 billion recently, and reduce the taxes necessary to finance any given expenditure. The new Fed policy benefits the general taxpayer at the expense of bankers, not a particularly deserving group, though not an underserving group either. The Fed should not dissipate its profits. The Congress and not the Fed should decide who should be the beneficiary of the Fed's money producing abilities.

The Fed's check clearing and collection facilities are rarely used, and consequently float rarely occurs, when the two parties to a check are local banks. In small towns with few banks, the two banking parties may informally exchange their claims against each other at the end of the day, the net debtor paying the other bank by transferring credit at the Fed. That is, at the end of the day bank A sends a messenger with all the checks drawn on bank B. The messenger returns with the checks bank B possesses that are drawn on bank A. The two banks compare totals. Assuming bank A is the net debtor, the banks instruct the Fed to debit bank A's account and credit bank B's. When the banks are nearby, sending checks to the Fed was a waste of time and resources and is more so now that the Fed charges for its check collection services.[7] Full cost pricing and profits are no longer dirty words at the Fed.

Basically the same principle is involved in large cities with many banks. Bilateral transfers are too expensive in large cities. Assuming 20 banks, messengers would have to crisscross the city 190 times if bilateral transfers occurred.[8] It is much simpler to have all messengers meet at a designated place called a clearinghouse, which may have a permanent location or be as transient as a floating crap game. The clearinghouse may be the back room of Security National this week, Fidelity Trust next week, and so on. Wherever the bank representatives meet, they complete Table 10–4. Some illustrative numbers are shown. For example, depositors brought to bank B $100 in checks drawn on bank A. Bank B's depositors wrote checks for $120 to depositors of bank A. Since each bank brings to the clearinghouse only checks drawn on other members of the clearinghouse, the sum of the "total credits" columns must equal the sum of the "total debits" rows.[9] The difference between the total credits and total

---

[7] Banks do not bear higher check processing costs by clearing directly. You don't just drop checks into a bag and take them to the Fed; the Fed insists checks be sorted.

[8] The number of pairwise combinations of N items is $N(N - 1)/2$. For $N = 20$, we get $20 \times 19/2 = 190$.

[9] Nothing profound is involved. Addition is commutative. Take a block of numbers. Add all the numbers row by row or column by column and you will get the same total.

**TABLE 10-4  Clearinghouse transactions**

| Checks drawn on | Checks received by | | | | Total debits | Net debits |
|---|---|---|---|---|---|---|
| | Bank A | Bank B | Bank C | Bank D | | |
| Bank A . . . . . . . . . . . . . | — | 100 | 65 | 150 | 315 | — |
| Bank B . . . . . . . . . . . . . | 120 | — | 50 | 165 | 335 | 50 |
| Bank C . . . . . . . . . . . . . | 75 | 45 | — | 35 | 155 | 15 |
| Bank D . . . . . . . . . . . . . | 160 | 140 | 25 | — | 325 | — |
| Total credits . . . . . . . . . | 355 | 285 | 140 | 350 | 1,130 | — |
| Net credits . . . . . . . . . . | 40 | — | — | 25 | — | 65 |

debits for any bank equals net credits (debits) if positive (negative). After completing the clearinghouse transactions table in a matter of minutes, the Fed is informed which bank accounts are to be credited and debited. In our example, banks A and D collect $40 and $25, respectively, and banks B and C are charged $50 and $15, respectively.

While not all checks give rise to Fed float, many do. Float is a short-run random source of the base. By definition of the word *random,* the Fed watches helplessly as float varies willy-nilly. Daily fluctuations in float are large but quarterly or even monthly averages of float are more stable.

## MISCELLANEOUS ASSET AND LIABILITIES

The Federal Reserve balance sheet contains a hodgepodge of small asset and liability accounts ranging from spartan steel desks and the latest generation computers to accrued wages and salaries. In addition, the Fed's net worth or capital account is quite small. These accounts are consolidated in the accounts "miscellaneous assets" and "miscellaneous liabilities and net worth." It is not worth analyzing these items in detail. Changes in these accounts often are accompanied by corresponding changes in the base. Occasionally, however, a transaction is recorded by offsetting entries in these small accounts, leaving the base unaffected.

The small account on the Fed's balance sheet called Treasury currency, which is mainly coins and a few greenbacks, is segregated from miscellaneous assets since the consolidated balance sheet subtracts this account from Treasury currency in circulation. The Fed maintains this stockpile of coins for the convenience of banks and the public.

## TREASURY DEPOSITS AT THE FED

As you are well aware, the Treasury collects billions of dollars in taxes annually. Nevertheless, in recent years tax receipts have invariably fallen short of federal expenditures. The Treasury sells bonds to finance the deficit. For all practical purposes the accounting entries associated with the two sources of Treasury receipts, taxes and bond sales, are identical.

We begin by outlining the rationale for the Treasury's current cash management policies, which avoid the instability of the Independent Treasury system while utilizing the Fed as a fiscal agent. We then explore alternative cash management policies.

The United States government may be viewed as a huge business employing millions of people and spending and receiving billions of dollars annually. Large firms have hundreds of demand deposit accounts, and the largest business of them all has thousands, called tax and loan (T&L) accounts. T&L accounts at thousands of commercial banks and the elaborate system of transferring funds from commercial banks to the Fed is explained by the lack of synchronization between Treasury receipts and expenditures and by a seemingly impartial system of selecting the commercial banks which will get the Treasury's business. Treasury receipts from taxes and bond sales initially are redeposited in the same bank against which a check is drawn. That is, the check which you mail to the Treasury on April 15 because insufficient taxes were withheld is forwarded by the Treasury to your bank.

FIGURE 10-6   **Treasury deposits tax or bond receipts in bank**

| | Your Bank |
| --- | --- |
| | Treasury tax and loan account + 100 |
| | Private check deposits            − 100 |

A small proportion of taxes is paid directly by individuals. Unincorporated enterprises and corporations forward withheld income and social security taxes and pay business income taxes at various times during the year. Regardless who makes payment for taxes, the banks credit the Treasury's account and debit the payer's account. An advantage of this system is the minimum impact of taxes and bond sales on individual banks. Government receipts do not redistribute deposits and reserves among banks.[10] To prevent possible loss to the Treasury from bank failures, banks are required to own U.S. securities as collateral against T&L accounts.

From the viewpoint of the entire banking system and the money supply, this system mitigates the effects of unsynchronized receipts and payments. Treasury receipts must *temporarily* reduce the money supply, which is defined to exclude Treasury deposits. Conversely, Treasury expenditures must *temporarily* increase the money supply. Therefore, whenever Treasury receipts are greater (less) than payments, the money supply falls (rises). According to the last balance sheet, the money supply

---

[10] The statement in the text is not completely accurate. Most, but not all, banks qualify as *special depositories,* that is, have T&L accounts.

falls by $100 if the Treasury is not spending during the tax payment period. Reserves, however, are unchanged when the Treasury keeps its funds in T&L accounts. Were the Treasury to deposit the tax receipts at the Fed, or place the receipts in a cash warehouse reminiscent of the Independent Treasury, the money supply *and* reserves would decline. See Figure 10–7.

FIGURE 10–7  Treasury deposits tax receipts at the Fed

| Commercial Banks | | Fed | |
|---|---|---|---|
| Deposits at<br> Fed  − 100 | Check<br> deposits  − 100 | | Deposits of<br> banks  − 100<br>Treasury<br> deposits  + 100 |

Larger (smaller) Treasury deposits at the Fed decrease (increase) the base. Figure 10–7 does not show the disruptive multiple contraction of private deposits that would follow the reserve loss. To prevent violent money supply fluctuations, the Treasury allows its T&L accounts to rise during tax payment periods.

In principle, the Treasury could make payments by writing checks against its T&L accounts. If it did this, Treasury receipts and expenditures would affect the money supply but not the monetary base. Treasury cash management is facilitated, however, by a single fiscal agent, the Fed. Treasury T&L accounts at the thousands of banks are feeder accounts for the Treasury's account at the Fed, against which all payments are made. Figure 10–8 illustrates the Treasury's cash management policies.

The relative size of the numbers in lines 1 and 2 reflects unsynchronized receipts and expenditures. Taxes are collected during some-

FIGURE 10–8  (1) Treasury deposits receipts at banks, (2) Transfers anticipated amount spent to Fed, and (3) Spends by drawing its deposits at the Fed

| Commercial Banks | | Fed | |
|---|---|---|---|
| (1) | Tax and loan<br> accounts  + 100<br>Private check<br> deposits  − 100 | (1) | |
| (2) Deposits at<br> Fed  − 20 | Tax and loan<br> accounts  − 20 | (2) | Treasury<br> deposits  + 20<br>Deposits of<br> banks  − 20 |
| (3) Deposits at<br> Fed  + 18 | Private check<br> deposits  + 18 | (3) | Treasury<br> deposits  − 18<br>Deposits of<br> banks  + 18 |

what widely spaced discrete time intervals while expenditures occur at a more or less continuous rate. During a tax collection period, receipts to T&L accounts are $100 (line 1) while anticipated expenditures are much less, only $20 in our example. *The Treasury transfers to its Fed account (line 2) an amount equal to anticipated expenditures.* The T&L account increase of $80 (lines 1 and 2) equals the amount receipts exceed anticipated expenditures. Assuming the Treasury correctly anticipates its payments, debits to Treasury deposits at the Fed exactly match credits, leaving the Treasury account and the base unchanged. In other words, Treasury expenditures of $20 are recorded by reversing the entries in line 2. Figure 10–8 assumes that the Treasury overestimates expenditures by $2; according to line 3 expenditures equal only $18. When the Treasury overestimates (underestimates) its expenditures, additions to Treasury deposits at the Fed are greater (less) than subtractions, Treasury deposits rise (fall), and bank reserves and the monetary base decrease (increase).

The Treasury's payment projection are often incorrect. If nothing else, the time interval between receipt and deposit of Treasury checks by individuals is not constant. More important, daily Treasury expenditures do vary substantially. It would be impractical to phone banks across the country every day to tell them the amount to be transferred from T&L accounts to the Treasury's account at the Fed. The Treasury has established a schedule indicating when transfers are to be made. Since the schedule covers some future time interval and is drawn up before the exact dates of payments are known, Treasury deposits at the Fed vary in spite of attempts to maintain a constant level. Nonetheless, the system of maintaining deposits in the banking system lessens the variation of the base associated with unsynchronous Treasury receipts and expenditures. Treasury deposits are similar to discounts in that (1) their variability is largely unintentional, (2) they are small relative to the base, and (3) during short periods of time they change significantly, both absolutely and relative to changes in the base necessary to achieve moderate (2 to 8 percent) annual rates of monetary growth.

In view of our subsequent discussion of fiscal policy, it is worth emphasizing that government spending and taxes only temporarily affect the money supply and need not have any permanent effect. Suppose the government shifts from a balanced budget to a deficit because either taxes are cut or expenditures rise. Assuming the Treasury sells bonds to the public in order to finance the deficit, the money supply decline during the bond sales program is quickly reversed when the proceeds are expended. Similarly, a Treasury surplus used to retire the national debt has no permanent effect on the money supply.

The Treasury practiced the cash management policy just outlined until 1967 and then adopted it again in 1978. In the interim the Treasury did not vary its T&L accounts in order to cushion the effect of unsynchronized receipts and expenditures on the monetary base. Instead, all receipts were almost immediately deposited at the Fed, causing the base to fall precipitously, *ceteris paribus*. The base rebounded slowly as the receipts were spent. Why did the Treasury manage its funds between 1967 and 1978 by imitating the Independent Treasury system? Critics finally convinced the Treasury in 1967 that commercial banks were robbing it, in a perfectly legal manner of course. By transferring to the Fed only the funds it anticipates spending, the Treasury's T&L accounts at banks were variable and, most important to bankers, quite large on average. *Banks earn income on the assets made possible by T&L accounts.* (Remember the balance sheet identity.) Synchronization problems aside, if the Treasury were to maintain deposits only at the Fed *while the Fed provides the same base,* the Fed's U.S. government securities account would increase by the average amount of T&L accounts at commercial banks.[11] This is precisely what the critics wanted. The Fed instead of commercial banks would earn the interest on the securities. The Independent Treasury system produced monetary instability when there was no central bank to offset withdrawals of cash and reserves from the banking system.

After 10 years of maintaining virtually all its deposits at the Fed, commercial banks finally recognized that the Treasury indeed was determined to tap every source of income. If the banks were again to have large T&L accounts, they had to devise a way of sharing with the Treasury the income made possible by these accounts. The Treasury favored a cooperative arrangement with the banks as it realized that the policy of immediately depositing receipts at the Fed had a disruptive effect on the base. A thorny legal issue arose: precisely how should the Treasury/banks income-sharing agreement be expressed so as not to suggest a kickback, collusion, or some other action illegal if one of parties were not the Treasury? Although interest payment on demand deposits was prohibited in 1978, the Solomons decided that banks could pay the Treasury interest on its T&L accounts because they no longer were demand deposits. T&L accounts are a "special" account. One advantage of being the regulator is having the ability to classify items to one's benefit. Unable for political reasons to exempt itself from the law prohibiting interest payment on demand deposits, the Treasury simply changed the name of its deposits, which now bear interest. The authorities extended this ploy to *consumers* by legalizing NOW accounts. Firms still cannot earn interest on their check deposits.

Selected nonbanks, that is, foreign governments and international organizations, also maintain accounts at the Fed. From the viewpoint of monetary control, nonbank deposits at the Fed are similar to Treasury deposits. Transfers of deposits from commercial banks to the Fed, whether by the Treasury or selected nonbanks, invariably affect the re-

[11] In other words, to prevent the reserve loss that would occur from Treasury withdrawals of T&L accounts from commercial banks to the Fed, the Fed can buy government securities from banks, thereby enlarging its portfolio at the expense of banks.

serve components of the base. Nonbank deposits are an uncontrolled use of the base. The Fed selects the organizations whose deposits it will accept. After doing this, the organization manages its deposit balances without Fed interference. Just as your deposits are not controlled by your bank, foreign deposits at the Fed are not controlled by the Fed.

Having completed discussion of the Fed's nonbase accounts, we now turn to the Treasury's balance sheet.

## GOLD, GOLD CERTIFICATES, AND OTHER INTERNATIONAL ASSETS

Gold has long been an important asset in settling international accounts and is the major Treasury asset. The Treasury's posture on gold over the past 50 years has covered the whole map. Due to repayments and other technical reasons the Treasury is occasionally alloted some gold nowadays. On balance, however, it is a seller of gold. The Treasury currently is unable to buy gold because its official price is much lower than the world market price.[12] Since there is no telling what the Treasury's position on gold will be as you read this book, and since official prices change by edict, a brief review of gold policy is in order before analyzing the effect of gold transactions.

Prior to 1933 the United States was on a gold standard. Gold circulated freely as money and was the basic form into which all other types of money could generally be converted. Gold certificates and other forms of currency circulated because they were more convenient than gold coins. Paper bills are less likely than gold coins to cause holes in your pockets. Anyone could buy or sell one fine ounce of gold at the Treasury for $20.67 paper money. The years 1933 and 1934 were ones of infamy for gold bugs. A series of Executive Orders devalued the dollar by 40.94 percent in terms of gold (to $35 per ounce of gold), demonetized gold coins, and transferred title of the Fed's gold to the Treasury in exchange for gold certificates. Private gold ownership was forbidden except in limited amounts for licensed purposes—for the manufacture of jewelry, teeth, and for a few other uses. The Treasury bought gold from domestic and foreign suppliers but sold unlimited amounts of gold at $35 per ounce only to official foreign organizations such as central banks. In terms of Figure 10–9, $D_{P+F}$ and $S_{P+F}$ are the private domestic and foreign demand and supply curves, respectively. Prior to 1933 the gold standard committed the Treasury to make up any excess supply or demand for gold at $20.67 per ounce. In our graph the Treasury purchased AB. The 1933 and 1934 Executive Orders raised the gold support price and reduced demand, illustrated by the dashed curve, by placing restrictions on gold usage.

---

[12] In January 1976, the "official" gold price was formally abolished at the International Monetary Fund meetings in Kingston, Jamaica. However, the history of gold makes it convenient to entertain the fiction of an official price.

Treasury gold purchases jumped to CD. Until 1967 incremental demand for gold at $35 per ounce was less than annual gold production or could easily be met from the coffers of the world's central bankers. Consequently, except for a few isolated instances, the free market price of gold stayed at the official price throughout this period, and central bankers on balance augmented their gold pool.

The modified gold standard of the 1930s remained essentially unchanged until 1967–68, when increases in the worldwide private demand for gold at $35 per ounce began to significantly outstrip the production of gold. In terms of Figure 10–9, higher wages and other costs made gold

**FIGURE 10–9  Gold standard demand and supply of gold**

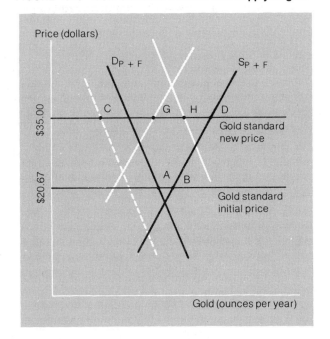

production more expensive, shifting the supply curve inward, and higher prices for other commodities at home and abroad made gold an attractive substitute, shifting the demand curve outward. The demand and supply curves intersected above $35. Although the Treasury did not sell gold to the private sector, other central banks did. As foreign central banks lost gold to meet their citizen's request, they made more frequent calls on the Treasury in order to replenish their dwindling gold supplies. The Treasury and the central banks of a majority of the world's leading countries were jointly drawn into a loosing proposition. Frustrated by their losses of gold to the private sector (GH in Figure 10–9), as they attempted to maintain the official price, the world's central bankers finally decided in March 1968, amid much fanfare, to throw in the towel. In brief, like spoiled children who had taken a licking, they picked up what chips were still theirs and refused to play any longer. They agreed in blood not to sell or buy any more gold to the nasty private speculators. All transactions within the charmed circle of central bankers took place at the pegged official price. As for the private speculators, they could do as they jolly well wished. With the sore losers out of the game, the free market price of gold fluctuates with the tides of private supply and demand, at times hitting unthought-of-heights. So long as the two circles do not come in contact with each other or with intermediaries, the official and free market prices go their separate ways, like a divorced couple.[13]

Policy changes have occurred more frequently in the past few years. On August 15, 1971, what many thought impossible became reality. In a televised speech President Richard M. Nixon announced that the Treasury would stop playing the gold game even within the charmed circle. The dollar became totally inconvertible as all U.S. Treasury gold purchases and sales were suspended. To realign foreign exchange rates, in December 1971 the Treasury devalued the U.S. dollar, that is, raised the official price of gold, to $38 per ounce. Since the Treasury maintained its hands-off-gold policy, the devaluation was largely symbolic. The dollar was further devalued in 1973 (to $42.22 per ounce of gold); ownership of gold no longer was a crime on January 1, 1975; and the Treasury resumed modest gold sales to the public. Treasury gold sales have been insufficient to drive the price of gold to anywhere near the official price, $42.22 per ounce. The official price of gold is the Treasury's *buying* price, at which no purchases are made. The Treasury has not let the official price interfere with its sales, which are made at market prices. In summary, the Treasury's gold position has shifted from (a) unlimited purchases and sales to all comers; to (b) unlimited purchases and sales to special groups; to (c) no transactions; and to (d) Treasury initiated sales but no purchases. While we are not forecasting a purchases and no sales policy, the only policy so far not followed by the Treasury, let us show the effect of gold purchases on balance sheets. Gold sales simply reverse the entries below.

Suppose miners, gold speculators, or foreign governments bring gold worth $100 to the Fed. The first line of the balance sheets in Figure 10–10

---

[13] Is gold that different from other commodities? Consider what would happen if your local supermarket advertised steak at $1.09 a pound. Earnest citizens would quickly clean the shelves of steak. Suppose the supermarket refused to restock the shelves. Who would be criticized, the supermarket for false advertising or the earnest citizens? The answer is clear, yet the gold mystique is so strong that in similar circumstances the private participants typically are derogatorily characterized as speculators, while the central bankers are defenders of the currency.

**FIGURE 10–10** **(1) Gold purchase, (2) Treasury issues gold certificates, and (3) Treasury sells bond**

| Treasury | | | | Federal Reserve | | | |
|---|---|---|---|---|---|---|---|
| (1) Gold | +100 | Treasury cash | +100 | (1) | | Treasury deposits | −100 |
| | | | | | | Deposits of banks | +100 |
| (2) | | Gold certifi- cates | +100 | (2) Gold certifi- cates | +100 | Treasury deposits | +100 |
| | | Treasury cash | −100 | | | | |
| (3) | | | | (3) | | Treasury deposits | +100 |
| | | | | | | Deposits of banks | −100 |

| Commercial Banking System | | | | |
|---|---|---|---|---|
| (1) Deposits at Fed | +100 | Check deposits | +100 |
| (2) | | | |
| (3) Deposits at Fed | −100 | Check deposits | −100 |

illustrates the impact of gold purchases. Unlike you and me, the Fed follows the 1930s laws and does not own gold, which is purchased on behalf of the Treasury. Thus, the Fed debits Treasury deposits and credits deposits of banks when the sellers of gold deposit the Fed's check in their commercial banks.[14] The Fed notifies the Treasury that it is the proud owner of $100 additional gold, and the Treasury debits gold and credits Treasury cash. While it may appear that the Treasury should credit Treasury deposits at the Fed instead of Treasury cash, the former account does not even appear on the Treasury's *monetary account* balance sheet, the incomplete Treasury balance sheet appropriate for analyzing the monetary base. The Treasury's deposits at the Fed arise from its fiscal (tax and borrowing) authority. When the Treasury purchases gold by drawing on its Fed deposits, the Treasury's fiscal net worth, which is not illustrated in Figure 10–10, decreases but its monetary net worth, Treasury cash, increases. Recall the earlier section indicating that Treasury cash is a misnomer.

---

[14] Private sellers of gold must deposit the Fed's check in commercial banks but foreign governments may have their deposit accounts at the Fed credited. However, foreign governments hold the proceeds of gold sales in their Fed accounts for only a short period, if at all. Gold is rarely sold to permanently increase foreign balances at the Fed. Foreign governments typically will purchase interest-bearing dollar-denominated assets such as Treasury securities with the proceeds of gold sales. When foreign governments do this, the first line of Figure 10–10 shows the impact of gold purchases.

Looking at line 1 of the Treasury and Fed balance sheets, *gold, a source of the base, increased and so did bank reserves*. The changes in the two uses, Treasury cash and Treasury deposits, cancel each other, the former increasing and the latter decreasing.

Gold purchases induce subsequent entries because the Treasury would be unable to pay its bills with the reduced deposits. It has two alternatives. First, the Treasury can have its account credited by selling the Fed claims on the gold, called gold certificates, as illustrated on line 2 of Figure 10–10. Issuance of gold certificates has no effect on the base. Table 10–2 shows that the Treasury now cannot afford the luxury of a large monetary net worth and has issued gold certificates equal to the gold stock. Second, the Treasury can replenish its balances at the Fed and maintain its monetary net worth by issuing bonds. As just indicated, tax and bond transactions do not appear on the Treasury monetary account balance sheet. Line 3 assumes that nonbanks draw on their check deposits to buy the bonds, which increases Treasury deposits at the Fed and reduces deposits of banks. Of course, bank purchases of the bonds would also reduce reserves. Issuance of bonds to finance gold purchases creates a wedge between the gold stock and certificates. The difference between gold and gold certificates is called sterilized gold, an appropriate term because gold purchases increase the base and the failure to issue gold certificates *while maintaining constant Treasury balances at the Fed* decreases the base. Sterilized gold is also called free gold as certificates equal to this amount can be issued. At various times the Treasury sterilized substantial amounts of gold to prevent reserve increases.

The mechanics of gold transactions would be simplified if the Fed bought gold directly. In such an event, the Fed would debit a gold account and credit deposits of banks. This is equivalent to the end result of lines 1 and 2, Figure 10–10. Can the Fed, like the Treasury, sterilize gold if its policies call for an unchanged quantity of reserves? Surely. The Fed instead of the Treasury sells bonds. In either case the private sector acquires additional bonds in exchange for gold. The possible desirability of sterilizing gold is no handicap to Fed ownership of this international asset. Perhaps the straightforward purchase of gold by the Fed is not practiced because it would diminish the mysterious aura of gold. In what is a monument to creative accounting, the Treasury buys gold by selling claims (certificates) on the gold to the Fed. What happens if the Fed wishes to exercise its claim and acquire gold? It cannot exercise the claim! If gold were purchased directly, it would be obvious to everyone that as far as its effects on the base are concerned, gold transactions are no different than purchase and sale of any other commodity.

The Fed follows the more direct approach when buying or selling other assets used to settle international balance of payments, for example, special drawing rights (SDRs) and foreign currency assets such as German mark or Swiss franc securities.[15] SDRs are created by the International Monetary Fund and are sometimes referred to as paper gold. These assets appear on line F of the Fed's balance sheet, Table 10–1. When the sellers of these assets deposit the Fed's check at commercial banks, the Fed debits special drawing rights certificates and credits bank reserve deposits.

Although the Treasury decided in mid-1971 to withdraw from the gold market, it purchased very small amounts of gold thereafter in response to prior commitments. Yet during the subsequent years the value of the gold stock reported in the Federal Reserve *Bulletin* rose significantly more than could be explained by the modest purchases. Have we uncovered some financial irregularity of interest to the General Accounting Office? No, the Treasury just partially tapped a potentially huge source of the base. Remember that in late 1971 and in 1973 the Treasury devalued the dollar in terms of gold. The higher official price of gold meant that the same physical quantity of gold was now carried at a higher value. If the Treasury had simply let its net worth increase or had issued gold certificates *and* let its deposits at the Fed increase, then the base would have remained constant. Consolidated assets (gold) increase but so do other liabilities (Treasury cash or Treasury deposits at the Fed). Instead, the Treasury issued gold certificates and paid its bills with the temporarily swollen deposits at the Fed. When the Treasury checks were deposited at banks, the base increased. In essence, the Treasury printed money to finance its expenditures. The official price of gold in 1981 was less than one tenth the market price. Will the Treasury raise the official price and use an accounting gimmick to finance its expenditures? Let the Treasury be aware that we are looking over its shoulder.

Under current policy the Treasury controls this source of the base. It cannot buy gold because its official and buying price is substantially below the world market price. The Treasury certainly would find eager buyers for the entire gold stock if it agreed to sell at the official price. The Treasury prefers small sales at world market prices. Most important, all the sales have been strictly at the Treasury's initiative. The Treasury talks to the Fed, which knows of planned gold sales well in advance. As matters now stand, the monetary authorities exert direct control over this source of the base. This may not be true in the future, and it certainly was not true prior to 1971. The association of gold with international transactions is enough to suggest that events in this country *and* abroad influence gold flows. However much one thinks the Fed determines events in this country, attributing to the Fed a major impact on foreign events is a flight of

---

[15] In fact, SDRs are handled somewhat analogously to gold. However, because we want to abstract from the allocation of SDRs by the IMF to the Treasury, which has no effect on the money supply, it is convenient to assume the Treasury does not participate in SDR sales by other countries.

fancy. People and gold responded to Nazism by fleeing to the United States. While the Fed has often been criticized, and justly so, associating the Fed with Nazism would be going too far. Throughout much of our history the Fed had little direct and immediate impact on gold flows. Unlike float, gold is a relatively long-lasting uncontrolled source of the base. The direction of gold flows is not reversed quickly. The United States gained gold throughout the 1930s and lost it during the 1960s.

## TREASURY CURRENCY OUTSTANDING AND TREASURY CURRENCY IN CIRCULATION

Treasury currency outstanding measures the net amount of Treasury currency issued, whether in circulation or still in the Treasury's vault. The rationale for this account has puzzled many. Treasury currency is an example of Treasury debt. Therefore the liability account "Treasury currency in circulation" in Table 10–2 is not surprising. But why is Treasury currency outstanding an asset? The answer relies on two facts: (1) the Treasury gets something when it creates money, as emphasized in Chapter 2, and (2) the Treasury has fiscal as well as monetary powers. What does the Treasury acquire when it prints and spends money? There is no unambiguous answer. The vast majority of the federal government's assets arise from its fiscal powers. Any attempt to segregate assets according to the source of finance, tax collection or money creation, is bound to be arbitrary. The Treasury is not different than you or me in this respect. Suppose you work part-time at the library and dining hall, and purchase a ticket to a rock concert and a record album. Who acquired the ticket, you the librarian or you the cook? And who owns the record? Clearly, any attempt to match the source of receipts and expenditures invites criticism. Instead of listing an arbitrary set of assets acquired by the Treasury as a monetary authority, the value of all assets so acquired are recorded in a common account, Treasury currency outstanding. That is, Treasury currency outstanding includes whatever assets were acquired with the Treasury currency in circulation. Name-calling does not solve much; a rose by any other name smells just as sweet. Balance sheets show assets and liabilities at some instant in time. When did the Treasury acquire what we do not know it acquired? When is Treasury currency outstanding debited? The only solution is to debit the account at the time currency is printed. Thus Treasury currency outstanding also includes currency printed but still on hand at the Treasury.

The above ideas are made more concrete by showing the accounting associated with Treasury currency creation. For simplicity, we assume money creation is costless. None of the principles illustrated are altered by recognizing the small cost of minting coins. The immediate impact of minting coins is shown on the first line of Figure 10–11. That is, line 1

**FIGURE 10–11** **(1) Treasury mints coins, (2) Treasury spends currency directly, (3) Treasury transfers currency to the Fed, and (4) Treasury spends deposits received in exchange for currency**

| Treasury | | Fed | |
|---|---|---|---|
| (1) Treasury currency outstanding +100 | Treasury cash +100 | (1) | |
| (2) | Treasury cash −100 Treasury currency in circulation +100 | (2) | |
| (3) | Treasury cash −100 Treasury currency in circulation +100 | (3) Treasury currency +100 | Treasury deposits +100 |
| (4) | | (4) | Treasury deposits −100 Deposits of banks +100 |

shows the effect of money creation while it is still in the Treasury's possession.

Keeping recently minted coins in the vault has no effect on any economic variable. The Treasury created an asset and credits its net worth since the currency (coinage) is not yet in circulation. A source and use of the base increase by the same amount. Of course, the Treasury does not mint coins to keep them in the vault; coins are minted to be spent directly or indirectly. Line 2 assumes the coins are spent directly on some item, increasing the currency component of the base. The coins more likely will be spent indirectly. The Fed maintains a stockpile of coins to meet the demands of banks and the public. Suppose a larger demand for coins depleted the Fed stockpile so it requests additional coins from the Treasury. Such a request is the most common impetus for currency creation. As expected, transporting cash from the Treasury to the Fed, as recorded on line 3, has no effect on the base. The Treasury's net worth fell because from its viewpoint more currency is in circulation. However, the currency is held by the Fed, which credits the Treasury deposits. Line 4 assumes the Treasury spends the deposits which were received in exchange for coins. As individuals deposit the Treasury checks, bank reserves increase.

As the name implies, Treasury currency is minted/printed exclusively by the Treasury. Therefore, Treasury currency outstanding, which changes when additional currency is created, is a controlled source that has a somewhat delayed effect on the base. During the short period between printing and disbursal, Treasury currency outstanding is neutralized by a use, Treasury cash. When the currency is spent directly or indirectly, the base increases.[16]

Although the Fed's stockpiling of Treasury coins and its own notes does not affect the base, this important housekeeping chore deserves more than the brief mention in the penultimate paragraph. The Fed's stockpile lets you transform any denomination of old limp currency into new crisp currency. Banks ship excess vault cash to the Fed, which credits their deposit account. Dirty bills are shredded, burned, and reissued. When banks are short on vault cash, the entries are reversed except that banks receive clean money. (This is *not* an example of laundering money, however.) Millions of dollars flow to and from the Fed daily as banks shift the composition of their reserves from vault cash to deposits and adjust the denominations of their vault cash.

## TREASURY HOLDINGS OF FED NOTES AND TREASURY CASH

The Treasury holds Federal Reserve notes for the same reasons individuals and firms do; Fed notes are a convenient means of payment for some transactions. We may ignore illustrating how this Treasury account changes since it does not appear separately in the consolidated Fed and Treasury balance sheet.

Analysis of all other accounts in a double-entry bookkeeping system obviates independent analysis of the final account, Treasury cash. We already indicated all the events which cause Treasury cash to adjust. It is desirable, nevertheless, to show that Treasury Cash does correspond to monetary net worth as alleged. A rearrangement of the Treasury's balance sheet, labeled Table 10–5, and our previous discussion imply that Treasury cash generally equals the Treasury's holdings of currency, including its own, and free gold, which was positive for many years but currently is zero. But its currency holdings and free gold equals the amount the Treasury qua monetary authority can spend without borrowing, which is what

---

[16] Since the Treasury always could issue coins, Figure 10–11 may *incorrectly* suggest that currency was elastic prior to the creation of the Fed. Currency was not elastic because the Treasury could readily and cheaply mint only a few types of coins, for example, pennies, while it specified that all types and denominations of currency could be convertible one for the other. If the Treasury attempted to place only additional pennies in circulation when the demand for currency in general increased, some pennies would quickly return to the Treasury in exchange for greenbacks and gold coins. The public wanted more currency, not just more pennies. Since greenbacks were restricted and gold coins could not be readily produced, the Treasury was unable to put the pennies in circulation and provide an elastic currency. The ability of the Fed to create complimentary notes that can be exchanged for Treasury currency makes total currency completely elastic today. This line of reasoning indicates that currency was less elastic prior to 1933 when the United States was on a strict gold standard. Paper money could not be expanded too fast then because individuals would exchange paper money for gold, drawing down the Treasury's limited supply.

**TABLE 10–5   A rearrangement of the Treasury monetary account balance sheet**

| | |
|---|---|
| (N) Treasury currency outstanding − | |
| (Q) Treasury currency in circulation | = Treasury currency at Treasury |
| + (O) Fed notes at Treasury | = Fed notes at Treasury |
| + (M) Gold − (P) gold certificates | = Free gold |
| Total | = (R) Treasury cash |

net worth or wealth measures. In other words, Treasury cash is the amount the Treasury could spend without printing additional currency (borrowing from the public) or reducing Treasury deposits at the Fed (borrowing from itself qua fiscal authority).

## SUMMARY

To save the reader from having to thumb back to the beginning of the chapter, we conveniently reproduce Table 10–3 with an additional column showing changes in sources and uses between December 1979 and January 1980. Economists cannot agree on terminology. Table 10–6 shows that the monetary base equation is also called the base, Federal Reserve credit, and related items.[17] If the table does not look much like an equation, on a long horizontal line write the sources (positive sign) and uses (negative sign) and place an equality sign before the base. Table 10–6 includes a memorandum not derived directly from the Treasury and Fed balance sheets. Banks report their vault cash positions to the Fed and Federal Deposit Insurance Corporation. From these reports and the Treasury and Fed balance sheets currency held by the public is calculated as a residual.

The reader should be able to construct the monetary base equation. The exact numbers in Table 10–6 are unimportant; they vary from day to day. What is important to gain from the table is knowledge about what transactions augment or reduce the base, the relative size of the accounts, and above all, why each account varies. Does float change because of con-

---

[17] The Fed publishes a table entitled member bank reserves, Federal Reserve credit and related items, or something similar. (The precise title of the table has varied recently.) The Fed table differs from our table by shifting currency held by the public *and* banks up "above the line" to join other uses. In terms of the balance sheet identity, Bank reserve deposits = Assets − Other liabilities − Currency held by the public and banks. Continued publication of this table over the past 20 years is a sign of a sclerotic Fed. The table was somewhat useful prior to 1960, when only deposits at the Fed counted as member bank reserves. Now that currency also counts as reserves, the Fed should not highlight one component of reserves. Again, even prior to 1960 the table was only somewhat useful. The Fed's table is convenient when one focuses on *member bank* deposits, but they are no different from nonmember deposits from the viewpoint of their effects on GNP. Our emphasis on money, which includes currency held by public and member and nonmember deposits, makes the monetary base table more appropriate.

**TABLE 10–6  Monetary base equation; the base, Federal Reserve credit, and related items December 31, 1979 and change from December 1979 to January 1980** ($ millions, monthly average of daily figures)

| | December 31, 1979 | Change, December 1979– January 1980 |
|---|---|---|
| Sources: | | |
| U.S. government securities ................... | $126,167 | −38 |
| Discounts to banks .......................... | 2,158 | −439 |
| Float ...................................... | 6,767 | −674 |
| Miscellaneous Fed assets ................... | 5,613 | −2 |
| Gold ...................................... | 11,112 | +44 |
| Special drawing rights certificates ............ | 1,800 | +264 |
| Treasury currency outstanding ............... | 12,947 | +65 |
| Total ................................. | $166,564 | −780 |
| Uses: | | |
| Treasury deposits .......................... | $  4,075 | +147 |
| Foreign and other deposits ................... | 1,841 | +92 |
| Miscellaneous Fed liabilities and net worth ..... | 4,957 | −269 |
| Treasury cash ............................. | 426 | +15 |
| Total ................................. | $ 11,299 | −15 |
| Monetary base = Sources − Uses .............. | $155,265 | $  −765 |
| Monetary base composition from Fed and Treasury balance sheets | | |
| Bank reserve deposits ...................... | $ 29,792 | −904 |
| Currency held by public *and* banks ........... | $125,473 | +139 |
| Monetary base composition from Fed, Treasury, and banks balance sheets | | |
| Bank reserves: Deposits at Fed and vault cash .. | | $  +735 |
| Currency in the hands of the public ........... | | $−1,500 |

scious Fed policy or because of some random factors? Is the gold stock immediately and directly affected by Fed and Treasury policy? Familiarity with Table 10–6 is essential in order to answer a controversial question in monetary economics: Can the Fed control the quantity of money?

The monetary base equation indicates that the monetary authorities do not have perfect control over the base, where perfect control means that a change occurs if, and only if, the Fed initiates some positive action. Treasury currency outstanding, being the amount of currency minted by the Treasury, and U.S. government securities, which is the cumulative net amount of open-market operations, are directly controlled by the monetary authorities. Gold currently is under Treasury control, but future gold policy is uncertain. The other accounts in Table 10–6 are sources or uses of the base which are not directly controlled by the Fed. These uncontrolled accounts typically are quite small; U.S. government securities is the overwhelming source of the base. However, monthly and even longer period *changes* in these accounts are significant compared to *changes* in the base. According to Table 10–6, the reduction in float accounted for nearly 90 percent of the decrease in the base between December 1979 and January 1980. In other months float is virtually unchanged, and discounts or Treasury deposits at the Fed explain large base changes. The Fed cannot set some dial, take a Rip Van Winkle nap, and expect the base or the money supply multiplier to remain constant until it awakens. The Fed has to continuously manipulate some dials to control the money supply.

### Defensive open-market operations

Open-market policy is the dial the Fed manipulates to counteract the effect of (1) uncontrolled sources and uses on the base and (2) currency ratio shifts on the money supply. Such open-market operations are called defensive. That is, *defensive open-market operations counteract uncontrolled factors and keep the base and money supply on target.* When the currency ratio increases and bank reserves fall, defensive open-market purchases replenish reserves and prevent a multiple contraction. When an uncontrolled source increases the base, the Fed sells securities to decrease the base. The Fed buys securities when uncontrolled uses reduce the base. Is the Fed successful? Can it counteract the uncontrolled factors and keep the base on target? Yes, provided the target period is not unreasonably short. The Fed cannot react instantly. Defensive open-market operation do not keep the base at its desired value minute by minute or hour by hour. Given an appropriate period, however, Table 10–6 correctly suggests that the base will equal its desired value. The U.S. government securities account overwhelms all other items in the monetary base equation. Additional evidence on control is presented in Chapter 13, where we analyze the meaning of control carefully and reintroduce the multiplier for a complete analysis of the money supply. Control of the base is only the first step in controlling money.

## QUESTIONS

1. How is the monetary base equation constructed? What is another name for the monetary base equation?

2. What are the Treasury's two monetary powers?

3. Are discounts at the Fed a source or use of the base? Are discounts important in explaining either the level or change in the base?

4. What is float? Why does it arise? What is its effect on the base? What events cause float to vary?

5. Describe the Treasury's current money management policy. What is the impact of Treasury receipts on individual banks and the banking system? Compare the Treasury's current money management policies with those of the mid 1970s.

6. Briefly summarize U.S. gold policy since 1930.

7. What is sterilized, or free, gold? How does one get free gold?

8. How can Treasury currency outstanding be an asset of the Treasury when the Treasury issued the currency?

9. Define Treasury cash. When will it be unaffected by gold purchases and currency creation?

10. For each of the following items state whether it is a source or use of the base. If it is a source or use, state whether an *increase* in the item causes the base to increase or decrease, and state whether the item is controlled or uncontrolled by the Fed. The items are: (*a*) check deposits at banks, (*b*) Eurodollars, (*c*) Treasury deposits at the Fed, (*d*) Treasury deposits at commercial banks (T&L accounts), (*e*) foreign deposits at the Fed, (*f*) U.S. government securities held by the Fed, (*g*) U.S. government securities held by commercial banks, and (*h*) gold held by dealers.

11. Define defensive open-market operations.

---

## appendix · Criticism of the Treasury's deposit management program

The Treasury's deposit management program as outlined in the chapter has become the source of a minor controversy in financial circles. Should the Treasury eliminate the impact of tax collections and bond sales on individual banks by depositing receipts at banks on which the checks are drawn? While this system seems most impartial, critics of the Treasury argue that it unduly favors large banks. The Treasury's current system does insure that banks which have the deposits of security buyers and corporations and other employers will get the government's banking business. Critics argue that this class of banks tends to be large, and that small banks are discriminated against.[1] If the Treasury were to distribute its T&L accounts among banks according to who bore the burden of the tax rather than who wrote a check for the tax, small banks would get a larger share of T&L accounts. While the current system may not be totally impartial, attempting to ascertain with any great accuracy who bears the burden of taxes is a hopeless task. What other reforms have been proposed? What bankers should get the government's business, allowing them to make more loans or acquire other assets?

Some have recommended that T&L accounts be maintained in banks that perform, or agree to perform, socially desirable functions. For example, T&L accounts might be held in minority banks or banks that lend to

---

[1] The Treasury has a schedule for withdrawals of deposits from banks to the Fed. The turnover of Treasury deposits is more rapid at large than small banks. Although large banks may initially acquire an unduly large proportion of Treasury deposit, the more frequent calls on T&L accounts at large banks tend to reduce average Treasury deposits. Nevertheless, critics argue the Treasury favors large banks.

minorities, banks that agree to use larger government deposits to make additional mortgages or loans for antipollution equipment, and so on. The government spends billions for various social programs. Deposits could be maintained where they will be most beneficial to society, perhaps thereby reducing tax burdens and the direct funding of social programs, or helping finance other socially desirable projects. While the critics' proposal is reminiscent of the Jacksonian "pet bank" scheme, it need not be equally sinister. The Treasury transferred its deposits from the Second Bank of the United States to politically selected private banks solely for the *personal* detriment of the former and aggrandizement of the latter. Critics of the Treasury's current deposit management policies are quite differently motivated. They are not interested in enhancing any particular bank and group of stockholders. Indeed, the critics want banks to distribute to society the benefits of enlarged deposits and loans.

The critics in turn have their critics. Some oppose the "reform" proposal on the grounds that determination of "socially desirable programs" is hardly objective. While this is indeed so, Congress makes such decisions daily in agreeing to fund one program and not another. Congress would continue to decide which programs are socially desirable, with banks simply acting as agents. Those posing as defenders of objectivism and the scientific approach often do so because they fear defeat for their pet programs and yet another victory for the opposition. Government is "too big" when it funds programs you oppose and cuts those you favor. A decision on the merits on the reform proposals should not depend solely on one's estimate of the likelihood that Congress will "correctly" evaluate socially useful programs. However large the concensus and however meritorious the programs funded, the reform proposal does run counter to the "sunshine" approach which keep things in the open for ready inspection. Taxpayers should be aware of the benefits and all costs of a project in order to accurately determine its desirability. When projects are funded indirectly, such as giving the government's business to those banks that support a project, it is difficult, if not next to impossible, to estimate total cost. If government deposits are used to make mortgages, for example, the cost of such a program is the smaller loans and higher interest rates which nonhomeowners pay as a consequence. Subsidizing new homeowners with taxes levied on the rest of society makes clearer precisely what is involved.

If the Treasury deposits proposal sounds farfetched, note that the government is already using the banking system to finance small businesses and other socially desirable groups. Direct loans by the Small Business Administration are small compared to bank loans guaranteed by that agency. Political rhetoric favoring the sunshine approach notwithstanding, the trend towards using government regulation, guarantees, and credit schemes as a means of allocating resources is explained precisely by their small budgetary impact and obscure effects. In Chapter 7 we met Fanny

Mae, Ginnie Mae, and Freddie Mac, the affectionate names of governmental agencies established to increase the resources allocated to housing by strengthening the mortgage market.[2] These low risk, government-sponsored agencies borrow funds cheaply and then lend indirectly to savings and loans and others at correspondingly low rates of interest. Billions of dollars of mortgages are acquired annually by these agencies with little or no budgetary impact. The aid to the construction industry is largely invisible because the mortgage interest covers the cost of borrowing. In view of recent trends, the surprising feature of the Treasury deposits proposal is its lack of implementation.

---

[2] The Federal National Mortgage Association is Fanny Mae, the Government National Mortgage Association is Ginny Mae, and the Federal Home Loan Mortgage Corporation is Freddie Mac.

# The instruments of monetary policy

Monetary policy often follows a tortuous path. It begins with the *three major instruments or tools of monetary policy: (1) open-market operations, (2) reserve requirements, and (3) discount policy.* The proximate or intermediate targets are the monetary aggregates and/or so-called money market conditions, such as short-term interest rates and marginal reserve measures. The goal variables or ultimate targets of monetary policy are GNP, the unemployment rate, and the consumer price index or some other major price index. Monetary policy follows a tortuous path because the proximate and ultimate targets are buffeted by forces other than the monetary instruments. The impact of some nonmonetary forces are immediate, while others affect the proximate and ultimate targets with a long lag. In order to fairly judge monetary policymakers in this complex environment, we must know more than the broad outlines of the policy instruments. Do the authorities have sufficiently sharp tools? This chapter scrutinizes the three major tools and glances at the links between tools and proximate goals. The next chapter examines the linkages more closely and the interrelationships between proximate targets.

## OPEN-MARKET OPERATIONS: AN INTRODUCTION

We begin, if only briefly, with the most important tool: open-market operations. The last chapter stated that open-market policy is the premier *defensive* tool, that is, the Fed uses open-market operations to offset the effect of uncontrolled factors on the base and money supply. But open-market operations are much more than a defensive tool. The Fed actively conducts some open-market operations in order to achieve the goal variables. What name should one give to these activist goal-oriented open-market operations, given that the passive, constancy-oriented operations are called defensive? Although the logic for "offensive" open-market operations is compelling, such terminology thoroughly vexes the Fed. The Fed prefers the term "dynamic open-market operations." That is, *dynamic open-market purchases and sales are conducted in order to achieve the goals*. Note that dynamic operations may be contractionary—sales—as well as expansionary—purchases. It is convenient to entertain the fiction that all uncontrolled factors are first offset by defensive operations before the Fed engages in dynamic operations. Viewed in this manner over 95 percent of all open-market operations are defensive. In point of fact, the uncontrolled sources and uses of the base are not offset if they work in the direction of the desired change. For example, suppose float increases by $400 million and, in view of the desired money supply and rates of interest, the Fed wants the base to increase by $500 million. In this case, there is no need for a $400 million defensive sale to counteract float *and* a $500 million dynamic purchase. A single $100 million purchase is adequate.

The balance sheet effects of open-market operations were illustrated almost from the beginning of the book.[1] Chapter 9 described the composition of the Federal Open Market Committee (FOMC). Significant mention of open-market operations had to be made along the way because it clearly is the most important monetary tool, so much so that monetary policy is often equated with open-market policy. Although the preeminence of open-market operations has been firmly established, the other tools are best analyzed first, reserving a thorough analysis of open-market operations as the capstone of the chapter.

## RESERVE REQUIREMENT POLICY

The establishment of uniform reserve requirements was one of the more important features of the Depository Institutions Deregulation and Monetary Control Act of March 1980. Prior to the act, the Fed set required reserves on demand, time and saving, and, occasionally, on other deposits of only its member banks. The reserve ratio was significantly less on time than on demand deposits. Member bank reserves had to be held in the form of deposits with Fed Banks or vault cash. Reserve requirements for nonmember banks were set by the 50 state bank commissioners, whose vigilance over their loss of power, or even its appearance, prevented cooperation and uniformity. In general, nonmember banks had lower reserve requirements, and at least part of the reserves could be held in the form of deposits at other banks or interest-earning liquid assets. Since large correspondent banks offered their depositors more and better services than the Fed did, and since the Fed let nonmember banks use its

---

[1] See Chapter 3, p. 67.

facilities indirectly through correspondents, the effective reserve requirement was much lower for nonmembers. That is, nonmember banks earned explicit interest on part of their reserves or received more services. Reserve requirements for nonbank depository institutions were set by the corresponding federal or state regulatory authority. Like nonmember banks, the required reserves for nonbanks were low and could be held in the form of deposits at other banks or liquid assets. For reserve requirement purposes, NOW and other similar checkable deposits were considered as time deposits by all regulatory authorities until 1980. Since other checkable deposits were highly restricted through 1980, their classification for reserve purposes was largely irrelevant then. The nationwide expansion of other checkable deposits in 1981 made their reserve classification an important issue.

The higher and stricter reserve requirements imposed by the Fed reduced bank profitability and discouraged membership. The ratio of member bank to total bank deposits fell from approximately 90 percent after World War II to 75 percent by 1979. The membership decline together with the expansion of NOW and similar accounts by nonbanks convinced the Fed that it was losing control over the quantity of money. Over the opposition of many nonmember banks and nonbank depositories, the Monetary Control Act set reserve requirements, subject to some Fed discretion, for *all* depository institutions. Reserves are held in the form of vault cash or deposits at the Fed.[2] Table 11–1 shows the

**TABLE 11–1  Depository institution reserve requirements after implementation of the Monetary Control Act, effective November 13, 1980**

| Type of deposit, and deposit interval | Percent |
|---|---|
| Net transaction accounts: | |
| Under $25 million | 3 |
| Over $25 million | 12 |
| Nonpersonal time deposits, by original maturity: | |
| Under 4 years | 3 |
| Over 4 years | 0 |
| Eurocurrency liabilities: | |
| All types | 3 |

reserve requirements after full phase-in and implementation of the Monetary Control Act. For nonmember banks and thrift institutions, there is a

---

[2] Nonmember banks and nonbank depositories (respondents) unfamiliar with the Fed may hold reserves in the form of complete pass-through deposits at member banks (correspondents). That is, the correspondent's required reserves increase by the full amount of the respondent's deposits. Such pass-through deposits are economically equal to deposits at the Fed.

phase-in period ending September 3, 1987. For member banks the phase-in period is about three years from the November 13, 1980 effective date, depending on whether their new reserve requirements shown on Table 11-1 are greater or less than the old reserve requirements. (The new requirements nearly always reduced member bank required reserves.) Net transaction accounts, which have the highest ratio, approximately equal net check deposits, as defined in M-1B (see Chapter 2), plus savings deposits on which the account holder is permitted to make withdrawals by telephone and preauthorized transfers (in excess of three per month). Telephone withdrawal and preauthorized transfer accounts, which were authorized nationwide *before* NOW accounts, are relatively small. Most probably, banks will be replacing them in the near future with checkable deposits. (Telephone withdrawal accounts are included in M-2 but not M-1B). As a good first approximation, therefore, check deposits and transaction accounts coincide.

Transaction account reserve requirements are graduated, 3 percent on deposits up to $25 million and 12 percent on the remainder. The lower reserve requirements for small depositories is a concession to the typical bank which was first brought under Fed required reserve policy by the Monetary Control Act. As Chapter 8 showed, nonmember banks on average are significantly smaller than member banks. The 3 percent required reserve ratio is sufficiently low as not to reduce the profitability of most nonmember banks, even if the Fed does not pay interest and provides few free services to its bank depositors. Indeed, in some cases the act reduced the reserves and increased the profits of small nonmember banks. Without the support of their small brothers and sisters, the numerically few but economically important large nonmember banks were brought kicking and screaming into the Fed's clutches. Although the Monetary Control Act significantly reduced the required reserve ratio of small member banks, these banks did not make out like bandits because the act also levied charges for services previously provided free.

Nonpersonal time deposits and Eurocurrency liabilities are also subject to required reserves. Nonpersonal time deposits are, with a few exceptions, time or saving deposits that are not transaction accounts and in which beneficial interest is held by a depositor that is not a natural person. For example, CDs held by corporations are nonpersonal time deposits. Eurocurrency liabilities basically are (*a*) net dollar borrowings by domestic banks from their foreign offices, (*b*) dollar assets sold by domestic banks to their foreign offices, and (*c*) dollar or foreign currency loans to United States residents by foreign offices of domestic banks. Some nonpersonal time deposits are small and, consequently, are included in M-2. However, most nonpersonal time deposits are included only in M-3 because they are large. Most Eurocurrency liabilities are not included in any of the monetary aggregates.

In addition to these basic reserve requirements the Board may, after consulting with the appropriate congressional committees, impose additional "emergency" reserve requirements on depository institutions at *any* ratio on *any* liability. Consultation does not necessarily imply approval, but it is unlikely that the Fed would implement emergency measures denounced by Congress. The Board may also set a supplemental reserve requirement of not more than 4 percent on transaction accounts. Supplemental reserve requirements may be imposed if they are deemed "essential" for monetary policy by five members of the Board. The fine difference between "emergency" and "essential" conditions is unspecified but important to bankers because emergency reserves, like basic reserves, do not earn interest while the supplemental reserves that are essential for policy participate in the Fed's earnings. The exact rate of interest earned by supplemental reserves is unspecified, but it will be positive. The Fed must justify to Congress any imposition of supplemental reserves. Emergency and supplemental reserves have not yet (mid-1981) been levied, and we expect they rarely will. Late 1976 was the last time the Fed Board changed required reserve ratios prior to changes dictated by the Monetary Control Act effective from November 13, 1980. Since the Board rarely chose to exercise its exclusive perogative over reserve requirements prior to the act, the current necessity for congressional consultation should reduce the frequency of changes even more.

Required reserves do not have to be met continuously. All institutions are allowed to average reserves over a one-week period beginning on Thursday. Until the late 1960s required reserves were concurrent with deposits. That is, average deposits this week determined average required reserves this week. Reserve requirements now are lagged, however. For depositories with total deposits exceeding $15 million, required reserves depend on deposits two weeks earlier. That is, daily required reserves, computed by multiplying the appropriate reserve ratio times end-of-day deposits, are averaged for each week beginning on Thursday (the "computation period"). The requirements are satisfied when the computation period's required reserves equal daily average reserves two weeks hence (the "maintenance period").[3] The lag is longer for institutions with total deposits under $15 million. These small depositories file a weekly report of deposits (computation period) only once each calendar quarter. The deposits during this one week computation period set the daily average required reserves for each week of a full calendar quarter (maintenance period) beginning one month after the computation period. For example, daily average deposits during the week beginning the third Thursday of January determine some small depositories weekly required reserves from the third Thursday of February through May. The one-week computation period per quarter was adopted in order to reduce the number of

---

[3] We are ignoring the fact that vault cash is not lagged because transfers of vault cash to the Fed rarely are prompted by required reserve considerations. Institutions with deposits under $15 million make up less than 4 percent of total deposits.

reports that small depositories must submit to the Fed. Of course, doing away with 12 reports of deposits each quarter makes the one submitted all important.

We have followed tradition by painting the reserve requirement as one that *must* be met. What penalties are incurred by failing to meet reserve requirements? Does the Fed chop bankers' hands—or worse? Officially at least, the penalty for reserve deficiencies is quite minor. Fed Banks are authorized to assess penalties for required reserve deficiencies at a rate of 2 percent per year above the discount rate. If banks could borrow unlimited amounts at the discount window, the penalty would be meaningless. However, discounting is restricted, as we shall see shortly. Since federal funds and other reserve adjustment assets sometimes cost more than 2 percent above the discount rate, and since banks rarely are short on required reserves, the 2 percent official penalty must understate the effective penalty. The higher effective penalty arises because the Fed has other regulatory powers, and failure to meet reserve requirements affects the administration of other regulations. For example, holding company applications would be denied any bank often deficient on reserves. Even if there were no other regulatory considerations, the Fed, like most other regulators, is sufficiently adept at harrassment to make compliance the course of least resistance. The Board ultimately may initiate cease and desist proceedings against reserve violators.

### Required reserves, liquidity, and solvency

What is the main purpose of reserve requirements? Originally, reserve requirements were viewed as important means of increasing the liquidity and solvency of banks. Although most people now are *mechanically* conditioned to deny that the main objectives of reserve requirements are more liquid and solvent banks, even bank regulators, when they let their guard down in informal discussions, revert to the old view about reserve requirements. Relatively low, say, about 10 percent, required reserves do *not significantly* increase a bank's liquidity and solvency. The two banking measures are improved only to a minor degree by reserve requirements.

Consider first the relationship between required reserves and liquidity, where for our purposes here liquidity means sufficient cash to be able to meet deposit outflows without selling earning assets. Suppose a depositor withdraws $10, causing total reserves to fall $10. Due to the lagged reserve feature, required reserves this week are *given* by prior deposits. Whether the bank is perfectly liquid or has to sell earning assets *this week* is independent of the reserve ratio, depending simply on its excess reserves. The bank would not have to sell earning assets if it had $10 in excess reserves. Excess reserves, and not required reserves, are the ultimate liquid asset. Can regulations require excess reserves? Of course not. Required excess reserves are a contradiction in terms. Taking a longer-run viewpoint, relatively low required reserves do provide some liquidity because, assuming no excess reserves, the amount of earning assets that must be liquidated two weeks hence is negatively related to the reserve ratio. For example, if the reserve ratio were twice as high, that is, 20 percent rather than 10 percent in our example, the $10 deposit outflow would require the sale of earning assets worth $8 instead of $9. Because reserve ratios are low, significant (100 percent in our example) reserve changes cause only minor (11 percent) changes in the amount of earning assets associated with deposit flows. Second, required reserves provide some liquidity because requirements are averaged over a week instead of having to be satisfied continuously. (The lagged feature is irrelevant for the arguments here.) In our example, the bank could operate with a $9 reserve shortage for a few days provided it had a positive excess some other days. In such a situation, we may view the $9 required reserves against $90 of other deposits as providing short-run liquidity which obviates the necessity for immediate sale of earning assets.

Let us now examine the relationship between required reserves and bank solvency. Look at the balance sheets for the two banks. On the basis of the two balance sheets, can you state with a high degree of confidence

**First National Bank**

| | | | |
|---|---|---|---|
| Reserves | 5 | Check deposits | 100 |
| Loans | 115 | | |

**Second National Bank**

| | | | |
|---|---|---|---|
| Reserves | 15 | Check deposits | 100 |
| Loans | 95 | | |

that the Second National Bank, with its high reserve ratio, is less likely to fail than the First National, assuming similar loan quality at both banks? No. Recalling the discussion of Chapter 8, what regulation has the greatest impact on reducing bank failures? If you could require a minimum ratio of items on the balance sheet, what ratio would you specify in order to minimize bankruptcy? Balance sheets should balance. The previous balance sheets purposely do not balance because we did not want to give away the answers to the questions. Capital adequacy requirements are the simplest and most effective means of reducing failures. Since capital (net worth) equals assets minus liabilities, and since insolvency occurs when assets are less than liabilities, the capital/asset ratio measures the maximum percentage loss the bank could incur prior to bankruptcy. Reserves do reduce the likelihood of failure somewhat because they are perfectly safe and lower the amount of risk assets. In our example, the First National's unillustrated capital account equals $20. Its loans (risk assets) could decrease in value approximately 17.4 percent ($20/

$115) before it is bankrupt. Although the Second National's reserve ratio is 15 percent, 10 percent more than the First National's, it is more likely to fail, *ceteris paribus*. Its loans could decrease in value only approximately 10.5 percent ($10/$95). As just stated, reserves have a minor effect on failures by reducing risk assets. For example, if the Second National's capital account also were $20 and its loans were $105 (so the balance sheet would balance), then it would remain solvent provided losses did not exceed 19 percent ($20/$105), somewhat higher than the 17.4 percent maximum loss for the First National.

### Monetary control and the existence of reserve requirements

The main purpose of reserve requirements is to aid monetary control. We first shall examine how the mere *existence* of reserve requirements aids monetary control and then shall examine how reserve requirement *changes* influence monetary and credit conditions. Recall that the Fed could not change reserve requirements prior to 1935; it rarely changed them between 1935 and 1980 when any variation did not have to be justified; reserve requirement variations are more unlikely now because the 1980 regulation specifies prior Congressional consultation. In view of this, reserve requirements would be a virtually worthless monetary instrument unless their mere existence facilitated monetary control. Yet, surprisingly, the primary benefits of constant, positive reserve requirements are often ignored while the secondary benefits of reserve variations are stressed. The existence of reserve requirements aids monetary control in three ways.

First, reserve requirements lessen the effect of all the uncontrolled sources and uses of the base on the money supply. The required reserve ratio appears in the denominator of the money supply multiplier, making the multiplier smaller. Since the money supply is the product of the multiplier and the base, required reserves reduce the volatility of the money supply due to variations in the base. Algebraically, $M = mB$, where the terms are as defined in Chapters 3 and 4. Required reserves lower m and, therefore, $\Delta M/\Delta B$. The higher the required reserve ratio, the smaller is the disruptive effect of uncontrolled sources of the base.

Second, required reserves reduce the effect on the money supply of fluctuations in the currency/check deposit ratio. For example, when the public decides to hold less cash, the banking system gains an equal amount of reserves which can support a multiple expansion. The size of the multiple expansion depends negatively on the required reserve ratio. The money supply is less responsive to currency/deposit fluctuations when the required reserve ratio is high. The extreme proposal of 100 percent required reserves, which seeks to transmogrify modern bankers into the goldsmiths of old with cash warehouses, is an attempt to eliminate altogether the effect of currency shifts on the money supply.

Finally, required reserves reduce the effect of fluctuations of the excess reserve ratio on the money supply. An example best illustrates this feature of required reserves. For simplicity, assume the second money supply case in Chapter 4, where individuals do not hold currency or time deposits. Check deposits are banks' only liability. In this case, the money supply equation is

$$M = \frac{1}{r_c + r_{ec}} B,$$

where $r_c$ and $r_{ec}$ are the required and excess reserve ratios, respectively. Suppose the bank determined excess reserve ratio fluctuates randomly between 0.05 and 0.1, and that the optimal money supply is $450. If there were no reserve requirements, that is, $r_c = 0$, then the optimal constant policy would set the base at $30. Excess reserve fluctuations, however, prevent continual attainment of the monetary target. With $r_c = 0$ and B = $30, the money equation shows that the money supply equals $600 when $r_{ec} = 0.05$ and $300 when $r_{ec} = 0.1$. On average, the monetary authority hits its target. The multiplier varies between 10 and 20. Now suppose a 15 percent reserve requirement is instituted. Given the same monetary target and excess reserve fluctuations, the Fed would increase the base to $100 in order to hit the monetary target on average. The important point, however, is the reduction in monetary fluctuations about the average due to the reserve requirements. When $r_c = 0.15$ and B = $100, the money supply equals $500 when $r_{ec} = 0.05$ and $400 when $r_{ec} = 0.1$. The imposition of reserve requirements reduces the range of monetary fluctuations from $300–$600 to $400–$500. In terms of the multiplier, the same fluctuations in the excess reserve ratio produce smaller variations in the multiplier when required reserves exist. In our example, the multiplier varied 100 percent (between 10 and 20) prior to the imposition of reserve requirements but only 25 percent (between 4 and 5) afterward. The required reserve ratio acts as an anchor stabilizing the money supply.

### Monetary control and reserve requirement changes

We shall not illustrate again the effect of reserve requirement variations. One point merits emphasis, however. Reserve requirement changes have no immediate impact on any item on banks' balance sheets or the money supply. Shortly thereafter, reserve variations do have an impact because banks are profit maximizers, subject to some constraints. Lower reserve requirements produce sterile undesired excess reserves. In order to earn more interest income, banks lower the loan rate and expand loans and deposits.

Are reserve requirement variations an effective way of changing money and interest rates? First, compared to other money policy instruments, the impact of reserve requirement variations is more widespread geographically and across institutions. Reserve requirements affect all depository institutions throughout the country. Open-market operations initially affect only those banks that have security dealers' accounts. While the final effects of open-market operations are filtered through the federal funds and government securities markets to all large banks quite rapidly and broadly, the final monetary impact on small banks and nonbank depositories is somewhat delayed for open-market operations compared to reserve requirement variations. Second, the current policy of specifying basic requirements which may be modified by emergency and supplemental measures suggests that neither frequent nor small reserve requirement variations are possible. Thus, reserve requirements are *not* sharp tools for short-run control. But if these characteristics often are desirable, reserve requirements are ideal when one needs a blunt instrument for long-run monetary variations. Precisely because reserve requirement changes are infrequent, have a large effect on the money supply, and must be justified, depository institutions and economic actors generally will interpret them correctly. In the parlance of economists, reserve requirements have desirable *announcement effects.* That is, since economic actors recognize that monetary policy at least indirectly affects their lives, they search for clues on the future posture of monetary policy. Inferences about the future derived from a policy action are its announcement effects. Policy tools which are used continually typically do not generate announcement effects. Some policy tools which are used infrequently engender false announcement effects; they suggest a fundamental change in policy when there is none. The Fed purposely has saved reserve requirements for the cleanup spot—other tools are the leadoff batters—so that its objective when changing requirements is clearly understood. Finally, the assumed permanency of reserve requirement variations may induce depository institutions to expand more rapidly into illiquid and long-term assets, which may have a greater economic impact than an equal expansion of liquid assets.

### Reserve requirement reforms

For many years the Federal Reserve advocated for three reasons the uniformity of reserve requirements across institutions. (Temporarily ignore the variability of requirements across deposit types.) First, uniform requirements eliminate the impact on the money supply of shifts in the public's preference for different types of institutions. As stated in Chapter 4, when reserve requirements are not uniform, "the" required reserve ratio in the multiplier can only be the average ratio. The shift of deposits from banks with low to high requirements would raise the average required ratio, reduce excess reserves, and generate a monetary contraction. Although reserve requirements still are not perfectly uniform, the

Monetary Control Act of 1980 significantly reduced the variability across institutions by bringing nonmember banks and all nonbank depositories within the fold. Moreover, graduation by size was substantially reduced. Second, uniformity across institutions was viewed as a prerequisite to the imposition of the high reserve requirements that facilitate monetary control. While this argument for uniformity is correct—the unprofitability of high reserve requirements induces banks with the option to escape them—the necessity for political compromise produced the precise opposite. That is, uniformity was accompanied by a general lowering of reserve requirements. Third, uniformity across institutions is desirable on equity grounds. Equals should be treated equally.

We introduce the next topic in the form of a problem. Suppose you are a Fed official with sole and complete authority over the required reserve ratio on nonpersonal time deposits maturing within 4 years. The current reserve ratio is 3 percent, but you can set it at any level between 0 and 100 percent. What ratio would you select and why? Do answer the question before reading on. The place to start is with the "why" question. We must specify the reason for reserve requirements before determing their optimal value.

Reserve requirements should be imposed in order to facilitate monetary control. Assuming M–1B is the appropriate monetary aggregate, then the reserve requirement on nonpersonal time deposits should be abolished. In that case, changes in nonpersonal time deposits would not affect the reserves available to support check deposits and produce monetary instability. In terms of the advanced money supply equation in Chapter 4, variations in t are irrelevant when $r_t = 0$. (Recall that t in Chapter 4 represents all nonmoney liabilities subject to reserve requirements.) If M–3 were the appropriate monetary aggregate, then nonpersonal time deposits, all of which are included in M–3, and transaction accounts, which approximately equal check deposits, should have identical reserve requirements. Uniformity of reserve requirements among the monetary components eliminates the effect of shifts in composition. Of course, this line of reasoning implies that reserve requirements should be extended to all the items in M–3. Current reserve requirements cannot be justified as the optimal values in order to control any monetary aggregate, unless the Fed has some secret and complex money supply measure such as M–1CKJ.

## DISCOUNT POLICY

Discount policy has two dimensions: (1) price, and (2) nonprice. The price dimension is simply the discount rate depository institutions pay on their borrowings at the Fed. The nonprice dimension places limits on the amount depositories can borrow at any given discount rate. The nonprice dimension, which has changed over time, has taken two main forms: (1) it used to require real bills as collateral, and (2) it now attempts to ascertain whether banks are borrowing for "need" or "profit." While formerly limited to member banks, the discount window was opened in 1980 to all depositories which are subject to reserve requirements.

Why are there two dimensions to discounting? The Fed feels two dimensions are necessary because (1) banks have different objectives than the Fed, (2) discounting is at the initiative of banks, and (3) the Fed favors discount rate stability. The Fed sets the discount rate with a view toward full employment and price stability. Are these the objectives of depository institutions? Of course not. They seek to make profits. At any discount rate banks may decide to borrow too much, given the Fed's objectives, so reserves and the money supply expand excessively. One solution is obvious: change the discount rate. The Fed, however, favors stable interest rates in general and a stable discount rate in particular. Given this objective, the other solution is to ration quantity through some nonprice dimension of discounting.

As stated earlier, discounting was the most important tool when the Fed was created in 1913. The Federal Reserve Act established reserve requirements but did not give the Fed the authority to change them. Open-market operations were largely dismissed because financial markets were underdeveloped. Although the issuance of government bonds in order to finance World War I significantly broadened the bond market, open-market operations remained a minor tool throughout the 1920s because it was contrary to the prevalent laissez-faire, antidiscretion philosophy of the time. Discounts are at the initiative of banks, although banks' behavior clearly depends on Fed policy. This made discounting compatible with the laissez-faire philosophy. Even those who favored a somewhat activist, discretionary policy still evaluated discounting positively because the banking initiative provided the Fed with information on the appropriate policy. At a time when few statistics were collected and when the statistics collected often were unreliable and dated, monitoring banks and their demand for loans was a good way of knowing the current and future state of the economy.

### The nonprice dimension: Real bills

The nonprice dimension of discounting was most pronounced when the Fed was created. In the early 20th century the Bank of England administered its discount window according to the precepts of the real bills or commercial loan theory. The creators of the Fed wanted it to emulate the Bank of England. Although the Fed abandoned strict adherence to the real-bills doctrine shortly after it came into existence in order to aid Treasury financings, the Fed practiced a flexible version of real bills at least until the early 1930s, and modern adaptations appear sporadically. Real bills as a theory of commercial bank management was discussed in Chapter 7. Basically, it says that banks will be liquid when they make short-term productive loans, that is, real bills. It also is a theory of central bank management. The real-bills doctrine states that a central bank will create the appropriate noninflationary amount of money when it discounts the real bills presented by commercial banks. The three fundamental assumptions of the real bills doctrine are:

1. The money supply is a constant multiple of the base.
2. Banks' requests for discounts at the Fed are a constant proportion of their inventory loans and other real bills.
3. Inventories and other goods financed by real bills are a constant proportion of total output.

If the base is provided solely by discounts so there is no gap between assumptions (1) and (2), it does follow, given the three assumptions, that the money supply changes will parallel income changes. Contrary to the assertion of the real-bills doctrine, proportionality between money and income does *not* guarantee price stability. On the other hand, many modern detractors of the real-bills doctrine are wrong in alleging that the real-bills doctrine always is destabilizing. Whether or not the real-bills doctrine is stabilizing depends on the source of the income change. Monetary policy which follows the precepts of the real-bills doctrine destabilizes an economy buffeted by demand shocks but stabilizes an economy buffeted by supply shocks. If income increases because demand increases, then the inflationary potential of a larger demand is augmented by monetary expansion. However, if income increases because supply increases, then the deflationary potential of a larger supply is averted by a real-bills policy.

Figure 11–1 illustrates these ideas. Suppose the initial demand and supply of commodities in general are represented by the solid curves in Figure 11–1. If for any reason demand now increases to D', income will increase. Banks will accommodate firms' need for higher inventories by discounting real bills and increasing the money supply. Monetary expansion further increases the demand for commodities, shifting the demand curve to D''. The real-bills doctrine is destabilizing in this case. It induces demand shifts in the same direction as the original disturbance. Now suppose the disturbance originates on the supply side. Supply shifts from S to S'. The higher income also leads to more loans and monetary expansion. Again, monetary expansion shifts demand, this time from D to D'. In this case the real-bills doctrine is stabilizing. The demand increase is necessary in order to keep prices stable.

What types of shocks, demand or supply shocks, tend to predominate? Is monetary policy conducted according to the real-bills doctrine stabilizing or destabilizing? Over time, both demand and supply shift out. The shocks illustrated by the shifting curves in Figure 11–1 are the deviations from the long-run supply and demand trends. Most economists during the

FIGURE 11–1   Real bills is destabilizing when demand shocks predominate but stabilizing when supply shocks predominate

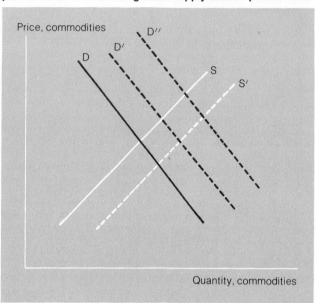

period from World War II to the 1970s thought that demand always was considerably more unstable than supply and, consequently, denounced the real-bills doctrine. While demand shocks did predominate immediately following World War II, more recent experience has shown that supply shifts cannot be totally ignored. Crop failures and oil embargoes and cartels are examples of (inward) supply shifts. Higher oil prices increase the quantity of commodities we must export to pay for our oil imports and reduce real income. If the monetary authorities had followed the real-bills doctrine, the money supply would have *fallen* with income. The higher oil prices would have been accompanied by lower prices in other sectors keeping the general level of prices more or less constant. Instead, the monetary authorities were unwilling to accept a reduction in our standard of living due to higher real prices for oil. Reacting almost as if higher OPEC prices and a lower standard of living were immoral, the inward supply was countered by monetary *expansion* and an outward shift in demand. If this had been the end of the story, the monetary expansion and inflation may have been worthwhile. At least output would not have fallen. However, the strengthened OPEC cartel which initiated the disturbance was not going to be outdone. OPEC raised oil prices in order to purchase more commodities. If the United States and other countries inflated, thereby temporarily reducing the real price of oil and the imports OPEC could acquire, then OPEC would raise prices again. An inflationary spiral got underway. Inward supply shifts were followed by outward demand shifts, which were followed by inward supply shifts and so on.

OPEC did not exist when the real-bills doctrine was widely accepted. However, in those days the economy was largely agricultural. The weather and other random factors have a much more important effect on the supply of agricultural economies. While we are not suggesting that supply was considerably more unstable than demand during the early 20th century, and that the real-bills doctrine was stabilizing, the real-bills doctrine is not as destabilizing as many postwar economists have suggested. Adam Smith, the father of the real-bills doctrine and economics in general, the creators of the Federal Reserve, and most early 20th century economists were not your run-of-the-mill dummies. They advocated the real-bills doctrine because it sometimes was stabilizing.

### The nonprice dimension: Need, not profit

The nonprice dimension has a new twist. The Fed no longer requires real bills as collateral.[4] The nonprice dimension is reflected today by the Fed's attempting to determine the reason for bank borrowing. According to the Fed, banks borrow either for "need" or "profit." Banks are allowed to borrow out of need but not for profit. In some sense all discounting is for profit. Arms-length transactions must make an economic unit better off or the transaction would not be made. No one forces banks to borrow at the Fed. They do so instead of selling liquid assets or issuing CDs because they are better off borrowing. Nevertheless, the Fed does *not* view banks as borrowing for profit when either (1) deposits are falling, or (2) "customer" loans are increasing. When either condition holds, banks are said to borrow out of need. Customer loans basically are loans to depositors, particularly small depositors. The Fed views banks as having an obligation to lend to their customers. According to Chapter 7, customer loans are obligations in the sense that failure to lend to depositors leads them to place their deposits elsewhere. Banks borrow for profit according to the Fed when discounts are financing security purchases or national loans. Surveillance against borrowing for profit explains why market interest rates often remain considerably above the discount rate.[5]

---

[4] Strictly speaking, only bank borrowings at the Fed which are secured by real bills are discounts or, as called years ago, rediscounts. Banks' borrowings at the Fed on the basis of their own promissory note secured nearly always by government securities are technically called advances, instead of discounts. Advances predominate by a wide margin. From an economic viewpoint, the two types of borrowings are identical.

[5] Some observers of the banking scene claim that such surveillance is unnecessary because banks are "naturally reluctant to borrow." Prior to the existence of the Fed, borrowing by banks was universally interpreted as a sign of weakness. Particularly in an age without deposit insurance, banks needed to project an image of strength and, consequently, rarely borrowed. The Federal Reserve, which looked at itself as a lender of last resort and not a

The Fed formalized somewhat its need concept and surveillance procedures in 1973 by establishing a seasonal credit privilege. To be eligible for this new borrowing privilege, deposit institutions must exhibit a seasonal pattern in loans and deposits that persists for at least eight weeks. The seasonal privilege is available to institutions with deposits under $100 million. The small depositories must arrange for the credit prior to the seasonal need. The primary beneficiaries are depositories in rural and resort areas.

### The relationship between the discount rate and money market interest rates

The Fed discount rate and money market interest rates, such as the three-month Treasury bill and federal funds rates, are highly positively correlated. See Figure 11–2. Why do the rates move together? What

**FIGURE 11–2   The discount rate and short-term interest rates**

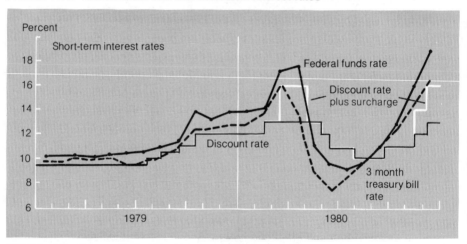

SOURCE: Federal Reserve Bank of New York, *Annual Report, 1980,* p. 10.

cause and effect relationship is responsible for the statistically positive correlation? The high positive correlation is due in part to a causal relationship from the discount rate to money market rates. First, higher dis-

permanent source of funds for banks, naturally strengthened banks reluctance to borrow through nonprice dimensions and surveillance. The strongest version of the reluctance hypothesis, which says that banks are naturally reluctant to borrow, is contradicted today by the liability management techniques of virtually all large banks. Strong reluctance now may be a characteristic of many small banks of little consequence. The weak version of the hypothesis has much truth: banks have become so accustomed to borrow less than the profit-maximizing amount from the Fed that suspension of surveillance procedures would induce little additional borrowing in the short run.

count rates discourage discounting, which reduces the monetary base. The initial effect of a lower base and money supply is higher market interest rates. Second, a higher discount rate sometimes provides the necessary political justification banks were seeking in order to raise interest rates. High interest rates are politically unpopular. For this and other reasons, banks sometimes ration credit. That is, the rate of interest is below its equilibrium value, and banks allocate credit on the basis of other variables. When the Fed raises its discount rate, banks can stop rationing credit and revert to employing the interest rate as an allocation tool. Banks can effectively respond to any criticism, "Look, we are simply following the example of the Fed." Since prices and interest rates are better allocation tools than years in business, asset size, skin color, sex, or yet other allocation devices, any reduction of credit rationing is a real plus for discount rate changes.

The positive association between the discount and market rates is also due to causation going the other direction, that is, from market interest rates to the discount rate. When business is booming and market interest rates are rising, the Fed must raise the discount rate in order to prevent the monetary expansion that would result from the positive relationship between discounting and the differential between the market and discount rate. In symbols,

$$D = (i_m - i_d , \ldots) \qquad (11-1)$$

where D is discounts, $i_m$ and $i_d$ are the market and discount rate, respectively, and the ellipses indicate that discounts depend on other factors besides the rate differential. While the Fed may inveigh against borrowing for profit and has set up some mechanical rules to detect such reprehensible conduct, the naked empirical truth is that discounts do depend on the rate differential. Aggregate deposit balance is associated with inflows and outflows at the micro level. When market rates exceed the discount, institutions incurring deposit outflows will borrow at the Fed, which will adjudge the banks needy. The Fed raises the discount rates in order to halt the reserve and monetary expansion.

Figure 11–2 shows that the discount rate lags behind market rates. For example, the federal funds rate fell in half (from approximately 18 percent to 9 percent) between April and July 1980. The decline in the discount rate was much more moderate (from 13 to 10 percent). The first reduction in the discount rate occurred on May 29, 1980, more than a month after the federal funds rate started its precipitous slide. Moreover, another reduction occurred on July 29, 1980, by which time the federal funds rate had started an upward climb which in December surpassed the April figure. While timing patterns are not infallible guides to causation, this lagged pattern suggests that causation generally runs from market rates to the discount rate. Two important implications follow from this finding. First, discount rate changes generally do not have expectational or announcement effects. Your TV anchorperson may announce in solemn tones that the Fed changed the discount rate. Most people will ignore the statement, not even knowing what it means. But how will the financially sophisticated who play the market interpret the Fed's action? They rarely will be surprised by discount rate changes. The discount rate lags market interest rates enough that sophisticated market participants have acquired earlier signals of the overall posture of monetary policy. Discount rate changes generally are viewed as technical adjustments to keep policy on course rather than as a change in policy.

We sprinkled the last paragraph with several "generally's" because the discount rate can have announcement effects. The most dramatic example of a discount rate change with an announcement effect occurred in late 1931. In 1930 and early 1931 the Fed repeatedly cut the discount rate, and justly so. The United States was in the midst of the worst depression in its history, so that any expansionary policy was welcome. In 1931 Britain went off the gold standard. The Fed was determined that the United States would remain on the gold standard, if necessary at the expense of employment and economic recovery. It feared, however, that foreigners might suspect that the United States would copy Britain. Talk is cheap. The Fed had to convince the public that it meant business about gold glittering. In one fell swoop the Fed more than doubled the discount rate. The market got the message that the Fed had new goals. The dollar strengthened, and the economy weakened further.

The second major implication of the lagged response of the discount rate to market interest rates is that discounting and, *ceteris paribus,* the money supply tend to be procyclical. That is, discounts and the money supply increase during booms because the greater borrowing during business expansions raises market interest rates. Needless to say, but said nevertheless, the appropriate policy is countercyclical. Money should contract, or expand less rapidly, during business expansions. To be sure, the procyclical pattern is not that long and strong because the Fed does not delay closing the interest rate differential inordinately.

### Discounting: Escape hatch or safety valve?

Open-market operations and discounting are negatively related in the short run. Whenever the Fed sells securities, thereby reducing the base and money supply and raising market interest rates, banks respond to the reserve loss by borrowing more, thereby offsetting some of the monetary and interest rate contraction. Open-market purchases also are partially offset in the short run by less discounting. Is the negative relationship between open-market operations and discounts a bane or a boon? This question has been debated for some time. As occasionally happens, the debaters get sidetracked on irrelevant issues and ignore the fundamentals. Most economists claim that the negative relationship makes discounting an escape hatch which reduces the effectiveness of open-market operations and overall monetary policy. The Fed must compensate for the negative relationship by engaging in larger open-market purchases and sales initially. A minority view the identical phenomenon as a safety valve. They view the larger open-market operations as positively beneficial. The debate degenerated into a semantic controversy because the debaters concentrated on irrelevant *averages*. The government securities market is so large that the Fed can readily compensate for *average* discounts. While this may keep the base on target on average, the negative relationship is not known exactly at all times. Discounting is at the initiative of banks, and their behavior is not always forecast correctly. Discounting, like other uncontrolled sources of the monetary base which cannot be predicted exactly, causes short-run fluctuations about the target. Unintentional fluctuations are *not* necessarily undesirable. The monetary authority may set such poor targets that deviations about the targets may be welcome. However, any random deviations from optimally set targets are undesirable, by definition. While the Fed's targets may well be nonoptimal, they probably are not so poor than uncontrolled deviations are an improvement. Discounting thus is an escape hatch instead of a safety valve.

Since analogies have always been popular in this debate, let me offer a new analogy while recognizing that no analogy is perfect. Suppose static interference hinders reception of a radio station. Is this desirable or not? Should you attempt to eliminate the interference? The answer largely depends on how much you enjoy the radio program. If the program is really worthwhile, you will attempt to eliminate the static immediately. On the other hand, the program may be so bad that the static dulls a cacophony of sound and actually improves matters.

### Reform proposals

Most of the reform proposals assume that the Fed is a sufficiently good fiddler, although certainly no concert violinist, that we want to listen to its music. The static from discounting is annoying. One proposal goes all the way: abolish discounts.[6] Let's hear the tune just as the Fed is playing it. The main criticism of this proposal focuses on its microeconomic consequences, particularly for small banks. Critics allege that small banks have few ways of adjusting their balance sheets and must rely on discounts at the Fed when they are buffeted by large shocks. The Fed accepts this position and has formalized and extended it to large banks. Besides the usual adjustment credit granted to banks with moderate short-run needs, in the 1970s the Fed established a new discounting category called special

---

[6] Milton Friedman, *A Program for Monetary Stability* (New York: Fordham University Press, 1959), p. 44.

circumstances, which basically is for banks with immoderate long-run needs. The main beneficiary of special circumstances discounting was the Franklin National Bank. Professor Friedman and others who want to abolish discounting claim that discounting is a vestige of the past. They concede that a few banks will be hurt by the proposal, but they claim that, contrary to years ago, virtually all banks, including small banks, have alternative credit sources. The Franklin National Bank case exemplifies the possibility that discounting may extend too much credit for too long and simply postpone the inevitable.

The second major reform proposal would tie the discount rate to market interest rates in the very short run. That is, this proposal would change discount rates frequently, say, weekly, in order to maintain a constant differential between the discount and market interest rates. Tying the discount and market rates would largely eliminate the procyclical effect of discounting. If this proposal were adopted, lack of knowledge of the precise relationship between discounts and the interest rate differential would be irrelevant. Since the differential would remain constant, its effect, whatever it may be, would also be constant. Of course, discounting depends on other factors besides the interest differential. (Recall the ellipses in equation 11–1.) The current proposal does not totally eliminate the unpredictable aspects of discounting.

The tying proposal has wide support. Its opponents are mainly domiciled at the Fed, which is somewhat surprising considering that the proposal would increase the likelihood of the Fed's hitting the target. The Fed has raised numerous "technical" issues such as how often should the discount rate be adjusted, to what specific market interest rate should the discount rate be tied, and what should the interest rate differential equal? While people not intimately involved in an operation often dismiss various real complications as mere technicalities, the issues raised by the Fed are important yet not readily answered. However, implementation of the proposal should not await determination of the *optimal* adjustment period, the *optimal* market rate, and the *optimal* differential. Improvements in any area should be adopted, and some (nonoptimal) tying scheme which improves the current administration of the discount mechanism can be readily found. One suspects that the Fed objects to the tying scheme because it reduces its discretionary power. No one who has savored power wants to be reduced to a robot.

The third proposal, which is a logical extension of the second, would have the Fed pay interest on commercial banks' excess reserves at the tied discount rate. In our discussion of the money multiplier and excess reserve ratio in Chapter 4, we said that excess reserves depend on market interest rates, among other variables. At that point we were implicitly assuming that excess reserves earned no interest so the market interest rate was the opportunity cost of excess reserves. If excess reserves earned interest at the discount rate, then the opportunity cost and excess reserve determinant would be the rate differential. Extention of the tying proposal to excess reserves would eliminate another important source of short-run monetary variations.

### Recent changes

All three proposals were made more than 20 years ago but remain just that, proposals, because of Fed opposition. The Fed is not against all change, however. With little prior notice it instituted the seasonal and special circumstances borrowing programs just mentioned. Compared to the traditional short-term adjustment discounts, the new programs offer longer term credit and, in the seasonal case, must be arranged beforehand. Perhaps in order to emphasize the special nature of these programs and to forestall more frequent discounting, the Fed in 1980 began applying a surcharge to short-term adjustment discounts by institutions with deposits of $500 million or more which borrow in successive weeks or in more than four weeks in a calendar quarter. The surcharge in mid-1981 was 3 percent.

Figure 11–3 presents some recent though limited empirical evidence on the magnitude of the effect of interest rate differentials on discounting. The horizontal axis measures the difference between the federal funds and the discount rates, which were graphed in Figure 11–2. The vertical axis measures discounts at the Fed. The regression equation, which best describes the relationship between the two variables, is illustrated along with the raw data for July through December 1980. The strong positive relationship would be eliminated by the tying proposal which keeps the interest rates differential constant.[7] More precisely, the tying proposal would eliminate about 75 percent of the variation in discounts. The unknown ellipses in equation 11–1 explain 25 percent of the variation in discounts.

## OPEN-MARKET OPERATIONS

The open-market story is told in two parts. One concerns the FOMC monthly meeting where policy is decided and the other the New York Fed's trading desk where operations are executed daily.

---

[7] The regression equation is

$$D = 9.03 + 1.92(i_{FF} - i_d), \qquad R^2 = 0.767 \qquad (11-1')$$

where D is discounts in $100 millions and $i_{FF} - i_d$ is the interest rate differential. The t statistic of the slope coefficient (1.92) equals 3.67, indicating that there is a high likelihood (over 95 percent) of a systematic relationship. The value of the $R^2$ indicates that approximately 75 percent of the variation in discounts is explained by interest rate differences. The results are only illustrative; the sample size could well be expanded.

**FIGURE 11–3  Relationship between the amount of discounts at the Fed and the difference between the federal funds and discount rates**

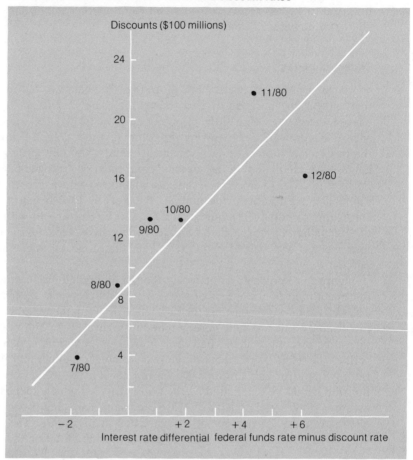

### FOMC meetings: They do it monthly

By the time the FOMC assembles at 9:30 A.M. around the 30-foot mahogany table in the Federal Reserve boardroom, each member is well prepared to deliberate. Since the last monthly meeting the members and nonvoting Fed Bank presidents have received daily, weekly, and occasional special reports which (1) describe past and prospective economic and financial developments, both domestic and international, and (2) present the staff's view of the direction of the economy and the probable effects of alternative policies.

Perhaps because some members fail to do their homework, or because the reports are so voluminous—up to 250 pages—that the members need a refresher, the meeting begins with the famous 5S, staff statistical "summary'' and slide show. For example, at the July 9, 1980, meeting the staff reviewed the behavior and rated the accuracy of existing forecasts of real GNP, the price index for gross domestic business product, the dollar value of total retail sales, unit sales of new automobiles, the index of industrial production, and so on. As we shall see later, the FOMC has a penchant for considering everything, and the large staff has to justify its existence. A special 5S is presented once each quarter. The senior staff unveils *detailed new* forecasts of the economy over the next year or so, given a continuation of monetary policy. Both the regular and special 5S end with a review of last month's monetary policy decisions, comparisons of the target and actual values of the monetary variables during the past months, and predictions of the effects of alternative policy proposals.

Armed with data about the present and forecasts of the future, decision making now begins. What shall we do? Which, if any, of the staff-prepared policy proposals should be adopted, and how should open-market operations be executed in order to implement the selected proposal? Your dedicated FOMC members again ask themselves, "What shall we do?" The specific items debated have varied considerably over time with changes in FOMC membership, economic trends, and special events.[8] Although the diversity of the debate over time does not invite ready summary, we can consider why policy disagreement occurs at any one time. Basically, monetary and other policymakers disagree because (1) goals are not precise and uniform, (2) forecasts of the value and the effect of nonpolicy variables are uncertain and subject to error, and (3) the effects of the policy variables are uncertain. If everyone's sole objective was 5 percent unemployment—a precise number, and not the vague "full employment"—and if it was known with certainty that unemployment would be 6 percent in the absence of monetary policy, and if it were certain that a 1 percent monetary expansion would reduce unemployment by an equal amount, then agreement on policy would be universal. But not even one of the three conditions for policy agreement is satisfied. We shall return at several points in the book to these *three conditions which make policy controversial and, simultaneously, exciting: (1) diverse goals, (2) general economic uncertainty, and (3) policy uncertainty.*

A decision, however difficult, must be reached. Following the debate, which the chair shapes and ends at its pleasure, each of the principals states what policy should be adopted. The chair then puts before the FOMC for final consideration and vote the policy directive that in the chair's mind best embodies the committee's views. (Chapter 9's mention of the power derived from chairing committees may be better appreciated now.) The chair's directive invariably is adopted although, for reasons to be stated shortly, in recent years dissenting votes are more common.

---

[8] An excellent inside source is Sherman Maisel, *Managing the Dollar* (New York: W. W. Norton, 1973). See pp. 6–10 and 37–41 for the importance of special events on open-market decisions.

### The FOMC directive: Summary and call for action

The directive, which has been lengthened over the years but still is less than a page, has three parts. The first briefly and incompletely reviews the data presented by the staff. The second part *briefly* states the *general* policy goals or ultimate targets. For example, at the November 18, 1980, meeting the expressed goals were:

> The Federal Open Market Committee seeks to foster monetary and financial conditions that will help to reduce inflation, encourage economic recovery, and contribute to a sustainable pattern of international transactions.

Perhaps because the goals are so general, the wording of this section changes somewhat but the substance remains constant throughout the years. For example, about 10 years before, on August 18, 1970,

> It is the policy of the Federal Open Market Committee to foster financial conditions conducive to orderly reduction in the rate of inflation, while encouraging the resumption of sustainable economic growth and the attainment of reasonable equilibrium in the country's balance of payments.

Immediately following the goal statement is the set of authorizations and instructions to the manager of the system open market account thought to be most compatible with the general goals. This section of the directive is the most important to economists and speculators. It also is the section which has changed most qualitatively and quantitatively. *Prior to June 1966 the instructions to the account manager were couched solely in terms of money market conditions.* Easier, constant, or firmer (sometimes called tighter) money market conditions were the order of the day. *Money market conditions are some combination of (a) free reserves, (b) the federal funds rate, (c) the three-month Treasury bill rate, and (d) something normally eloquent central bankers can only describe as the "tone and feel of the market." Free reserves, which may be positive or negative, are excess reserves minus discounts at the Fed.* Negative free reserves are often called net borrowed reserves. During the 1950s and early 1960s, free reserves were the most important determinant of money market conditions by far. Yes, "monetary" policy operating instructions prior to 1966 were (1) extremely vague (easier or firmer) and (2) directed solely at money market conditions, and not money itself, or even a closely related item such as the base or reserves. Operating instructions based heavily on free reserves were severely criticized, particularly by Professors Karl Brunner and Allan Meltzer in a 1964 study.[9] We shall formally examine the relationship between free reserves, money, and interest rates in the next chapter. Suffice it to say here that free reserve instructions make the money supply procyclical. The natural tendency for excess and free reserves to fall dur-

---

[9] See *The Federal Reserve's Attachment to the Free Reserves Concept* (Washington, D.C.: House Banking and Currency Committee, 1964).

ing a boom had to be counteracted by open-market purchases and monetary expansion in order to maintain the specified money market conditions. Monetary expansion during booms hardly is the appropriate policy.

Largely in response to the critics, the operating instructions were modified in June 1966 to include what has been called a proviso clause. The account manager was directed to keep "money market conditions at about their recent ranges; *provided*, however, that if required reserves expand considerably more than seasonally expected, operations shall be conducted with a view to attaining some . . . firming of money market conditions."[10] For the first time the account manager was instructed to consider explicitly, if only conditionally, an item, required reserves, well known to be closely related to money. Shortly thereafter, the proviso clause mentioned bank credit, which is virtually identical to total deposits. At the January 1970 meeting, which followed Professor Arthur Burns's nomination to the Fed chair but preceded his installation, the proviso at long last mentioned money explicitly. Less than two months after assuming office, at the March 1970 FOMC meeting, Professor Burns succeeded in bringing money out of the shadows to center stage. The FOMC sought "to promote some easing of conditions in credit markets *and* somewhat greater growth in money over the months ahead" (Our emphasis). Money *officially* was on par with credit market conditions in 1970. Compared to money market conditions, credit market conditions place much greater weight on interest rates and play down free reserves.

Given our objective of learning the broad pattern of shifts in open-market operating strategy, the next important change occurred in the mid-1970s when the Fed specified annual money supply growth rates each quarter. For example, at the beginning of April the Fed specified the desired rate of monetary growth for the year ending the following March. The Fed thus officially had a longer run operating target, the annual money supply, and two short-run targets, the money supply and short-term interest rates. In fact, interest rates ruled the roost and money was a decidedly secondary constraint, as administration of the long-run monetary target illustrates. "Base drift" and the "forgiveness principle" characterized administration of the long-run target. To illustrate this, suppose that at the April meeting the FOMC adopted a range for annual monetary growth ending the following March of 4 to 6 percent. Suppose further the money supply actually increased by 9 percent during the second quarter. The FOMC in July would use the second quarter's swollen money supply as the base in computing desired monetary growth rates for

---

[10] Federal Reserve, *Annual Report, 1966*, p. 151. Our italics. The directive of the February 1966 meeting of the FOMC instructed the account manager to operate "with a view toward a gradual reduction in reserve availability." Subsequent meetings determined that the account manager and many committee members interpreted "reserve availability" as free reserve availability, although the proponents of the reserve clause had in mind total or required reserves, which are approximately equal.

the year ending next June. In this manner the base used to measure monetary growth kept shifting up. The forgiveness principle was in effect because the long-run money targets remained virtually constant in spite of large short-run deviations. The excess expansion (9 percent in our example) was *not* corrected by downward revisions of the long-run target values (4 to 6 percent).

The Full Employment and Balanced Growth Act of 1978, better known as the Humphrey-Hawkins Act, eliminated base drift and the forgiveness principle and effectively made the Fed consider the money supply. The Humphrey-Hawkins Act *requires* the FOMC to establish *calendar-year* growth ranges for monetary and credit aggregates in February of each year. The base in computing growth rates is the average value during the previous year's fourth quarter. The FOMC *must* review these ranges in July, although it may reconsider the one-year ranges at any time.[11] The Committee, however, may *not* change the period to which the one-year ranges apply. The base period (the fourth quarter) remains the same throughout the year. Under Humphrey-Hawkins a day of reckoning does arrive when we can see whether the target was hit. There was no day of reckoning prior to Humphrey-Hawkins. Monetary growth rates were always set for "next year," which kept shifting and never arrived. One always looked forward and did not look back on a given *calendar* period as Humphrey-Hawkins requires. Humphrey-Hawkins eliminated base drift and the forgiveness principle.

The greater accountability requirements of Humphrey-Hawkins forced the Fed to amend its errant ways in the historic October 6, 1979, FOMC meeting. February 1979 was the first time the Fed was required to specify money growth ranges under the 1978 Humphrey-Hawkins Act. Using the 1978 fourth quarter as a base, the FOMC stated that in 1979 the money supply was going to grow between 1.5 and 4.5 percent. Look at Figure 11–4, where we show the actual money supply and desired money supplies assuming 1.5 and 4.5 percent growth. The actual money supply in the beginning of 1979 was considerably below the desired level. The Fed took the shortfall in stride; it had several months to correct the situation. From March through September monetary growth accelerated dramatically. By late September it became clear that with three months remaining the Fed would not hit its stated annual objective if it continued its course of action. What an embarrassment! At the very inception of the mandate to specify monetary growth ranges for a given calendar period, the Fed was not meeting its own stated objective because it was overly concerned about interest rates. *At the October 6, 1979, FOMC meeting the Fed revised its strategy.*[12] *The meeting was "historic" for two reasons. First,*

---

[11] At the time of the mid-year review, the FOMC also sets tentative ranges for the monetary aggregates for the next calendar year.

[12] The Fed also revised its targeted money stock upwards, on the grounds that it overestimated the growth of other checkable deposits. Simple revision of the targeted values was insufficient, since it is widely known that targets constantly revised are always hit.

**FIGURE 11–4  Actual money supply and desired money supplies, given 1.5 to 4.5 percent target growth rate, 1979**

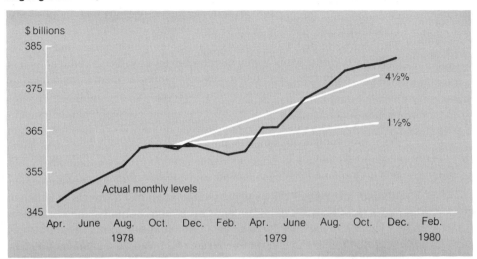

SOURCE: Federal Reserve Bank of St. Louis *Review*, March 1980, p. 9.

*the Fed stated in blood that it would pay much more attention to the money supply and less attention to the federal funds rate. Second, to underscore its commitment to the money supply, the Fed said it would begin controlling the supply of bank reserves more directly.*

Take a look at part of the official operating directive of the November 18, 1980, FOMC meeting:

> At its meeting in July, the Committee agreed that these objectives [reduction of inflation, etc.] would be furthered by growth of M–1A, M–1B, M–2, and M–3 from the fourth quarter of 1979 to the fourth quarter of 1980 within ranges of 3½ to 6 percent, 4 to 6½ percent, 6 to 9 percent, and 6½ to 9½ percent respectively.
>
> In the short-run, the Committee seeks behavior of reserve aggregates consistent with growth of M–1A, M–1B, and M–2 over the period from September to December at annual rates of about 2½ percent, 5 percent, and 7¾ percent, respectively, or somewhat less, provided that in the period before the next regular meeting the weekly average federal funds rate remains within a range of 13 to 17 percent.

Although official statements often do not tell the whole story, this directive, nevertheless, is sufficiently accurate for comparative purposes. Summarizing the important differences between this and earlier directives:

1.  Monetary aggregates (M–1A through M–3) are "long-run" (one-year) operating targets. The Fed did not set long-run targets in 1970, when it had only a month horizon. By the mid-1970s the Fed had a long-run

operating target, but it placed little effective constraint on policy because the target applied to the forever moveable "next year." The *calendar-year* monetary growth ranges required by Humphrey-Hawkins made the constraint more effective.

2. The short-run operating targets are monetary aggregates and the federal funds rates. Money market conditions have been reduced to the federal funds rate, and the monetary aggregates are considered. In order to achieve the targeted monetary aggregates, the account manager now is supposed to focus on reserves. The targeted short-run and long-run rates of monetary aggregates may differ.

3. Tolerance ranges of "about X percent" are specified. Thus, the directive, while not absolutely precise, is more definite than years ago when easier or firmer conditions were prescribed.

Although insufficient time has passed to accurately judge the strength of the Fed's October 1979 commitment to the money supply, the Fed seems to be living up to its word. It does pay *more* attention to the money supply and *less* attention to the federal funds rate. Note, however, that the money supply still is *not* the Fed's only operating target. Monetary growth came to a halt in October and November 1979 but, because the Fed had other targets, monetary growth resumed in December although the money supply already exceeded its desired level. The M–1B growth ranges were raised to 4–6.5 percent in 1980. The 1980 pattern of actual monetary growth relative to the target growth ranges is a near clone of the 1979 pattern although the Fed was operating throughout 1980 under the new operating procedure which focuses on reserves more directly! Look at Figure 11–5. In 1980, however, the Fed did hit, although just barely, the upward range by reducing the money supply in December. To repeat, more time must pass before the October 6, 1979 FOMC meeting is or is not adjudged historic.

With the FOMC's instructions in mind, the manager of the system open-market account, who is a senior vice president of the New York Fed, returns to New York and manages operations until the next meeting.

### Managing the account

Exhibit 11–1 puts you in the trader's desk and shows you how to do it.[13] Would you like to work at the New York Fed? Many find the purchase and sale of Treasury bills worth billions exhilirating, and jobs at the Fed are scarce.

---

[13] Exhibit 11–1 is taken unabashedly from Paul Meek, *Open-Market Operations* (Federal Reserve Bank of New York, 1978). Meek, monetary adviser in the New York Fed Bank's Open-Market Operations and Treasury Issues Division, tells the inside story better than anyone. The Meek pamphlet and numerous other publications are available free from the Federal Reserve Bank of New York, 33 Liberty St., New York, N.Y. 10045.

**FIGURE 11–5   Actual money supply and desired money supplies, given 4 to 6.5 percent target growth rate, 1980**

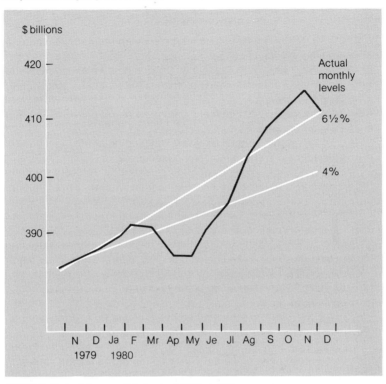

SOURCE: Federal Reserve *Bulletin,* April 1981, p. 278.

Exhibit 11–1 says it all, except for other means of supplying and absorbing reserves besides cash delivery transactions, which involve delivery and payment the same day. A "regular" delivery transaction involves delivery and payment the next business day. Years ago, outright transactions—either cash or regular—predominated, but they currently account for less than 5 percent of open-market operations. The Fed now supplies reserves mainly by making *repurchase agreements* with dealers, where the Fed purchases securities and the dealer agrees to repurchase the same securities at the original price plus interest within an agreed period of up to 15 days. Repurchase agreements are made only at the Fed's initiative. Conversely, the Fed can absorb reserves temporarily through matched sale-purchase, also called reverse repurchase. These transactions involve the Fed first selling Treasury bills and subsequently purchasing the same issue at a predetermined price. Outright transactions can stir hurried consultations as dealers attempt to ascertain whether the transactions are dynamic or defensive. Repurchase or reverse repurchase transactions clearly are short run.

**EXHIBIT 11-1**

---

### The trading desk: They do it daily

Each day presents a new challenge to the account manager and his colleagues. Yet each day has much in common with every other day. It is Tuesday before Thanksgiving. On this day, as on all days, the manager must bear in mind the directive adopted at the last FOMC meeting. Suppose the short-run instructions call for growth of total reserves consistent with a 3–5½ percent growth of M–1B provided the federal funds rate is between 9 and 13 percent.

The trading room's business day begins at 9:00 A.M. News tickers are pounding out the overnight financial news. Securities traders are re-orienting themselves by scanning yesterday's closing quotations on the board facing the open end of the trading desk. Two officers hurry to a 10th floor conference room for separate meetings with representatives of three dealer firms. Fed officers directly responsible for open-market operations meet with the dealers on a rotating basis every business day. The dealers comment on market developments as well as matters of particular interest to their firms. The Fed officers listen and ask questions. The meetings, brief and to the point, are conducted in market jargon. The dealers leave at 9:15. Two senior partners of a second dealer firm enter the conference room. They comment on the market's inactivity during the last few days and other matters. On leaving at 9:30, the two senior partners bump into the vice president of a New York wholesale bank, who covers much the same material. At 9:45 the Fed officers take the elevator down to their eighth floor offices to prepare for the daily Treasury call.

Shortly after 10:15 each day, the fiscal assistant secretary of the Treasury and the account manager use a direct telephone line to compare notes on the immediate outlook for the Treasury's balances at Reserve Banks. Their objective is to coordinate changes in Treasury balances with the system's management of bank reserves. Scheduled transfers from tax and loan accounts to the Treasury's Fed account are $350 million but an expenditure drain of $600 million is projected. The net effect is a $250 decrease in Treasury deposits and increase in unborrowed reserves.

At 10:45 the account manager joins the desk officer in reviewing a research report, received only moments before, which projects factors affecting bank reserves and the base over the next six weeks. The projections are based upon the behavior of factors over the same calendar period during the past several years. The projections indicate that during the next week float will decline $1.5 billion in accordance with end-of-month patterns. A seasonal rise in currency in circulation increases the need to expand reserves.

The projections are just that, projections, and not certainties. The officers get a feel of the market by looking at the federal funds and

**EXHIBIT 11-1 (*continued*)**

Treasury bill rates for signals of the timing and magnitude of the reserve pressures actually at work on this particular day. Two clerks update the quotation board with the latest "runs" of prices and yields obtained by telephone from dealers. The Fed's traders anticipate from their conversations with dealers what the board shows: interest rates are a shade higher. The officers begin to formulate the day's plan of action. The manager writes out the day's program. Meanwhile, a staff call is made to the Board in Washington and to the office of one of the Reserve Bank presidents currently on the FOMC. Today is San Francisco's turn. The officers hurry to an adjoining office to participate in the key telephone conversation—the 11:15 conference call—that formalizes the day's strategy.

"Washington and San Francisco are standing by," announces the telephone operator, completing the three-way telephone hookup that enables the account manager to review developments with the staff of the Board and the Reserve Bank president on call. Participating in the conversation at the New York end today are the president of the bank, the manager of the system account, and the officers of the securities department. Seated directly behind a telephone microphone, the manager speaks:

> Yesterday, we had a shortfall of reserves that more than offset what we put in. We look for a sharp decline in reserves today and tomorrow as currency in circulation increases and float drops. This will be offset somewhat by a decline in Treasury deposits. The uncontrolled tightening is confirmed by the Federal funds rate, which opened at 12⅛ percent bid, ⅝ percentage point above yesterday's close. In view of the expected stringency in reserves, the account plans to purchase as much as $500 million of Treasury bills.

The Board participant and San Francisco Reserve Bank president may express their views and report about possible money supply revisions. The call is usually completed by 11:30. A Board staff member promptly summarizes the call in a memorandum sent to each Board member, and a telegram is sent to each Reserve Bank president.

With the decision made and explained to Fed officials outside New York, the manager turns to the officers and securities traders who sit before telephone consoles linking them to the more than 30 dealers in U.S. securities. "We're going to ask for offerings of all types of bills for cash," the manager says. Each person is quickly assigned two to four dealers to call.

Joan, a Fed trader, presses a button on her telephone console, sounding a buzzer at the corresponding console of a government securities dealer.

**EXHIBIT 11–1** (*concluded*)

---

"Jack," Joan says, "we are looking for offerings of all bills for cash delivery."

Jack replies, "I'll be back in a minute." The salespersons of his firm quickly contact customers to see if they wish to make offerings. Jack consults the partner in charge about how aggressive he should be in offering the firm's own holdings.

Ten minutes later Jack calls back. "Joan, I can offer you for cash $5 million of January 5 bills to yield 8.85 percent—$20 million of January 26 bills at 8.90—$10 million of March 23 bills at 9.05—and $30 million of May 30 bills at 9.14."

Joan says, "Can I have those offerings firm for a few minutes?"

"Sure. It's firm for 20 minutes."

Within minutes the "go-around" is completed. The traders have recorded the offerings obtained from their calls on special preprinted slips. The officer-in-charge arrays the individual dealer offerings on an inclined board atop a stand-up counter. A tally shows that dealers have offered $1.8 billion of bills for cash sale, that is, with delivery and payment today. The officer then begins circling with a red pencil the offerings that provide the highest rate of return—lowest price. An associate keeps a running total of the amounts being bought. When the desired amount—$500 million—has been circled, the individual slips are returned to the traders, who quickly telephone the dealers.

"Jack, we'll take the $5 million of January 5 bills at 8.85 and the $30 million of May 30 bills at 9.14, both for cash; no, thanks, on the others," Joan says.

Only the paper work remains. The traders write tickets, which provide the basic authority for the Bank's government bond department to receive and pay for the specific Treasury bills bought. The Federal Reserve credits to the dealers' banks immediately add $500 million to reserves and the base. A large part of the increase in reserves is transferred the same day over the Fed's wire network from the dealers' checking accounts to the reserve accounts of banks in other cities: $10 million is wired to Hartford by a dealer to pay off an insurance company loan, $25 million to a San Francisco bank to redeem securities held by it, and so on. Thus, reserves spread quickly across the country. And banks gaining reserves may redistribute part of them temporarily by lending them in the federal funds market.

---

## SUMMARY

The three main monetary policy instruments are open-market operations, reserve requirements, and the discount mechanism. To the novice the three instruments are simply alternative means of accomplishing the same end. If the Fed wants less money and higher interest rates, it simply sells securities in the open-market or raises reserve requirements or raises the discount rate. While the three tools can be used interchangeably to achieve the same *general* targets, the sophisticated student of the financial system knows that the *specific* effects of the tools vary considerably. For example, the novice says that the Fed simply raises reserve requirements in order to reduce monetary growth. But can the Fed raise requirements? How will the general public and depository institutions react to the announcement of higher reserves? Will the reserve requirements be broadly based or fall on selected institutions? Will the reduced profitability from higher reserves cause a reduction in the number of financial institutions and higher service charges? The answers to similar questions about open-market operations are quite different.

## QUESTIONS

1. Define defensive and dynamic open-market operations.

2. With the passage of the Monetary Control Act, what financial institutions are subject to the Fed's reserve requirement ratios? What liabilities have reserve requirement ratios, and what do the ratios equal? What assets count as reserves?

3. What are the main means of enhancing bank (a) solvency, and (b) liquidity? How, if at all, do required reserve ratios affect bank solvency and liquidity?

4. State three ways by which the mere existence of reserve requirements aids monetary control.

5. What are the advantages of uniform reserve requirements applicable to all depositories?

6. Discuss the real-bills doctrine of central banking. What are its basic assumptions? Does it tend to stabilize or destabilize the economy?

7. How does one distinguish between borrowing for profit or need? Does the positive association between amount discounted and the difference between market interest rates and the discount rate necessarily imply that borrowing is for profits?

8. Explain the causal relationships which produce a positive association between the discount rate and short-term money market rates.

9. State and evaluate critically various proposals to reform the discount mechanism.

10. State in chronological order the main changes in the authorization and operating instructions given to the manager of the system open-market account.

11. What two changes in the operating instructions of the October 6, 1979, FOMC meeting have led many people to claim the meeting was historic?

# Monetary policy: Strategy, targets, and independence

# 12

Both this and the next chapter amplify and extend the discussion on the strategy of monetary policy begun at the end of the last chapter. Although the topics are similar, the chapter divisions are justified on the grounds that they provide convenient stopping places. The student more interested in the ultimate goals of monetary policy may skip both chapters and proceed directly to Chapter 14. Most students interested in Federal Reserve decision making should read this chapter, particularly if they omit Chapters 19 and 20 on the so-called IS–LM model. The next chapter admittedly is for the specialist.

This chapter is difficult and imprecise, filled with qualifying statements and much hemming and hawing. Yet the difficulty and imprecision are inevitable, given the topic. Brace yourself: economists and other policymakers are not omniscient. The fundamental theme of this chapter is that the economic structure is uncertain. Given this disheartening but undeniable fact, optimal policy is not easily ascertained, if indeed it exists at all. Different *opinions* about the structure of the economy yield different policy prescriptions. This is not to say that all opinions are equally valid. Uncertainty does not mean total ignorance about the economic structure. This chapter first rationalizes the two-stage strategy whereby an operating or intermediate target is selected. We then describe and attempt to grade several of the previously and currently most popular monetary policy targets. In view of the topic's difficulty and indefiniteness, we shall hit only the highlights. The last section shifts from "what" and "why" questions to "who." In particular, it discusses the pros and cons of an independent Federal Reserve.

Some simplification is absolutely necessary. We shall assume universal agreement on a well-defined ultimate goal, which may be one dimensional or a unique, feasible combination of various variables.[1]

## ECONOMY POLICY IN AN UNCERTAIN ECONOMIC STRUCTURE

Monetary policy and economic policy in general involve the manipulation of certain policy tools or instruments (the cause variables) in order to achieve some ultimate targets or goals (the effect variables). Temporarily place policymakers in their paradise: assume they always can achieve their goals even though the policy tools do not have an immediate and direct impact on the goals. When will they be in this paradise? Two conditions are sufficient. First, changes in the policy instruments must have a perfectly predictable effect on the goals. Second, the effect of any other variables on the goals must be perfectly predictable at all times. Figure 12–1 presents a simple schematic representation of some of these

**FIGURE 12–1  Policymaking in a certain environment**

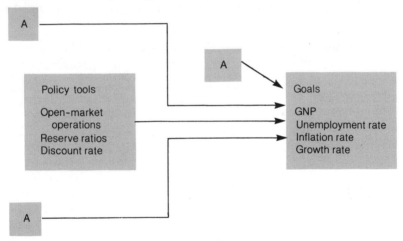

ideas. Time is being measured along the horizontal axis. The causal policy tools precede the goals by some distance because their impact is neither immediate nor direct. Policy works with a lag. The precise, if lagged, relationship between the tools and goals is illustrated by a solid line connecting the two. The figure shows the monetary policy tools and goal variables, but the analysis is applicable to other policies as well. Autonomous, from the viewpoint of the policymaker, factors also influence

---

[1] Chapter 21 analyzes some of the problems associated with multiple goals. Except when confusion may arise, we follow traditional practice of not distinguishing between "goal" as a variable (say, GNP) and "goal" as a specific value of the variable (full employment GNP).

the goals. The lags of the various autonomous factors, represented by A in Figure 12–1, may be either shorter or longer than the policy lag. Provided the policymaker can predict the value and impact of the autonomous variables exactly, then the goals still can be achieved exactly. However, the relationship between tools and goals will no longer be simple. When the autonomous factors are expansionary, the instruments must be set lower than normal. Numerous instrument settings are compatible with given goals, depending on the value of the autonomous variables.

The policymaker's world is not paradise, however. Precisely because ideal conditions do not exist, policymaking is controversial, as the section on open-market operations emphasized. Even assuming away disagreement about goals, controversies arise because of uncertainty or imperfect knowledge about the economic structure, in particular uncertainty about the relationship between instrument and goal and uncertainty about the value and impact of autonomous variables. The question marks about the autonomous variables and the multiple broken lines between variables in Figure 12–2 attempt to portray the uncertain world of the policymaker.

Given our uncertain world, what operating strategy should the policymaker follow? What method of operation maximizes the likelihood

FIGURE 12–2  Policymaking in an uncertain environment

| | **Monetary aggregates** | **Money market conditions** | **Interest rates and credit** |
|---|---|---|---|
| Suggested operating targets | Money supply<br>Monetary base<br>Total reserves<br>Unborrowed reserves | Free Reserves<br>Federal funds rate<br>Treasury bill rate | Long-term bond rate<br>Treasury bill rate<br>Liquidity (Fed's L) |

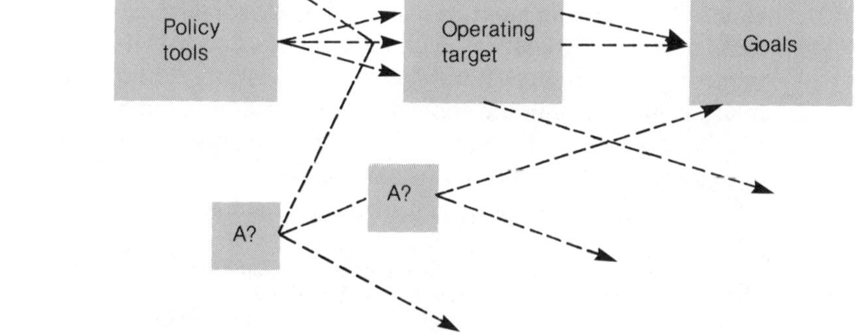

of hitting the goals, given one's estimate of the relationship among the variables? One operating strategy focuses *directly* on the goals. For various reasons most people recommend a two- (or more) stage strategy outlined in the previous chapter. The policymaker focuses on at least one operating or intermediate target which the policymaker treats, for purposes of a short-run operating guide, as if it were the true goal or ultimate target.[2] The (at least) two-stage monetary policy strategy is depicted in Figure 12–2 by a box between the instruments and goals. The intermediate target should be a *readily observable* variable which responds to the policy instruments *before* the goals respond. The top portion of Figure 12–2 identifies some candidates for the monetary policy operating target. Given the goals and the policymaker's best estimate of the autonomous variables and the economic structure, the optimal value of the intermediate target is selected. The policymaker then focuses on this variable and adjusts the instruments to hit the optimal value. Periodically, the value of the intermediate target is adjusted to reflect different goals or different estimates of the autonomous variables.

The two-stage strategy is proposed mainly because it provides information about the autonomous variables in an economy characterized by (1) data lags and (2) structural lags. Accurate estimates of some variables are available virtually immediately. For example, interest rate data are virtually contemporaneous, and relatively accurate estimates of today's money supply are known within a week. Data lags for other variables are considerably longer. A calendar quarter is the shortest period for GNP estimates, and reasonably accurate estimates are first available approximately two months after the quarter ends. Even if the policy instruments had an immediate impact on the goals, data lags imply that policymakers will be unable to achieve the goals because they cannot compensate for the unknown effect of the autonomous variables. A readily available intermediate target may signal the behavior of the autonomous variables and indicate how policy should be adjusted. For example, suppose some autonomous variable reduces both the operating target and goal variable, where the operating variable is readily observable, by definition, but the autonomous and goal variables are observed with a long lag. By concentrating on the intermediate variable, the authorities are forewarned in this case that a more expansionary policy is necessary.[3] The admonition to ball players to keep one's eye on the ball is a good one, provided the ball can

---

[2] Much of the literature on monetary policy strategy and targets and indicators is confused and confusing. A notable exception, both in terms of its high quality and conclusion against uncritical acceptance of intermediate targets and indicators, is Benjamin Friedman, "Targets, Instruments, and Indicators of Monetary Policy," *Journal of Monetary Economics,* October 1975, pp. 443–73.

[3] Particularly when the distinction between targets and indicators is blurred, control by the authorities is supposed to be a characteristic of a good target. If this were the case, the targets would *not* provide information about the exogenous variables and thereby would defeat one of their main functions. We shall discuss indicators later.

be seen before it crosses the plate. If one cannot see the ball, then one should search for clues as to when to swing.

Of course, the instruments do not have an immediate impact on the goal; structural lags exist. Even if there were no data lag with respect to the goal variable, the existence of structural lags implies that the authorities will be unable to compensate for the unpredicted effect of autonomous variables. Focusing on an intermediate target is desirable because the autonomous variables are not totally random over time, that is, they are *not* serially *un*correlated. For example, the policy instrument as well as the autonomous variables influence the intermediate target before they influence the goal. Suppose today's policy instruments and autonomous variables affect the intermediary target next month and the goal next year. Today's autonomous variables are related to prior autonomous variables, that is, the autonomous variables are serially correlated. The strength and consistency of the relationship between current and prior autonomous variables depends on the length of the lag. Consequently, monitoring the intermediate target yields better information on the proper setting of the instruments necessary to compensate for today's autonomous variables. In our example, the current value of the intermediate (goal) variable depends upon last month's (year's) autonomous variables. The current value of the autonomous variables, which the policy instruments must counteract in order to achieve the goal next year, is more closely related to last month's value than last year's value. Therefore, focusing on the intermediate variable instead of the goal may provide better information on the current value of the autonomous variables and increase the likelihood of setting the policy instrument at the value proper for the goal.

Another justification for the two-stage strategy is different degrees of uncertainty about economic linkages between instruments and goal. If the policymaker is reasonably certain about the relationship between the target and goal, then in the short-run the policymaker may treat the target as if it were the goal and concentrate his or her energies on the difficult task of hitting the optimal value of the intermediate target.[4]

The major issues in this two-stage strategy are:

1.  Assuming a single operating target, which one is the best? The candidates are money market conditions, particularly free reserves, interest rates, and the money supply.
2.  Are multiple targets, either at the same or different points in the chain linking instruments and goals, feasible and desirable? In terms of Figure 12–2, may one have numerous items in one intermediate target box and several boxes at different horizontal positions.

---

[4] The two justifications for a two-stage strategy—the information content of the operating target and a reasonably certain relationship between operating target and goal—may be mutually contradictory.

The answers to these questions depend heavily on one's estimate of the structure of the economic system.[5] Because only estimates (guesses?) of the economic structure are available, we give both the pros and cons to the answers presented more or less in chronological order of their popularity.

## FREE RESERVE STRATEGY

The section on open-market operations in Chapter 11 stated that prior to 1966 monetary policy, as summarized by the open-market directive, focused exclusively on money market conditions. When defining terms, the Fed stated that money market conditions included the federal funds rate, three-month Treasury bill rate, and the elusive tone and feel of the market. Whatever weight these variables may have had in some official definition of money market conditions, in reality money market conditions were equivalent to free reserves, which are excess reserves minus discounts at the Fed. Large (small or even negative) free reserves indicated easy (firm) money market conditions.

The Fed never stated explicitly why free reserves became the target. Nevertheless, the argument for free reserves is seemingly based on its being a good predictor of future money supply and interest rate movements and, ultimately, income and prices. Open-market purchases or increases in uncontrolled sources of the base have a positive immediate impact on excess reserves and, therefore, on free reserves. Banks' initial reaction may be partial repayment of their discounts. This has no effect on free reserves. Drawing down excess reserves to repay discounts keeps the difference between the two constant. The high free reserves generated by the open-market purchase are only temporary. Banks will shortly make loans and create deposits, causing lower interest rates and a larger money supply.

What is wrong with a free reserve target? The Fed totally ignored, or at least significantly underestimated, the effect of the autonomous factors on free reserves, which is somewhat surprising since one reason for an operating target is the information it yields about the autonomous variables. The significant underestimate made the money supply procyclical and reduced the normally moderating behavior of interest rates. For example, suppose firms suddenly become more pessimistic about the future and start spending less. A recession gets underway. The spending decline is accompanied by a reduction in the demand for credit and lower market interest rates. Recalling the determinants of excess reserves and dis-

---

[5] The "structure of the economic system" certainly does incorporate those very complex relationships between money, interest rates, real output and prices, which take up the bulk of Chapter 14 onward. Consequently, the reader may well want to return to this chapter after reading most of the book, say, after Chapter 20. Nevertheless, some aspects of the structure of the economic system are sufficiently simple to justify an early look at monetary policy.

counts, what will happen to free reserves? Lower market interest rates increase banks' demand for excess reserves and reduce discounts, particularly since the discount rate lags market rates. Both large excess reserves and small discounts increase free reserves.

The Fed did not realize that banks' demand for free reserves depended significantly on market rates. Consequently, the larger free reserves alarmed the Fed. It feared that it was expanding the monetary base too rapidly and that the money supply would be rising and interest rates falling too rapidly in the near future. The Fed responded by *selling* securities, which reduced the money supply and prevented a rapid interest rate decline. Of course, in time the Fed realized that a recession was under way and that the larger free reserves were not expansionary because the demand for free reserves had risen. However, the lagged awareness of market interest rate effects on free reserves and the general underestimate of the effects made the money supply procyclical about turning points and reduced the interest rate fluctuations which help stabilize the economy.

A free reserve target was equally objectionable during the expansionary phase of a business cycle. As the boom got under way and market interest rates rose because firms were borrowing more, the demand for free reserves fell, often to negative levels. Unaware of the business boom and decline in the demand for free reserves, the Fed responded by open-market purchases in order to maintain free reserves at the constant target value. The open-market purchase increased the money supply and partially offset the higher market rates which help stabilize the economy during booms. The Fed's commitment to free reserves should not be questioned just because it is as silly as the deaf man who heard the mute person say that the blind woman saw the crippled person run—on water.

## MONEY AND INTEREST RATES: MULTIPLE TARGETS

The last chapter stated that both before and after the historic October 6, 1979, FOMC meeting the Fed officially had two short-run operating targets, monetary growth rates and the federal funds rate. The meeting was "historic" because the *effective* target shifted from interest rates to money. We asserted without proof that the Fed generally cannot hit both targets simultaneously. This section presents the proof and some empirical data supporting a behavioral shift.

Figure 12–3 draws the demand and supply of money as functions of interest rates. We do not wish to get into an excursus on the shape of these curves. Good old-fashioned common sense supports the proposition that the amount of loans and money supplied by banks increases and the amount demanded by the public decreases when interest rates rise.[6] Al-

---

[6] We do not want to suggest that money is a loan (credit). However, we are aware that the reader may recognize the similarity between Figures 5–3 and 12–3. Figure 12–3 purposely has interest rates (plural) on the vertical axis because the argument against multiple targets is independent of the specific interest rate selected.

**FIGURE 12–3  The Federal Reserve generally cannot control both interest rates and money**

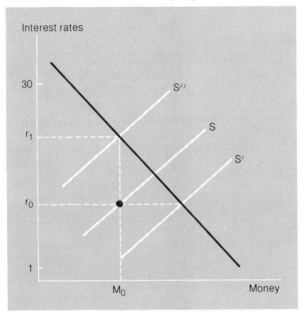

though the Fed expresses the monetary target as a growth rate, there is a one-to-one relationship between growth rates and current values, given the previous period base quantity. From a diagrammatic viewpoint, money levels are more convenient than growth rates. Suppose $r_0$ and $M_0$ are the Fed's multiple interest rate and money targets, respectively. Are the multiple targets feasible? Generally, no. The Fed's instruments influence the supply curve. Lower reserve requirements, for example, shift the supply curve outwards from S to S'; banks are able to supply more money at any interest rate. The Fed can set the instruments so that the supply curve goes through the point $(M_0, r_0)$. However, the Fed's instruments do not directly influence the demand curve. Except in the fortuitous situation where the demand curve passes through the point $(M_0, r_0)$, these two targets are incompatible. The supply curve S leads to small errors in both targets. Figure 12–3 shows that one could hit either target exactly at the expense of larger errors in the other target.

The Fed's targets are not precise, as we have been assuming so far, but are ranges. (We explore shortly the rationale for ranges.) General Custer trained his men to be sharp shooters by using big targets. Similarly, wide ranges increase the likelihood of attaining multiple targets. For example, the money supply $M_0$ is feasible according to Figure 12–3 provided the interest rate can range between 1 and 30 percent. In this case, interest rates are not an effective target, in the sense that it does not constrain use of the instruments. When multiple targets are specified, the width of the targets and the frequency and size of errors provide clues concerning the effective target. They are not infallible clues for various reasons. For example, presumably no one knowingly selects unattainable targets; the Fed mistakenly thought $(M_o, r_o)$ was feasible. One target may be hit more frequently simply because it is easier to predict.[7] Nevertheless, when the size of the *relative* ranges and errors differ significantly over time, we may reasonably assume shifts in the main operating target.

Figures 12–4 and 12–5 support a shift in operating targets as announced at the October 6, 1979, FOMC meeting. Prior to the meeting, the FOMC

**FIGURE 12–4   1979 federal funds rate, actual and FOMC target range**

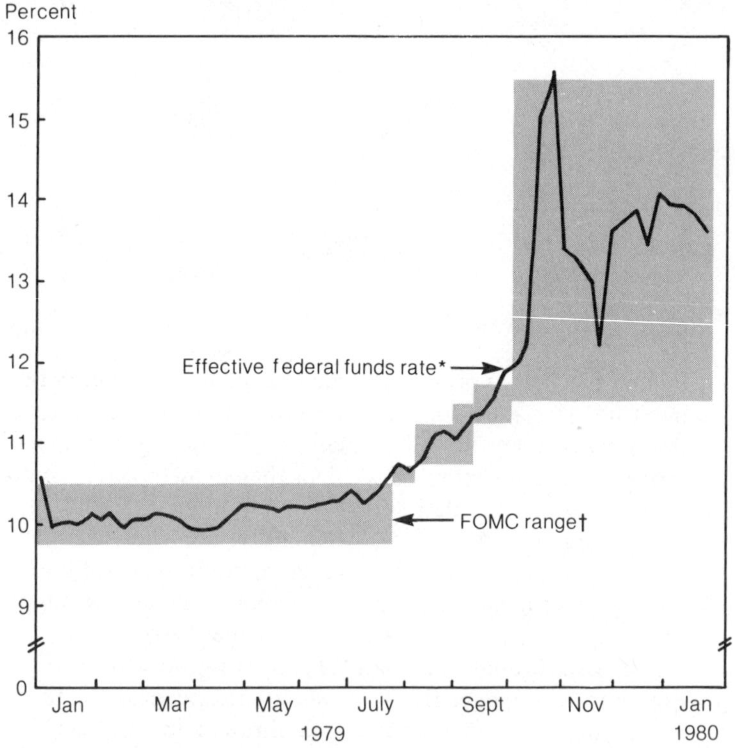

* Weekly averages of effective daily rates
† At each meeting during 1979 the FOMC established a range for the federal funds rate. These ranges are indicated for the first full week during which they were in effect
**SOURCE:** Richard Lang, "The FOMC in 1979: Introducing Reserve Targeting," Federal Reserve Bank of St. Louis *Review*, March 1980, p. 12.

---

[7] Even the measurement of targets is controversial. Why should money be seasonally adjusted? Is the seasonal pattern *created* by the Fed and then expunged by seasonally adjusting? Is the commitment to interest rates disguised by seasonally adjusting money but not interest rates?

**FIGURE 12-5    1979 money growth rates, actual and FOMC target range**

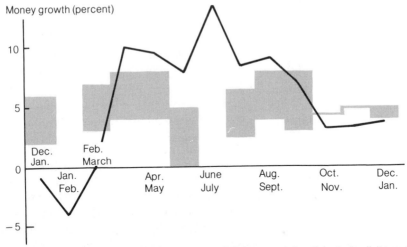

**Note:** Monetary targets were not specified for January/February and June/July. An implicit target range existed from October to December since the Fed specified growth rates "in the order of" some percentage.
**SOURCE:** Federal Reserve Bank of St. Louis *Review*, March 1980, pp. 4, 11; and various Federal Reserve *Bulletins*.

range for the federal funds rate was no more than three quarters of one percent, and the target always was hit. Moreover, the range was relatively constant across the monthly FOMC meetings. In contrast, the FOMC tolerance ranges for monetary growth rates before October 1979 were quite wide—at least 4 percent—and the Fed hit the range only in one month, and then barely so. The Fed did not even specify money growth rates for January/February and June/July 1979. The FOMC ranges for money fluctuated considerably across the monthly decision-making periods. Roles were significantly reversed after October 1979. The FOMC range for fed funds was widened to 4 percent. The Fed hardly deserves congratulations for hitting the funds target more or less continuously since it now was practicing the General Custer principle. The October 1979 and immediately subsequent meetings did not specify a *range* for money growth; growth rates "in the order of" a certain number were specified. By January 1980 a range, albeit smaller than previously stated, was again specified. Although the Fed did not hit the unique money targets during the October to December 1979 periods, the difference between target and actual values during the period was consistently less than the difference between mid-range and actual values prior to October. The Fed reduced the size of the money target *and* became more accurate, in total contradiction of the Custer principle.

What is the main target today? At this writing (mid-1981), monthly "Records of Policy Actions of the FOMC" in the Federal Reserve *Bulletin* suggest that the Fed has weakened somewhat in its new resolve to focus quite sharply on money and is reverting to weighing interest rates more heavily, though still much less so than before October 1979. The reader interested in more current data should consult the *Bulletin*.[8]

We have been implicitly assuming that interest rates and money are concurrent targets. That is, in terms of Figure 12–2 we have assumed the two targets are in the same box. While this is a valid interpretation of Fed policy, the Fed also suggested prior to October 1979 that the federal funds rate was a target anterior to money. In other words, the Fed claimed both the two-stage strategy just outlined *and* a three-stage strategy where it focused on the funds rate to hit the target money supply, which in turn would hit the ultimate goal. Are interest rate and money targets feasible when the former is anterior? In general, no, largely for the same reasons that concurrent interest rate and money targets generally are infeasible. If nothing else, the federal funds rate and money do not have even the same dimensions. The Fed recognized the folly of its particular three-stage strategy and shifted to reserves as an anterior target.

> The principal reason advanced for shifting to an operating procedure aimed at controlling the supply of bank reserves more directly was that it would provide greater assurance that the Committee's objective for monetary growth could be achieved.[9]

No two targets, either synchronous or nonsynchronous, are perfectly compatible at all times unless they are identical, such as a short and long-run money supply target. Nevertheless, a dollar aggregate like reserves is far preferable to interest rates as an anterior target for money. The next chapter shows that something even better than reserves exists.

## MONEY OR INTEREST RATES

"The question is," said Humpty Dumpty," which is to be master—that's all."[10] Which shall be master, money or interest rates? The Fed's operating strategy is not developed in total isolation. It largely reflects the prevalent economic thinking of the time. For many years most academic economists favored an interest rate target. Advocates of a money target long were a small, if vocal, minority. Their numbers grew rapidly and by 1980 they dominated the profession. This is not to say that so-called monetarists dominate the economics profession, and Keynesians are a

---

[8] The importance of personalities in monetary policy is great indeed. The last chapter stated that Professor Burns' appointment to the Fed chairmanship in 1970 occasioned the *first* mention of money in a FOMC directive. The October 1979 meeting followed by only three months the appointment of Chairman Paul Volcker. He, however, had been a permanent committee member as president of the New York Fed Bank.

[9] Federal Reserve *Bulletin*, December 1979, p. 974.

[10] Lewis Carroll (Charles Dodgson), *Through the Looking Glass* (New York: Elsevier and Everyman's Library).

minority. Monetarism and Keynesianism are convenient *multi* dimensional lables. *A money target instead of an interest rate target indeed is a cardinal tenet of monetarism.* Nevertheless, many supporters of a money target would be uncomfortable in the monetarist camp. The eclectic middle sides with the monetarists on this issue.

We sketch a scenario where the majority's position is the correct one.[11] Assume firms become pessimistic about the future sales outlook and respond by reducing investment spending today. The expectations pattern tends to be self fulfilling. The reduced investment spending by firms causes producers of plant and equipment to lay off employees and reduce their output. With increased unemployment and lower incomes, the sales of all firms drop, just as had been expected. Since some investment spending is financed by borrowing, lower investment spending reduces the demand for loans and interest rates fall. What happens to the money supply? It also falls slightly, other things being equal. According to Chapter 4, the money supply multiplier falls as the desired excess reserve and time/check deposit ratios rise in response to lower interest rates. The base also falls as banks find it less profitable to borrow at the Fed. How should the Fed respond to high unemployment and low production levels? Clearly, the Fed should restore the previous level of aggregate demand by increasing the quantity of money and bank credit and, thereby, lowering interest rates. If the money supply were the Fed's policy target, the appropriate response is sure to follow. Observing a fall in the money supply which is contrary to the desired policy, the Fed undertakes some combination of large open-market purchases, reserve requirement reductions, and discount rate reductions. However, if the rate of interest were the policy target, the Fed may well be lulled into sitting on its hands. Lower interest rates are necessary to restore full employment, but the decline in aggregate demand and high unemployment have simultaneously lowered interest rates. Observing that interest rates already have fallen, the Fed may believe its job has been done and fear an even greater reduction in interest rates—the appropriate policy to restore full employment—would simply be inflationary.

Keynesian advocates of an interest rate target still exist because they are correct on occasion. Assume greater uncertainty about the economy which induces individuals to want more liquid money and less illiquid bonds. As the public sells its bonds in the hope of acquiring cash, the interest rate tends to rise. If the interest rate were the Fed's target, then it immediately would purchase securities in the open market to prevent the higher interest rates. This is the appropriate policy in this case. Given society's constant outlook about goods and services, a constant interest rate is necessary to maintain output. Higher interest rates would have reduced spending and income. If the Fed had focused on the money

---

[11] A formal proof using IS–LM analysis concludes Chapter 20.

supply, it would have remained largely idle because the sale of bonds mainly shuffles bonds and money among the public with little impact on the total. In this case, the higher interest rates would not be counteracted and would reduce spending and income.

If interest rate movements predominantly reflect changes in the demand for money as the last paragraph assumed, then interest rates would be good targets. On the other hand, if interest rates were influenced by a myriad of factors, then observation of their fluctuations tells us that something happened, but what? The monetarist argument against interest rates states that money demand is stable and interest rates pick up too many signals, making interpretation of their fluctuations extremely difficult. Monetarists stress the importance of inflationary expectations on interest rates. (Recall Chapter 5's analysis which indicated that as first approximation interest rates rise by the expected rate of inflation.) If, instead of the last paragraph's larger money demand, interest rates had risen due to higher inflationary expectations, and if the Fed had responded identically by *increasing* the money supply, then monetary policy fuels inflationary expectations. Resist the temptation to argue that the Fed would not act in this manner in this case. If the Fed knew what case it was, it would not need a target.

## OPEN-MARKET INSTRUCTIONS: VAGUENESS VERSUS PRECISION OR ART VERSUS SCIENCE

Whatever the operating variable may be, should its targeted value be specified precisely or vaguely? Recall that a shift towards greater precision is one of the major changes in open-market directives. Still, the directives generally specify fairly wide ranges. Why is the Fed so imprecise about its target? *First, policy vagueness facilitates reaching a consensus.* We said that policy disagreements stem from differences over (1) goals or ultimate targets, (2) forecasts of the state of the economy and the effect of nonpolicy variables, and (3) forecasts of the effect of the policy instruments on the goals. Yet policymakers rarely discuss such differences explicitly. Exposing the source of policy disagreements typically strengthens the disagreements and paralyzes decision making. Because precise policy proposals usually must be justified more rigorously, preciseness exposes sources of policy disagreement and reduces the likelihood of arriving at a consensus. If positions do not have to be justified, committee members may arrive at the same conclusion for different reasons. For example, someone who believes that a deep recession is imminent and that the policy instruments are very powerful will favor a "moderate" policy. But those who believe that a small stimulus is sufficient and that the policy instruments are relatively weak will also favor a "moderate" policy. Thus, two people come to the same conclusion for different reasons. Moreover, disagreement implies that compromises may be necessary. Compromises are more easily reached when committee members believe others are flexible. Precise targets suggest inflexibility and generate hostile reactions from other committee members. These ideas are partially confirmed by the greater number of dissenting opinions now that the directives are somewhat more precise.

Second, there is the General Custer principle: large targets make sharp shooters. Imprecise targets shield the Fed from the criticism that it does not hit its target. Moreover, the compatibility of vague targets with many goals not only facilitates decision making within the Fed but lessens outside criticism that the Fed is pursuing undesirable goals. It is much easier to deny charges when you admit nothing beforehand. As a result of frequent accusations of being overly concerned about inflation and paying too little attention to unemployment, the Fed feels constantly under siege. Vague responses are characteristic of any organization that feels threatened.

Finally, vague answers often are equated with expert answers to difficult questions, while precise answers allegedly are given to easy questions by those suffering from tunnel vision. The need to maintain the aura that monetary policy cannot be reduced to a few simple rules and requires great breadth of vision is especially important to an independent Fed. In other words, the long tenure of Fed Board members and other aspects of Federal Reserve independence, which will be discussed shortly, can be justified only if monetary policy is an art practiced by wise people above the political fray. The Fed has convinced others and, more important, itself that monetary policy is an art instead of a science.[12] Life is so complex that the FOMC demands the famous staff statistical summary and slide show before it begins deliberations. After a long pause and a deep draw on a pipe or a cigar which fouls the air with curls of white smoke, your typical Fed officials begin their responses to senators' questions with, "Things are not so simple." While such an opening line might encourage follow-up questions—after all, no one should be embarrassed asking questions about things that are not so simple—the opening line is designed to justify subsequent gobbledygook that unfortunately thoroughly intimidates most questioners and convinces them that Fed officials have the wisdom to deal with these not so simple issues.

## POLICY INDICATORS

Let us now switch gears and look at one aspect of *market* behavior. The Fed cannot directly focus on the millions of market participants. There simply are too many. The Fed must infer the behavior of millions from a few prices and quantities. Individual economic units are luckier. Ignoring the Treasury's minor monetary powers, there is only one monetary au-

---

[12] Maisel, *Managing the Dollar*, p. 168.

thority. The effects of monetary policy on many large economic units are sufficiently strong yet uncertain and variable that it is profitable for them to search for indicators of monetary policy.[13] Indicators of current policy are valuable because policy works with a lag and because it presages future policy, that is, policy is serially correlated. A combination of ease of observation, the profit motive, and just plain curiosity has produced thousands of Peeping Toms. What is the Fed up to? Defining terms formally, the *monetary policy indicator is the variable which best measures the effect of monetary policy on the goal variable.* Each economic unit here specifies its goal, which, in principle, could be virtually any variable. For example, a gold dealer wants to know the effect of Federal Reserve policies on the price of gold, which is his goal variable. The indicator literature invariably assumes, however, that some aggregate output or employment measure is the goal. These socially oriented goals are assumed because, as one might expect, the indicator problem has been discussed most extensively by academic economists, who seem motivated more by curiosity and a desire to heap blame or lavish praise than by profits.

While the Fed makes mere observation of its actions easy—it releases weekly data on its open-market operations and the base, and the discount rate and reserve ratios are known continuously—construction of an indicator which interprets and summarizes the Fed's actions is difficult. A good indicator should possess two characteristics. First, the indicator should be dominated by the Fed's actions. Second, the indicator should be closely related to the goal. Unfortunately, there is no perfect indicator, in the sense that one cannot find a variable which changes only when the Fed acts and which has a one-to-one relationship with aggregate output. If a perfect indicator existed, the Fed, and only the Fed, would influence output. Second best situations often are complex and indefinite, and this case is no exception. The most frequently suggested indicators are "adjusted" reserves; the "adjusted" monetary base; a short-term interest rate, particularly the federal funds rate; a long-term interest rate; and the money supply, where reserves or the base are adjusted for reserve requirement changes. For example, if reserve ratios are reduced by 10 percent, the adjusted base rises 10 percent.

In general, a trade-off exists between the two properties of a good indicator. The more strongly is a variable dominated by the Fed, the weaker typically is its relationship with the goal. This is so because short lags between policy instruments and indicators reduce the time non-Fed variables can influence the indicator. However, this increases the number of non-Fed variables that can come between the indicator and goal, given any structural lag between Fed instruments and the goal.

---

[13] We accept Benjamin Friedman's minority viewpoint ("Targets, Instruments, and Indicators of Monetary Policy") that the *monetary authority* does not need an indicator. The *public* needs an indicator. Anterior targets and indicators are conceptually distinct although the same variable may fulfill both functions.

A concrete example is helpful. The Fed's portfolio of securities, which measures net cumulative open-market operations, satisfies the first characteristic perfectly. The Fed, and only the Fed, is responsible for open-market operations. However, float has the same effect as open-market operations on banks' ability to lend and create deposits. Consequently, reserves or the base, which incorporate float, should be better related to the goal, but neither is perfectly controlled by the Fed. There has been a tendency over time for the preferred aggregate to shift closer toward Federal Reserve control and from interest rates to a monetary aggregate. Many who favored the money supply several years ago now prefer the adjusted base, thereby not attributing to the Fed any influence on the multiplier except through the reserve ratio. Proponents of long-term interest rates have largely shifted to short-term interest rates or adjusted reserves.

## SHOULD THE FEDERAL RESERVE BE INDEPENDENT?

Some hot topics become old hat so quickly that they burn less energy than some tepid issues which smolder year after year. The independence of the Fed has been one tepid issue from the moment of the Fed's existence until today. The independence of the Fed within the structure of the federal government is illustrated in several ways. First, the tenure of Board members is 14 years, and they can be removed from office only for cause. Board members cannot be removed from office simply because their views are unpopular or because they belong to the wrong party. The term of office is sufficiently long to minimize the threat of covert political pressure. Moreover, the terms of office are staggered to prevent presidential "packing" of the Fed. The president does not even get to appoint the Fed chair immediately.[14] Second, Federal Reserve operations produce so much income that it is not dependent on congressional appropriations. Third, the Board reports and is accountable to Congress not the executive. For many years the Board avoided virtually any contact with the administration. The need for coordination has recently lead to the inclusion of the Fed chair in the Quadriad and similar meetings of main economic policymakers.

The independence of the Fed is far from absolute, particularly in the long run. Congress created the Fed and gave it the authority to execute the monetary responsibilities Congress has under the Constitution. At any time Congress may change the structure of the Fed or even abolish it. Aware of this, the Fed is sensitive to contemporary political opinion.

Defending the independence of the Federal Reserve at the 1976 commencement exercises at Bryant College, former Fed Chairman Arthur

---

[14] The chair's term of office is four years. If not reappointed to the chair, the person may continue serving the remaining portion of the 14-year term.

Burns said that the major justification for an independent Fed is "the need for a strong monetary authority to discipline the inflationary tendencies inherent in modern economies."[15] While inflation itself is not a goal of any administration, decision makers prone to political pressure tolerate too high inflation rates in order to accomplish other goals.

> Under our scheme of governmental organization the Federal Reserve can make the hard decisions that might be avoided by decision makers subject to day to day pressures of political life.
>
> *   *   *   *   *
>
> Such a step [monetary policy lodged in the presidency] would create a potential for political mischief or abuse on a larger scale than we have yet seen. Certainly, if the spending propensities of federal officials were given freer rein, the inflationary tendency that weakened our economy over much of the past decade would in all likelihood be aggravated.[16]

There are three main arguments against the Fed's independence. First, an independent Fed is undemocratic. In a democratic society policy goals are formulated by elected officials. To the extent an appointed agency substitutes its goals for those of elected officials, a fourth branch of the Constitution has been indirectly created. Second, even if everyone shared common goals, attainment of the goals requires coordinated policy, which independence largely precludes.[17] Third, an independent Fed is not much more likely to curtail inflation. The same Chairman Burns, who while in office said that an independent Fed was absolutely essential in the battle against inflation, reflected with anguish after leaving office in 1979 that "viewed in the abstract, the Federal Reserve System had the power to abort the inflation at its incipient stage 15 years ago or at any later point, and it has the power to end it today. It did not do so because the Federal Reserve was itself caught up in the philosophic and political currents that were transforming American life and culture."[18]

## SUMMARY

Monetary policy in the postwar period has been characterized by relative constancy of goals but significant diversity in operating strategy. Prior to 1965 free reserves unquestionably were the intermediate or operating target which the Fed sought to control in order to achieve its goals. A free reserve policy produces a procyclical monetary policy. Whenever aggre-

---

[15] Arthur Burns, "The Independence of the Federal Reserve System," *Challenge,* July 1976, p. 23. Reprinted with permission of publisher M. E. Sharpe, Inc., Armonk, New York, 10504.

[16] Ibid., pp. 21 and 23.

[17] A formal proof of the need for policy coordination is presented in Chapter 21.

[18] Arthur F. Burns, "The Anguish of Central Banking," the 1979 Per Jacobsson Lecture, Belgrade, Yugoslavia, p. 14. Reprinted by the American Enterprise Institute.

gate demand increases, free reserves tend to fall. In order to maintain the targeted value of free reserves, the Fed purchases securities, causing interest rates to fall and the money supply to expand. Severe criticism finally dislodged the Fed's attachment to free reserves. The Fed then officially started wearing bifocals; its two proclaimed targets were interest rates and money. Just as one cannot simultaneously focus through both lenses of bifocals, the Fed generally cannot control both interest rates and money. Throughout the 1970s interest rates were the effective operating target, as Keynesians recommended. The relative ascendancy of monetarism and relative decline of Keynesianism is reflected in a shift from an effective interest rate policy to a money supply policy. Time is too short to tell how firmly rooted monetarism is at the Fed.

## QUESTIONS

1. What conditions must exist in order for policymakers to achieve their ultimate goals?
2. What are the fundamental justifications for a two-stage policy strategy which focuses on an operating target?
3. Define free reserves. State the rationale for a free reserves operating target. When will free reserves be a poor operating policy, that is, produce a procyclical monetary policy?
4. Demonstrate that the Fed generally cannot hit an interest rate and money supply target simultaneously.
5. What type of information is helpful in determining which of two stated operating targets is the effective operating target?
6. When is the money supply preferable to interest rates as an operating target? Are interest rates ever a better operating target than the money supply?
7. Whatever the operating target may be, why does the Fed specify a target range instead of a specific value?
8. What is meant by an indicator of monetary policy? What two characteristics should an ideal indicator possess?
9. In what ways is the Federal Reserve independent?
10. List the arguments for and against an independent Federal Reserve.

# Can the Federal Reserve control the quantity of money?

# 13

The last chapter stated that the Fed cannot control money and interest rates simultaneously. We further claimed that the reason the Fed was quite wide of the short-run money mark was because it indeed chose to exercise some control over interest rates. There exists another possibility we did not consider: the Fed simply cannot control the money supply. This possibility should be analyzed because the money supply is the *only* long-run (annual) target, yet the Fed barely hit its big monetary target, as we indicated in the last chapter. (The target growth range for M–1B was 4 to 6.5 percent.) Can the Federal Reserve control money? This is one of the basic questions of money and banking which must be answered affirmatively.

Control of the money supply by the Federal Reserve is the subject of unnecessary controversy because of (1) the linking of logically distinct but practically joint arguments, and (2) the failure to acknowledge unequivocably the existence of side constraints and costs. Two tenets of monetarism are: The Fed *should* control the money stock, and the Fed *can* control the money stock. The last chapter indicated that situations arise where the Fed should control interest rates instead of the money supply. While acknowledging this possibility, monetarists claim such situations are so infrequent that a monetary target is far superior to an interest rate target. The response to monetarists by most economists, particularly those within the Federal Reserve System, has verged on the illogical until quite recently. Most Fed officials preferred to claim lack of control rather than debate whether money or the rate of interest is the appropriate target. In other words, the Fed generally chose to link the monetarists' logically distinct propositions—the Fed can and should control money— and based its defense against the should-control proposition by denying the can-control proposition. Denial of the can-control proposition was largely based on the existence of many factors influencing the money supply. Presumably, the Fed cannot counteract these other factors.

In its more exact moments, the Fed acknowledges that the answer to the can-control issue is not clearly negative. The Fed then alleges only that the costs greatly exceed the benefits of monetary control, where the main costs are associated with the interest rate fluctuations necessary to control money. Fluctuations in the rate of interest or other variables generally are imperfectly predicted, misallocate resources, and unquestionably increase the cost and difficulty of planning, particularly for financial institutions. However, neither the Fed nor anyone else has been able to measure the magnitude of the cost of variable interest rates. Without measurement, the cost-benefit argument against the should-control proposition must remain speculative. Perhaps because the cost-benefit argument is speculative, the Fed generally is careless in expressing its opposition to monetary control. It's much simpler to claim that money cannot be controlled. If the can-control question is negative, then the should-control question is moot.

## CONTROL, TIME, AND UNCERTAINTY: THE GENERAL CASE

Before answering the chapter's title question, let us state two fundamental principles about policymaking and control applicable to both fiscal and monetary policy. (1) Control must be discussed within some time frame of reference determined by the policymaker's ultimate goal. (2) In an uncertain world perfect control of an intermediate target (for example, the quantity of money) does *not* guarantee attainment of the ultimate goal (for example, some desired value of GNP). Consequently, perfect control is an unreasonable requirement. Control is said to exist when the actual value of the intermediate target approximately equals the desired value, given the ultimate goal.

### Control and the time period

Fundamental principles surely are stated succinctly, so let us elaborate. Suppose that in view of the economic goals the Fed wants the money supply to remain constant. Suppose further that in spite of Federal Reserve efforts to keep the money supply constant, the various uncontrolled factors affecting the base and multiplier cause the money supply to follow an erratic path. The daily and even weekly money supply varies substantially but the average money supply during calendar quarters remains constant. Does the Fed have control over the money supply in this case? Clearly the answer depends on the appropriate time interval of the analysis. No, the Fed does not control daily and weekly money balances, but it does control quarterly average balances. What is the appropriate time interval of analysis? If weekly fluctuations in the quantity of money had no effect on the goal variable, what mattered being the quarterly average quantity of money, then the Fed does control money. Of course, if weekly fluctuations had significant effects on the goal, then the Fed does not control money. The question of control is inseparable from the effect of the intermediate target on the goal; the target variable matters not in its own right but because of its effects on the goal. Economic policy is for practical people. Policymakers are judged on their ability to control variables which have a significant effect on the ultimate goal.

### Control and exogenous factors

Regardless of the appropriate time period, policymakers never can hit the targeted value to the last decimal place. If there were an exact and predictable relationship between the target variable and the goal, then lack of perfect control is the sole reason for not achieving the goal. For example, suppose the goal is a $3 trillion annual income (GNP), the full employment level of GNP. If income always were five times the money supply, then the money target is $600 billion, and actual income always differs from the goal by five times the difference between the actual and targeted money supply. No one seriously believes that the relationship between any target variable, monetary or otherwise, and the ultimate goal is exact and predictable. The monetary authority at best knows the average relationship between monetary policy and the goal. Strikes, oil embargoes, and government spending, which may be viewed as exogenous variables from the viewpoint of the monetary authority, have an effect on income. Income occasionally will be greater than $3 trillion because the exogenous forces are expansionary. Conversely, depressive exogenous forces cause income to fall short of the goal even when the money supply is $600 billion. Since perfect control over the policy variable does not guarantee achievement of the goal at all times, requiring perfect—to the last decimal—control is unreasonable. Control, without any qualifying adjective, exists when the differences between the actual and target values of money are sufficiently small. In such cases monetary errors explain only a small proportion of the discrepancy between the actual and goal values of GNP, the major discrepancy being due to exogenous forces.

The statement that monetary control exists when the difference between the actual and targeted values of the money supply is "sufficiently small" lacks precision. But that is exactly the point. Control of a policy variable is not a matter of yes or no but of degree. Barring the absolute, the existence of control cannot be proven but is the subject of agreement among reasonable people.

### The monetary control period

How are these general principles related to the question of control over the quantity of money? No one believes that reasonable (up to 2.5 percent) daily monetary fluctuations have any effect whatsoever on goal variables. (Of course, 2.5 percent daily is identical to over 900 percent annually, so we are talking about changes larger than typically observed.) Indeed, one is somewhat hard pressed to find individuals who believe that the observed fluctuations in the monthly average money supply have affected GNP. Money growth rates alternating monthly between 4 and 6 percent surely have virtually the same effect on GNP as a steady 5 percent growth per month. Discrepancies between the actual and targeted values of quarterly average money supply do cause GNP to deviate from its desired value, but the importance of even quarterly discrepancies should not be exaggerated. To be conservative and err on the side against monetary policy, and because the Fed specifies monthly money growth ranges, assume months are the appropriate time period of analysis.[1]

## AN OPERATING STRATEGY TO CONTROL MONEY

Precisely what operating strategy should the Fed follow? Numerous operating strategies have been proposed, but we shall discuss only one which gives quite accurate results. As has been stressed, the money supply may be expressed as the product of the multiplier and the base, $M = m \cdot B$. Given some target money supply, the preferred operating strategy predicts the multiplier and, given this prediction, selects the value of the base consistent with the desired money supply. How the desired money supply value was selected is irrelevant for the can-control problem at hand. Under this regime the base becomes the target and the money supply is the goal.[2] With its prediction of the multiplier in hand, the FOMC operates on the base to attain some specified monthly average money supply. Intramonthly fluctuations in the base are tolerated; the FOMC focuses on the monthly average base. Monetary control requires both (1) hitting the monetary base target, and (2) predicting the multiplier

---

[1] Although the Fed often specifies a bimonthly monetary growth target, the bimonthly target is set *after* the first month has passed. This is identical to setting monthly targets. We return to the monthly targets in Chapter 23, where we discuss policy credibility and rational expectations.

[2] This is simpler than the equivalent notion of the base as anterior intermediate target and the money supply as posterior intermediate target.

relatively accurately. Expressing these ideas in terms of the general form of the money supply equation,

$$\text{Desired money supply} = \text{Predicted multiplier} \times \text{Target base}, \quad (13\text{--}1)$$

$$\text{Actual money supply} = \text{Actual multiplier} \times \text{Actual base}, \quad (13\text{--}2)$$

$$\frac{\text{Desired money supply}}{\text{Actual money supply}} = \frac{\text{Predicted multiplier}}{\text{Actual multiplier}} \times \frac{\text{Target base}}{\text{Actual base}} \quad (13\text{--}3)$$

The actual money supply approximately equals the target value when the actual base approximately equals the target value and the multiplier is predicted relatively accurately.[3]

### Control of the base

Could the Fed control money if it adopted the strategy outlined here? The answer nowadays is a loud yes, as the remainder of this section demonstrates. Consider first the Fed's ability to hit the monthly average monetary base target. As Chapter 10 said, uncontrolled accounts are pushing the base in one direction today and another tomorrow. Some of the uncontrolled sources and uses of the base fluctuate significantly within a month but are more stable from month to month. Float is an example of such an account. Monthly fluctuations in other uncontrolled accounts, for example, Treasury deposits at the Fed, can be as large as intramonthly fluctuations. Nonetheless, defensive and dynamic open-market operations can completely offset uncontrolled factors and hit a monthly base target.[4] How can we be so definite? First, under this strategy the Fed knows just what has to be done. The (actual) monetary base is derived exclusively from the Fed and Treasury balance sheets, which are available daily. While the Fed may well tolerate *intra*monthly variations of the monetary base, as the end of a month approaches the Fed knows virtually exactly the *monthly average* actual base, which is compared with the monthly

---

[3] The reader may wonder why the opposite strategy is not proposed. That is, why not operate on the multiplier by changing reserve requirements and predict the base? From the viewpoint of monetary control, an important difference between the multiplier and base is the data lag. The Fed is virtually continuously aware of any changes in the base, which is a liability of the monetary authorities. At the beginning of each day the Fed and Treasury have balance sheets figures for the end of the previous day and, therefore, can compute the base. The Fed does not have to predict the base; it knows the value of the base. The multiplier includes ratios of items on banks' balance sheets, which are available to the authorities on a preliminary basis only after a time lag in some cases of several days, and highly accurate information may be available only after several months. For this reason and others, attempts to control the multiplier in the short run by frequently changing reserve requirements make little sense. This is not to deny that reserve requirement changes nearly always have a rapid effect on the multiplier, the possible exception being during a multiplier trap to be discussed shortly. The point, however, is that the resultant effects of reserve requirements changes are known accurately only after a lag.

[4] Defensive and dynamic open-market operations were defined at the end of Chapter 10 and beginning of Chapter 11.

average target base.[5] Second, the account manager can purchase or sell the appropriate amount of securities to close any gap between desired and actual values. Look again at the relative size of the accounts in the monetary base equation, Table 10–6, and the summary of Chapter 10. Fed holdings of U.S. government securities are ten times larger than any uncontrolled account. Moreover, the total trading volume of U.S. government securities is approximately $12 billion daily. A moderate annual rate of monetary growth (say, 6 percent) requires approximately a $0.5 billion monthly increase in the monetary base. Uncontrolled factors rarely change the base by more than $5 billion per month. Therefore, the maximum *monthly* volume of defensive and dynamic open-market operations, $5.5 billion, is less than half the *daily* trading volume of U.S. government securities. The base target can be hit precisely easily enough.

### Predicting the multiplier

Since the Fed can control the base, controlling the money supply then revolves on the Fed's ability to forecast the multiplier. Figure 13–1 shows

**FIGURE 13–1   The money supply multiplier**

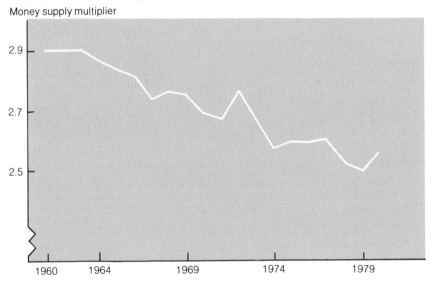

SOURCE: *Economic Report of the President, 1981.*

the value of the money supply multiplier for an almost 20-year span. Although the multiplier varied considerably during this long period, hit-

---

[5] We are not suggesting that the account manager should take a vacation until the end of each month and ignore all beginning-of-month random forces. The text simply emphasizes that hitting a monthly average target is consistent with significant intramonthly variation.

ting a high of 2.91 in 1960 and a low of 2.53 in 1979, it is reasonably stable over short periods. Chapter 4 indicated that the multiplier depends on income, interest rates, and numerous other variables. For purposes of short-run predictions, a much simpler relationship may yield sufficiently accurate forecasts of the multiplier. Albert Burger has proposed the following forecasting equation.[6]

$$\text{Predicted money multiplier} = 0.29 + 0.89 \text{ lagged money} \\ \text{multiplier} + 0.04 \text{ lagged Treasury bill rate percentage} \quad (13\text{--}4) \\ \text{change}$$

This forecasting equation takes as inputs variables that the Federal Reserve knows accurately. For example, to predict the December 1981 money multiplier with this equation, the Fed must know only the November 1981 multiplier and the Treasury bill rate in October and November. In essence, this is a very mechanical method that does not attempt to incorporate information the Fed might have about expected movements of such key factors as Treasury deposits in the forecast month. Moreover, although the Fed sets reserve requirements, this forecasting equation assumes reserve requirement changes surprise the Fed. The predicted multiplier using equation (13–4) does not depend on reserve requirements during the period. Surely this leads to prediction errors; the actual multiplier in, say, December 1981 does depend on the December 1981 reserve requirements. While alternative forecasting equations should be able to perform as well as this simple, mechanical method, its virtue is precisely its simplicity, which facilitates implementation.[7] When the monthly forecasted multiplier given by equation (13–4) is compared with the actual multiplier, the forecasting errors are quite small. The average forecasted multiplier/actual multiplier ratio is less than 1.001 or, equivalently, the average forecasting percent error is less than 0.1 percent.[8]

---

[6] "Money Stock Control," in *Controlling Monetary Aggregate II: The Implementation* (Boston: Federal Reserve Bank of Boston, 1973). Equation (13–4) was constructed to forecast the old M–1 multiplier. Since old M–1 and new M–1A are virtually identical, the equation should forecast M–1A approximately as well. Moreover, a similar equation with somewhat different coefficients should forecast M–1B accurately. Recent structural changes might reduce the predictability of any multiplier.

[7] For an even simpler, more mechanistic but still relatively accurate (though not as accurate as equation (13–4) method of forecasting the multiplier, see Anatol Balbach, "How Controllable is Money Growth?" Federal Reserve Bank of St. Louis *Review*, April 1981, pp. 3–12.

[8] The calculated errors are for the period 1964–71 and should be updated after the full effect of recent structural changes are felt. While the structural changes may have increased prediction errors, the 1964–71 period used to test the equation also was a difficult period for monetary control. Reserve requirements were changed seven times, and Reg Q ceilings caused the time/check deposit ratio to vary significantly.

James Johannes and Robert Rasche, in "Predicting the Money Multiplier," *Journal of Monetary Economics*, July 1979, pp. 301–25, claim that various statistical problems in a Box-Jenkins ARIMA model of the multiplier occur because of reserve requirement changes. As a result, they construct a net monetary base series, which is adjusted for reserve re-

Since the money supply is the product of the multiplier and base, and since the monthly average value of the base can take any value the Fed wants, the average ratio of the desired value to the annual value of money also is less than 1.001. See equation (13–3). The monthly average difference between the desired and actual money supply is less than 0.1 percent. Is this difference between desired and actual values sufficiently small that the Fed can claim control of the money supply? While recognizing that there is no definite answer, we would answer the question affirmatively. Yes, the Fed can control the money supply! GNP will differ from its goal value mainly because the Fed (like others) incorrectly estimates the target money supply, and only in small part because the Fed cannot hit the incorrectly estimated monetary target.

## QUALIFYING COMMENTS

We said several times in the last section that the Fed can control money *nowadays,* and we believe control will continue in the future. However, as Chapter 9 indicated, monetary control is a relatively recent phenomenon. Indeed, lack of control was one of the main reasons Congress passed the Federal Reserve Act in 1913. But a central bank is *not* a sufficient condition for monetary control. The operating strategy, laws and regulations, and the structure of the financial system all influence the degree of monetary control. For example, the Fed could not control money when its operating targets were free reserves and the federal funds rate.

### A reserve target for money

Assuming the Fed was unconcerned about interest rate fluctuations, could it control the money supply, given its current operating strategy? Our answer is a slightly qualified yes. We chose to express the money supply as the product of "the" multiplier times the base. The money supply may also be expressed as the product of any number of reserve measures and a multiplier m', where the value of m' depends on the specific reserve measure. For example, we show in the Appendix that if M = mB, where, as usual, M is the money supply, m is the (base) multiplier, and B is the base, then

$$M = \frac{(1 + k)m}{1 + k - mk} R \qquad (13\text{–}5)$$
$$= m'R$$

---

quirement changes, and a corresponding net adjusted multiplier. They forecast the adjusted multiplier directly and by components using ARIMA models. We prefer the forecasting equation (13–4) because ARIMA models are complex and because our approach determines a base target at the *beginning* of each month independently of events during the month. Accurate predictions of an adjusted multiplier do not necessarily imply accurate monetary control since the corresponding adjusted base target may be difficult to attain. Accurate multiplier predictions are only one element of monetary control.

where R is total reserves, k is the currency/check deposit ratio and the other terms are as just defined. The Fed prefers equation (13–5). Because it prefers equation (13–5), the Fed's current strategy seeks the value of total reserves consistent with the given target value of the money and the predicted total reserve multiplier m'.[9] The Fed's current strategy is quite similar to our preferred strategy outlined in the last section, where the (base) multiplier is predicted, and the base is the operating target for the money supply. Although the two strategies are quite similar, the monetary base target is somewhat better. Precisely because the money supply is better controlled by focusing on the monetary base instead of total reserves, from the beginning we viewed money as the product of the (base) multiplier and the base although our equations in Chapter 4 are formally equivalent to equation (13–5).

The base is better than reserves as a monetary control target for two reasons. First, since the base is constructed exclusively from Treasury and Federal Reserve balance sheets, it is known with certainty subject to at most a one day lag. Balance sheets can be constructed daily. The data lag for reserves is longer. Banks' *deposit* reserves are known also subject to a maximum one day lag, but the currency component is uncertain for a week until banks submit their required reports. While the weekly data lag for reserves is quite short for many purposes, a week's lag is significant for purposes of short-run monetary control. One cannot be certain of hitting the monthly reserve target when the actual value is unknown for a week. Second, for reasons that are not obvious, the base multiplier m is forecast better than the reserve multiplier.[10]

**The lagged reserve rule**

Recalling Chapter 11, the lagged rule sets required reserves this week on the basis of deposits two weeks ago. In determining the timeless equilibrium money supply of Chapter 4 we justifiably could ignore the lagged provision. For purposes of short-run control where timing is crucial, the type of reserve ratio, lagged or contemporaneous, does matter. The remainder of this section shows how the lagged reserve rule increases the interest rate instability associated with any monetary control policy.

---

[9] Total reserves are the operating target across FOMC meetings but unborrowed reserves are the day-to-day target. "Under the approach adopted in October 1979, the FOMC sets short-run targets for monetary expansion. . . . A path for total reserves is calculated based on the expected relationship between reserves and the money stock—the so-called reserves-money multiplier. . . . A path for nonborrowed reserves then is calculated by making an allowance for the portion of total reserves expected to be provided through borrowings at the Federal Reserve Bank discount windows." Board of Governors of the Federal Reserve System, "Monetary Report to Congress Pursuant to the Full Employment and Balance Growth Act of 1978," February 25, 1981, p. 25.

[10] Burger, "Money Stock Control." The Fed, however, has recently claimed that there is no clear evidence that one multiplier is predicted more accurately than the other. "Monetary Policy Report to Congress," p. A29.

Assume the Fed does not engage in open-market operations or in any other way counteract bank actions, irrespective of the reserve rule. The unit of analysis is the aggregate banking system. Suppose the demand for business loans increases this week. Under either reserve system, banks accommodate their customers and create additional deposits. Deposit expansion under a contemporaneous reserve rule increases required reserves, which banks first attempt to acquire by borrowing in the federal funds market. This raises the federal funds rate and interest rates generally. However, the federal funds market simply shuffles reserves among banks without affecting the total. The higher interest rates do induce banks to discount at the Fed and demand less excess reserves. In this manner they meet their higher reserve requirements. Contrast this situation with the lagged reserve rule, where banks can create deposits this week without any restraining influence from *predetermined* required reserves. Although current reserves place no constraint on current loan and deposit expansion, the expansion is finite because banks realize that required reserves rise in the future, at which time the cost of reserves may be high. Nevertheless, without the discipline of coincident requirements, deposit expansion under the lagged rule is likely to be greater. Because deposits and required reserves increase more in the lagged case, two weeks hence the federal funds rate, and interest rates generally, must rise more than they did in the coincident case in order to increase discounts and reduce excess reserves more. The lagged reserve rule increases the interest rate volatility associated with any degree of monetary control or, more likely, reduces the degree of monetary control exercised, given the Fed's aversion to interest rate volatility.

The Fed now recognizes that the lagged reserve rule, which was introduced when credit market conditions were the operating target, reduces the degree monetary control and is considering reverting to contemporaneous reserves. The Fed does not act precipitously, however.

## MONEY SUPPLY LIQUIDITY TRAP

A money supply *liquidity trap* is the extreme case of lack of monetary control. The same term will be used in the discussion of money demand but the concepts are quite different.[11] A *money supply* liquidity trap refers to a situation where the Federal Reserve encounters great difficulties in changing the quantity of money *relatively rapidly*.[12] The control con-

---

[11] A *money demand* liquidity trap occurs when monetary expansion, rapid or otherwise, has no effect on aggregate demand because additional money is hoarded.

[12] U.S. Congress, *Hearings on H.R. 5327* (Banking Act of 1935). 74th Congress, 1st Session, (Washington, D.C.: House Committee on Banking and Currency, 1935); George Horwich, "Effective Reserves, Credit, and Causality in the Banking System of the 'Thirties," in *Banking and Monetary Studies,* ed. Dean Carson (Homewood, Ill.: Richard D. Irwin, 1963); Karl Brunner and Allan H. Meltzer, "Liquidity Traps for Money, Bank Credit, and Interest Rates." *Journal of Political Economy,* January/February 1968. *Traps* can be

troversy concerns how closely the target can be hit; the trap controversy concerns the possibility that *no* monetary change can be effected in the near future. The discussion usually is phrased in terms of monetary increases because the possibility of a trap was first raised to excuse the Fed's conduct during the 1930s, when surely the appropriate policy was a large and rapid monetary expansion. Yet, the money supply fell by approximately one third between 1929 and 1933, when the economy hit bottom and slowly began climbing upward. Prices rose approximately 2.3 percent annually between 1933 and 1935, but they still were 20 percent lower than 1929 prices. Unemployment in 1936 was 16.9 percent. Only medicine men would have doubled reserve requirements, as the Fed did, in order to cure an "inflationary bias."[13] Apologists for the Fed argued that its misguided actions were of little consequence because any attempt at rapid monetary expansion was doomed to failure.[14]

To ascertain the validity of the apologists' claim, consider first how the Fed changes the money supply. The general instruments of monetary control are (1) open-market operations, (2) the discount rate, and (3) reserve requirements. The first two instruments affect the base, while the latter affects the money supply multiplier. A money supply trap exists if the Fed encounters difficulty changing (1) the multiplier through reserve requirement changes—a multiplier trap—*and* (2) the base through discounts and open-market operations—a base trap.[15]

### A money supply trap in 1929–1933

A multiplier trap clearly existed in the 1929–33 period. The Fed did not have the authority to change reserve requirements! Did a base trap also exist? Whether or not the Fed could have prevented the sharp fall in the money supply during the Great Depression is debatable. At that time the Fed was subject to various "reserve" requirements in terms of gold and real bills. That is, gold and real bills had to equal specified percentages of the Fed's currency in circulation and bank reserve deposits. (All reserve

defined differently, sometimes causing misunderstanding. Brunner and Meltzer's study is the most complete *comparative statics* study of traps. They largely ignore the question of the time involved in moving from one money supply to another. Here, the speed of adjustment rather than the ultimate effect determines whether or not a trap exists.

[13] In the late 1970s a woman finally was appointed to the Board of Governors of the Federal Reserve System. Reserve requirement policy in the 1930s was discussed in Chapter 4's section on excess reserves.

[14] The apologists allege even more frequently that a money demand liquidity trap existed so monetary expansion, even if successful, would have no effect on aggregate demand and output. The chapters on income theory consider this possibility.

[15] We ignore the implausible case where a change in the base (multiplier) would induce an exactly countervailing change in the multiplier (base), keeping the money supply constant. There may be some interaction between the two determinants of money but, lacking perfect offset, the money supply responds to changes in either determinant. Our multiplier trap has also been called a bank credit trap.

requirements for the Fed were repealed by the late 1960s.) During the Great Depression commercial bank excess reserves were relatively low and discounts were still significant, though less than in the 1920s. Some economists claim that the Fed could not have engaged in massive open-market purchases because banks would have repaid their discounts, and the Fed would have failed to meet its required reserve ratios. While the *immediate* impact of open-market purchases on the base indeed is largely negated by repayment of discounts, *ceteris paribus,* the offset effect is relatively short lived. After an extensive analysis, Professor Milton Friedman concluded that the evidence does not support the existence of a liquidity trap in the early 1930s.[16] The Fed's excess "reserves" were sufficiently large, and the offset effect due to discounts was sufficiently short lived that massive open-market purchases were possible. Moreover, the *ceteris paribus* condition does not have to hold. The Fed could have lowered the discount rate.[17] The money supply could have increased in the Great Depression. Only a lack of determination prevented the Fed from increasing it.

### A money supply trap in the late 1930s

By the late 1930s when the Fed incorrectly *increased* reserve requirements, banks were swollen with excess reserves, and discounts had fallen to an inconsequential amount. Whether a multiplier trap ever occurred when the Fed had the ability to change reserve requirements is debatable, but at no point in U.S. history were economic conditions more favorable for such an occurrence than during the late 1930s. Banks do have a desired excess reserve ratio, which implies that reserve requirement changes *in either direction* ultimately affect the money supply. However, we saw in Chapter 4 that banks reacted slowly to the reserve requirement increase. If the Fed had instead lowered requirements, the additional excess reserves probably would have had little impact on the money supply in the short run. Sometimes banks temporarily demand the extra excess reserves, and bank credit does not expand. When interest rates and the demand for loans are extremely low due to poor business conditions, as was true during the late 1930s, all credit-worthy borrowers have been satisfied. Finding additional borrowers takes time. Alternatively stated, an increase in actual excess reserves may initially raise the desired ratio because banks do not have ready borrowers. Ultimately, borrowers are found, the desired excess reserve ratio returns to its original level, and

---

[16] Milton Friedman and Anna Schwartz, *A Monetary History of the United States, 1867–1960* (Princeton: Princeton University Press, 1963). For a contrary view, see E. A. Goldenweiser, *American Monetary Policy* (New York: McGraw-Hill, 1951). Goldenweiser was the director of the Fed's Division of Research and Statistics.

[17] Recall that instead the Fed *raised* the discount rate for balance of payment purposes. See the section on discounts in Chapter 11.

deposits increase to eliminate the undesired excess reserves. Recall, however, that many banks are involved in the money supply process, taking time for the expansion process to be completed. Banks often ration credit during prosperous periods and, consequently, have a ready pool of credit-worthy borrowers.

In the late 1930s the United States might have been in a multiplier trap. Higher reserve requirements between June and December 1936 were accompanied by a temporary monetary expansion rather than contraction. Reserve requirements fell between December 1937 and June 1938 but check deposits remained virtually unchanged.[18] *Temporarily* the money supply multiplier was more or less fixed, and lower required reserves were accompanied by a higher demand for excess reserves. However, to our knowledge no one has claimed a base trap existed during the late 1930s. Any claims about a base trap are limited to the Great Depression. Massive open-market purchases were possible and would *not* have resulted in a reserve deficiency for the Fed. The Fed only held approximately 7 percent of marketable U.S. government securities outstanding, which by 1938 was larger than the money supply.[19] The Fed also had more than an adequate amount of gold certificates by the late 1930s. Large open-market purchases were possible and would have increased the money supply.[20] Mistakes rather than inability characterize Federal Reserve policy during the 1930s.

## SUMMARY

This short chapter applies, extends, and summarizes many ideas expressed in earlier chapters. For example, Chapter 11 described the lagged reserve rule, and this chapter states one of its most important implications. Chapter 4 presented a history of the Federal Reserve's misguided reserve requirement policy and of the excess reserve situation in the late 1930s. The possibility of a slow adjustment process was mentioned then, and its full implications are drawn now. This pulling together of material is occasioned by the importance of the chapter's main topic: Can the Federal Reserve control the quantity of money? Yes, the Fed can control money today. With an affirmative answer we are ready to explore monetary *policy,* and not simply monetary *disturbances.*

Although the total financial system was not one of this chapter's main

---

[18] See Table 4–2.

[19] Board of Governors of the Federal Reserve System, *Banking and Monetary Statistics* (Washington, D.C.: National Capital Press, 1943), pp. 35, 512.

[20] Open-market purchases must increase the quantity of money provided at least some of the securities are sold by the public. If banks sell all the securities and demand the additional reserves the multiplier falls sufficiently so that the money supply remains constant in spite of the increase in the base. However, banks never are the only sellers of securities. Sales by banks alone implies that they are indifferent between earning assets and reserves while the public is not.

topics, we should reemphasize at this time the importance of the financial system, which is the second main strand of thought running through the previous chapters. In the process of creating money, banks lend. Because the banking system is the major lender, the structure and performance of the banking industry were singled out for special attention. But banks are only one group of lenders. We expanded our sight to include nonbank intermediaries such as savings and loans, credit unions, life insurance companies, and retirement funds because as a group their loans exceed bank loans by approximately 50 percent. While a direct finance market where ultimate borrowers and lenders meet does exist, banks and non-bank intermediaries play a key role in a financial system which transfers funds and, ultimately, resources among economic units. A smoothly functioning financial system is absolutely essential to improve the allocation of resources both among economic units and over time and to reap the advantages of specialization.

## QUESTIONS

1. Discuss the relationship between policy control, the time period, and policy goals.
2. What are the implications for policy control of exogenous factors influencing the goals?
3. What is the appropriate monetary control period?
4. Describe the preferred operating strategy for monetary control discussed in the text. How does it compare with the operating strategy outlined by the FOMC at the October 6, 1979, meeting?
5. Explain how the lagged reserve rule increases interest rate variability for any monetary control rule.
6. Define a money supply liquid trap, a base trap, and a multiplier trap. Which, if any, of these traps existed in 1929–33 and in the late 1930s?

---

appendix · The bank reserves multiplier

We expressed the money supply, M, as the product of "the" multiplier, m, and the base, B.

$$M = mB \qquad (13A\text{--}1)$$

This appendix shows that the money supply may also be expressed as the product of a multiplier m′ and reserves, R, where m′ is given by equation (13A–2),

$$M = m'R = \frac{(1 + k)m}{1 + k - mk}R, \qquad (13A\text{--}2)$$

and k is the currency ratio, C/DC.

By definition, the base equals reserves plus currency, which may be expressed as the product of the currency ratio and deposits.

$$B = R + C = R + kDC \qquad (13A-3)$$

Making use of the money definition

$$M = DC + C = (1 + k)DC \qquad (13A-4)$$

Substituting equations (13A–3) and (13A–4) in (13A–1) gives

$$M = m(R + kDC) = m\left(R + \frac{kM}{1 + k}\right) \qquad (13A-5)$$

Rearranging equation (13A–5) gives (13A–2).   Q.E.D.

# PART 4

# Monetary theory

# National product and income accounts

# 14

The basic questions of monetary economics are: (1) can the Federal Reserve control the quantity of money, (2) does money affect the total amount spent, and (3) how is the amount spent translated into prices and quantities of goods acquired? Up to now we basically have been concerned with the first question. The following chapters answer the second and third questions. Prior to launching into monetary theory, however, let us examine the precise meaning of such terms as total spending, income, GNP, saving, and investment. The so-called national product and income accounts are the subject of this chapter.

It must be emphasized from the outset that this chapter makes no pretense of offering income or monetary theory. It presents no behavioral relationship concerning the determinants of total spending or income and does not attempt to explain why and by how much money affects total spending. Just as we first had to know precisely what money is before analyzing the Fed's control of money, so we must know how total spending or income is measured before explaining why it equals a certain value this year. Thus, this chapter provides the background for the theoretical chapters that follow. Since the purpose of this chapter is simply to provide necessary background material, we resisted the temptation to present a complete discussion of the national income and product accounts. Many technical items like the difference between net national product and national income are ignored when these items are unimportant for our theoretical models. We describe the measurement of only those economic variables whose determinants will subsequently be analyzed.

## THE NATURE OF GROSS NATIONAL PRODUCT

Gross national product, popularly known as GNP and represented in algebraic equations by Y, is the market value of all goods and services produced by a nation's economy during a stated period of time. Production is measured at its point of *final* fabrication or sale during the period. GNP is available on a quarterly basis and usually is expressed at an annual rate. That is, if GNP in January–March 1980 equals $650 billion, annualized GNP during this period is $2.6 trillion per year. GNP is not available for periods shorter than a quarter, but of course, GNP for longer periods is readily computed by adding quarterly figures. The term *gross* indicates that the nation's entire output is measured, including that amount which simply replaces capital goods worn out during the period. GNP avoids double counting by measuring the value of output at its point of final fabrication or sale during the period. Perhaps in order to be brief, many authors state that GNP is the market value of *final* goods and services. While brevity is desirable, the brief statement causes some readers to believe incorrectly that unfinished goods are not included in GNP. The value of goods in process of production is included in GNP. Assume a simple economy where the only production during the period is a semifinished auto. GNP is not zero but equals the value of the partially completed auto. Consider another example. Suppose a farmer produces wheat, which is sold to a miller who produces flour, which in turn is sold to a baker who sells bread to consumers. Wheat and flour are transformed in a subsequent production stage in this example, and GNP does not measure these items. Only the market of bread is included in GNP. However, if the period had ended *before* the baker had an opportunity to bake bread, the flour would enter GNP. By counting the market value of goods and services only at their point of final fabrication or sale during the period, GNP measures total output once and only once.

Table 14–1 presents data on GNP and related measures for selected years following World War II. Column (1) shows the annual market value of GNP (Y, for short), with quantity or output, y, valued at the level of prices, P, prevailing during the year. In symbols, $Y \equiv Py$. Changes in the market value of GNP reflect the behavior of both output and price, two variables with quite different welfare implications. Perhaps because a comparison of market values hides as much as it reveals, market values are called nominal values. Columns (2) and (3) break down nominal GNP into output and price; the product of column (2) and column (3), with the decimal shifted two places to the left, equals column (1). Column (2) shows the value of GNP for each year at constant (1972) prices. Since column (2) eliminates the effect of price changes from nominal GNP, it is an indicator of output and called real GNP. Column (3) is an index of prices of all goods and services included in GNP. It measures the general level of prices during the year as a percentage of the general level of prices

**TABLE 14–1   Nominal GNP, real GNP, and the GNP price index, annual values and percentage changes** (selected years between 1946 and 1980)

| Year | (1)<br>Nominal<br>GNP<br>(billions<br>of $)<br>$Y \equiv Py$ | (2) y<br>Real GNP<br>at constant<br>1972 prices<br>(billions<br>of $) | (3) P<br>GNP<br>price<br>index<br>(1972 =<br>100) | (4)<br>Nominal<br>GNP,<br>per-<br>centage<br>change | (5)<br>Real<br>GNP,<br>per-<br>centage<br>change | (6)<br>GNP<br>price index,<br>percentage<br>change |
|---|---|---|---|---|---|---|
| 1946 ........ | 209.8 | 478.3 | 43.8 | — | — | — |
| 1947 ........ | 233.1 | 470.3 | 49.6 | 11.1 | −1.7 | 12.9 |
| 1948 ........ | 259.5 | 489.8 | 53.0 | 11.3 | 4.1 | 6.9 |
| 1949 ........ | 258.3 | 492.2 | 52.5 | 0.5 | 0.5 | −0.9 |
| 1956 ........ | 421.7 | 671.6 | 62.8 | — | — | — |
| 1957 ........ | 444.0 | 683.8 | 64.9 | 5.3 | 1.8 | 3.4 |
| 1958 ........ | 449.7 | 680.9 | 66.0 | 1.3 | −0.4 | 1.7 |
| 1959 ........ | 487.9 | 721.7 | 67.6 | 8.5 | 6.0 | 2.4 |
| 1966 ........ | 756.0 | 984.8 | 76.8 | — | — | — |
| 1967 ........ | 799.6 | 1011.4 | 79.1 | 5.8 | 2.7 | 3.0 |
| 1968 ........ | 873.4 | 1058.1 | 82.5 | 9.2 | 4.6 | 4.4 |
| 1969 ........ | 944.0 | 1087.6 | 86.8 | 8.1 | 2.8 | 5.1 |
| 1973 ........ | 1326.4 | 1255.0 | 105.7 | — | — | — |
| 1974 ........ | 1434.2 | 1248.0 | 114.9 | 8.1 | −0.6 | 8.7 |
| 1975 ........ | 1549.2 | 1233.9 | 125.6 | 8.0 | −1.1 | 9.3 |
| 1976 ........ | 1718.0 | 1300.4 | 132.1 | 10.9 | 5.4 | 5.2 |
| 1977 ........ | 1918.0 | 1371.7 | 139.8 | 11.6 | 5.5 | 5.8 |
| 1978 ........ | 2156.1 | 1436.9 | 150.1 | 12.4 | 4.8 | 7.3 |
| 1979 ........ | 2413.9 | 1483.0 | 162.8 | 12.0 | 3.2 | 8.5 |
| 1980 ........ | 2627.4 | 1480.7 | 177.4 | 8.8 | −0.2 | 9.0 |

**SOURCE:** *Economic Report of the President, 1981.*

in 1972. Columns (4)–(6) show the annual percentage change of columns (1)–(3). The percentage change of nominal GNP approximately equals the sum of the percentage changes of real GNP and prices. Annualized quarterly data for GNP are graphed in Figure 14–1.

Examination of Table and Figure 14–1 reveals several important facts about the post-World War II period.

1.   Nominal GNP has increased more or less continuously, the sole exception being 1949. Both higher prices and higher real GNP account for the growth of nominal GNP, with prices being somewhat more important. In 1980 real GNP and the price index were approximately 3.10 and 4.05 times, respectively, their levels in 1946. The few years of declining real GNP witnessed increases in nominal GNP as prices rose faster than output fell. The upward march of nominal GNP was interrupted in 1949, and prices fell that year.

2.   The upward trend of real GNP—3.5 percent annually between 1948 and 1980—has been less consistent. Real GNP fell in seven years, and four of those years have been after 1969. The largest annual percentage decline

**FIGURE 14–1    Gross national product**

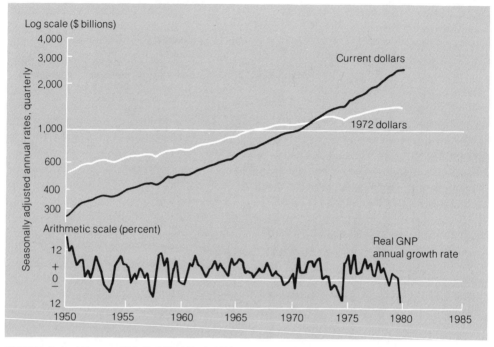

SOURCE: Federal Reserve, *Historical Chart Book, 1980.*

of real GNP in the postwar period occurred in 1947, when it fell nearly 2 percent. Two successive years of declining GNP occurred in 1974–75. Compared to the pre-war period, recent downturns have been shorter and more moderate. The average annual rate of decline of real GNP between 1929 and 1933 was approximately 8 percent, and output fell by 5.5 percent in 1938. Nowadays, "bad times" often are characterized by a failure of real GNP to grow fast enough rather than by a decline in GNP. Changes in GNP are reflected in the unemployment rate. While the 8.5 percent unemployment rate in 1975 was excessive, the average unemployment rate in 1930–33 was 18.3 percent.

3. In no other period in the history of the United States has inflation, measured by the percentage change in the GNP price index, been so persistent. Prices fell only once, in 1949. Moreover, the rate of inflation seems to be escalating. The average inflation rate was 2 percent between 1956–65, 5.7 percent in the following decade, and 7.2 between 1976–80. Prior to the 1970s, there was a tendency to dismiss high rates of inflation as the inevitable consequences of unusual events, particularly wars. Prices rose sharply following World War II as price controls were phased out, during the height of the Korean conflict, 1951, and during the prolonged Vietnam War, 1965–70. However, the uncomfortably high rates of

inflation in 1974–75 and 1978–80 cannot be explained by a war that requires low unemployment rates for the mobilization effort. The term *stagflation* was coined to describe 1974–75, years of declining or slowly growing GNP, high unemployment, and high inflation. The relationship between output and inflation is discussed in Chapter 23.

## WHY GNP IS IMPORTANT

Economic statistics are a growth industry. Every year governmental units, private firms, and nonprofit institutions flood the nation with more economic statistics, some of so little value that one wonders if they were collected simply to keep statisticians employed. Most economics statistics, however, are quite useful, and their announcement generates much attention. GNP is one of the statistics watched most widely and closely. Why is this so? Goods and services are not produced out of thin air but require the use of labor and capital. While technical progress causes output to grow over time even if labor and capital are constant, higher levels of output at any one time necessitate higher employment and capacity utilization. GNP may be viewed as an indicator of the rate of use of factors of production and, to some extent, the importance of GNP is derived from this property. High GNP is associated with high employment or, equivalently, low unemployment. But GNP is more than just a proxy for unemployment, a statistic which is readily available. GNP is a measure of welfare.

The quantity of commodities acquired for current and future use is a measure of an individual's welfare during a period. No one would argue that this is the perfect measure of welfare. Most people would feel worse off when those around them are starving, even if they could continue to eat caviar. In other words, the welfare of most individuals depends on the distribution of income. Intangibles such as the weather also can affect welfare. The mere sight of a polluted stream and deforested mountain probably reduces welfare. While it is not difficult to list 20 additional reasons why the quantity of commodities acquired is an imperfect measure of welfare, construction of the ideal welfare measure is difficult, if not impossible. How does one measure your welfare loss due to the poverty around you? How do we balance your loss against the gain to antisocial sadists from the misery of their neighbors? Faced with such difficult questions, we are forced to rely on a rough-and-ready measure of welfare such as the quantity of goods and services acquired during a time period. This is easily measured and surely is an important component of the ideal measure.[1]

---

[1] Yes, we purposely slid over another difficult question, the services yielded by durables. If one is willing to disregard this difficulty, we also should be forgiven for ignoring the depreciation of capital goods and equating welfare with the gross value of goods and services acquired.

From an aggregate viewpoint, that is, from the viewpoint of society as a whole, the only commodities that can be acquired during some time period are the goods and services produced. There is no net acquisition of "used" commodities, that is, commodities produced in a previous period. You can sell your used car and 19th century stamp collection or better yet, you can give me the items. Have the two of us together acquired anything? No, I now own the items and you do not. If a car is manufactured during the period, society as a whole *must* acquire a car. Someone other than the manufacturer either buys the car or the manufacturer keeps it, and in the latter case we view the car manufacturer as acquiring the car, perhaps involuntarily. Unlike purchases of used cars, the acquisition of a car produced during the period is not counterbalanced by someone parting with a car they owned before the period began.

The definition of purchases is sufficiently important to bear repeating. Purchases are acquisitions by the public *and* producers. A firm that produces a commodity and does not sell it to someone else purchases the commodity for itself. Defining purchases in this manner makes total purchases equal production. Some of the goods produced are voluntarily purchased by the manufacturer to replenish inventories. Manufacturers involuntarily purchase commodities when they are unable to find buyers. Goods purchased by manufacturers, whether voluntarily or involuntarily, are available to satisfy society's future wants. Some of the ideas in this paragraph are summarized by the equation,

$$E \equiv Y \equiv Py \tag{14–1}$$

where E represents total expenditures for current goods and services, including acquisitions by producers themselves which add to their inventories. The identity symbol emphasizes the expression is true by definition.

## GNP AS EXPENDITURES FOR PRODUCT

Total expenditures may be broken down in many ways. For example, total spending equals the spending of farmers, carpenters, and all others; expenditures of economic units east and west of the Mississippi River; expenditures on red, blue, and other commodities. If we were simply interested in definitions and measurement, every breakdown of total spending would be equally satisfactory. However, definitions and measurement are only a first step; we ultimately want to explain *desired* expenditures. How much do people want to spend? Given our ultimate objective of explaining GNP, breaking down total spending is useful only if the components are predictable and react to different factors. Classifying economic units as either east or west of the Mississippi River is a waste of time since rivers have little, if any, effect on spending. The breakdown you select reflects your views concerning the predictability of the components and the difference in their determinants. If you believe that farmers and carpenters react to different factors than the rest of the population, and if you can predict the spending of farmers, carpenters, and all others, then this is the appropriate breakdown for you.

One classificatory scheme with a long history but made especially popular by Lord Keynes views GNP as the sum of spending by major types of economic units, households, firms, government, and foreign. All economic units belong to one of the four classes, and terms are defined so the following is always true:

$$C + I + G + X - Z \equiv E \equiv Y \qquad (14\text{--}2)$$

where

$C$ = Consumption, household expenditures on current goods and services.

$I$ = Gross domestic investment, firms' current purchases to maintain and increase the capital stock.

$G$ = Government expenditures on current goods and services.

$X$ = Exports, foreign purchases of current goods and services.

$Z$ = Imports, purchases by domestic units of foreign goods and services.

What are some examples of the various spending categories? Consumption includes three broad classes of purchases: consumer durables, nondurables, and services. Consumer durables include such things as new cars, stereos, and refrigerators. Nondurable goods include food, beverages, and clothing. Examples of consumer services are haircuts and admissions to rock concerts. Purchases of which of the following goods would be included in consumption: an ocean-view lot, a used car, and a Louis XIV antique desk? Not being current goods, none are included in consumption.

Gross domestic investment, henceforth simply called investment, is the acquisition of current goods that maintain and increase the capital stock, which includes houses and apartment buildings, producer's plant and equipment, and inventories. Because structures and producer's plant and equipment have a long life, purchases of these items are readily measured directly. Acquisition of inventories is measured by the change of inventories on hand during the period. Gross investment is the sum of depreciation, the expenditures necessary to maintain a capital stock that is used up during the production process, and net investment, increases in the stock of capital goods. The term *domestic* indicates that we include here purchases to maintain and increase the capital stock at home and not the capital abroad. Most investment is made by economic units which everyone agrees are firms. However, households seemingly purchase new houses, so is it correct to say that investment is firms' current purchases to maintain and increase the capital stock? We attribute a schizophrenic personality to households, which become firms when they purchase a house. Why do we lump purchases of houses with business plant and equipment as investment? Because the factors which influence purchases of houses are quite similar to the determinants of business plant and equipment.

Business inventories are the buffer account which makes total production equal sales. Suppose firms are producing more than the other economic units are purchasing. The "purchase" of the "unsold" goods by the producer is manifested in higher inventories and, therefore, investment. Inventories and investment fall when sales to households, government, and foreigners outstrip production. Suppose there is a sudden surge in new car sales. The surge was so sudden that car manufacturers do not have time to hire more workers and produce additional cars. How does this event affect GNP? Consumption increases and the inventory component of investment decreases by an equal amount leaving GNP unchanged, at least for the moment. Subsequently, GNP may increase as firms produce more to meet the enhanced demand.

Construction of houses, apartment buildings, shopping centers, office buildings, and factories is investment. Equipment increases when General Motors purchases a current computer, and inventories increase when IBM keeps the computer. In either case, investment occurs. Ask a person on the street for a good example of investment and he or she will probably mention purchases of General Motors and IBM common stock, a government bond, or a savings and loan deposit. Are these purchases examples of investment? No. Investment is the acquisition of final goods and services by firms in order to maintain and increase the capital stock. Your purchase of IBM stock is not an example of investment for two reasons. First, only firms (including schizoid households acting like firms) invest; if an individual's spending is part of GNP, it is consumption. Second, IBM stock is a financial instrument and not a final good or service. Even if a firm were to purchase IBM shares, it would not be investing in an economic sense. A firm invests when it purchases IBM computers instead of IBM stock. It is unfortunate that the term *investment* has a different meaning on the street than in economic classrooms. Nevertheless, our coining a new term for firms' acquisition of capital goods would only confuse matters because the term *investment* has a long economic history.

Government expenditures on current goods and services are illustrated by purchases of armaments and the salaries of bureaucrats and teachers. Spending at all levels of government, local, state, and federal, are included. Transfer payments such as social security and welfare payments are not included in the expenditure side of GNP because the recipients, however deserving, do not provide the government with goods and services during the period. Private charitable contributions are not consumption, and collective contributions to the elderly and poor are not government expenditures.

Exports, foreign purchases of current goods and services, need little discussion. Wheat sales to Russia and the hotel expenses of foreign tourists are examples of exports. One may wonder why imports are subtracted to get GNP. Remember GNP is the output and expenditures for goods and services produced by a nation. The domestic sectors also purchase foreign goods, which are already included in consumption, investment, and government spending. Therefore, imports must be subtracted from exports in order to arrive at *national* product. For example, suppose you order a custom-made suit from Hong Kong. How does the purchase affect the GNP accounts? Consumption *and* imports increase, leaving GNP constant. If you had ordered a domestic suit instead, consumption and GNP increase. In principle, imports could be excluded from the other spending categories, thereby making it unnecessary to subtract imports from exports. Following such an approach would entail high data collection costs, however, because many imported goods are indistinguishable from domestic goods once they are off the docks. Do you know if your shirt was made in the United States or abroad? Besides this very practical reason for including purchases of imported goods in the domestic spending categories (for example, consumption) and then subtracting total imports, one often wants a readily available summary of the net transactions with the rest of the world. Exports increase a nation's claims against the foreign sector. For example, sales by IBM of computers to a British firm might lead to larger IBM deposits in London banks. The larger deposits can be used to finance future purchases from British firms. Imports have the opposite effect; the claims of the rest of the world increase when we import. Net exports, exports minus imports, is a measure of foreign investment.[2] Just as investment is the acquisition of domestic capital goods which will yield services in the future, net exports give rise to claims against the rest of the world which can be used in the future to purchase goods and services.

Figure 14–2 graphs the dollar amount of the major components of real GNP, and Table 14–2 expresses them as a percentage of GNP. Since real GNP increased markedly during the period, the increase in every spending component is hardly surprising. Figure 14–2 has a ratio or logarithmic scale, so the slopes of the expenditure lines measure the rate of growth. Not every component has grown at the same rate, causing the percentages in Table 14–2 to vary.

1.  Consumption is by far the largest component of GNP. Households currently purchase approximately 65 percent of total production, a percentage that has declined somewhat in the postwar period. The decline was quite clear until 1968, but since then consumption has rebounded.

---

[2] Net exports is not the only measure of foreign investment. Gifts, often called aid, from private citizens or the government to foreigners also increase the claims against a country. Net exports minus gifts to foreigners is traditionally called net foreign investment.

**FIGURE 14–2  Major components of gross national product**

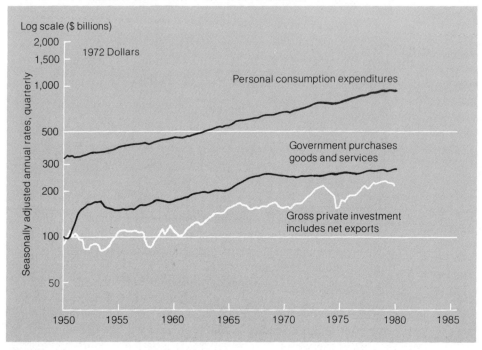

SOURCE: *Federal Reserve Historical Chart Book, 1980.*

**TABLE 14–2  GNP as expenditures for product, 1946–1980**

| Year | Real GNP ($ billions) | Con-sump-tion (percent) | Invest-ment (percent) | Govern-ment expendi-tures (percent) | Exports (percent) | Import (percent) | Net exports (percent) |
|------|------|------|------|------|------|------|------|
| 1946 ...... | 478.3 | 68.6 | 14.6 | 13.1 | 7.1 | 3.4 | 3.7 |
| 1948 ...... | 489.8 | 67.4 | 17.7 | 12.4 | 6.5 | 4.0 | 2.5 |
| 1950 ...... | 534.8 | 67.1 | 18.8 | 13.5 | 4.9 | 4.2 | 0.7 |
| 1952 ...... | 600.8 | 62.5 | 15.0 | 21.8 | 5.2 | 4.6 | 0.6 |
| 1954 ...... | 616.1 | 64.4 | 14.4 | 20.7 | 4.9 | 4.4 | 0.5 |
| 1956 ...... | 671.6 | 63.2 | 16.8 | 18.9 | 5.7 | 4.7 | 1.0 |
| 1958 ...... | 680.9 | 64.5 | 13.8 | 21.2 | 5.2 | 4.6 | 0.6 |
| 1960 ...... | 737.2 | 64.2 | 15.1 | 19.8 | 5.5 | 4.6 | 0.9 |
| 1962 ...... | 800.3 | 62.9 | 15.1 | 20.9 | 5.4 | 4.5 | 0.9 |
| 1964 ...... | 876.4 | 63.0 | 15.2 | 20.4 | 5.9 | 4.5 | 1.4 |
| 1966 ...... | 984.8 | 61.7 | 16.5 | 21.7 | 5.7 | 5.0 | 0.7 |
| 1968 ...... | 1058.1 | 61.7 | 15.1 | 22.9 | 5.7 | 5.5 | 0.2 |
| 1970 ...... | 1085.6 | 63.0 | 14.3 | 22.3 | 6.4 | 6 0 | 0.4 |
| 1972 ...... | 1185.9 | 62.6 | 16.1 | 21.6 | 6.2 | 6.5 | −0.3 |
| 1974 ...... | 1248.0 | 62.9 | 15.2 | 21.4 | 9.8 | 9.3 | 0.5 |
| 1976 ...... | 1300.4 | 64.1 | 14.2 | 21.2 | 9.5 | 9.1 | 0.4 |
| 1978 ...... | 1436.9 | 63.5 | 16.5 | 20.5 | 9.7 | 10.2 | −0.5 |
| 1980 ...... | 1480.7 | 63.6 | 15.0 | 20.4 | 13.0 | 11.9 | 1.1 |

SOURCE: *Economic Report of the President, 1981.*

The consumption percentages today and in the mid-1950s are approximately equal.

2. Investment as a proportion of GNP fell slightly in the postwar period. The decline is partially masked by its volatility. Investment is a small fraction of GNP, averaging approximately 15 percent, so any fall is a large proportional change. For example, if the investment/GNP ratio falls 2 percentage points from 15 to 13 percent, this is more than a 13 percent (2/15) decline in the relative importance of investment.

3. Following World War II government expenditures for goods and services fell precipitously, from approximately 39 percent of GNP in 1945 to 13 percent in 1946. The percentage remained at the low level until the Korean War, when government expenditures rose to approximately 22 percent. While wars invariably increase government spending, a unique feature of the Korean War was the failure of total government spending to revert to its prewar level. The decline in the relative importance of defense expenditures was countered by other federal expenditures and especially state and local government spending, so total government spending remained steady at 20 to 22 percent. Because investment and government expenditures are small fractions of GNP, a small decline in the investment share of GNP and an increase in the government shares translate into a large change in the relative importance of these two expenditure categories. In the late 1940s government expenditures were less than investment, but government expenditures were approximately 35 percent larger than investment by the 1970s.

4. Imports and to a lesser extent exports increased sharply compared to GNP. Most developed economies were in shambles following World War II. As a result, imports to the United States were unusually low and exports by the United States were unusually large. Net exports in the late 1940s were approximately 2 to 3 percent of GNP. In the 1950s and 1960s exports more or less kept pace with GNP, imports grew somewhat faster, and net exports seldom exceeded 1 percent. Foreign trade veritably exploded in the 1970s. The export share of GNP nearly doubled, substantially surpassing the high percentage of exports following World War II. More and costlier oil is the most important factor behind the import rise. Wheat sales one year, an oil embargo the next year, and higher oil prices another year have made net exports more volatile, but there is no indication of a significant long-run change in the importance of net exports. The higher prices of oil and other imported goods have given foreigners the wherewithal to buy U.S. exports. Net exports should remain small and, most probably, positive. While net exports were negative in four years of the 1970 decade, the positive net exports of 1975 alone almost wiped the slate clean.

Henceforth, we refrain from explicitly analyzing net exports, which shall be subsumed in investment. That is, investment now is gross domestic investment and net exports. Incorporating net exports in investment substantially simplifies the theoretical models presented in subsequent chapters without introducing fundamental errors. Net exports are a small proportion of GNP and, as we mentioned earlier, net exports are a measure of foreign investment. Thus, the investment measure now includes domestic and foreign investment.

## GNP AS INCOME

Expenditures on goods and services produced by a nation are received by producers which (*a*) pay households for supplying labor and other factors of production, (*b*) pay taxes, and (*c*) retain some of the receipts. Since we are measuring *national* product, all the income accrues to the three domestic sectors. The households also pay taxes, which may be thought of as government income. Thus, the total amount spent is distributed and becomes income. Symmetry with the expenditure side suggests that GNP viewed as the distribution of receipts be expressed as the sum of household disposable income (household income minus taxes), business disposable income, and government income or, more simply, taxes. We then have income and expenditures of three domestic sectors. However, the subsequent theoretical models disregard the division of private income between households and business. Since we view the GNP accounts as an aid to the theoretical models, we immediately consolidate the household and business sectors when looking at GNP as the distribution of receipts. The division of income between the private sector and government is important.

$$Y \equiv Py \equiv Y_d + T \tag{14-3}$$

where $Y_d$ is private disposable income, and T is taxes. Since private disposable income is GNP minus taxes, equation (14–3) is true by definition. Household disposable income is approximately 85 percent of private disposable income; business income, which includes depreciation allowances, makes up the remainder. Subsequent exposition is simplified by talking as if disposable private income accrues entirely to the household sector.

The following example illustrates that GNP may be viewed as production, spending, or income. Assume that the only goods produced are $100 worth of gizmos. Households and government purchase $65 and $25, respectively. For simplicity, assume no foreign sector. Only labor services, which are provided by households, are needed to produce perfect gizmos. Labor income is $110, out of which households pay $20 in taxes. Therefore, household disposable income is $90. What does GNP equal— $90, $100, $110, or possibly some other amount? Thinking of GNP as the value of goods and services produced, it clearly equals $100. Households and government purchase gizmos worth $90. Business spending or investment includes inventory accumulations which make production equal total spending. Since firms produced $100 gizmos and sold $90 to other sectors, inventory accumulation is $10. Total spending, including possibly undesired inventory investment, is $100. Household disposable income is $90, and government income or taxes is $20. If GNP is also total income, does it equal $110? No. Just as the spending side includes a residual account, the inventory components of investment, the income side also includes a residual account, business income. Since it cost firms $110 to produce gizmos worth $100, business income is $-$10. Including the business loss of $10, total income is $100. Private (household and business) disposable income is $80, and taxes are $20.

Household disposable income equals household receipts for supplying factors of production minus taxes. For example, disposable income includes wages and salaries, which are payments for labor service, and interest and dividends, payments for capital services. Household income as computed by the Commerce Department, the publisher of the GNP accounts, does not correspond with the Internal Revenue Service (IRS) concept of household income. Capital gains from the sale of common stock and other assets are considered by the IRS to be income, albeit taxed at a rate different than other income. Does the Commerce Department include capital gains in disposable income? No, capital gains are not household receipts for supplying factors of production.

Transfer payments, which are not included in government expenditures, are treated as negative taxes and subtracted from gross tax revenues to get net taxes. The effect of government on the private income stream is measured by net taxes. Taxes reduce private disposable income, and social security benefits, relief payments, and other transfers increase disposable income. The symbol T in equation (14–3) represents net taxes.

Table 14–3 shows the income side of GNP. Column 1 lists GNP. Column 2, private disposable income, plus column 3, net taxes, sum to 100. The income share declined in the postwar period, falling from approximately 84 percent of GNP in the late 1940s to 80 percent in the 1970s. Of course, net taxes followed a converse pattern. What explains the uproar about higher taxes? Again, the decline in the personal income share does not seem that great but net taxes, starting from a low base, rose substantially. The net tax share of GNP increased by a quarter from approximately 16 to 20 percent. Moreover, government is redistributing a larger proportion of GNP. Gross taxes and transfer payments as a proportion of GNP have risen more sharply than net taxes. See columns 4 and 5. Those paying substantially higher taxes are quite vocal while the recipients of government transfer payments are relatively silent.

## EQUILIBRIUM CONDITIONS

Stating truisms and definitions is not a waste of time if it provides some insight to the solution of a problem. Seemingly trite observations like

TABLE 14–3  GNP as income from production, 1946–1980

| Year | (1)<br>Nominal<br>GNP<br>($ billions) | (2)<br>Private<br>disposable<br>income<br>(percent) | (3)<br>Net taxes<br>(percent) | (4)<br>Gross taxes<br>(percent) | (5)<br>Transfer<br>payments<br>(percent) |
|---|---|---|---|---|---|
| 1946 ...... | 209.8 | 84.3 | 15.7 | 24.3 | 8.6 |
| 1948 ...... | 259.5 | 84.4 | 15.6 | 22.2 | 6.6 |
| 1950 ...... | 286.5 | 83.7 | 16.3 | 23.6 | 7.3 |
| 1952 ...... | 348.0 | 79.3 | 20.7 | 26.0 | 5.3 |
| 1954 ...... | 366.8 | 78.6 | 21.4 | 27.2 | 5.8 |
| 1956 ...... | 421.7 | 79.9 | 20.1 | 26.1 | 6.0 |
| 1958 ...... | 449.7 | 81.6 | 18.4 | 25.7 | 7.3 |
| 1960 ...... | 506.5 | 79.6 | 20.4 | 27.5 | 7.1 |
| 1962 ...... | 565.0 | 79.7 | 20.3 | 27.8 | 7.5 |
| 1964 ...... | 637.7 | 80.0 | 20.0 | 27.3 | 7.3 |
| 1966 ...... | 756.0 | 78.8 | 21.2 | 28.2 | 7.0 |
| 1968 ...... | 873.4 | 77.8 | 22.2 | 30.3 | 8.1 |
| 1970 ...... | 992.7 | 78.6 | 21.4 | 30.9 | 9.5 |
| 1972 ...... | 1185.9 | 78.7 | 21.3 | 31.4 | 10.1 |
| 1974 ...... | 1434.2 | 78.8 | 21.2 | 32.2 | 11.0 |
| 1976 ...... | 1718.0 | 80.9 | 19.1 | 31.4 | 12.3 |
| 1978 ...... | 2156.1 | 79.5 | 20.5 | 32.3 | 11.8 |
| 1980 ...... | 2627.4 | 81.0 | 19.0 | 31.7 | 12.7 |

SOURCE: *Economic Report of the President, 1981.*

peanuts sold equal peanuts bought and the price paid by buyers is the price received by sellers ultimately led to an important conclusion: supply and demand determine quantity and price. Quantity and price remain constant when *desired* sales equal *desired* purchases. An increase in demand normally causes a higher quantity and price. The same is true for GNP, which is nothing other than the sum of all commodities. Expressing GNP as spending and production emphasizes that actual GNP depends on the interaction of demand *and* supply for all commodities. The general price level and real GNP remain constant if *desired* total expenditures equal *desired* production. If desired expenditures or desired production were to increase, GNP could rise. The equilibrium condition is

$$C + I + G = Y \qquad (14\text{–}4)$$

Equations (14–2) and (14–4) look quite similar but they make entirely different statements. Equation (14–2) says that during any time period *actual* expenditures on current goods and services equal *actual* production. Equation (14–4) says that prices and output remain constant when *desired* spending equals *desired* production. Compact expression is the purpose of algebraic equations, but algebra is almost too compact in this case. We try to indicate the very different statements being made by equations (14–2) and (14–4) by using the identity symbol (≡) when refer-

ring to actual magnitudes and the equality symbol (=) when referring to
desired magnitudes. Many authors do not make even this distinction;
then, actual and desired magnitudes are distinguished only by the verbal
discussion surrounding the equations.

Does equation (14–4) hold at all times? Is desired spending always
equal to desired production? Is the economy always at equilibrium? Of
course not. Suppose desired spending is greater than desired production.
What will happen in this case? Output and/or prices will increase. In
subsequent chapters we analyze whether output, prices, or some combination of the two will increase. For the moment, assume prices are rigid
and only output increases. Why does output increase when desired expenditures exceed desired production, and why do actual expenditures
always equal actual production? For simplicity, assume no government or
foreign sector. Suppose desired consumption is $80, and desired inven-
tory accumulation investment is $30. Actual and desired production dur-
ing the period is $100. Therefore, desired expenditures exceed production
by $10. What happens? Firms stand ready to meet the demand of house-
holds, who succeed in purchasing commodities worth $80. Since produc-
tion equalled $100 and consumption is $80, actual inventory investment is
$20, which is $10 less than the desired amount. Actual expenditures
equal actual production. Why did *firms* produce commodities worth $100
when *firms and households* wanted to purchase commodities worth $110?
Economic units are unaware of the plans of other economic units. If firms
knew that desired consumption was $80, they would have produced com-
modities worth $110 in order to invest $30. Presumably, firms thought
desired consumption was $70. How do firms react to their underestimate
of demand? They increase production; prices are rigid, by assumption.
Since actual investment was $10 less than desired investment when pro-
duction was $100, firms might produce commodities worth $110, anticipating that the previous $10 short-fall in investment will be corrected. This
probably is not the end of the story as the higher production, employment,
and household income could well cause consumption to rise above $80.
Subsequent chapters discuss in full the so-called multiplier. For our purposes the story can end here; we simply wanted to show why production
increases when it is less than desired spending. Summarizing this
example,

$$C + I + G > Y \qquad \text{desired values}$$
$$80 + 30 + 0 > 100 \qquad \text{desired values}$$
$$80 + 20 + 0 \equiv 100 \qquad \text{actual values}$$

Can the following inequality hold?

$$C + I + G < Y. \qquad (14–5)$$

Certainly. Indeed, the unusual case is represented by equation (14–4).
Most of the time the economy is not in equilibrium; prices and/or output

often are changing. The law of symmetry usually holds in economics. Reversing the argument in the preceeding paragraph, prices and/or output fall when inequality (14–5) holds.

## SUMMARY

During a given period of time the goods and services produced must be acquired by some group, possibly producers themselves. The GNP accounts tell us how much was produced and what group acquired the goods and services. Production in the United States nearly tripled during the postwar period. The proportion of commodities acquired by household and businesses decreased while government expenditures increased its share of GNP. The GNP accounts do not tell us why production is one amount and not a different amount. They also do not tell us if GNP will be increasing or decreasing. Nevertheless, an understanding of the GNP accounts is a necessary first step. We must know where we are before analyzing why we are there and where we are going. The following chapters examine the determinants of desired expenditures and production. What do desired expenditures equal? How can we change desired expenditures? These questions are of utmost importance because actual production and prices respond to desired values. If desired expenditures exceed actual expenditures and production, production and/or prices will increase as firms respond to the demand for commodities. When production ultimately equals desired expenditures, everyone can be satisfied and the price/output structure will be maintained.

## QUESTIONS

1. State the main trends in post-World War II nominal GNP, real GNP, and the GNP price index. How do the postwar trends compare with prewar trends?
2. In what sense does GNP measure the value of "final" goods and services? Does final mean finished (ready for ultimate use) or last (not processed further *during* the period)?
3. Is GNP an ideal measure of welfare? Explain your answer.
4. What are the traditional components of total expenditures? What types of items are included in each component?
5. Which of the following items is an example of investment: (a) purchase of 19th-century gold coins, (b) construction of a vacation home, (c) purchase of land to build a vacation home, (d) purchase of oriental rugs, (e) purchase of common stock, (f) purchase of a new U.S.-made car by a car rental firm, and (g) purchase of a new car by a teacher?
6. What are the main trends in the relative importance of the GNP expenditure components?
7. Give some examples of differences in the income concept of the GNP account and the IRS tax code.

8. What explains the differences in the trends of the government expenditures component of GNP and total government spending for whatever reason?

9. Can actual expenditures exceed actual production? Can desired expenditures exceed production? What adjustments occur when expenditures exceed production?

appendix · The saving-investment relationships

The saving-investment identity emphasizes that GNP is both spending and income and that households and government must refrain from acquiring commodities if firms are to maintain and increase the capital stock. Combining equations (14–2) and (14–3) of the text with exports (X) and imports (Z) subsumed in investment (I), we express GNP as both spending and income.

$$C + I + G \equiv Y \equiv Y_d + T \tag{14A–1}$$

The production process gives rise to a circular flow of receipts. Firms pay households for labor services and other factors of production used to produce commodities. In addition, firms and households pay taxes. Firms do not run out of funds and the process continues because households and government use their income to acquire commodities. Households typically do not consume their entire income because they derive utility from current *and* future consumption. Households save in order to provide for the future. Private saving, $S_p$, is defined as disposable income minus consumption.

$$S_p \equiv Y_d - C \\ \equiv Y - T - C \tag{14A–2}$$

Saving is often called a *leakage* because it equals the amount that does not flow back to the business sectors from households. Private saving measures the household sector's accumulation of financial assets, including money, which must inevitably occur when income and expenditures are not equal.

Look at equations (14A–1) and (14A–2). Subtracting C from both sides of (14A–1) and substituting (14A–2) in (14A–1), one gets

$$I + G \equiv S_p + T \tag{14A–3}$$

In words, the purchases of current commodities by firms and government (I + G) must equal the commodities households do not purchase because they save and are taxed ($S_p$ + T).

If there were no government so that $G \equiv T \equiv 0$ and private saving equaled total saving, then inspection of equation (14A–3) shows that investment equals saving. The same is true when government exists, provided we recognize that government saving is an element of total saving. Analogous to households, the difference between government receipts and expenditures is called government saving, $S_G$.

$$S_G \equiv T - G \tag{14A-4}$$

Household saving has always been positive, which certainly is not true of government saving. It sometimes is convenient to have distinct terms for negative and positive government saving. Negative government saving is called a deficit, and positive government saving, which was quite common years ago, is a surplus. Also analogous to households, a surplus leads to an accumulation of *net* financial assets, that is, the purchase of assets or, more likely, the retirement of debt. Deficits have the opposite effect of net financial assets.

Total saving, S, is the sum of private and government saving. Adding equations (14A-2) and (14A-4), we get

$$\begin{aligned} S &\equiv S_p + S_G \\ &\equiv (Y - T - C) + (T - G) \\ &\equiv Y - C - G \end{aligned} \tag{14A-5}$$

Equations (14A-1) and (14A-5) readily imply that

$$I \equiv S \tag{14A-6}$$

Call equation (14A-6) the pure saving-investment equation, and equation (14A-3) is the modified saving-investment equation. Equation (14A-6) has a real and a financial interpretation. First, the real interpretation says that firms acquire those current goods which are not purchased by households and government. Second, households and government jointly acquire the financial claims issued by firms. (Of course, the government may incur a deficit, so that households also acquire government debt.) Since different groups save and invest, financial instruments must be associated with the saving-investment process.

Since equations (14A-3) and (14A-6) follow from (14A-1), the following statements are identical: during any given period of time (*a*) spending on current goods and services equals income, (*b*) total saving equals investment, (*c*) private saving plus taxes equal investment plus government expenditures.

The pure version of the saving-investment identity, equation (14A-6), was preferred years ago to the modified version. Government was viewed as providing society with goods and services which are currently used up. For example, government expenditures include payments for the police protection society receives during the period. Consumption goods are also exhausted during the period. Total saving then corresponds to currently produced commodities not exhausted and available for the future. Equation (14A-6) also was associated somewhat more closely with finance. Saving is a leakage, and injections of investment are necessary to maintain the circular flow. Firms' receipts from consumption and government expenditures are less than their income payments. Firms acquire the funds to augment the circular flow by issuing financial claims.

The traditional view about government expenditures is not altogether accurate. Highways and bombers, which have long, useful lives, also are examples of government expenditures. Therefore, total saving may underestimate the provision for future needs. For this reason and because the analysis of fiscal policy is easier when taxes and government expenditures appear explicitly rather than being subsumed in total saving, equation (14A–3) has gained in popularity. Equation (14A–3) views government expenditures and investment as contributing equally to economic growth.

Just as the actual expenditures-production identity is equivalent to the actual saving-investment identity, the *equilibrium* condition can be expressed by the equality of desired spending and production or by the equality of *desired saving and desired investment*. When desired saving and investment are equal, price and real output remain constant. We do not bother to prove this as one only need interpret equations (14A–3)–(14A–6) as representing desired magnitudes. However, we do derive the relationship between desired saving and investment when desired spending is greater than income. Suppose

$$C + I + G > Y = Y_d + T \qquad (14A–7)$$

Rearranging (14A–7)

$$I > Y_d - C + T - G = S_p + S_G = S, \text{ or}$$
$$I + G > Y_d - C + T = S_p + T \qquad (14A–8)$$

In words, when desired spending is greater than income, then desired investment exceeds total desired saving or, equivalently, desired investment plus government expenditures exceeds private saving plus taxes. Again the law of symmetry applies. Reverse the inequality in (14A–7) and what is the relationship between desired saving and investment? Desired saving exceeds investment when expenditure demand is less than supply.

How does one characterize a situation where price and output are decreasing? Is aggregate demand less than production, does desired total saving exceed investment, or does desired private saving plus taxes exceed investment plus government expenditures? All three approaches are correct and formally equivalent although they do emphasize different factors. Prior to the 1930s aggregate demand and production were believed to be in balance most of the time, and government spending and taxes were quite low. Economists in those days emphasized the effect of policy on the composition of goods satisfying current and future needs. Therefore, the equilibrium relationship was expressed almost exclusively by the equality of desired saving and investment. While many continue to express the equilibrium condition in the same manner, the aggregate demand-production approach is more popular today. Keynes in the 1930s stressed the likelihood of deficient aggregate demand. Restoring full employment was the primary policy objective; how policy affects the composition of output was of secondary importance. This led to expressing equilibrium as the equality of aggregate demand and production. While we think Keynes exaggerated the possibility of chronically deficient aggregate demand and unemployment, we favor the aggregate demand-production approach because of its similarity with microeconomics. Everyone knows that the price and/or quantity of peanuts or any other commodity fall when supply exceeds demand. You probably realized before reading this chapter that the same principle applies to commodities in general. Ask what happens when saving exceeds investment and you will get a correct answer less often. Microeconomics did not prepare us to think about equilibrium as the lack of expenditures by households being made up by business and government expenditures. Moreover, while the saving-investment approach may have financial institutions lurking in the background because of its emphasis on sectoral income and expenditure imbalances, the saving-investment approach does not necessarily bring them to center stage, as we shall see later. We recognize, however, that some will disagree, and for that reason have this appendix and one in Chapter 17.

**15**

The relationship between money, the rate of interest, income, and prices is one of the fundamental but difficult and controversial issues all monetary economic books must tackle. This relationship is the subject of the remainder of this book. Years ago less space would have been given to this topic. Most economists were confident that they understood how our economic system functioned. John Maynard Keynes thought his colleagues were wrong. Believing that a forceful presentation of his new economic framework was imperative for success, Keynes lashed at his predecessors and contemporaries in his *The General Theory of Employment, Interest, and Money,* published in 1936. "Thus I cannot achieve my objective of persuading economists to re-examine critically certain of their basic assumptions except by a highly abstract argument and also by much controversy."[1] Keynes was persuasive, and rightly so. His work was pathfinding. However, Keynes may have been too persuasive and critical. In the euphoria of discovering a new economic framework, Keynes's followers totally ignored its limitations. Keynes asks "forgiveness if, in the pursuit of sharp distinctions, my controversy is itself too keen."[2] His followers did not forgive their predecessors. They heaped abuse on classical economics, the label Keynes gave to pre-1936 orthodox economics.[3] The disciples became more dogmatic than the master. Keynes recog-

---

[1] John Maynard Keynes, *The General Theory of Employment, Interest, and Money* (New York: Harcourt Brace Jovanovich, 1936), p. v. By permission of Royal Economic Society and Macmillan, London and Baskingstoke.

[2] Ibid.

[3] In economics, as elsewhere, the word "classical" has ever-changing meanings. Prior to 1936, believers of the labor theory of value were classicists, while marginalists were neoclassicists. Since value theory is unimportant to understand early monetary economics, we accept Keynes' classification of all pre-1936 orthodox economics as classicists.

nized some strong points in classical economics but Keynesians could see none. By the mid-1950s Keynesian economics ruled supreme, except at the University of Chicago and a few satellite universities.

Revolutionary excesses eventually are corrected. Theoretical and empirical academic research and economic policy failures exposed some weakness in Keynesian economics and some strengths in classical economics. Initially, studies presenting evidence against Keynesian economics were viewed as the work of crackpots, or even demons. But the mounting evidence could no longer be ignored. By the 1970s most economists accepted some aspects of both classical and Keynesian economics. Milton Friedman, the leading modern exponent of classical ideas, said, "In one sense, we are all Keynesians now; in another no one is a Keynesian any longer."[4] The days of stock answers to difficult economic questions fortunately are gone.

## THE SCIENTIFIC METHOD AND THE ROLE OF TIME IN ECONOMICS

In what sense are we all Keynesians now, and in what sense is no one a Keynesian any longer? How can economists subscribe to both classical and Keynesian theory? We are all Keynesians now and no one is a Keynesian any longer in the sense that recent empirical evidence supports some Keynesian propositions previously denied by classicists while simultaneously contradicting other Keynesian propositions. We can subscribe to both theories because, contrary to the picture Keynes painted, classical and Keynesian economics are complementary in some respects. We must rely on both theories to understand our economy's adjustments over time. The remainder of this section elaborates on these answers. To some extent it repeats Chapter 1, which briefly discussed economic theory in general and compared classical and Keynesian economics. The scientific method and the basic difference between classical and Keynesian economics are sufficiently important to justify some repetition prior to a detailed examination of both models.

Adjustments to some disturbance take place over time. A change in government expenditures or some other initial condition does not cause sharp, if perhaps somewhat delayed, once-and-for-all jumps in dependent variables such as income, prices, and the rate of interest. Instead, the dependent variables respond more or less continuously over time. An ideal theory readily predicts the exact time path of the economic variables. Indeed, theories are judged mainly on the basis of their explanatory and predictive powers. The frequently heard statement, "It is good in theory but not in practice," illustrates a complete misunderstanding of theory. Good theory is practical theory. In addition, the accurate predic-

---

[4] Milton Friedman, *Dollars and Deficits* (Englewood Cliffs, N.J.: Prentice-Hall, 1968), p. 15.

tions of good theory are general and sufficiently simple to be readily understood and generated relatively cheaply. For example, a highly complex theory which requires one year's computer time to predict the effect on Mali's economy of my once-in-a-lifetime trip to Timbuktu is bad theory, however accurate. It is not simple and general. Agreement on the properties of good theories—accuracy, simplicity, and generality—is widespread.

For various reasons mentioned in Chapter 1, economists encounter difficulties in testing the validity of theories by measuring empirically the precise relationship among economic variables. With numerous empirical studies reporting different relationships, the accuracy of any theory is debatable. The results of one empirical study may suggest theory A is accurate and theory B is wrong, while another empirical study concludes the opposite. Both the classical and Keynesian theories presented in this book enjoy considerable empirical support. The reader largely must accept this on faith, however. This book summarizes and evaluates only a few empirical studies of the relationship among economic variables. Our main objective is a critical evaluation of the assumptions and logical structure of the classical and Keynesian models. We hope that such a critical evaluation may suggest how future empirical studies should proceed. Knowledge of assumptions and their correspondence to reality may well provide a clue about future definitive empirical results. Empirical economics not grounded in theory and history flourishes in a chaos congenial to its mentality.

In some respects classical and Keynesian economics are competing *general* theories which analyze the relationships among many variables. Neither is a specific theory concerning only one relationship, say, the effect of interest rates on the demand for money. Keynesian and classical economics contain many elements. Originally, some of the elements of the two theories were diametrically contradictory. For example, classicists stated monetary expansion always causes proportional nominal income changes, and early Keynesians suggested money has no effect on nominal income. Economists currently are both classicists and Keynesians in the sense that some of the diametrically contradictory elements of the two theories have been disavowed in light of better empirical evidence. Although the empirical evidence is still diverse and inconclusive, it is much less so now than years ago. The accumulating empirical evidence contradicted extreme positions. In response, the theories have been modified to make them more similar. Everyone now concedes that money matters; the magnitude of monetary effects is a current issue between classicists and Keynesians. In other words, economists have reached a concensus on true or false questions but disagree on multiple choice questions regarding how much, how long, how often, and so on.

Consensus on some issues and the cooling of passions have led to a better understanding of classical and Keynesian economics. We now realize that elements of the two theories previously thought to be contradictory are complementary. As stated, the effects of some change in initial conditions are distributed over time, and an ideal theory *readily* predicts the exact time path of the economic variables. Our world is less than ideal in many respects. Dynamic theories describing motion are complex. Simplicity dictates some approximation to movement over time. Economists attempt to capture the movement over time by a series of snapshots just as a movie is a series of still pictures. Classical and Keynesian models are examples of snapshots. Time and motion seemingly do not exist. Given some set of assumptions, supply and demand curves are constructed. The static, snapshot models then determine equilibrium values at one moment in time and compare alternative equilibria as the assumptions are changed. These models do not describe in detail how one moves from one equilibrium to another.

How well do static, snapshot models describe dynamic changes over time? The adequacy of a single static model and the number of static models necessary to describe reasonably well changes over time depends on the extent and consistency of the changes. For example, suppose one wants to record the changes that occur in a forest during a year. A movie camera continually filming in order to capture every flutter of the leaves is unnecessary for most purposes. Four snapshots, one during each season, gives an adequate description of the forest throughout the year. Changes occurring in a desert might be summarized by two snapshots before and after a rainfall. Figure 15–1 illustrates an economic example. At time zero some "shock" (change in initial conditions) occurs and disturbs variables X and Z. The dotted and dashed lines in Figure 15–1 show the time path of X and Z changes, respectively, measured from their initial values. In other words, the lines show the differences between the values of X and Z over time and their initial values. The snapshot at some moment gives us one dot or dash while a movie films the entire dotted or dashed line.

Any single dot describes relatively accurately the position of the entire dotted line. One snapshot, static model satisfactorily describes X changes. The same is not true of Z changes. One snapshot at time A, showing that the shock reduces Z, is deceiving, since it ignores that the shock ultimately increases Z. One snapshot at time C, is equally deceiving since one might well conclude the shock always causes Z to increase. We need at least two snapshots, at times A and C, to describe the time path of Z, and possibly three snapshots, at times A, B, and C. Many economic variables have a time path like Z.

The classical model is a *long-run* static model. It takes a snapshot at time C. For 160 years, from 1776 to 1936, economists had only a long-run model taking its snapshot at time C. We owe Keynes a huge debt. The Keynesian model is a short-run model, taking its snapshot at time A. The debate immediately following Keynes' pioneering study centered on which model, the long-run classical or short-run Keynesian, best de-

FIGURE 15-1 The time path of X and Z changes measured from their initial values, the lines showing the difference between the values of X and Z over time and their initial values

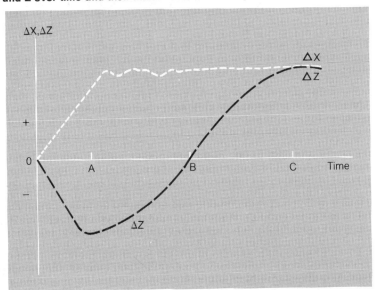

scribed the average change over time. Should we take *one* snapshot at time A or C? One had to choose sides; fence straddling was forbidden. The debate was silly. Fence straddling is now respectable. To describe changes over time we need both classical and modern Keynesian economics purged of extreme positions shown to be incorrect. While classical and Keynesian economics compete in some respects, they also are complementary, together approximating changes over time. Our economic film is still quite jerky. Two or three snapshots—a Keynesian short-run, a classical long-run and possibly an intermediate run linking the short and long—describe movement over time. Movies (economic dynamics, technically speaking) are too difficult to develop.

Because Keynesian economics was wrapped in criticism of classical economics, we begin with the latter. Pride of place should not be misinterpreted as favoring classical economics. Both schools of thought are correct. While classical economics comes first, Keynesian economics is given more space.

## CLASSICAL ECONOMISTS

Name at least three classical economists. Most people cannot do so. Can you? Classical economists were not a faceless horde of old fuddy-duddies. Who were the leading orthodox economists prior to 1936? Adam

Smith (1723–90) is the father of economics.[5] His principal claim to fame, *The Wealth of Nations,* was published in 1776. Thus the United States and economics share a common birthday. The book firmly established the advantages of specialization and the division of labor, and was, on the whole, skeptical of government interference with the free play of private initiative. Smith's byword was *laissez faire.*

The new science of economics attracted David Ricardo (1772–1823). After earning a fortune on the London Stock Exchange, Ricardo devoted a greater portion of his time to scientific and literary pursuits. His *Principles of Political Economy and Taxation* proved him a master of abstract reasoning and monetary problems. Ricardo elaborated the doctrine of comparative advantage so fundamental to international trade.

John Stuart Mill's (1806–73) *Principles of Political Economy* (1848, in two volumes) was not equivalent to your current principles texts. It was the main graduate theory book for over half a century. It laid out virtually the entire body of deductive economic analysis, together with applications to concrete problems. Mill's *Principles* was the economics best seller until Samuelson's *Principles of Economics.*

The principle apostle of Adam Smith on the European continent was Jean Baptiste Say (1767–1832), best known for his celebrated law of markets. After being translated from the French, Say's *Treatise* quickly became one of the most popular economics textbooks in early 19th-century America, largely because it was easier reading than Adam Smith's *Wealth of Nations.* Say the successful popularizer was unable to communicate with that select circle of professional economists who demand precise and clear expression of complex theory. He spent more than a decade attempting to clarify and explain the law of markets, with little success. We will return to the law of markets shortly.

Leon Walras (1834–1910), seeking the general principles which underlie the working of an exchange economy, firmly established the mathematical method in economics. Advocacy and use of mathematical methods and criticism of laissez-faire dogma were cardinal sins in France. The French economist found refuge at the University of Lausanne, Switzerland. Unfettered by dirty applications (relevance?), Walras titled his main work *Elements of Pure Political Economy.*

Alfred Marshall's (1842–1924) *Principles* (1890) was the last economics book to encompass the entire theoretical thought of its time. Marshall was the master of partial-equilibrium analysis, other things being equal. In his hands supply and demand supplemented with elasticities and the short and long run reached new heights. Marshall's *Principles* was discussed, dissected, interpreted and reinterpreted and yet survived intact, obviously a testimonial to his genius.

---

[5] Although Smith is the father of economics, most histories of economic thought courses begin with Plato, Aristotle, and St. Thomas Aquinas. More likely claimants to the paternity title are Sir William Petty, Richard Cantillon, and David Hume.

Keynes's favorite whipping boy was his contemporary, Arthur Cecil Pigou (1877–1959), who succeeded Marshall to the most prestigious British chair. Pigou almost single-handedly created the fields of public finance and welfare economics. He described how taxes, subsidies, and government regulation can reconcile differences between economic self-interest and society's well-being due to monopolies and external effects such as pollution. He antagonized Keynes by stressing monetary over fiscal policy as a cure for the Great Depression.

Many more classicists could be named, but we conclude the list with an internationally recognized American classical economist. Irving Fisher (1867–1947) of Yale was mainly interested in the relationship between money, interest, and business activity. Fisher is credited with enunciating the proposition that nominal interest rates rise by the expected rate of inflation. (See Chapter 5.) His equation of exchange and expression of the quantity theory of money are discussed shortly.

Every profession honors its superstars. Baseball has its Hall of Fame, and Hollywood has the Academy Awards. Current superstars like Paul Samuelson and Milton Friedman can (and did) win a Noble prize. How did the profession previously honor its superstars? It attached their names to a conundrum (Ricardo-Tooke), law (Say and Walras), effect (Fisher and Pigou), condition (Marshall-Lerner), and revolution (Keynes)![6]

Some of the most influential economists prior to 1936 espoused unorthodox views and, therefore, are not classicists. Robert Malthus, Thorston Veblen and, of course, Karl Marx were unorthodox economists. Some diversity is consistent with a school of thought like classical economics, but a school implies wide acceptance of basic assumptions and a similar outlook. Deny certain basic assumptions and you are unorthodox, a euphemism for crackpot, regardless of the validity of your views or influence. Straying too far from a narrowly conceived discipline of economics is almost guaranteed to place a person on the unorthodox list. Thorston Veblen and Karl Marx were too interested in sociology and political processes to be orthodox. We shall identify the modern exponents of the classical school later.

## ESSENTIAL FEATURES OF CLASSICAL ECONOMICS

Economists like other social scientists do not live in a vacuum. Theory, application, and politics interact. A laissez-faire philosophy and politics spawned the theory of comparative advantage and a free trade policy. Theories are constructed to explain current issues and policies, and current issues test the validity of theories. This principle explains the newer offerings of many economic departments, which include courses in the

---

[6] Tooke was a classicist, but Abba Lerner is a staunch early Keynesian. His and Marshall's condition concerns the delicate balance of import and export elasticities essential to exchange rate stability.

environment, pollution, and women's issues. Moreover, important developments in one area of economics influence the analysis in other areas. What were the most important economic events between 1776 and 1936? There is no correct answer but surely everyone would include the Industrial Revolution, growth of income in selected countries accompanied by stagnation in others, and increased international trade partially due to colonization. As the interaction of theory and application suggests, the early classical economists emphasized international economics and what is now called development economics. This emphasis influenced classical monetary analysis in the early as well as later period when interests widened. Indeed, classical monetary economics is incomprehensible without a lengthy digression on growth and development.

What were the causes of the Industrial Revolution and growth of income in selected European countries, Canada, and the United States? We do not expect a definitive answer to a much debated question. But before reading the next paragraph pause at least a few minutes and list some important factors.

What sources of income growth did you list? Most classicists and modern development economists mention a larger capital stock generated by saving and, of course, investment. Capital is one of the factors of production. Its growth increases income. Capital accumulation takes the form of more factories, machines, and supporting transportation and communications systems. Growth of the labor force, another factor of production, is mentioned less frequently because it may cause divergent movements of income per capita and total income. A larger population and labor force may well reduce income per capita as additional workers tilling the same soil produce less than the average worker. Nevertheless, additional workers produce something, and GNP rises. Current total income would be much lower had the United States closed its borders in 1776. Growth requires not just more but better factors of production. Innovations and inventions, often called technological progress, increase the productivity of labor and capital goods. Education and technical and vocational training are other extremely important sources of income growth. The importance of a better educated and generally more skillful labor force is particularly obvious after a war, when seemingly devastated countries quickly return to their status as world powers. Primitive tools are more useful than the latest generation computers in unskilled hands. Entrepreneurship, a willingness to take risks and that little understood talent for management and organization, produces better mouse traps. The so-called Protestant ethic which causes people to work hard is an additional cause of income growth.

We could expand the sources of growth but our purpose has been served. Actual output and income is determined by the intersection of supply and demand, and output changes when supply or demand change (the curves shift). The sources of growth can be classified as supply factors and demand factors. Reread your and our lists of the sources of growth. Would you classify the overwhelming proportion of sources as supply or demand factors? Does output and income grow mainly because supply or demand increases? Supply factors are dominant. A larger capital stock and labor force, technological progress, a better educated labor force, a stronger entrepreneurial spirit, better organization and management, and a continual willingness to work all increase supply. As stated, actual income and output is determined by the intersection of demand and supply. The classicists thought demand was insatiable. *Income increased mainly because the supply curve shifted outward and one moved along a demand curve.*

Income and output growth was hardly uniform in the classical period, like today. Most countries grew little if at all. Although early economic statistics are sketchy and not very reliable, it appears the distribution of income among countries was more skewed in 1936 than 1776. Why did some countries stagnate while others grew? Unfortunately, supply conditions prevented growth in most countries. Are Chinese, Indian, Haitian, and Bolivian tastes really that different from Western European, Canadian, and American tastes? Are Indians so mystical that they want few consumer goods? Of course not. Income stagnated in India and most countries in spite of an almost universal desire for consumer goods. True, income does not grow when the population prefers to commune with nature and gambol through the woods wearing ashen cloth and eating wild berries. But this idyllic picture hardly represents underdeveloped countries, where labor typically works harder and longer but produces less because capital, skills, and entrepreneurship are scarce.

Suppose you were an economic advisor to an underdeveloped country. What growth policies would you prescribe? Would you recommend that the government encourage saving by creating government-sponsored financial intermediaries, build roads, support education and technical and vocational training, and dislodge bottlenecks hampering industry and agriculture? Alternatively, would you recommend a massive welfare program financed by additional money creation and a wide-ranging advertising campaign to whet appetites for luxuries? The choice of policies is obvious: prescribe the former and proscribe the latter. One set of policies stimulates aggregate supply while the latter stimulates demand. But aggregate demand is not deficient in underdeveloped countries. Supply constrains output. However desirable income redistribution may be, massive welfare payments increasing aggregate demand have little effect on output growth.

### Say's Law

This fundamental classical belief that demand is insatiable is succinctly summarized by Say's Law: *supply creates its own demand*. Brevity often causes confusion. Adding a short phrase would make Say's Law less controversial. The validity of many propositions depends on the time period of the analysis. History shows that supply creates its own demand *in the long run*. Look at Figure 15–2. The concept of full employment or

**FIGURE 15–2   Actual and full-employment trend GNP, 1900–1980**

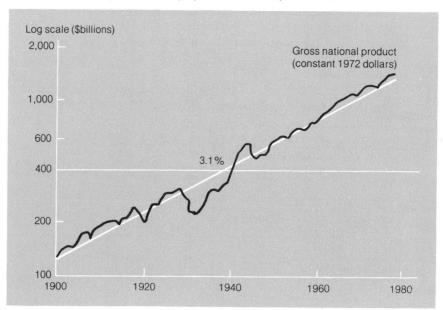

maximum potential output is not precise. Nonetheless, examination of long historical records shows actual output paralleling full employment output, with the former sometimes falling short and occasionally overshooting the latter. Classicists were optimistic that history would repeat itself. Demand will remain insatiable. The upward movement of productive capacity will drag demand along. Social critics unaware of Say's Law implicitly accept it when they claim manufacturers create a "need" for their products.

There is a business cycle, and recessions do occur.[7] No proof beyond recessions is necessary to establish that *supply does not create its own*

---

[7] Characterization of similar events varies over time. Economic downturns in classical times were crises and panics. Herbert Hoover thought this term too emotional and frightening. He said a *depression* accurately described economic conditions during his administration, 1929–33. The economy lacked vigor and spirits were low, but people were not hysterical and irrational. Following World War II, Herbert Hoover's calming depression became too alarming. The economy never was depressed, just recessed. By the 1970s recessions were outlawed by the political party in power. We now have rolling readjustments and pauses.

*demand in the short run.* When methodical and philosophical divisions were keen among economists, quotation after quotation was dissected in an attempt to determine the time period implicit in Say's statement. True, one can find passages in Say's work suggesting that supply creates its own demand in the short run.

Say was not a great thinker and influencial policymaker. He merits more than a toenote in history of economic thought textbooks precisely because of his deficiencies. Keynes rescued him from oblivion by appending his name to a law often quoted to ridicule classical economists. But were all classical economists dummies? Were they so oblivious to the real world that they alone failed to recognize recessions obvious to all? We think not. David Ricardo, the leading economist around 1800, certainly was a practical man, making a fortune on the London Stock Exchange. John Stuart Mill was much more influential than Say; Mill was perhaps the most influential economist between 1830 and 1870. A child prodigy who suffered repeated bouts of psychological depression, Mill was not the most practical of men. Yet even he recognized the existence of economic depressions and the limitations of Say's Law in the short run.

> Although he who sells, really sells to buy, he need not buy at the same moment when he sells: and he does not therefore necessarily add to the *immediate* demand for one commodity when he adds to the supply of another. The buying and selling [in a monetary economy] being now separated, it may very well occur, that there may be, at some given time, a very general inclination to sell with as little delay as possible, accompanied with an equally general inclination to defer all purchases as long as possible . . . [W]hen there is a general anxiety to sell, and a general disinclination to buy, commodities of all kinds remain for a long time unsold, and those which find an immediate market, do so at a very low price. . . . It is true that this state can be only temporary, . . . and is generally followed by more than common briskness of demand.[8]

We believe the Mill passage correctly represents sometimes contradictory and unclear classical views. Some may think that we are overly generous to classical economists. At this late date, however, let us study classical theory for its truths and ignore any possible errors. This is not a book in the history of economic theory; classical theory, like every other theory, is worthy of detailed study only if it is accurate. The classical model presented here assumes Say's Law does hold in the long run but not in the short run.

Granting that classicists recognized that Say's Law holds only in the long run is not much of a concession. The important point is: how long is the long run? What calendar period of time corresponds with the economic concept of the long run? Classical economists unfortunately never

---

[8] J. S. Mill, *Essays on Some Unsettled Questions of Political Economy* (London: John W. Parker, 1844), pp. 70–71. Italics in original.

answered the timing questions explicitly. The short period and long period mark off particular initial conditions (that is, assumptions), reactions, and adjustments such as the market clearing and price flexibility. The short period is chronologically shorter than the long period, and that is all classicists stated. (Fortunately, the periods were not reversed to really confuse matters.) Short-run static models predict changes at some point in time closely following some shock and simultaneously help in understanding the entire time path of the changes. Long-run static models predict the ultimate change. Consider Figure 15–3, which plots the change, relative to

**FIGURE 15–3  The time path of Z and Z′ changes measured from their initial values**

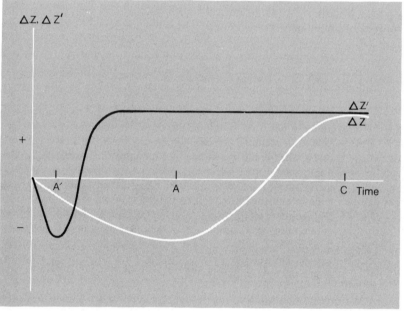

the initial value, of Z and Z′ over time. The maximum decrease and subsequent increase is identical for Z and Z′. However, Z′ is quite stable. Variable Z′ adjusts more rapidly than Z. The calendar time of the short run for Z′ and Z is approximately A′ and A, respectively. Calendar time A approximates the short run for variable Z and the long run for Z′. Observing Z′ for the first time at time A misses the sharp initial decline. Times A and C are the long run for Z′ and Z, respectively. The clock time of the short and long period is not a theoretical question. Empirical analysis—looking at the facts—is essential.

Although never stated explicitly, classical writings hint at the clock time of the short and long period.[9] Some classicists wrote as if Say's Law held at all times. Why? As they interpreted the empirical evidence, the short run is chronologically short and matters little. Adjustments occur relatively rapidly. Recessions are temporary. Output quickly rebounds to the maximum potential supply. Prices and interest rates fluctuate but quickly return to equilibrium. One can ignore situations where Say's Law does not hold if the long run were one month. Fleeting moments are not worth analyzing. On the other hand, Say's Law is irrelevant if the long run is a century. If we were pressed to estimate (guess?) the length of the classical short run, our hesitant answer is one to two years. In fact, the average duration of recessions has been 18 months. Classicists were shocked by the Great Depression, which began in 1929. By 1933 the economy definitely should have returned to full employment. Instead, the economy just hit bottom after a protracted decline. Full employment was another eight years away!

The Great Depression was too painful to be dismissed as a unique case. Adjustment to full employment sometimes is very slow. Nonetheless, extreme cases can be overemphasized. Even if the short run always were about 10 years, as was the case in 1929, can we ignore the long run? Can we ignore policies which have effects 10 years hence? Perhaps some, but not all. Our favorite education example of Chapter 1 illustrates your agreement that not all effects beyond 10 years can be ignored. The rate of return on education is negative for those with only a ten year horizon.

### Quantity theory of money

What role does money play in the long run classical model? Money determines prices. It does not affect long run real output because monetary policy influences only the demand for commodities. Aggregate supply is unrelated to the quantity of money. Money, particularly the fiat variety, would be miraculous indeed if it had any effect on a nation's ability to produce. No nation would invest and sacrifice current consumption in order to increase future output if printing costless money could accomplish the same objective. The leaders of less developed countries are not ignorant. They are aware of their ability to produce an infinite amount of

---

[9] Failure to answer timing questions is not a uniquely classical sin and continues today. Recall your typical microeconomic principles course. Theories of the firm and industry emphasize the short and long run. The amount of capital and number of firms are fixed in the short run but vary in the long run. No principles or advanced theory text states the calendar time during which capital and the number of firms are fixed. The length of the short run might well depend on the specific industry. The short run probably is chronologically shorter in the garment industry than the steel industry, where efficient production requires larger and technologically more sophisticated plants. While the amount of capital and number of firms distinguish the short run from the long run in microeconomics, market clearing and flexible prices distinguish the short run from the long run in monetary economics.

fiat money. They refrain from doing so because it will have no ultimate impact on a nation's ability to produce. Monetary expansion *consistently* increases aggregate demand, which ultimately influences prices alone. *The classical doctrine that monetary changes have a predictable effect on demand and, ceteris paribus, cause proportional price changes is called the quantity theory of money.* This is the second fundamental belief of classical economics.

Nominal income (and output) is the product of prices, P, and real income, y. *An alternative expression of the quantity theory of money is: monetary changes consistently cause proportional nominal income changes but leave real income unchanged.*

## NEOCLASSICAL ECONOMISTS

Many current economists accept the two fundamental theorems of classical economics: (1) Say's Law, that is, supply creates its own demand in the long run, and (2) the quantity theory of money, that is, money has a strong and predictable effect on demand and tends to cause proportional price changes. The modern economists who unfailingly accept the two fundamental propositions are called neoclassical economists. Until about 1970, neoclassical economists were sufficiently homogeneous in their beliefs that they typically were considered a single group, monetarists. Since 1970, however, two splinter groups have arisen, supply-side economists and rational-expectations economists. Thus, three groups now reside in the neoclassical camp: monetarists, supply siders, and rational expectationists.

The monetarists are not only the oldest but also far and away the largest neoclassical group. As such they form the standard against which the other two are measured. The leading monetarist clearly is Milton Friedman, a long-time professor at the University of Chicago and now at Stanford University's Hoover Institution of War, Peace, and Revolution. Although Friedman and monetarism are almost synonymous, other internationally respected monetarists include Phillip Cagan of Columbia University, Karl Brunner of the University of Rochester, and Allan Meltzer of Carnegie-Mellon, to name a few. The Federal Reserve Board of St. Louis is a long-time advocate of monetarism within the System.

The supply siders are the smallest neoclassical group but became highly influential with the election of President Ronald Reagan. The best known academic supply sider is Arthur Laffer of the University of Southern California. Many members of the Reagan administration are alleged to be supply siders. Contrary to monetarists, supply siders believe that fiscal policy, particularly tax policy, can significantly influence real output through its effects on *supply,* hence their name. Note that supply siders are good bearers of the classical torch. Tax policy influences output because taxes affect supply, which creates its own demand. While taxes may also affect demand, this is only incidental and totally unnecessary according to supply siders. If taxes only influenced demand, then output would be unchanged. Monetarists deny that fiscal policy has an *appreciable* effect on either demand or supply and, therefore, output.

Among the leading members of the rational expectations school are Robert Lucas of the University of Chicago and Thomas Sargent and Neil Wallace of the University of Minnesota. The Federal Reserve System is not monolithic. The Federal Reserve Bank of Minneapolis advocates rational expectations as strongly as the St. Louis Fed advocates monetarism. The rational expectation approach is quite complex and not summarized quickly without making it sound foolish. With our apologies then to the rational expectations school, whose views will be presented more fully in Chapter 23, rational expectations comes close to accepting the strong Keynesian interpretation of Say's Law, that is, supply creates its own demand at all times. Of course, rational expectations advocates recognize that output sometimes is below full employment. They claim that such situations occur because suppliers underestimate demand and produce too little, and not because demand is lacking. Markets clear at all times according to the rational expectations school. The school further claims that estimates of demand are unbiased, that is, overestimates at some points are matched by underestimates at other points. Stated somewhat differently, expectations are rational when they are not systematically wrong. Therefore, while output below full employment for a *short* time is consistent with rational expectations, prolonged depressions or expansions indicate systematically incorrect estimates and contradict rational expectations. Compared to monetarists, the rational expectations school claims the economy is much more stable. Major recessions and booms contradict rational expectations but do not necessarily contradict monetarism.

**AGGREGATE SUPPLY**

Unless stated otherwise, the composite neoclassical model presented in this and the next chapter is acceptable to all three groups. The remainder of this chapter takes a close look at supply, the piper which plays the tune in neoclassical economics. What determines supply in the long run? After answering that question, we extend somewhat our discussion of the quantity theory of money. However, the reader must await the next chapter for a complete presentation of the quantity theory and the adjustments which make demand equal supply. This chapter presents the basics.

**The production function**

Goods and services do not fall like manna from heaven. An often long and complicated production process transforms inputs, also called factors of production, into goods and services, or output. The relationship between factors of production (inputs) and output is called the production function. Land, capital, and labor are factors of production. For simplicity, however, assume homogeneous labor is the only variable factor and a standard commodity output, gizmos. Gizmos are extremely versatile. They are eaten (consumption), produce little gizmos (investment), and are hurled at the enemy (government expenditures). We may think of the production function as the technological relationship showing how much is produced as alternative amounts of labor are employed. Figure 15–4 graphs a production function. Output, y, is on the vertical axis, and labor, L, is on the horizontal axis. The curve is upward sloping at first and then

**FIGURE 15–4  Production function relationship between output and input**

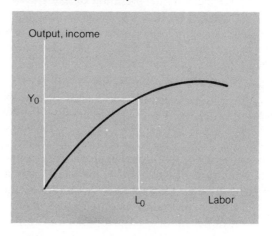

**FIGURE 15–5  Supply and demand for labor as functions of the real wage**

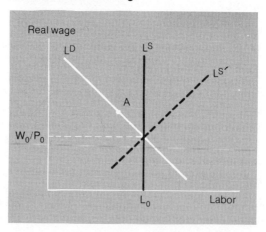

downward sloping. At least initially additional workers should produce more output. After employment becomes quite large, additional workers actually reduce output as congestion becomes severe and management of large numbers becomes chaotic. As economists, however, we can ignore the downward sloping portion reflecting congestion and mismanagement. Profit-oriented firms will never hire that many workers. By definition the curve's slope is the change in income or output, measured on the vertical axis, divided by the change in labor, measured on the horizontal axis. The slope, $\Delta y / \Delta L$, measures the marginal physical product of labor, $MPP_L$, the additional output produced by an additional worker. Figure 15–4 illustrates a declining marginal physical product of labor; the curve becomes flatter. The existence of fixed factors explains the declining marginal physical product of labor. As additional workers till the soil and are supervised less closely by a limited number of managers, each additional worker becomes less productive.[10]

The height of the production function depends positively on the quantity of capital, the quality of the labor force, and the degree of technological advancement and entrepreneurship. The production function shifts when the just enumerated factors change. For example, technological progress and a more skillful labor force shift the production function upward more or less smoothly and continuously over time. Dramatic changes in the annual or decadal rate of technological progress are common in selective industries but rare economywide. Analysis of these shifts is left to development and managerial economists. For simplicity, we usually ignore production function shifts.

### The demand for labor

In many respects labor is no different from other commodities. The demand and supply of labor determine the number of workers employed and, in conjunction with the production function, output. Consider first the demand for labor. What is the objective of firms? Why do firms produce?

Prior to World War II profit maximization was the only objective economists considered. Although most economic texts still assume profit maximization is the objective at all times, post-World War II economists have discussed other objectives, such as sales maximization (market share) subject to some minimum profit constraint. The new theories were constructed to better describe the "real world," particularly in the short run.[11] Attempts to maximize profits at every moment can be counterproductive. Suppose you owned a restaurant. Would you loudly announce

---

[10] Recalling principles of economics, what name is given to this fundamental law of production? The law of diminishing returns.

[11] Herbert Simon won the 1978 Nobel Prize in economics largely for his nonprofit-maximizing theories of the firm.

a temporary 20 percent price surcharge whenever the waiting line was long, and parade in front of the restaurant with a sale sign whenever it was empty? Alternatively, would you purposely cut costs and food quality some days? Such actions may maximize profits in the short run but are almost guaranteed to drive you out of business. Tomorrow's demand depends on a firm's behavior today. Consequently, characterization of firm's behavior and objectives depends on the time period. Future evaluation of the Phillips curve, which claims there is a permanent tradeoff between inflation and unemployment, examines the relation between objectives and time. For now just accept that in the long run the profit-maximization assumption is realistic. Firms cannot ignore competitive pressure forever. Firms continually seeking objectives besides profit maximization eventually will be bankrupt as new and more profit-conscious firms enter an industry. Indeed, the desire "to make a buck" is so strong that entry in competitive industries tends to eliminate economic profit. Firms earn only accounting profits, a normal rate of return on capital.

Assuming profit maximization, firms hire workers until the additional cost equals the additional revenue generated by workers.[12] In a competitive industry the additional costs of labor is the wage rate, W. Competitive firms can hire any amount at the existing wage rate. The revenue generated by an extra worker is the product of the commodity price, P, times the marginal physical product of labor. Expressing the profit-maximizing condition algebraically,

$$W = P \cdot MPP_L, \text{ or } MPP_L = \frac{W}{P}. \qquad (15-1)$$

Profit-maximizing firms equate the marginal physical product of labor and the real wage, W/P. Equation (15–1) generates the negatively sloped demand curve for labor graphed in Figure 15–5. As stated earlier, the marginal physical product of labor declines as additional workers are hired. This implies that the real wage firms are willing to pay declines as additional workers are hired. Alternatively stated, as the real wage falls firms find it profitable to hire more, if less productive, workers. This certainly corresponds with common sense. When labor costs are high relative to the price of gizmos, that is, the real wage is high, firms will demand little labor.

### The supply of labor

The neoclassical supply of labor reflects the maximization of a leisure/commodities preference (utility) curve. Individuals derive satisfaction from both leisure and commodities which are plotted on the horizontal

---

[12] Technically speaking, profit maximization equates the marginal cost of labor and its marginal revenue product.

**FIGURE 15–6  Opportunity locus. The real wage determines the commodities/leisure trade-off**

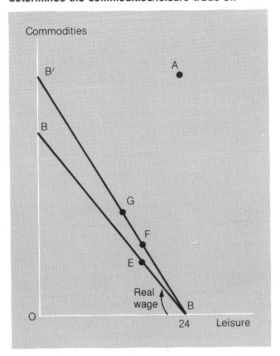

and vertical axes, respectively, of Figure 15–6. Most people would like 24 hours of leisure daily and an unlimited quantity of commodities, represented by point A in Figure 15–6. What people "like" and what they can achieve do not coincide. Economics, the study of scarcity, says individuals cannot enjoy unlimited amounts of both. Every day has 24 hours which must be divided between leisure and work. All work and no play makes Jack a dull boy, and all play and no work makes Jack starve. Jack forgoes some leisure and works in order to purchase commodities now and in the future. The real wage determines the quantity of commodities Jack can purchase by sacrificing leisure and working. For example, if the wage rate is $6 per hour and the price of commodities (gizmos) is $4, work effort and the sacrifice of an hour's leisure allows Jack to purchase 1.5 gizmos. The $6 nominal wage does not measure the rewards of work effort in terms of commodities. The real wage, and *only* the real wage, sets the opportunity locus (trade-off curve) between leisure and commodities given by line BB in Figure 15–6. Ignore line BB′ for the moment. In this example Jack could loaf all day and be broke, enjoy 23 hours of leisure (work 1 hour) and be able to purchase 1.5 gizmos, enjoy 22 hours of leisure and be able to purchase 3 gizmos, and so on. The absolute value of the slope of the opportunity locus BB equals the real wage, 1.5 in our example. Workers select that leisure (and work, since leisure and work must equal 24 hours per day) and commodities combination on the trade-off curve which maximizes their preferences. Without drawing indifference curves, assume utility maximization occurs at point E. *The work decision in the long-run neoclassical model is uniquely determined by the real wage which sets the trade-off curve, given workers' preferences for leisure and commodities.*

How do changes in the real wage affect the amount of labor supplied? Monetarists and supply siders differ on this question. All price changes have so-called income and substitution effects. Higher real wages allow one to enjoy more commodities (leisure) for any given quantity of leisure (commodities)—the income effect—and increase the cost of leisure in terms of commodities foregone—the substitution effect. In terms of Figure 15–6, a higher real wage rotates the opportunity locus upward to BB', which illustrates that the higher real wage makes one better off. Aside from the intercept, every point on BB' is above and to the right of BB. Since leisure is desirable, one tends to acquire more leisure (work less) when real wage rises. However, the higher real wage has increased the cost of leisure in terms of commodities foregone, which tends to reduce the amount of leisure demanded and, therefore, increase labor supplied. In terms of Figure 15–6, the opportunity has become steeper besides shifting upward. Monetarists claim that the negative (positive) income effect on work effort (leisure) approximately equals the positive substitution effect so that labor supplied is virtually independent of the real wage. Figure 15–6 illustrates a case to total independence; a higher real wage causes a person to move from point E to F, which is directly above E. The monetarist position is illustrated by the solid vertical supply curve in Figure 15–5. Supply siders on the other hand say that the substitution effect dominates. Higher real wages induce *greater* (less) *work effort* (leisure). The supply siders' position is illustrated by point G in Figure 15–6 and the dashed upward sloping supply curve in Figure 15–5.

Disagreement within the neoclassical camp about the slope of the labor supply curve sometimes obscures the fundamental similarity: *all neoclassicists claim that labor supply simply depends on the real wage.* The disagreement concerns only the precise relationship between labor supplied and the real wage. For example, suppose wages were to double. Would *any* neoclassicist predict *unequivocally* that the amount of labor supplied will increase? No. What happened to prices? If prices also doubled so the real wage were unchanged, the same amount of labor services would be supplied. Proportional wage and price changes do not change the real cost of leisure and the rewards of work. The opportunity locus remains fixed. The same work effort maximizes labor's preference relationship between leisure and commodities. Thus the supply of labor in classical monetary theory, like the supply and demand curves for all products in traditional microeconomics, is grounded on maximization principles. Firms and consumers *ultimately* maximize profits or preferences, yielding supply and demand curves.

Preference maximization, just like profit maximization, is unrealistic in the short run. Contracts, custom, and misperception of wages and prices prevent short-run preference maximization. For example, employment contracts at a specified money wage are quite common. As prices and, therefore, the real wage change, many individuals are obligated by contracts to work the same number of hours. Fortunately, we no longer live in a slave society. Contracts elapse. In the long run contracts do not constrain preference maximization. Subsequent chapters analyze the short-run determinants of labor supply. The purpose of this brief paragraph is to warn against the uncritical application of a theory for all time and space. Most long-run neoclassical assumptions are unrealistic in the short run.

### Labor market equilibrium and the aggregate supply curve

Look at Figure 15–5. The demand and supply of labor uniquely determine a real wage and amount of labor effort. This is true regardless of the shape of the supply curve. Given the existing capital stock, quality of labor, and degree of entrepreneurship as represented by the production function, Figure 15–4, the level of output and income is determined. Note well what happens: *output is determined independently of consumer and other demands for commodities.* Firms' quest for profits and individuals' preferences for leisure and commodities in conjunction with existing technology, capital, labor force quality, and entrepreneurship determine output, that is, supply determines output. The unique supply is illustrated by the vertical aggregate supply curve, AS, in Figure 15–7. The vertical line illustrates that the unique output is consistent with any price level, provided the nominal wage adjusts to keep the real wage constant.

The equilibrium employment naturally is a point on the labor supply curve and represents full employment, in the sense that everyone willing to work at the wage/price structure is doing so. Suppose the economy temporarily found itself at the disequilibrium point A. The real wage is too high, and unemployment exists equal to the horizontal distance between A and the labor supply curve. What will happen? Wages fall or, more likely, wages do not rise as fast as prices. In any case, real wages fall as the army of the unemployed—to borrow a very unclassical phrase—fight for the existing job. A lower real wage induces firms to hire more workers. The real wage continues to fall until everyone willing to work at the wage/price structure is doing so. Full-employment equilibrium is reached at $(W_0/P_0)$.[13]

---

[13] Full employment and related concepts are analyzed in greater detail in Chapter 23.

FIGURE 15-7   Classical economics and the quantity theory of money

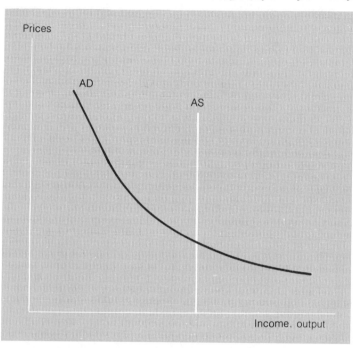

## THE QUANTITY THEORY AND AGGREGATE DEMAND

Classical economists had a very simple money demand equation which neoclassicists no longer accept. However, within the context of the entire classical/neoclassical model where commodity supply is independent of commodity demand, the simple classical money demand equation and a more complex equation yield the same conclusions.[14] Since simplicity is desirable, let us accept the classical money demand equation. Classicists viewed money solely as a medium of exchange. In other words, they had only a transactions demand for money. The amount of money one holds according to classicists is proportional to one's transactions and income. In symbols,

$$M = kPy \qquad (15-2)$$

where P is prices, y is real income or output, and k is the factor of proportionality linking money (M) and nominal income (Py). Assuming a given money supply, equation (15–2) also represents the equilibrium relationship in the money market because at equilibrium demand equals supply. Equation (15–2) is called the cash balance or Cambridge k version of

[14] The form of the money demand relationship is extremely important in Keynesian economics where aggregate supply is not fixed.

the quantity theory because economists from Cambridge University favored its use.

Irving Fisher and others favored the velocity version of the quantity theory. Cambridge economists look at money while it was being held in anticipation of spending. Fisher's velocity version, however, looks at money directly as it is being spent and changing hands. The average rate at which people want to spend money, that is, the average desired rate of turnover of money, is called desired velocity, V. Money multiplied by velocity then equals total desired spending, which at equilibrium equals the value of output and income.

$$MV = Py \qquad (15\text{--}3)$$

For example, suppose velocity is 6 per year. Then a \$1 billion money supply can generate annual income payments of \$6 billion because the average dollar is spent six times during the year. Clearly, V and k are reciprocals, $V = 1/k$ and $k = 1/V$. If the average dollar is spent 6 times per year, then the average dollar is held 1/6 of a year. Classicists thought that velocity or its reciprocal, the transaction coefficient k, could be treated as if it were a known constant. That is, the quantity theory says that k or V and, therefore, the demand for money, is stable, predictable, and independent of the quantity of money.

The aggregate demand curve shows the relationship between output and price when the nonlabor markets of the economy are in equilibrium, given the money supply, fiscal policy, and other exogenous variables. When the money market equation takes the classical form, the equation is sufficient to give the equilibrium relationship between output and price. In this special case, the aggregate demand curve AD simply graphs the classical equation (15–3) or (15–2) for a given V or k and money supply. The aggregate demand curve is a downward sloping curve. A given money supply which turns over a fixed number of times per period can finance a given volume of transactions. If the price per item rises, the number of items which can be purchased falls. The intersection of aggregate demand and supply determine the price level.

## MONETARY AND FISCAL POLICY

Suppose the quantity of money changes. How does the economy respond? Since velocity and its reciprocal, k, are independent of the quantity of money, inspection of equations (15–2) and (15–3) indicates that monetary expansion shifts the aggregate demand curve upward and outward proportionally. People have more money than they need for current transactions and, consequently, spend the additional money balances. Since the supply of commodities is independent of the quantity of money in the long run, the enhanced demand simply raises prices proportionally without affecting output.

Money may not affect output in the long run, but does it influence other economic variables besides the price level? In particular, does the quantity of money have any *long-run* effect on the rate of interest? No. The demand for automobiles and other commodities depends to some extent on the rate of interest. Therefore, if monetary expansion permanently lowered the rate of interest, the demand for commodities would permanently exceed the supply of commodities, which is independent of money. Such a situation is impossible; equilibrium eventually prevails. In the long run the rate of interest also is independent of the quantity of money.

Now assume fiscal policy instead of monetary policy is expansionary. More specifically, assume personal income tax rates are reduced, and the government issues bonds to finance the same level of expenditures. What is the long-run effect of the tax reduction? Neoclassicists agree that tax cuts have no effect on *aggregate demand*. When velocity can be treated as a constant, tax reductions which do not change the quantity of money cannot change nominal income (Py) and, therefore, do not shift the aggregate demand curve. To be sure, lower taxes increase *disposable income,* which tends to produce more spending. However, the government sells additional bonds to raise the money necessary to pay for its expenditures. Although not illustrated in Figure 15–7, the additional bond sales drive up interest rates and reduce spending. Because tax reductions and equal bond sales by the Treasury have no effect on money, the interest rate effect must exactly cancel the disposable income effect when velocity is constant.

Do personal income tax reductions affect aggregate supply? To answer this question we must consider the effect of taxes on the production function and the demand and supply of labor, the relationships which underlie the aggregate supply curve. The production function is a *technological* relationship, and profit-maximizing firms hire workers until the *technologically* determined marginal physical product of labor equals the real wage. Consequently, taxes do not affect either the production function or the demand for labor. Taxes may influence the supply of labor, however. When the leisure-commodities opportunity locus and supply of labor were derived, we implicitly ignored taxes or, equivalently, assumed tax rates were constant. A reduction in tax rates has the same effect on the opportunity locus as an increase in (pretax) real wages, since after-tax wages determine the commodities one can purchase. The monetarist's vertical labor supply claims that the amount supplied is fixed irrespective of the real wage. Since the amount of labor supplied does not increase when pretax real wages increase, labor supply is unaffected by taxes. Consequently, equilibrium employment and the aggregate supply curve are unaffected by the tax cut.

Supply siders, however, claim that labor supplied is highly responsive to the real wage rate. Since lower tax rates and higher pretax real wages have the same impact on the commodities that can be purchased by workers, tax cuts shift the supply of labor rightward according to supply siders.[15] Equilibrium employment increases, and the vertical aggregate supply also shifts rightward. Output increases only because aggregate supply increases. If tax reductions had shifted the aggregate demand curve upward, prices would rise but output would remain fixed so long as taxes do not shift aggregate supply.

## SUMMARY

Economic theory, policy, and history are interrelated. Theories are constructed to explain important economic events, and economic and social policy is strongly influenced by theory. As Keynes so eloquently stated, "Practical men, who believe themselves to be quite exempt from any intellectual influences, are usually the slaves of some defunct economist. Madmen in authority, who hear voices in the air, are distilling their frency from some academic scribbler of a few years back."[16] Keynes wrote *The General Theory* to free practical men from slavery to classical economics which, according to Keynes, "is misleading and disastrous if we attempt to apply it to the facts of experience."[17] While Keynes undoubtedly was the brightest mid-20th-century economist, his criticism of classical economics was too harsh. Classical economics may be incomplete and is incapable of analyzing every problem. However, it does explain many facts well, which justifies its study. Dispel any idea that the study of classical theory is prompted by a sense of history or the desire to pay homage to our ancestors. To repeat, we study classical economics because it explains some aspects of the past and accurately predicts the future. The two basic propositions of classical economics which all current neoclassicists accept are (1) Say's Law, and (2) the quantity theory of money. We showed how supply factors alone determine output in the long run. Although money may have a predictable effect on aggregate demand, money can only affect prices when output is determined by supply.

Keynes was more successful than even he had envisaged. *The General Theory* almost immediately made many practical men the slaves of Keynes, a testimonial to the ideas contained in the book. But slavish devotion to either Keynesian or neoclassical economics is wrong. Both Keynesian economics with its emphasis on the short run and neoclassical economics with its emphasis on the long run are necessary to understand the unfolding over time of the effects of money and other policy variables. Keynesian and neoclassical economics are competitive in some respects but, on balance, are better viewed as complementary, jointly providing an

---

[15] The supply siders' Laffer curve, which shows the relationship between tax receipts and tax rates, is presented in the appendix. By permission of Royal Economic Society and Macmillan, London and Baskingstoke.

[16] Keynes, *The General Theory*, p. 383.

[17] Ibid., p. 3.

approximation to a dynamic theory. Subsequent chapters on Keynesian economics show that monetary and fiscal policy can influence output in the short run. In the long run, however, monetary policy influences prices alone, and fiscal policy without supply-side effects simply alters the composition of output. More government spending implies fewer private goods from a fixed supply.

**QUESTIONS**

1. In what sense are we all Keynesians now, and in what sense is no one a Keynesian any longer?

2. What are the main properties of good theories?

3. In what way are classical and Keynesian economics complementary?

4. Name at least three classical economists and state their major accomplishments.

5. Explain the two fundamental beliefs of classical economists?

6. What three groups of economists make up the neoclassical school? What are the main differences between the three groups?

7. Explain how neoclassicists derive output independently of demand. What are the fundamental assumptions underlying the neoclassical supply and demand for labor? What variable determines the amount of labor supplied and demanded?

8. Write the cash balance (Cambridge k) and velocity versions of the quantity theory equation. Define terms and indicate how they are related.

9. What is the effect of monetary changes in the long-run neoclassical model? What assumption is made about k(V)?

10. What is the long-run effect of lower taxes according to (1) monetarists and (2) supply-side economists?

## appendix · Taxes and the Laffer curve

Tax receipts equal the product of the tax rate and tax base. In the case of the income tax, the base is income, of course, so that

$$T = t \cdot Y \qquad (15A-1)$$

where T is tax receipts, t is the income tax rate, and Y, as usual, is nominal income. For simplicity, we are assuming proportional instead of progressive taxes. Clearly, if either the income tax rate or income is zero, tax receipts also are zero. Does the government get all the income if the tax rate were 100 percent? Yes, but in that case all the income is nothing. Aside from a few workoholics, a confiscatory 100 percent tax rate totally

**FIGURE 15A-1   Laffer curves**

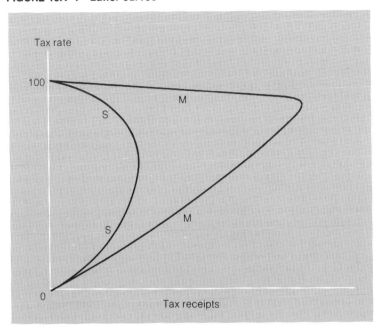

eliminates the incentive to work. Income in equation (15A–1) cannot be considered a constant; it depends on the tax rate. Since tax receipts are zero when the tax rate is zero or 100 percent, and since we observe that the government does collect taxes when the tax rate is positive but less than confiscatory, the relationship between tax receipts and tax rates must first be positive and then negative, as is illustrated in Figure 15A–1. Tax receipts are maximized at some intermediate tax rate below 100 percent. The backward bending curves in Figure 15A–1 are Laffer curves. The Laffer curve typically is drawn as a semicircle or, at least, a nice smooth curve such as SS. However, the curve MM in Figure 15A–1 also satisfies the condition that tax receipts are positive except when the tax rate is zero or 100 percent.

The text stated that supply siders claim that tax reductions increase work effort. In terms of equation (15A–1), a smaller t allegedly increases Y. The more extreme supply siders go further. Lower tax rate increase work effort and income so much that tax receipts actually increase.[1] The economy supposedly is on the backward bending portion of the curve!

---

[1] Tax receipts increase when the percentage increase in income exceeds the percentage decrease in the tax rate. Note that a positively sloped labor supply curve, so that taxes have a negative effect on work effort, does not by itself guarantee that the economy is on the backward bending portion of the curve.

What type of labor supply curve in Figure 15–5 is implied by Laffer curve MM? Curve MM implies the labor supply curve is vertical until the real wage is extremely low. There is a proportional (straight line) relationship between tax receipts and tax rates until rates approach 100 percent because work effort and income are constant. Laffer curve MM represents the monetarist position; the labor supply curve is vertical about wage and tax rates likely to be observed. (No one should be forced to qualify every statement for ephemeral possibilities because of fear of being interpreted too literally. What would happen if the wage rate were one mill is irrelevant.) Monetarists join their Keynesian colleagues in claiming that tax rate reductions tend to lower tax receipts. Of course, inflation and other factors increase nominal income and tax receipts, so that one may want to lower tax rates.

# Neoclassical economics: A detailed analysis

# 16

This chapter is for those from Missouri, the show-me state. (Non-Missourians may proceed directly to Chapter 17 without loss of continuity.) With the aid of graphs we attempt to justify some major propositions of neoclassical economics outlined in the previous chapter while simultaneously illustrating secondary issues. We primarily will analyze:

1. The determinants of velocity, with emphasis being placed on the reasons for treating it as a constant.
2. Rate of interest and price adjustments which equate aggregate demand to a given full-employment income without need of monetary or fiscal policy.

The quantity theory of money hypothesis that prices tend to be proportional to the quantity of money hinges on velocity being exogenous. The last chapter, however, offered no rationale for treating velocity and the transactions coefficient as constants. Moreover, the last chapter stopped short of attempting to justify Say's Law. We did show that supply determines a unique level of output. We still must show how the desired expenditures of households and firms adjust in the long run to equal the supply-determined output, without need for government intervention. The automatic adjustment process may be so slow, however, that one may wish to supplement it with short-run discretionary policy. The concluding section evaluates the relationship between the effectiveness of short-run monetary and fiscal policy and the cause of temporary deficiencies in expenditures.

Appendix A contains a numerical example of the entire classical model. Instead of saving the appendix for dessert, some may prefer to turn to it after completing each section and compare piece by piece the graphic approach in the text and the numerical example in the appendix. Indeed, one can immediately turn to the first part of the appendix, which numerically derives the aggregate supply curve presented graphically in the previous chapter.

## COMMODITY THEORY OF MONEY

Monetary expansion through the debasement of coins was a recurrent phenomenon during the Middle Ages. Since inflation invariably followed debasement and monetary expansion, the public quite naturally believed the two events were related. The precise relationship, however, was unclear for many years. So-called *commodity theorists* argued that money's value or purchasing power depended on the commodity value of the money substance itself. Debasement reduces the gold or other commodity content of coins, by definition, and according to the commodity theorists makes money less valuable by raising the general price level of commodities. The fact that the quantity of money increases was thought irrelevant. The commodity theorists argued that replacing full-bodied gold coins with an equal amount of coins with less gold content or paper money would be highly inflationary. Such a theory may sound incredibly naive to the modern reader long since accustomed to inconvertible paper money. But the commodity theory was difficult to disprove for many years as debasement was the principal means of monetary expansion. It probably still has a few adherents. Many supported the 1934 devaluation of the dollar (lowering the gold content of the dollar or raising the dollar price of gold) as a direct means of raising the depressed U.S. price level. Quantity theorists viewed debasement as incidental to monetary expansion. They claimed that monetary expansion, however achieved, caused inflation. The Spanish discovery of gold in the New World settled the controversy between commodity and quantity theorists. The influx of Spanish gold coins, which were not debased, raised prices throughout Europe as the quantity theorists predicted and contrary to the commodity theory.

## QUANTITY THEORY OF MONEY

Although the quantity theory of money is one of the oldest and most widely publicized economic theories—it almost invariably is presented in principles texts—it also is one of the most misunderstood. Look at Figure 16–1, which graphs quarterly velocity between 1960 and 1980.[1] Velocity has been far from constant; it has a strong upward trend. Many people,

---

[1] The velocity of M–1A and M–1B coincided until the early 1970s, and the differences in the two velocities since then are imperceptible. Velocity did not increase sharply through the 20th century. It rose moderately in the early decades and fell significantly between 1930 and 1945.

FIGURE 16–1   Income velocity of money, 1960–1980

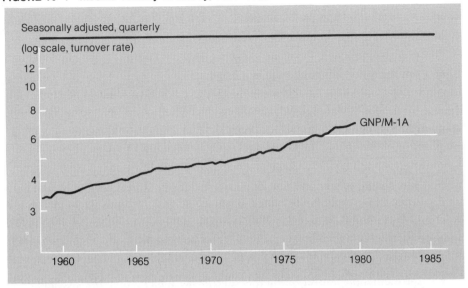

economists included, claim that Figure 16–1 contradicts the quantity theory. In fact, the graph seemingly confirms one aspect of a properly understood quantity theory. One reason for the confusion is a misunderstanding of the word *constant* as used by quantity theorists. Constant does not mean unchanging to quantity theorists. Instead, the alleged constancy of velocity is a shorthand expression for (1) the stability and predictability of velocity, and (2) the independence of velocity and the quantity of money. Because this special meaning of constant can be confusing, in the last chapter we carefully stated that "velocity may be treated *as if* it were a constant" or, "velocity is exogenous," that is, determined outside the system. (Exogenous does not mean unchanging; the weather is exogenous but variable.) In view of the confusion regarding the quantity theory and this chapter's admittedly Missourian orientation, we begin with basic principles and tolerate some slight repetition of the last chapter so that the full quantity theory is available in one place.

### Equations of exchange and quantity theory equations

The quantity theory of money is mainly a theory of the price level. It also is a theory of money demand and of the effects and importance of money versus other factors. Thus, the quantity theory encompasses many elements. One thing the quantity theory is not: it is not a theory of money supply. It assumes the central bank has perfect control of the money supply, which can be set at any desired value.[2] We usually assume government fiat money, a simplification with little effect on the conclusions. The other financial asset besides money is a standard bond whose yield is "the" interest rate. The essential difference between money and bonds is that the former is the medium of exchange. Any financial asset which is not a medium of exchange is a bond.

The two versions of the quantity theory, Fisher's velocity approach and the cash-balance approach associated with A. C. Pigou and other Cambridge University economists, differ more in appearance than substance. All classical economists viewed money as the medium of exchange. Indeed, classical economists virtually ignored any other function of money. They gave only lip service to money's role as a temporary abode of purchasing power and unit of account. Money is held simply to carry out some reasonably well-defined purchasing plan. According to classicists, money is not held for contingencies (temporary abode of purchasing power) or because its *dollar* price is fixed (unit of account). Thus, classicists had a "pure" transactions demand for money.

The *starting* point of Fisher's velocity version of the quantity theory is the elementary observation that all transactions involve the exchange of a nonmoney commodity and money. During any given period of time, the value of money expenditures equals the value of all commodities sold. Alternatively stated, the value of all goods purchased and sold are equal, and money is used to purchase every good. Fisher's equation of exchange expresses this truism algebraically.

$$MV_T \equiv P_T T \qquad (16-1)$$

where M is money, $V_T$ is the transactions velocity or average rate of transactions turnover of money, $P_T$ is the price index of all commodities sold, and T measures the quantities of all goods sold during the period. In one sense the equation of exchange is somewhat of a misnomer. It is an identity or truism and not the traditional equilibrium equation. To repeat, the equation of exchange simply says that the observed money expenditures equal the value of all commodities sold. Such a truism may be the starting point of a theory, but is not a theory with predictive content. Nevertheless, let us examine the truism more carefully.

Fisher called the right-hand side of equation (16-1) the sale-of-goods side. Each sale is regarded as the product of a price and quantity. As stated several times in the preceeding paragraph, all sales are measured. Thus, $P_T T$ includes the value of GNP as well as sales of second-hand commodities, bonds, and labor services. Money is exchanged in every transaction. Clearly $P_T$ and T are rather special kinds of indexes of price

---

[2] Wicksell's cumulative process analyzes the short-run interaction between aggregate demand and the money supply in an economy with a passive central bank which lets commercial banks dictate monetary policy. Thus, Wicksell should not be considered a quantity theorist.

and quantity, respectively. The left-hand or money side expresses total expenditures as the product of money times its velocity. In principle, velocity can be measured by attaching to every dollar bill a beeper, which would signal the central bank's computer every time the dollar bill changed hands. At the end of the time period, the computer would tally how many transactions were made with each dollar, that is, whether it turned over 0, 1, 2, . . . times. The weighted average of these numbers of turnover is velocity. Principle may correspond with reality in the future. Today, actual velocity is computed by dividing total sales by money. Velocity is that number which makes the equation true. Suppose total transactions per year are $200 and the money stock is $25. What does velocity equal? The average rate of money turnover is 8 per year.

The exchange truism is the foundation of the Fisherian quantity theory equation, which is an equilibrium equation. The equilibrium relationship was expressed by Fisher as

$$MV_T = P_T T. \qquad (16-2)$$

The variables are similar to equation (16–2) except that they represent *desired* instead of actual values. For example, $V_T$ in equation (16–2) is the possibly unobserved desired rate of turnover. Actual velocity, which is readily computed, need not equal desired velocity just as the quantity of bread purchased need not equal demand. To further distinguish the truism from the equilibrium statement, equations (16–1) and (16–2) used the identity ($\equiv$) and equality ($=$) symbols, respectively. Equation (16–2) says algebraically that individuals are just satisfied with their money balances and the money market is in equilibrium when the rate people want to spend and, thereby, reduce their money balances—$MV_T$—equals the rate they add to their money balances through the sale of goods—$P_T T$. When desired subtractions equal desired additions the amount remains constant, a feature of equilibrium.

The ambiguities of the concepts of "total quantities" (T) and the "general price level" ($P_T$)—particularly those arising from the mixture of intermediate, final, and capital asset transactions—were never satisfactorily resolved. Nevertheless, the early classicists used total transactions because it could be approximated by bank debits, the value of all checks written. Reasonably accurate banking and financial statistics antedate most other statistical series. The more recent development of GNP statistics has stressed the importance of current production and income rather than gross transactions. As a result, the quantity equation has more recently tended to be expressed in terms of GNP instead of transactions. Instead of equation (16–1) we have

$$MV \equiv Py \qquad (16-3)$$

where M represents, as before, money; V is income velocity, the average number of times during the period that money is used in making GNP

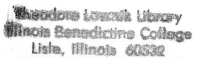

expenditures; P is the GNP price index; and y is real GNP. A GNP version of the equilibrium equation (16–3) may also be written.

$$MV = Py \qquad (16\text{–}3a)$$

Equations (15–7) and (16–3a) are identical.

Fisher's equation looks at the means of payment in motion, moving from one person to another. Cambridge economists preferred to look at the means of payment at rest. Money is held for some period of time before it is spent on current goods and services. The quantity of money can be expressed as the product of its average holding period for nominal GNP expenditures times nominal GNP.

$$M \equiv kPy \qquad (16\text{–}4)$$

Defining the Cambridge k as "the average time period money is held" makes clear the reciprocal relationship, even when the algebraic equations are unwritten. If the average dollar is spent 7 times during the year ($V = 7$), then $1/7$ year measures the length of time the average dollar is held ($k = 1/7$).

Provided one recognizes the truisms expressed algebraically by equations (16–3) and (16–4), V and k may be defined more mechanically without objection. Rearranging equations (16–3) and (16–4),

$$V \equiv Py/M, \qquad (16\text{–}3')$$

$$k \equiv M/Py. \qquad (16\text{–}4')$$

Velocity is the ratio of nominal income to money and k is the ratio of money to nominal income. These mechanical definitions will be used later. Remember, however, that the identities were not written to merely define k and V but express the truism that money is held for some time interval and then spent. The Cambridge k, like velocity, could be measured independently by the beeper technique. Instead, it is derived from independently measured money and income data.

Just as the actual velocity equation of exchange, (16–1), provided the foundation for the desired velocity version of the quantity theory of money, (16–2), so (16–4) led to the Cambridge version of the quantity theory of money.

$$M = kPy \qquad (16\text{–}5)$$

Equation (16–5) expresses the equilibrium relationship in the money market. The left-hand side is the exogenously determined money supply. The right-hand side is money demand, which is the product of the desired length of time people want to hold their money income multiplied by income. More simply, money demand is some desired proportion, k, of nominal income. The equality of demand and supply at equilibrium gives equation (16–5).

## Velocity versus the Cambridge k

Although equations (16–3a) and (16–5) are mathematically equivalent, Pigou and his Cambridge cohorts insisted that their equation (16–5) was much clearer from an economic viewpoint than Fisher's equation (16–3a). Like other equilibrium equations, (16–5) has demand on one side and supply on the other. The left-hand side of equation (16–3a) has MV, which is neither money demand nor supply. Fisher, of course, disagreed with the Cambridge economists' assessment of the economic clarity of equations (16–3a) and (16–5). Fisher thought it best to think of equilibrium as occurring when desired additions equal desired reductions. Since both approaches are correct while emphasizing different elements, the use of both is convenient. Some problems are more easily analyzed by considering money in motion than at rest, and vice versa.

Fisher's quantity theory equation incorporates a basic neoclassical belief: money has an important effect on spending. True, money is used to purchase every good, but this is insufficient justification for expressing desired reductions in money balances as the product of money and velocity. All purchases are made by some economic unit, that is, a household, firm, or government. One could just as easily express total spending and the reduction in money balances as the sum spent by the different units C + I + G. The formally equivalent statement selected reflects one's economic belief. Fisher thought that household, firms, and government spending patterns were sufficiently similar to justify consolidation in one spending class. He emphasized the most important determinant: money.

## Prerequisites of a theory

A theory must specify the determinants of the variables and describe their interrelationship. Simply noting that MV = Py or M = kPy at equilibrium tells us virtually nothing. Suppose the money supply doubled. The equation says that at the new equilibrium either velocity is cut in half (or, equivalently, k doubles), prices double, real output doubles, or some combination of velocity, prices, and output change. An example is helpful. Suppose M = 100, V = 5, P = 1 and y = 500 so MV = Py is 100 · 5 = 1 · 500. Now double the quantity of money, M = 200. A new equilibrium exists when velocity is cut in half, V = 2.5, and prices and real output are unchanged, 200 · 2.5 = 1 · 500. Instead of velocity falling, prices could double. Another possible equilibrium is M = 200, V = 3.5, P = 0.7 and y = 1000, so monetary expansion reduces velocity and prices but increases output. Clearly, an endless number of combinations satisfies the equilibrium equation. The quantity theory is anything but wishy-washy. It analyzes the determinants of and interaction among the variables and yields definite predictions.

We already know the determinants of two variables in the quantity theory equation. The quantity of money is perfectly controlled by the Fed, at least as a first approximation. Money is a causal factor and does not respond to any of the variables in the equation. When the central bank changes the quantity of money, the other variables must respond. Equilibrium output and real income does not respond to monetary changes, however. Output is determined by the supply and demand for labor and the production function. Do monetary changes affect velocity, V, or its mathematical equivalent, the transactions coefficient, k? No. *In general, V and k are relatively stable and independent of the quantity of money.* We examine shortly how classicists arrived at this very important conclusion. The implication of an "as if" fixed transactions coefficient is that prices and money change proportionately. $M = \bar{k}P\bar{y}$, where the bars over k and y indicate these variables are fixed, or at least independent of money. Double money and prices double.

## DETERMINANTS OF THE TRANSACTIONS COEFFICIENT, VELOCITY, AND TRANSACTIONS DEMAND

Precisely what factors influence the desired income transactions coefficient, k, and why can it be considered a constant? In other words, the demand for money is proportional to income. What are the determinants of the proportionality factor, k, and why can it be considered a constant? Fisher and his followers often gave the impression that money is a hot potato. Households want to spend or lend their money holdings as soon as possible. Money per se has no utility, in contrast to commodities and bonds. Nevertheless, velocity is not infinite, and money is held longer than a split second because of institutional and technological factors. Thus, classicists had a very mechanical approach to the transactions coefficient, velocity, and money demand. One technological factor limiting velocity is the speed of transportation and communications. Trains in 1900 and now faster airplanes carry checks from New York to California. Even if money were spent immediately, transit time lags limit the rate of money turnover. For example, if all payments went through the mails which took a week for delivery, velocity could be no greater than 52 per year, and a dollar is "held" at least $1/52$ of the year. As transportation and communications improve through time, Fisher said velocity would rise and the transactions coefficient would fall.

A second determinant of velocity is the degree of synchronization of receipts and expenditures. Households and business firms would hold little or no money if they were assured that a sufficient amount of money would flow to them just at the moment expenditures are anticipated. But receipts and expenditures are not perfectly synchronized. Households may be paid weekly or monthly. Paydays are a joyous occasion but not enough to spend everything immediately and starve the rest of the pay period. The holding period of money falls and velocity rises as receipts and expenditures are better synchronized. Imagine an author who receives $3,000 royalty checks each quarter and spends it all evenly during the quarter. Our author's money balances have the sawtooth pattern illustrated in Figures 16–2. The author begins the quarter with $3,000 and is

**FIGURES 16–2   Transactions balances**

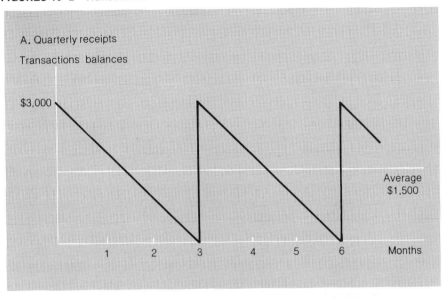

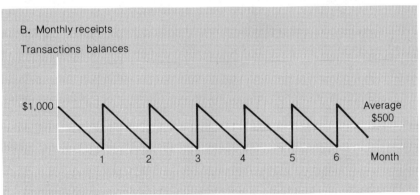

penniless as the quarter ends. The process repeats itself each quarter, so annual income and expenditures are $12,000. Average money balances are $1,500, and annualized k is ⅛ ($1,500/$12,000). Some of the money is spent instantaneously, and some is held a full quarter. On average, money is held one and a half months or, equivalently, one eighth of a year. Velocity is eight times a year. Now suppose the author receives royalty

checks monthly so receipts and expenditures are more closely synchronized. At the beginning of each month the author receives $1,000,
which is spent evenly throughout the month. Annual income and expenditures remain $12,000. Our author's money holdings are now illustrated in
Figure 16–2B. The average dollar is spent every half month. Annual velocity is 24, or k = $^1/_{24}$.

Discussion of the total transactions version of the equation of exchange
($MV_T \equiv P_T T$) was not motivated alone by a desire to know the history of
economic thought. It helps explain why specialization and the degree of
vertical integration is a determinant of the income velocity of money.
Money is used in all transactions, whether one purchases final goods and
services or intermediate goods and financial assets. Less vertical integration increases intermediate goods transactions, by definition, as some
firms produce or purchase raw materials and others manufacture final
goods and services. A vertically integrated baking industry purchases
wheat and sells bread, eliminating independent millers. As firms become
more specialized and production becomes less vertically integrated, the
volume of non-GNP transactions increases. Since money is held for GNP
and non-GNP transactions, greater specialization increases the money/
income (GNP) ratio k, because more money must be held for the nonin-
come (GNP) transactions. In other words, transactions velocity, that is,
the number of times the average dollar changes hands for whatever reason, measures the "work" money performs. Specialization does not affect
the total work money can perform but does decrease (increase) the
amount of work money performs for GNP (non-GNP) purposes. Therefore, specialization reduces income (GNP) velocity. For example, suppose all transactions initially are associated with GNP, and on the average, money is spent weekly. Income (GNP) and transactions velocities
both are 52 per year. Assume firms suddenly specialize and intermediate
transactions are as large as GNP transactions. Money should continue to
change hands every week. However, the average dollar purchases final
goods and services only every other week; money is being spent for
intermediate goods. Total transactions velocity remains at 52 but income
velocity falls to 26 per year. In terms of the algebraic equations,
$MV_T \equiv P_T T$ and $MV \equiv Py$. Dividing the transaction equation by the income equation gives $V_T/V \equiv (P_T/P)(T/y)$. Specialization and less vertical
integration raises T/y but should have no effect on the relative prices of
different types of goods. With $P_T/P$ unchanged, less vertical integration
implies that $V_T/V$ rises. Money is used in all transactions, and its rate of
turnover on all transactions is unchanged. With $V_T$ constant, the increase
in $V_T/V$ requires a smaller V. Of course, the lower income velocity is
equivalent to the just stated increase of the Cambridge income k.

Finally, Fisher recognized that velocity depends on the availability of
credit. Many individuals during Fisher's time had accounts at grocery and
general stores. They signed for groceries and paid the grocer on their

paydays. Credit synchronizes receipts and payments more closely and increases money's rate of turnover, or reduces its average holding period. Our world has become much more formal and legalistic. Informal credit accounts at individual stores have given way to plastic credit cards issued by national companies. The growth of total credit has been substantial but less than the growth of credit cards as informal credit sources dried up. The increasing availability and use of credit enters the quantity theory equation by raising velocity.

Recognition of credit effects on velocity seemingly forces attention on the rate of interest, which may be viewed as the price of credit. However, Fisher and his velocity approach followers stopped short of considering the relationship between velocity and interest rates. Velocity and the demand for money were very mechanical in Fisher's hands. Slow trains and unsynchronized receipts and payments limited the rate of turnover of money. Fisher was blinded by concentrating on money in motion rather than at rest, or so others have suggested. Whatever may be the reason for Fisher's failure, the Cambridge economists, who preferred the cash balance version of the quantity to Fisher's velocity version, *sometimes* recognized that k, desired money holdings relative to income, depends on the rate of interest. Of course, this implies velocity also depends on interest rates since k = 1/V. Consistency is the hobgoblin of little minds, and Marshall, Pigou, and other Cambridge economists had great minds. On their best days, Cambridge economists stated explicitly and clearly the negative relationship between desired money holdings and interest rates (positive relationship between velocity and interest rates).[3] On other days, and there are many, Cambridge economists overlooked the effect of interest rates on the money/income ratio. Inconsistencies and contradictions on specific issues can be found among members of any school of thought. Unlike a master and disciples who uncritically tow the line, schools of thought are characterized by a generally accepted viewpoint punctuated by occasional dissent. On balance, classical economists believed k and V and, therefore, the demand for money were independent of interest rates.

In summary, classicists thought the demand for money is proportional to income where the factor of proportionality, k, depended on technological and institutional factors such as the transportation and communications system, the synchronization of receipts and payments, vertical integration, and the availability of credit measured by the breadth of financial markets and institutions. These technological and institutional factors are exogenous, that is, influence variables within the system but are not influenced by the included variables, particularly the quantity of money. Therefore, when considering the effect of monetary policy the income transactions coefficient and velocity may be treated as constants.

---

[3] A. C. Pigou, "The Value of Money," *Quarterly Journal of Economics,* 32 (November 1917): 38–65.

## THE MODERN QUANTITY THEORY AND KEYNESIAN
## TRANSACTIONS DEMAND

Virtually no one fully accepts every aspect of the classical quantity theory of money. Yet virtually everyone accepts some aspect of it, and virtually every aspect is accepted by someone. Keynesian economists believe that the classical money demand equation and the analysis of the determinants of velocity are important elements of total money demand. Keynes claimed, however, that classicists had only a transaction demand for money. He mentioned another element to money demand, as subsequent chapters will describe. Indeed, the Keynesian second element to total money demand prompted our mention in the last section of the possibility of interest rates influencing the demand for money. Current empirical evidence strongly supports the validity of the Keynesian second element or, at least, indicates that the classicists erred in assuming money demand is independent of the rate of interest. The demand for money certainly does depend on the rate of interest. This does not deny, however, the usefulness of the classical quantity theory as a partial explanation of total money demand, as Keynes recognized.

Neoclassical economists on the other hand totally repudiate the specific form of the classical money demand. Neoclassicists do not emphasize that money is the medium of exchange. In fact, they totally ignore the services performed by money. Neoclassicists look at money as simply one of many assets. This asset approach inevitably leads to the assumption that money demand depends on wealth or some proxy of wealth, such as Friedman's permanent income.[4] Moreover, with the possible exception of Professor Friedman, every neoclassicist includes an interest rate term in the demand for money.[5] As mentioned in the last chapter, however, from the viewpoint of the entire neoclassical model the precise form of the money demand relationship is irrelevant. The same quantity theory conclusions follow whether or not money demand depends on current income or wealth and the rate of interest, as we demonstrate rigorously in later chapters.[6] Since the form of the classical quantity theory equations (16–2) and (16–5) are particularly simple, let us attribute them to neoclassicists as well as classicists and proceed directly to the important quantity theory conclusions, which neoclassicists wholeheartedly embrace.

---

[4] Permanent income is a weighted average of current and lagged income, where the weights decline exponentially.

[5] Friedman's position on the interest elasticity of the demand for money is not altogether clear. Virtually everyone interpreted, correctly, I believe, his "The Demand for Money: Some Theoretical and Empirical Results," *Journal of Political Economy,* August 1959, as saying that the demand for money is independent of the rate of interest. However, Friedman said, "We have been misinterpreted wrongly, I believe, as saying that (the Cambridge) k is completely independent of interest rates." ("A Theoretical Framework for Monetary Analysis," *Journal of Political Economy,* March–April 1970, p. 216.)

[6] This is not true for the Keynesian model. Within the Keynesian model the effects of monetary and fiscal policy do depend crucially on whether or not money demand depends on the rate of interest.

## QUANTITY THEORY CONCLUSIONS

As indicated earlier, an exogenously determined desired velocity in conjunction with output determined by the supply and demand for labor and production function yields a strong conclusion: monetary changes cause proportional price changes. Using bar superscripts to denote "constants," double money and prices double when $M\bar{V} = P\bar{y}$. Assumptions and conclusions of the quantity theory of money seem straightforward but must be interpreted carefully. First, the quantity theory says all prices, including the wage rate or price of labor services, respond proportionally to money. This follows from the assumption of a constant output. Employment and output remain constant only if the real wage is unchanged, that is, commodity prices and wages change proportionally. (See Figures 15–4 and 15–5.) Thus the price effects of money should be interpreted broadly to include wages. Second, velocity and income are constant in the sense that their equilibrium values and growth over time are independent of the quantity of money. They do change over time. Classical economists were confident the production function illustrated in Figure 15–4 would shift upward over time so that the output produced by a given labor force would rise. Moreover, over time the demand and supply for labor would increase. Thus, output rises over time because each worker is more productive and more workers are hired. Somewhat less confidently, Fisher and other classicists thought velocity would rise slightly over time with technological change and transportation improvements. Greater specialization and less vertical integration could reduce velocity, however. Assuming velocity grows less rapidly than output, prices would fall if the money supply remained constant. Monetary expansion is necessary to maintain a constant price level in a growing economy. For example, suppose velocity is fixed and output doubles over time. Prices would fall 50 percent if the money supply were constant. Money is needed to finance transactions. When output and the number of transactions doubles, the prices associated with each transaction must fall in half in order to maintain proportionality between a fixed quantity of money and the total value of transactions. A constant price level requires a doubling of the money stock in this case. Monetary expansion prevents prices from having to fall 50 percent, and prices are twice as high as they would have been. If constancy through time of velocity and output is sometimes alleged, it is only for convenience. Thereby, we can avoid the cumbersome statement, "Monetary changes cause price changes proportional to what they otherwise would have equaled," and simply state, "Monetary changes cause proportional price changes."

The velocity version of the quantity theory, equation (16–3a), yielded the aggregate demand curve of Figure 15–7. Figure 16–3 graphs the cash balance version of the quantity theory, $M = kPy$. The price level is on the horizontal axis and money is on the vertical axis. The solid ray from the origin graphs the money demand curve, given the average money

**FIGURE 16-3   The quantity theory: Money demand and supply**

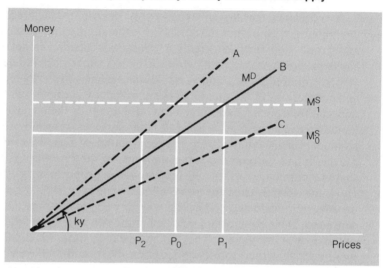

holding period, k, and real income. Ignore for the moment the dashed lines from the origin. The slope of the ray is ky or, equivalently, y/V. ($M^D$ = kPy, and $\Delta M^D$ = ky$\Delta$P. In words, the difference equation says that the change in money demand equals ky multiplied by the price change. $\Delta M^D$ = ky$\Delta$P is equivalent to $\Delta M^D/\Delta P$ = ky, which is the slope of the ray since money and prices are on the vertical and horizontal axes, respectively. In terms of velocity, the slope of the ray is y/V since k = 1/V.) The solid horizontal line $M_0^S$ represents the initial money supply set by the central bank. Equilibrium as shown by the intersection of the two lines determines the price level, $P_0$. Now suppose monetary expansion shown by the line $M_1^S$. The money demand curve does not rotate in response to monetary policy. Real income and the average holding period of money balances are independent of the quantity of money. The economy moves along the money demand curve and prices rise proportionally to $P_1$.

The classical analysis of the determinants of output and velocity makes an even stronger assertion than the independence of output and velocity and money. Output and velocity growth through time are *highly predictable* besides being unrelated to (independent of) the quantity of money. An example best illustrates that independence without predictability is of little value to policymakers. Suppose annual velocity and output depend on the rainfall in Kankakee, Illinois, the won-lost record of the Washington Redskins, and the December 31 winning number in the New York lottery. The central bank then could confidently assume that annual velocity and output is independent of the quantity of money. We are unaware of theories linking money to rainfall, sports, and games of chance. The independence of output and velocity and money tells the central bank that prices, and only prices, respond to money. In terms of Figure 16–3, independence means that the money demand curve does not rotate as supply changes. (Recall that the slope of the money demand curve is y/V.) However, the demand curve could rotate for other reasons. Will the demand curve remain the solid line B? In this admittedly unrealistic example, rainfall, sports, and games of chance determine velocity and output and, therefore, the position of the money demand curve. Neither the central bank nor anyone else can reliably predict rainfall, sports, and games of chance. The money supply compatible with some desired price level is uncertain when velocity and output change randomly and rotate the money demand curve from B to A to C in Figure 16–3. The central bank will achieve its price objective if it can predict the position of the demand curve, and if the demand curve does not move when the central bank changes the money supply.

Consider another situation. Suppose Disney World initiates a new "ride." With a class A ticket you can throw rotten tomatoes at Donald Duck. Under what conditions would you be likely to hit the old lecher? Ideally, Donald would remain still. Even if this were not the case, your chances of hitting him are good if he moves predictably—say, smoothly from one side of the stage to the other—and independently—Donald does not duck. You would be lucky indeed to hit him if he moved randomly and reacted to your toss.

Velocity and output do not depend on rainfall or Donald Duck's behavior. The level and growth over time of velocity and income depend on technology, population and the labor supply, and institutional factors. These determinants of income and velocity change relatively smoothly over time. Indeed, it is the smoothness of these changes which make velocity and output growth highly predictable. Suppose real income rises faster than velocity, which increases the slope of the money demand curve and makes it steeper. In other words, y rises faster than k falls. The demand curve rotates from B to A in Figure 16–3. The steeper curve indicates more money is demanded at every price level. Assuming a fixed money supply $M_0^s$, the equilibrium price level falls. Can the central bank maintain the desired price level $P_0$? Yes, indeed. The central bank will have been able to *predict* the change in demand and increases the money supply to $M_1^s$. Drawing graphs and rotating the demand curve should not, but sometimes does, obscure the fact that its position is not controlled by the central bank, but must be estimated instead.

Look at Figure 16–1 again. It seemingly confirms the quantity theory assumptions that velocity is stable, changes smoothly over time, and is predictable. Velocity does not appear to jump randomly. Instead, the upward trend is relatively smooth so next quarter's velocity is reasonably well predicted by extrapolation. We realize that the terms *seemingly confirms, relatively smooth,* and *reasonably well predicted* are imprecise, and someone may not accept our interpretation. At this point, however, more precise measures are too disruptive to the flow of thought. Remember neoclassical theory concerns the long run; velocity changes smoothly and predictably in the long run. A precise evaluation that concludes that *quarterly* velocity is unpredictable does not necessarily contradict the quantity theory. Such a precise evaluation simply implies the long run is longer than a quarter. Velocity per one, two, or five years could be stable and predictable even if quarterly velocity is not. The empirical Chapter 22 presents better evidence on the question of timing and other neoclassical/Keynesian controversies. The imprecise evidence contained in Figure 16–1 is presented to dispel at an earlier stage the sometimes entrenched idea that neoclassical economics is a fairy tale in never-never land. The path of quarterly velocity is not perfectly smooth but not so random that the long run is the indefinite future.

Prices in many countries are rather erratic. Prices rose and fell prior to World War II but, at least in the United States, have risen almost continually in the postwar period. The rate of inflation has not been uniform, however. How do neoclassicists explain variable rates of inflation? The central bank has an unsteady grip on the money stock. Velocity and output growth are highly predictable. Prices would follow a steady course if the monetary authority maintained a steady policy. For example, suppose full-employment output outstrips any velocity increase. In symbols, y is rising faster than V. If the money stock remained constant, prices would fall steadily and gradually. Rapid and uniform rates of monetary expansion are associated with high and uniform rates of inflation. However, the monetary authority accelerates and decelerates monetary growth, and inflation accelerates and decelerates. Variations in the rate of inflation are almost exclusively due to variations in money growth.

## THE COMMODITIES MARKET AND AGGREGATE EXPENDITURES

The neoclassical analysis of the commodities market is designed to explain how expenditures are equated to the output determined by workers' willingness to work and firms' quest for profits. Before discussing the more difficult adjustment process, the determinants of aggregate expenditures are explained. Figure 16–4 graphs aggregate expenditures, C + I + G, or, more simply, E, on the vertical axis and aggregate output, y, on the horizontal axis.

The unique aggregate supply determined by the labor market is the solid vertical line labelled $y_0$. Temporarily ignore the broken lines. The 45° line contains all the points equidistant to the axes, by definition, so it is the equilibrium line. Along this line supply equals demand. *The neoclassical belief that supply creates its own demand implies that an aggregate demand curve, EE, will intersect the 45° line at the same point it is intersected by the vertical supply line.* Figure 16–4 illustrates this neoclassical belief; the

**FIGURE 16-4  Aggregate expenditures and output**

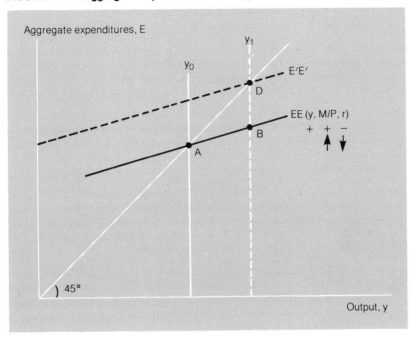

solid EE goes through point A. Figure 16–4 also illustrates that aggregate expenditures, particularly the consumption component, depends positively on income. The aggregate expenditure curve slopes upward but its slope is less than one, that is, it is flatter than the 45° line. Demand increases as income increases but not by the full income increase. Since income is already determined by supply conditions, a more thorough explanation of income effects is unnecessary at this point and postponed until the chapters on Keynesian economics.[7] Note well, however, that the neoclassical belief that supply creates its own demand does *not* imply that the 45° line is also the aggregate demand curve. The 45° line would represent aggregate demand if you believed that supply in and of itself causes an equal demand. But neoclassicists do not allege this. In terms of Figure 16–4, the neoclassical belief in Say's Law means that when supply shifts to the broken line $y_1$, the expenditure curve also shifts to maintain equilibrium. The supply increase by itself causes a less than equal increase in demand as the economy moves from A to B, which is below D. The other determinants of expenditures will also change, however, causing the expenditure curve to shift upward and intersect the 45° line at point D.

---

[7] The consumption decision is an important determinant of equilibrium income in the Keynesian model.

What factors besides income influence expenditures? The second determinant of expenditures is wealth approximated by real money balances, $M_0/P$. Wealth or net worth is a stock, and income and spending are flows. Wealth is measured at some moment while income is measured during some time interval. Capital goods, which we shall ignore, net bond holdings, and real money balances compose a single economic unit's wealth. From the viewpoint of society as a whole, net bond holdings are zero in a closed economy. Bonds are the assets of creditors but the equal liability of debtors. Society's wealth is independent of the value of bonds outstandings. Ignoring the capital stock, society's wealth equals its real money balances.[8] The wealth or real balance effect on consumption spending is often called the Pigou effect in honor of its popularizer. How does wealth affect spending? Suppose you win the grand prize in the Maryland lottery and become an instant millionaire. Will you spend a different amount now that you are wealthier, other things being equal? Most people will spend more. The Pigou effect says more money or a lower price level has a direct and positive effect on demand.

The determinants of expenditures are shown explicitly in Figure 16–4. The signs beneath the variables indicate their effect on spending. Some may prefer to look at the arrows, which indicate the direction that the curve shifts. For example, expenditures and real money balances are positively related, so larger money balances shift the expenditure curve upward.

Aggregate expenditures depend negatively on the rate of interest for two reasons. First, some households who had been planning to borrow in order to finance a major expenditure will be deterred by high finance costs. Moreover, those households already planning to save will be encouraged to save more. Households refrain from current consumption and save in order to provide for the future. The rate of interest measures the tradeoff between current consumption and future consumption made possible by saving. For example, suppose the rate of interest is 8 percent (.08 written as a decimal) and gizmos cost $1. By saving $1 today one can purchase 1.08 next year.[9] As the rate of interest rises and current consumption can be substituted for more future consumption, the typical household consumes less and saves more.

---

[8] We are implicitly assuming that all money is fiat money. Demand deposits are assets of depositors and liabilities of banks and not part of society's wealth. Therefore, society's wealth is less than its real money balances when demand deposits exist. In this case wealth equals the monetary base. Since the money supply equals the money supply multiplier times the base, $M = mB$, wealth equals the money supply divided by its multiplier. We are also assuming the public views any government bonds as their own and that they are simultaneously an asset and liability.

[9] We are assuming the rate of inflation is zero. The distinction between real and nominal interest rates was discussed in Chapter 5.

### INVESTMENT AND THE RATE OF INTEREST

While households respond somewhat to the rate of interest, it mainly affects firms' investment spending. Investment is the acquisition of new capital goods such as machines which, when combined with other factors of production, produce a stream of commodities in the future. The investment decision entails two calculations: compute the rate of return on the investment and then compare it with the rate of interest. The rate of return on an investment and the yield on bonds are computed in a similar manner. Suppose the price of the capital good is $P_K$ in general ($100 as a specific example) and the anticipated net revenue at the end of the year is $R_1$ ($110). Net revenue is the anticipated additional revenue from the sales of commodities produced with the machine minus all costs of production—labor and raw materials, for example—except the initial cost of the machine (depreciation) and interest. For simplicity assume the machine disintegrates at the end of the year. The rate of return on the investment—or the marginal efficiency of investment—is that rate of discount which equates the price of capital goods and the present value of the net revenue.

$$P_K = R_1/(1 + rr)$$
$$\$100 = \$110/(1 + 0.1)$$
(16–6)

In terms of equation (16–6), the marginal efficiency of investment is rr, 0.1 stated as a decimal, or 10 percent, in our specific example.

Profit-maximizing firms compare the marginal efficiency of investment and the rate of interest. (Remember we are abstracting from the myriad of interest rates and assuming a homogeneous bond which yields "the" rate of interest.) If the marginal efficiency of investment, possibly adjusted downward for the riskiness of anticipated future sales, is greater than the rate of interest the investment will be undertaken whether the firm must borrow or has sufficient money on hand. In this respect firms are no different from you and me. We would borrow at, say, 8 percent when we can invest the proceeds at 10 percent. Firms with sufficient money on hand to finance the investment view the rate of interest as an opportunity return; it is the return that firms sacrifice by using the money themselves rather than lending it to someone else. Firms maximize profits by undertaking all investments yielding returns greater than the opportunity return. If the marginal efficiency of investment just equals the rate of interest, the investment is a matter of indifference; if the marginal efficiency of investment is less, the investment should not be undertaken.

The marginal efficiency of investment schedule, more simply called the investment schedule, shows the amount of desired investment at alternative interest rates, r. The downward-sloping line labeled I(r) in Figure 16–5 is the investment schedule. Why is the investment schedule down-

**FIGURE 16–5  Investment schedule**

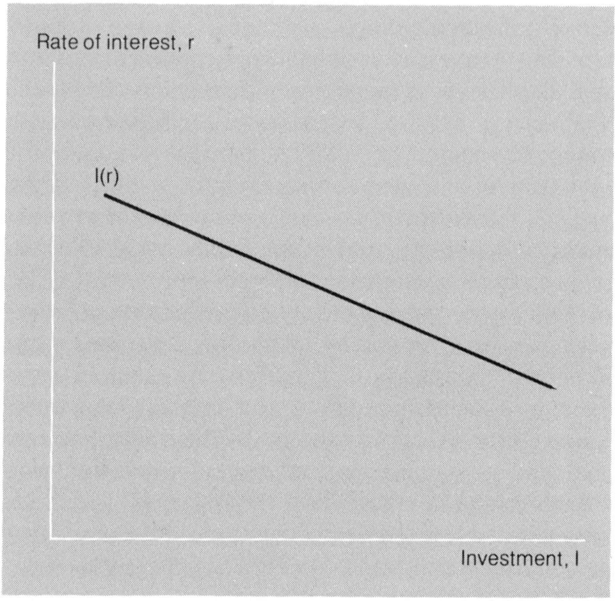

ward sloping? Alternative investments can be ranked by their rate of return. Few investment projects yield rates of returns greater than or equal to some arbitrarily high rate of interest and, therefore, investment by profit-maximizing firms is low. As the rate of interest falls, more investments yielding at least equal rates of return are undertaken. An alternative, and in some respects preferable, explanation for the negative relationship between investment and the rate of interest is based on the substitutability of factors of production. For example, one can mow a yard with an inexpensive lawn mower and substantial labor effort or with a more capital intensive sit-down mower and less labor effort. The optimal capital stock associated with any given output is negatively related to the rate of interest, other things being equal. At low interest rates profit-maximizing firms substitute capital for labor until the rate of return on capital equals the rate of interest. Net investment is the additional capital stock during the period. As the rate of interest declines, firms undertake more investments and move towards the larger optimal capital stock.[10]

---

[10] An analogy may aid in differentiating between the ranking of alternative investments and optimal capital stock explanations for a downward-sloping investment schedule. Why is the aggregate demand curve for, say, tea downward sloping? Two explanations are possible. First, each person may demand a fixed quantity of tea but the price people are willing to pay varies. As the price of tea falls, more people buy tea. The ranking of alternative investment approach is analogous. It ignores the substitutability of capital and labor and assumes each new project is associated with a fixed capital stock. An alternative explanation says that as

Neoclassicists claim the investment schedule I(r) is relatively flat because the rate of return on capital declines gradually. Substantially larger net investment is undertaken in order to increase the capital stock sufficiently and equate the rate of return on capital with lower interest rates. In drawing the investment schedule or any other demand curve, we assume all other factors affecting demand are given and unchanged. The investment schedule shifts as firms' estimates of net revenue, $R_1$, vary. Looking at equation (16–4), higher anticipated net revenue raises the rate of return on investment and shifts the investment schedule upward. The future is uncertain. Waves of excessive optimism and pessimism regarding future sales would dramatically shift the investment schedule. Our discussion of the quantity theory suggests that classicists discounted this possibility. The economy is basically stable. In the past firms usually have found ready buyers and they expect this pattern to continue. Quite moderate shifts of the investment schedule are the rule according to neoclassicists and, anticipating somewhat future chapters, the exception according to Keynes.

How are these properties of the investment schedule reflected in Figure 16–4's aggregate expenditure curve? The sensitivity of investment to the rate of interest causes slightly lower interest rates to shift the expenditure curve significantly upward. The relative stability of the investment curve says that expenditure curve shifts due to firms' behavior are quite moderate except when the rate of interest changes. Although neoclassicists believe that large government spending is unnecessary, they clearly recognize that it is a component of demand and has the potential for shifting the expenditure curve.

## LONG-RUN EQUILIBRIUM

Having specified the determinants of expenditures we can now attempt to explain how full-employment supply creates its own demand without any government action. Exposition of this difficult argument is facilitated by assuming full-employment output is produced at all times. The next section on short-run changes allows output to fall below full employment temporarily before rebounding back up to full employment. Take heed that our attempt to justify Say's Law is only partially successful. Neither the classicists nor anyone following them has been able to "prove" that demand will equal full-employment output. At best one can present a plausible explanation of the process by which demand adjusts towards supply. Whether demand will finally equal supply cannot be proven. While this may sound deficient, neither Keynes nor anyone else has

---

the price of tea (the rate of interest) falls, each person buys more tea (net investment expands) and substitutes tea (capital) for coffee (labor). Our emphasis on GNP and gross investment would add depreciation to this explanation for net investment.

"proven" the opposite, that is, demand will not equal full-employment output.

The adjustment process relies heavily on Walras's Law, which places a restriction on demand and supply curves due to the budget constraint. Demand and supply curves are not wishful-thinking curves; they do indicate the quantities requested from a fairy godmother. Demand and supply curves recognize that we live in a quid pro quo economy. If we demand more of one commodity, we must demand less of another or supply more of a third commodity in order to acquire the funds to make the purchase. For example, if we demand more apples we must demand fewer oranges, reduce our money holdings, or supply more bonds (borrow). Suppose there are n goods and services which include money, bonds, factors of production, and consumer items. Formally stated, Walras's Law says that the sum of the demand and supply for all n goods and services are always equal. Mathematically,

$$\sum_{i=1}^{n} P_i D_i \equiv \sum_{i=1}^{n} P_i S_i, \text{ or } \sum_{i=1}^{n} P_i(D_i - S_i) \equiv 0,$$

where $D_i$ and $S_i$ are demand and supply, respectively, and $P_i$ is the price for the ith good. The ith market is in equilibrium when $D_i - S_i = 0$. An alternative statement of Walras's Law is: if $n - 1$ markets are in equilibrium, the nth market must also be in equilibrium. Disequilibrium is never limited to a single market.

Suppose the economy is at full-employment equilibrium as represented by the broken lines $y_1$ and $E'E'$ in Figure 16–4. Now assume firms' investment opportunities decline and consumers suddenly become bearish and save more. The investment schedule in Figure 16–5 shifts leftward and the aggregate expenditure curve in Figure 16–4 shifts downward, becoming the solid line EE. The unchanged full-employment output temporarily exceeds demand by BD. How is demand again equated to full-employment output? According to Walras's Law, a decline in the demand for commodities cannot be the only change. The firms and consumers who were previously purchasing commodities must be doing something with their funds. In our highly aggregated model the only alternatives to commodities are bonds and money. Neoclassicists typically assume that lower investment will be accompanied by a reduction in the demand for loanable funds (less borrowing). When consumers become bearish and save more, they typically supply loanable funds with their additional saving. Both the reduced demand and enhanced supply of loanable funds reduce the rate of interest, which shifts the aggregate expenditure curve back up to $E'E'$. A lower rate of interest is sufficient for full employment.

The second and more complicated case supposes firms and households hoard the funds previously spent on investment and consumption. In other words, the reduced demand for commodities manifests itself in a larger demand for real money balances. At any price and income level more money is demanded. The money demand curve in Figure 16–3 shifts from B to A and becomes steeper as the Cambridge k increased, or velocity decreased. At the initial price level $P_0$ the demand for money exceeds supply $M_0^S$ so individuals hoard income receipts and do not purchase commodities. There is no reason for the rate of interest to fall as the additional saving is not lent. Prices fall, however, as aggregate demand is less than output. The price decline from $P_0$ to $P_2$ in Figure 16–3 satisfies society's demand for additional real money balances. The same amount of *nominal* money balances is satisfactory at the lower price level. Hoarding stops. The nominal quantity of money demanded again equals the fixed nominal supply at $P_2$. Aggregate expenditures fell to EE because society wanted additional real money balances. When prices fall and society has its additional real balances, the expenditure curve shifts back to its initial position.[11]

We therefore have two alternative ways to maintain full employment: interest rate or price level movements. Which alternative is most likely? Interest rate movements. The demand curve for money is quite stable. It rarely shifts. *Spending shifts are typically associated with shifts in lending instead of the demand for money. The rate of interest typically adjusts expenditures and full-employment output, but sometimes price level variations are necessary.*

Do changes in the quantity of money have any permanent effect on the rate of interest? No. From earlier sections we know that in the final analysis monetary changes do not affect either real balances or income, two of the three determinants of aggregate expenditures. Therefore, the equilibrium rate of interest must be independent of the quantity of money in order for the commodities market to be in equilibrium. If monetary expansion were to permanently lower the rate of interest, aggregate expenditures would permanently exceed the fixed supply of commodities. Such a permanent disequilibrium is an impossibility.[12] Money may have short-run but not long-run effect on the rate of interest.

---

[11] We are implicitly assuming that the *real* demand and supply of loanable funds is independent of the price level. The *nominal* demand and supply of funds is proportional to the price level. If the loan market contains a real balance effect, the shifts in saving and money demand will lower both interest and prices. The truly interested student might read Don Patinkin, *Money, Interest, and Prices: An Integration of Monetary and Value Theory*, 2d ed (New York: Harper & Row, 1965), an encyclopedic text on neoclassical economics. In terms of Patinkin's graph, we are assuming the BB curve is flat. Appendix B discusses some quite advanced issues about saving, investment, the rate of interest, and Walras's Law.

[12] Note that the argument in the text is based on the rate of interest necessary to equate aggregate *expenditures* and output and is independent of the relationship between money demand and the rate of interest. If the money supply doubles, prices double, and the rate of interest remains constant, then money demand equals the doubled supply whether or not money demand depends on the rate of interest.

## THE SHORT RUN

Classicists and neoclassicists pay little attention to the short run because they believe the economy adjusts rapidly toward full employment. In his monumental 515 page book, *The Purchasing Power of Money,* Irving Fisher devoted just a 19-page chapter to the so-called transition period—the short run.[13] Again suppose that consumers spend less and save more so that, in terms of Figure 16–3, the aggregate expenditure curve shifts downward from $E'E'$ to EE and is less than the $y_1$ full-employment output. Without any government action, full-employment equilibrium is restored through either a lower interest rate if households lend the additional saving or a lower price level if households hoard. The economy may adjust rapidly but not instantaneously, however. What relationships exist in the short run before all adjustments have occurred? Consider the possibility that the additional saving is lent. The *equilibrium* interest rate falls. However, the *market* interest rate may not fall rapidly enough and may remain above the new equilibrium for some time. A "sticky" rate of interest means that demand shifts back to $E'E'$ in Figure 16–4 only after a long lag. Full-employment output will be greater than spending for some time. Were firms to continue producing full-employment output, undesired inventories would accumulate. If the market rate of interest is sticky and does not fall rapidly enough, output will temporarily fall below full employment as firms attempt to reduce the accumulating undesired inventories. Should the government pump up demand by undertaking additional expenditures financed by borrowing? Such a policy prevents the market interest rate from having to fall as the government borrows (sells bonds equal to) the additional amount the private sector is saving and lending. Larger government expenditures would shift the aggregate expenditure curve back to $E'E'$ and compensate the downward private spending shift. Classicists generally opposed government expenditures as a means of achieving full employment. First, classicists doubted the market interest rate was sticky and did not fall rapidly enough to restore full employment. Second, even if interest rates were sticky, the appropriate policy is not greater government expenditures which prevents the interest rate from having to fall. Classicists were harsh disciplinarians. If the rate of interest will not fall by itself, beat it down. How is this accomplished? By monetary expansion, which temporarily lowers the rate of interest. Monetary expansion increases further the already swollen supply of credit and dislodges the temporarily sticky interest rate. Laissez-faire classicists spurned government expenditures because they thought most government expenditures were wasteful. Society derived little benefits from the goods and services acquired by the government. Full employment achieved by

---

[13] New York: Macmillan, 1926. Chapter 4.

additional government-sponsored ditch digging and pyramid building is not preferable to unemployment.

Regardless of its benefits, government expenditures are inappropriate when the additional saving is hoarded. In this case, society saves more because it wants additional real money balances. Sticky prices instead of interest rates cause problems. The interest rate is unchanged not because it is sticky but because the additional saving is hoarded, leaving the supply of credit constant. Hoarding shifts the money demand curve upward from B to A in Figure 16–3. If prices do not fall rapidly enough to increase real balances and shift the demand curve back to E'E' in Figure 16–4, output will decline as it is greater than demand at the constant rate of interest. Firms will not let inventories accumulate for long periods. The central bank can prevent a recession. If society cannot "manufacture" the additional real balances demanded because prices are sticky, the central bank simply increases the nominal money supply. In terms of Figure 16–3, the shift of the money demand curve is countered with an upward shift of the money supply. Society now has the additional money balance it wants, and the expenditure schedule shifts back and intersects the 45° line at full-employment output.

Government expenditures cannot prevent recessions induced by hoarding and sticky prices. Government spending financed by bonds has no effect on the money supply and is hardly likely to dislodge a downwardly sticky price level. Only larger real balances achieved through monetary expansion or deflation can restore equilibrium. In terms of Figure 16–4, additional government spending does tend to shift the expenditure curve from EE up to E'E'. There is an important difference, however, between this sticky prices case and the previous sticky interest rate case. In the previous case, the government bond sales necessary to finance the expenditures did *not* raise interest rates, by definition of "sticky" interest rates. In this case, however, the bond sales do raise interests. Prices, and not interest rates, are sticky. The negative financial effects of government spending counteracts its positive direct effect. The net effect is an expenditure curve invariant to government spending.

Classical economists doubted that either monetary or fiscal action was necessary to restore full employment. Interest rates and prices are sufficiently flexible. Nevertheless if, by chance, the economy did not adjust rapidly enough so a recession occurred, monetary policy was the appropriate medicine. Fiscal policy simply is powerless on occasion (that is, when saving is hoarded), and when powerful (that is, saving is lent) it absorbs scarce resources better used by the private sector. Monetary policy always is capable of generating full-employment demand without a resource cost (assuming fiat money).

The viewpoints and conclusions in this section were attributed to classicists. Do neoclassicists accept these classical viewpoints? Totally.

## SUMMARY

Classicists believed that the demand for money was proportional to income. They analyzed the determinants of the factor of proportionality and concluded it could change over time. However, they also concluded that at any one time the proportionality factor or, equivalently, velocity, was predictable and independent of the quantity of money. Neoclassical economists can no longer believe that money is proportional to income; the data flatly contradict the belief. However, they do believe that money has a predictable and independent effect on (nominal) income or, at least, has a more predictable effect than fiscal policy. Just because money has a predictable effect on income is not a sufficient condition for an active monetary policy. The economy is basically stable; interest rate and price adjustments normally bring the economy back to full employment quite rapidly. Discretionary policy usually is unnecessary. However, if discretionary policy is adopted, monetary policy is the appropriate choice.[14] Fiscal policy usually can do the job. However, when people are not spending because they want more ready purchasing power (real balances) but prices are sticky, then only the monetary authorities can satisfy the public's demand and restore full employment.

## QUESTIONS

1. Define the commodity theory of money. When was it widely advocated?
2. Explain the difference between the equation of exchange and the quantity theory of money equation.
3. In what sense is velocity, or the transaction coefficient k, a constant according to classicists and neoclassicists?
4. What are the main differences between the velocity and cash balance approaches to the quantity theory of money?
5. List the determinants of velocity according to classical economists and state their effect (positive or negative) on velocity.
6. State the main differences and similarities between the classical and modern quantity theories.
7. Draw two graphs. Place velocity and time on the axes of one graph and the change in velocity and the change in the quantity of money on the axes of the second graph. On each graph, draw two scatters of points, one which tends to confirm and another which contradicts the quantity theory of money.
8. Explain why investment is negatively related to the rate of interest. What is the neoclassical view concerning the shape and position of the investment schedule?
9. Define the Pigou effect and Walras's Law.

---

[14] We shall discuss lags and the controversy between discretionary policy and a monetary rule after the Keynesian model has been presented.

10. Assume aggregate expenditures decline. According to neoclassicists, what types of automatic adjustments restore full-employment equilibrium? Which adjustment is most likely, and why?

11. Assume some "stickiness," that is, the automatic adjustments are long delayed, so that output would tend to decline. Under what conditions can (a) monetary and (b) fiscal policy maintain full employment? Considering resource costs and program benefits, which policy should be adopted according to neoclassicists?

## appendix A · A numerical example

A numerical example of the classical model is offered here. Suppose the production function is

$$y = 25L - 0.1L^2 \qquad \text{production function} \quad (16A\text{--}1)$$

where y is output or real income, and L is labor. The derivative of the production function is the marginal physical product of labor, which is defined as the change in output per unit change of labor.

$$\Delta y/\Delta L = 25 - 0.2L \qquad \text{marginal product of labor} \quad (16A\text{--}2)$$

(Those unfamiliar with calculus and unwilling to accept equation (16A–2) on faith should read footnote 1. Since calculus is not a prerequisite for this book, we use difference rather than differential notation.) Graphically, the marginal product is the slope of the production function. The slope becomes flatter and the marginal product falls as more workers are hired. For example, at $L = 50$ equation (16A–2) shows that marginal product is 15; at $L = 100$ it is 5. (Ignore values of L greater than 125. Firms never hire so many workers that they trip over each other and have negative marginal products.) Profit-maximizing firms hire workers until the marginal product equals the real wage. Setting (16A–2) equal to the real wage and rearranging gives the demand for labor.

$$25 - 0.2L^D = W/P \qquad \qquad \text{labor demand} \quad (16A\text{--}3)$$
$$L^D = 125 - 5\,W/P$$

The demand for labor is negatively related to the real wage. Assume labor supply is positively related to the real wage.

$$L^S = 94 + 1.2\,W/P \qquad \text{labor supply} \quad (16A\text{--}4)$$

---

[1] Suppose the quantity of labor changes. The new quantity of labor may be expressed as the old quantity plus the change, $L + \Delta L$, and similarly for output. Substituting $y + \Delta y$ and $L + \Delta L$ for y and L in equation (16 A–1), we get $y + \Delta y = 25(L + \Delta L) - 0.1 (L + \Delta L)^2 = 25 (L + \Delta L) - 0.1 (L^2 + 2L\Delta L + \Delta L^2)$. Subtracting equation (16A–1) from the last equation and dividing by $\Delta L$ gives $\Delta y/\Delta L = 25 - 0.2L - 0.1\Delta L$. As $\Delta L$ becomes small so we are at the margin, the ratio $\Delta y/\Delta L$ approaches $25 - 0.2L$.

The equilibrium condition in the labor market gives the quantity of labor and real wage.

$$L^D = L^S \qquad\qquad\qquad \text{labor equilibrium}$$
$$L^D = 125 - 5W/P = 94 + 1.2\ W/P = L^S \qquad\qquad (16A-5)$$
$$W/P = 5; \quad L^D = L^S = 100$$

Substituting the equilibrium quantity of labor in the production function gives a unique full-employment output.

$$y = 25\ (100) - 0.1\ (100)^2 = 1,500 \qquad\qquad (16A-1')$$

Output is derived independently of the demand for commodities.

Let us now turn to the quantity theory of money. Suppose money balances are held on the average for 0.40 of the period ($k = 0.40$). Money demand, $M^D$, is

$$M^D = kPy = 0.40P(1,500), \quad \text{money demand} \quad (16A-6)$$

or if one prefers the Fisher "money demand" relationship,

$$M^DV = Py;\ M^D(2.5) = P(1,500), \qquad\qquad (16A-6')$$

where (16A–6) and (16A–6′) make use of the fact that $y = 1,500$. Suppose the money supply, $M^S$, is 1,200.

$$M^S = 1,200 \qquad \text{money supply} \quad (16A-7)$$

Setting money demand and supply equal

$$M^D = M^S \qquad\qquad\qquad \text{money equilibrium}$$
$$M^D = 0.40P(1,500) = 1,200 = M^S \qquad\qquad (16A-8)$$
$$P = 2; \quad M^S = M^D = 1,200$$

The quantity theory equation determines prices, which are proportional to the money supply. Consequently, real money balances are independent of the money supply. Real balances are 600 (1,200/2). The nominal wage is 10 since the real wage is 5. See equation (16A–5).

Suppose aggregate expenditures are

$$E = 625 + 0.6y + 0.1M/P - 17r \quad \text{aggregate expenditures} \quad (16A-9)$$

Setting expenditures, E, equal to output, y,

$$625 + 0.6y + 0.1M/P - 17r = y \quad \text{commodities equilibrium} \quad (16A-10)$$

But the equilibrium values of real income (1,500) and real money balances (600) were determined earlier. On substituting these values in equation (16A–10) and rearranging, the equilibrium condition in the commodities market gives the rate of interest.

$$625 + 0.60(1,500) + 0.1(600) - 17r = 1,500$$
$$r = 5 \qquad\qquad (16A-10')$$

There is a supply and demand for bonds which can be ignored. According to Walras's Law the bond market is in equilibrium when the labor, money and commodities markets are in equilibrium.

Suppose the money supply doubles so that $M^S = 2,400$. What are the new equilibrium values of the variables? Money does not enter until equation (16A–6). Therefore, the equilibrium output, real wage, and labor demanded and supplied are unaffected. Solving equations (16A–6) through (16A–8), prices double, $P = 4$. Real balances still equal 600, or 2400/4. Since output and real balances are unaffected by the monetary expansion, inspection of equation (16A–10) shows that the interest rate also is unaffected. Monetary changes only influence prices (including nominal wages).

Suppose instead that the aggregate expenditure curve shifts down so that it now equals $608 + 0.6y + 0.1M/P - 17r$. (Retain the original money supply assumption, that is, $M^S = 1,200$.) What are the new equilibrium values of the variables? In essence, the supposition changes equation (16A–9) and those that follow. Since equations (16A–1) through (16A–8) determine income and real balances, the shift only changes the equilibrium interest rate, which now equals 4 (!) percent. (This numerical exercise was constructed a *long* time ago!) Walras's Law states that some other demand of supply also changed. Presumably, the unspecified supply and demand for loanable funds (bonds) also changed.

Finally, assume that instead of the initial relationship, the money demand relationship is, $M^D = 0.5Py$, *and* the aggregate expenditure relationship is, $E = 610 + 0.6y - 0.1(M/P) - 17r$. What are the new equilibrium values of the variables? The reader who has followed the example this far knows the general approach to the problem but still wants his or her answer confirmed. In this case, only prices/wages change.[2] The new price (wage) level is 1.6 (8). This is the hoarding case. The public spends less because the demand for money balances increased.

---

## appendix B · Saving, investment, and the rate of interest

Viewed in isolation, it appears that many interest rates could equilibrate the commodities market since aggregate demand is a function of output and real money balances in addition to the rate of interest. For example, the specific commodities market equilibrium equation used in Appendix A was

$$625 + 0.6y + 0.1M/P - 17r = y.$$

---

[2] The reader is warned that every possible mechanical modification of money demand and aggregate expenditures does not change the solution for the price level alone. Modification of two or more demand and supply relationships is a necessary but not sufficient condition for Walras's Law, which must be satisfied at all times.

The left-hand side, a function of income, y, real money balances, M/P, and the rate of interest, r, is aggregate expenditure demand and the right-hand side is aggregate output supply. Many values of y, M/P , and r will satisfy this equilibrium equation. For example, the set y = 1,500, M/P = 600, and r = 5 satisfies the equation but so does y = 2,000, M/P = 2,260 and r = 3, and so on. Within the context of the entire neoclassical model, however, only one rate of interest equates expenditures and output. The order of the markets analyzed in the text was not selected at random. The labor market determines real output. Given real output and velocity, the quantity theory equation yields the price level and real money balances. In the mechanical equation-solving sense, expenditures and output determine the rate of interest because the equilibrium values of the other determinants of aggregate demand are estimated elsewhere or exogenous, and the rate of interest is the remaining variable to be solved.[1] Indeed, the rate of interest does not appear in the labor and money market equations. It is assumed that the equilibrium interest rate is economically feasible. (Negative interest rates are not economically feasible.)

The fact that the equilibrium rate of interest in neoclassical economics can be ascertained by looking at the commodities market equilibrium relationship has baffled many modern economists. In some respects the neoclassical mode of expression has contributed toward misunderstanding neoclassical thought. Until quite recently, neoclassicists preferred to express the commodities market equilibrium relation as the equality of saving and investment instead of the equivalent equality of aggregate demand and output. The saving and investment approach highlights the fact that aggregate equilibrium does not require each economic unit to be in equilibrium and that borrowing and lending is occurring in the background. For example, the aggregate economy is in equilibrium provided the excess commodity supply of savers, whose income exceeds spending by definition, equals the excess commodities demand of investors, who spend more than their income. After recognizing that every economic unit is not spending an amount exactly equal to its income, the logical next step is to inquire what households do with their saving and how firms acquire funds to invest. *One possibility* has savers demand bonds (lend) and investors supply bonds (borrow). Clearly, this demand and supply of bonds affect the rate of interest. Many have incorrectly concluded from the last two sentences that savers must *always* demand bonds and investors *always* supply bonds if the equilibrium rate of interest can be ascer-

---

[1] Restating the textual discussion somewhat more technically, in a truly general equilibrium static model where every price is an argument in all the excess demand functions one cannot say that any one market determines a price. However, the neoclassical model is not a truly general equilibrium system but can be solved recursively. "Aggregate expenditures and output determine the rate of interest" is a shorthand statement for a particular recursive structure where the noncommodity market equilibrium equations yield solutions for all the variables except the rate of interest. One then solves the commodities market equilibrium condition for the rate of interest.

tained by the commodities market as well as the bond market. Since savers can hoard instead of demanding bonds, many claim the neoclassical model is absurd. This invalid criticism of neoclassical economics stems from a failure to recognize restrictions placed on equilibrium relation by Walras's Law.

When the economy is in equilibrium, the rate of interest determined by saving and investment also equates bond supply and demand. For simplicity, assume the government's budget balances; it neither borrows nor lends. Also assume savers and investors are distinct groups so savers do not invest, and conversely. Suppose a typical household's money balances at the beginning of the period are $1,500. Income during the period is $1,000 and consumption is $800. What happens to the household's $200 saving? In our simplified aggregate model with standard bonds (loans) and money the household has two alternatives: it can demand bonds or it can hoard. Hoarding occurs when the demand for money is greater than the supply. The household hoards in this example when the demand for money is $1,700, $200 more than the household has.

$$\text{Saving} = \text{Bond demand} + \text{Hoarding}$$

Firms must finance their investments by either supplying bonds or dishoarding, i.e., running down their money balances.

$$\text{Investment} = \text{Bond supply} + \text{Dishoarding}$$

Looking at the two equations above indicates that, in general, saving does not equal bond demand and equality of saving and investment does *not* imply equality of bond supply and demand. But equilibrium is hardly the general case and implies certain restrictions. Given an aggregate money supply, money market equilibrium implies that hoarding, if any, just equals dishoarding. To the extent that one group is trying to build up its money balances, another group must be running them down if total money demand is to equal a fixed total supply. Therefore, when the money market is in equilibrium, the rate of interest which equates saving and investment also equates bond supply and demand. Look at the last two equations again. This is an illustration of Walras's Law. If the money and commodities markets are in equilibrium, then the last market, the bond market, must also be in equilibrium.

# Keynesian economics: Fundamental assumptions and the basic model

# 17

The methodological approach adopted in discussing classical economics is repeated here: fundamental assumptions of Keynesian economics are stated before getting down to nuts and bolts. There is altogether too much emphasis in economics on the nuts and bolts of curve shifting and intersection points without any appreciation of fundamental assumptions, which often yield clues regarding the generality and predictive content of the model. For example, the intersection of the neoclassical curves says that output and unemployment are independent of the rate of monetary expansion, which solely influences the price level. Nevertheless, a central bank aware of the assumptions of neoclassical theory would not slam the brakes on the money supply if it were unwilling to sustain some temporary unemployment. The neoclassical curves are not appropriate at all times, only in the long run. Do not get me wrong, the nuts and bolts are important, but only *after* the fundamental assumptions are well understood. If, contrary to my expectation, you have time to read only part of this chapter, by all means read the first section on fundamental assumptions. The nuts and bolts tend to be forgotten sooner—though let us hope not before the final exam—and are less important in understanding the basic policy issues which divide economists and politicians.

The second section builds the basic $C + I + G = y$ Keynesian model. Although recent empirical evidence suggests the basic model explains facts relatively poorly, it is pedagogically useful to begin with a basic model which reviews your principles course, and then add more nuts and bolts to construct the advanced Keynesian model of the next chapters. Moreover, the basic model was "the" Keynesian model, or at least a good approximation of it, until the mid-1950s, and a small but dying breed of staunch Keynesians still believe the evidence supports the basic model. (The advanced model has much stronger empirical support in our mind.) In any case, the same fundamental assumptions underlie this chapter's basic Keynesian model and next chapter's advanced model.

## FUNDAMENTAL ASSUMPTIONS

In many respects neoclassical and Keynesian economics are competing theories. Chapters 15 and 16 highlighted those neoclassical assumptions denied by Keynesians. We hope that our stress on differences will not obscure the similarities too numerous to list. Anticipate this section and simultaneously test your knowledge of neoclassical economics by listing the highlighted neoclassical assumptions and then inverting them.

John Maynard Keynes was a man of many talents. He was the leading British academic economist of the 1930s, editor of the scholarly *Economics Journal,* advisor to British governments, and still found time to systematically spend part of each day making money, in the street sense of the word. No, his talents were not that diverse; he was neither a forger nor banker and did not "create" currency or demand deposits. Keynes was a first-rate theorist not given to wasting his talents on minor issues or economically optimal but politically unacceptable policies. He was a practical man who tackled the big issues. Of course, the big issue in the early 1930s was the Great Depression. Keynes's contemporaries, the classicists, were a patient lot who preached caution. The economy adjusts rapidly, and prosperity was around the corner. Keynes thought otherwise. His famous dictum—in the long run we are all dead—expresses his belief that the economy adjusts very slowly, the ultimate effect of some disturbance being realized many decades from now. Given this belief, Keynes naturally emphasized the short run and ignored the long run.

### Keynes's Law

What determines output and real income in the short run? Classicists gave but passing attention to this vital question, so Keynes had to answer it virtually "from scratch." If Say's Law summarizes classical economics, Keynes's Law is: demand creates its own supply. Say's Law is correct in the long run, and Keynes's Law is essentially correct in the short run. You may not be able to squeeze blood out of a turnip, but our economy is not a turnip. It is more like a restaurant, extending an analogy used earlier. Suppose a restaurant which traditionally has been half full suddenly receives a three-star rating from the premiere food critic. Crowds storm the restaurant to discover what they had been missing. Some of the new patrons will be seated immediately and their demands are met. Others form a queue. Management spots the queue and tells the waiters to prevent customers from lingering after dinner so the latecomers can be served. Water glasses are not refilled and ashtrays are not cleaned. The restaurant traditionally stays open to midnight to serve the after-theater set and the few Spaniards unable to adapt to the "barbaric" custom of eating dinner before 11:00 P.M. However, a skeleton crew usually is sufficient to satisfy this meager demand, and most workers leave at 10:00 P.M. Our critics's review upset normal operations. If the waiters were unable to prevent lingering and the queue still exists at 10:00 P.M., the staff is asked to work overtime. Management does everything possible to justify the food critic's review. Demand creates its own supply in the short run. Firms do not attempt to maximize profits in the short run but instead strive to maintain or even increase their market share by meeting demand.

Homey examples of general principles are often eschewed by professionals because counterexamples are likely. After turnips are harvested, no amount of demand, however large, will increase supply until the following season.[1] True, the quantity of *every* product may not be determined by demand in the short run, but Keynes's Law applies to a sufficiently large number of industries as to characterize reasonably well the entire economy. Moreover, the statistical evidence tends to support the proposition that demand creates its own supply in the short run. But statistics is such an arcane science beset by difficulties that the inability to construct homey examples supporting the statistical "evidence" is a sign that something is definitely amiss.

You often will find Say's Law listed in the index of money and banking or history of economic thought books, but as far as we know, you will never find Keynes's Law. We dubbed the assumption that demand creates its own supply Keynes's Law. This assumption underlies all Keynesian models. The commodities market is in equilibrium when desired expenditures, E, the sum of consumption, investment, and government expenditures, equal desired production. In symbols, the equilibrium condition is

$$E = C + I + G = y$$

Keynesian economics concentrates exclusively on specifying the determinants of the expenditure components. Then the equilibrium equation is used. Absolutely no attention is given to the determinants of desired production.[2] Why? One must simply specify desired expenditures because demand creates its own supply.

In terms of Figure 17–1, a graph we used previously to illustrate Say's Law, Keynesian economics analyzes the aggregate expenditure curve,

---

[1] We shall accept this as a counterexample, although it implicitly assumes, perhaps unrealistically, that the short run is less than one year.

[2] Chapter 23 presents a model with an aggregate supply curve derived by assuming that labor demand is a function of the real wage but labor supply depends on nominal wages. This intermediate model is neither neoclassical nor Keynesian in our mind. Of course, if one prefers to call the intermediate model a very sophisticated Keynesian model, then the text accurately describes only the simple C + I + G and advanced IS–LM Keynesian models.

**FIGURE 17–1   Fundamental Keynesian graph, unspecified supply adjusts to demand**

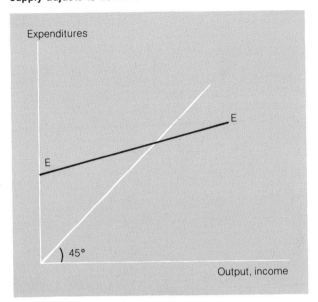

EE. Aggregate expenditure is measured on the vertical axis, and output is on the horizontal axis. The upward-sloping aggregate expenditure curve illustrates the dependence of demand on output. After specifying the position of the EE curve, one looks where it crosses the 45° line to ascertain the equilibrium level of income since along the 45° line demand equals output. An aggregate output or supply curve is ignored; it is assumed that such a curve will intersect the 45° line whenever the expenditure curve does.

An alternative statement of Keynes's Law is: supply is perfectly elastic in the short run so prices are independent of demand. The horizontal SS line in Figure 17–2 is the perfectly elastic supply curve at a price $P_0$. Temporarily ignore the dashed line S'S'. The demand curve DD has the usual shape; more output is demanded at lower prices. As demand increases from DD to D'D', more is produced—demand creates its own supply—but prices remain constant. Our restaurant keeps prices fixed while it attempts to justify the food critic's review. As we argued, Keynes's Law is essentially correct, and the virtually continuous upward march in the price level does not necessarily contradict it. The observed price level depends on the interaction of demand and supply. Prices rise because the horizontal supply curve shifts upward to S'S' and not because demand increases. Keynesian economics is silent about the position and shifts of the supply curve. If pressed, a Keynesian might state briefly and quickly that past wage contracts and possibly past demand may affect the

**FIGURE 17-2 Keynesian aggregate demand and supply**

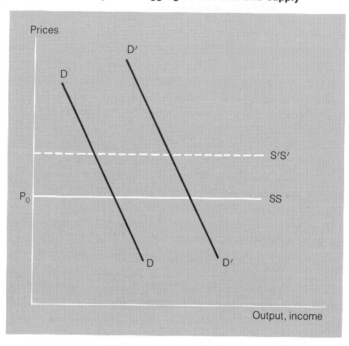

present supply curve. However, the past is a given in the present, so the supply curve is exogenous. To simplify the analysis, shifts of the exogenous supply curve are never considered and, therefore, prices are assumed to be fixed. Keynesian economics analyzes the demand curve. What determines its position and how do various policies shift the demand curve? A flat supply curve does not imply that Keynes's answer to these questions is incorrect.

The Keynesian perfectly elastic supply, fixed-price assumption is unrealistic. Prices do rise as everyone is aware. We cannot even allege the assumption is correct after the lapse of sufficient time; the Keynesian model describes short-run reactions. In Keynes's defense, however, no model is entirely realistic and general. Specifying the determinants of a marginally upward-sloping supply curve adds somewhat greater realism but complicates the analysis significantly since the interaction of supply and demand could not be ignored. Keynes thought and the empirical evidence confirms that aggregate price adjustments lag behind aggregate quantity adjustments.[3] As a first approximation, Keynes let only quantity adjust.

---

[3] Following Marshall, traditional *microeconomics* correctly assumes that the microeconomic short-run supply curve is steeper than the long-run curve. However, the converse is true in the aggregate. The firm or industry analyzed in microeconomics adjusts quantity in the short run by employing different quantities of a few variable factors of

## Recession prone economies

What calendar period corresponds with the short run during which demand creates its own supply and prices are independent of demand, or approximately so? How long do price adjustments lag behind quantity adjustments? Keynes clearly realized that the calendar length of the short run depends on the initial conditions, the most important being the rate of unemployment.

Prices are sticky in a downward direction. While truly extreme downturns like 1929–33 are associated with price declines, more moderate downturns do not induce firms to lower prices and clear their shelves of excess inventories. Instead, firms hold the line on prices and hope for a rebound in demand. At high rates of unemployment the demand rebound has a long-lasting effect on output. The calendar length of time of the short run is positively related to the rate of unemployment. At low rates of unemployment an increase in desired expenditures has a short-lived effect on output, and prices rise soon after. Full employment, a slippery economic concept described in detail in Chapter 23, is not some technological minimum level of unemployment and maximum output. No one defines full employment as zero unemployment. Actual output has occasionally been greater than full-employment output, particularly during wars. There always is some slack in the economy—not everyone is working seven days a week—and Keynes's Law is always correct, if only for a short calendar period when the economy is at "full employment."

Now Keynes was a practical man. Why did he analyze the short run during which demand creates its own supply and prices are independent of demand? According to Keynes, the short run was much more than a fleeting moment and worthy of analysis because aggregate demand is chronically deficient. Recessions and depressions punctuated by an occasional boom are the norm. If this were *not* the case, the Keynesian analysis of the responsiveness of aggregate demand to fiscal and monetary policy would be largely a matter of curiosity with little practical significance. If the unemployment rate typically was low and output was high, then fiscal or monetary policy induced changes in aggregate demand would have short-lived effects on output. In this case, the effects of price changes, which would occur soon after demand shifts, should not be ignored. The world in 1936 was ripe for Keynesian economics. Although the economy touched bottom in 1933, unemployment still equaled approximately 17 percent in 1936. Prices between 1933 and 1936 were more or less stable, albeit at a low level. Policies stressing demand expansion were bound to gain wide currency.

production. In the long run all factors are variable, new firms enter the industry, and resources are drawn from other firms and industries, making the microeconomic supply curve flatter. From the viewpoint of the entire economy, however, resources are fixed; there are no "other" firms and industries which the aggregate economy can utilize. The aggregate economy is more elastic in the short run when misperceptions, contracts, custom, and other such factors impede profit and utility maximization.

### The L-Shaped Supply Curve

Complex ideas are difficult to state succinctly and even more difficult to represent graphically. The Keynesian aggregate supply curve is often drawn as a reverse L.

**FIGURE 17–3  Modified Keynesian aggregate supply**

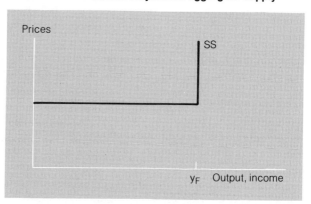

In some respects Figure 17–3 does capture Keynes's ideas. Recall that Keynes said that (1) quantity always responds first to changes in demand, and (2) the lagged price response, if any, depends on the existing level of output. According to Figure 17–3, increases in demand up to some point, labelled $y_F$ for full-employment income, cause output to increase but have no effect on price. When output already is $y_F$, further increases in demand simply raise prices. While there certainly is a strong semblance between Keynesian thought and Figure 17–3, the latter does not capture Keynesian thought perfectly. In particular, Figure 17–3 denies the valid proposition that quantity always responds to changes in demand, if only for a short calendar period of time. The flat aggregate supply curve in Figure 17–2 does show this valid Keynesian proposition. However, the flat aggregate supply curve fails to illustrate the lagged price response when output is quite high. Indeed, it is precisely this failure which leads many Keynesians to draw a reverse L-shaped supply curve. For the moment we prefer to view the supply curve as perfectly flat throughout. This seems best, provided one realizes the length of time the curve remains flat and does not shift upward is a function of where one is on the curve. Figure 17–3 may be viewed as mixing elements of both classical and Keynesian economics, which may not be objectionable if only one model is to be used for all time and space. It resembles the now old-fashioned view that there is a permanent tradeoff between inflation and unemployment, as discussed in the final chapter. Our approach with two sharply different time periods and models facilitates understanding the modern view that the unemployment-inflation relationship shifts over time.

Keynesian economics assumes that monetary policy and interest rates are of secondary importance. Indeed, monetary policy might be useless as a means of stimulating the economy out of a deep depression. Fiscal policy in the form of government expenditures and taxes is the key policy for controlling aggregate demand. This fundamental Keynesian assumption shines through in the manner desired expenditures are expressed: the sum of government expenditures and other items. Money is not highlighted because it has an indirect and secondary effect on aggregate demand.[4] This Keynesian assumption is debatable; some empirical studies confirm and some deny it. At least the advanced Keynesian model in the next chapter is sufficiently general that this assumption can be relaxed by changing the slopes of various curves.

In summary, Keynesian economics describes short-run adjustments. It assumes:

1. Demand creates its own supply.
2. Prices are fixed.
3. The economy is basically recession prone with an occasional boom pulling the economy out of its normally lethargic state.
4. Monetary policy is of secondary importance. Fiscal policy is the key policy for controlling aggregate demand.

Assumptions 1 and 2 are not independent; either one largely implies the other. While assumption 3 is not an integral component of the Keynesian *theoretical models* it provides the foundation for many Keynesian *policy prescriptions*. Assumption 4 is unrelated to the other assumptions. While the advanced Keynesian model can be purged of assumption 4, doing so violates Keynes's thought and a widely accepted, easy way of labeling economists as Keynesians or monetarists. Economists who interpret the diverse and sometimes contradictory evidence as supporting assumption 4 are often called Keynesian, whatever their other beliefs.

## THE BASIC KEYNESIAN MODEL: DETERMINANTS OF SPENDING

What variables influence desired spending? Although Keynesian economics emphasizes fiscal policy, it is silent about the determinants of government expenditures. In Keynesian models government spending is an exogenous variable. Government spending influences income and, in the advanced IS–LM model of the next chapter, the rate of interest, but government spending itself is not influenced by income and the rate of interest. The causation goes from government expenditures to income, and not vice versa. Only fiscal policymakers can change government spending. Exogenous variables and parameters are denoted by lower-case

---

[4] Recall that Fisher and other classicists expressed desired expenditures as the product of money and velocity. Might you prefer the Fisherian expression if you interpreted the empirical evidence as confirming the importance of money?

letters or capital letters with a subscript zero. As a particular example assume government spending equals 200.

$$G = G_0 = 200 \qquad (17\text{--}1)$$

Assuming prices are fixed, nominal and real values coincide as the price index equals unity.

### The investment schedule

Keynes accepted the classical/neoclassical formal analysis of investment but reversed the importance of anticipated net revenue and the rate of interest.[5] Recall that the rate of return on an investment is that rate of discount which equates the cost of the investment and the present value of the anticipated net revenue stream. Profit-maximizing firms undertake all investments with rates of return greater than or equal to the market rate of interest. Neoclassicists claim that investment is quite sensitive to the rate of interest because the net revenue stream declines gradually as firms invest more and the capital stock grows. Substantially larger net investment is undertaken in order to increase the capital stock sufficiently and equate the rate of return on investments with lower interest rates. Keynes questioned this. He thought investment opportunities were quite limited and the rate of return dropped sharply during any period of time. Keynes's main quarrel with the classicists, however, was their lack of attention to the uncertainty of the future net revenue stream generated by investments. Many investment projects have a long life. Estimates of net revenue 5, 20, and 40 years hence are necessary to calculate the rate of return on an investment. According to Keynes, these distant estimates of net revenue are so uncertain that they are unduly influenced by a mob psychology. "In estimating the prospects of investment we must have regard, therefore, to the nerves and histeria and even the digestions and reactions to the weather of these upon whose spontaneous activity it largely depends."[6] The "state of confidence" is alternately euphoric and melancholic and anticipated net revenues and the rates of return on investment rise and fall. The state of confidence is the primary and the rate of interest is a decidedly secondary determinant of investment. Figure 17–4 summarizes Keynes's thought. The investment schedule is very steep—the rate of return on investment drops sharply during any time period—and over time shifts from A to B to C with changes in the state of confidence. In contrast, the neoclassicists claim the investment schedule is relatively flat and stable.

---

[5] Those who skipped Chapter 16 can read just the section on investment, which stands by itself. See pp. 439–41.

[6] J. M. Keynes, *The General Theory of Employment, Interest, and Money*, (New York: Harcourt Brace Jovanovich, 1936), p. 162. By permission of Royal Economic Society and Macmillan, London and Baskingstoke.

**FIGURE 17–4  Investment relatively unresponsive to the rate of interest shifts with changes in the state of confidence**

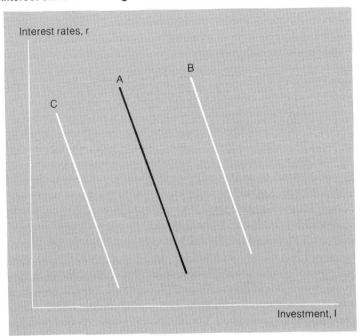

The state of confidence so important to investment may be measured indirectly or by surveying firms, but we do not know its determinants. Thus, it becomes an exogenous variable in the model. The state of confidence is the cancer of the economic system: whether or not you have it is extremely important; you can tell whether you have it; we are uncertain of its causes. Keynes thought the exogenous state of confidence was so important compared to the rate of interest that expressing investment as a function of the rate of interest might be misleading. Look at Figure 17–4 again. What explains changes over time in the amount of investment? Variations in the state of confidence, which shift the investment schedule, are much more important than interest rate variations causing movements along an investment schedule. All economic models are simplifications, and basic models are only first approximations. The basic Keynesian model ignores the effect of interest rates on investment; investment depends solely on the state of confidence.

Another interpretation of the simple Keynesian model says investment also depends on the rate of interest, but the rate of interest is fixed. Whichever interpretation one prefers—investment depends solely on the state of confidence or investment depends on the state of confidence and a fixed rate of interest—investment is an exogenous variable. As a specific example assume desired investment equals 150.

$$I = I_0 = I(r_0) = 150 \qquad (17-2)$$

### The consumption function

According to Keynes, current disposable income, total income minus taxes, definitely is the most powerful determinant of desired consumption and private saving. The Keynesian consumption function in general and as a specific example is

$$\begin{aligned} C &= a + b(y - T) \\ &= 65 + 0.75(y - T) \end{aligned} \qquad (17-3)$$

The parameter a (65) is the level of consumption independent of *disposable* income. It may be interpreted as the minimum consumption necessary to maintain body and soul. The parameter b (0.75) measures the change in consumption per unit change in disposable income and is called the marginal propensity to consume disposable income, $MPC(y_d)$.

$$MPC(y_d) = \frac{\Delta C}{\Delta y_d} = b = 0.75$$

Keynes accepted the classical assumption, which has since been repeatedly confirmed by the data, that households consume only a fraction of incremental disposable income. As income increases, households consume and save more. The parameter b lies between zero and one, $0 < b < 1$. Keynes disagreed with his classical teachers about the effects on desired consumption of interest rates and wealth measured by real money balances. Keynes thought that interest rates and wealth effects on consumption were sufficiently small that they could be ignored altogether or consolidated with other factors and considered to be exogenous. Current statistical estimates of interest rate and wealth effects are more mixed than the estimates of other economic hypotheses. However, even those who have estimated significant interest rate and wealth effects probably agree that disposable income is the most important determinant of short-run consumption.[7] Regardless of the outcome of the statistical debate, equation (17–3) does represent the beliefs of Keynes.

---

[7] This statement certainly is true when wealth is approximated by real money balances. Some economists employ more comprehensive measures of nonhuman wealth which include the capital stock. Even when allowance is made for the fact that wealth is greater than quarterly or annual income, the wealth coefficient typically is smaller and less significant. Professor Friedman and others have related consumption to permanent income, which represents the return on total human and nonhuman wealth and is measured empirically by a weighted average of current and past incomes. When consumption depends on permanent income, the validity of the statement in the text depends on the rate of decline of the weights attached to past incomes in computing permanent income, the calendar length of the Keynesian short-run and other economic and semantic issues—for example, consumption here measures all household expenditures rather than Friedman's flow of services from durable goods—beyond the scope of a money and banking book.

Taxes reduce disposable income and consumption. Since this is review material—all principles books present the basic model—let us introduce greater realism by immediately including an income tax as well as the standard lump sum or autonomous tax. The tax equation is

$$T = T_0 + ty$$
$$= 20 + 0.2y \tag{17-4}$$

where $T_0$ is the autonomous (independent of income) tax and t is the income tax rate. Property taxes, estate and inheritance taxes, franchise fees, and transfer taxes are examples of autonomous taxes. Substituting the tax equation in the consumption function gives

$$C = a - bT_0 + b(1 - t)y$$
$$= 65 - 0.75(20) + 0.75(1 - 0.2)y = 50 + 0.6y \tag{17-3'}$$

While a(65) is the value of consumption independent of *disposable* income, $50 = a - bT_0$ is the value of consumption independent of total *national output and income,* y. Call b(1 − t) the marginal propensity to consume national income, MPC(y). When national income increases one unit, taxes increase by t and disposable income increases by (1 − t), of which b is spent. Of course, when the marginal tax rate equals zero, changes in disposable and national income are equal and so are the marginal propensities to consumer disposable and national income.

Figure 17–5 graphs the consumption function, labelled C. Consumption is on the vertical axis and the horizontal axis measures national income and output since this is the variable to be solved. We are interested in national income instead of disposable income. Temporarily ignore the other lines. The intercept of the consumption line C measures autonomous consumption, $50 = a - bT_0$, and the slope of the line is 0.60 = b(1 − t), the marginal propensity to consume national income.

## EQUILIBRIUM RELATIONSHIPS

Having specified the three components of desired total spending, we can now determine algebraically the equilibrium level of output and real income because demand creates its own supply. Setting aggregate demand equal to income and making use of equations (17–1)–(17–4), we solve for income in terms of the parameters and exogenous variables.

$$C + I + G = y$$
$$a - bT_0 + b(1 - t)y + I_0 + G_0 = y$$
$$y = \frac{1}{1 - b(1 - t)} (a - bT_0 + I_0 + G_0) \tag{17-5}$$
$$= \frac{1}{1 - 0.75(1 - 0.2)} (65 - 0.75(20) + 150 + 200)$$
$$= 1,000$$

**FIGURE 17-5  Aggregate expenditures and income**

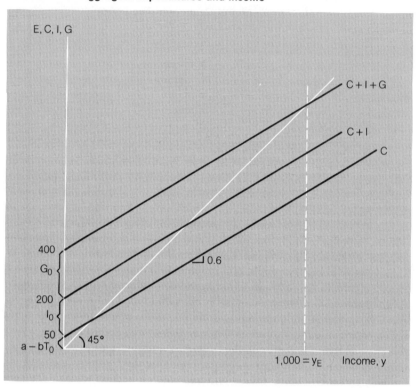

The terms in parentheses in the third line of equation (17–5) are total exogenous or autonomous spending. (Look at equations (17–1)–(17–4) and calculate desired total spending when y = 0). Equilibrium real— and nominal with the price level fixed at unity—income equals autonomous spending times the inverse of one minus the marginal propensity to consume *national* income. As written, equation (17–5) suggests an alternative expression. The marginal propensity to consume national income is less than unity. Therefore, $1/(1 - b(1 - t))$ is greater than unity and called the multiplier. Income is the product of the multiplier and autonomous spending.

Figure 17–5 graphs the spending relationships. Exogenous investment and government expenditures are added to consumption by shifting the curve upward to C + I and C + I + G. The intercept of the total expenditures curve, E = C + I + G, is total autonomous spending, $400 = a - bT_0 + I_0 + G_0$, and its slope is $0.60 = b(1 - t)$, the marginal propensity to consume national income. All the points equidistant to the axes lie along the 45° (degree) line, by definition. The total expenditures curve intersects the 45° line at income $y_E = 1,000 = (a - bT_0 + I_0 + G_0)/1 - b(1 - t)$, and this is the equilibrium level of income. Consider why any other level of income and output is not an equilibrium. Suppose income were below $y_E$. At income levels below the equilibrium, aggregate expenditures exceed supply. The C + I + G curve is above the 45° line. Assuming firms satisfy the demand of households and government, actual investment is less than desired. Inventories are declining, or not increasing as fast as desired. Firms respond by increasing production and national income. Demand creates its own supply. Conversely, when income is greater than $y_E$, demand is less than supply. Firms' inventories are increasing at an undesired high rate, and output is curtailed.

One should be aware of the correspondence between the algebraic and graphic methods. As previously stated, total autonomous spending, or total desired expenditures when income equals zero, is the term in parentheses in equation (17–5) and the intercept of the aggregate demand curve E = C + I + G in Figure 17–5. The slopes of the 45° line and demand curves are 1 and $0.60 = b(1 - t)$, respectively, so the multiplier, $2.5 = 1/(1 - 0.60) = 1/(1 - b(1 - t))$, is the inverse of the difference between these two slopes. The intercept of the total expenditure curve E is the gap between aggregate demand and output at zero output. As output increases by one unit, the gap is reduced by less than one unit because demand responds to output. In our example, as output increases by 1, demand increases by $0.60 = b(1 - t)$ so the gap between demand and output is reduced by $0.40 = 1 - b(1 - t)$. Thus, the multiplier, $2.5 = 1/0.40 = 1/(1 - b(1 - t))$, measures the number of units of output necessary to close the *gap* by 1 unit. At equilibrium the gap must be closed. Equilibrium output is the product of the multiplier (gap closing factor) and autonomous expenditures (gap).

## THE MULTIPLIER AND FISCAL POLICY

Income $y_E$ may be the short-run equilibrium level of income but is it the full-employment level of income? Keynes thought not. Generally, income would be substantially below full employment. Investment opportunities are strictly limited and households are not spendthrifts. When income equals $y_E$ the private sector is stuck. Of course, if the private sector were not stuck, $y_E$ would not be an equilibrium. Prices are assumed fixed but even if they were to fall, demand would not increase. Look at the Keynesian spending equation again. Does C, I, or G depend on the price level? No. Moreover, interest rate adjustments do not bring the economy to full employment. Interest rates are fixed or have no effect on spending. How does one get out of this depressing situation? One could hope and pray for a return of entrepreneurial spirits. A more effective way is available: increase government expenditures. What size increase is necessary? How responsive is income to government spending? A mechanical answer to such questions often is readily available and is a convenient starting point.

Look at equilibrium equation (17–5) again. Let income and government expenditures change so that

$$\frac{\Delta y}{\Delta G} = \frac{1}{1 - b(1 - t)} = \frac{1}{1 - 0.75(1 - 0.2)} = 2.5 \qquad (17\text{–}6)$$

The multiplier of autonomous expenditures in the equilibrium income equation also equals the government spending multiplier, defined as the change in income per unit change in government expenditures, $\Delta y/\Delta G$. Government only needs to nudge the economy in order to maintain full employment. For example, suppose the gap between equilibrium and full-employment income is 100. How much additional government spending is necessary to close the full-employment gap in our example? Just 40, since the marginal propensity to consume national income is 0.6 and the multiplier is 2.5.

The mechanical answer often is a convenient starting point but one must go beyond mechanics and understand the economic rationale. The fundamental reason for the multiplier is the dependence of spending on income. The exposition is more easily followed with the aid of Table 17–1

**TABLE 17–1   The multiplier: An illustration**

| Time period | Desired spending | | | | Output y | Actual I |
|---|---|---|---|---|---|---|
| | C | I | G | C + I + G | | |
| 0 | 650 | 150 | 200 | 1,000 | 1,000 | 150.0 |
| 1 | 650 | 150 | 201 | 1,001 | 1,000 | 149.0 |
| 2 | 650.6 | 150 | 201 | 1,001.6 | 1,001 | 149.4 |
| 3 | 650.96 | 150 | 201 | 1,001.96 | 1,001.6 | 149.64 |
| 4 | | | | | 1,001.96 | |
| . | | | | | | |
| . | | | | | | |
| . | | | | | | |
| ∞ | 651.5 | 150 | 201 | 1,002.5 | 1,002.5 | 150.0 |

and Figure 17–6, an enlargement of Figure 17–5 around the equilibrium. The initial equilibrium values at time period 0 are shown in the first row of Table 17–1 and are represented by the line C + I + G in Figure 17–6. In period 1 the government spends $1 more, shifting the aggregate demand and curve upward to C + I + G + $1. Output, however, remains constant at $1,000. Firms do not anticipate perfectly government or other demand so current output depends on prior demand, as the downward-pointing

**FIGURE 17-6  Aggregate expenditures and income**

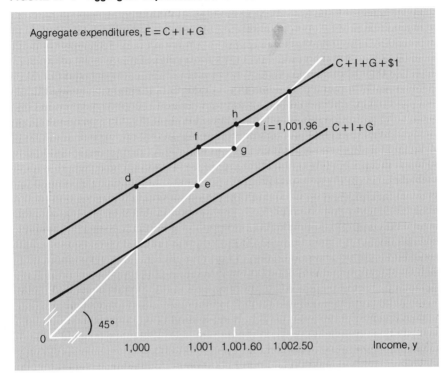

arrows in Table 17–1 indicated. The row for time period 1 in Table 17–1 corresponds with point d in Figure 17–6. At point d desired spending exceeds output, and firms' actual inventory investment is $1 below the desired level.

In the next period firms hire additional workers to meet the additional government demand and possibly pay larger dividends if the government purchase enhances firms' earnings. In any case, output and income increase $1.00 to $1,001 in period 2, and we move to point e in Figure 17–6. If the private sector did not respond to higher incomes, this would end the story. But the private sector does respond. Although national income increased $1.00, disposable income increases ($1 − t) = $0.80 since the tax rate is t = 0.20. Households spend b = 0.75 times their larger disposable income or an additional b(1 − t) = $0.60, that is, consumption in period 2 increases from $650 to $650.60. The induced consumption spending is represented graphically by sliding along the curve from point d to f in Figure 17–6. At point f demand again exceeds output. In period 3 firms hire yet more workers to meet this newly induced household demand, and output and income increases an additional b(1 − t) = $0.60 to $1,001.60. We now are at point g. The newly hired workers producing consumer goods also pay taxes; their disposable income is $b(1 - t)^2 = \$0.48$; they spend $b^2(1 - t)^2 = \$0.36$. We move to point h, where demand is $\$1,001.96$. Successive rounds of additional income and induced spending follow with each successive round of additional income getting smaller and smaller as $b(1 - t)$ is less than one. Eventually, the additional government expenditures increase income by $1/(1 - b(1 - t))$.[8] The argument is symmetric; lower government spending reduces income by the multiplier.

This successive rounds explanation of the government spending multiplier is analogous to the disaggregate bank-by-bank explanation of money supply expansion. Indeed, the closeness of the analogy prompted us to immediately express equilibrium income as the product of a multiplier and exogenous variables.[9] The money supply expansion problem had an aggregate explanation, and so does the government spending multiplier. When government spending increases, the demand for commodities exceeds supply. Firms increase supply, which induces greater household consumption equal to $b(1 - t)$ times the additional supply. The additional saving or *net* increase in supply available to satisfy government demand equals $1 - b(1 - t)$ times the higher gross output. The government demand must be satisfied at equilibrium and, consequently, $\Delta G = (1 - b(1 - t))\Delta y$. Therefore, the multiplier is $1/(1 - b(1 - t))$.

Government spending is just one component of autonomous spending. Investment and some consumption expenditures also are autonomous. Clearly, the multiplier argument does not depend on the specific autonomous spending component. The parameters $a$, $-bT_0$, $I_0$, and $G_0$ enter equation (17–5) in the same manner. While the multiplier of every type of autonomous spending is $1/(1 - b(1 - t))$, the autonomous tax multiplier is smaller because taxes do not have a dollar-for-dollar effect on autonomous spending. Higher autonomous taxes reduce disposable income dollar for dollar, but the change in consumption independent of national income is $-b$. Therefore, $-bT_0$ appears as the autonomous spending term in equation (17–5). The lower autonomous consumption due to taxes, $-b$, is multiplied by the same number to get the autonomous tax multiplier, i.e., $\Delta y/\Delta T_0 = -b/(1 - b(1 - t))$. Additional government spending is more expansionary than an equal tax cut. In terms of Figure 17–5, the expenditure curve is shifted upward more by government spending than an equal autonomous tax cut.

An equal increase in both government expenditures and *autonomous* taxes is expansionary as the expenditure curve rises by $1 - b$. Income

---

[8] This successive rounds explanation of the multiplier is formally called period analysis. After n rounds or periods, $\Delta y = \Delta G + b(1 - t)\Delta G + (b(1 - t))^2\Delta G + \ldots + (b(1 - t))^{n-2}\Delta G$. At the limit the sum of this geometric series is $\Delta G/(1 - b(1 - t))$.

[9] Similar modes of expression should not be confused with a necessary relationship between the two. The monetary base does not equal autonomous spending, and the money supply and government spending multipliers depend on entirely different factors.

increases by $(1 - b)/(1 - b(1 - t)) = \$0.625 = \$2.50 - \$1.875$. Clearly, if income taxes were abolished so $t = 0$, then *equal changes in government expenditures and taxes which keep the government's budget balanced cause equal income changes. A succinct statement of this originally startling conclusion is: the balanced budget multiplier is unity.* In our example the income increase is less than the government expenditure and *autonomous* tax increase because the government runs a surplus. The equal expenditure and autonomous tax increase initially leaves the budget balanced, but a surplus is generated as income expands and income taxes are collected. If autonomous taxes had been raised less than government expenditures, so that total (autonomous plus income) taxes equalled expenditures, then we would observe the balanced budget multiplier. (See question 6 at the end of the chapter.)

Multiplier analysis suggested to Keynes that government fiscal policy could stabilize the economy in spite of highly volatile investment. First, the mere existence of income taxes imparts some stability. The income tax is an example of an *automatic stabilizer:* a policy which automatically reduces the variability of disposable income and, thereby, induced spending and output. For example, suppose national output and income increase $1 in response to larger desired investment. A multiplier effect is now set in motion as the newly hired workers respond by spending more. If income taxes did not exist, the $1 additional national income translates into $1 additional disposable income, and in this round consumption increases by $b. With a tax rate of t, however, disposable income increases by $1 - t. Since consumers continue to spend the same function of their *disposable* income, consumption increases by $b(1 - t)$ in this case. The changes in disposable income and consumption are smaller in each spending round when taxes exist. The marginal propensity to consume *national* income and the investment multiplier, $1/(1 - b(1 - t))$, are negatively related to the income tax rate. In our example, with $b = 0.75$, the 20 percent income tax rate reduces the multiplier from 4 to 2.5. Graphically, income taxes make the consumption function in Figure 17–5 flatter.

Anything less than confiscatory taxes ($t = 1$) mitigates but does not altogether prevent magnified income fluctuations due to volatile investment. Keynes thought discretionary fiscal policy could counteract the income fluctuations which the tax system did not automatically eliminate. Whenever investment falls, the government preferably spends more or, alternatively, cuts autonomous taxes and tax rates. Conversely, contractionary fiscal action curbs the occasional boom. In this manner GNP is kept on target. *The necessity of fine tuning, that is, active fiscal demand management is one of Keynes's key messages.* Government spending should be high on average and flexible in order to counteract the economy's natural tendency towards recessions and the mercurial state of confidence of investors.

## Case study: A basic Keynesian interpretation of the Great Depression[10]

The reactions of government to the Great Depression, interpreted according to the basic model in Table 17–2, illustrate the novelty of Keynes's message that fiscal policy is a tool to manage aggregate demand. Between 1929 and 1933 real GNP fell approximately 30 percent, or $62.1 billion in 1958 prices. The unemployment rate rose from approximately 3 to 25 percent. The problem was a lack of demand, which is understated by the figures just mentioned. Between 1929 and 1933 the labor force grew, technology improved, and full-employment output rose. Therefore, the gap between full-employment and actual GNP widened by more than the 30 percent decline in real GNP. Table 17–2

**TABLE 17–2  Real (1958 prices) and percentage changes of GNP and autonomous spending between 1929–1933 and average values of parameters**

|  | Real change (billions) | Percentage change | Average values |
|---|---|---|---|
| GNP | −62.1 | −30.5 | — |
| Investment | −36.6 | −87.5 | — |
| Autonomous consumption $\begin{bmatrix} a \\ -bT \end{bmatrix}$ | 0.0 | 0.0 | — |
|  | +0.5 | +5.9 | — |
| Government spending | +1.3 | +5.9 | — |
| Income tax rate | — | — | 0.028 |
| Multiplier, $1/(1 - b(1 - t))$ | — | — | 1.78 |

supports the Keynesian belief that a volatile investment is a major cause of business cycles. Investment virtually collapsed during the Great Depression, falling approximately 87 percent, or $36.6 billion in 1958 prices.[11] The second component of private autonomous spending, consumption independent of *disposable* income and represented by the parameter a, is assumed to have remained constant.

Although Keynes's book which spelled out in detail the rationale for fiscal policy was published after the Great Depression, Keynesian ideas were sufficiently well developed during the Depression that some economists and bankers advocated an expansionary fiscal policy. However, the government was non-Keynesian and did little to counteract the collapse of investment. Income tax rates were so low, approximately 3 percent, that they contributed little automatic stability.[12] Real autonomous tax collections declined $1.2 billion and augmented autonomous

---

[10] This section accepts the parameter estimates of Robert J. Gordon, *Macroeconomics* (Boston: Little, Brown, 1981), pp. 84–87.

[11] Investment includes net exports. We are assuming actual and desired values coincide.

[12] Seventy percent of net taxes in 1929 were estimated to be autonomous. The income tax rate was estimated by dividing 30 percent of net taxes by GNP.

consumption by $0.5 billion since tax reductions increase disposable income. Even this minor contribution to demand was largely fortuitous. Tax rates on property and other nonincome variables were raised significantly. Indeed, tax rates were raised in 1932 more than in any previous peacetime year. The value of property and other autonomous variables fell so much that autonomous tax receipts fell in spite of rate increases. Government spending was only slightly more expansionary, increasing $1.3 billion. The total contribution of fiscal policy to autonomous demand, that is, the sum of government spending and the consumption effect of autonomous taxes, was $1.8 billion, or about 5 percent of the decline in investment. Government stood by idly; fine tuning was not attempted in the Great Depression. Total autonomous spending fell $34.8 billion, $36.6 minus $1.8 billion. Fortunately, the marginal propensity to consume private disposable income, b, was not that high and the multiplier effect of autonomous spending on income was relatively low.[13] The multiplier was 1.78, so GNP declined by $62.1 billion, $34.8 billion times 1.78.

How did the government rationalize its actions, or lack of them, in terms of the basic model? Policymakers alleged that the state of confidence of investors was negatively related to the government deficit. If additional government spending and larger deficits so impaired the state of confidence as to lead to an equal reduction in investment, then government spending would have no effect on income. Such a situation seems extremely doubtful but cannot be ruled out. When one considers an enigma like the state of confidence, virtually anything is possible. One could argue that additional government expenditures will be interpreted as a sign of determination to combat depressions and thereby enhance the state of confidence. Keynes took a middle-of-the-road position, assuming investment is independent of government expenditures. In this case government expenditures can counteract variations in the private demand for commodities.

## MODIFICATIONS OF THE BASIC MODEL WHICH HIGHLIGHT
## ESSENTIAL FEATURES

Let us modify slightly the basic Keynesian model. In particular, assume government spending is only partially autonomous, $G_0$. It also has an induced component, $gy$,

$$G = G_0 + gy$$
$$G = 200 + 0.15y$$

(17–1')

---

[13] Table 17–2 implies that the marginal propensity to consume total private, both household *and* business, disposable income is about 0.45. This is much lower than the propensity to consume household disposable income, which is greater than 90 percent. As stated in Chapter 14, the models presented here do not segregate private income.

where g (0.15) is government's marginal propensity to spend. What is the justification for assuming that government spending is partially induced. A mere glance at the historical data presented in Chapter 14 is sufficient justification; government spending has paralleled the upward trend of income. Even those totally unaware of the historical record would expect government spending to be positively related to income. We can consider two extreme cases of government: (1) it is totally unresponsive to the wants of the public and simply attempts to enlarge itself, or (2) it represents perfectly the wants of the public. If the former were the case, government spending would be positively related to income because the income tax system provides government the wherewithal to spend. The government may well believe there is an upper limit to its spending which can be financed by bond sales and money creation. Spending beyond the limit must be financed by taxes. As income rises, the government earns a *fiscal dividend,* that is, tax receipts rise with income even though tax rates are unchanged. What happens to the fiscal dividend? It is spent, however foolishly, by a government determined to enlarge itself.

Now consider the other extreme. Suppose government represented perfectly the wants of the public. Would the fiscal dividend also be spent in this case? At least partially. The consumption function says that as incomes rise, households want more sporting equipment, books, cars, and other consumer goods. The same should be true of goods and services provided by government. As incomes rise households should want more and better parks, schools, highways, and defense. While many may wish that the government not spend the entire fiscal dividend, virtually everyone wants some additional government goods and services, making g, government's marginal propensity to spend, positive. Most governments are a blend of the two extremes and, therefore, government spending is positively related to income.[14]

How does this modification of government's behavior change our results? The equilibrium level of income is still given by setting aggregate expenditures equal to income. Using equation (17–1'), (17–2) and (17–3'), equilibrium income in terms of the parameters and exogenous variables is:

$$C + I + G = y$$
$$a - bT_0 + b(1 - t)y + I_0 + G_0 + gy = y$$
$$y = \frac{1}{1 - b(1 - t) - g}(a - bT_0 + I_0 + G_0) \qquad (17\text{–}7)$$
$$y = \frac{1}{1 - 0.75(1 - 0.2) - 0.15}(60 - 0.75(20) + 150 + 200)$$
$$= 1,600$$

The terms in parentheses in the third line of equation (17–7) are total exogenous spending. The term $1/(1 - b(1 - t) - g)$ is greater than one and

---

[14] When government spending depends on tax receipts, the tax system need no longer be an automatic stabilizer.

may be called a multiplier. Income is the product of a multiplier and autonomous spending.

Compare equation (17–7) with (17–5), where the latter gives the equilibrium level of income when government spending is entirely autonomous. The two equations are quite similar. In each case equilibrium income is the product of autonomous spending and a multiplier. The multipliers differ slightly, however. Why is this so? What do b(1 − t) and b(1 − t) + g represent in the two cases? These terms are the *respending propensities,* that is, the sum of the marginal propensity to spend national income by each sector. The original basic model assumed only one sector, households, have a marginal propensity, b(1 − t), to spend national income. The modification adds government's respending propensity, g. Since we are retaining the assumption that investment is independent of income, the total, household plus government, respending propensity is b(1 − t) + g. *The multiplier always is the inverse of one minus the total respending propensity.*

A comparison on the basic and modified models highlights the essential features of Keynesian economics. Autonomous spending is the driving force of the system. Autonomous spending brings forth an equal amount of output and income in the first round and induces respending and additional income in subsequent rounds. In the modified model, respending at each round equals b(1 − t) + g × income in the previous round. The respending multiplies upward the value of autonomous spending. *National income always is the product of autonomous spending and a multiplier which is the inverse of one minus the respending propensity.*

## SUMMARY

The basic Keynesian model solves the equilibrium level of income with the aid of only one equilibrium equation, C + I + G = y. Graphically, only one figure is necessary. Only one equation or graph is necessary because all desired spending, C + I + G, is either autonomous or dependent on income. That is, the general form of C + I + G is A + Ry, where A is autonomous spending and R is the marginal propensity to spend national income, respectively. Ry is total induced spending, that is, spending dependent on income. When desired spending takes this form we can set spending equal to output and get a unique equilibrium value of y.

$$A + Ry = y$$
$$y = \frac{A}{1 - R}$$

What name do we give to the reciprocal of 1 − R? R, which lies between zero and one, is the marginal propensity to spend, so the reciprocal of 1 − R is the multiplier. Income is the product of autonomous spending and the multiplier. If spending depended on the rate of interest or any other endogenous variable, the equilibrium equation would contain two variables and generally not yield a solution for income.

Each spending category in the basic model has an autonomous component: $a - bT_0$ for consumption, $I_0$ for investment, and $G_0$ for government expenditures. The basic model assumes only one sector, households, have a marginal propensity to spend national income, $b(1 - t)$. The equilibrium level of income is

$$y = \frac{A}{1 - R} = \frac{a - bT_0 + I_0 + G_0}{1 - b(1 - t)}$$

The basic model can be readily modified by adding an induced component to government expenditures and investment. This changes the specific form of the multiplier without altering the fundamental structure of the model and the multiplier concept. To repeat, what cannot be added without abandoning the single equation solution is another variable influencing spending.

The investment component of autonomous spending is the engine of magnified income variations which can be neutralized by government spending varying counter to investment. Fiscal policy rules the roost. It is *the* stabilization tool. What role does money play in the basic Keynesian model? Absolutely none. Money is not a type of autonomous spending and has no direct effect on spending. Money may influence interest rates and other variables but, by definition, this has no effect on *autonomous* spending.

The advanced Keynesian model developed in the next chapters assigns money a minor supporting role, not surprisingly. Basic models are recognized to be first approximations which give the flavor of advanced models. It would hardly make sense to have a basic Keynesian model where money does not matter at all and an advanced Keynesian model where only money matters. The advanced model is very flexible, however. While Keynesians do assume the shapes of the curves in their advanced model are such that money has little effect on income, the shapes of the curves can be changed easily enough to radically change this conclusion. Even if one interprets the evidence as indicating that money matters a great deal and, accordingly, changes the shapes of the Keynesian curves in the advanced model, knowledge of the basic Keynesian model is important because it dominates the thought of some policymakers and so forcefully emphasizes the importance of demand in the short run.

## QUESTIONS

1. State the basic assumptions of Keynesian economics?

2. Define (*a*) Keynes's Law, (*b*) the marginal propensity to consume national income, (*c*) fiscal dividend, (*d*) automatic stabilizer, (*e*) responding propensity, (*f*) autonomous spending, and (*g*) fine tuning.

3. How do neoclassical and Keynesian views about investment differ?

4. Assume the following spending equations.

$$C = 30 + 0.75y$$
$$I = 100$$
$$G = 150$$

    *a.* What does autonomous spending equal?

    *b.* What is the value of the marginal propensity to consume national income? What is the value of the multiplier?

    *c.* What is the equilibrium level of income?

5. Some have modified the basic Keynesian model by including an induced income-dependent spending component to investment and government spending. That is, the investment and government expenditure relationships are

$$G = G_0 + gy \qquad\qquad (17\text{-}1')$$
$$I = I_0 + vy \qquad\qquad (17\text{-}2')$$

where g and v are the marginal propensities to spend by government and firms, respectively. The consumption relationship,

$$C = a - bT_0 + b(1 - t)y. \qquad\qquad (17\text{-}3')$$

    *a.* Determine equilibrium income in terms of autonomous spending and the parameters.

    *b.* What is the value of the autonomous spending multiplier?

    *c.* State the economic rationale for the multiplier and, in so doing, explain why the multiplier in this case with induced investment and government spending differs from the multiplier shown in equation (17-8).

    *d.* Why may government expenditures and investment depend on income?

6. Assume the standard basic model with completely autonomous investment and government expenditures so spending is given by equations (17-1)-(17-4). Equilibrium income is

$$y = \frac{1}{1 - b(1 - t)} (a - bT_0 + I_0 + G_0)$$

    *a.* Assume $1 additional government expenditures. What does the income change equal?

    *b.* Assume autonomous taxes increase by $(1 - t). For example, if the income rate, t, is 0.20, autonomous taxes increase by $0.80. What does the income change equal?

    *c.* Suppose both (*a*) and (*b*) above occur. What does the income change equal? What does the total, autonomous plus income, tax change equal?

    *d.* Define the balanced budget multiplier. Does (*c*) above illustrate the balanced budget multiplier?

7. How, if at all, does recognition that government spending depends positively on income affect the automatic stabilizer properties of the fiscal system?

appendix · The saving-investment approach

We presented the basic Keynesian model in order to provide the reader with a convenient review. In spite of our preference for the expenditure approach, we offer this appendix so that the chapter serves its intended purpose for those who were taught the saving-investment approach. Warning: The material in subsequent chapters is considered to be new, so that the saving-investment approach appears for the last time.

Let us derive the expression for equilibrium income in terms of the parameters and exogenous variables given in the text. As stated in the appendix to Chapter 14, at equilibrium private saving plus taxes equal investment plus government spending.

$$S_p + T = I + G \qquad (17A-1)$$

The right-hand side simply is the sum of two exogenous variables. What does the left-hand side equal? After paying taxes, income is consumed or saved. That is, private saving is disposable income minus consumption.

$$S_p = y_d - C = y - T - C \qquad (17A-2)$$

Call private saving plus taxes modified saving, $S_M$, because it would equal saving if government did not exist, as equation (17A-2) readily confirms.

$$S_M = S_p + T = (y - T - C) + T = y - C \qquad (17A-3)$$

Modified saving is the leakage from the spending stream. Substituting the consumption equation (17-3′) given in the text,

$$
\begin{aligned}
S_M &= y - a + bT_0 - b(1 - t)y \\
&= -a + bT_0 + (1 - b(1 - t))y \qquad (17A-4) \\
&= -65 + 0.75(20) + (1 - 0.75(1.0 - 0.2))y = -50 + 0.4y
\end{aligned}
$$

The autonomous component of modified saving is the negative of autonomous consumption, and the sum of the marginal propensities to consume and save (modified) equal unity. As national income increases by a unit, saving increases by $1 - b(1 - t)$, or 0.4 in our example. The S line in Figure 17A-1 graphs the saving relationship.

The injections to the spending stream are desired investment plus government expenditures, represented by a horizontal line $I + G$ since they are independent of income. At equilibrium, leakages or the output not purchased by households equals the injections from firms and government. Setting the modified saving equation (17A-4) equal to investment plus government expenditures, we get

$$
\begin{aligned}
I_0 + G_0 &= S_M \\
I_0 + G_0 &= -a + bT_0 + (1 - b(1 - t))y \qquad (17A-5)
\end{aligned}
$$

$$y = \frac{1}{1 - b(1 - t)} (a - bT_0 + I_0 + G_0) = 1{,}000$$

**FIGURE 17A–1  Saving equals investment plus government expenditures**

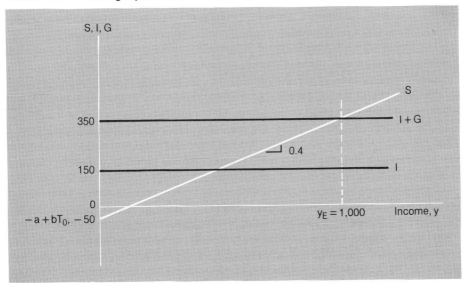

In words, equation (17A–5) says that income equals the multiplier, which is the inverse of the marginal propensity to save national income, times autonomous spending. Equations (17–5) and (17A–5) are identical, and their graphical representations, Figures 17–5 and 17A–1, are more or less complements showing the same equilibrium income. The gap between the $I + G$ and $S_M$ curves is 400 when income is zero. The slope of the $S_M$ curve and the rate the gap between the two curves is being closed is $0.40 = 1 - b(1 - t)$.

# Keynesian money demand and an introduction to the advanced model

# 18

The advanced Keynesian model extends the basic model by incorporating interest rate effects. While Keynes did not abandon the importance of the state of confidence as a determinant of investment, he met the classicists halfway in his advanced model by including the rate of interest. Output and income still are determined by investment and the other components of aggregate demand, which now depends on the rate of interest in addition to income and autonomous elements. Monetary policy can now play an indirect role. If monetary policy can change the rate of interest, and if investment is responsive to the rate of interest, then monetary policy can effect GNP. As stated earlier, Keynes thought monetary policy was relatively insignificant compared to fiscal policy.

While recognition of interest rate effects opens a crack for monetary policy, it could foreclose the use of fiscal policy as a stabilization tool. Fiscal policy has an indirect negative effect on investment. For example, suppose a recession exists and government spends more and cuts taxes in order to stimulate the economy. The expansionary fiscal policy probably has no direct effect on investment. However, the expansionary fiscal policy creates a budget deficit which somehow must be financed. Assuming the Federal Reserve maintains a neutral policy and does not accommodate the Treasury by open-market purchases and monetary expansion, bond sales to the public are the only means of financing the deficit. The sale of bonds by the Treasury or anyone else tends to lower bond prices, or, equivalently, raise the rate of interest. In this manner fiscal policy has an indirect negative effect on investment. The higher interest rates associated with budget deficits could reduce investment by an amount equal to the increase in government expenditures, in which case fiscal policy has no effect on aggregate demand. Keynes recognized this possibility but discounted it. As he interpreted the economic data, the negative indirect effect of fiscal policy on investment was quite small.

Monetarists disagree with Keynes. As they interpret the data, money has a strong positive, if indirect, effect on aggregate demand, while fiscal policy has such a strong negative indirect effect on investment as to render it virtually useless. Perhaps because measurement of indirect effects is the issue, the Keynesian-monetarist controversy may remain unresolved longer than other economic controversies. Under the circumstances, knowledge of alternative outcomes and the circumstances under which they occur is highly desirable.

With the aid of graphs the next section elaborates on the aggregate demand, rate of interest, and income interrelationship mentioned in the first two paragraphs. We then consider the demand and supply of money, which determines the rate of interest. Reviewers of *The General Theory* proclaimed that Keynes's theory of the demand for money was a milestone marking the death of an incomplete and inadequate classical transactions theory and the birth of the asset approach. With the passage of time quick reviews were superseded by exegetical tomes, and praise of Keynes's *specific* money demand theory became fainter, if not totally absent. Nevertheless, Keynes's specific theory is presented in considerable detail. Some knowledge of the history of economic thought is desirable, and whose theory should we know if not that of the most influential 20th century economist? Moreover, knowledge of the admittedly somewhat erroneous *specific* money demand theory is essential to understand numerous Keynesian policy proposals. Note well that only the *specific* Keynesian explanation is flawed; the originally revolutionary *general* Keynesian belief that money demand depends on the rate of interest is now almost universally accepted. The final section analyzes monetary and fiscal policy within the aggregate demand and rate of interest nexus.

## AGGREGATE DEMAND AND THE RATE OF INTEREST

To highlight the differences between the basic and advanced Keynesian model, let us ignore any possible modifications of the basic model. In particular, let us assume consumption depends only on income, and government expenditures are entirely exogenous. The consumption function, C, is graphed first in Figure 18–1A, and then government expenditure is added, shifting the curve upward to C + G. A fundamental difference between the basic and advanced Keynesian models is the investment relationship. Keynes accepted the classical explanations for a negative relationship between investment and the rate of interest. For example, as stated in Chapter 16, the downward-sloping investment curve may be viewed as an ordering of investment projects by its rate of return, which is equated to the rate of interest, r, by profit-maximizing firms. As the rate of

**FIGURE 18-1   Aggregate expenditures and the rate of interest**

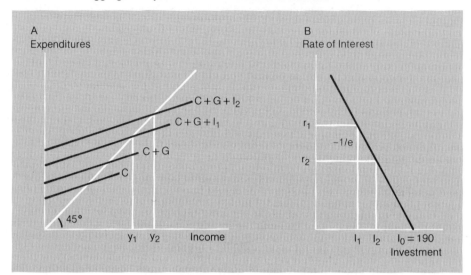

interest falls, firms find it profitable to undertake additional investments that yield lower rates of return. The general form of the investment relationship and a specific example are given by equation (18-1).

$$I = I_0 - er$$
$$= 190 - 5r \tag{18-1}$$

$I_0$ is autonomous investment which may be viewed as a measure of firms' state of confidence. The parameter e(5) measures the responsiveness of investment to the rate of interest, that is, $\Delta I / \Delta r = -e$. The basic model, a first approximation, says e = 0; the advanced Keynesian model says e is small, relative to autonomous investment, but not zero.

Figure 18-1B graphs the investment function.[1] Given equation (18-1), a mathematician would have investment on the vertical axis and the rate of interest on the horizontal axis. Economists, however, traditionally reverse the axes.[2] This makes somewhat more difficult the achievement of a

---

[1] The slope of Figure 18-1B does not correspond with our numerical example, which was selected so that the equilibrium interest rate is much smaller than the equilibrium income. We believe this gives the numerical example a greater semblance of reality although, of course, if one interpreted investment and the other components of aggregate demand as being measured in trillions of dollars and the interest rate in percentage points, then the reverse would be true. Correspondence of measurement units between the numerical example and the graph would make the latter less helpful.

[2] To help explain the workings of the economy, Leon Walras used algebra and hardly any graphs, while Alfred Marshall used graphs and hardly any algebra. The influence of these two economists was so strong that economists who offered both algebraic and graphical examples adopted Marhall's graphs and Walras's algebra even though the two economists reversed variables. Walras focused on quantities demanded and supplied at a given price or

major objective of this book: development of equal proficiency in the algebraic and graphical approaches and, therefore, employment of both interchangeably. How are the parameters represented graphically? The investment curve intersects the horizontal axis at $I = I_0 = 190$. (Look at equation (18–1.) When $r = 0$, as is true by definition along the horizontal axis, $I = I_0 = 190$.) Since the rate of interest and investment are on the vertical and horizontal axes, respectively, the slope of the investment curve, $\Delta r/\Delta I$, is $-1/e$. (Look at equation (18–1) again. The change in investment per unit change in the rate of interest, $\Delta I/\Delta r$, equals $-e$. Taking the inverse, $\Delta r/\Delta I$ is $-1/e$.) Thus, the algebraic measure of the sensitivity of investment to the rate of interest corresponds with the inverse of the slope in the graphical approach. When investment is very responsive to the rate of interest, that is, e is large, then the investment curve is flat (the absolute value of the slope is small). Although slope and elasticity are not identical concepts, they often are equated in monetary/macroeconomics.[3] A flat (steep) curve is said to be elastic (inelastic). According to our new terminology, the investment curve is elastic when investment is sensitive to the rate of interest. Figure 18–1B is drawn relatively steep (inelastic) because it is assumed investment is *not* very responsive to the rate of interest. If the rate of interest influenced investment more strongly, then the investment curve would be flatter (more elastic).

The rate of interest is not a parameter in the advanced Keynesian model; it is an endogenous variable to be determined by the economic system. As a result, equality of aggregate expenditures and income does not yield a unique equilibrium level of income. Investment and aggregate expenditures and, therefore, the equilibrium level of income take many values, depending on the rate of interest. Look at Figures 18–1A and 18–1B. Assume the rate of interest is $r_1$ percent so investment is $I_1$. Shifting the C + G curve upward by $I_1$, the aggregate expenditure curve $C + G + I_1$ corresponding to rate of interest $r_1$ intersects the 45° line at $y_1$. (Although investment and income are measured in the same units, that is, dollars, the scale differs between Figures 18–1A and 18–1B so both figures can be approximately the same size even though investment is a

rate of interest while Marshall theorized in terms of the demand and supply price or rate of interest for a given quantity. For example, Walras focused on the amount of investment that would occur at a rate of interest. In his algebraic examples, investment is on the left-hand side and the rate of interest is on the right. If he had had graphs, which he did not, Walras surely would have had investment on the vertical axis and the rate of interest on the horizontal. Marshall had the rate of interest on the vertical axis and investment on the horizontal axis because he focused on the rate of interest necessary to induce some given amount of investment. If Marshall had used equations, he surely would have placed the rate of interest on the left-hand side.

[3] The slope is the ratio of changes, that is, $\Delta y/\Delta x$, while the elasticity is the ratio of *percentage* changes, that is, $\Delta y/y \div \Delta x/x$, or $x\Delta y/y\Delta x$. Slope and elasticity clearly are not equal. A straight line has a constant slope but its elasticity is variable. Two parallel lines have identical slopes but different elasticities. Nevertheless, monetary/macroeconomists typically equate slope and elasticity because they usually compare two lines at the point of intersection. At such a point, the flatter line is more elastic and vice versa.

small component of income.) Suppose the rate of interest falls to $r_2$ percent. According to Figure 18–1B, firms invest more, which shifts the expenditure curve in Figure 18–1A to $C + G + I_2$. The equilibrium level of income rises to $y_2$. Aggregate demand and, therefore, the equilibrium level of income is negatively related to the rate of interest. We must know the rate of interest to determine the equilibrium level of income.

## THE DEMAND AND SUPPLY OF MONEY

Keynes looked at the money market to determine the rate of interest. He assumed decisions are made sequentially. Households first decided on the basis of their disposable income how much to consume and save. Having made this decision, households then allocate their saving between financial assets. To simplify the analysis Keynes assumed there were only two assets, money and long-term bonds. The private sector and government issue long-term bonds but all bonds are viewed as identical. Sequential decision making suggested to Keynes that the specific asset market to be analyzed in order to determine the rate of interest is a matter of indifference. For example, suppose money demand exceeds supply. How can the Keynesian household acquire additional money balances? The Keynesian household must borrow; it does not consume less and save more because this decision depends simply on disposable income. The excess demand for money and additional borrowing cause higher interest rates. Compared to classicists, Keynes restricted the scope of economic behavior. The classicists admitted that consumers may save more and hoard because an excess demand for money exists. Excess supply situations according to Keynes even more strongly illustrate that either asset market may be analyzed. Suppose that the money supply increases so that supply now exceeds money demand. The excess supply normally will be directly and immediately associated with additional lending and lower interest rates. This is so because in most economies the money supply expands through open-market purchases and bank loan and check deposit expansion. Clearly, this will be associated with falling interest rates, at least initially. Even if the government expands supply by printing additional fiat money, the same result occurs. Having previously decided how much to consume and save, households buy bonds or, equivalently, lend the additional money. Keynes preferred to analyze the supply and demand for money instead of bonds.

Keynes was much less certain than classical economists that the monetary authorities could control the money supply, partly because he emphasized the short run while they emphasized the long run. The Keynesian money *supply* liquidity trap says that the monetary authorities sometimes cannot rapidly change the quantity of money. Nevertheless, in his complete economic model Keynes ignores the money supply trap and assumes that the monetary authorities attempt and, in fact, do control the quantity of money. The classical money supply hypothesis was adopted in order to reduce the sources of different classical and Keynesian conclusions. The money supply, $M^S$, is an exogenous variable, $M_0$.

## TRANSACTIONS AND PRECAUTIONARY DEMAND FOR MONEY

Any misgivings Keynes may have had about the money supply equation were minor compared to his criticism of the classical demand for money. Recall that the classicists viewed money strictly as a medium of exchange and had only a transactions demand for money. Keynes accused them of major sins of omission instead of commission. He wholeheartedly endorsed the classical transactions demand for money but castigated them for overlooking other important elements of money demand. In addition to being a medium of exchange, money also is a temporary abode of purchasing power and unit of account. The three functions or services performed by money suggest that *total money demand is the sum of three components: the transactions demand, the precautionary demand, and the speculative demand for money.*

More recent research shows that Keynes should have embraced the classical transactions demand somewhat less warmly. After recognizing that money is the medium of exchange, the classicists immediately leaped to the conclusion that money demand is proportional to income, a proxy for transactions, where the factor of proportionality depends on such factors as the regularity and frequency of payment, the rapidity of communications and transportation, and the degree of vertical integration.[4] The demand for the medium of exchange certainly should be related to income but why should it be proportional to income instead of depending on the square root of income or income squared? The classicists and Keynes offer no justification for the proportionality assumption.

William Baumol's and James Tobin's inventory theoretic approach to the transaction demand, which is summarized in Appendix A, states that the transaction demand depends on the square root of income. More important, according to Baumol and Tobin the demand for money for transactions purposes also depends positively on brokerage costs and negatively on the interest rate. The dependence of money demand on the interest rate is a major Keynesian conclusion repeatedly confirmed empirically but denied by classicists. The intuitive rationale for including brokerage costs and the rate of interest parallels the discussion of these two variables as determinants of desired excess reserve.[5] Suppose our author is paid $3,000 quarterly and spends the entire amount evenly during the quarter. The sawtooth pattern A in Figure 18–2 need not represent

---

[4] The classicals transactions demand for money was presented in Chapter 16, p. 428.

[5] Cf. Chapter 4, pp. 83–85.

**FIGURE 18-2 Transactions balances under different assumptions about bond purchases and sales**

(A) Transactions balances when $3,000 are received at the beginning of each quarter and spent at a constant rate. No bonds are purchased or sold.
(B) Transactions balances when $3,000 are received at the beginning of each quarter and $1,500 are immediately used to buy bonds, which are sold at midquarter. Spending occurs at a constant rate.
(C) Transactions balances when $3,000 are received at the beginning of each quarter and an immediate $2,000 bond purchase is followed by a $1,000 bond sale in month 1 and another sale in month 2. Spending occurs at a constant rate.

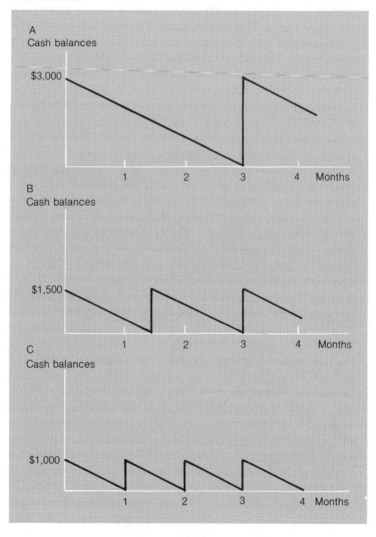

the individual's cash balances, as the classicists implicitly assumed.[6] Although money is received, the author could buy and sell bonds and not hold money for any significant period of time. Sawtooth pattern B represents the cash balances of an individual who used half, $1,500, of the quarterly salary to buy bonds and then sells the bonds at midquarter. What bond purchase strategy would make transactions balances follow sawtooth pattern C? An immediate $2,000 bond purchase followed by a $1,000 sale one month hence and another $1,000 sale two months hence yields pattern C. Note that the same cash pattern occurs when the individual is paid monthly and does not enter the bond market. Which of these three, or possibly yet other, cash patterns is selected? The Baumol-Tobin inventory theoretic approach assumes profit maximization.[7] Pattern B is preferred to A when the brokerage cost of buying and selling bonds worth $1,500 is less than the interest earned on the bonds during the first half of the quarter. Lower brokerage costs and higher interest rates encourage individuals to buy and sell bonds more frequently and economize on average transactions balances. At sufficiently high interest rates the individual would select pattern C, where average cash balances are only $500.

The studies by Baumol and Tobin notwithstanding, we shall assume as did Keynes and the classicists that the transactions demand for money, $M_T^D$, is proportional to income and independent of the rate of interest.

$$\frac{M_T^D}{P} = k'y \qquad \text{or} \quad M_T^D = k'Py$$

$$\frac{M_T^D}{P} = .2y \tag{18–2}$$

To emphasize that Keynes unlike the classicists viewed the transactions demand as only one component of total money demand, the factor of proportionality is $k'$ instead of the Cambridge k. Although the price level is assumed fixed, the effect of relaxing this assumption in later chapters is more easily understood when the price level appears explicitly in equation (18–2). The price level is 1 in our numerical example, and $k' = .2$. Why is the simple proportionality assumption substituted for the more complicated Baumol-Tobin square root formula? Simplicity is desirable, provided no serious errors are introduced. Substituting income for its square root is no serious error.[8] Omitting the rate of interest could be a serious

---

[6] See Figure 16–2 and the surrounding discussion on the determinants of velocity.

[7] The Baumol-Tobin analysis is described as inventory theoretic because it is based on the principles underlying optimal inventory control. Inventories are held to bridge gaps between production and sales. Money is held to bridge gaps between receipts and expenditures.

[8] Postwar data suggests the square root model is only marginally more accurate than the classical proportionality model. The square root and proportionality models imply the income elasticity of money demand is 0.5 and 1.0, respectively. Goldfeld's postwar study estimates the income elasticity is 0.68, and most longer run studies have estimates close to unity. S. Goldfeld, "The Demand for Money Revisited," *Brookings Papers on Economic Activity*, no. 3 (1973).

error. However, as we shall see shortly, Keynes introduced the rate of interest in his speculative demand. Given that the interest rate appears in the speculative demand, nothing is gained by adding an interest rate term in the transactions demand, and the analytic convenience of attaching a different motive to each variable would be lost.[9]

The precautionary demand is typically mentioned for the sake of completeness and then is often dismissed because, like the rate of interest in the transactions demand, its effects are captured elsewhere. We shall follow this traditional approach. The demand for money for precautionary purposes emphasizes that money is a temporary abode of purchasing which is particularly useful because general uncertainty about the future is the rule. Let us divide uncertainty into two classes: uncertainty about interest rates (bond prices) and uncertainty about any other factor, called general uncertainty. General uncertainty includes uncertainty about such things as one's job, salary, health; the availability of specific commodities; and the value of total expenditures. A serious illness could drastically reduce one's income and simultaneously increase total expenditures. The house or car of your dreams may suddenly come on the market and require quick purchase. The precautionary motive for money demand says that individuals faced with general uncertainty will hold a temporary abode of purchasing power in order to protect themselves against unfavorable events and take advantage of favorable events. What variables determine the amount of precautionary balances demanded? One obvious variable, the degree of general uncertainty, is extremely difficult to measure. Keynes said income is the main determinant which can be measured.

The precautionary demand depends positively on income because for any degree of uncertainty the rich have more to lose from unfavorable events and also have more favorable opportunities. Mr. Rich and I may feel equally uncertain about our jobs but he suffers a greater loss if he is fired. The possible sale of a $1 million mansion excites Mr. Rich but is totally immaterial to me; my precautionary balances are designed to take advantage of a possible hamburger sale at the supermarket. While we could add another income term in the money demand expression in order to capture the precautionary motive, this only complicates matters and adds nothing new. The transactions motive already suggests that money demand is positively related to income.

## SPECULATIVE DEMAND AND LIQUIDITY PREFERENCE

Two of Keynes's major hypotheses were: (1) there exists a speculative demand for money, that is, households will demand money instead of the alternative asset, a perpetuity, even if they do not foresee any likelihood of near term expenditures and (2) the speculative demand for money

---

[9] Of course, no one actually segregates dollar bills by the motive for holding them.

depends negatively on the rate of interest. The speculative demand is also called the asset demand, and the graph of the speculative money demand is traditionally called the liquidity preference curve. Figure 18–3 graphs several downward-sloping liquidity preference curves. The speculative

**FIGURE 18–3 Liquidity preference curves**

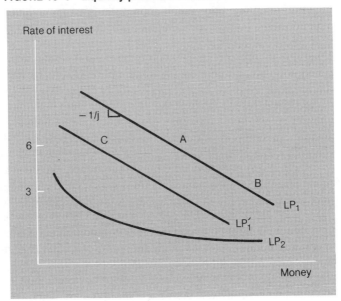

demand was crucial to Keynes because it implies that monetary policy *may* be totally ineffective. Consider the converse. Suppose there is no speculative demand but only transactions and precautionary demand so no one holds more money than dictated by planned expenditures and an allowance for uncertain expenditures. Suppose further that the authorities increase the quantity of money. In this case the money balances will be spent. Transactions and spending must increase if money demand is to again equal money supply. If a speculative demand exists, then monetary equilibrium could be achieved by less than proportional transactions and income changes. Indeed, if the entire monetary expansion is absorbed as additional speculative balances, then monetary policy has no effect on spending. Policy is effective to the extent that money market equilibrium is achieved through adjustments in transactions demand instead of speculative demand.

Two explanations for speculative money demand are popular, Keynes's expected return explanation which emphasizes the unit of account property of money and Tobin's portfolio risk explanation. The two explanations stem from the relaxation of different crucial assumptions which led classicists to omit the speculative demand. While both explanations deduce the negatively sloped liquidity preference curve, the Keynesian explanation deduces two other properties of speculative demand which have important policy implications. For this reason and because of Keynes's unique place in the history of economics, the Keynesian explanation is presented here while Tobin's explanation is relegated to Appendix B.

After deciding how much money to hold for planned and probable expenditures, assume an economic unit has sufficient wealth to acquire a portfolio of additional money and perpetual bonds. Classicists assumed economic units were strict profit maximizers. The money-bonds portfolio decision is based solely on the expected total return, which is the sum of the interest (coupon) and capital returns. That asset with the highest expected total return is selected. Currency earns no interest. While the interest return on other types of money, for example, check deposits, is positive in some countries and in some time periods, let us assume for simplicity that interest on all types of money is zero. This guarantees that the interest return is less on money than bonds, as indeed is normally the case. The second component of total yield is the capital yield, the difference between future and current dollar values. Being the unit of account, the capital yield on money *must* be zero. A $20 bill today is still a $20 bill a year hence; it may purchase fewer commodities because the dollar value of other commodities rises while the value of a $20 bill remains constant.[10] Bonds are not the unit of account. Holders of either bonds or money suffer real purchasing power losses as the prices of commodities rise, and bond holders incur additional nominal capital losses when interest rates rise. Assuming the perpetuity pays $1 per period, the expected total dollar return on bonds, $R_T$, during the period is

$$\begin{matrix} \text{Expected total} \\ \text{dollar return} \end{matrix} = \text{Coupon} + \text{Expected capital return}$$
$$R_T = 1 + (1/r_E - 1/r_0), \qquad (18\text{--}3)$$

where $1/r_E$ is the expected end-of-period price of bonds, and $1/r_0$ is the current bond price. (Equation (18–3) makes use of the inverse relationship between bond prices and interest rates. That is, $r_E$ is the expected rate, and $1/r_E$ is the expected bond price.)

Classicists recognized the uncertainty of bonds but assumed that the expected or average capital yield was zero. In other words, they assumed the expected future rate of interest always equalled the current rate. Lack of a speculative demand is the inevitable *correct* conclusion from these classical assumptions. In this case expected profit (and return) maximizers do not hold any speculative money balances because money offers no

[10] While the unit of account function is served by many interest paying accounts such as savings deposits and leads to the broad $M_3$ definition of money, Keynes's argument does not depend on the assumption that the return on money is zero. The essential feature of the unit of account is certainty of return, if any, and capital value.

return while the expected total return on bonds equals the coupon. The crucial assumptions which led classicists to reject the existence of a speculative demand for money are: (1) economic units are expected profit maximizers and (2) expected future and current interest rates are equal, so that the expected capital yield on bonds is zero. Drop either of these two assumptions and the unit-of-account property of money can imply an aggregate speculative demand that is negatively related to the rate of interest.

Keynes denied the second classical assumption and let the expected future interest rate diverge from the current rate. The classical long-run time period almost requires the equality of actual and expected interest rates and bond prices. A divergence between the current and expected future value tends to narrow over time, so that in a long-run equilibrium, which by definition precludes any narrowing or other changes, current and future value will coincide. For example, suppose the current rate of interest is 8 percent and the expected future interest rate is 10 percent. While such a time situation certainly could exist for a short period of time, interest rates surely are not always overestimated. Individuals learn; eventually expectations will be revised downward if the current rate remains at 8 percent. The revised expectations cause other behavioral changes, for example, lower expected interest rates may induce greater investment. Revisions stop and constancy occurs when the actual and expected interest rates are equal. In the long run the expected total return on bonds coincides with the coupon yield as the expected capital yield vanishes. In the Keynesian short run, however, the expected total return on bonds may well be negative. *Speculative money balances are held by those economic units expecting future interest rates sufficiently above the current rate that the expected capital loss is greater than the interest yield, making the total return on bonds negative.* Continuing our example, when the current interest on consols paying $1 per period is 8 percent, their price is $12.50. A profit-maximizing individual who expects the rate of interest to rise to 10 percent, and bond prices to fall to $10, will hold money because the $2.50 capital loss exceeds the $1 coupon. Money may not bear interest and as the unit of account cannot offer a capital yield, but this is preferable to expected losses on bonds. When the rate of interest is very high, nearly everyone will be expecting lower interest rates and capital gains from higher bond prices. Therefore, nearly everyone prefers bonds at high interest rates, and the speculative demand for money is very small. As the rate of interest falls, the expected rate of more and more households will exceed the current rate of interest. These households sell their bonds to avoid the expected capital losses and hold speculative money balances. At very low interest rates nearly everyone is expecting higher rates, and speculative money balances are large. *Given society's set of expectations, speculative money demand is negatively related to the rate of interest.*

### Properties of the Keynesian liquidity preference curve

Keynes's explanation of the speculative demand in terms of discrepancies between current and normal interest rates further suggests that the liquidity preference schedule is unstable and ultimately becomes flat. Each of these properties of the liquidity preference schedule has important policy implications. Consider first why the schedule is unstable. The Keynesian explanation assumes a given aggregate set of expected future interest rates. Test your knowledge of the importance of the given expected rate by answering the following: how, if at all, will the liquidity preference $LP_1$ curve in Figure 18–3 be affected if everyone suddenly revises their expectation, and when are revisions likely? The liquidity preference curve shifts in the same direction as the revision in the expected rate. Lower expected rates shift $LP_1$ downward to $LP_1'$. Temporarily ignore the curve labelled $LP_2$. Lower expected rates and higher expected bond prices tend to raise the return on bonds, given any current rate of interest, and reduce the amount of money demanded. To counteract this tendency and induce households to demand the same amount of money, the current interest rate (bond price) must be lower (higher). Instead of considering the rate of interest necessary to induce the same amount of money demanded—the vertical shift of the $LP_1$ curve—analyze the problem in terms of the amount of money demanded at every interest rate—the horizontal shift of the $LP_1$ curve. When lower future interest rates and larger capital gains are expected, at every current rate of interest and price of bonds some holders of speculative money balances will now expect a positive return on bonds and switch from money to bonds. The liquidity preference curve shifts leftward from A to C.[11]

When is the expected rate of interest likely to change and shift the liquidity preference curve? Households' expected rate of interest and the position of the liquidity preference curve is based in large part on past and current experience, as suggested by our discussion of the equivalence of expected and actual values in the long run. This implies that *moving along a liquidity preference curve causes it to shift.* For example, suppose the rate of interest had been 6 percent in the past so most households are expecting the rate of interest to be approximately 6 percent in the future. This expectation gives $LP_1$. Suppose the rate of interest falls from 6 to 3 percent, a rate of interest most households consider abnormally low. One moves from point A to point B on $LP_1$ in Figure 18–3 as households, demand more money to avoid the expected loss on bonds when the rate of interest rebounds upward. If the rate of interest is maintained at 3 percent, however, it will no longer seem abnormally low. The normal interest rate will be revised downward and the liquidity preference curve shifts to $LP_1'$. Movements in the current rate of interest are not the only source of

---

[11] The two equivalent ways of viewing the shift are presented for the reader's convenience. Select the approach you find easier.

variation in the normal rate. Playing a role analogous to entrepreneurs' state of confidence in the investment schedule, Keynes thought households' normal rate of interest is little understood and highly variable, causing a continually shifting, unstable liquidity preference curve.

Abstracting from instability and assuming the normal rate of interest is fixed, the Keynesian explanation of liquidity preference says that the liquidity preference curve eventually becomes flat. Technically speaking, *at some low rate of interest liquidity preference becomes perfectly elastic, and a money demand liquidity trap exists*. The liquidity trap, illustrated by $LP_2$ in Figure 18-3, sets a floor on the rate of interest.[12] At some sufficiently low interest rate the economy enters a liquidity trap because everyone expects higher interest rates and avoids capital losses by holding only money. The demand for money becomes absolute. If the monetary authority were to increase the money supply, the additional money balances would be willingly held. In a liquidity trap money does not influence spending and, therefore, income. The liquidity trap is a dilemma the monetary authorities want to avoid.

The post-Keynesian portfolio explanation of liquidity preference in terms of interest being the reward for risk is silent about the stability and slope of the schedule. It is compatible with the linear liquidity preference relationships in Figure 18-3. Let us assume this is the case and consider instability and the liquidity trap later as special cases. The algebraic form and a specific example of a linear total money demand function is

$$\frac{M^D}{P_0} = k'y + h - jr \qquad (18-4)$$
$$M^D = .2y + 116 - 2r$$

The first term, $k'y$, is the transactions demand, and $h - jr$ represents the linear downward-sloping liquidity preference. The parameter $j$ measures the responsiveness of speculative demand to the rate of interest. Since Figure 18-3 has the rate of interest on the vertical axis, and money demand on the horizontal axis, the slope of the liquidity preference curve, $\Delta r/\Delta M^D$, is $-1/j$. If $j$ is large, the slope of the linear liquidity preference curve in Figure 18-3 is small (flat), indicating that a small change in the rate of interest leads to a large change in liquidity preference.

## MONETARY POLICY

We are now ready to integrate the analysis of the commodities and money markets in order to ascertain the effects of monetary and fiscal policy. Aggregate expenditures and equilibrium income depend on the rate of interest. Look at Figure 18-4A, which is similar to Figure 18-1A.

---

[12] The term *liquidity trap* without qualifying adjectives henceforth always is a money *demand* liquidity trap.

**FIGURE 18–4   Aggregate expenditures, money, and the rate of interest**

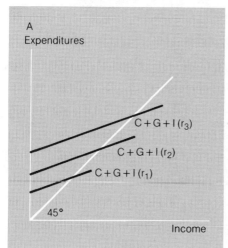
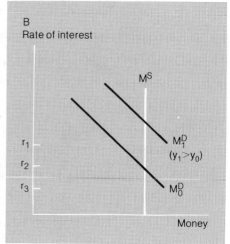

The negative relationship between investment and the rate of interest is illustrated indirectly by three aggregate demand curves, a higher curve corresponding to a lower rate of interest. Given the rate of interest, we can ascertain equilibrium income. Let us turn to the money market, graphed in Figure 18–4B. The equilibrium rate of interest is determined by the intersection of the liquidity preference curve and the vertical money supply. However, the position of the liquidity preference curve in Figure 18–4B depends on income. Higher incomes increase the amount of money demanded for transactions and precautionary purposes, shifting liquidity preference upward and rightward from $M_0^D$ to $M_1^D$, and raising the equilibrium rate of interest. Many interest rates equate the demand and supply of money, depending on the level of income. Money market equilibrium does not yield a unique rate of interest which can be substituted in the aggregate demand equation. In this respect the two markets are on equal footing. Recall that many levels of income equal aggregate demand, depending on the rate of interest. Commodities market equilibrium does not yield a unique level of income which can be substituted in the money demand equation. The upshot is that *the overall equilibrium income and rate of interest are determined simultaneously*. One cannot calculate the equilibrium rate of interest first and then income, or vice versa. Both the commodities and money market curves depend on the rate of interest and income. The simultaneous solution to the two variables indicates interaction or feedback effects between the commodities and monetary sectors. Any increase in aggregate demand generates monetary effects, and monetary expansion and interest rate movements generate income effects.

We now tackle a major question: What are the effects of monetary policy, and how do they occur? Our answer will make use of Figure 18–5, which definitely should be familiar by now. The initial equilibrium income and rate of interest are generated by the solid lines. Being an equilibrium,

**FIGURE 18–5  Monetary expansion**

Monetary expansion shifts the money supply line from $M_0^S$ to $M_1^S$. The rate of interest falls from $r_0$ to $r_1$. Investment increases, shifting the aggregate demand curve from A to B. Induced spending and the multiplier effect causes movement from B to C. Higher income and transaction demand shifts liquidity preference rightward to $M^D(y_1)$. The interest rate rises from $r_1$ to $r_2$. Adjustments continue until an equilibrium is reached. Equilibrium income increases from $y_0$ to $y_e$ and the rate of interest falls from $r_0$ to $r_e$.

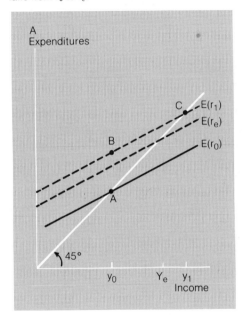
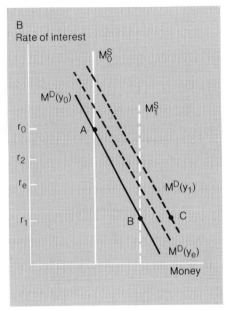

the solid lines are compatible. That is, the solid aggregate demand curve $E(r_0)$ is drawn for the equilibrium interest rate $r_0$, and the liquidity preference curve $M^D(y_0)$ occurs when income is $y_0$. Assuming the equilibrium income $y_0$ is less than full-employment income, the Fed increases the quantity of money. Simply stating that this would increase income is decidedly incomplete, ignoring many important intermediate steps. We want to know more than the direction of the final outcome. Income may increase, but will the increase be large or small? Magnitude effects and other issues can be readily answered later if we now consider carefully the interactive adjustment process and sequence of events leading towards equilibrium. Discussion of the channels of monetary policy and the dynamic process linking money and income—answering the "how" question mentioned in the opening sentence of this paragraph—is difficult but important.

Monetary expansion shifts the money supply line from $M_0^S$ to $M_1^S$. Looking at the expansion from the viewpoint of the money suppliers, the Fed successfully purchases bonds only if it bids bond prices up and, thereby, lowers interest rates. Similarly, commercial banks with additional (excess) reserves expand loans and deposits by reducing the loan rate. Looking at the expansion from the other side, the public will sell bonds to the Fed and hold additional money balances only if the interest rate falls. Bank borrowers spend their deposits, and the rate of interest must decline to induce the recipients to hold the enlarged money supply. We move along the liquidity preference curve $M_0^D$ to $M_1^S$, and the rate of interest falls from $r_0$ to $r_1$. Speculative balances *initially* absorb the entire monetary expansion. Lower interest rates generate the second step in the sequence of events: investment increases. The aggregate demand curve shifts upward as more investments become profitable at the lower interest rate. Incomes increase as firms hire more workers to produce machinery and other investment goods. The newly hired workers respond by consuming more, the third step in the sequence of events. We can graphically view the second step shifting the aggregate demand curve upward from point A on $E(r_0)$ to point B on $E(r_1)$ while the third step causes a movement along the upward sloping $E(r_1)$ to point C. The higher level of income increases the amounts of money demanded for transactions purposes, shifting the liquidity preference from $M^D(y_0)$ to $M^D(y_1)$. This is the fourth step in the sequence of events. Given a fixed money supply, the enlarged transactions demand necessarily reduces the amount available for speculative purposes and causes the rate of interest to jump upward to $r_2$, which still is below its initial level. The partial recovery of the rate of interest from its very depressed level chokes off some new investment and shifts the aggregate demand curve downward, but still above $E(r_0)$. Income falls somewhat below $y_1$. This reacts back on the liquidity preference curve. The interactive adjustment process may be quick or continue for some time. Ultimately, however, equilibrium prevails. *Monetary expansion increases* (to $y_e$) *equilibrium income and decreases* (to $r_e$) *the equilibrium rate of interest. Monetary policy is symmetric. A monetary contraction reduces income and raises the rate of interest.*

## FISCAL POLICY

Assume an increase in government spending financed by the sale of bonds. When the private sector purchases the bonds, private deposits and the money supply, which is defined to exclude government deposits, decline. As the government spends the proceeds of the bond sale, the money supply returns to its original quantity. Abstracting from these very short-run effects—the government typically sells bonds and acquires funds immediately prior to its spending program—more government demand shifts the aggregate demand curve upward from $E_0(r_0)$ to $E_1(r_0)$ in Figure 18–6A but has no immediate effect on the money market curves of Figure 18–6B. Additional government spending depletes the inventories of firms,

**FIGURE 18–6  Fiscal expansion**
Fiscal expansion shifts the aggregate expenditure curve upward from $E_0(r_0)$ to $E_1(r_0)$. Induced spending and multiplier effects cause a movement along $E_1(r_0)$ to 45° line. Higher income and transaction demand shifts liquidity preference rightward to $M^D(y_1)$. Interest rate rises from $r_0$ to $r_1$. Investment decreases, shifting the aggregate expenditure curve below $E_1(r_0)$. Adjustments continue until equilibrium is reached. Equilibrium income increases from $y_0$ to $y_e$ and the rate of interest rises from $r_0$ to $r_e$.

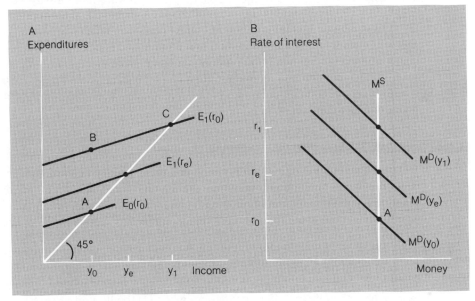

which respond by hiring more workers to restock their inventories and meet the government demand. Production and income increase directly. However, this sets in motion an adjustment process or sequence of events which may make the immediate and ultimate effects radically different. The first step is favorable to government spending. Workers recently hired by producers of government goods now have higher incomes and consume more. A multiplier effect is underway as more workers are hired to produce consumer goods for the government workers. This induced spending and multiplier effect is represented in Figure 18–6A by a movement along $E_1(r_0)$.

The higher level of income increases the amount of money demanded for transactions purposes, shifting the liquidity preference curve from $M^D(y_0)$ to $M^D(y_1)$. This is the second step in the sequence of events. Since the money supply is fixed, the larger transactions demand reduces the amount available for speculative purposes. The third step is an increase in the rate of interest to $r_1$, which is sufficiently high to make individuals satisfied with their smaller speculative balances. The fourth and final step is lower investment as some projects are no longer profitable at the higher rate of interest. The aggregate demand curve retrogresses somewhat and stands between $E_0(r_0)$ and $E_1(r_0)$. The curtailment of investments by government spending distinguishes the advanced from the basic Keynesian model and reduces the size of the multiplier. There may be multiple rounds of this sequence of events. That is, the investment reduction and somewhat lower income reduces consumption from its temporarily very high level, the transactions demand for money falls below $M^D(y_1)$, and so on. The economy is stable, however. These feedback effects between the sectors become smaller and smaller, and equilibrium is often reached in a small number of rounds. *Government spending increases equilibrium income* (to $y_e$) *and the rate of interest* (to $r_e$). The higher interest rate frees money from speculative purposes so that the fixed total money supply can finance larger transactions.

## MONETARY AND FISCAL POLICY MULTIPLIERS

The adjustment process or sequence of events leading toward equilibrium facilitates understanding when the *positive* interest rate effect of monetary policy on income and the *negative* interest rate effect of fiscal policy on income are large.[13] Expansionary monetary policy reduces the rate of interest, which increases investment and income. Money has a large effect on income when, *ceteris paribus*, (1) monetary policy changes the rate of interest significantly, and (2) rate of interest changes produce significant investment changes. In terms of the slopes of the curves, money has a significant effect on income when (1) the liquidity preference schedule is steep so the rate of interest is sensitive to the quantity of money and (2) the investment schedule is flat so investment spending responds significantly to the rate of interest. These two conditions which produce a large positive effect for money cause fiscal policy to have a small effect on income. Monetary policy reduces interest rates but fiscal policy raises them. The interest rate effect of fiscal policy significantly reduces its multiplier when, *ceteris paribus*, (1) the liquidity preference schedule is steep so the rate of interest must rise significantly to reduce speculative balances and create transactions balances and (2) the investment schedule is flat so the higher interest rates choke off a large amount of investment. The interest rate effects which create a large monetary policy multiplier create a small fiscal policy multiplier.

---

[13] Money has a *negative* effect on the rate of interest, which in turn has a *negative* effect on investment. Therefore, the effect of money on spending and income is positive, the product of two negatives.

## SUMMARY

The rate of interest, which is ignored in the basic Keynesian model, links the real and financial sectors in the advanced model. The rate of interest enters the real sector in a neoclassically oriented investment function. At low interest rates more investment projects are profitable. Monetary policy causes interest rate movements and, therefore, affects investment and income. While the role Keynes assigned to the rate of interest in the real sector was quite standard, the speculative motive and dependence of money demand on the rate of interest is a crucial Keynesian contribution once financial variables are recognized and no longer implicitly assumed to be fixed. If there were no speculative money demand so that money demand is independent of the rate of interest, then money supply, income, and transactions would be tied rigidly. If money were held simply for transactions purposes, only income changes could equilibrate money demand to exogenous money supply changes. Fiscal policy has no effect on the money supply. Once financial effects are considered, fiscal policy can influence income and transactions only if some speculative money balances can be transferred to transactions balances. Keynes stated that this transfer does indeed occur. He explained the existence of speculative balances in terms of a divergence between the current and future expected rate of interest. As the interest rate rises and bond prices fall, more profit-maximizing economic units avoid speculative money balances and prefer the high appreciation potential of bonds. Additional government spending raises the rate of interest, which releases some speculative balances and provides the additional transactions balances necessary to finance a higher level of income.

## QUESTIONS

1. What are the main differences between the basic and advanced Keynesian models?

2. Suppose the investment equation is $I = I_0 - er$. How is the slope of the investment schedule related to "e"?

3. Explain intuitively why the transactions demand for money should depend on brokerage costs and the rate of interest.

4. Discuss the precautionary demand for money. What function or service performed by money does it stress? What variables influence the amount of money demanded for precautionary purposes?

5. What is meant by the speculative or asset demand for money? What are the implications for monetary policy of the speculative demand for money?

6. Discuss Keynes's derivation of the speculative demand for money. What assumptions led classical economists to deny the existence of the speculative demand for money? Which assumption did Keynes drop? As explained by Keynes, is the speculative demand a short or long-run phenomenon? Explain.

7. What are the two main properties of the downward-sloping Keynesian liquidity preference curve?

8. Define a (money demand) liquidity trap. When may it tend to occur? What is the relationship between the current and expected rate of interest in a liquidity trap?

9. What is the effect of monetary policy on income and interest rates in the advanced Keynesian model? Sketch the adjustment process or sequence of events associated with monetary *contraction*?

10. What is the effect of fiscal policy on income and interest rates in the advanced Keynesian model? Sketch the adjustment process or sequence of events associated with *reductions* in government spending.

---

## appendix A · Inventory theoretic approach to the transactions demand for money

Money is a medium of exchange. Ignore any other services money may perform, so it is held only for transactions purposes. For simplicity, let all transactions be included in national income. Given these assumptions, how much money will an economic unit demand? The classicists *assumed* the average amount of money held would be proportional to income, where the proportionality factor k depended on such factors as the degree of synchronization of receipts and expenditures. The assumption seemed reasonable and had been made for so long that even Keynes accepted it unquestioningly. William Baumol and James Tobin are the doubting Thomases of monetary economics.[1] They were unwilling to assume that money demand is proportional to income. The demand for all other goods is derived from maximization or minimization principles. Why treat money differently? Extending cost minimization behavior to money demand, Baumol and Tobin found that money demand increases less than proportionally with income. In particular, money demand depends on the square root of income. More important, transactions demand depends negatively on the rate of interest. The remainder of the appendix proves the last two sentences.

Assume an individual will spend the amount y at an even rate during the time period. Our individual begins the period without any money and does not receive any income. To acquire money and spend y, the individual either sells bonds previously purchased or borrows. Assuming uniform and constant interest rates during the period, a cost minimizer is indifferent

---

[1] William Baumol, "The Transaction Demand for Cash: An Inventory Theoretic Approach," *Quarterly Journal of Economics,* November 1952, pp. 545–56; and James Tobin, "The Interest Elasticity of Transactions Demand for Cash," *Review of Economics and Statistics,* August 1956, pp. 241–47.

between the two ways of acquiring cash. We suppose bonds (assets) are sold. While a total of y bonds must be sold sometime during the time period, the cost minimizer decides when and how many bonds should be sold each time. For example, all y bonds could be sold at the beginning of the period, or y/2 bonds could be sold at the beginning and halfway through the period, or y/3 bonds could be sold at the beginning of each third, and so on. Express the number of times bonds are sold as y/X, where X equals the amount of bonds sold each time, called the lot size. For example, if you spent \$100 during the period (y = 100) and sold \$20 bonds each time (X = 20), then you sold bonds five times during the period.

The two components of total cost, brokerage cost and interest opportunity cost, are related to the lot size in opposite ways. Each bond purchase or sale entails a brokerage cost, b, which is the sum of commission payments to brokers and the opportunity cost of one's time spent making the bond transaction. Assuming for simplicity that the brokerage cost is independent of the amount sold, total brokerage costs are by/X, the product of the cost per sale, b, times the number of sales, y/X. Total brokerage costs clearly are reduced by selling less frequently and increasing the lot size. Brokerage costs are minimized by selling bonds worth y at the beginning of the period. Algebraically, by/X decreases when X increases and is minimized when y = X, given that y ⩾ X.

Minimizing brokerage cost maximizes interest opportunity cost, however. When all the bonds are sold immediately and initial cash holdings equal spending during the period, interest income is totally foregone. By selling bonds more frequently and holding less cash and more bonds, interest opportunity cost is reduced. Since the cash acquired by selling X bonds periodically is expended at constant rate, average cash balances are X/2. Interest opportunity cost is rX/2, the product of the rate of interest, r, and average cash balances. Letting W represent total cost,

$$\text{Total cost} = \frac{\text{Brokerage}}{\text{cost}} + \frac{\text{Interest opportunity}}{\text{cost}}$$
$$W = \frac{by}{X} + \frac{rX}{2}. \tag{18A-1}$$

Equation (18A–1) shows that brokerage cost is negatively and interest opportunity cost is positively related to the lot size of bond sales, X.

The decision variable is lot size. Costs are minimized by setting the derivative with respect to X equal to zero.

$$\frac{dW}{dX} = -\frac{by}{X^2} + \frac{r}{2} = 0 \tag{18A-2}$$

Those unfamiliar with the calculus will have to accept without proof that Equation (18A–2) holds when costs are minimized. Solving equation

(18A–2) for the average cash balance, X/2, and, by definition, the transactions demand for money, $M_T^D$,

$$M_T^D = \frac{X}{2} = \sqrt{\frac{by}{2r}} \qquad (18A-3)$$

The transactions demand depends on the square root of brokerage cost and income and is negatively related to the rate of interest.

If the justification for the name *inventory theoretic* is unclear, consider the following example. A retailer sells at a constant rate commodities worth $1,000 per period. The retailer buys a batch of commodities from the wholesaler and maintains an inventory due to acquisition costs such as the cost of writing orders, inspecting the commodities on arrival, and paying the wholesaler's bill. Many of these acquisition costs are fixed. For example, the bookkeeping costs of paying a $30 and $300 bill are identical. Suppose acquisition costs per purchase are $12.50. The placement of large orders does tie up one's funds in large sterile inventories instead of interest earning securities. The interest opportunity cost of large inventories must be balanced against low acquisition costs. Suppose the rate of interest is 10 percent, or 0.1 written in decimal form. What is the optimal order size and, therefore, average inventory? Although some names have been changed—brokerage costs became acquisition costs—the retailer clearly faces the same problem as the person minimizing the cost of transactions balances. Substituting the numbers in this example in equation (18A–3)

$$\frac{X}{2} = 250 = \sqrt{\frac{12.50\ (1,000)}{2\ (0.1)}} \qquad (18A-4)$$

The order size X is 500, and the average inventory is 250.

---

# appendix B · Liquidity preference, risk, and portfolio theory

Keynes's explanation of liquidity preference has been criticized on two main grounds: (1) it is invalid in the long run and (2) it implies only one asset is held while we observe portfolio diversification. James Tobin's explanation of liquidity preference is free of these criticisms while still stressing that money is a unit of account whose dollar price in the future is certain, that is, money is a risk-free asset.

### Keynesian liquidity preference

Let us review Keynes's explanation given in the text. Assume expected *profit-maximizing* households have wealth which will not be spent during the period. They must decide which asset, money or bonds, to hold. The bond coupon payment always is greater than any interest payment on money so, for simplicity, assume money earns no interest. The dollar value of money is fixed but bond prices can vary. A profit maximizer will hold speculative money balances only if interest rates are expected to rise enough so that the capital loss on bonds exceeds the coupon payment. At any moment in time the expected future rate may exceed the current rate, and speculative balances may be positive. In the long run, however, the current and expected future rate coincide, invalidating Keynes's explanation for speculative balances. Constancy of the rate of interest and other economic variables characterizes long-run equilibrium, by definition. Those holding speculative balances because they expect higher future rates of interest in the long run forego income. A profit maximizer will not suffer opportunity losses forever. Mistakes are eventually corrected, and the expected rate coincides with the constant long-run rate of interest. While it is true that other features of the Keynesian model stress the short run, economists wanted a general explanation for liquidity preference instead of one valid only in the short run.

Even in the short run where interest rates may diverge, the Keynesian explanation implies behavior contradicted by observation. Rewriting the text's equation (18–3) for your convenience,

$$\begin{matrix} \text{Expected total} \\ \text{dollar return} \end{matrix} = \text{Coupon} + \begin{matrix} \text{Expected capital} \\ \text{return} \end{matrix}$$

$$R_T \quad = \quad 1 \quad + \quad (1/r_E - 1/r_0) \qquad (18B\text{–}1)$$

where $r_E$ and $r_0$ are the expected and current rate of interest, respectively. A profit maximizer will prefer bonds (money) when equation (18B–1) is positive (negative). A unique switching point exists. Setting equation (18B–1) equal to zero,

$$R_T = 1 + (1/r_E - 1/r_C) = 0, \qquad (18B\text{–}2)$$

where $r_0$ became $r_C$ to signify the critical current rate which makes a profit maximizer indifferent between money and bonds, given the expectation of the future. Solving equation (18B–2) for the critical rate,

$$r_C = r_E/(1 + r_E). \qquad (18B\text{–}2')$$

The critical rate, $r_C$, is always less than the expected interest rate. (The denominator in equation (18B–2′) is greater than unity.) To be indifferent between money and bonds, the current interest rate must be less than the expected future rate, that is, interest rates must be expected to rise. For example, if $r_E = 0.1$, then the critical rate is approximately 0.09. An expected interest rate increase from approximately 9 percent to 10 percent causes a capital loss equal to the coupon payment.

Equation (18B–2) is rarely satisfied, and normally the household is not indifferent to money and bonds. Looking at equations (18B–1) and (18B–2), we see that the return on bonds is positive and no speculative balances are held when the rate of interest is above the critical rate. Only money is held below the critical rate. The lines ABCD and AEFG in Figure 18B–1A graph the liquidity preference curves of persons R and S, respectively. Who expects higher interest rates, and who is wealthier? Person S expects

**FIGURE 18B–1  Liquidity preference curves (A) personal curves and (B) aggregate curve**

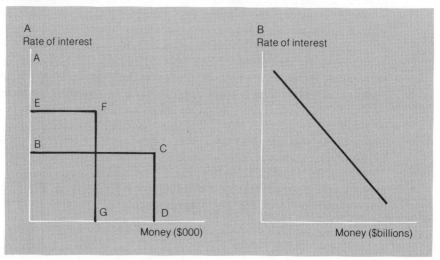

higher future rates than person R and has a higher critical rate. Because higher rates and lower bond prices are expected, person S continues to hold sterile money balances when person R no longer does. Person R is wealthier and can demand more money; BC is longer than EF. If expectations were uniform, each individual liquidity preference curve would be kinked at the same point, and the aggregate curve would have the same shape. Expectations are not uniform, however. The aggregate liquidity preference in Figure 18B–1B is a downward sloping curve precisely because expectations differ. According to Keynes, the aggregate curve is *not* downward sloping because each person holds more money as the interest rate falls. Instead, more people are suppose to sell all their bonds and hold only money. We do not observe this pattern of assets. Nearly everyone holds a diversified portfolio whose composition is relatively constant. Households do not put all their eggs in one basket.

### Risk and return analysis

In search of a justification for speculative money demand in the long run and for portfolio diversification, James Tobin assumed that individuals calculate a probability distribution of future interest rates where the average or expected future rate is assumed equal to the current rate.[1] Since neither a capital gain nor loss is anticipated, the expected total return on bonds equals the coupon payment, which is greater than the zero return on money. Individuals need not hold bonds exclusively because they maximize a utility function which depends on two variables, expected return (income) and risk. Expected return increases utility but risk decreases utility. The typical household is risk averse. It prefers a guaranteed $1 million to 50 percent changes of receiving nothing or $2 million. Although the expected return is $1 million in either case, the second case is risky. The household requires a higher expected return, perhaps $1.2 million achieved by increasing to 60 percent the probability of receiving $2 million, to be indifferent between the guaranteed and risky cases. Money does not yield a return but, being the unit of account, its return and price are certain. Bonds are risky. Although one may expect the future interest rate to equal the current rate, the expectation may not be realized. Contrary to expectations, the interest rate may rise (fall), causing capital losses (gains). Individuals normally hold both assets to earn some return and avoid some risk. The rate of interest may be viewed as the reward bondholders earn for bearing risk. Given their preferences for return and risk, households hold fewer risky bonds and more safe money as the rate of interest and reward for bearing risk fall. Alternatively stated, the rate of interest is the opportunity cost of holding a safe asset like money. As the rate of interest and opportunity cost of safety fall, households demand additional safe money balances. The remainder of this appendix uses graphs and algebra to prove the assertions made here and extends the analysis beyond liquidity preference proper to portfolio theory. Warning: Difficult material ahead. Proceed slowly.

The individual's basic problem is selecting the asset combination which maximizes a utility function dependent on the expected return and risk of the asset portfolio. The asset portfolio's expected return, E, is on the vertical axis of the top portion of Figure 18B–2, and risk, as measured by the standard deviation of returns, is on the horizontal axis. Indifference or constant utility curves are labelled $U_i$. In traditional microeconomics indifference curves are downward sloping because the two axes measure "goods" providing positive utility. In this case, however, a "bad," risk, is on one axis. To maintain constant utility, additional risk must be compensated by additional return. The indifference curves of risk averters are upward sloping.[2] A larger number subscript signifies greater utility. An individual would like to be at the far northwest portion of the graph. The opportunity locus, which here is the equivalent of the budget constraint in

---

[1] James Tobin, "Liquidity Preference as Behavior Towards Risks," *Review of Economic Studies,* February 1958, pp. 65–86. Tobin won the 1981 Nobel Prize largely on the basis of this article and his work on portfolio theory.

[2] What is the shape of the indifference curves for a Keynesian risk-neutral person who attempts to maximize return? The indifference curves would be horizontal.

FIGURE 18B-2 Portfolio expected return, risk, and the speculative demand for money

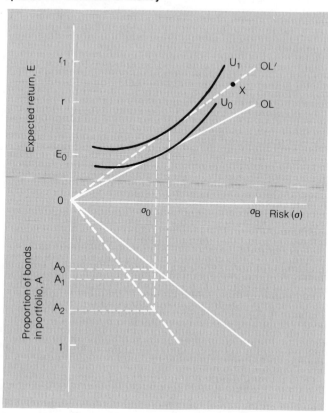

traditional microeconomics, limits the level of utility attainable. Let A be the proportion invested in bonds. Anticipating interest rates and the capital value of bonds will be constant, the expected total return on bonds equals the current rate of interest, r. The asset portfolio's expected return, E, depends on the proportion of bonds held.

$$E = Ar \qquad (18B-3)$$

Since the zero yield on money is certain, portfolio risk, $\sigma$, also depends only on the proportion of bonds.

$$\sigma = A\sigma_B, \qquad (18B-4)$$

where $\sigma_B$ is the riskiness of bonds. The solid line in the bottom portion of Figure 18B-2 graphs equation (18B-4) for a given $\sigma_B$. The maximum portfolio return and risk, which occur when the portfolio is fully invested in bonds, that is, $A = 1$, are r and $\sigma_B$, respectively. Solving equations (18B–3) and (18B–4) for A, the solid opportunity locus labeled OL in Figure 18B–2 is

$$E = (r/\sigma_B)\sigma. \qquad (18B-5)$$

The locus shows the asset portfolio's return and risk as the proportions of bonds and money vary, where the proportions can be ascertained from the bottom figure. The slope, $\Delta E/\Delta\sigma$, of the opportunity locus is $r/\sigma_B$ because bonds increase portfolio return by r but also increase risk by $\sigma_B$. Maximum attainable utility occurs when the indifference curve is tangent to the opportunity locus. The utility maximizing portfolio return and risk are $E_0$, and $\sigma_0$, respectively, and the proportion of bonds in the portfolio is $A_0$. (The proportion of money is $1 - A_0$ since we are assuming two assets.)

Now assume the rate of interest rises from r to $r_1$. The increase is viewed as permanent and does not affect the riskiness of bonds. The solid bond proportion/portfolio risk line in the lower portion remains applicable but the opportunity locus rotates counterclockwise to OL′ as its slope steepens to $r_1/\sigma_B$. As illustrated in Figure 18B–2, the highest attainable indifference curve now is $U_1$. The proportion of bonds increases from $A_0$ to $A_1$ and, therefore, the proportion of money decreases as the rate of interest rises. The speculative demand and rate of interest are negatively related.

Consider some secondary and specialized issues. Suppose the government levies a proportional tax with full loss offset. That is, any loss is fully deductible against other income or a proportion of the loss is refunded. Possible gains are reduced but so are possible losses. This type of tax reduces the riskiness of bonds by the tax rate. Assuming a 20 percent tax rate, the bond proportion/portfolio risk line in the bottom portion of Figure 18B–2 rotates clockwise by the tax rate and becomes the broken line. The expected return also is lower by the tax rate. Therefore, the solid opportunity locus is unaffected by the tax. Equation (18B–5) and the slope of the locus depend on the interest rate/risk ratio, which is constant when both terms fall proportionally. Since the tax affects neither the indifference curves nor the opportunity locus, the utility maximizing *after-tax* return and risk remain constant at $E_0$ and $\sigma_0$, respectively. To achieve this result, the individual increases the proportion of bonds from $A_0$ to $A_2$, given the new risk curve. The tax system effectively makes the government and citizen partners. The government shares the return and risk. To maintain the preferred position after taxes, the citizen increases the pre-tax portfolio return and risk by holding more bonds and less money. The United States' tax system is progressive and loss offset exists but, depending on the specific case, may not be complete. While the assumptions of the model are not entirely realistic, the model still may help explain the increasing demand for high risk "tax shelters."

### Portfolio theory

Let us now drop the assumption that there is one risky asset and that expected future and current rates of interest coincide. In the single risky asset case, the asset is labeled a bond. When multiple risky assets are assumed, standard terminology differs for some reason now forgotten, and the risky assets are called stocks. Each person forms a probability distribution of rates of return for each stock and then calculates the expected (average) return and risk (dispersion) of return. A person may expect capital gains and losses, causing the expected total return to diverge from the current return. The utility maximizer first selects his optimum stock portfolio and then the optimum combination of money and the stock portfolio. What are some characteristics of the optimum stock portfolio? Looking at Figure 18B–2, a steeper opportunity locus allows one to reach a higher indifference curve. The optimum stock portfolio is that one stock or combination of stocks which has the highest estimated ratio of expected return to risk because this ratio equals the slope of the opportunity locus. Suppose investing 70 percent of total stocks in stock G and 30 percent in stock H gives the largest return/risk ratio and generates the broken opportunity locus in Figure 18B–2.

The optimum stock portfolio typically will differ from person to person because stocks are appraised differently. Those who expect a +50 percent return on IBM stock will be buying IBM from those who expect a −50 percent return. A different appraisal is the *only* reason stock portfolios will differ. Your optimum stock portfolio, which gives the steepest opportunity locus and makes possible the highest indifference curve, depends simply on your estimates of expected return and risk. It is independent of the utility function. A very risk-averse pin-stripe banker and a mildly risk-averse nurse with identical estimates of stock performance will select the same stock portfolio, 70 percent stock G and 30 percent stock H in our example. Preferences for expected return and risk determine the specific point selected on the opportunity locus and, thereby, the proportion of the stock portfolio and money. For example, suppose the indifference curves drawn in Figure 18B–2 belong to our banker, who maximizes utility by holding $A_1$ (say, 40) percent of total assets in stock and $1 - A_1$ (say, 60) percent money. The unillustrated indifference curve for the less risk averse nurse would be much flatter and tangent to the opportunity locus at a point such as X, where the proportion invested in stock is higher, say 80 percent. (A vertical line from X will intersect the solid portfolio composition/risk line in the bottom portion at a point below $A_1$.) The conservative banker holds fewer stocks. The nurse who prefers more risk does *not* pick riskier stocks—the stocks of both the nurse and banker are divided between G and H in the same 70 versus 30 percent proportion. The nurse simply buys more of the optimum stock portfolio. A gambler borrows to buy the stock portfolio, in which case we can view his or her money holding as being negative. The optimum stock portfolio is leveraged up or down to attain the preferred return/risk combination.

Mark Twain said, "Put all your eggs in one basket and—WATCH THAT BASKET." Most people would disagree. They have many obligations and cannot spend their entire day searching for THE stock. Even those whose job is finding undervalued stocks admit that their evaluations may be wrong. Mutual funds and trust officers select widely diversified stock portfolios. While it is well known that diversification reduces risk, some are unaware that the risk reduction can be achieved *without* any sacrifice of expected return. Look at Table 18B-1. The first column shows

**TABLE 18B-1   Diversification reduces risk without changing expected return**

| | Returns on stock V, 50 percent likelihood each outcome | Returns on stock W, 50 percent likelihood each outcome | Returns on equal holdings of stocks V and W, 25 percent likelihood each outcome |
|---|---|---|---|
| | −5 ⟨ −5 / 15 | −5 / 15 | −5 / 5 |
| | 15 ⟨ −5 / 15 | −5 / 15 | 5 / 15 |
| Expected return | 5 | 5 | 5 |

the two equally likely rates of return, −5 and +15 percent, earned on stock V and its expected return. The return on stocks V and W are identical, and V and W are independent. The top portion of column 2 has four entries but only two are different. Column 3 shows that diversification reduces risk as returns are more closely centered about the expected value. Equal investments in stocks V and W reduce from 50 to 25 the likelihood of −5 and +15 percent rates of return. The expected return remains 5 percent. If portfolio diversification reduced both risk and return, it would be far less prevalent.

# The advanced Keynesian model: IS–LM

# 19

This is a bridge chapter. It formalizes with graphs and algebra the advanced model presented verbally in Chapter 18 and provides the foundation for Chapter 20. The formal model is called IS–LM for reasons which will be clear shortly. Those who prefer graphs and algebra to prose will now be able to master Chapter 18. That group is outnumbered by sufferers of math anxiety. We are not asking the majority to endure for the benefit of the few "math types" what at this point may seem excessive formality and unnecessary rigor. The formal and rigorous IS–LM model does more than summarize Chapter 18. Its main function is to provide the foundation necessary for the analysis in subsequent chapters of various complex issues. Besides summarizing the past and equipping us for the future, this chapter answers fully one of the most important questions of monetary economics: When will monetary and fiscal policy have a large effect on GNP? This question, one of the most important dividing Keynesians and monetarists, was only partially answered in the last chapter.

## THE IS CURVE: AGGREGATE EXPENDITURES EQUAL INCOME

Equations (19–1) to (19–3) state the general forms and specific examples of the expenditure relation for the three sectors, households, firms, and government.

$$C = a + by,$$
$$= 50 + 0.6y, \tag{19–1}$$

$$I = I_o - er,$$
$$= 190 - 5r, \tag{19–2}$$

$$G = G_o,$$
$$= 200. \tag{19–3}$$

At this point the notation and justification for equations (19–1) to (19–3) need little explanation. For simplicity, we have assumed no taxes are levied so b(=0.6) equals the marginal propensity to consume national and disposable income. Fiscal policy corresponds with government spending. Panels A and B of Figure 19–1 are identical to figures in Chapter 18. The consumption function graphed in panel A has intercept a(=50) and slope b(=0.60). Adding the fixed government expenditures $G_0$(=200) gives the C + G line. Panel B graphs the investment function I, where its slope is − 1/e. Ignore the dashed curves in all three panels. Assume the rate of interest is $r_1$ percent so investment is $I_1$. Shifting the C + G curve upward by $I_1$, the aggregate expenditure curve C + G + $I_1$ corresponding to rate of interest $r_1$ intersects the 45° line at $y_1$. Point $X_1$ in panel C of Figure 19–1 shows the equilibrium income when the rate of interest is $r_1$ percent. Suppose the rate of interest falls to $r_2$ percent. According to Figure 19–1B firms invest more, shifting the aggregate expenditure curve in Figure 19–1A to C + G + $I_2$. Point $X_2$ in Figure 19–1C shows the equilibrium income, $y_2$, when the rate of interst is $r_2$ percent. Proceeding in this manner for all possible rates of interest, one gets the IS curve in Figure 19–1C. *The IS curve is a downward sloping curve showing all the interest rate-income combinations which equate aggregate expenditures and income.* The IS curve in panel C consolidates the consumption, government, and investment relationships graphed in panels A and B.

Nearly all downward sloping curves are demand curves. Consequently, is the IS curve a demand curve? No, and it is not a supply curve either. *The IS curve is an equilibrium curve.* Equality of aggregate expenditures and income is the equilibrium condition in the commodities market. The IS curve is downward sloping because lower interest rates increase the investment component of aggregate expenditures, and at equilibrium aggregate expenditures equal income.

The IS curve derives its name from the saving-investment approach to income determination. The commodities market is in equilibrium when expenditures equal income or, equivalently, when investment equals saving, hence IS. As stated in appendixes, we think the expenditures-income approach is easier and more insightful.

Figure 19–1C graphs the IS curve. The general algebraic equation for the IS curve and a specific numerical example is

$$
\begin{aligned}
y &= \frac{a + I_0 + G_0}{1 - b} - \frac{er}{1 - b} \\
&= \frac{50 + 190 + 200}{1 - 0.6} - \frac{5r}{1 - 0.6} \\
&= 1{,}100 - 12.5r
\end{aligned}
\tag{19–4}
$$

Wait! How did we get equation (19–4)? What is the IS curve? The IS curve is the commodities market equilibrium curve. Therefore, set the sum of equations (19–1), (19–2), and (19–3), that is, C + I + G or aggregate

**FIGURE 19–1  Construction of the IS curve**
The IS curve is a downward sloping curve showing all the interest rate-income combinations which equate aggregate expenditures and income.

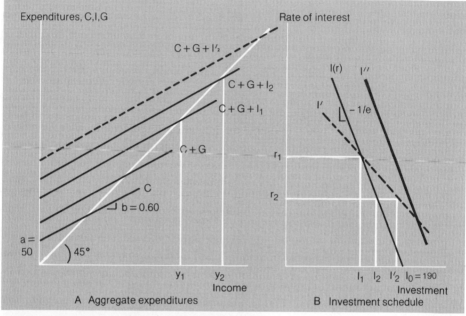

A  Aggregate expenditures

B  Investment schedule

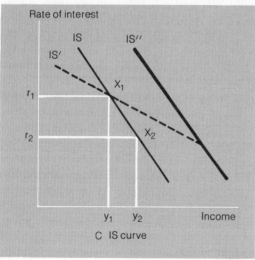

C  IS curve

expenditures, equal to y. Then rearrange and one gets equation (19–4). The term b is the marginal propensity to consume national income and, in this case, the total respending propensity since investment and government spending are assumed to be independent of income. The inverse of $1 - b$ is the familiar multiplier. According to the IS equation (19–4), income is (1) autonomous spending times the multiplier minus (2) the investment curtailed by the rate of interest, er, also multiplied upward. The second component distinguishes the basic and advanced Keynesian models; in the advanced model the equilibrium level of income depends on the rate of interest. In the basic model the IS curve is a vertical line at the unique income level because either the rate of interest and investment are autonomous or investment is totally unresponsive to the rate of interest, that is, the parameter e is zero.

## THE SLOPE OF THE IS CURVE

When the IS curve is flat, small interest rate changes lead to large income changes. What factors determine the slope of the IS curve? The algebraic approach readily yields the answer. Assuming the autonomous components in equation (19–5) are constant, first calculate the income change when the rate of interest changes.

$$\Delta y = \frac{-e\Delta r}{1 - b} \qquad (19\text{–}5)$$

The IS curve plots the rate of interest on the vertical axis and income on the horizontal axis. Therefore, the slope of the IS curve is $\Delta r/\Delta y$, which according to equation (19–5) is

$$\frac{\Delta r}{\Delta y} = \frac{-(1 - b)}{e} \qquad (19\text{–}5')$$

The IS curve is flatter (the absolute value of the slope is smaller) as the marginal propensity to consume national income, b, is larger and the responsiveness of investment to the rate of interest, e, increases. In terms of the curves used to construct the IS curve, the IS curve is flat when (1) the investment schedule is flat (elastic), and (2) the consumption function is steep.

Figure 19–1 aids visualizing the determinants of the IS curve's slope. Consider the interest sensitive, elastic investment schedule illustrated by the dashed line I′ in panel B. Compared with the relatively inelastic investment schedule, a decline in the rate of interest from $r_1$ to $r_2$ causes a greater increase in investment ($I'_2$ instead of $I_2$) and a larger upward shift in aggregate expenditures ($C + G + I'_2$ instead $C + G + I_2$). The same interest rate decline causes a larger income increase when investment is interest elastic. The flat investment curve in panel B generates the flat IS curve in panel C. For any *given* upward shift of an expenditure curve in panel A, the slope of the curve determines the magnitude of the income increase. Imagine a steeper aggregate expenditure curve because the marginal propensity to consume is larger. In this case a given upward shift of expenditures will intersect the 45° line farther out, and the IS curve is flatter.

The economic rationale for these algebraic and graphical results follows quite readily. The IS curve shows all the interest rate-income points where aggregate demand equals income. When the investment component of aggregate demand is responsive to the rate of interest, then small interest rate changes lead to large expenditure and income changes and a flat IS curve, other things being equal. The last explanation implicitly considered the income change necessary to maintain equilibrium when the rate of interest changes. Now consider the opposite situation. An increase in income produces an excess supply in the commodities market because the marginal propensity to consume is less than unity. The larger is the MPC, the smaller is the excess supply. Consequently, a small decline in the rate of interest is sufficient, other things being equal, to eliminate the excess supply of commodities when the MPC is large. Perhaps more simply, the IS curve tends to be flat when the MPC is high because the income multiplier of any interest rate induced aggregate expenditure change is large.

## SHIFTING THE IS CURVE

Do changes in the rate of interest or income shift the IS curve? No! Look at Figure 19–1C again, which graphs the IS curve. What variables are on the axes? The rate of interest and income. Therefore, changes in these variables cause the economy to move *along* an IS curve but do not shift the IS curve.

The IS curve summarizes much information. It incorporates the C, I, and G curves. Any shift in these underlying curves causes the IS curve to shift. The solid IS curve in Figure 19–1C corresponds with the solid investment line in Figure 19–1B. Now assume investment increases; a technological breakthrough or heightened expectations cause firms to invest more at every rate of interest. The dotted I″ line in Figure 19–1B represents the new investment relationship. At every rate of interest a larger amount would be added to C + G in Figure 19–1A, so the C + G + I total expenditure curve intersects the 45° line at a higher point. The dotted investment line gives the dotted IS″ line. Clearly, either consumption or government spending shifts have the same effect on the total expenditure curve as the investment shift. *Increases in autonomous consumption, investment, or government spending shift the IS curve upward and rightward.* Although not shown graphically the converse is true. Less investment or government spending shifts the IS curve downward and leftward. Going beyond graphics, the economic rationale for the IS shift readily follows from its definition. The IS curve shows all the interest rate-income combinations where income equals aggregate demand. When the latter increases at every rate of interest, the equality will be maintained only if income rises—the IS curve shifts rightward. One could equally well view the curve shifting upward. At every income level, the rate of interest must be higher in order to keep demand constant in spite of a heightened investment outlook—the IS curve shifts upward.

The basic Keynesian model assumes that either aggregate demand is independent of the rate of interest or the rate of interest is constant. Assuming the rate of interest is constant so $\Delta r = 0$, the first difference form of the IS equation (19–4) is $\Delta y/\Delta I_0 = \Delta y/\Delta G_0 = 1/(1 - b)$, which is precisely the basic Keynesian multiplier when taxes are ignored. In terms of the graph, horizontal shifts of the IS curve hold the rate of interest constant. *The magnitude of the horizontal shift of the IS curve equals the autonomous spending change times the basic Keynesian multiplier.* In other words, the horizontal shift of the IS curve per unit change in autonomous spending equals the basic multiplier. For example, assume investment is $1 more at every rate of interest. The IS curve shifts rightward and income increases by the multiplier because of induced spending. Of course, the rate of interest need not, and typically does not, remain constant, in which case the income change is different than the multiplier. The importance of these rate of interest indirect effects which divide Keynesian and monetarists will be studied in detail later.

Fiscal policy shifts the IS curve. More (less) government spending shifts the IS curve rightward (leftward). How does monetary policy affect the IS curve? Monetary policy has no effect on the IS curve; that is, monetary policy does not shift the IS curve because spending here does not depend *directly* on the quantity of money. Again, look at the equation for the IS curve, (19–4). The quantity of money does not appear anywhere. Autonomous consumption, investment, and government expenditures are included in equation (19–4) and changes in these variables shift the IS curve. Since money does not appear in equation (19–4), changes in the quantity of money do not shift the IS curve. Monetary policy determines the rate of interest and, therefore, which point on the IS curve the economy finally attains.

## POINTS OFF THE IS CURVE

Could the economy ever be at point A, which is off the IS curve in Figure 19–2? If you recall the definition of the IS curve, the correct answer is obvious. The IS curve is the commodities market equilibrium line; it shows all the interest rate and income combinations where aggregate expenditures equal income. Therefore, the previous question asks: Could the commodities market ever be out of equilibrium? Phrased this way, the answer is clearly yes. Indeed, disequilibrium points such as point

### FIGURE 19–2   The IS curve aids forecasting income

The IS curve divides interest rate-income combinations into those where income will be rising and those where income will be falling. Arrows indicate direction of income change.

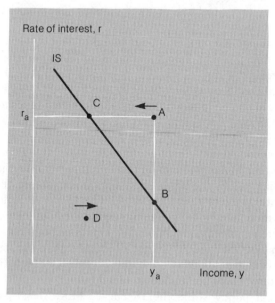

A are the rule, at least in the Keynesian short run. Income typically is changing so that, by definition, it is not in equilibrium, and the economy is off the IS curve. The points on the IS curve in Figure 19–2 are far fewer than the points off the curve.

If the economy is rarely on the IS curve, why have we spent so much time describing it? All equilibria like the IS curve are guides to successful forecasting, which sometimes decides the fate of governments and private fortunes.[1] Most people know the current state of the economy. The important issue is: How will the economy behave in the future? To predict future changes we must compare the current situation relative to the equilibrium alternatives given by the IS curve. The IS curve is important because it divides the interest rate-income combinations where income will be rising from those where income will be falling. Suppose the economy is at point A in Figure 19–2 so income is $y_a$. Is an expansion or contraction likely? Although we cannot determine the final equilibrium at the moment, we know income will be falling. The vertical line through point A intersects the IS curve at point B so, by definition, income is the

---

[1] We are implicitly assuming the system is stable, a reasonable assumption in a highly aggregated model.

same at points A and B, and the rate of interest is higher at point A. At point B on the IS line aggregate demand equals income. Since the rate of interest is higher at point A than point B, expenditures must be less than income, and income will be falling as shown by the horizontal arrow. (Income is on the horizontal axis.)

This time let us compare points A and C. By construction, the rate of interest is the same at points A and C, and income is lower at point C. At point C on the IS curve expenditures equal income. Investment plus government expenditures are the same at point A and C since the rate of interest is the same. However, a marginal propensity to consume less than unity implies expenditures are less at A than C. Therefore, income exceeds aggregate expenditures. At point A unintended inventory accumulation occurs, and output falls. The horizontal arrow indicating income variations points leftward. Point A is one arbitrary point. The identical analysis is applicable to any other point above and to the right of the IS curve. *For any interest rate-income combination above and to the right of the IS curve, income will be falling.* Applying the same type of argument, the reader should verify that *for any interest rate-income combination below and to the left of the IS curve, income will be rising.* The horizontal arrow at point D faces rightward. *Of course, when the economy is on the IS line, income is constant, a requirement for equilibrium.* The IS line, the product market equilibrium line, cannot be used to predict the behavior of interest rates; it solely predicts product and income changes.

## THE LM CURVE

Although we discussed everything anyone wanted to know about IS but was afraid to ask, the interest rate-income point toward which the economy gravitates is still unknown. All is not lost. Economists are excellent matchmakers: a downward-sloping curve is invariably united with an upward-sloping curve to produce a unique point. Not wishing to break tradition, it is time we introduce the LM curve, the money market equilibrium curve which yields another relationship between income and the rate of interest. Equations (19–6) to (19–8) give algebraic and numerical money market equations.

$$M^S = M_0 = 300 \qquad \text{supply} \qquad (19\text{–}6)$$

$$\frac{M^D}{P_0} = k'y + h - jr \qquad \text{demand} \qquad (19\text{–}7)$$
$$M^D = 0.2y + 116 - 2r$$

$$\frac{M_0}{P_0} = k'y + h - jr, \text{ or,} \qquad \text{equilibrium} \qquad (19\text{–}8)$$
$$r = \frac{h - (M_0/P_0) + k'y}{j}$$
$$= -92 + 0.1\,y$$

Briefly recapping these equations which were introduced in Chapter 18, equation (19–6) assumes the money supply is totally exogenous, an assumption that will be dropped later. Total money demand, equation (19–7), has two components, transactions, k'y, and speculative, h − jr. In the numerical example the price level is set at unity. Setting supply equal to demand gives the money market equilibrium equation (19–8), called the LM equation because money demand originally was written as L (for liquidity) instead of $M^D$.

The demand and supply equations are graphed in Figure 19–3A. The solid vertical line is the money supply. The slope of any liquidity preference curve is −1/j. Its position depends on the level of income. Higher incomes increase the amount of money demand for transactions purposes and shift the liquidity preference curve rightward. The extent of the rightward shift depends positively on k'. Inspection of Figure 19–3A shows that as income increases the rate of interest which equilibrates the money market rises. The solid LM curve in Figure 19–3B graphs the money market equilibrium relationship, given the solid vertical supply. *The LM curve is an upward-sloping curve containing all the income and interest rate combinations that equate money demand and a given money supply.* It is upward sloping because as income increases, the amount of money demanded for transactions increases. In order to maintain equilibrium in the money market, the amount demanded for speculative purposes must fall. This happens when the rate of interest rises.

### Slope of the LM curve

Our lengthy discussion of IS should have given us insights about the factors influencing the slope and position of the LM curve and the changes that occur when the economy is off the LM curve. Although IS and LM are not related economically, they are analytically similar. The second line of equation (19–8) writes the LM relation in a manner which readily yields its slope, $\Delta r/\Delta y$. Differencing equation (19–8)

$$\Delta r/\Delta y = k'/j. \qquad (19\text{–}8')$$

Equation (19–8') states that the slope of the LM curve depends positively on the transactions coefficient k' and negatively on the interest rate coefficient j. In other words, the LM curve is steep when k' is large and j is small. When speculative money demand is relatively unresponsive to the rate of interest and the liquidity preference curve is steep, that is, its slope, −1/j, is large, then the LM also is steep.

What is the economic rationale for equation (19–8')? The LM curve is the money market equilibrium curve. As we move up the LM curve the amount of money demanded for transactions purposes increases and the amount demanded for speculative purposes decreases so the sum of the two equals the fixed money supply. When k' is large so that any given

**FIGURE 19–3 Construction of the LM curve**
The LM curve is an upward sloping curve showing all the interest
rate-income combinations which equate money demand
and supply.

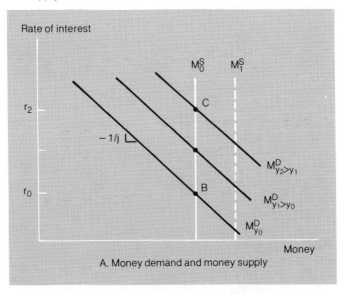

A. Money demand and money supply

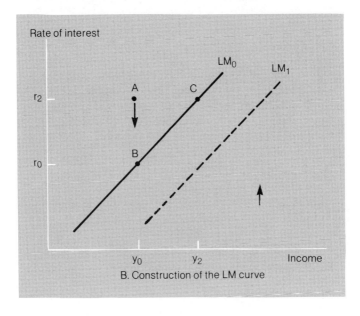

B. Construction of the LM curve

income increase causes a large increase in the amount of money demanded for transactions purposes, then, *ceteris paribus,* the rate of interest will have to rise significantly to produce a large decrease in the amount demanded for speculative purposes. *The LM curve is steep (flat) when k' is large (small).* When the liquidity preference curve is relatively steep so that a higher rate of interest causes only a small reduction in the amount demanded for speculative purposes, then *ceteris paribus,* a small increase in income and transactions demand will equilibrate the money market. *The LM curve is steep (flat) when the liquidity preference curve is steep (flat).*

### Shifting the LM curve

The axes of the LM curve like the IS curve measure income and the rate of interest. If either of these variables changes the economy moves along the LM curve, which does not shift. The LM curve shifts when the underlying curves, money supply and money demand, shift. For example, assume a larger money supply represented by the broken vertical line in Figure 19–3A while the solid demand curve remains fixed. The graph readily shows that for any given income and liquidity preference curve, a lower rate of interest equates money demand and supply. The larger money supply gives the dashed LM curve. *Monetary expansion shifts the LM curve downward and rightward. The converse is true: monetary contraction shifts the LM curve upward and leftward.* At this point we should no longer need graphical aids for the converse case and can proceed directly to the economic rationale. The LM curve is the money market equilibrium curve. When the money supply is curtailed, less must be demanded if equilibrium again recurs. Given any income level (horizontal coordinate) and transactions demand, the equilibrium amount demanded for speculative purposes must fall, which occurs when the interest rate rises. The LM curve shifts upward. We can also view monetary contraction as shifting the LM curve leftward. Given any interest rate (vertical coordinate) and speculative demand, the equilibrium amount demanded for transactions purposes must fall, which occurs when income decreases.

According to ordinary supply and demand, equal but opposite shifts have the same effect on price. For example, an increase in demand has the same effect on price as an equal decrease in supply. The analog of price in the LM analysis is an income-interest rate combination. *A reduction in money demand has the same effect on the LM curve as monetary expansion. A decrease (increase) in money demand shifts the LM downward (upward) and rightward (leftward).* While not illustrated in Figure 19–4A in order to prevent excessive clutter, visualize each liquidity preference curve shifting leftward the same distance the money supply was shifted rightward. The new demand curves and initial (solid) money supply also produce the dashed LM curve. When money demand falls, lower interest rates, which increase the amount demanded for speculative purposes, or a higher level of income, which increases the amount demanded for transactions purposes, is necessary if the amount demanded again equals the constant money supply.

### Points off the LM curve

Could the observed rate of interest and income correspond to a point off the LM curve? Could demand not equal the supply of money? The questions are identical, and the answer is yes. Suppose the economy is at point A in Figure 19–3B while, given money demand and supply, the solid LM curve is appropriate. What will happen to income and the rate of interest? Since we do not know the position of A relative to the unspecified IS curve, we cannot tell how income will be changing. We can safely predict that the rate of interest will fall. Why? A vertical line connects points A and B on the solid LM curve. At point B the money supply just satisfied the transactions and speculative demand. By construction, income and the transactions demand for money are equal at points A and B. The rate of interest is higher, and the amount of speculative demand is lower, at point A than at B. Since money demand and supply are equal at point B on the LM curve, money demand is less than supply at point A. There is an excess supply of money. In the Keynesian analysis the excess supply of money is used to buy bonds or, equivalently, make loans. The rate of interest falls. Indeed, the lower rate of interest eventually induces households to demand the temporarily excessive money supply.

The problem may also be analyzed by comparing points A and C, which is the point on the LM curve horizontal to A. Income and the transactions demand for money are less at point A than C. Therefore, larger speculative balances are available at A. By construction, the rate of interest and amount of money demanded for speculative purposes are identical at A and C. The amount of money available for speculative purposes at A exceeds the amount demanded. Households attempt to rid themselves of the temporarily excessive money balances by buying bonds, which drives the rate of interest down. Point A is an arbitrary point. The same argument is valid for any other point above and to the left of the LM line. *All income-interest rate combinations above and to the left of the LM line represent situations where the demand for money is less than the supply, and the rate of interest falls.* The reader should be able to explain why the converse is true. *All income-interest rate combinations below and to the right of the LM line represent situations where the demand for money exceeds supply, and the rate of interest rises. Once on the LM line there is no tendency for the rate of interest to change because the demand and supply of money are equal.* The vertical arrows in Figure 19–3B indicate the direction of interest rate (vertical axis) changes.

## IS AND LM: GENERAL EQUILIBRIUM

The IS curve is the commodities market equilibrium curve. Given the appropriate interest rate, expenditures can equal virtually every level of income. The LM curve is the money market equilibrium curve. The demand and supply of money are equal at virtually every interest rate, given the appropriate income level. The intersection of the IS and LM curves in Figure 19–4 represents general equilibrium. A unique interest rate and

FIGURE 19–4   IS and LM: General equilibrium

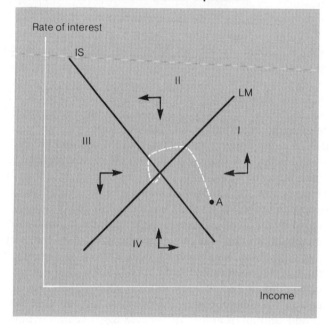

income equates both aggregate demand and income and the demand and supply of money. The algebraic and numerical solutions for the general equilibrium income and rate of interest are found in the appendix.

Since the economy rarely is at equilibrium, one should analyze the adjustment process or sequence of events leading toward equilibrium. The adjustments that occur when the economy is out of equilibrium are summarized by the arrows in Figure 19–4. The intersection of the IS and LM curves forms four quadrants, labelled I, II, III, and IV in Figure 19–4. Quadrant I is upward and rightward of the IS curve and simultaneously downward and rightward of the LM curve. Recalling the previous discussion and Figures 19–2 and 19–3B, in quadrant I income exceeds aggregate demand and the demand for money is greater than the supply. Therefore, income falls (the horizontal arrow points left), and the rate of interest rises (the vertical arrow points up). Similar reasoning applied to the other three quadrants gives the counterclockwise pattern of arrows in Figure 19–4. (The reader is strongly urged to pause and explain the direction of the arrows in quadrants II to IV.) Rotating the arrows counterclockwise 90° gives the arrows in the next quadrant. A final helpful if abhorrent reminder of the pattern formed by the arrows—linking the arrows forms a reverse swastika.

Suppose we are temporarily at point A in Figure 19–4. The dotted curve is one possible equilibrium adjustment path which conforms with the pattern of the arrows. The theory does not specify the precise adjustment path. We could move directly and rapidly from A to the equilibrium without circling it. Alternatively, the adjustment process could be represented by a series of vertical and horizontal lines which form a cobweb pattern. That is, the rate of interest and income might change sequentially instead of simultaneously. While subsequent sections generally assume such a path because of the pedagogical convenience of allowing only one variable to change at a time, the adjustment path illustrated here is more realistic. About point A the rising interest rate is simultaneously reducing the excess demand for money and investment, which causes income to fall. Equilibrium is the center of a vortex.[2] At least one of the variables always adjusts toward equilibrium, and sometimes both variables move toward equilibrium. For example, at every point in quadrant I income is approaching its equilibrium value. The rate of interest is adjusting toward equilibrium 50 percent of the time because half the points in quadrant I are below the equilibrium rate of interest. However, 50 percent of the points in quadrant I are above the equilibrium rate of interest yet interest rates continue to rise. The dotted curve illustrates the possibility of overshooting. Income at A is too high but falls more than ultimately necessary. The illustrated adjustment path passes through quadrant III, where income is below the equilibrium. The more or less rhythmical short-run income fluctuations which characterize industrial economies may be the result of overshooting during the adjustment process instead of continually shifting equilibria.

## MONETARY POLICY: THE MONEY MULTIPLIER

Suppose equilibrium income is below full-employment income as Keynes assumed to be the typical case. The Fed correctly increases the quantity of money. What are the effects of the monetary expansion? The rate of interest falls, which stimulates demand and output. This is illustrated in Figure 19–5, where you are asked to temporarily ignore the dashed IS curve. Monetary expansion shifts the LM rightward but has no

---

[2] Those who enjoy games can draw the IS–LM curves so that the economy is unstable and equilibrium acts as a center of centrifugal force. While such games may be fun, they do not help us understand our economy.

**FIGURE 19-5   Monetary expansion shifts the LM curve rightward**
Monetary expansion increases income and lowers the rate of interest. Income increases more when the IS curve is elastic (flat).

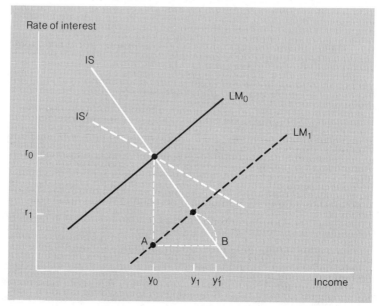

effect on the solid IS curve since aggregate expenditures do not depend *directly* on the quantity of money. The rate of interest falls from $r_0$ to $r_1$ and income rises from $y_0$ to $y_1$.

The size of the money multiplier, which henceforth is defined as the ratio of the income change to the money change, that is, $\Delta y/\Delta M$, is one of the most important and controversial issues in monetary macroeconomics.[3] Indeed, the effectiveness of monetary policy sometimes is measured solely by the size of the money multiplier, something empirical economists have been unable to pin down closely. Before considering other criteria of policy effectiveness equally or more important than the size of the multiplier and before presenting the empirical results, let us analyze the determinants of the money multiplier. What conditions must exist for the multiplier to be large? When is the multiplier small? The answers to these questions proceed directly from the adjustment process or sequence of events which follows monetary expansion. Therefore, reconsider the sequence of events outlined in the previous chapter and summarized in Table 19-1. The adjustment path represented by dots in the IS–LM Figure 19-6 is consistent with Table 19-1. The economy initially at point $(r_0,y_0)$ is "shocked" by monetary expansion. The LM curve shifts downward and the new equilibrium is $(r_1,y_1)$. Monetary policy

---

[3] Do not confuse this multiplier with the money *supply* multiplier analyzed in Chapters 3 and 4. The two multipliers are not related in any way.

**TABLE 19-1  Adjustment process or sequence of events following monetary expansion. Signs are reversed for monetary contraction.**

1. $+ \Delta M^S \rightarrow - - \Delta r$
   Monetary expansion first lowers the rate of interest enough to induce society to demand the larger money supply.

2. $- - \Delta \rightarrow + + \Delta I$
   After some lag the lower rate of interest stimulates investment.

3. $+ + \Delta I \rightarrow + \Delta y \rightarrow + \Delta C \rightarrow + + \Delta y$
   The larger investment demand leads to increased production and income, which in turn induces consumption and more income.

4. $+ + \Delta y \rightarrow + \Delta M_T^D \rightarrow - \Delta M_A^D \rightarrow + \Delta r \rightarrow - \Delta I$
   The larger income increases the amount of money demanded for transactions purposes. To maintain equilibrium, the amount demanded for speculative purposes, $M_A^D$, must fall, which occurs when the rate of interest rebounds upward from its very depressed level. The partial recovery of the rate of interest curtails somewhat the investment and income boom.

Final result:           $+ \Delta M^S \rightarrow - \Delta r$
                                    $+ \Delta y$

does not shift the IS curve. The initial equilibrium point is on the old and new IS curve so there is no immediate tendency for income to increase. However, point $(r_0, y_0)$ is upward and leftward of the now relevant LM' curve so the rate of interest falls—step 1 in Table 19-1. Assuming adjustment in the money market is complete before the commodities market reacts, we move down vertically to point A. The lower interest rate transfers the entire monetary expansion into speculative balances. Point A is off the IS curve, however. Aggregate expenditures exceed output because the rate of interest is too low. The swollen demand for investment goods causes firms to hire more workers, who then consume more. The movement from points A to B captures steps 2 and 3 in Table 19-1. The economy is now on the IS curve but off the LM curve. Higher income and output increase the amount demanded for transactions purposes. Without further expansion of the money supply, the larger transactions component must be associated at equilibrium with a reduced speculative component. The rate of interest rebounds upward and reduces the amount demanded for speculative purpose. While we could assume the economy proceeds vertically from B to the LM curve, a truncated adjustment process is sufficient for our purposes of understanding the determinants of the multiplier. The higher rate of interest reduces somewhat the investment boom. The economy moves from point B to $(r_1, y_1)$ because we now assume the commodities and money markets adjust simultaneously.

The money multiplier has four determinants. Table 19-2 shows the determinant that influences the changes at each step of the adjustment process outlined in Table 19-1. Follow the adjustment process. The rate of interest must fall so money demand equals supply. What graph has money on one axis and the rate of interest on the other? Liquidity prefer-

TABLE 19–2 **Determinants of the money multiplier, $\Delta y/\Delta M$.**
**The money multiplier tends to be large when the following**
**conditions hold.**

1. Liquidity preference is inelastic (steep), so
   $+ \Delta M^S \rightarrow$ large $- - \Delta r$
2. Investment schedule is elastic (flat), so
   $- - \Delta r \rightarrow$ large $+ + \Delta I$
3. Marginal propensity to consume is large so,
   $+ + \Delta I \rightarrow + \Delta y \rightarrow$ large $+ \Delta C \rightarrow$ large $+ + \Delta y$
4. Transactions demand coefficient is small so
   $+ \Delta y \rightarrow$ small $+ \Delta M_T^D \rightarrow$ small $- \Delta M_A^D \rightarrow$ small $+ \Delta r \rightarrow$ small $- \Delta I$.

ence. What determines how much the rate of interest must fall? The slope
of the liquidity preference curve. When liquidity preference is *not* responsive to the rate of interest and its slope $(-1/j)$ is absolutely large and steep,
then the rate of interest falls substantially and, *ceteris paribus*, the monetary expansion causes a large increase in spending and income. How
sensitive is spending to the rate of interest? The more responsive is investment to the lower interest rate (e is large) and the flatter and absolutely
smaller is its slope $(-1/e)$, then, *ceteris paribus*, the larger is the increase in
investment and income. Consumption responds to income. *Ceteris paribus*,
the higher is the marginal propensity to consume, the more spending is
induced and the higher is income. Finally, the larger income increases the
amount of money demanded for transactions purposes, which tends to
raise the rate of interest and have a negative feedback effect on income. A
small transactions coefficient k′ reduces the negative feedback effect and
increases the money multiplier. When k′ and the amount of money demanded for transactions purposes is small, then, *ceteris paribus*, a larger
amount is available for speculative purposes, the interest rate is lower,
and income is larger.

How is the information presented in Table 19–2 illustrated graphically
in terms of the IS–LM curves? Look at Figure 19–5, which illustrates IS
curves with different slopes. Monetary policy shifts the LM curve and the
economy slides along an IS curve. Clearly, *the money multiplier is larger
when the IS curve is flat.* For the steep IS curve the new equilibrium is $y_1$,
which is less than $y_1'$, the equilibrium for the flat IS curve. When is the IS
curve flat? An entire section was devoted to this question precisely because the money multiplier depends heavily on the slope of the IS curve.
The IS curve is flat when the investment schedule is flat (elastic) and when
the marginal propensity to consume is large.

### Liquidity preference, LM curves, and the money multiplier

Illustrating with IS and LM curves the relationship between the elasticity of the liquidity preference curve and the money multiplier is somewhat

more difficult. Indeed, it is sufficiently difficult to be a good test of mastery of IS–LM. Assume two economies, A and B, which are alike in every respect except for the liquidity preference relationship illustrated in Figure 19–6A. Money demand is less responsive to the rate of interest in economy A. What shapes do the IS and LM curves take in economies A

**FIGURE 19–6  The money multiplier increases when liquidity preference becomes inelastic (steep)**

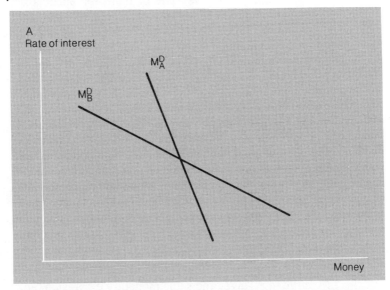

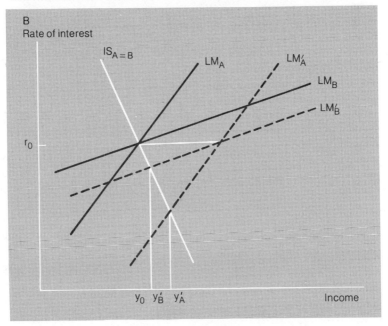

and B, and how do they respond to monetary changes? The answers are illustrated in Figure 19–6B. Since economies A and B are assumed identical in every respect except for the liquidity preference curve, the IS curves for the two economies coincide because, by assumption, the aggregate expenditure curve is identical. The LM curves, which summarize money demand and supply relationship, do not coincide. Recalling our earlier discussion, the slope of the LM curve partially reflects the slope of the liquidity preference schedule. The demand for speculative money balances is quite responsive to the rate of interest in economy B and its LM curve is quite flat. Along an LM curve larger speculative balances are associated with smaller transactions balances because total money demand is fixed and equals the *given* money supply. In economy B any given increase in the rate of interest (vertical axis) causes a large reduction in the speculative demand, so income (horizontal axis) must increase significantly to generate a large compensatory change in transactions demand. The significant increase of the variable on the horizontal axis for a given change of the variable on the vertical axis implies the curve is flat. The speculative demand and LM curves are inelastic in economy A. Assuming the unique IS curve intersects the two LM curves at their common point, the initial equilibrium income and rate of interest, $y_0$ and $r_0$, are the same in the two economies.

Let output be less than full employment. The monetary authorities in both economies respond by increasing the quantity of money by the same amount. The shift of the LM curve in economy B is illustrated by $LM'_B$ in Figure 19–6B. Income in B increases to $y'_B$. What is the new position of the LM curve in A, given the same monetary expansion, and where will it intersect IS? The almost universal immediate response says the LM curve in A shifts downward and intersects the IS at the same point, $y'_B$. Incomes in both economies were equal and increase equally. If this was your immediate reaction, check yourself. Why was Figure 19–6 constructed? We are trying to show graphically that the money multiplier depends on the slope of the liquidity preference schedule. The new LM curve in A does not intersect the IS curve at $y'_B$; if it did, the money multiplier would *not* depend on the slope of the liquidity preference schedule.

When economies differ only in the responsiveness of money demand to the rate of interest, then monetary expansion shifts the LM curves by the same *horizontal* distance, as illustrated in Figure 19–6B. Why does monetary expansion shift the LM curves by the same horizontal distance in this case? Given any monetary expansion, the total amount of money demanded must increase when the economy reaches a new equilibrium. The increase could occur because only transactions demand, only speculative demand, or some combination of the two components increases. Algebraically,

$$\Delta M^S = \Delta M_T^D + \Delta M_A^D,$$

where the terms are as previously defined. Consider our economy's demand for money at two points along a horizontal line. By virtue of being along a horizontal line where the rate of interest is constant, the speculative demand at the two points is identical, that is, $\Delta M_A^D = 0$. The transactions demand differs, however. Given any horizontal distance (income difference) between the points, the magnitude of the transactions demand difference depends on the transactions coefficient $k'$. In our economies A and B the transactions coefficients are identical; by assumption, only the slope of the liquidity preference differs. Therefore, the same horizontal distance produces the same change in money demand. Because income is on the horizontal axis and has the same effect on money demand in our two economies, the LM curves shift by the same horizontal distance. Looking at Figure 19–6B, *the money multiplier is large when speculative money demand and, thereby, the LM curve are steep.*

The careful reader recalls that the slope of the LM also depends on the transactions coefficient $k'$. In particular, the LM curve is flat (steep) when $k'$ is small (large), *ceteris paribus*. Transactions demand is $k'y$. When $k'$ is small, income must change significantly in order to produce the change in transactions demand which compensates for changes in speculative demand and the rate of interest. According to Table 19–2, the money multiplier is large when $k'$ is small. Therefore, *the money multiplier is large when the LM curve is flat due to a small transactions coefficient.* We reserve for Appendix A the graphical demonstration of the relationship between the money multiplier and transactions coefficient. The last two italicized sentences imply that *there is no consistent relationship between the slope of the LM curve and the money multiplier.* The money multiplier is large when the LM is (1) steep due to an inelastic speculative money demand or (2) flat due to a small transactions demand coefficient. The money multiplier is small when the LM curve is steep due to a large transactions demand coefficient. One has to know why the LM is steep before one can state whether the multiplier will be large or small.

## FISCAL POLICY: THE MULTIPLIER

In general, fiscal and monetary policy are alternative means of controlling aggregate output. Assuming current output is below maximum potential output, the government can stimulate the economy by spending more and financing the resultant deficit by bond sales. Figure 19–7 illustrates the effects of fiscal policy. Additional government spending shifts the IS curve rightward, as indicated earlier, but has no effect on the LM curve because the underlying money demand and supply curves do not depend directly on government spending. Assume the steep LM is appropriate; the flat curve will be shortly explored. The final result is a higher income and rate of interest.

The size of the fiscal multiplier is no less important and controversial

**FIGURE 19-7  Government spending shifts the IS curve rightward**
Additional government expenditures increases income and the rate of interest. Income increases more when the LM curve is elastic (flat).

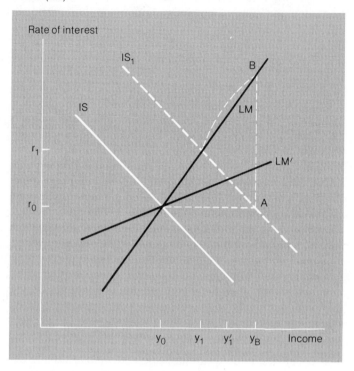

than the money multiplier. After our careful analysis of the determinants of the money multiplier, the reader should be able to ascertain relatively quickly the economic rationale for the determinants of the government spending multiplier. The determinants follow directly from the adjustment process or sequence of events generated by additional government expenditures, which was outlined in the last chapter and summarized in Table 19-3. The dotted curve in Figure 19-7 is a graphical representation of the adjustment path consistent with Table 19-3. The movement from the initial equilibrium point $(y_0, r_0)$ to point A in Figure 19-7 illustrates line 1 in Table 19-3. In response to the larger government demand, firms hire more workers and incomes rise. The newly hired workers consume more and incomes rise further. Point A is on the IS' curve but off the LM curve. More money is demanded to finance the larger volume of transactions. Money market equilibrium is restored by a reduction in speculative balances achieved by higher interest rates due to the government bond sales financing the deficit. Step 2 and 3 in Table 19-3 are illustrated by the

**TABLE 19-3 Adjustment process or sequence of events following additional government expenditures. Signs are reversed for fiscal contraction.**

1. $+ \Delta G \rightarrow + \Delta y \rightarrow + \Delta C \rightarrow + + \Delta y$
   Firms hire workers to satisfy the government's demand, and these workers consume more, causing additional production and income.
2. $+ + \Delta y \rightarrow + \Delta M_T^D$
   Higher incomes increase the amount of money demanded for transactions purposes.
3. $+ \Delta M_T^D \rightarrow - \Delta M_A^D \rightarrow + \Delta r$
   Given a fixed money supply, a larger transactions demand means less money is available for speculative purposes, and the rate of interest rises.
4. $+ \Delta r \rightarrow - \Delta I$
   The higher rate of interest chokes off some investment.

Final result: $+ \Delta G \rightarrow + \Delta r$
$+ \Delta y$

movement from A to B on the assumed relevant LM curve. The higher interest rates reduce the amount invested and income falls. While so far we have been assuming adjustment in one market is complete before the other market adjusts, that is, the adjustment path is perfectly horizontal or vertical, we now relax the assumption and have both markets adjust simultaneously so the economy proceeds directly from B to the new general equilibrium point $(y_1, r_1)$.

When will the government spending multiplier be large? Look at Table 19–4 in conjunction with Table 19–3. The workers producing airplanes or

**TABLE 19-4 Determinants of the government expenditures multiplier, $\Delta y / \Delta G$. The government expenditures multiplier tends to be large when the following conditions hold.**

1. Marginal propensity to consume is large so,
   $+ \Delta G \rightarrow + \Delta y \rightarrow$ large $+ \Delta C \rightarrow$ large $+ + \Delta y$
2. Transactions demand coefficient is small so,
   $+ \Delta y \rightarrow$ small $+ \Delta M_T^D$
3. Liquidity preference is elastic (flat) so,
   $+ \Delta M_T^D \rightarrow - \Delta M_A^D \rightarrow$ small $+ \Delta r$
4. Investment schedule is inelastic (steep) so,
   $+ \Delta r \rightarrow$ small $- \Delta I$

other goods demanded by the government now earn an income and consume more. A high marginal propensity to consume induces more demand and higher income. The amount of money demanded for transactions purposes increases. Given a fixed money supply, the amount demanded for speculative purposes falls, interest rates rise, investment falls, and income is curtailed somewhat. The ultimate investment downturn is less and the fiscal multiplier is larger, *ceteris paribus,* when the transactions coefficient k′ is small so only modestly more transactions balances and modestly less speculative balances are necessary. The interest rate rise necessary to produce any given decline in speculative balances depends on the slope of the liquidity preference schedule. Interest rates rise less and the fiscal multiplier is larger when liquidity preference is elastic. How sensitive is investment to the rate of interest? This is measured by the elasticity of the investment schedule. While the investment schedule is highly inelastic, the negative impact on investment is small and the fiscal multiplier is large, *ceteris paribus.*

### Fiscal policy and the LM curve

The effect of some of the determinants of the government expenditures multiplier are illustrated graphically in Figure 19–7. Since government expenditures shift the IS curve but not the LM curve, it is immediately obvious that the fiscal multiplier is large when the LM curve is flat. In Figure 19–7 income rises to $y'_1(>y_1)$ when the LM is relatively flat. Recalling our earlier discussion, the LM curve is relatively flat when the transactions coefficient is small and the liquidity preference curve is flat. In this case larger incomes—on the horizontal axis—necessitate little additional transactions money balances, and the equal reduction is speculative money balances, given the fixed money supply, is achieved by marginally higher interest rates—on the vertical axis—when the liquidity preference curve is flat. The relationship between the fiscal multiplier and its other two determinants, the marginal propensity to consume and slope of the investment, is considerably more difficult to illustrate graphically and, therefore, is reserved for Appendix A. The difficulty occurs because these multiplier determinants simultaneously affect the shape and magnitude of the shift of the IS curve. A heuristic explanation should be satisfactory at this point. Income is on the axis of the IS–LM graph; consumption is the spending component dependent on income. This causes the magnitude of the horizontal shift of the IS curve to depend positively on the marginal propensity to consume. Clearly, the larger is the marginal propensity to consume and the horizontal shift of the IS curve, the larger is the income increase and fiscal multiplier.

The advanced Keynesian, IS–LM, fiscal multiplier is smaller than the basic Keynesian multiplier. The basic Keynesian model ignores monetary repercussions on investment. In terms of Table 19–3, the adjustments process stops at step 1 as the rate of interest is implicitly held fixed. In the basic model the multiplier equals the horizontal shift of the IS curve since along a horizontal line the rate of interest is held constant. In the advanced model the higher interest rates reduce investment and the multiplier. Assuming the steep LM curve is appropriate so equilibrium income is $y_1$, the distance $y_B - y_1$ in Figure 19–7 measures the so-called *"crowding out" effect, the offsetting reduction in private spending and income that follows expansionary fiscal policy due to money market repercussions and higher interest rates.* The sale of government bonds to finance government expenditures reduces the funds available to private firms. As drawn in Figure 19–7, the direct effect of government expenditures does not crowd out an equal amount of private spending so, on balance, government spending still has a positive effect on income.

## MONETARISTS AND KEYNESIANS ON THE SLOPES OF THE INVESTMENT AND LIQUIDITY PREFERENCE CURVES AND THE SIZE OF THE MONEY AND GOVERNMENT EXPENDITURE MULTIPLIERS

Table 19–5 summarizes Tables 19–2 and 19–4. It indicates the relationship between monetary and fiscal multipliers and their determinants. Both

**TABLE 19–5  Relationship between multipliers and their determinants**

|  | Size of money multiplier | Size of government spending multiplier |
|---|---|---|
| Investment schedule |  |  |
| Elastic | Large | Small |
| Inelastic | Small | Large |
|  | Monetarist | |
|  | Keynesian | |
| Liquidity preference |  |  |
| Elastic | Small | Large |
| Inelastic | Large | Small |
| Large MPC | Large | Large |
| Small transactions coefficient | Large | Large |

multipliers are positively related to the marginal propensity to consume and negatively related to the money transactions coefficient. Perhaps because these two determinants have the same general effect on both multipliers, empirical estimates of the marginal propensity to consume and the money transactions coefficient are not that controversial. Let us concentrate on the two controversial determinants, the elasticities of the investment and liquidity preference schedules. Monetarists, like their classical predecessors, claim the investment schedule is relatively elastic and the liquidity preference schedule is inelastic, if it exists at all. Although monetarists emphasize the long run where demand affects prices but not output, they accept the Keynesian proposition that output responds to demand in the short run. Monetarists' beliefs about the elasticities have prompted them to allege, as Table 19–5 indicates, that the money multiplier is large and the government spending multiplier is small. This is one of the major tenets of monetarism. Keynes turned matters upside down. He said the investment schedule was relatively inelastic and the liquidity preference curve was elastic, so money has little effect on demand and output. The authorities should rely on fiscal policy to manage demand and output.

Is the money multiplier, in fact, large or small? Who is correct, the monetarists or the Keynesians? While understanding the logical structure of Keynesian economics is facilitated by an uninterrupted analysis of theoretical issues before evaluating the empirical studies, these questions are so important that at least a brief answer now is appropriate. A more detailed summary of the empirical literature is presented later. The evidence on the size of the multipliers is inconclusive largely because two research strategies are followed. Keynesians estimate large scale structural models, that is, postulate many demand and supply equations and estimate them statistically. The Keynesian econometric models are like our IS–LM only more complicated. For example, instead of one consumption equation, there are equations for durables, nondurables, and services, which depend on somewhat different variables. After each equation is estimated statistically, the model is thrown into a computer to simulate the response of the economy. The computer grinds out predictions based on the many estimated equations and their interactions. The large-scale models generally find that the investment schedule is quite inelastic and liquidity preference sufficiently elastic that the government spending multiplier is considerably larger than the money multiplier. Monetarists do not attempt to estimate supply and demand equations. They get to the "bottom line" and relate income directly to money and government spending. These bottom line studies show that the money multiplier is large and the government spending multiplier is virtually zero. Monetarists and Keynesians co-exist because we do not know why two reasonable research strategies should yield diametrically different answers.

## QUESTIONS

1. Define the IS curve. Carefully explain why the IS curve is downward sloping. What factors lead to a flat IS curve? What factors cause the IS curve to shift rightward?

2. What does the magnitude of the horizontal shift of the IS curve equal?

3. Could the economy ever be off the IS curve? If so, explain what adjustments will occur.

4. Substitute LM for IS and reanswer questions 1 to 3.

5. Assume the quantity of money increases. Carefully explain and illustrate an adjustment path where for two rounds one market fully adjusts before the other market reacts. Illustrate an adjustment path where overshooting occurs.

6. List the four parameters which determine the size of the money multiplier. What is the economic rationale for the direction of the relationship between each parameter and the multiplier?

7. Is there a consistent relationship between the size of the money multiplier and the slopes of (a) the IS curve, and (b) the LM curve? Explain your answer.

8. Answer questions similar to 5 to 7 for government spending instead of the quantity of money.

9. Compared to the IS–LM multipliers, (a) is the basic Keynesian government spending multiplier larger or smaller and (b) is the money-nominal income multiplier of the quantity theory larger or smaller? Explain your answer. (Assume any parameter which appears in two models has the same value.)

---

## appendix A · Multipliers, IS–LM curves, and the model's parameters

We first examine the effect of the money transactions coefficient $k'$ on the IS–LM curves. Assume two economies, A and B, which are alike in every respect except that the transactions coefficient is greater in economy B, $k'_B > k'_A$. What are the shapes of the IS–LM curves in the two economies, and how do they shift when monetary policy changes? The answers are illustrated in Figure 19A–1. The IS curves for the two economies coincide; the IS curve is independent of money demand, the sole difference between A and B. The LM curve is steeper in economy B. For a unit increase in income (horizontal axis), the amount demanded for transactions increases more in economy B, by assumption. To maintain equilibrium the speculative demand must decrease more in B and, therefore the interest rate (vertical axis) must rise more since the speculative demand is assumed equally responsive to the rate of interest. Assume the unique IS curve intersects the two LM curves at their common point.[1] Monetary expansion in economy B shifts its LM curve to $LM'_B$, and income increases to $y'_B$. Given the same monetary expansion in A, where is its new LM curve located? If we can ascertain one point on the new LM curve we can draw the entire curve because monetary expansion causes parallel shifts. The LM curves of the two economies shift *vertically* the same distance. The point $(y_0, r_1)$ is on $LM'_B$ and $LM'_A$. The rate of interest is on

---

[1] We are also assuming a fixed element to transactions demand so that the LM curves intersect.

**FIGURE 19A-1  The money multiplier is large when the LM curve is flat due to a small transactions coefficient**

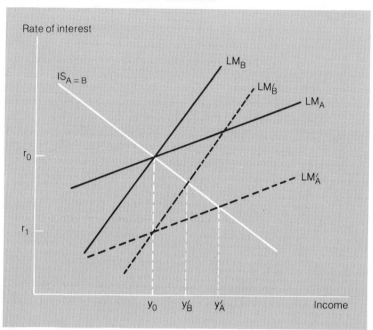

the vertical axis, and the extent of the vertical shift of the LM curve depends on the responsiveness of money demand to the rate of interest, as measured by the slope of the liquidity preference curve. If the liquidity preference curve is steep, then the LM shifts down more because the interest rate has to fall more to produce a given change in the amount of money demanded. The same responsiveness of money demand to the interest rate is illustrated graphically by equal vertical shifts of the LM curve. The vertical shift is independent of the transactions coefficient because along a vertical line the transactional demand and income are constant, by construction. The same vertical shift implies that the $LM_A$ curve shifts horizontally a greater distance. Looking at Figure 19A-1, the flat LM curve intersects the IS curve further to the right, that is, $y'_A > y'_B$. When the LM curve is flat because the transactions coefficient is small, the money multiplier is large.

We now examine the effect of the elasticity of the investment schedule on the size of the government spending multiplier. Continuing our partial equilibrium approach, let the elasticity of the investment schedule be the only difference between our hypothetical economies A and B. Figure 19A-2 draws the same LM curve for A and B. Let the investment schedule be less elastic in A than B. In economy A any given interest rate

**FIGURE 19A–2  The government spending multiplier is large when the IS curve becomes steep due to an inelastic investment schedule**

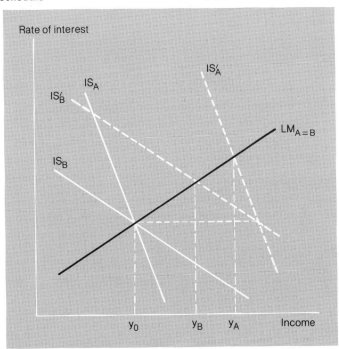

change leads to a smaller change in investment demand and, at equilibrium, income. The elasticity of the IS curves mirror the investment schedules. Government spending financed by bonds shifts the IS curve outward. The extent of the horizontal shift is the same in both economies, as Figure 19A–2 illustrates. Income increases more in economy A where the investment schedule is relatively inelastic. The magnitude of the horizontal shift depends only on the marginal propensity to consume, which is assumed equal in both economies, because along a horizontal line the rate of interest and its effects are being held constant.

---

## appendix B · The algebra of IS–LM

The appendix continues the algebraic approach that was dropped in the text. Algebra is an extremely powerful tool. We first show the similarity between the basic and advanced models. Then mere inspection of the algebraic equations reveals the relationship between multipliers and the various parameters.

Let us rewrite for convenience the IS and LM equations. The IS curve (equation (19–4)) is

$$y = \frac{a + I_0 + G_0}{1 - b} - \frac{er}{1 - b} \tag{19B–1}$$

The LM curve (equation (19–8)) is

$$r = \frac{h - (Mo/Po) + k'y}{j} \tag{19B–2}$$

The general (money and commodities market) equilibrium solution, which is represented graphically by the intersection of the IS and LM curves, is determined algebraically by solving equations (19B–1) and (19B–2) simultaneously.

$$y = \frac{a + G_0 + I_0 - e(h - M_0/P_0)/j}{(1 - b) + (ek'/j)} \tag{19B–3}$$

$$r = \frac{k'(a + I_0 + G_0) + (1 - b)(h - M_0/P_0)}{j(1 - b) + ek'}$$

We certainly do not expect anyone to memorize the general equilibrium income formula. Nevertheless, the rationale for equation (19B–3) parallels the rationale for the much simpler income formula of the basic Keynesian model. Look at equation (19B–2) again. If income were zero, the rate of interest would equal $(h - M_0/P_0)/j$. Investment, equation (19–2) in the text, would then equal $I_0 - e(h - M_0/P_0)/j$. Therefore, what does the numerator of equation (19B–3) measure? The numerator is total "autonomous" spending, the spending which would occur if income were zero. But income is not zero because firms respond to spending. The income generated by meeting the initial autonomous spending induces additional spending, and more rounds of income and spending. How much additional spending is induced per additional dollars of national income? The induced effect on consumption is the positive marginal propensity to consume, b, but the induced effect on investment is negative. As income increases by a dollar, the transactions demand for money increases by $k'$. To maintain equilibrium in the money market, the rate of interest must rise by $k'/j$. (Look at equation (19B–2). What is the slope of the LM curve?) This reduces investment by $ek'/j$. The respending propensity in this case is $b - (ek'/j)$. The denominator of equation (19B–3) is precisely one minus the respending propensity. Just as in the basic Keynesian model, the IS–LM equilibrium level of income is autonomous spending times the multiplier, which is the inverse of one minus the respending propensity. The IS–LM income formula is more complicated because autonomous and induced spending include interest rate effects.

Suppose equilibrium income is below full-employment income. What is the effect on income of (a) monetary policy, and (b) government spending? Differencing the general equilibrium income equation (19B–3) first with respect to money and then with respect to government spending gives the multipliers.

$$\frac{\Delta y}{\Delta M} = \frac{e/Po}{j(1-b)+ek'},$$ (19B–4)

$$\frac{\Delta y}{\Delta G} = \frac{1}{(1-b)+(ek'/j)}.$$ (19B–5)

Inspection of (19B–4) confirms that the money multiplier is large when

1a. j is small. (j is $\Delta M^D/\Delta r$, so that a small j means the liquidity preference schedule is steep.)
1b. e is large. (e is $\Delta I/\Delta r$, so that a large e means the investment schedule is flat.)
1c. b is large. (b is the marginal propensity to consume.)
1d. k' is small. (k' is the money demand transactions coefficient.)

Inspection of equation (19B–5) indicates that the government spending multiplier is smaller in the IS–LM model than in the basic model since (ek'/j) is positive. The government spending multiplier tends to be large when

2a. b is large.
2b. k' is small.
2c. j is large.
2d. e is small.

After 1a–1d, the economic interpretation of 2a–2d should be clear.

# Analysis of selected issues within the IS–LM framework

This chapter uses the IS–LM machinery constructed in the previous chapter to analyze selected issues in monetary theory. The issues are analyzed in order of difficulty, from the easiest to the most difficult. The reader is warned that the last section is a challenge. Some may prefer to read a few sections, skip to the next chapter and later, if at all, return to this chapter. Too much IS–LM at one sitting has been known to cause indigestion.

## EXTREME CASES: CONSTANT VELOCITY, LIQUIDITY TRAP, AND A VERTICAL INVESTMENT SCHEDULE

The classical assumption that velocity is fixed because money demand has only a transactions component implies the vertical LM curve illustrated in Figure 20–1. Algebraically, the Cambridge version of the classical case states

$$M = kPy \qquad (20-1)$$

In the classical long run, k and y were considered fixed, and the money supply determined the price level. In the Keynesian short run, k and P are considered fixed, in which case the money equation (20–1) uniquely determines real income. Of course, this is precisely what a vertical LM curve illustrates; the vertical LM has only one value of income. The rate of interest does not appear in equation (20–1) and, thereby, is irrelevant, which again is precisely what a vertical LM curve implies. Suppose the government spends more and finances its expenditures by selling bonds. As we learned in the previous chapter, the IS curve shifts out to IS' but

**FIGURE 20–1    Classical money demand or constant velocity**
The classical transactions demand produces a vertical LM curve and
makes fiscal policy totally ineffective.

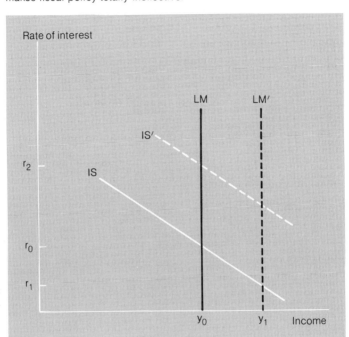

the LM curve remains fixed. Equilibrium income also remains fixed at $y_0$, and the interest rate rises to $r_2$. In order to finance a larger volume of transactions, the money supply must increase or some speculative balances must be transferred into transactions balances. Government spending does not affect the money supply. In the normal Keynesian case, fiscal policy is effective because it raises the rate of interest and thereby transfers money from speculative to transactions purposes. *When money is held simply for transactions and there are no speculative balances which can be transferred, additional government expenditures raise the interest rate but only succeed in reducing investment and private spending by an equal amount. The "crowding out" effect is complete.*

Restating some of these arguments in terms of velocity, along a normal upward-sloping LM curve velocity is variable. The LM curve is constructed for a fixed money supply. As one moves up the LM curve and income increases, velocity also increases. In the normal case government expenditures influence income because the economy lands on a point higher up the LM curve where velocity is greater. The vertical LM illustrates constant velocity. When the money supply and velocity are constant, government spending has no effect on demand and income. Algebraically, velocity and the inverse of the Cambridge k in the normal Keynesian case are

$$V = \frac{1}{k} = \frac{Py}{M} = \frac{y}{(M/P)} = \frac{y}{k'y + h - jr} = \frac{1}{k' + \dfrac{h - jr}{y}} \quad (20\text{-}2)$$

where, using earlier notation, the real demand for money, M/P, is $k'y + h - jr$. Expansionary fiscal policy reduces the term $(h - jr)/y$—the numerator becomes smaller and the denominator larger. According to equation (20-2), this increases velocity and, equivalently, reduces the Cambridge k, which is not a constant equal to the transactions coefficient $k'$.

Monetary policy is effective in the classical case. Expansionary monetary policy shifts the LM outward, and the new equilibrium income increases, $y_1 > y_0$. The rate of interest falls from $r_0$ to $r_1$. Knowing the reason for the interest rate decline readily explains why, contrary to the situation being considered, monetary policy will be completely ineffective at certain times. In the classical money demand case, the rate of interest does *not* fall in order for speculative demand to absorb the larger supply. The rate of interest has no direct effect on money demand. The rate of interest falls because this is the only way in the IS–LM model that aggregate demand and income can increase and, thereby, absorb the additional money supply into transactions balances. The interest rate is the only channel of monetary policy, that is, the only link between the real and monetary sectors. Given this, monetary policy is totally ineffective when either (1) the rate of interest does not respond to monetary policy or (2) aggregate demand and income are independent of the rate of interest. These cases are essentially the basic Keynesian model, which may be viewed as a special case of the more general IS–LM model.

The rate of interest does not respond to monetary policy when the economy is in a liquidity trap because, by definition, the rate of interest is already at its minimum. Any increase in the quantity of money is hoarded. Figure 20–2A illustrates liquidity preference curves subject to a liquidity trap, and Figure 20–2B graphs corresponding LM curves. The minimum interest rate is $r_{LT}$, at which liquidity preference curves become perfectly elastic. Given a low level of income relative to the quantity of money, the economy will be in a liquidity trap. Looking at Figure 20–2A, at income $y_0$ the transactions demand is so low compared to the money supply $M_0^S$ that the resultant large quantity of speculative balances drives the rate of interest to its minimum value. As income and the transactions demand increase, the liquidity preference curve shifts rightward and intersects the $M_0^S$ above $r_{LT}$. Correspondingly, the LM curve is flat at $r_{LT}$ for a stretch but eventually slopes upward. Assuming the solid IS curve in Figure 20–2B so the economy is in a liquidity trap, increasing the money supply from $M_0^S$ to

**FIGURE 20–2**

In a liquidity trap money demand is perfectly elastic.

A liquidity trap or a vertical IS curve make monetary policy totally ineffective.

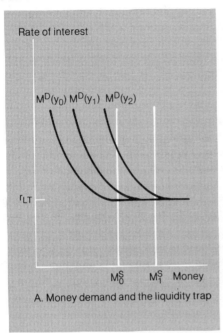

A. Money demand and the liquidity trap

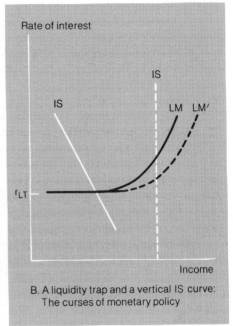

B. A liquidity trap and a vertical IS curve: The curses of monetary policy

$M_1^S$ in Figure 20–2A simply makes money more redundant. Monetary expansion extends the flat portion of the LM curve without influencing the rate of interest. While Keynes viewed the liquidity trap as a theoretical possibility of little practical importance, many of his followers thought the economy would often be mired in a liquidity trap, thereby making monetary policy totally ineffective.

*The liquidity trap is the total denial of the quantity theory, which says that velocity is independent of the quantity of money. When the economy is in a liquidity trap, velocity is totally dependent on the quantity of money.* If the trap exists and nominal income, Py, is independent of the quantity of money, the quantity theory equation MV = Py is satisfied only if velocity is perfectly flexible. Double the money supply and velocity is cut in half.

Figure 20–2B also illustrates the second case when monetary policy is totally ineffective. The dashed vertical IS curve occurs when investment is independent of the rate of interest, as the basic Keynesian model alleges. Assuming the economy is not in a liquidity trap, monetary expansion reduces the rate of interest but demand and income do not respond. The rate of interest falls enough to absorb into speculative balances all the additional money.

## AN INTEREST RESPONSIVE MONEY SUPPLY

In view of our thorough discussion of the influences of the private and banking sectors on the money supply in the short run, we should relax the assumption that the Fed controls the money supply perfectly. In the highly aggregated IS–LM model we can capture to some extent the nonpolicy induced effects on the money supply by adding a positive interest rate term to the money supply equation.

$$M^s = M_0 + j'r \tag{20-3}$$

The money supply now is the sum of two components, an exogenous term measuring the Fed's influence, $M_0$, and an endogenous term measuring interest rate effects on the money supply. The money supply depends positively on the rate because higher interest rates cause a reduction in the time deposit and excess reserve ratio and induce banks to borrow more at the discount window. The upward-sloping money supply line in Figure 20–3A graphs equation (20–3). In this case, "an increase in the money

**FIGURE 20-3  Money supply responsive to the rate of interest**
An interest responsive money supply produces an upward sloping LM curve even if money is held only for transactions purposes.

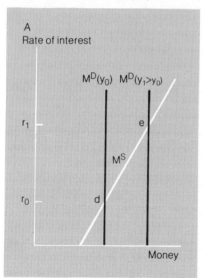

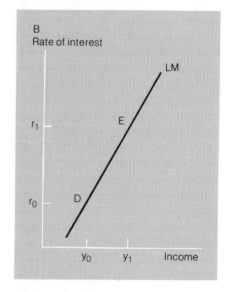

supply" means an increase in the exogenous component, which shifts the money supply line rightward. Even assuming a perfectly inelastic classical money demand, inspection of Figure 20–3 shows that the LM curve is positively sloped when the money supply is partially endogenous. Instead of drawing from speculative balances, higher incomes and transactions can now be financed by the private expansion of the money supply. The LM curve is positively sloped when either (1) money demand and interest rates are negatively related or (2) money supply and interest rates are positively related.

An interest responsive money supply relationship has important implications for fiscal and monetary policy. First, a classical money demand does not necessarily make fiscal policy totally ineffective. With the Fed inactive on the sidelines, deficit spending raises the rate of interest and induces banks to provide the necessary transactions balances. Second, the money multiplier is reduced by the interest responsiveness of the money supply. In the previous chapter we indicated that the money multiplier decreases as money demand becomes more interest responsive. Introducing a positive money supply relationship is analytically equivalent to making the negative money demand relationship more elastic. What matters is the responsiveness of the money *market* to the rate of interest; whether the amount of money supplied increases or the amount of money demanded decreases as the rate of interest rises is irrelevant. Note that the exogenous and endogenous money components move in different directions. Total monetary expansion is less than the exogenous expansion induced by the Fed because the Fed's expansionary policy reduces the rate of interest, which causes the private sector to contract the money supply. This is why the money multiplier, defined as the change in income divided by the exogenous money supply change, is smaller when the money supply contains an endogenous component.

## MONEY AND THE RATE OF INTEREST AT FULL EMPLOYMENT

The IS–LM model is quite flexible. It can be used to analyze the effect of various events under different assumptions. For example, we just saw that the effect of monetary and fiscal policy in the Keynesian short run depends crucially on the form of the money demand function and the resultant LM curve. We illustrate the flexibility of the IS–LM model by analyzing the effect of money on the rate of interest, which may be puzzling the reader because at various points in this book we have espoused virtually every position. In the early chapters we indicated that a sufficiently strong and *prolonged* monetary expansion raises the nominal rate of interest because individuals who anticipate inflation and a declining purchasing power of the dollar attempt to maintain their real return. The chapters on neoclassical economics stressed that a *solitary* monetary injection simply raises prices and wages, without influencing the rate of interest. A few chapters later we discovered that according to Keynes monetary expansion reduces the rate of interest. At each point we emphasized the validity of the different positions, and we are not going to retract anything now. Consider first why neoclassical and Keynesians disagree about the effect on the rate of interest of a solitary monetary injection and then consider the effect of a sustained monetary expansion.

The neoclassical and Keynesian conclusions follow logically from their assumptions. Which assumption is crucial, causing the different conclusions? The assumptions of neoclassical and Keynesian economics differ in several respects. The IS–LM model shows that the crucial assumption is the length of the time period and, consequently, the current level of income relative to full-employment income. In Chapter 16 we asserted, and now we have the tools to prove rigorously, the neoclassical conclusion that the rate of interest does not depend on the quantity of money in the long run even if money demand depends on the rate of interest.

Figure 20–4 graphs the now familiar IS and LM curves. A new wrinkle is the dashed vertical line at $y_F$, full-employment income. We begin by assuming the economy is at a long-run equilibrium where the current level of income given by the intersection of the solid IS and LM curves equals full-employment income. Suppose the Fed mistakenly increases the quan-

**FIGURE 20–4  Money and the rate of interest at full employment**
A solitary monetary injection and a temporary inflation have no effect on the rate of interest even if the demand for money depends on the rate of interest. Permanent inflation raises the rate of interest.

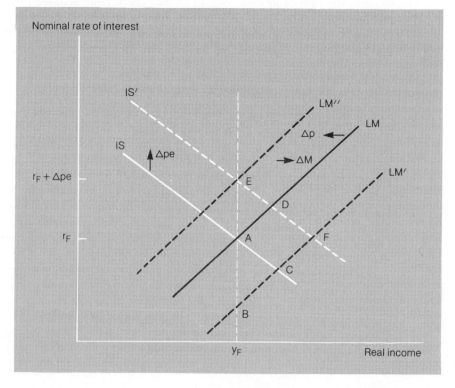

tity of money so the appropriate curve now is LM'. What happens? As we indicated earlier, full employment is not the technologically maximum output which occurs when everyone is working overtime. At least 3 percent unemployment—and quite possibly considerably more—and a 40-hour work week is compatible with full employment output, which is best viewed as the long run economically sustainable output. Given this, the adjustment process outlined in the last chapter remains valid for the initial stage. That is, the interest rate first falls precipitously from A to B. This is the *liquidity effect* of the monetary expansion. The depressed interest rate stimulates investment demand and then rebounds somewhat as output adjusts to the higher level of demand. The economy moves from B to C, where labor is working overtime and output exceeds full employment. Firms meet the demand at existing prices without regard for current profits, which may actually decline somewhat as overtime pay raises wage costs.

Point C is only a short-run equilibrium; current output exceeds full employment. Workers who initially accepted overtime eagerly now desire a return to their typical work schedule. Output tends to regress toward the full-employment level. Firms note that the monetary expansion and higher demand is permanent and attempt to restore their profit margins by raising prices. Allowing sufficient time to elapse for prices to rise makes it incumbent to distinguish between nominal (dollar) income and real (fixed price) income, where the latter is measured on the horizontal axis. *Higher prices* and nominal income, given any real income, *shift the LM curve upward and leftward*. Money performs various services and is held for various reasons. The number of dollars needed is proportional to the price level. For example, an individual may hold money to buy one gizmo. The amount of money needed to buy one gizmo clearly depends on the price of gizmos. At any real income and output level more money will be necessary for transactions purposes when prices are higher and, consequently, less will be available for speculative purposes from the given money supply. Individuals are satisfied with lower speculative balances when the interest rate is higher—the LM curve shifts up. The inflationary pressure pushing the LM up persists so long as the rate of interest remains below $r_F$, the rate consistent with full employment. The LM curve returns to its initial position when the price increase is proportional to the monetary expansion, that is, when the quantity of real money balances equals its initial value. At that point the *temporary* inflation stops.

In Figure 20–4 the economy moves from point C back to A. Although money *demand* depends on the rate of interest, as illustrated by the upward-sloping LM curves, the long-run equilibrium rate of interest does not depend on the *quantity* of money. At long-run equilibrium aggregate expenditures equal full-employment output. Since money does not affect full-employment output, it cannot ultimately affect the rate of interest, which is a determinant of aggregate expenditures. The upward movement of the rate of interest from B to C and from C to A is called the *real income* and *actual price effect*, respectively, of the monetary expansion. The sum of the real income and actual price effects is the *nominal income effect*. William Gibson estimated the liquidity effect lasts approximately two months, after which interest rates start to rise. Interest rates fully rebound to their initial level and the (nominal) income effect is complete well within a year.[1]

Suppose the expansion was not an isolated event; the Fed persistently pursues an expansionary policy. Inflation no longer is a temporary phenomenon. Inflation persists and society comes to expect it. In this case the rate of interest rises, with the economy settling at point E instead of A in Figure 20–4. Expected inflation shifts the investment schedule and IS curve upward. Investment involves the purchase of plant and equipment to produce future goods. By definition, inflation raises the price of future goods relative to current goods and, therefore, increases the rate of return on investment. For example, assume a $100 machine, which for simplicity is the only factor of production, yields 105 gizmos one year hence. In a stable environment the gizmos are expected to fetch $1 each, making the rate of return on the machine 5 percent. Inflation is a monetary phenomenon and does not influence the machine's real rate of return. It continues to produce 105 gizmos. However, the price of gizmos next year is higher in an inflationary environment. Assuming firms expect a 5 percent inflation so the gizmos will sell $1.05 instead of $1, the nominal rate of return rises to approximately 10 percent. Abstracting from progressive taxes and other complications, as a first approximation the IS curve shifts upward by the expected rate of inflation, and the real rate of interest remains constant. This rise in the rate of interest from A to E is called the *inflationary expectations* or *Fisher effect*.

If the price increase were proportional to the monetary expansion so the real quantity of money remained constant and the initial LM curve prevailed—the outward movement due to the monetary expansion being just counteracted by the inward movement due to inflation—the higher IS curve would intersect the LM at point D beyond full employment. This cannot be the permanent solution. Outputs greater than full employment are temporary. For some time period inflation will outpace the monetary expansion, real money balances will fall, and the LM curve rises above its initial position to LM″ in Figure 20–4. Inflation is characterized by high nominal interest rates and tight money in a real sense. There are more dollars around—indeed, this is the cause of the inflation—but there are fewer dollars relative to the prices of commodities. While this conclusion may seem paradoxical, further reflection suggests its reasonableness. The purchasing power of money sinks during an inflation. Like passengers on the Titanic, money holders attempt to jump ship, preferring commodities

---

[1] William Gibson, "Interest Rates and Monetary Policy, *Journal of Political Economy*, June 1970, pp. 431–54; and "Price Expectations Effects on Interest Rates," *Journal of Finance*, March 1970, pp. 19–34.

to money. This further sinks the purchasing power of money. Society economizes on its real money holdings because their cost is high. Eventually, however, the rate of inflation just equals the rate of monetary expansion, and the LM curve is stabilized at its higher position. A solitary monetary injection permanently raises prices proportionally but has no permanent effect on the rate of inflation, which is temporarily positive as prices adjust upward. Similarly, continued monetary growth eventually raises the rate of inflation equally, but temporarily inflation exceeds its permanent rate. While inflation induces people to reduce their command over commodities held in the form of money, the reduction of real balances is not continual.

## GOVERNMENT SPENDING AT FULL EMPLOYMENT

Although we emphasize monetary policy, our Figure 20–4 facilitates the ready analysis of fiscal policy at full employment. Is expansionary fiscal policy, like expansionary monetary policy, inflationary at full employment? Yes, according to much of the popular press and many politicians. Economists of all stripes, however, have been much more reluctant than journalists and politicians to claim that expansionary fiscal policy *per se* is the source of our inflation. Professor Friedman goes further than some economists. He categorically denies that fiscal policy causes inflation. His well-known opposition to government spending is based on other reasons. Friedman said, "Inflation is always and everywhere a monetary phenomenon."[2] Who is correct, Friedman or the journalists and politicians?

In answering the question, let us rule out any supply-side effects due to fiscal policy because their existence is speculative and, in any case, they already were discussed in Chapter 15. (From now to the concluding sections of Chapter 23, where we meet up with rational expectations economists again, we shall assume all neoclassicists are monetarists.) By ruling out supply-side effects, monetary and fiscal policy are placed on equal footing. Although we stated several times that different *quantities* of money have no effect on aggregate supply, Chapter 23 indicates that different *rates of growth* of money and, therefore, different inflation rates do affect aggregate supply.

### Government spending and a vertical LM curve

We stated in Chapter 16 that Professor Friedman's position on the effect of interest rates on the demand for money is not altogether clear.[3] Nevertheless, virtually everyone has interpreted him as stating that the

---

[2] Milton Friedman, *Dollars and Deficits* (Englewood Cliffs, N.J.: Prentice-Hall, 1968), p. 39.

[3] See footnote 5, Chapter 16.

demand for money does not depend on the rate of interest. Although Friedman rejects the classical transactions approach to money and favors the asset approach, which views money simply as one of many assets, within the IS–LM model his denial of interest rate effects is equivalent to acceptance of the classical transaction demand, $M = kPy$. That is, according to Friedman, the LM curve is the dashed vertical line in Figure 20–4 at $y_F$. (The price level associated with the money supply cannot be illustrated in this graph with the rate of interest and real income on the axes.) An increase in government spending which shifts the IS curve to IS' only raises the rate of interest in this special case. Private spending is curtailed by the amount of additional government spending. Real output is ultimately constant at full employment, and so is the price level because the constant velocity implies a rigid link between the value of expenditures and money. Given Friedman's assumptions, inflation is strictly a monetary phenomenon.

### Government spending and an upward sloping LM curve

Perhaps, as Friedman claims, his position on the interest rate elasticity of the demand for money has been almost universally misinterpreted because, although he and monetarism are virtually synonymous, nearly every other monetarist includes an interest rate term in the demand for money and, consequently, draws upward-sloping LM curves. When the LM curve is upward sloping, government spending does induce higher prices. An increase in government spending financed by bonds shifts the IS curve to IS' while the solid LM curve remains fixed, assuming the Fed follows a hands-off policy. Point D in Figure 20–4 cannot be a permanent equilibrium. While firms temporarily meet the government demand and move to point D, they subsequently revert to their previous production plans and raise prices, causing the LM curve to shift upward to LM". Because the higher interest rate necessary to reduce private demand by the amount of additional government spending also reduces the amount of money demanded for speculative purposes in this case, prices rise and transactions money demand increases enough to equate total money demand and the fixed supply. Government spending increases velocity and prices in the long run, given a Keynesian (non-Friedman monetarist) money demand.

While the Keynesian money demand does allow government spending to be a source of inflation, it is not a likely major source. In Figure 20–4, full-employment output is held fixed so that the larger government spending increases government's percentage of GNP. It is the larger government share rather than the larger absolute amount spent that causes inflation. Additional government spending which just keeps pace with a rising full employment is no more inflationary than additional money which parallels income growth. In terms of Figure 20–4, an increase in government spending which shifts the IS curve out is not inflationary when the full-employment and LM lines shift out equally. IS and LM curves shifted rightward by the same distance continue to intersect at the same interest rate. While we can very confidently expect the *absolute* amount of government spending to increase annually, the government spending share of GNP is less likely to change significantly. Chapter 14 showed that the government share rose in the early 1950s and has remained relatively constant since then. Thus, government spending is a *temporary* source of inflation; government spending is inflationary when its share of GNP is increasing. In order to continually shift the IS curve relative to full employment, the government's share of output must continually rise, which is impossible. Adding the words "sustained" makes Friedman absolutely correct: sustained inflation is always and everywhere a monetary phenomenon.

### Fiscal policy and accommodative monetary policy

Why do many journalists and politicians claim that government spending is a major, sustained source of inflation? Are they just plain wrong? Not exactly. We analyzed the effects of changes in government spending *per se*. In the "real world," however, many variables change simultaneously, and it is extremely difficult to disentangle their separate effects. Nonspecialists often attribute to government spending the effects of other variables which usually move together with it. What variables usually increase when the government's GNP share increases? One variable is the money supply. We saw in Chapter 11 and 12 that until quite recently money market conditions and interest rates were the Fed's operating target. The money supply fluctuated willy-nilly while interest rates were kept fixed, at least in the short run. Although the Fed is paying much more attention to the money supply today, it certainly has not altogether abandoned its fixation on interest rates. As a result, monetary policy tends to accommodate fiscal policy. To prevent the higher interest rates associated with additional government spending, the Fed increases the money supply.

While the Treasury is selling bonds to finance additional spending, the Fed is conducting open-market purchases. For a short time at least, the Fed successfully keeps interest rates down. In terms of Figure 20–4, expansionary fiscal policy alone pushes the economy to point D. The accommodative monetary policy pushes the economy out further to point F. Point F is beyond full employment and cannot be a position of long-run equilibrium. Prices rise, which increases the amount of money demanded and shifts the LM' curve upward. Assuming the Fed accepts the inevitability of higher interest rates and does not expand the money supply further, the temporarily accommodative monetary policy makes fiscal policy more inflationary than it would otherwise be. Prices must rise more to shift up to LM″ the accommodative policy LM′ instead of the constant policy LM.

## THE REAL BALANCE EFFECT AND THE NEOCLASSICAL ADJUSTMENT PROCESS

Neoclassicists believe that the economy will not be stuck below full employment permanently. Natural forces propel the economy toward full employment. The neoclassical adjustment process of Chapter 16 is now presented within the IS–LM framework. Assume the economy is at full employment and, for simplicity, let money demand take the classical form. Given the quantity of money and the transactions coefficient, the price level has adjusted so that the classical LM equation $M_0 = kPy$, is satisfied at full-employment income $y_F$. The vertical line in Figure 20–5 is

**FIGURE 20–5  The real balance effect and adjustments toward equilibrium**
The real balance effect shifts the IS curve rightward, guaranteeing that monetary policy can produce full employment.

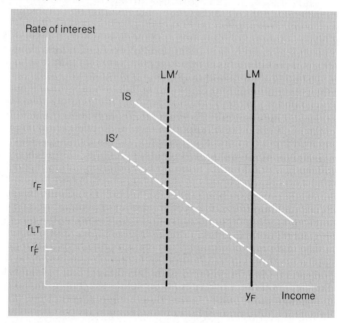

the classical LM curve. Suppose this happy state of affairs is disturbed by a reduction in aggregate demand. The IS curve shifts inward to IS′. The classicists assumed, and Keynes concurred, that individuals typically would buy bonds with the funds previously being spent. Since neither money demand nor supply shifts, the LM curve remains fixed.[4] (Ignore the dashed LM curve.) Interest rates are quite flexible in both directions. Looking at Figure 20–5, it appears that a downward movement in the rate of interest to $r_F'$ is sufficient to maintain full employment.

At this point Keynes parted company with his classical mentors. First, Keynes stressed the unit of account function of money and the speculative demand for money, in which case the LM is upward sloping but not vertical. Clearly, an IS curve shifted downward would intersect a positively sloped LM curve at an income below $y_F$. Interest rate adjustments are insufficient to maintain full employment when society holds speculative money balances. Some other adjustment is necessary. Second, even if money is held for transactions purposes only and the LM curve is vertical, Keynes thought aggregate demand was so limited that the full-employment rate of interest was unfeasible. For example, a negative rate of interest would be necessary if the IS curve shifted inward so much that it crossed $y_F$ below the horizontal axis. If demand were so limited, interest rate adjustments would be insufficient to maintain full employment. Negative interest rates never have and never will be observed. Why lend and be paid back less when one can hold money? The rate of interest must be above some minimum positive value—the liquidity trap rate of interest $r_{LT}$. In his less pessimistic moments Keynes thought the full-employment rate of interest was positive, though below the liquidity trap rate of interest. Whichever is the case, Keynes thought the economy would be mired at underemployment equilibrium unless the government undertook expansionary fiscal policies.

The situation would be worse if consumers hoarded the funds previously spent on commodities instead of buying bonds. The decreased demand for commodities now is associated with an equal increased demand for money. Recalling that an increase in the demand for money has the same effect as a decrease in supply, in this case both the IS and LM shift inward by the same amount. The dashed curves in Figure 20–5 are applicable. The equilibrium rate of interest stays constant while income falls below full employment. The issue here is not whether interest rate adjustments are sufficient; the rate of interest has no reason whatsoever to adjust. While neoclassicists play down the likelihood of this hoarding case, they do not feel that it occasionally violates the basic proposition that the economy contains endogenous forces driving the economy toward full employment. If full employment is the amount firms and workers want and are willing to produce, and if current output is less than that amount, then neoclassicists say that eventually—certainly not

---

[4] A bond market equilibrium curve similar to the commodities (IS) and money (LM) market equilibrium curve exists, and it shifts along with the IS curve because the demand for bonds also changed. We can ignore the bond market equilibrium curve because the intersection of the IS and LM curves is sufficient to determine the equilibrium interest rate and income. The bond market curve passes through the IS–LM intersection point.

immediately—wages and prices will fall. If workers *never* are willing to lower their wage demands, are they really unemployed and willing to work? Neoclassicists think not. What amount of unemployment the rate of interest cannot reduce at first will ultimately be eliminated by a decline in the price level. Lower prices shift the LM curve outward. A given quantity of money can finance more transactions when the price of each transaction is lower. The LM curve returns to its initial position, restoring full employment.

Figure 20–5 may make it appear that the rate of interest must fall along with prices. Is the magnitude of the interest rate decline feasible, or are we just back at a previous case Keynes thought likely? As drawn in Figure 20–5 the solid LM curve and broken IS curve intersect at a rate of interest below the liquidity trap rate, $r_{LT}$. Is the economy doomed to underemployment even if prices decline? Neoclassicists say no. Professor Pigou in particular thought, and modern empirical studies confirm, that consumption depends on wealth in addition to current income. While it is true that money is only one component of wealth in virtually every society, let us ignore other assets and equate wealth with money.[5] The Pigovian consumption function is:

$$C = a + b(y - T) + b'(M/P)$$

where $b'$ measures the real balance (wealth) or Pigou effect. Real money balances have a *direct* effect on consumption and aggregate demand. The real balance effect says that as prices fall and real money balances increase the IS curve shifts outward. The outward shift of *both* the IS and LM curves as prices decline eliminates the need for interest rate adjustments.

The importance of the real balance effect as an *endogenous* propeller toward equilibrium may well be academic. Over time prices have become less flexible downward. Monetary authorities may be unwilling to rely on the quite possibly long delayed automatic price adjustments. This does not diminish the importance of the real balance effect as an *exogenous* propeller toward equilibrium. If the price level is sticky and fails to produce additional real money balances, the Fed should intervene. Either lower endogenous prices or more exogenous money increases real balances and aggregate demand even in a liquidity trap. Money no longer exclusively affects aggregate demand indirectly via the rate of interest. *The real balance effect says consumption depends directly on money so that monetary expansion shifts the IS curve outward.* The real balance effect brings money to the forefront and denies that monetary policy is ever totally impotent.

## MONEY SUPPLY VERSUS INTEREST RATES: INSTABILITY OF IS–LM

For many problems it is convenient to ignore uncertainty and assume an omniscient policymaker. However, the controversy regarding the

---

[5] See footnote 8, Chapter 16.

money supply versus interest rates as the intermediate target of monetary policy, a controversy we discussed intuitively in Chapter 12, can be analyzed rigorously only if uncertainty is introduced explicitly within the IS–LM framework.[6] The discussion is simplified by assuming the Fed can control perfectly the rate of interest or money supply so the financial variables may be viewed as policy tools as well as operating targets. Let the interest rate be strictly a tool/operating target, the value of which is dictated solely by the ultimate goal. That is, no particular interest rate is desirable by itself. Let full-employment income, represented by $y_F$ in Figure 20–6, be the ultimate goal which the policymaker attempts to achieve

**FIGURE 20–6  Unstable aggregate demand**
When aggregate demand is uncertain and the IS curve is unstable, a money supply policy is superior to an interest rate policy.

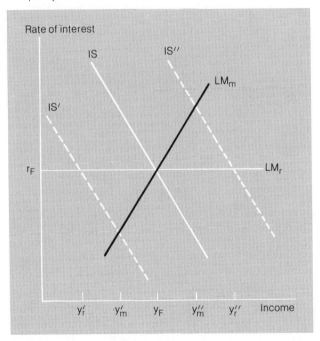

by selecting the money supply or rate of interest. For simplicity, assume that incomes on either side of full employment are equally undesirable. Society foregoes commodities when income is less than full employment, and incomes above full employment cause inflation. The goal is $y_F$, and the dispersion of actual income about $y_F$ measures failure to achieve the goal. The further is income from $y_F$, the less successful is the

---

[6] This section is based on William Poole's pathfinding "Optimal Choice of Monetary Policy Instruments in a Simple Stochastic Model," *Quarterly Journal of Economics,* May 1970, pp. 197–216.

policymaker. Of course, complete success (zero failure) occurs when income always is $y_F$, that is, the dispersion is zero.

We first show that in a certain world the choice between the money supply and rate of interest as intermediate targets may be decided on the basis of personal prejudice or the toss of a coin because attainment of full employment is independent of the intermediate target. When certainty exists, aggregate expenditures and money demand are known because there are no unknown random forces causing deviations from the average. Stated somewhat differently, in a certain world the predicted demands are always realized. In terms of the IS–LM graph, certainty exists when we always know exactly the shape and position of the IS curve and, given the money supply selected, the LM. Suppose the certain aggregate demand yields the solid IS curve in Figure 20–6. The central banker who prefers an interest rate policy would peg it at $r_F$, confident that the resultant income would then be $y_F$. Those who prefer a money supply policy would select a money supply $M_F$ which in conjunction with the certain money demand would produce an LM curve which intersects the certain IS curve at $y_F$. (See $LM_m$ in Figure 20–6.) The policymaker generally cannot control both the rate of interest and money supply. Certainty implies, however, that the relationship between the two is known and constant. If the authorities peg the interest rate at $r_F$, the resultant money supply must be $M_F$. If the money supply is $M_F$, the interest rate must be $r_F$. Which variable the authority cares to emphasize is irrelevant.

Most policymakers are no dumber than the rest of us. The goals are not attained at all times because we live in an uncertain world. We simply do not know all the factors which influence aggregate and money demands, much less their precise effects. Even if the structure of the economy were known with certainty, policy lags explain the authorities' failure to keep the economy at full employment consistently. Today's interest rate and money supply influence aggregate demand in the future, making accurate prediction of the future values of the other determinants of aggregate demand necessary if the goal is to be achieved. Crystal balls are cloudy at best. Even if interest rates and money had an immediate effect on aggregate demand, the inability to monitor demand continuously produces deviations from the goal. This quarter's GNP is uncertain until next quarter. Current money demand also is uncertain. We do not know where we are until we have left. Although the policymaker is uncertain about (1) the current state of the economy, (2) future behavior of the economy, and (3) the structure of the economy and the effects of policy, some decision must be made now. It is hardly surprising that the goal often eludes the policymaker.

Let's give the policymaker a break. Assume money demand is known, and the authorities are uncertain about only aggregate demand. *Average* aggregate demand and its dispersion is known, but the average value may not be realized at any one time. For example, the policymaker may know that aggregate demand averages 100 but at any one time could be between 80 and 120. We may view the IS as a band instead of a line. This is represented graphically by an unstable average IS curve shifting outward and inward. Average aggregate demand produces the solid IS. For un-known reasons—those elusive animal spirits—firms and consumers may be especially bullish. The high aggregate demand produces IS″ instead of the normal IS. At other times low aggregate demand yields IS′. The band formed by IS′ and IS″ measures the instability of aggregate demand and the uncertainty the policymaker faces. In such a "real world" setting the authorities are unable to maintain the economy at full employment. While complete success is unattainable, the policymaker chooses a course of action which is correct on the average. The specific course of action selected now matters.

Suppose a money supply policy is selected. Given the solid average IS and a known money demand, the authorities optimally select the money supply which produces $LM_m$, as was true when total certainty existed. The policymaker awaits the outcome of his action. He can confidently predict the position of the LM curve since money demand is known with certainty by assumption. Aggregate demand and the position of the IS curve are uncertain but finally manifest themselves. Income averages $y_F$ but is not constant. Given the optimal money supply, the inflationary income $y_m''$ occurs when aggregate demand is above normal, and the reces-sionary income $y_m'$ occurs when aggregate demand is below normal. The distance between $y_m'$ and $y_m''$ measures the failure of a money supply pol-icy.[7] Interest rates are allowed to vary when the authorities select a money supply policy.

Suppose an interest rate policy is adopted instead. The interest rate is set at $r_F$, which is correct on average. The flat $LM_r$ in Figure 20–6 is not a traditional LM curve. It is a money market equilibrium curve but the money supply is not being held constant. Indeed, as we move out along $LM_r$ the money supply is increasing in order to maintain the rate of inter-est constant in spite of higher income and transactions requirements. Figure 20–6 shows that an interest rate policy lets income fluctuate from $y_r'$ to $y_r''$, which is wider than the fluctuations which occur under a money supply policy. *When aggregate demand is uncertain and the IS curve is un-stable, a money supply policy is superior to an interest rate policy.* The inter-est rate policy effectively creates a liquidity trap and the basic Keynesian multiplier. The central banker with a firm grip on the money supply in-evitably lets the rate of interest fluctuate, and the interest rate fluctuations

---

[7] If it appears that a superior money supply policy exists, you probably are implicitly trying to create a certain world. True, $y_F$ could be maintained indefinitely by counteracting any movement of the IS by an opposite movement of the LM. But this is exactly the certainty case just considered where the policymaker knows the IS and then positions the LM to achieve full employment. The essential aspect of uncertainty is decision making *before* some outcome is known.

moderate aggregate demand. The central banker determined to maintain a rate of interest provides no moderating influence and must let the money supply follow aggregate demand.

The opposite case is represented by Figure 20–7. Aggregate demand now is certain and money demand is uncertain. In this case the IS curve is

**FIGURE 20–7   Unstable money demand**
When money demand is uncertain and the LM curve is unstable, an interest rate policy is superior to a money supply policy.

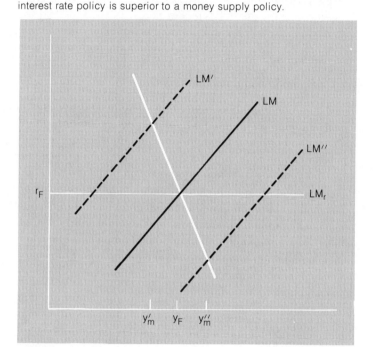

fixed. A money supply policy leads to LM fluctuations from LM′ to LM″. The optimal money supply and average money demand generate LM, which intersects the IS at $y_F$. A money demand larger (smaller) than expected generates LM′ (LM″), given the fixed money supply. A money supply policy lets income fluctuate from $y'_m$ to $y''_m$ in Figure 20–7. *When aggregate demand is certain and the IS curve is stable, an interest rate policy is superior to a money supply policy.* Indeed, an interest rate policy maintains income precisely on target. An interest rate policy still loses control of the money supply. In this case, however, lack of monetary control is desirable. By concentrating on the rate of interest and ignoring the money supply, the latter dutifully trails money demand and exactly neutralizes its fluctuations. Money supply increases (decreases) equal money demand increases (decreases).

Uncertainty is not limited to one area. Both the real and monetary relationships are uncertain. Which policy is superior in this case? As one might have surmised, the relative degree of uncertainty and instability of IS and LM determine the superior policy. *If money demand is known with greater certainty than aggregate demand so the LM is more stable than the IS, then a money supply policy is superior to an interest rate policy, and conversely.* This is illustrated in Figure 20–8, where the LM shifts less

**FIGURE 20–8  Unstable aggregate demand and money demand**
When money demand is more certain than aggregate demand and the LM curve is more stable than the IS curve, income fluctuations are minimized by stabilizing the money supply instead of the rate of interest.

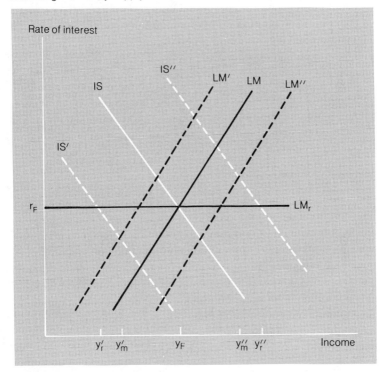

than the IS. When a money supply policy is followed, income fluctuates from $y'_m$ to $y''_m$, which is less than the $y'_r$ to $y''_r$ income fluctuations which occur when an interest rate policy is adopted.

Monetarists espouse a money supply policy while Keynesians espouse an interest rate policy. Are these policy prescriptions in accord with the remainder of monetarist and Keynesian theory? We have emphasized that compared to their Keynesian colleagues, monetarists interpret the economic data as indicating that the *entire* economic system is quite stable.

That is, monetarists expect the IS *and* LM curves to remain within a narrow band while Keynesians expect wide fluctuations. Our emphasis on this disagreement between monetarists and Keynesians is not misguided and explains other policy differences. It is important to note, however, that *overall* economic stability is not an issue in the money supply versus rate of interest debate. At issue here is the *relative* stability of aggregate demand versus money demand. Classicists and their modern disciples have long emphasized that velocity and money demand is one of the most stable economic relationships, more stable than aggregate demand. Their preference for a money supply target is consistent with their view about velocity. The basic Keynesian model stressed the volatility of investment, which at first glance would seem inconsistent with an interest rate policy. Those familiar with Keynes's explanation of the speculative demand realize that his theory and policy prescriptions are not *necessarily* contradictory. According to Keynes, money demand also is unstable. The expected future rate of interest is a critical variable in Keynes's explanation of the speculative money demand. Keynes was uncertain how expectations of the future are formed. Even if expectations of the future depend solely on current and past values, any change in the current rate of interest then affects the expected future rate and causes the liquidity preference and LM curves to shift.[8] The monetary authority may as well select an interest rate policy if the LM is as unstable as the IS.

## QUESTIONS

1. When is the (*a*) money multiplier and (*b*) government spending multiplier zero? Give economic explanations for your answers and illustrate them with IS–LM graphs.

2. Define a (money demand) liquidity trap. Draw liquidity preference and LM curves which illustrate a liquidity trap.

3. How does recognition of a positive relationship between the rate of interest and the amount of money supplied influence (*a*) the slope of the LM curve, (*b*) the size of the government spending multiplier, and (*c*) the size of the (exogenous) money multiplier?

4. Discuss the pattern of interest rates over time when the rate of monetary growth *decelerates*.

5. With the aid of an IS–LM graph, illustrate the liquidity, real income, actual price, and expected price effects on the rate of interest of monetary *contraction*.

6. Assuming full employment, under what conditions does an increase in government's share of GNP simply raise interest rates? When is government spending *per se* inflationary? Explain the consequences of additional government spending when its interest rate effects are neutralized.

---

[8] See Appendix A, Chapter 18.

7. Illustrate with IS–LM curves the real balance effect of a monetary *contraction*. Discuss the significance of the real balance effect for monetary policy.

8. Since prices rarely fall, the real balance effect is a theoretical nicety of no practical significance. Critically evaluate the statement.

9. Carefully explain and illustrate with IS–LM graphs the relationship between uncertainty about aggregate expenditures and money demand on the one hand and interest rates or money supply operating targets on the other hand.

10. How do monetarists and Keynesians justify their preferred operating target?

# PART 5

# Monetary policy and inflation

# Issues in monetary policy 21

This chapter discusses selected issues in monetary policy. Each section is more or less independent of the others. We make no pretense of being encyclopedic, and some may even quarrel with our selection of issues to be covered. Some issues such as leads and lags cannot be easily handled in the static neoclassical and Keynesian models and are presented here for the first time. We also expand on certain topics mentioned briefly earlier. All theories are simplifications; the world is too complex to attempt to explain everything. In this "second pass" some simplifying assumptions are dropped to broaden the applicability of the analysis.

## RULES VERSUS DISCRETION

The so-called rules versus discretion debate concerning the conduct of monetary policy might be labeled laissez-faire versus fine tuning. This is a debate between the two extreme wings of the economics profession. Professor Friedman and other staunch monetarists support a rules policy. Indeed, they more than support it; a rules policy is near the top of any list of the tenets of monetarism. *A rules policy has the money supply grow at a constant rate dictated by long-run objectives and, therefore, monetary changes are independent of the past and near future predicted values of goal variables such as GNP.* All prescribed policies are not rules, as here defined. For example, policymakers who *methodically* and *automatically* reduce the rate of growth of money by some fraction of last period's rate of growth of GNP would *not* be following a rules policy because the rate of growth of money would be variable and dependent on past GNP. Constancy alone does not qualify as a rule. A constant interest rate policy also is not a rules policy. The opposite of rules, discretionary policy, was advocated especially strongly by the economic advisors of the Kennedy and Johnson administrations, some of whom after savoring power prefer to be in exile in Washington's prestigious "think tanks" rather than return to academia. *Discretionary policy is characterized by frequent changes dependent on past and near future predicted values of the goal variables.*

Proponents of a monetary rule advocate a fiscal policy consistent with the philosophy underlying their approach to monetary policy. A rules approach to fiscal policy sets tax *rates* and spending *programs* which do not vary in response to the business cycle. Tax receipts and the number of people who qualify for such spending programs as unemployment compensation would automatically vary during the cycle. The budget would swing from a surplus during the expansion to a deficit during the contraction but balance over the business cycle. Discretionary fiscal policy would vary tax rates and spending programs so the budgetary swings over the business cycle would be substantially greater. Moreover, advocates of discretionary fiscal policy deny the desirability of balancing the budget over the business cycles. Perpetual deficts varying in size according to the state of the economy are acceptable. Because many of the same points are at issue in the debate regarding the conduct of monetary and fiscal policy, we prefer the more general laissez-faire versus fine tuning to rules versus discretion, where the latter is almost exclusively associated with the monetary policy debate.

The money supply can grow at many constant rates—10 percent, 5 percent, 0 percent (in which case the money supply remains fixed), $-5$ percent, and so on. What should be the specific rate of monetary growth? What long-run objective governs the specific rate? In the final analysis the rate of monetary growth simply affects the long-run rate of inflation. Proponents of a monetary rule invariably oppose high rates of inflation; price stability or even a mild deflation is preferable. Given these desired rates of inflation, a straightforward application of the quantity theory equation says the money supply should grow at approximately 4 percent. For small changes, the percentage form of the quantity theory equation is

$$\frac{\Delta M}{M} + \frac{\Delta V}{V} = \frac{\Delta P}{P} + \frac{\Delta y}{y}$$

The equation says that the sum of the percentage change of money and velocity—the left-hand side—equals the sum of the rate of inflation and real income growth—the right-hand side. For example, if there are 5 percent more dollars and each dollar is spent 2 percent faster the price and/or quantity of commodities rises 7 percent. Assuming velocity remains constant and real output grows 4 percent annually on average, long-run price stability requires a 4 percent rate of monetary expansion. Suppose our assumptions are incorrect and velocity increases by 1 percent and real output grows 3 percent annually on average. In this case the same 4 percent rate of monetary expansion would generate an underlying 2 percent rate of inflation. Monetarists would not be upset by this outcome; the economic differences between a long-run mild deflation, price stability, and mild inflation are minor. The main thing is not to change the rate of monetary expansion and the corresponding long-run rate of inflation, which should be relatively low at most. With 4 percent being perhaps the preferred rate of monetary growth, any constant growth rate between 1 and 7 percent is acceptable, given the likely changes in velocity and real output. Monetary growth outside this range is likely to generate too much deflation or inflation.

### Justifications for a rules policy

Why do Professor Friedman and others favor rules? On what basis do they prefer rules over discretion? Rules are advocated on several grounds. First, an obvious point which, nevertheless, bears stating. *Advocates of a monetary rule believe that money matters in the sense that it has an important effect on aggregate demand.* While the precise moderate (between 1 and 7 percent) rate of monetary growth may be unimportant because aggregate demand only affects the rate of inflation in the long run, a monetary policy which influences aggregate demand causes real output fluctuations in the short run. If money did not matter and had little effect on aggregate demand and output in the short run, the way monetary policy was conducted would be irrelevant. Those who believe money does not matter, do not take the rules versus discretion debate seriously. The belief that money matters is a necessary but not sufficient condition to advocate a rules policy. Other arguments in favor of a rules must be marshalled.

*The second justification says that a monetary rule is the only way to make the Fed consider the money supply.* The only good Fed is a shackled Fed. The Fed frequently employed a target or intermediate variable other than the money supply. For example, the Fed often attempted to stabilize interest rates. As we demonstrated in the last chapter, a policy of stabilizing interest rates magnifies business cycles caused by shifts in aggregate demand. An increase in aggregate demand which tends to overheat the economy also raises the rate of interest as borrowing and the demand for money increase. The higher interest rates reduce some of the expansionary pressure. If the Fed stabilizes interest rates, the moderating influence on the economy of higher interest rates during the boom is lost, by definition. The Fed's attention has not been riveted on interest rates exclusively. During the late 1920s the Fed was alarmed by stock market speculation fueled in large part by low margin bank loans. Lacking the power to single out loans for stock purchases, a determined Fed embarked on a general contractionary policy which reduced total bank loans and the money supply, along with stock market loans. The general contractionary policy did indeed have the desired negative effect on the stock market, and much more. To cleanse the stock market from the speculative influences of the late 1920s, the money supply fell and helped precipitate the Great Depression of the 1930s. The cure was worse than the disease. Monetarists are pessimistic that the Fed will learn from history. The economy is doomed to more booms and busts as the rate of interest, stock market, and other target variables continue to blind the Fed from watching the money supply. Even if discretionary *monetary* policy were preferable to a rule, the Fed would quickly abandon *monetary* policy and practice an interest rate or some other policy. The Fed's October 1979 resolve to pay greater (but not total) attention to the money supply may not be long lasting. A rule forces the Fed to consider only the money supply. While a rule may be second best in principle, it is the best attainable policy.

Monetarists typically are not suave politicians willing to settle for the attainable. Even if the unlikely occurred and the Fed learned from history, *rules are preferable to discretionary policy because* (a) *the economy is basically stable and* (b) *policy lags are long and variable.* Conditions (a) and (b) imply that a discretionary policy will magnify the business cycle. At this point a graph is helpful. Figure 21–1 abstracts from the upward trend and assumes full-employment income remains constant at $Y_F$. The

**FIGURE 21–1**
Discretionary policy represented by the dashed curve magnifies instability. The rules policy represented by the solid curve is preferred because the economy is basically stable and policy lags are long and variable.

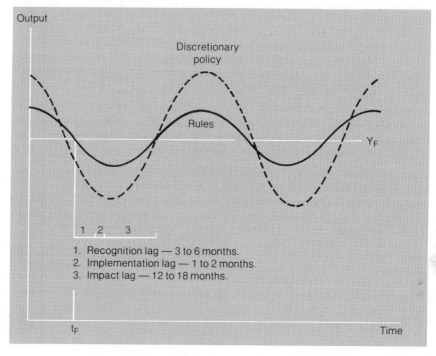

1. Recognition lag — 3 to 6 months.
2. Implementation lag — 1 to 2 months.
3. Impact lag — 12 to 18 months.

solid sine curve intersecting $Y_F$ represents the path of income assuming a monetary rule. We assume for simplicity that the real income path is independent of the specific rule rate of monetary growth, which influences only the long-run rate of inflation. A monetary rule is a neutral policy which neither magnifies nor dampens the normal expansions and contractions of the economy. In a stable economy the expansions and contractions are mild and short. In terms of Figure 21–1, the maximum vertical distance between the solid curve and $Y_F$ measures the amplitude of the business cycle, and the horizontal distance between alternate intersections of $Y_F$ measures the length of the cycle. Since the "mild" and "short" cycles which characterize stable economies are relative concepts, the solid sine curve by itself is at most suggestive of stability. The curve representing income under a neutral policy must be compared with policy lags and the income pattern discretionary policy generates.[1]

### Monetary policy lags

The total policy lag may usefully be divided into three components which vary in length by type of policy and degree of economic knowledge.

1. Recognition lag. The recognition lag is the time interval between the need for policy action and its recognition by policymakers.
2. Implementation lag. The implementation lag is the time interval between the recognition that policy action is necessary and its implementation.
3. Impact lag. The impact lag is the time interval between the implementation of policy and its impact on the economy.[2]

Ideally, the recognition lag would be a lead; the policymaker should anticipate the need for policy action so there is sufficient time for the implementation and impact of policy. While the recognition lag has declined over time, and it may be shortened somewhat more as the collection of statistics and their analysis improve, a lag still exists. The recognition lag now typically is between three and six months. In some cases, however, the recognition lag lies outside this range. In 1979 many economists were forecasting that a recession was "around the corner." They tenaciously stuck to their forecasts and month after month were proven wrong as the forthcoming statistics showed no end to the expansion. By the beginning of 1980 they had sufficient egg on their faces and reversed their long-standing prediction to a continuation of the modest

---

[1] In other words, (a) the economy is basically stable and (b) policy lags are long and variables are not independent statements. Recessions are mild relative to the havoc monetary mismanagement could cause, the policy lags are long relatively to the time it takes a temporarily depressed economy to bounce back unassisted.

[2] Sometimes the recognition and implementation lags are consolidated and called the inside lag, and the impact lag is called the outside lag. The inside lag then is the time interval between the need for policy action and its implementation.

expansion. The change in forecasts could hardly have been more ill advised. Several months later the Commerce Department announced that the contraction in the second quarter of 1980 exceeded any contraction in the postwar period. The earlier forecasts at long last materialized. Armed with the new information, virtually every forecaster claimed in August 1980 that a recession was under way. However, the forecasters were again wrong. Real GNP rose in the third quarter of 1980, and the National Bureau of Economic Research (NBER), the official arbiter of recessions and expansions, announced in 1981 that the recession ended and expansion began in July 1980. The 1980 recession is the shortest on record, lasting just six months, from January to July 1980. The 1980 recession also is unusual in that it contradicts the traditional definition of a recession as at least two consecutive quarters of declining real GNP. Although real GNP rose in the first quarter of 1980, the decline in the second quarter was sufficiently great that the NBER classified the first half of 1980 as a recession.

While the upper limit of the recognition lag may well decrease, the lower limit is unlikely to fall much below three months. Policymakers, like most individuals, are risk averse; it simply is too risky politically and financially to base one's actions on predictions instead of fact. Even though expansionary policy may be appropriate during a boom because the impact lag is so long that the policy will not take hold until the subsequent recession, such policy timing is likely to earn one ridicule because either the impact lag is often ignored or the projected recession does not occur. GNP must first fall before expansionary policy can be safely contemplated. This is true for both monetary and fiscal policymakers, neither of whom has a monopoly on accurate crystal balls and statistics. The length of the recognition lag is independent of the type of policy.

*The implementation lag which follows the recognition lag is largely institutionally determined.* In the United States the implementation lag for monetary policy is approximately one to two months. The Federal Open Market Committee meets approximately monthly in Washington, and telephonic conferences revising the instructions given to the account manager at the last meeting are relatively common. While policy can be initiated virtually immediately after the need is recognized, it may take up to two months to fully implement the policy change in order to minimize the short-run perceived and actual disruptive effects of money on the rate of interest. If the implementation lag for monetary policy is short and predictable, the lag for fiscal policy is the precise opposite, long and variable. Distributional and stabilization issues become inexorably intermeshed. When a tax cut to stimulate the economy is necessary, we fight only to restore our rightful share, while our adversaries are determined to further enrich themselves at our expense. With everyone attempting to increase his share, undoubtedly simply to compensate for previous injustices, even an across-the-board tax cut is considered unfair and discriminatory.

It takes time for coalitions to form and resolve the distributional impact of a tax cut needed for stabilization purposes. In a parliamentary system like Great Britain, where the executive branch is the leadership of the party controlling the legislature and votes by party line are the rule, the fiscal policy implementation lag is quite short. In the United States, however, where the separation of powers is a fundamental concept underlying the Constitution and votes by party line are the exception, the implementation lag can be so long that countercyclical fiscal policy should be attempted only when its desirability is utterly obvious. During a crisis, coalitions are formed more rapidly and the implementation lag is shorter. While everyone recognizes that the implementation lag in the United States is excessively long and variable, attempts to shorten the lag have been unsuccessful. The Democratic Kennedy and Johnson administrations requested from the Democratic Congress the authority to impose across-the-board tax changes. Party ties not withstanding, Congress balked, ever zealous of safeguarding its powers.

The impact lag is perhaps the most controversial. After analyzing the data, Professor Friedman concludes that the monetary policy impact lag is long—about 12 to 18 months—and quite variable. Other monetarists, however, find that the impact lag is considerably shorter. For example, the St. Louis Fed, whose model is described in detail in the next chapter, finds that money has a significant impact on GNP virtually instantaneously, and the impact grows monotonically throughout a year. On the other hand, some large-scale Keynesian structural models find that it takes a full year before monetary policy has any effect, and the full effect is not realized until four years afterwards. Detailed estimates of the impact lag of monetary and fiscal policy are presented in the next chapter. For now, suffice it to say that the estimates are quite diverse.

The various monetary policy lags as estimated by Professor Friedman are graphed in Figure 21-1. Although income is falling before time $t_F$, an expansionary policy is undesirable since resources are more than fully employed before $t_F$ and inflation threatens. An expansionary policy should bolster aggregate demand at time $t_F$ when the economy naturally starts to fall below full employment. However, the need to bolster aggregate demand is recognized approximately 6 months later. It takes the Fed about a month or two to increase the money supply, and aggregate demand responds about 15 months later. The total lag—the time interval between the start of a recession and the expansionary effect of monetary policy on aggregate demand—averages about two years but is quite variable. The economy is stable in the sense that the average length of time it takes an unassisted economy to rebound to full employment approximately equals the total lag of monetary policy. The effects of the expansionary monetary policy normally are felt precisely when they are unnecessary. The ex-ante countercyclical policy becomes an ex-post procyclical policy. Instead of dampening the business cycle, discretionary monetary policy tends to magnify it. The dashed sine curve illustrates the time path of real income when discretionary policy is pursued.

As the average length of the monetary policy lag decreases, discretionary policy is more likely to dampen business cycles, *ceteris paribus.* Compared to Professor Friedman, the St. Louis Fed and other monetarists assert the monetary policy lag is considerably shorter. Nevertheless, monetarists are united in opposing discretionary policy. The likelihood that monetary policy will dampen business cycles depends on the variability of the policy lag in addition to its average value. Monetarists believe that the variability is sufficiently large that discretionary policy is undesirable even if the average lag is relatively short. A graph like Figure 21–1 cannot illustrate the variability of the lags; only the average values of the time paths and lags can be portrayed. While Figure 21–1 illustrates Professor Friedman's view that monetary policy is misdirected on average—the dashed average discretionary curve and the solid average rule curve are in phase but the amplitude of the former is greater—neither Professor Friedman nor anyone else believes monetary policy is *always* destabilizing. Indeed, the case against discretion does not require monetary policy to be destabilizing even most of the time. In other words, in an uncertain and variable world discretionary policy is undesirable even if it is correct on average. Discretionary policy is advantageous only if it is countercyclical more often than it is procyclical. This is so because the loss from not achieving the goal is typically measured by the square of the difference between the actual value of the variable and the goal value. For example, assume the goal is a $100 GNP while actual GNP is $95. The loss from not achieving the goal is $25 = 5^2$ (the loss units are not dollars). Now suppose discretionary policy is implemented. Because the policy lag is unpredictable, GNP fluctuates between $90 and $100 instead of always equalling $100. The average effect of the policy is zero; half the time it successfully attains the goal but the other half it decreases GNP by $5 and makes matters worse. Nevertheless, discretionary policy is inferior to a neutral policy. One period there is no loss as GNP equals $100, but the loss the next period is $100 = 10^2$ as GNP equals 90. The mean loss under a discretionary policy is 50, more than the 25 loss under a neutral policy.

*Finally, monetarists offer various philosophical/political arguments in favor of rules.* The late Professor Henry Simon virtually alleged that discretion would enslave us and rules would set us free.

> There is imminent danger, however, that actual governmental policies will undermine irreparably the kind of economic and political life which most of us prefer to the possible alternatives. This danger manifests itself . . . in measures and policies which involves delegation of legislative powers and the setting-up of *authorities instead of rules.*
>
> It is this danger of substituting authorities for rules which especially deserves attention among students of money. An enterprise system cannot function effectively in the face of extreme uncertainty as to the action of

monetary authorities or, for that matter, as to monetary legislation. . . . We seem largely to have lost sight of the essential point, namely, that definite, stable, legislative rules of the game as to money are of paramount importance to the survival of a system based on freedom of enterprise.[3]

Behind all the philosophical/political arguments is the belief that rules minimize the likelihood of high rates of inflation. While monetarists believe that the effects of moderate (say, up to 5 percent) inflation are not that significant, they believe that high rates of inflation at least fray the social and political fabric of society and more probably tear it asunder. For example, any comprehensive attempt to explain the rise of the Third Reich cannot ignore the inflation of the early 1920s, which left many Germans feeling betrayed. High rates of inflation have occurred only when discretionary policy prevailed. A government is unlikely to announce that it *permanently* will increase the money supply by, say, 100 percent and hope to achieve approximately the same rate of inflation. Even when governments have announced such high rates of monetary growth, they invariably are seen as temporary and often are reductions from even higher rates of monetary expansion. While it seems plausible that rules effectively will end hyperinflation, there is little historical evidence to support this proposition since no country has adopted a rules policy.

Considering polar cases is useful as it focuses attention on basic issues. We must point out, however, that many economists and politicians favor an intermediate policy which allows officials discretion when there is a relatively large deviation from the goal. For example, an intermediate policy might specify that the money supply should grow at 4 percent provided the rate of unemployment is within 2 percentage points of the full-employment rate. When the unemployment rate deviates from the full-employment rate by more than 2 percent, officials should do whatever necessary to ensure a speedy return to full employment. Such an intermediate policy is thought to raise significantly the likelihood that discretionary policy will, in fact, be countercyclical because the length of time it takes the economy to close any gap between the actual and goal values of a variable is positively related to the size of the gap. Attempts to smooth every little wiggle are likely to be counterproductive. Thus, the intermediate policy is a call for benign neglect except when there exists a clear and present danger.

## CHANNELS OF MONETARY POLICY

What are the channels of monetary policy? What is the monetary policy transmission mechanism? Before answering the questions, we should note

---

[3] Henry Simons, "Rules Versus Authorities in Monetary Policy," *Journal of Political Economy*, February 1936. Reprinted by permission of The University of Chicago Press. © 1936 by the University of Chicago. All rights reserved.

that all disciplines develop a vocabulary which occasionally seems designed to confuse the uninitiated. Economists' *investment* is one example, and *channels of monetary policy* is another. On first hearing the term, nearly everyone *incorrectly* associates the channels of monetary policy with the instruments of monetary policy, for example, open-market operations. Those who hope to earn their union card in economics cannot, however, avoid such confusing terms. You will never be considered a master economist unless you talk like one. The channels of monetary policy refers to the linkages between money and income or the means by which monetary changes cause aggregate demand and income changes. Empirical research has confirmed three channels of monetary policy: (1) interest rates, (2) credit rationing, and (3) wealth.

In the Keynesian models, the rate of interest is the only channel of monetary policy. In particular, money affects income because money influences the rate of interest, which in turn influences firms' investment. Early researchers attempted to quantify this channel by interviewing business executives, who stated the rate of interest had only a minor effect on investment. What one says and what one does often do not coincide, and interviews can be biased. In any case, subsequent statistical analysis has assigned to the rate of interest a greater importance on firms' plant and equipment decisions. The immediate effect of the rate of interest on investment is small indeed as the interviews suggested, but the effect grows over time. The rate of interest has a delayed effect on the desired capital stock, and the investment necessary to acquire the desired capital stock is lagged in order to lower costs. For example, stretching the construction period of a steel mill from one to three years substantially reduces costs. Considerably more responsive than plant and equipment, however, is the housing component of investment. The government's attempts to insulate the housing industry from the roller coaster pattern of interest rates in recent years have been marginally successful. The rate of interest remains an important determinant of housing. Finally, the interest rate channel is more pervasive than Keynes indicated. Econometric studies find that durable consumption and state and local government spending also are somewhat responsive to interest rates. Professor Friedman goes even further. He alleges that interest rates influence all types of spending including nondurables and services. The diversity of interest rates coupled with their all pervasive effects has led Professor Friedman to the somewhat paradoxical position of favoring the rate of growth of money over any one interest rate as a measure of "the" rate of interest channel.

### Credit rationing

The rate of interest is only one term or provision in any loan contract. The amount of the loan, term to maturity, and collateral are a few other terms. Neoclassical and Keynesian models assume a standard loan with terms which remain constant over time except for a rate of interest, which adjusts in response to the demand and supply for money and credit. In other words, the rate of interest is assumed to be the sole means of allocating the available money and credit. The simplification is reasonably accurate most of the time but occasionally is wide of the truth. *Credit rationing occurs when the rate of interest remains fixed and the other terms of a loan are adjusted to allocate the supply of money and credit.* Credit rationing may preclude one from receiving credit regardless of how high an interest rate one is willing to pay. There is no denying the existence of credit rationing. One sometimes hears that banks and other depository institutions are not making loans. While the statement is not literally correct—loans are maturing continuously and being renewed—it quickly conveys to the potential borrower the fact that credit is being rationed. The previous relationship between the borrower and the bank, the size of the borrower, the color of the borrower's skin, or some other factor is paramount in determining whether a loan is granted in such cases. By changing the magnitude of credit rationing monetary policy affects aggregate demand while the rate of interest remains constant.

While the extent of credit rationing at any one time is difficult to measure, a consensus states that credit rationing is positively related to the level and change in the rate of interest and will decline significantly in the 1980s. Since interest rates typically are high and rising during a boom, credit rationing is procyclical, being prevalent during booms and virtually nonexistent during depressions. Usury laws, Regulation Q ceilings on deposits, and other institutional factors explain the positive relationship between credit rationing and interest rates. Consumer loans and mortgages typically were subject to usury laws, which were adopted by most states because of an alleged need to protect naive consumers from sophisticated lenders. Having protected the individual consumer, many states sought to protect the collective whole by extending usury laws to state and local borrowing. The usury laws probably harmed consumers individually and collectively more than they helped them. When the rate of interest hit the usury law maximum, state and local governments were forced to postpone expenditures, and consumer credit and mortgages were rationed as these interest rates could not rise further, by definition. Consumers willing to pay higher rates saw credit flowing to firms instead. Many state legislatures were cognizant of the value (lessness ?) of usury laws, and throughout the 1960s and 1970s raised the maximum rate shortly after it became binding. By 1980, Congress passed legislation which virtually abolished state usury laws on mortgages. This complemented the gradual dismantlement of Regulation Q mentioned earlier. Henceforth, savings and loan associations in particular will be able to pay depositors and charge homeowners whatever interest rate is necessary.

Credit rationing is not altogether a thing of the past. At times the Fed wants to lessen the visibility of a program severely restraining the economy and specifically asks bankers to refrain from raising their loan rates. Asked not to use the rate of interest as an allocation device, bankers ration credit. Bankers need not be cajoled to ration credit. They are mindful that poll after poll shows that low interest rates are an ultimate goal for most individuals, and not simply a means of achieving some desired GNP or other goal. When market interest rates rise, banks temporarily maintain their loan rates at the expense of higher profits. Too sharp and rapid an increase in loan rates is sure to incur the wrath of Congress and may produce lower long-run profits. Banks bide their time and ration credit. A higher Federal Reserve discount rate can reduce the time period credit is rationed since bankers can rightfully claim that they are just emulating the Fed.

### Wealth effects

The third channel of monetary policy is the wealth effect. As we indicated earlier, consumption depends on wealth, so that money influences aggregate demand if it affects wealth. Does money affect wealth? When money is fiat money exclusively and is injected into the economic system by transfer payments instead of open-market purchases, then monetary expansion clearly increases society's wealth as someone has additional assets and no one incurred a liability or lost assets. These assumptions were implicit in our discussion of the real balance of Pigou effect. However convenient the assumptions may be, they certainly are unrealistic for an economy like the United States where open-market purchases are the main monetary policy instrument. Some economists have argued that monetary expansion effected by open-market purchases does not generate a wealth effect. At first glance the argument seems plausible. Look at matters from the viewpoint of the seller of the bond. He has additional money but his holdings of government bonds decrease by an equal amount. The composition of the seller's assets changes but his total assets and wealth remain constant. *Those who argue that monetary expansion effected by open-market purchases does not generate a wealth effect err because they concentrate on the wealth of the bond seller alone and ignore how the purchase affects the wealth of the rest of society. We will show that an open-market purchase increases the value of common stocks and, if monetary and fiscal policy are properly measured, necessitates a tax reduction or transfer payment with a present value equal to the open-market purchases. Higher valued common stocks and lower net taxes increase wealth, consumption, and income.*

Common stocks are the ownership claims on firms' plant and equipment and other assets. Being ownership claims, common stocks do not cancel in an aggregate balance sheet and are one component of society's wealth. Higher stock prices enrich stockholders without impoverishing anyone. As a first approximation, the price of common stock equals the capitalized or present value of the firm's earnings stream. Recalling our earlier analysis of interest rates and present values, lower (higher) interest rates raise (reduce) stock prices. The negative relationship between stock prices and the rate of interest is not based exclusively on the premise that stock prices equal the present value of earning streams. Stocks and bonds are substitutes. When interest rates fall and bond prices rise, common stocks appear cheap at current prices, and their dividend yield seems high. Individuals purchase stocks and raise their prices sufficiently so that they no longer are cheap. Therefore, if monetary expansion lowers the rate of interest, then wealth and, subsequently, consumption and income increase.

While it is useful to distinguish the interest rate induced wealth effect from the direct interest rate effect, neither channel is operative when the economy is in a liquidity trap. Moreover, the procyclical nature of credit rationing suggests that rationing is virtually nonexistent in a liquidity trap and, as such, less rationing is an ineffective channel of aggregate demand expansion. It is the banks which seek creditworthy customers during a liquidity trap. Nevertheless, the budgetary aspects of open-market purchases creates a wealth effect which renders monetary policy effective during a liquidity trap, provided fiscal policy is properly measured. Fiscal policy traditionally is measured by the size of the full-employment budget deficit.[4] Since taxes in particular are positively related to income, tax receipts fall and the actual budget deficit increases during a recession. This does *not* indicate fiscal policy is expansionary; the actual budget deficit widens but the *full-employment* budget deficit remains constant, assuming the same full-employment income. Fiscal policy is expansionary and the full-employment budget deficit increases when either tax *rates* are reduced or spending programs increase.

An open-market purchase which increases the monetary base and money supply simultaneously produces an expansionary monetary policy and contradictory fiscal policy because the full-employment budget deficit falls. An open-market purchase reduces the government's net interest payments and debt as the Fed now owns the government securities and returns the interest payments to the Treasury. If the full-employment budget balanced prior to the open-market purchase, it will swing into a surplus following the Fed's purchase. *The Treasury's lower interest expense and bond principal redemptions must be countered by additional expenditures in other areas or lower taxes for an open-market purchase to produce a pure change in monetary policy without influencing fiscal policy.* For simplicity, suppose the Treasury had budgeted the immediate redemption

---

[4] For other measures of fiscal policy see, Alan Blinder and Robert Solow, "Analytical Foundations of Fiscal Policy," in *The Economics of Public Finance* (Washington, D.C.: Brookings Institution, 1974).

of the bonds instead of simply rolling them over.[5] Assuming the Treasury does not cut taxes, a fiscally neutral open-market purchase obliges the Treasury to return to society the money saved by the acquisition of the securities by its partner the Fed. The recipients of the Treasury's largess are wealthier and spend more.[6]

Note again that the open-market purchase neither increases nor decreases the wealth of the seller of the security. The seller exchanges a, say, $100 bond for $100 cash. The rest of society is the beneficiary. The security is worth $100 because its owner is promised future income payments. The seller of the security *voluntarily* sacrificed future income payments in exchange for cash, which produces no measured income but yields liquidity and other services which the former bondholder values. The *voluntary* transaction cannot reduce the bondholder's well being, and his spending will not decrease. Freed by the open-market purchase from having to pay the bondholder, the Treasury now can either make gifts to the rest of society or cut taxes without any budgetary impact. Abstracting from distributional effects, additional gifts are equivalent to tax cuts. When gifts are made, gross taxes are unchanged but net taxes are reduced. The rest of society is better off and spends more. This wealth effect argument did not refer to the rate of interest and, therefore, resuscitates monetary policy from the liquidity trap. A real balance or wealth effect occurs even if the monetary base increases by an open-market purchase which reduces the public's holdings of government bonds.

## COOPERATIVE MONETARY AND FISCAL POLICY: MULTIPLE GOALS AND POLICY UNCERTAINTY

So far we largely have viewed monetary and fiscal policy as substitutes. One group says the money multiplier is large and predictable while the fiscal multiplier is small and variable, and another group says the opposite. One group says policymakers should rely on monetary policy, while another group advocates fiscal policy. Is there ever a need for monetary *and* fiscal policy to be complementary? Do we ever need both policies simultaneously? Must policy be coordinated because only a unique combination of monetary and fiscal policy will achieve the goal? The answer to all three questions is "yes." *Both monetary and fiscal policy are necessary*

---

[5] The assumption that the securities would have been redeemed is clearly unrealistic but in no way affects our conclusion.

[6] The interraction between stocks and flows makes it possible to attribute the additional spending to higher incomes. For example, suppose I give you $1 this year. While you are forever $1 wealthier than you otherwise would be, your income this year rises by $1, but next year's income is unchanged. Suppose further that you spend more this year. Did you spend more because your income or wealth increased? There is no definitive answer. Moreover, any higher spending next year may be attributed to higher lagged income. Nevertheless, in this example we prefer to attribute any additional spending to wealth because the source of the additional spending is constrained in time instead of occurring continuously.

*when either (1) society has multiple goals or (2) policy effects are uncertain.*

We have been implicitly assuming so far that society has a single goal such as full-employment income, and that the effects of policy are known. In such a case, monetary and fiscal policy can be substitutes. If income is below full employment, the income goal generally can be attained by either additional money or government spending. Even "extreme" cases such as a money demand or investment schedule totally unresponsive to the rate of interest do not require both monetary and fiscal policy. In these extreme cases one policy is completely ineffective and reliance must be placed exclusively on the other. *Given the single-mindedness and perfect-knowledge assumptions, monetary and fiscal policy are complementary only if there exists some constraint to the use of policy.* For example, suppose private autonomous expenditures fell by $30 but the institutional structure limits the government spending increase to no more than $10, and the maximum monetary expansion increases aggregate demand by $20. In this case both monetary and fiscal policy are necessary.

While the institutional structure does limit the use of fiscal policy, monetary policy is not so constrained except in the shortest of short runs. Just look at the monetary record of Germany in 1922 and Hungary in 1945. Nevertheless, even if we can ignore constraints, lags, and lack of knowledge of the structure of the economy, both monetary and fiscal policy are necessary because society has multiple goals. The assumption that full-employment income is the only goal is unrealistic. As we mentioned earlier, economists traditionally allege society's goals also encompass economic growth, price stability, and exchange rate stability, and many polls indicate a low rate of interest is an independent goal of the general populace. While some may claim polls are biased and the rate of interest should not be an independent goal because the interest paid by one group is interest received by another group, let us assume the rate of interest is the second goal in order to be able later to illustrate the argument with IS–LM curves.[7] Whatever its merits as an independent goal, the rate of interest does influence significantly the widely accepted goals of economic growth and exchange rate stability. Low rates of interest stimulate economic growth by increasing investment and the capital stock but lower the exchange rate and worsen the balance of payments.

Suppose the interest rate already is sufficiently low that the goals are a higher income and constant rate of interest. (Further reductions in the rate of interest are undesirable because of its impact on the balance of payments.) In this case neither monetary nor fiscal policy alone can achieve both goals. Expansionary monetary policy increases income *and* lowers interest rates. Expansionary fiscal policy increases income *and* raises

---

[7] Lenders are reluctant to tell pollsters that a *high* rate of interest is a goal for fear of appearing antisocial. Thus, the views of borrowers are overweighted.

interest rates. For income to increase while the rate of interest remains constant, both monetary and fiscal policy must be expansionary. This is illustrative of an important economic principle: the number of independent policy instruments generally must equal the number of goals.[8] If we have three goals we need three instruments; four goals, four instruments; and so on. While proving this principle is difficult, the reader familiar with a somewhat similar principle in mathematics may be more willing to accept this economic principle. Generally, how many equations are needed to solve for two variables? Two. Many values of the variables x and y satisfy the equation $x + 2y = 5$. If $x = 0$, then $y = 2.5 = (5/2)$ satisfies the equation, and if $y = 0$, then $x = 5$ satisfies the equation. Letting one variable equal zero is the analog of using only one policy to achieve the goal. The two equations $x + 2y = 5$ and $x + 3y = 7$ have a unique non-zero solution: $x = 1$ and $y = 2$. The number of equations and variables are the analogs of goals and instruments, respectively. Both instruments (variables) x and y must be "used", that is, cannot equal zero, in order to solve the two equations (goals). No values of x and y satisfy the three equations $x + 2y = 5$, $x + 3y = 7$, and $x + 4y = 8$. Two instruments cannot satisfy three goals.

An IS–LM graph illustrates the previous paragraph. (Those who ignored the IS–LM analysis may proceed directly to the next paragraph.) Look at Figure 21–2. The solid IS and LM curves representing the initial position of the economy show income is $y_0$ and the rate of interest is $r_0$. Suppose the objective is $y_F$ while any rate of interest is acceptable. This is illustrated by the vertical line, any point on which is equally desirable. Either expansionary monetary policy which shifts the LM curve from the solid to the dashed position or expansionary fiscal policy which shifts the IS curve to the dashed position is sufficient. Now assume an interest rate goal so only one point on the $y_F$ line is acceptable. Barring the fortuitous where either $r_g$ or $r_m$ is the interest rate goal, neither monetary nor fiscal policy alone is sufficient. If the multiple goal is $r_0$ and $y_F$, expansionary monetary and fiscal policy are necessary as indicated by the dotted IS and LM curves. The attainment of multiple policy goals requires cooperation.[9] Only one pair of IS and LM curves goes through any one point.

### The need for cooperation

Attainment of multiple goals may require seemingly perverse and foolish actions by one policymaker. This is best demonstrated by an algebraic/numerical example. Since the principle to be illustrated here is

---

[8] The Noble Prize winner Jan Tinbergen first elucidated this principle in *On the Theory of Economic Policy* (Amsterdam, 1952).

[9] In Chapter 20's section on fiscal policy at full employment, there were two instruments, monetary and fiscal policy, but three goal variables—real income, the price level, and the rate of interest.

**FIGURE 21–2**
Both monetary and fiscal policy are necessary to achieve a specific income/rate of interest combination such as ($y_F$, $r_0$). In general, the number of policy instruments must equal the number of goals.

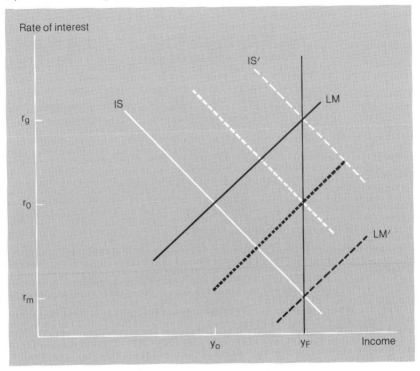

not particular to monetary or fiscal policy, we use general notation. Let the goal variables be $y_1$ and $y_2$. Given the current values of the variables, the desired changes in $y_1$ and $y_2$ are 3 and 6, respectively. Algebraically,

$$\Delta y_1^d = 3 \quad \text{and} \quad \Delta y_2^d = 6 \qquad (21\text{--}1)$$

where the superscript represents "desired."

There also are two policy tools, $x_1$ and $x_2$. The effects of the tools on the goals, which we assume are known with certainty, are shown below.

$$\Delta y_1 = \Delta x_1 \quad \text{and} \quad \Delta y_2 = \Delta x_1,$$
$$\Delta y_1 = 3\Delta x_2 \quad \text{and} \quad \Delta y_2 = 5\Delta x_2. \qquad (21\text{--}2)$$

The equations above are multipliers, although written somewhat differently than usual. For example, the $x_2$ multiplier on $y_1$ is 3. Both $x_1$ and $x_2$ have positive effects on $y_1$ and $y_2$, and society wants both $y_1$ and $y_2$ to increase. Given this, one's "gut" reaction is that both policy tools should increase. However, neither policy tool can accomplish both goals simultaneously. Looking at equations (21–1) and (21–2), $x_1$ has the same effect on goals $y_1$ and $y_2$, but society wants the change in $y_2$ to be twice the change $y_1$. If $\Delta x_1 = 3$ so $\Delta y_1 = 3$ and the first goal is satisfied, then $\Delta y_2 = 3$, which is only 50 percent of $\Delta y_2^d$. A unitary increase in $x_2$ fulfills the $y_1$ goal but leaves the $y_2$ goal a unit short, that is, $\Delta y_2 = 5$ instead of 6. The tool $x_2$ does come close to achieving both goals, but close is not good enough. It appears both $x_1$ and $x_2$ should increase. How much should the two tools be increased in order to fulfill the goals exactly?

The reader has been given a difficult *technical* problem. However, we have assumed the even more difficult *political* and *economic* problems were solved. The political problem is the achievement of a consensus on specific goals given here by equation (21–1). For example, everyone favors full employment but what specifically is full employment? Is it 4 percent unemployment, 6 percent, or some other number? Policies proposed when unemployment is, say, 5 percent clearly depend on one's estimate of full employment. A consensus on many economic policies is difficult because they are zero sum games, that is, the benefits to our group or in one area are offset by equal losses elsewhere. After a consensus finally has been reached the effect of the instruments on the goals must be ascertained. Economists spend a lifetime estimating imperfectly the type of information assumed to be known with certainty in equation (21–2). Having been given the outcome of the political process, equation (21–1), and of economic investigations, equation (21–2), the technician sets the dials at appropriate levels.

What answer did you get? By how much must $x_1$ and $x_2$ change to achieve the goal? The answer is the solution to the equations

$$3 = \Delta x_1 + 3\Delta x_2$$
$$6 = \Delta x_1 + 5\Delta x_2 \qquad (21\text{–}3)$$

Equations (21–3) are derived from equations (21–1) and (21–2). The goal or desired change, the left-hand side of (21–3), is set equal to the sum of the changes due to $x_1$ and $x_2$, the right-hand side. Solving equation (21–3),

$$\Delta x_1 = -1.5 \quad \text{and} \quad \Delta x_2 = 1.5$$

When one looks in isolation at the policymaker responsible for $x_1$, he appears to be doing the wrong thing. One wants variables $y_1$ and $y_2$ to increase, and $x_1$ causes both variables to increase, yet the policymaker decreases $x_1$. Policymaker $x_1$ is acting correctly however. Simultaneous achievement of the goals requires reducing $x_1$. Policymakers should not be judged in isolation.

### Policy uncertainty

The estimates of the government spending and money multipliers are numerous and diverse. No policymaker should assume that he has a pipeline to the Truth making his estimates perfectly accurate. Even if there were a single goal, the use of both monetary and fiscal policy is desirable because the effects of policy are uncertain.[10] The joint use of monetary and fiscal policy does not guarantee the goal will be fulfilled, but it does reduce the likelihood of large errors. Consider the following example. Suppose the goal is to increase y by 8, that is, $\Delta y^d = 8$. For simplicity, assume the relationships between the goal and two tools, $x_1$ and $x_2$, are similar. The expected $x_1$ and $x_2$ multipliers are 4 but the actua! values in each case are uncertain. The probabilities are one third that the $x_1$ and $x_2$ multipliers will be 2, 4, or 6. Mathematically,

$$E(\Delta y/\Delta x_1) = E(\Delta y/\Delta x_2) = 4$$
$$Pr(\Delta y/\Delta x_1 = 2) = Pr(\Delta y/\Delta x_1 = 4) = Pr(\Delta y/\Delta x_1 = 6) = \tfrac{1}{3}$$
$$Pr(\Delta y/\Delta x_2 = 2) = Pr(\Delta y/\Delta x_2 = 4) = Pr(\Delta y/\Delta x_2 = 6) = \tfrac{1}{3}$$

If *either* $x_1$ or $x_2$ is used, the policymakers increase the tool by 2 units so the expected change in y equals the desired change. The probabilities are one third the actual change may be either 4, 8, or 12.

$$\text{Given } \Delta x_1 \text{ or } \Delta x_2 = 2, \quad E(\Delta y) = 8, \text{ and}$$
$$Pr(\Delta y = 4) = Pr(\Delta y = 8) = Pr(\Delta y = 12) = 1/3 \quad (21\text{–}4)$$

Now assume the policymakers increase *both* $x_1$ *and* $x_2$ by one unit so the expected change also equals 8.

$$(21\text{–}5)$$

---

[10] The uncertainty considered here differs from the uncertainty present in the analysis of the money supply versus interest rate controversy. The earlier uncertainty was about the state of the economy as represented by aggregate demand and money demand. The uncertainty currently considered deals with the effects of policy. In terms of the IS–LM curve, we previously were uncertain about the position of the IS and LM curves. We now consider uncertainty regarding the magnitude of the shifts of the curves in response to government spending and monetary policy.

Regardless of the value of $\Delta y/\Delta x_1$, each of the three possible values of $\Delta y/\Delta x_2$ is assumed equally likely.[11] The probability that $\Delta y = 4$ is $\frac{1}{3}$ when either $x_1$ or $x_2$ is employed. When both policies are used, the probability that $\Delta y = 4$ is reduced to $\frac{1}{9}$, where the latter is the product of the equal $\frac{1}{3}$ probabilities that $\Delta y/\Delta x_1 = 2$ and $\Delta y/\Delta x_2 = 2$. A comparison of equations (21–4) and (21–5) shows that reliance on both policies instead of one alone reduces the likelihood of large errors and the variability of the goal.

While probably not immediately apparent, equations (21–4) and (21–5) are another illustration of the advantages of portfolio diversification. The policy tools correspond with assets in this case. Neither an investor nor a policymaker in an uncertain world should place all his eggs in one basket. The use of both policies spreads the risk, that is, minimizes the likelihood of unfavorable outcomes.

## MONETARY AND FISCAL POLICY: COOPERATION OR SUBSERVIENCE?

The last section on the theory of optimal policy assumed policymakers have common, if multiple, goals and argued for coordinated, simultaneously executed monetary and fiscal policy. The history of policy may suggest that actual policy often is not coordinated in any meaningful sense. The suggestion is partially correct, and partially wrong. The abstract theory of policy argued for coordination but did *not* state how the two policies should be related. We showed that at times both policies should move in the same direction, while at other times coordinated policy adjusts instruments in different directions. Optimal coordination, however, cannot explain all disparate policy movements. Policymakers often cannot agree on the goal variables, and when they finally reach agreement on the variables, the specific target values still are at issue. For example, one policymaker's target rate of unemployment may be 4 percent while another aims for 6 percent. Different goals may manifest themselves by uncoordinated, disparate policy movements or by the dominance of one policymaker over another. Are monetary and fiscal policy, in fact, coordinated and, if so, do they move in the same or opposite direction? If policymakers disagree on the goals, does policy become uncoordinated or does one policymaker become subservient to the other? An episodical and incomplete history is all that can be presented without undue length.

### The 1940s: Pegging interest rates

One could argue that monetary policy did not exist throughout the 1940s. As mentioned earlier, the monetary authorities were instructed to

---

[11] Our assumption that policies $x_1$ and $x_2$ are independent simplifies the analysis but is not crucial. The use of both policies reduces variability provided the policies are not perfectly positively correlated.

let the money supply vary as necessary in order to peg interest rates. The Fed bought whatever government bonds the private sector refused at the pegged interest rate structure. This policy was adopted for the pure convenience of the Treasury. Interest rates were set at a low level in order to minimize the Treasury's interest expense and deficit. The effect of the rate of interest on other sectors and goals was irrelevant, at least until the late 1940s.

Pegging interest rates makes fiscal policy and the money supply move in the same direction. Expansionary fiscal policy tends to raise the rate of interest, which is held constant by increasing the money supply. Pegging interest rates lets the Treasury concentrate exclusively on its other objective, with the Fed taking care of the interest rate. It is unlikely, however, that such a division of labor will lead to successful attainment of the other objective. The Fed compensates for any effect the Treasury has on the rates of interest but, in so doing, the Fed affects the Treasury's other goal, requiring further action by the Treasury. Since the relationship between the rate of interest and another goal such as full-employment income does not remain constant over time, constant or pegged interest rates imply that the other objective must be sacrificed at times.

During World War II and shortly thereafter, a pegged interest rate structure was consonant with the Fed's objective. The extremely low pegged rates helped finance the war, and everyone was 100 percent behind the war effort. Raising interest rates after the war was eschewed as unpatriotic. Those who had purchased bonds and helped the war effort would incur capital losses from higher interest rates. The Fed also favored a continuation of the low interest rate policy because it would avert the major postwar depression many were forecasting. Montgomery Ward has earned a permanent place in the history of business for not expanding and falling far behind Sears because it forecast a depression. The postwar depression did not materialize by 1950, however, and forecasts were revised. In that year the United States became embroiled in the Korean War. Sharply higher defense expenditures and other increases in aggregate demand combined with the low pegged interest rates now produced an inflationary situation. At this point the Federal Reserve and Treasury sharply disagreed on goals. The Treasury was willing to sacrifice price stability for low interest rates, but the Fed was not so disposed.[12] It claimed that patriotism now called for high interest rates. While this would produce a nominal capital loss, high interest rates would arrest inflation and real capital losses to bondholders. By wrapping its objectives in flag and country, the Fed regained its independence—or at least stopped being totally subservient to the Treasury—in the famous Federal Reserve—Treasury Accord of 1951.

---

[12] See Chapter 20's section on fiscal policy at full employment.

### The 1950s: Even keel

The post-Accord, 1950s policy of "even keel" made the Fed a servant of the Treasury only for short periods, which if repeated sufficiently often become a long period. Even keel means that the Fed keeps interest rates approximately constant—downward interest movements are tolerable but upward movements are taboo—in the week or so before and after major Treasury financings. As we mentioned in Chapter 6, new Treasury issues in the 1950s were marketed at prespecified terms instead of being auctioned. Few bonds would be sold if market interest rates rose subsequent to the announcement of the bond's terms but prior to the sale date. Given the Treasury's phobia of "failed" issues, the Fed was coerced to even keel before the issue date, and it continued doing so afterwards so that the new bondholders would not suffer an immediate capital loss and be less receptive to government bonds in the future.

Occasional even keeling hardly ties the Fed's hands, but protracted periods of even keel approach a policy of pegging interest rates. Given that much of the large Treasury debt was relatively short term, Treasury financings occurred quite frequently. Therefore, even keel did significantly constrain Fed behavior, though much less than prior to the Accord. With the passage of time, however, the Fed asserted greater independence, and even keel constraints on monetary actions became less important for various reasons. First, the Fed believed that the market could tolerate sharper interest rate movements during periods of Treasury inactivity. Second, the 1950s was a relatively prosperous period, and the Eisenhower administration generally adopted a balanced budget or small deficit. Consequently, the ratio of the national debt to income fell, and "major" financings requiring even keel became less frequent. By the late 1950s monetary policy continued to accommodate fiscal policy largely because such action was congruent with the Fed's objectives.

### The 1960s: The beginnings of cooperation

The 1960s differed from the earlier periods insofar as the Treasury and Fed considered themselves coequals, with each openly critical about the other's policy. Monetary and fiscal policy often moved in different directions. By the early 1960s it became evident that the persistent United States balance of payments deficit was not a transient phenomenon. At the same time the unemployment rate was excessively high. As indicated in Chapter 5, the Fed attempted to cure the twin evils of high unemployment and a balance of payments deficit by Operation Twist, that is, raising short-term and lowering long-term interest rates. The Treasury believed that the Fed was overly concerned with the balance of payments deficit. Besides twisting the yield curve, the Treasury wanted the Fed to reduce the overall level of interest rates and, thereby, unemployment, at the expense of the balance of payments if necessary. The Fed refused. Institutional constraints hampered fiscal policy. The Treasury in the early 1960s could not implement an expansionary fiscal policy, which may have reduced both unemployment and the balance of payments deficit.

The sizable reduction of personal and corporate income tax rates proposed by President John F. Kennedy in late 1962 was finally enacted by Congress in 1964 after his death. The sizable tax reduction, which became effective in steps in 1964 and 1965, is a classic example of too much, too late. The tax cut was proposed in 1962 when the unemployment rate exceeded 5.5 percent; it was fully implemented in late 1965 when the unemployment rate was 4.4 percent. Moreover, the Vietnam War buildup began in earnest in 1965. A combination of war expenditures and the tax cut swung the full-employment budget from a $3.2 billion surplus in the 4th quarter of 1963 to a $14.9 billion deficit by the end of 1965.[13] At this point even the Treasury feared that the fiscal stimulus was too great to be consistent with price stability. With the Treasury unable to turn off the fiscal spigot, the Fed, always more concerned than the Treasury about inflation and the balance of payment, was only too willing to apply the monetary brakes. The money supply grew by 1 percent in 1966. *Coordinated policy subject to constraints had the monetary and fiscal instruments move in different directions.*

The Fed may have overreacted in 1966. The halt in monetary growth produced a "credit crunch" and record high interest rates; disintermediation occurred; the stability of intermediaries was threatened; and residential construction nose dived. Fortunately, however, the economy only suffered a minirecession as monetary policy was able to reverse itself quickly in 1967. Monetary policy became more or less neutral. Given the size of the fiscal stimulus, the monetary restraint consistent with price stability would have had too large an impact on intermediaries and housing. Inflation became a reality.

In June 1968, a full three years after the rise in federal expenditures due to the Vietnam War and the Great Society, Congress finally passed the Revenue and Expenditure Control Act, which levied a 10 percent income tax surcharge and placed a ceiling on federal expenditures. The full-employment budget shifted from a $30 billion deficit in the second quarter of 1968 to a modest surplus a year later. The Federal Reserve and others feared a fiscal overkill so the monetary growth rate was accelerated. Monetary and fiscal policy again moved in opposite directions although largely sharing the same goals. By mid-1969, however, it became clear

---

[13] Robert J. Gordon, *Macroeconomics* (Boston: Little, Brown, 1978), Appendix B. The actual federal budget approximately balanced in 1965 in spite of the tax cut. This has led supply-side economists to claim that the economy was on the backward bending portion of the Laffer curve. The tax cuts supposedly were deflationary because they raised output much more than demand. However, an inflationary tax cut is consistent with a subsequent budget surplus provided an acceleration effect is sufficiently strong.

that fiscal policy was not having its intended negative effect on aggregate demand, perhaps because the tax increase, a surcharge, was only temporary. The Fed reversed itself. The monetary growth rate plummeted from 8 percent annually in late 1968 to 6 percent in the first half of 1969, and 1 percent in the second half of 1969. The Fed again may have overreacted. While other factors besides monetary policy can explain recessions, the recession of 1969–70 was underway.

The 1970s was one of the most dismal decades in the economic history of the United States. The discomfort index, the sum of the rates of unemployment and inflation, hovered around 20 percent some years. Large deficits and high rates of monetary growth were chronic. Economists without a knowledge of the history of the 1940s and 1950s were surprised to learn that, unlike 1966 and 1968, monetary policy accommodated fiscal policy. Many rediscovered that in order to prevent sharp *short-run* interest rate movements, monetary and fiscal policy must move in the same direction. However, the *long-run* effect of accommodating the deficit by increasing the rate of monetary growth is inflation and higher nominal interest rates. What were record high mortgage rates in 1966 would seem extremely low to new homeowners in 1980. The less said about the 1970s, the better for economists.

## CHARACTERISTICS OF EFFECTIVE POLICY

What are the criteria for evaluating policy effectiveness? Under what conditions is a policy, monetary or otherwise, likely to achieve its objective? What characteristics must an effective policy instrument possess? The characteristic most often listed first by others and implicitly stressed by us so far is the size of the multiplier. While a large multiplier is not always desirable, *the effectiveness of a policy generally is positively related to its multiplier, that is, the magnitude of its effect on the goal.* Why is policy effectiveness positively related to its multiplier? Clearly, policy is totally worthless if the multiplier is zero. Provided the multiplier is positive, however small, it is less clear that a large multiplier enhances the policy's effectiveness. Suppose the money multiplier equals 50 in economy A and 2 in economy B, and income is $100 below the full-employment level in both economies. Is monetary policy more effective in economy A? In economies A and B the monetary authorities would increase the money supply by $2 and $50, respectively, and achieve the goal. Why is policy more effective in A because the money supply must increase by only $2 instead of $50? Monetary expansion during any time period may be constrained for various resources. *The existence of constraints on policy changes implies that a large multiplier enhances policy effectiveness.* In our example, if the constraint limiting the money supply change were $30, the goal could be achieved in economy A but not in economy B.

## The resource cost of monetary and fiscal policy

Any policy uses resources. Because of this fact, the size of the multiplier is an important criterion of policy effectiveness. Policies differ in the amount of resources used. Any type of spending, private or government, uses resources equal to the amount spent. In contrast to the dollar-for-dollar relationship between government spending and resource cost, there is virtually no resource cost to tax and monetary policy. The resource cost of tax policy includes the time spent in reaching a consensus on the specific tax provisions, the cost of printing new forms, the time spent by taxpayers familiarizing themselves with new tax laws, and so on. These costs typically are a small percentage of tax receipts. Similarly, the annual cost of monetary changes are small and may be ignored as a first approximation.[14] Additional government spending next year is much more costly in terms of resources than equal tax cuts or monetary increases.

What are the implications of the different resource costs incurred by the various policies? In an ideal world, government spending would not be used for stabilization purposes, so fiscal policy would be limited to tax policy. Stabilization policy would rely on monetary policy or tax policy exclusively, if attempted at all. Government would spend for allocation purposes exclusively. That is, government spending uses resources but it also yields society benefits. Society values the police and fire protection, schools, roads, and other goods and services provided by government. Resources are allocated correctly when the marginal benefit of government spending equals marginal cost. In an ideal world, government spending programs would be expanded to the point where the benefit from an additional dollar spent equals unity, which is the marginal resource cost. The direct benefit of tax and monetary policy are small and like their cost may be ignored. Once the appropriate allocation of resources and goods

---

[14] We are not contradicting our earlier assertion that currency is fiat money but checkable deposits are full-bodied money. The present value of the cost of checkable deposits maintained forever equals the amount of the deposits. However, the text here considers the annual cost of deposits. Annual banking costs and revenues are a small fraction of their assets and deposits.

Money and government spending have different dimensions; the former is a stock while the latter is a flow. This makes a meaningful comparison of costs difficult. The dollar-for-dollar relationship between government spending and resource cost is independent of the time period. For example, whether the government spends $1 during a calendar quarter or decelerates its spending rate to spend the same amount during a year, resources worth $1 are used. On the other hand, the cost of maintaining money in existence clearly depends on the time period. The cost of a larger money supply for a calendar quarter is one fourth the cost of a larger money supply for a full year. Should we compare $1 government spending with the cost of maintaining an additional dollar in circulation for a quarter, a year, or forever? While a full answer is beyond the scope of this book, the answer depends in part on the goal and the time pattern and ultimate size of the multiplier between policy and goal. By comparing annual costs, we are implicitly assuming that within a year money and government spending have roughly the same effect on income, which is the goal and has the dimension of a flow.

and services between the private and government sectors has been determined, the government selects that monetary and tax policy combination which will pay for its expenditures and promote full employment with price stability. If aggregate demand falls and discretionary policy is advisable, the government should cut taxes or increase the quantity of money in order to stabilize the economy. The benefits from expanding government spending beyond the current *optimum* do not justify the cost, by definition. While this argument appears to be a powerful weapon for opponents of government spending, the sword cuts both ways. Government programs which have been selected appropriately must not be cut during inflationary periods. We must not let national defense and our schools deteriorate during inflation, just as we must recognize the folly of a public works project to build pyramids when we and our neighbors are unemployed.[15]

### Resource costs and the effectiveness of government spending

We do not and will not live in an ideal world. Countercyclical government spending has been and will continue to be employed. Considering the cost and benefits of government spending, is a large or small government spending multiplier desirable? The answer clearly depends on how one evaluates government spending, but the precise relationship between one's evaluation of government spending and the size of the multiplier of effective policy is contrary to the initial reaction of many. Because tastes and opinions differ, government is spending the correct amount and *aggregate* marginal benefits equal cost even though some believe government is profligate and others denounce it for penny pinching. Government spending is considered effective when the size of the multiplier is *negatively* related to one's evaluation of the benefits from government spending.[16] For those who believe that government spends beyond the point where benefits equal cost, a *large* multiplier enhances the effectiveness of government spending because the resource cost of achieving full employment is low. For example, if income is $100 below full employment and government builds pyramids or otherwise spends foolishly to lift the economy out of a recession, government would waste and the private sector would forego $10 if the multiplier were 10. Government waste rises to $50 if the multiplier were 2. If your analysis of the data indicates the government spending multiplier is small and you consider government spending beneficial, then you should grade government spending highly. In this case the government can provide society with parks, clean air, and other worthwhile products because the private sector's responding pro-

---

[15] Technically speaking, the opportunity cost of government spending is zero only if unemployment exists *and* it cannot be reduced by monetary or tax policy.

[16] We are implicitly assuming the economy is more prone to recessions than overemployment.

pensity and the multiplier are small, which is all to the good because the private sector would have acquired electric toothbrushes, gas guzzlers, and other silly products.

Although there is no logical connection between one's evaluation of the benefits of government spending and one's empirical estimate of the government spending multiplier, the two are *positively* related. Conservatives like Professor Friedman believe much government spending is wasteful, and the government spending multiplier is small. Liberals like Professor John Kenneth Galbraith believe the benefits of government spending far outweigh the cost, and the government spending multiplier is large. Therefore, both conservatives and liberals believe that government spending is inefficient, at least in its resource effects. Everyone feels frustrated by government spending. Conservatives who oppose government spending would like the government multiplier to be large so that only a little "wasteful" spending would push the economy to full employment. The desired and estimated values of the multiplier do not coincide. While conservatives would like a large government spending multiplier, they estimate the multiplier to be small. Precisely because it is small, we must tolerate significant government waste in our quest for economic stability. On the other hand, liberals who support government spending would like the government multiplier to be small so that we could reap substantial benefits from government spending before being constrained by full employment. The desired and estimated values of the multiplier do not coincide. Liberals would like a small government spending multiplier, but their estimates indicate it is large. Precisely because it is large, we must forsake significant government benefits in our quest for economic stability.

The big-bang-for-a-buck philosophy was made most explicit by the Defense Department in the 1950s. A weapons system which could cheaply kill all our enemies 100 times over was an efficient system. We prepared for global warfare and discounted local skirmishes. This bang-for-buck philosophy is so deeply enrooted that those whose empirical studies estimate a large government spending multiplier often uncritically allege government spending is effective. A large multiplier definitely enhances policy effectiveness when the maximum policy change is constrained. Reflecting on the resource cost of government spending indicates, however, that a large multiplier enhances policy effectiveness only if one believes that the benefits of government spending are quite small so the amount of low benefit/high cost government programs cannot expand much. Moreover, a large multiplier definitely is undesirable when the policy is uncontrolled. Suppose the money multiplier were one trillion. The danger to livelihoods due to float and other uncontrolled sources of the monetary base would rival the danger to life due to accidental nuclear warfare. If the arguments against a large multiplier are almost as persuasive as the pro arguments, why did we stress the multiplier in earlier chapters? As we shall see shortly, the size of the multiplier is positively associated with most other policy characteristics which unquestionably enhance effectiveness. It is for this reason that the multiplier was stressed in the first pass at difficult problems where some simplification was essential. The multiplier is not unimportant in its own right but its main importance stems from its positive relationship with other effectiveness characteristics.

### Policy predictability

In an uncertain, unpredictable world THE multiplier is the AVERAGE multiplier. A policy will not have the same effect at all times; the effect of any policy will be variable. *To be effective and have a high likelihood of attaining the goal, the variability of policy must be small relative to its average effect.* In other words, policy is reliable when the t-ratio of the multiplier is large, that is, the ratio of the average multiplier to the variability (standard deviation) of the multiplier. Thus, the bang-for-buck or (average) size of the multiplier criterion is positively related to a policy's reliability.

Table 21–1 illustrates that deviations from the goal will be small and policy is reliable when the t-ratio is large. The table assumes there are

**TABLE 21–1  Policy is effective when the variability of the multiplier is small relative to its average value**

| Probability | Possible multiplier values | | |
|---|---|---|---|
| | $\Delta y/\Delta A$ | $\Delta y/\Delta B$ | $\Delta y/\Delta C$ |
| 1/3 | 2 | 4 | 1 |
| 1/3 | 3 | 5 | 3 |
| 1/3 | 4 | 6 | 5 |
| | Average multiplier; variability (standard deviation) | | |
| | $3; \sqrt{2/3}$ | $5; \sqrt{2/3}$ | $3; \sqrt{8/3}$ |
| | Possible values of $\Delta y$ given current shortfall of 15 | | |
| | $\Delta A = 5$ | $\Delta B = 3$ | $\Delta C = 5$ |
| 1/3 | 10 | 12 | 5 |
| 1/3 | 15 | 15 | 15 |
| 1/3 | 20 | 18 | 25 |

three policy instruments, A, B, and C, none of which has a perfectly predictable multiplier effect on the goal. Each policy yields three equally likely (probability = ⅓) multipliers. For example, one third of the time the multiplier of policy A is 2, one third of the time it is 3, and one third of the time it is 4. The information in the first three rows is summarized by row 4, which shows the average or expected multiplier followed by its standard deviation, a measure of variability. Policy B has a larger average multiplier than either policy A or C, and the standard deviation of policies A and B are equal and smaller than the variability of policy C. (The range, a more easily computed but inferior measure of variability, also shows that C is more variable than either A or B, which are equally variable.) Therefore, B, A, and C is the ranking of the policies ordered by the t-ratio, a measure of predictability. Assuming the goal variable y is 15 units below the desired value, the last three rows of Table 21–1 indicate the possible outcomes when policy is adjusted to be correct on average. For example, $\Delta A = 5$ because the average A multiplier is 3, and the y shortfall is 15. The rankings ordered by the t-ratios and closeness to the goal of $\Delta y = 15$ coincide. Policy B is most reliable; its average multiplier is large relative to its variability.[17]

A third criterion of policy effectiveness is short time lags, the importance of which was emphasized in the rules versus discretion debate. As a first approximation, the recognition lag is identical for all policies. *Effective policies have a short implementation and impact lags.*[18]

Policies often are not coordinated even though coordination is essential to the achievement of multiple goals. When policy is uncoordinated, a policymaker with one instrument cannot attain multiple goals and may not even attempt to achieve the highest ranking goal because of the policy's undesirable side effects on secondary goals. *Effective policy is free of undesirable side effects.*

The brevity of the last two paragraphs should not be interpreted as indicating that short time lags and the lack of undesirable side effects are relatively unimportant. The brevity is due to their prior analysis.

## SUMMARY

The basic Keynesian model's portrayal of the simplicity of implementing policies that maintain continuous full employment contrasts sharply with reality. Policymakers encounter numerous difficult problems. The first thing any policymaker must do is determine the goals. Precisely what is he or she attempting to accomplish? Monetary and fiscal policymakers have often disagreed on goals. In the 1940s a strong Treasury brought the Fed under its complete control, while in the 1960s the Fed and Treasury acted as coequals when they disagreed and cooperated when they shared common goals.

---

[17] We are not suggesting that a policymaker should rely on policy B exclusively. A previous section stated that multiple policies should be employed when their effects are uncertain. The greater reliability of B implies the policymaker will prescribe larger doses of B than A and C, and the substitution for B of an independent distribution identical to either A or C reduces aggregate reliability.

[18] Sometimes the lengths of the two lags are listed as separate criteria, in which case a short implementation lag is called policy reversibility.

Cooperation is essential to achieve multiple goals. Cooperation also is essential when the effects of the policies themselves are uncertain. The next chapter illustrates this uncertainty by presenting a small sample of the diverse estimates of the monetary and fiscal policy multipliers. The use of multiple policies when uncertainty exists reduces the likelihood of large deviations from the goal, just as a diversified portfolio reduces the likelihood of large losses.

Professor Friedman and most monetarists believe that the variability in the magnitude and timing of monetary policy, in combination with an average lag of one to one and a half years, precludes the effective use of monetary policy as a stabilization tool. No one is questioning the Fed's motives or *relative* ability. Monetarists just claim that effective stabilization policy is beyond the ability of any group and, consequently, a rules policy should be adopted.

## QUESTIONS

1. Distinguish between monetary policy conducted according to (*a*) rules and (*b*) discretion.
2. Contrast the proposed fiscal policy of the advocates of (*a*) rules and (*b*) discretionary policy.
3. What long-run objective governs the rate of growth of the money supply?
4. Explain why monetarists prefer a rules policy.
5. List and define the three lags that occur when using discretionary policy.
6. List the three channels of monetary policy. Which channel operates in Keynesian models?
7. What is credit rationing? In what portion of the business cycle is it more prevalent?
8. When does monetary expansion increase society's wealth?
9. What is the basis for the contention that the wealth effect occurs even when the monetary base increases by an open-market purchase?
10. How many instruments are needed to attain a set of goals? Illustrate your answer with an IS–LM graph, given the goal is a lower interest rate and constant income.
11. In an uncertain world, what is the benefit of using both monetary and fiscal policy?
12. Discuss the relationship between monetary and fiscal policy in the 1940s, the 1950s, and the 1960s.
13. If you believe that the benefits of government spending are extremely small, would you prefer a large or a small government spending multiplier? Explain.
14. What are the criteria by which one judges the effectiveness of monetary or fiscal policy?

# An empirical summary of the money-income relationship

**22**

Economic theory does not pin down the monetary and fiscal policy multipliers. It is time we look at the empirical evidence. The evidence is inconclusive largely because two a priori reasonable research strategies yield different results. *One research strategy estimates large-scale structural models, that is, postulates many demand and supply equations and estimates them statistically.* The large-scale econometric models are like our IS–LM, only more complicated. Our IS–LM model has a total of eight equations, six demand and supply equations—consumption, investment, government spending, taxes, money demand, and money supply—and two equilibrium equations—IS and LM. Some large-scale structural models have more than 900 equations. Instead of one consumption equation, there are equations for durables, nondurables, and services, each of which is influenced by somewhat different variables. We might expect the rate of interest to have a greater effect on durables, such as automobiles, than on services. The really large models further disaggregate durables, nondurables, and services. After all the equations are estimated statistically, the model is thrown into a computer to simulate the estimated response of the economy to the autonomous variables, particularly monetary and fiscal policy variables. The computer grinds out predictions based on the many estimated equations and their interaction.

The second research strategy cuts through the thicket of supply and demand equations and gets to the bottom line immediately. *Reduced form models relate income directly to monetary and fiscal policy variables and, occasionally, other exogenous variables such as labor strikes.* The simplicity of reduced form models makes possible their presentation.

$$\Delta Y_t = a_0 + \sum_{i=0}^{n} b_i \Delta M_{t-i} + \sum_{i=0}^{n} c_i \Delta G_{t-i} + \sum_{i=0}^{n} d_i \Delta T_{t-i} \qquad (22\text{--}1)$$

The reduced form equation (22–1) relates the change in income in any time period t to current and lagged changes in money, government spending, and taxes.[1] (A 900-equation structural model must for now remain a figment of the imagination.) Equation (22–1) may be viewed as a modified version of equation (19B–3), which expresses the equilibrium value of income after solving simultaneously the IS–LM equations. The modifications to equation (19B–3) include (1) expressing the variables as first differences (changes) instead of levels, (2) introducing lagged terms, and (3) dropping the nonpolicy exogenous variables, such as autonomous consumption, in order to focus on the policy variables. (Statistically speaking, the nonpolicy exogenous variables are included in the error term, which makes the $R^2$ of the estimated equation less than unity.) By not estimating any supply and demand equations, reduced form models make no attempt to answer "how" and "why" questions, but focus exclusively on "what." The builders of reduced form models realize that the policy variables affect many endogenous variables besides income, and that the effect on income may not be direct. Nevertheless, they believe that better answers are acquired by concentrating on one issue—the what question.

There are pros and cons to the two types of models. From a purely methodological and statistical viewpoint, however, there is no reason to believe that either type of model would produce biased estimates of the effects of monetary and fiscal policy. That is, a theoretical statistician would predict that the two research methodologies yield similar answers. Why should structural models per se systematically estimate a larger or smaller money multiplier than reduced form models? They should not, yet they do. And largely because they do, we have our two main schools of economists, monetarists and Keynesians.

1. Compared to structural models, reduced form models typically find that monetary policy has a larger multiplier and that fiscal policy has a smaller multiplier. Indeed, some reduced form models find that within a year fiscal policy has no effect on income.
2. Compared to structural models, both monetary and fiscal policy have shorter lags in reduced form models. The full impact of both policies occurs within a year in some reduced form models while structural models have up to four year lags.

## DIFFERENT EMPIRICAL ESTIMATES: A MYSTERY OR TALE OF TORTURE?

The admonition "seek and ye shall find" is nowhere more true than in empirical work. Economists who believed a priori that money matters constructed reduced form models and discovered strong empirical evi-

---

[1] We encountered a similar equation in Chapter 2. One empirical test of the definition of money selects the money measure that performs best in the equation.

dence for their position. Similarly, most structural models were estimated by fiscalists whose a priori beliefs were confirmed. A nasty thought inevitably comes to mind: Are the different results from the structural and reduced form models a real economic mystery or have some clever people tortured the data until they confessed? The data have been tortured, that is, much experimentation preceded the reported results. This *partially* explains the different results. However, the remaining difference is sufficiently large that we appear to have a real economic mystery.

Before presenting evidence supporting the mystery viewpoint, we must point out that empirical work is not for the squeamish. Empirical studies *must* torture the data to some extent. Empirical studies begin with a hypothesis which is to be confirmed or denied; they do not seek illustrations of known facts. Because empirical studies are *searches* for *possible* explanations that have no natural tendency to reveal themselves, some experimentation is necessary. For example, our hypothesis may state that variables X and Y are related, other things being equal. Empirical studies then attempt to ascertain the type of relationship, if any. Is the relationship linear, quadratic, logarithmic, or yet some other form? Is the relationship between current values alone or should lagged values be included? What are the other things that must be held constant in order to ascertain the relationship between variables X and Y? Even if, by chance, we initially postulate the best answers to these questions, how would we know they were the best unless we subsequently found worse answers? The question is not should we torture the data, but did we torture them enough or too much? Because the data finally confess what we want to hear does not necessarily imply excessive torture. True, seek and ye shall find. We are also exhorted to leave no stone unturned.

There are two main reasons for believing that a mystery exists. First, the single equation reduced form model can be relatively easily examined for signs of excessive torture and, quite predictably, was so examined by Keynesians who found the initial results contrary to their a priori beliefs. The model was tested and retested in order to ascertain whether it satisfied the canons of proper statistical methods and whether the results were sensitive to the calendar time period of the analysis. We shall mention some of the less abstruse statistical arguments shortly. The statistical retesting discovered some contusions but no signs of gross torture. The upshot was a narrowing of the difference between the two types of models. However, no amount of retesting has been able to close the gap totally.

Second, monetarists' preference for reduced form models and Keynesians' preference for large-scale structural models are consistent with their philosophical viewpoint and general outlook about the structure of the economy expressed long *before* any empirical studies. For example, monetarists Henry Simons in 1936 and Milton Friedman in 1953 came out for monetary rules largely because they thought the economy was too complex and uncertain for discretionary policy.[2] When computational and statistical advances made empirical work feasible in the 1960s, in accord with their earlier statements monetarists spurned large scale models because they require more knowledge than available. Empirical studies answer the questions asked; they do not pose questions or make suggestions. No data series has ever whispered, "Hey, bunkie, include me in your explanation of the demand for variable X." Monetarists say that the (incorrect) exclusion of variables due to lack of knowledge makes the estimates of the included variables highly suspect.[3] Keynesians on the other hand are more confident about their ability to ask good questions and include the appropriate variables. Moreover, their perceived need for regulation and intervention in many areas necessitates large scale structural models.

## THE ST. LOUIS MODEL[4]

Milton Friedman and David Meiselman constructed the first reduced form model.[5] Pathfinders in any area rarely have the last word. They are no exception. Numerous critics were quick to point out several flaws in their study which, if corrected, invalidated their conclusion that the results were "strikingly one-sided" in support of monetary policy and against the Keynesian government spending multiplier, and, more generally, any autonomous spending multiplier.[6] Just as the dust was settling, Leonall Andersen and Jerry Jordan from the St. Louis Federal Reserve Bank published a reduced form equation free of many of the flaws the critics were harping about but which was even more "strikingly one-

---

[2] Henry Simons, "Rules Versus Authorities in Monetary Policy," *Journal of Political Economy,* February 1936, pp. 1–30; and Milton Friedman, "The Effects of a Full-Employment Policy on Economic Stability: A Formal Analysis," in *Essays in Positive Economics* (Chicago: University of Chicago Press, 1953), pp. 117–32. Variable (uncertain) lags is one reason for a monetary rule.

[3] Technically speaking, omitted variables lead to biased estimates when they are correlated with the included variables, which is quite likely to be the case with the time series data used by structural models.

[4] First warning: Proceed directly to Chapter 23 if you did not read the Appendix to Chapter 2.

[5] "The Relative Stability of Monetary Velocity and the Investment Multiplier in the United States," in Commission on Money and Credit, *Stabilization Policies* (Englewood Cliffs, N.J.: Prentice-Hall, 1963), pp. 165–268.

[6] Ibid., p. 166. Some of the more important critiques were Donald Hester, "Keynes and the Quantity Theory: A Comment on the Friedman-Meiselman CMC Paper," *Review of Economics and Statistics,* November 1964; Albert Ando and Franco Modigliani, "Velocity and the Investment Multiplier," and Michael de Prano and Thomas Mayer, "Autonomous Expenditures and Money," *American Economic Review,* September 1965. Replies by Friedman and Meiselman and rejoinders also appear in the journal cited. One of the main flaws of the Friedman-Meiselman study was the use of *actual* spending and taxes. This reduces the measured impact of fiscal policy due to the "reverse causation" argument, which will be discussed shortly.

sided.''[7] Andersen then teamed up with his St. Louis colleague Keith
Carlson and expanded the reduced form approach to other variables besides income.[8] Equation (22–1) is the St. Louis Fed reduced form equation for nominal GNP. The regression estimate of this equation is presented in Table 22–1. Tax variables initially were included, but the esti-

**TABLE 22–1  Regression of quarterly nominal GNP changes on money and government spending changes***

| Variable | 0/t | 1/t − 1 | 2/t − 2 | 3/t − 3 | 4/t − 4 | Sum |
|---|---|---|---|---|---|---|
| $\Delta M$ ......... | 1.22 | 1.80 | 1.62 | 0.87 | 0.06 | 5.57 |
| | (2.73) | (7.34) | (4.25) | (3.65) | (0.12) | (8.06) |
| $\Delta G$ ......... | 0.56 | 0.45 | 0.01 | −0.43 | −0.54 | 0.05 |
| | (2.57) | (3.43) | (0.08) | (−3.18) | (−2.47) | (0.17) |
| $R^2 = 0.66$ | | | | | | |

* Regression coefficients and t values in parentheses by time lag period.
**SOURCE:** L. Andersen and K. Carlson, "A Monetarist Model for Economic Stabilization," Federal
Reserve Bank of St. Louis *Review*, April 1970, p. 11. The money supply is old M–1, and government
spending is measured assuming full employment. The estimate of the constant term is 2.67.

mated coefficients were very small and statistically insignificant. The data
are quarterly. The lag structure, namely the value of n in equation (22–1),
is an empirical question estimated here to equal 4. GNP this quarter
depends on monetary and fiscal policy in the current and four prior calendar quarters and on the unspecified exogenous factors. The full effect of
both policies is felt in 5 quarters.

The dimension of the variables is the change (first difference), so the
coefficients are estimates of the money and government spending multipliers.[9] Because regression coefficients show the effect of one variable
holding the other variables constant, and because money and taxes (al-

---

[7] "Monetary and Fiscal Actions: A Test of Their Relative Importance in Economic
Stabilization" Federal Reserve Bank of St. Louis *Review*, November 1968, pp. 11–24.

[8] L. Andersen and K. Carlson, "A Monetarist Model for Economic Stabilization,"
Federal Reserve Bank of St. Louis *Review*, April 1970, pp., 7–25.

[9] The estimates in Table 22–1 are based on data from 1953 to 1969. Benjamin Friedman
published updated (through 1976) estimates of the St. Louis equation. His conclusion, and
the article's title, was "Even the St. Louis Model Now Believes in Fiscal Policy," *Journal
of Money, Credit, and Banking*, May 1977, pp. 365–67. The long-run government spending
multiplier is approximately 1.5 according to Benjamin Friedman. However, extension of
the sample period makes the first difference form violate the least squares assumption of
homoscedasticity. When all variables are expressed in their percentage change instead of
change (first difference) so that the estimated coefficients are elasticities instead of multipliers, the least squares assumption of homoscedasticity seems to be satisfied, and the
estimates are very similar to those presented in Table 22–1. (See Keith Carlson, "Does the
St. Louis Equation Now Believe in Fiscal Policy?" Federal Reserve Bank of St. Louis
*Review*, February 1978, pp. 13–19.) Because the "old" results created such a stir when first
published, and because multipliers are much more commonly used than elasticities, we
present the old results instead of the equivalent new results.

though not shown here) initially were included, the government budget constraint implies that these are estimates of *deficit financed* government spending multipliers. The coefficients are impact multipliers. For example, the coefficient for $\Delta M$ in the middle column says that, other things being equal, the GNP change this quarter is 1.62 times the money change lagged two quarters, or, equivalently, the GNP change two quarters hence equals 1.62 times the current monetary change.

Table 22–2 is derived from Table 22–1 to highlight the cumulative (sometimes also called dynamic) multipliers, which equal the sum of the

**TABLE 22–2  St. Louis model's money and government spending multipliers**

| Quarters elapsed | 0 | 1 | 2 | 3 | 4 | 5+ |
|---|---|---|---|---|---|---|
| Money multiplier: | | | | | | |
| impact ......................... | 1.22 | 1.80 | 1.62 | 0.87 | 0.06 | 0.00 |
| cumulative ..................... | 1.22 | 3.02 | 4.64 | 5.51 | 5.57 | 5.57 |
| Government multiplier: | | | | | | |
| impact ......................... | 0.56 | 0.45 | 0.01 | −0.43 | −0.54 | 0.00 |
| cumulative ..................... | 0.56 | 1.01 | 1.02 | 0.59 | 0.05 | 0.05 |

impact multipliers to that date. For example, suppose the quantity of money increases $1 this quarter, everything else remaining constant. Nominal GNP increases $1.22 the same period and $1.80 the next period, so the cumulative increase by next period is $3.02. An easily remembered *approximation* to Table 22–2 is available. A $1 increase in the quantity of money causes nominal GNP to increase approximately $1.5 this quarter and in each of the two subsequent quarters. The money multiplier attains its long-run value of approximately 5.50 in a year. GNP increases by approximately the amount of government spending within six months, remains at the same level for another quarter, and then falls during the next six months, so by the end of 15 months GNP virtually reverts to its original value. Government spending crowds out an almost equal amount of private spending in slightly more than a year. The St. Louis equation says that government spending changes the composition of output but not the total.

The last chapter stated that magnitude or multiplier effects per se are not the be all and end all of policy. Which policy is more predictable and reliable? Reliability is measured by the t values shown in parentheses. (Recall that the t value is the ratio of the regression coefficient (average measure) to its standard deviation (variability measure).) Except for the fourth quarter after the monetary expansion, at which time an equilibrium has been reached for all practical purposes, Table 22–1 indicates that quarter-by-quarter monetary policy is more reliable than fiscal policy. The difference in the reliability of the two policies is most dramatic when viewed over the entire year. See the t-ratios for the column labeled Sum in Table 22–1. In summary, the St. Louis equation finds that, relative to fiscal policy, monetary policy is much (1) stronger, (2) faster, and (3) more reliable.[10]

## LARGE-SCALE STRUCTURAL MODELS

Some of the better known large-scale structural models and the number of their equations are: BEA (Bureau of Economic Analysis), 346; DRI (Data Resource, Inc.), 1,009; Wharton, 937; and MPS (MIT-Penn-Social Science Research Council, which formerly was called the Fed-MIT-Penn model).[11] Figures 22–1 and 22–2 show the cumulative or dynamic money and government spending multipliers, respectively, given by these large scale models and, for comparison purposes, by the St. Louis model.[12] While in their more conciliatory moments Keynesians claim that everyone now believes that "money matters," surely the builders and users of the BEA must be nonbelievers. According to the BEA model, money affects *neither* prices *nor* output since nominal GNP multipliers are being estimated. The BEA model says there *is* a liquidity trap.

The DRI, MPS, and Wharton model estimates of the one-year forward money multiplier are a remarkably similar 0.5, and the two-year forward multipliers are about 1.25. At this point the three models part company. Monetary policy is gaining steam according to the MPS and Wharton models, while the DRI model says monetary policy is petering out, with the nominal GNP/money multiplier falling to approximately two thirds. The money multiplier in the MPS model climbs to approximately 3.5 at the end of four years.[13] The Wharton money multiplier gains steam so slowly that it still is hovering somewhat above unity at the end of four years. Given the difficulty of knowing even the direction, expansionary or

---

[10] The St. Louis equation only measures the impact lag. However, everyone agrees that the implementation lag is much shorter for monetary policy.

[11] Harry Kelegian and Bruce Vavrichek, "An Evaluation of the Forecasting Properties of Macro Economic Models, with Special Emphasis on Model Size," in a forthcoming book edited by Jan Kmenta and James Ramsey. The numbers, which include the exogenous variables, are only meant to be suggestive. These models are revised relatively frequently.

[12] Gary Fromm and Lawrence R. Klein, "The NBER/NSF Model Comparison Seminar: An Analysis of Results," in *Econometric Model Performance: Comparative Simulation Studies of the U.S. Economy*, ed. L. Klein and E. Burmeister (Philadelphia: University of Pennsylvania Press, 1976), pp. 402, 405. Except for the St. Louis multiplier, the results presented on their p. 405 are unborrowed reserve multipliers. Money is an endogenous variable in the large scale models. For comparability, the dynamic unborrowed reserve multipliers for each period have been multiplied by 0.135, the ratio of unborrowed reserves to the money supply in 1970. While the adjustment factor could be allowed to vary over time due to lags in the money supply response to Fed action, the fundamental patterns in Figures 22–1 and 22–2 are unaltered by such refinements.

[13] Figure 22–1 does not show multipliers beyond four years. However, we should note that given a sufficiently long time, the MPS money multiplier rivals St. Louis's. The five-year forward MPS multiplier is nearly 5.

FIGURE 22-1  **Cumulative nominal GNP/money multipliers predicted by various models, by quarters elasped from date on monetary change**

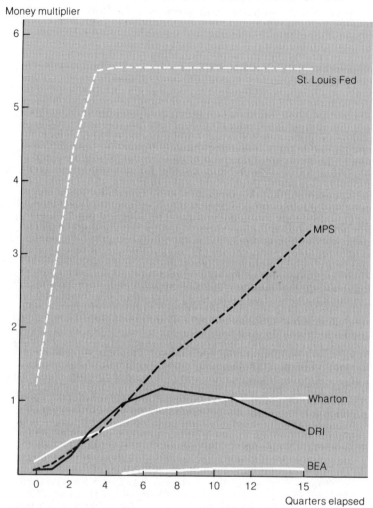

Money multiplier

**SOURCE:** Gary Fromm and Lawrence Klein, "The NBER/NSF Model Comparison Seminar: An Analysis of Results," in *Econometric Model Performance: Comparative Simulation Studies of the U.S. Economy*, ed. L. Klein and E. Burmeister (Philadelphia: University of Pennsylvania Press, 1976), p. 405. All results except St. Louis' have been multiplied by 0.135 to convert unborrowed reserves to money. The St. Louis estimates are from L. Andersen and K. Carlson, a "Monetarist Model" for Economic Stabilization," Federal Reserve Bank of St. Louis *Review*, April 1970. See our Table 22-2.

contractionary, of appropriate policy a year hence, much less four years hence, the model builders—who have time for little else—and the users—who pay significant sums for the models' forecasts—might believe that money matters but, if so, money matters *very* little indeed to them.

The structural model estimates of fiscal policy are somewhat more

**FIGURE 22-2  Cumulative nominal GNP/government spending multipliers predicted by various models, by quarters elapsed from date of spending change**

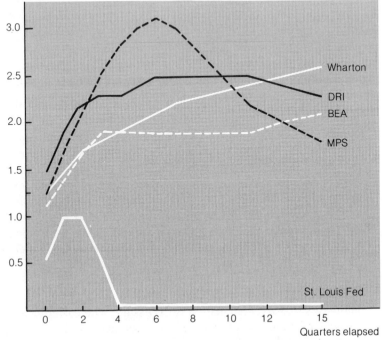

SOURCE: Gary Fromm and Lawrence Klein, "The NBER/NSF Model Comparison Seminar: An Analysis of Results," in *Econometric Model Performance: Comparative Simulation Studies of the U.S. Economy*, ed. L. Klein and E. Burmeister (Philadelphia: University of Pennsylvania Press, 1976), p. 402. The St. Louis estimates are from our Table 22-2.

uniform. First, the contemporaneous government spending multiplier of all the structural models is marginally greater than unity. Firms fully meet the government's demand in the quarter, and some spending is induced. In contrast, the St. Louis model says that within the initial quarter firms partially meet government spending out of inventories and expand somewhat—the contemporaneous government spending multiplier is positive but less than 1.0. Second, structural models estimate the government spending multiplier is approximately 2 at the end of the year. Third, the government spending multiplier beyond a year wanders more or less aimlessly, with the average estimate remaining at approximately two after four years. Even the structural models claim that the early Keynesian textbook examples of a marginal propensity to consume out of GNP of 0.75 and government spending multiplier of 4.0 are way too high.

One of the main problems of large-scale models is their failure to yield estimates of policy reliability. After all the equations are estimated statistically, multipliers are calculated by changing a policy variable and throwing the model into a computer, which calculates the predictions based on *all* the estimated equations *and* their interaction. Because monetary and fiscal policy interact with so many other variables, which then influence GNP, measures of the standard deviation of the multipliers are meaningless.[14] Without a measure of variability, t-values or other measures of policy reliability cannot be constructed.

## A RECONCILIATION OF STRUCTURAL AND REDUCED FORM RESULTS[15]

Empirical studies of the demand for money, which we shall not present, unanimously (Friedman notwithstanding) confirm that the demand for money does depend on the rate of interest. At the same time, the studies show that the demand for money is not very sensitive to the rate of interest. More important, there is virtually no evidence that the demand for money becomes more elastic at lower rates of interest and eventually approaches a liquidity trap.[16] The empirical money demand studies in conjunction with the advanced Keynesian IS–LM model, which remains the most popular theoretical model, imply that the St. Louis estimates of the government spending multiplier and the structural model estimates of the money multiplier are implausibly low. How can one reconcile the empirical money demand and multiplier estimates?

Before attempting such a reconciliation, let us convince any doubting Thomases that a reconciliation is necessary. The easier case is the inconsistency of an interest sensitive money demand and a virtually zero government spending multiplier. Government spending, like any other spending, financed by bond sales drives up interest rates. When higher interest rates reduce the amount of money demanded, the same money stock can finance more transactions and a higher GNP. The government spending multiplier should be positive. In terms of IS–LM curves, when the demand for money depends on interest rates, the LM curve is positively sloped, and not vertical. An increase in government purchases, which shifts the IS curve outward, produces a higher output.

Now consider why the typical structural model estimate of a 1.25 money multiplier after two years is implausibly low. Velocity, being the ratio of nominal GNP to money, measures the rate at which *average*

---

[14] Standard deviations could be computed but they would be so large that every t-ratio would be insignificant, and comparisons of policy reliability would be meaningless.

[15] Second warning: Proceed directly to Chapter 23 if you do not have a strong statistical background.

[16] For an excellent summary of the empirical money literature, see chapters 6–8 of David Laidler, *The Demand for Money: Theories and Evidence,* 2nd ed. (New York: Dun-Donnelly, 1977). Goldfeld apparently also was thoroughly convinced that there is no liquidity trap. He methodically analyzed every unsettled issue about money demand in 1973 and 1976 and did not explore the possibility of a trap. Stephen Goldfeld, "The Demand for Money Revisited," *Brookings Papers on Economic Activity* 3(1973): 577–638, and "The Case of the Missing Money," *Brookings Papers on Economic Activity* 3(1976): 683–730.

money balances are spent. It equalled 4.56 in 1970. The money multiplier, being the ratio of nominal GNP changes to money changes, measures the rate at which *marginal* money balances are spent. *Actual* velocity and the structural model *estimates* of the multiplier imply that money is becoming less productive in terms of expenditures, that is, the marginal product of money is less than the average product. How would a declining productivity of money be reflected in its demand? The demand for money must exhibit either (1) diseconomies of scale, or (2) a liquidity preference curve which becomes much more elastic at low interest rates, so that larger proportions of money end up as idle speculative balances. Diseconomies of scale mean that (transactions) money demand increases more than proportionally with expenditures, which would be necessary if money is becoming less productive. Alternatively, a liquidity trap must be close at hand for velocity to greatly exceed the multiplier. In a liquidity trap the multiplier is zero, by definition, but velocity is positive—some output is produced even in a great depression. Empirical money demand studies confirm neither of these two conditions. The demand for money exhibits neither diseconomies of scale nor increasing interest elasticity at low rates.[17]

The St. Louis Fed says its fiscal policy multiplier estimates are consistent with an interest elastic money demand provided the IS–LM framework is expanded to include (1) interest rate induced wealth effects, and (2) portfolio diversification effects. Because higher interest rates reduce common stock values, which along with other components of wealth influence consumption positively, the higher interest rates produced by government expenditures curtail consumption in addition to investment. Moreover, a *permanent* increase in government spending necessitates a *perpetual* stream of government bonds. This causes a portfolio imbalance. To diversify portfolios, the demand for money increases at any given interest rate.[18] In term of the IS–LM graph, additional government spending shifts the IS outward, but recognition of portfolio diversification effects means that the LM will continually shift inward. The increased demand for money and inward LM shift curtails GNP considerably because the IS curve is relatively flat due to the interest rate induced wealth effect.

---

[17] Again, Friedman notwithstanding. Friedman's finding that money is a luxury, that is, the "income" elasticity of money demand exceeds unity, does imply that long-run marginal velocity is less than the average. However, because his income measure is permanent income, which changes by a fraction of nominal income changes in the short run when permanent and nominal incomes do not coincide, marginal velocity can exceed the average. The St. Louis money multiplier estimate is consistent with constant or slightly increasing economies of scale, which is the result most money demand studies find. Milton Friedman, "The Demand for Money: Some Theoretical and Empirical Results," *Journal of Political Economy,* June 1959, pp. 327–51.

[18] We are not attributing the higher money demand to a wealth effect because monetarists argue that government bonds, like private bonds, are not wealth because they generate future tax liabilities. Moreover, attributing wealth effects to government bonds would cut both ways; it would increase money demand and consumption.

Surprisingly, advocates of large-scale models have not attempted to reconcile their typical money multiplier estimates and empirical money demand studies. Instead, they have focused on the so-called reverse causation argument, which says that money and GNP are related because GNP changes cause monetary changes, the reverse of the causation pattern normally alleged. There certainly is an element of truth to the reverse causation argument. We saw in Chapters 11 and 12 that the Fed often attempts to stabilize interest rates. When an autonomous increase in demand raises GNP and interest rates, the Fed must expand the money supply to moderate the interest rate rise. If reduced form models for the postwar United States were the sole evidence for a money/income relationship, then the reverse causation argument would carry great weight. However, there is strong evidence of a money/income relationship long before the Fed existed and in many other countries.

The reverse causation argument can be extended. If the significant statistical relationship between money and income does not necessarily mean that money influences GNP, then the insignificant statistical relationship between fiscal policy and GNP is consistent with fiscal policy influencing GNP. For example, suppose firms' "animal spirits" are low, and investment and GNP tend to fall. Suppose further that fiscal policy becomes expansionary and *does* counteract the exogenous change in demand. GNP and fiscal policy would be statistically unrelated. GNP would be constant period after period while fiscal policy would be extremely variable. However, in this case it would be wrong to conclude that the lack of statistical relationship means that fiscal policy is impotent. GNP remains constant only because fiscal policy does influence it and compensates for the exogenous factors. The paradox is: the better a policy stabilizes the economy by counteracting the effect of exogenous factors, the more worthless the policy appears statistically. While this may explain to some extent the small fiscal policy coefficient in the reduced form models, it cannot be the whole explanation. The implementation lag of fiscal policy is just too long for one seriously to believe that it offsets a major amount of exogenous GNP variations. Moreover, this extension of the reverse causation argument also suggests that the monetary coefficients could be too low. After 1951, which precedes the starting date for all the models, the Fed pegged interest rates only in the short run. Interest rates do rise, albeit with some lag, in an expansion, and monetary policy is countercyclical.

### Prediction errors

Let us take another tack to the question: which model gives the best multiplier estimates? There simply is no definitive answer. Nevertheless, the model's *overall predictive performance* in the post-model-building pe-

riod provides one *tentative* answer.[19] We shall accept the multiplier estimates of the model which best predicts income. For example, suppose a
model is estimated in late 1975. Beginning with the first quarter of 1976,
the actual values of exogenous variables and the actual initial values of
lagged endogenous variables are substituted in the model, which is run
forward to predict nominal GNP one, two, three, or more quarters in the
future. The process is repeated for the second quarter of 1976, and so on.
Figure 22–3 shows the prediction errors by the number of quarters ahead
forecasted.[20] Errors for the DRI and MPS models could not be computed.

**FIGURE 22–3   Nominal GNP prediction errors of various models, by
number of quarters ahead forecasted**

Prediction errors ($ billion)

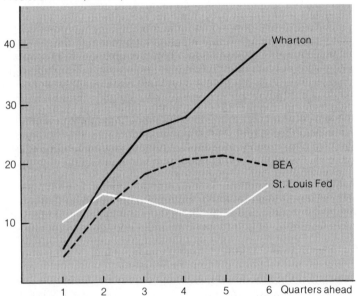

**SOURCE:** Gary Fromm and Lawrence Klein, "The NBER/NSF Model Comparison
Seminar: An Analysis of Results," in *Econometric Model Performance: Comparative
Simulation Studies of the U.S. Economy*, ed. L. Klein and E. Burmeister (Philadelphia: University of Pennsylvania Press, 1976), p. 387. Prediction errors are the
root mean square error.

---

[19] "Testing a model by means of a test period that occurs after the model was built is the
only way to discriminate between the (inferior) models that have been chosen to fit primarily
the random and non-enduring features of the premodel-building data, and the (superior)
models that have been chosen to fit primarily the systematic and enduring features of the
economy." (Carl Christ, "Judging the Performance of Econometric Models of the U.S.
Economy," in Klein and Burmeister, *Econometric Model Performance*, p. 324). Parenthesis
in original.

[20] Error here refers to the root mean square error.

The figure indicates that bigger does not necessarily mean better. The BEA and Wharton forecasts one quarter ahead were significantly more accurate than the St. Louis forecast. The errors of the large scale models were approximately only 50 percent the initial St. Louis error. However, the forecasts of the large models, particularly the Wharton model, deteriorate badly as the forecast period lengthens. The five quarter ahead forecast errors of the BEA and Wharton models were approximately two and three times, respectively, as large as the St. Louis error. On balance, the St. Louis model is the qualified winner in the nominal GNP forecasting sweepstakes. If for no other reason, the qualification is necessary because relative prediction errors may well depend on the forecast period.[21] The St. Louis model could predict accurately five years ago and inaccurately today. Even if there were unqualified proof that the St. Louis model always was the overall best forecasting model, the model's multiplier estimates need not be the most accurate. GNP could be forecasted accurately because overestimates of the effects of one policy are being compensated by underestimates of another policy. While we may never know the size of the money multiplier, the St. Louis estimate at least deserves serious consideration.

## SECTORAL DETAIL IN THE MPS MODEL

Let us make some use of the main benefit provided by large models and take a quick glance at sectoral detail. We scrutinize only the MPS (MIT-Penn-Social Science Research Council) model because it develops the financial sector more fully than the other large models do. The MPS model includes the three channels of monetary policy mentioned in Chapter 21: (1) interest rate (per se) effect, (2) wealth effect induced by interest rates, and (3) credit rationing.[22] Figure 22–4 and Table 22–3 show the *direct* effect, by channel, on four major aggregate demand components of a $1 billion increase in unborrowed reserves. Direct effect here means that induced spending/multiplier repercussions and feedbacks from GNP to the financial sector are purposely not measured. Figure 22–4 shows that

---

[21] This indeed seems to be the case. The errors shown in Figure 22–3 generally are for the late 1960s and early 1970s. The paper by Kelejian and Varvrichek, "An Evaluation of the Forecasting Performance of Macro Economic Models," shows that between 1976 and mid 1978 the prediction errors of the St. Louis Fed model approximately equaled the average error of seven large scale models. Among the large scale models, bigger is not necessarily better. Kelejian and Vavrichek recognize that the sample number of predictions for any one model was quite small, which makes their conclusions tentative. One effect of the small sample size is a decidedly nonmonotonic relationship between forecast errors and the length of the forecast period. The theoretical section of their paper illustrates that superior forecasting does not necessarily imply superior structural specification. Model validation and forecasting performance are separable issues.

[22] The (direct) interest rate effect usually is called the cost of capital effect. The latter may be viewed as a refined version of the former made necessary by "real world" complications, primarily taxes, investment tax credit, depreciation, relative price changes, and inflation.

**FIGURE 22–4  Direct effect on final demand of a $1 billion increase in unborrowed reserves**

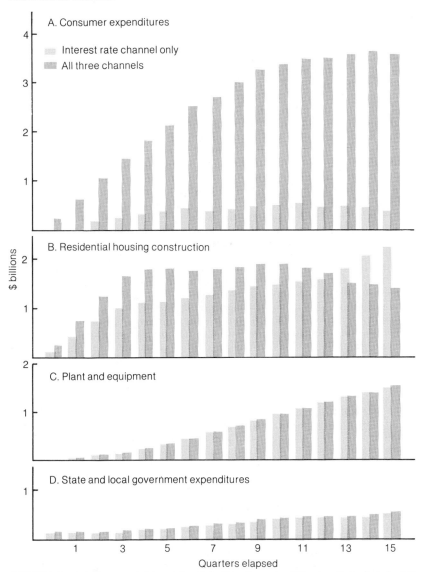

**SOURCE:** Frank deLeeuw and Edward Gramlich, "The Channels of Monetary Policy," *Federal Reserve Bulletin,* June 1969.

interest rates (per se) have a minor effect on consumption, mainly through automobile purchases and other durables. However, about 40 percent of the impact of monetary policy occurs through interest rate induced wealth effects on consumption. Monetary policy influences interest rates, which influence stock prices, which in turn influence consumption. Assigning a

**TABLE 22–3   MPS model percentages of total direct effect of monetary policy on GNP, by sectors, policy channel, and calendar quarters after policy implementation**

| | Consumption expenditure | | | Investment | | | |
|---|---|---|---|---|---|---|---|
| | | | | Housing construction | | | Plant and equipment |
| Quarter | Interest rate | Wealth | Total | Interest rate | Credit rationing | Total | Interest rate |
| 4 ...... | 8.6 | 34.3 | 42.9 | 28.6 | 17.1 | 45.7 | 5.7 |
| 8 ...... | 7.4 | 42.6 | 50.0 | 24.1 | 9.3 | 33.4 | 11.1 |
| 12 ...... | 7.4 | 44.1 | 51.5 | 22.1 | 4.4 | 26.5 | 16.2 |
| 16 ...... | 5.7 | 45.7 | 51.4 | 31.4 | −11.4 | 20.0 | 21.4 |

| | State and local government interest rate | Total | | | |
|---|---|---|---|---|---|
| Quarter | | Interest rate | Wealth | Credit rationing | Total* |
| 4 .......... | 5.7 | 48.6 | 34.3 | 17.1 | 100.0 |
| 8 .......... | 5.6 | 48.2 | 42.6 | 9.3 | 100.0 |
| 12 .......... | 5.8 | 51.5 | 44.1 | 4.4 | 100.0 |
| 16 .......... | 7.1 | 65.6 | 45.7 | −11.4 | 100.0 |

* May not sum due to rounding.
**SOURCE:** Frank deLeeuw and Edward Gramlich, "The Channels of Monetary Policy," *Federal Reserve Bulletin*, June 1969.

separate channel to this indirect interest rate effect emphasizes its strength and indirectly castigates those who neglected it for many years.

Table 22–3 shows that while housing contributes nearly half of the early impact of monetary policy, its importance gradually declines over time. This pattern is attributed largely to the rationing channel and to the more rapid effect of interest rates on housing than on plant and equipment. In periods immediately following the policy change, market interest rates fall relative to the sluggish deposit rates of financial intermediaries. Deposit flows are stimulated, and financial intermediaries awash with deposits reduce credit rationing. As time goes on, the normal relation between market and deposit rates and between mortgage rates and other loan terms are restored. As this happens, the rationing effect diminishes. In fact, by the end of four years the rationing effect changes direction. The delayed increase in demand by the other sectors puts pressure on the direct finance market, reduces deposit flows, and increases credit rationing, which reduces housing construction. The more rapid effect of interest rates on housing than plant and equipment may be explained by the shorter construction period of the former. By the end of four years monetary policy has the same impact on both types of investment.

Construction expenditures of state and local governments like consumer expenditures are influenced somewhat by the rate of interest. Only the federal government is totally insensitive to the rate of interest.

## SUMMARY

The questions "How much do monetary and fiscal policy matter?" and "In what ways do monetary and fiscal policy matter?" are central issues underlying many specific problems in the private and public sectors. Because the questions are so important, the answers deserve careful scrutiny. It is discouraging to report that virtually every empirical study has an implausible element. For example, we suggested that the wealth effect induced by interest rate might explain the virtually zero fiscal policy multipliers in the St. Louis model. The MPS model does indeed find strong evidence for a wealth effect. However, it also finds that the fiscal policy multiplier is positive. The large-scale structural model estimates of the money multiplier are inconsistent with the huge body of empirical money demand studies. If the studies summarized here contain an implausible element, they also are methodologically reasonable and contain many plausible elements. There is no need to be disheartened. A discipline is vibrant and controversial only if it is in a mild state of disarray. Besides, every new answer only brings a new question.

## QUESTIONS

1. Briefly describe and compare the methodological approach of large-scale structural models and reduced form or bottom line models.

2. Outline the conclusions of large-scale structural and reduced form models concerning the magnitude and speed of the impact of monetary and fiscal policy.

3. Which research approach, large-scale structural or reduced form models, is favored by (a) monetarists and (b) Keynesians?

4. State two reasons for believing that the difference in the results of large scale structural and reduced form models are not simply due to the excessive manipulation of the data in order to confirm preconceived beliefs.

5.* Summarize the findings of the St. Louis Fed model concerning the (a) strength, (b) speed, and (c) reliability of monetary and fiscal policy.

6.* Answer the last question for the average large-scale structural model.

7.** Carefully explain why the St. Louis estimates of the government spending multiplier and the structural model estimates of the money multiplier are implausibly low, given the value of actual velocity and the typical estimate of the demand for money.

8.** Define reverse causation. Explain the extension of the reverse causation argument which states that effective stabilization tools tend to be statistically insignificant.

9.** Compare the prediction errors of the St. Louis model on the one hand and the average structural model on the other.

10.** State the findings of the MPS model concerning the relative importance of the channels of monetary policy and the sectors affected by monetary policy.

# The unemployment-inflation conundrum

# 23

The famous microeconomic trade-off curve between guns and butter was eclipsed in popularity in the early 1960s by another trade-off curve, the so-called Phillips curve. Named after the late British economist A. W. Phillips, the curve purports to show a *permanent* trade-off between the rate of inflation and the rate of unemployment.[1] That is, Phillips stated that the rate of unemployment could be permanently lowered at the cost of a higher rate of inflation. Phillips' 1958 study was perhaps the single most influential economic study since Keynes's *General Theory*. It dominated the thinking of academics and policymakers for a decade. The influence of the Phillips curve was relatively short lived, however. In his 1968 American Economic Association presidential address, Professor Milton Friedman questioned the existence of a *permanent* trade-off.[2] He stated that there is only a short-run or *temporary* trade-off between inflation and unemployment. The strength and speed of the impact of Friedman's critique rival Phillips' original study. What seemed like an immutable truth in 1958 was questioned in 1968 and totally repudiated by 1978. Virtually no one now believes there is a permanent trade-off of any consequence between inflation and unemployment, given probable inflation rates. (The trade-off during hyperinflations and major deflations is highly speculative due to the limited number of observations.) This chapter looks

---

[1] A. W. Phillips, "The Relationship between Unemployment and the Rate of Change of Money Wage Rates in the United Kingdom, 1861–1957," *Economica*, November 1958, pp. 282–99.

[2] Milton Friedman, "The Role of Monetary Policy," *American Economic Review*, March 1968, pp. 1–7.

at the rise and fall of the Phillips curve and other theories about the unemployment-inflation relationship.

It has been our custom to look closely at the concept and measurement of a variable before analyzing its determinants. Being rather far along in the book to change strategies, the chapter begins by noting some problems in measuring inflation and unemployment, and the diversity hidden by the aggregates. This is followed by an analysis of the working of labor markets and the meaning of that very popular but extremely slippery concept of "full employment." Although in previous chapters we emphasized output and prices instead of unemployment and inflation for ease of exposition and other reasons, we now show the implications of the output-price relationships derived earlier for the unemployment-inflation relationship. We show that the relationship we derived contrasts sharply with the Phillips curve and differs in detail but not substance with the Friedman view that the trade-off between unemployment and inflation vanishes in the long run. A review of the sources and costs of inflation concludes the chapter.

## MEASUREMENT OF INFLATION AND PRICE INDEXES

*The three main broadly based price indexes are: the GNP price deflator, the consumer price index (CPI), and the producer price index (PPI), which is the successor to the wholesale price index (WPI). Inflation is measured by the percentage change of one of these indexes,* most often the CPI.

All price indexes are ratios of the current price of a "market basket" to the price of the basket at a base year. Algebraically, $P_t$, the price index at time t, is

$$P_t = \left( \sum_{i=1}^{n} q^i P_t^i \Big/ \sum_{i=1}^{n} q^i P_0^i \right) \times 100 \qquad (23\text{--}1)$$

where the base period has subscript zero and the summation is over the n commodities, q, in the market basket. As a matter of convention, the ratio is multiplied by 100 so that the base year index is 100. Equation (23–1) is identical to the following,

$$P_t = \sum_{i=1}^{n} \left( \frac{q^i P_0^i}{\Sigma q^i P_0^i} \right) \frac{P_t^i}{P_0^i} \times 100 \qquad (23\text{--}2)$$

Equation (23–2) suggests another definition for a price index: A price index is a weighted average of the ratios of current to base year prices, where the weights equal the ratio of the value of the commodity $(q^i P_0^i)$ to the total value of all commodities $(\Sigma q^i P_0^i)$. Expressing the rate of inflation in terms of the index,

$$\text{Inflation at time t} = \frac{\Delta P_t}{P_t} \times 100 = \frac{P_t - P_{t-1}}{P_t} \times 100 = \pi_t \quad (23\text{--}3)$$

where $P_t$ is one of the indexes. From 1971 through the end of 1981, the base period for the CPI and PPI was 1967, but beginning in 1982 price indexes are scheduled to use a 1977 base. Since prices rose from 1967 to 1977, shifting to a 1977 base reduces the price *index* for 1982. That is, 1982 prices are not as high when compared to 1977 instead of 1967. However, shifting base periods will have no effect on the rate of inflation in 1982 or any other period.[3]

The market basket, that is, the $q^i$ in equations (23-1) and (23-2), either continually shifts and depends on current conditions or remains fixed, at least in the short run. For the GNP deflator, current output is the continually shifting market basket, the price of which is being evaluated. That is, the GNP deflator is the ratio of current output valued at current prices (nominal GNP) to current output valued at base year prices (real GNP). In contrast to the GNP deflator, the CPI and PPI indexes use fixed weights.[4]

The names of the indexes reflect their differences in terms of market-basket coverage and the stage in the distribution system when measurement occurs. The market basket of the (U.S.) GNP deflator is all U.S.-produced goods measured at their final stage of production. The CPI measures the price of the typical basket of goods and services purchased by urban households at the retail level. In other words, the CPI is a weighted average of retail prices, where the weight of each commodity equals the proportion spent on the item by a typical urban household. The CPI is overall a narrower price index than the GNP deflator. For example, the CPI does not measure the prices of government expenditures and investment goods, except residential housing. However, unlike the GNP deflator, the CPI does measure the prices of imported goods. (Remember that imports have no direct impact on GNP, which measures *national* output.)

The PPI measures prices received by producers. Unlike the GNP deflator and CPI which measure prices at the final stage of the production process exclusively, the PPI lets prices percolate their way through the system. This is accomplished by having three PPI, one for crude mate-

---

[3] For example, the 1977 CPI (1967 base) was 181.5. What was the rate of inflation between 1967 and 1977? Since the 1967 CPI (1967 base) is 100, by definition, the rate of inflation for the decade is 81.5 percent. In 1982, when the base period is shifted to 1977, the 1977 CPI will be 100, by definition, but the 1967 CPI (1977 base) will be 55.1 or (100/181.5) × 100. (To convert any year's CPI from a 1967 base to a 1977 base, divide by the 1977 CPI (1967 base) or 181.5 in our example.) Using 1977 base indexes and substituting in Equation (23-3), the inflation rate is ((100 − 55.1)/55.1) × 100 = 81.5, which is the same answer we got using 1967-based indexes.

[4] The fixed weights need not, and in the CPI do not, reflect expenditures in the base period (1977 for the CPI). The basket for the CPI was determined by consumer expenditures in 1972–73. Thus, the CPI measures the current cost, relative to the cost in 1977, of purchasing the consumer goods of 1972–73. Price indexes which use fixed and current period baskets are called Laspeyres and Paasche indexes, respectively. Thus, the CPI is a Laspeyres index, and the GNP deflator is a Paasche index. A fixed (1972) weight GNP price index is available but it is used much less frequently than the current weight GNP deflator.

rials, one for intermediate materials, and one for finished goods. For example, the PPI–crude materials rises when the price of wheat paid by millers increases. PPI–intermediate materials rises when millers raise the price of flour to bakers. PPI–finished goods rises when bakers raise their prices to supermarkets. The CPI measures prices only at the supermarket and other retail outlets. Because the PPI measures prices at early stages of production, the PPI and, more particularly, some of its subindexes of commodities, often are harbingers of subsequent GNP deflator and CPI movements.

### The diversity of price movements

Over long periods of time the choice of the broadly based index used to measure inflation matters little, as Table 23–1 shows. As the time period

**TABLE 23–1  Average annual percentage change**

| Time period | CPI | PPI-intermediate materials | GNP deflator |
|---|---|---|---|
| 1950–1980 | 4.1 | 4.4 | 4.0 |
| 1960–1980 | 5.1 | 5.4 | 4.7 |
| 1970–1980 | 7.6 | 9.4 | 6.6 |
| 1978 | 7.7 | 6.8 | 7.3 |
| 1979 | 11.3 | 12.7 | 8.5 |
| 1980 | 12.4 | 15.1 | 8.2 |

| | CPI components | | |
|---|---|---|---|
| | House-hold fuels | Homeownership: Financing, taxes, and insurance | Used cars | Apparel and upkeep |
| 1978 | 5.3 | 13.5 | 2.0 | 3.5 |
| 1979 | 35.1 | 19.8 | 7.8 | 4.4 |
| 1980 | 37.9 | 28.2 | 3.7 | 7.0 |

**SOURCE:** *Economic Report of the President, 1981;* Bureau of Labor Statistics, *Consumer Price Index Detailed Report.*

becomes shorter, the specific index selected does significantly influence *the* rate of inflation. For example, the rate of inflation in 1980 was more than 50 percent higher when measured by the CPI instead of the GNP deflator. That is, 12.4/8.2 = 1.51, so that 12.4 is more than 50 percent larger than 8.2. (Of course, the CPI inflation rate was *not* 50 percentage *points* greater than the GNP deflator measure of inflation.)

The significantly higher rate of inflation in 1979 and 1980 when measured by the CPI instead of the GNP deflator is partially explained by the explosion of oil prices, which had a greater effect on the CPI than the GNP deflator for two reasons. First, since the United States imports a significant amount of oil, the weight of oil products is greater in the CPI than in the GNP deflator. In other words, the ratio of *national* production to *total* consumption is smaller for oil products than most other products. Second, the GNP deflator measures only domestic oil prices, which were regulated during the late 1970s and rose less than imported oil prices. Whichever index one selects, one fact is unmistakable: the rate of inflation accelerated between 1950 and 1980.

The broadly based price indexes in turn mask a significant degree of price diversity. Table 23–1 shows that annually between 1978 and 1980 the financing, taxes, and insurance cost of homeownership has consistently grown faster than the CPI index, while used-car and apparel prices have consistently lagged behind other consumer prices. Household fuels show an erratic pattern. They lagged behind the general index in 1978 and veritably exploded in 1979 and 1980.

### The CPI as a cost-of-living indicator

The CPI is the most widely discussed price index. It also is the most important in terms of direct impact. Over 50 percent of all households are *directly* affected by the CPI. Receipts ranging from negotiated wage escalator clauses, social security, and food stamps to indexed rents and alimony payments are tied directly to the CPI. The index affects virtually all other households indirectly through inflationary expectations and wage settlements. Although the CPI often is called a cost-of-living index, it need not be one for you for various reasons. That is, if the rate of inflation measured by the CPI is, say, 10 percent, the nominal income increase necessary to maintain *your* standard of living need not equal exactly 10 percent. First, because all prices do not rise proportionally, the CPI is not a cost-of-living index when your consumption pattern differs from the market basket. Although the market basket represents the average consumption pattern, virtually no household is average and purchases the market basket. Higher prices for Iranian caviar have no effect on the CPI but significantly reduce the standard of living of Mr. Gourmand Megabucks, III. The unreliability of the average for individual economic units is not peculiar to the CPI. The average household in 1980 had 2.75 people, yet no such household exists. Second, even if consumption patterns were identical over a long period of time, the existence of durables with more or less constant sales implies that consumption patterns differ in the short run. For example, suppose that every year half the population buys a coat that lasts two years. Assuming coat prices fall relative to the prices of other goods, the inflation rate measured by the CPI overestimates the rise in the cost of living for the half of the population that purchases coats this year and underestimates the rise for the half that does not purchase coats.

While the previous arguments are against the unthinking application of the CPI to every household, the following arguments indicate the CPI inflation rate is an upward biased estimate of the cost of living. That is, for most people the change in the CPI overstates cost-of-living increases. The CPI is biased upward because it uses fixed weights in the short run, which delay introduction of new products in the index and assume lack of substitution. The current CPI market basket was introduced in 1978 and is based on a detailed survey of consumer expenditures in 1972–73. The current market basket replaced a market basket introduced in 1964 based on a 1960–61 survey of consumer expenditures.[5] Given these dates, new products introduced between 1961 and 1973 first appeared in the CPI market basket in 1978, and products introduced after 1973 have yet to appear in the index.[6] There is approximately an average 10-year lag between the introduction of a product and its appearance in the CPI. Since new products replace old products because the public feels that they provide more services per dollar, and since new products typically fall in price relatively to old products—look at the prices of hand calculators and other electronic products in the 1970s—the long lag in the appearance of new products in the CPI biases it upward.

The fixed weights also bias the CPI upward because they implicitly assume lack of substitution, although downward-sloping demand curves imply that households buy less of those goods which increase in price. The CPI assumes we are continuing to drive gas guzzlers and keeping our houses as warm in 1981 as we did in 1972–73, when consumers were last surveyed. The serious deterioration of fixed-weights indexes over time ultimately forces periodic revisions. A basket which still heavily weighed horseshoes and tallow is hardly a market basket.

Firms periodically introduce new models of old products. The BLS (Bureau of Labor Statistics), which constructs the CPI, attempts to adjust prices for quality changes. For example, higher automobile prices caused by tougher safety and pollution standards are adjusted downward. In most cases the necessary adjustments cannot be accomplished relatively easily and are ignored. The use of fixed weights and inadequate adjustment for quality changes is estimated to impart a 1 to 2 percent upward bias to the CPI.[7]

A combination of the general upward bias of the CPI as a cost-of-living index and the different expenditure pattern of the elderly, which may have accentuated the bias for them, explains some of the attempts to untie

---

[5] Because the base periods (1967 and 1977) for the CPI do not coincide with either the dates new market baskets were introduced (1964 and 1978) or the dates of the surveys (1960–61 and 1972–73) which generated the baskets, we prefer to call the CPI a fixed-weight index instead of a base-weight index, as is traditional.

[6] The shift in January 1982 to a 1977 base will not affect the weights.

[7] Although the weights of major commodity groups are fixed in the CPI, some substitution within groups is tolerated, particularly when some products are not available.

social security payments from the CPI. The CPI recognizes that the majority of households are buying homes on credit by including a significant interest-cost component. The elderly generally rent or own their homes outright; it is difficult to get a 30-year mortgage at age 65. Because interest costs rose significantly during the 1970s but the elderly were not purchasing this type of "commodity," the CPI overestimated the cost of living for them.[8]

## MEASUREMENT OF EMPLOYMENT AND UNEMPLOYMENT

The employed, E, are those who are working; the unemployed, U, are those who are able and willing to work but are not; the labor force, LF, is the sum of the employed and unemployed. The unemployment rate, u, is the percentage of unemployed in the labor force.

$$u = \frac{U}{E + U} \times 100 = \frac{LF - E}{LF} \times 100 \qquad (23-4)$$

Not everyone is working or seeking employment. Somewhat more than a third of the population over age 16 is not in the labor force. Provided we can spend all day thinking abstractly and do not have to dirty our hands with measurement and everyday problems, these definitions seem precise and totally adequate. What could be easier than measuring employment and unemployment? Employment is the doughnut, and unemployment is the hole. The president of a Fortune 500 company is employed; those who worked in a plant that just burned to the ground now are unemployed; an 80-year-old person who moved to Florida is not in the labor force. While most people can be readily categorized as employed, unemployed, or not in the labor force, the number whose classification at any one time is problematic is not inconsequential compared to the unproblematic changes over time. In the postwar period unemployment rates have varied by three to four percentage points between cyclical lows and highs, so that a 2 percent classification error could set in motion unnecessary compensatory policies.

BLS quite correctly has not let unresolved conceptual issues and the need to be somewhat arbitrary stop it from calculating unemployment statistics. A good, if imperfect, measure is better than none at all. On what basis are individuals, in fact, classified as employed and unemployed? (Those over 16 who fit neither the employed nor unemployed category are

---

[8] Although any durable good produces problems for builders of price indexes, the handling of home-ownership costs in the CPI is especially difficult and controversial. The BLS itself is aware of the problem but has been unable to find the solution. See BLS, *The Consumer Price Index: Concepts and Content over the Years,* Report 517 (Washington, D.C.: U.S. Government Printing Office, 1978). For a technically sophisticated but readable article on the contribution of housing to recent inflation see Alan Blinder, "The Consumer Price Index and the Measurement of Recent Inflation," *Brookings Papers on Economic Activity* 2 (1980): 539–65.

classified as not in the labor force.) Each month's unemployment statistics are based on interviews of a scientifically selected sample of approximately 50,000 households. People are employed if during the week preceding the interview they (a) worked at least one hour either as paid employees or in their own business or farm, (b) worked at least 15 hours as unpaid workers in a family enterprise, or (c) had a job or business but were not at work because of illness, bad weather, strikes, or personal reasons. People are unemployed if they did not work at all during the week preceding the interview and (a) actively looked for work sometime during the previous four weeks or (b) were waiting to report to a new job or to be recalled from a temporary layoff within the next 30 days. Actively looking for work is demonstrated by (a) registering at a public or private employment agency, (b) placing or answering advertisements, (c) interviewing prospective employers, or (d) asking friends or relatives about possible job opportunities. Those not in the labor force typically are too old, sick, students, or women with strong family responsibilities.

Figure 23–1 graphs the national unemployment rate since 1948 and the trend line. The lowest annual unemployment rate (2.9 percent) occurred at the 1953 business cycle expansion induced by the Korean War, and the highest rate (8.9 percent) was during the 1975 cyclical trough. The trend (from a 1980 viewpoint) in postwar unemployment is unmistakably upward. The poor performance of the economy in the 1970s accounts for this upward trend. A trend line computed a decade earlier would have been virtually flat.

**EXHIBIT 23–1**

---

### Teasers on employment and unemployment

The following examples illustrate that classification is not clear cut. Suppose two young people are preparing for their careers. A bright young woman who wants to be an economist goes to college. Another more mechanically inclined and dexterous woman needs practical experience and is an apprentice plumber. Do both belong in the same category, whatever that may be? Should the college student be placed in the employed category when she accepts a 10-hour-a-week job? Consider an example closer to my heart. In what category should a teacher belong during the summer when he is not teaching? Suppose a manufacturing firm has habitually laid off low-seniority workers whenever demand was slack and rehired them when demand picked up. A young man aware of the firm's policy accepts a job and intends to climb the seniority ladder. Senior workers are very well paid and not laid off. Suppose that after several months' employment the young factory worker is laid off at the beginning of the summer. Should he and the school teacher be placed in the same category? Or is the laid off factory worker apprenticing for a well-paid job, and should he be in the same category as the plumber or college student?

**FIGURE 23-1  National unemployment rate, 1948-1980**

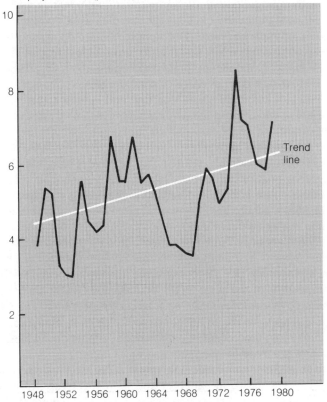

Unemployment rate (percent)

**SOURCE:** *Economic Report of the President, 1981.*

**TABLE 23-2  Unemployment and the labor force, 1954 and 1975**

| | Unemployment rate, 1975 | Share of labor force | |
|---|---|---|---|
| | | 1954 | 1975 |
| Panel A: | | | |
| Both sexes, 16 to 19 years | 19.9 | 6.2 | 9.5 |
| Both sexes, 20 to 24 years | 13.6 | 8.6 | 14.5 |
| Females, 25 years and over | 7.0 | 24.5 | 29.0 |
| Males, 25 years and over | 5.5 | 60.7 | 46.9 |
| Panel B: | | | |
| Nonwhite females, 20 years and over | 11.5 | 3.9 | 4.7 |
| Nonwhite males, 20 years and over | 11.7 | 6.1 | 5.7 |
| White females, 20 years and over | 7.5 | 24.4 | 30.9 |
| White males, 20 years and over | 6.2 | 59.3 | 49.2 |

**SOURCE:** Bureau of Labor Statistics, *Handbook of Labor Statistics.*

### The diversity of unemployment rates

Although a sample of approximately 50,000 households may seem small, it significantly exceeds the samples used by other countries and by public opinion pollsters. The sample is large enough to yield reliable unemployment rates by age-race-sex groupings.[9] Just as the broadly based CPI masked significant price movement diversity, the national unemployment rate is an average of widely different unemployment rates. Figures 23–2 and 23–3 show that age and race are the main classificatory variables which produce diverse unemployment rates, with sex being an important but secondary classificatory variable. Figure 23–2 emphasizes the relationship between age and unemployment. Unemployment has always been negatively related to age, and Figure 23–2 shows that the negative relationship is becoming more pronounced. The teenage unemployment rate is high and getting higher compared both to young adults and adults. Figure 23–3 shows unemployment rates relative to the rate for white males 20 years and over.

The diversity of unemployment rates by demographic groups suggests a *mechanical* explanation for some of the upward trend in the national unemployment rate. The aggregate unemployment rate depends on the composition of the labor force. When groups which traditionally have high unemployment rates make up a larger proportion of the labor force, then the aggregate unemployment rate will rise even if unemployment rates by groups remain constant. Compositional effects do, in fact, largely explain the upward trend in aggregate unemployment. The share of the labor force for the groups whose unemployment rates are illustrated in Figures 23–2 and 23–3 is shown in panels A and B, respectively, of Table 23–2. Both 1954 and 1975 were recession years. Table 23–2 shows that the proportion of teenagers, young adults, and females increased markedly during the postwar period, and the proportion of nonwhites increased somewhat.

---

[9] The sample is also large enough that one can produce alternative unofficial unemployment statistics in order to partially compensate for conceptual difficulties. For example, in the official unemployment statistics the college students living at home and looking for a part-time job and the household head looking for a full-time job are treated identically. Both are unemployed. Yet the labor force time lost and the hardship of the unemployment on others is quite different in the two cases. BLS reports separately the number of full-time and part-time jobholders and jobseekers, head and nonhead of household unemployment, etc. From these reports one can calculate various unofficial unemployment percentages which place the college student and household head in different categories.

Incidentally, how did you answer the teasers in Exhibit 23–1? For purposes of the official aggregate unemployment statistic, BLS classifies the economics undergraduate as out of the labor force, provided she is not looking for a job. Acceptance of the part-time job changes her status to employed, which is also the status of the apprentice plumber. A teacher with a contract for the following academic year is classified as employed during the summer although he may not be working. The factory worker who received an indefinite layoff and does not look for a job is out of the labor force. (Indefinite layoff means no fixed recall date. It does not necessarily mean that the probability of recall to the job at any time is very small.) If the layoff specifies recall within 30 days, he or she is unemployed.

**FIGURE 23-2   Selected unemployment rates, 1949–1980**

Unemployment rate (percent)

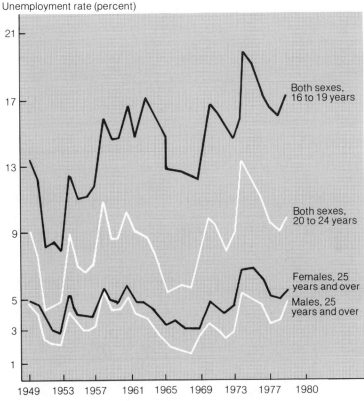

**SOURCE:** Bureau of Labor Statistics, *Handbook of Labor Statistics, 1981.*

The Council of Economic Advisers estimated that the aggregate unemployment rate in 1980 would be one percentage point lower if the labor force composition equalled that of 1950.[10]

Some critics claim that such adjustments of the aggregate rate are designed to make the economy's performance appear better than is warranted. Why should we implicitly accept the higher unemployment rates of some groups as natural and unavoidable?

## FULL EMPLOYMENT AND LABOR MARKETS

Let us assume that unemployment and employment are well defined. Does the higher unemployment rate of teenagers, nonwhites, and females

---

[10] See the *Economic Report of the President,* particularly the 1977 and 1978 issues. The decline in the birth rate in the 1960s will lead to a smaller proportion of teenagers and young adults in the 1980s so that compositional changes will then tend to reduce the unemployment rate.

FIGURE 23-3  **Ratios of unemployment rates by race and sex to the unemployment rate of white males, 1954–1980** (all people 20 years and over)

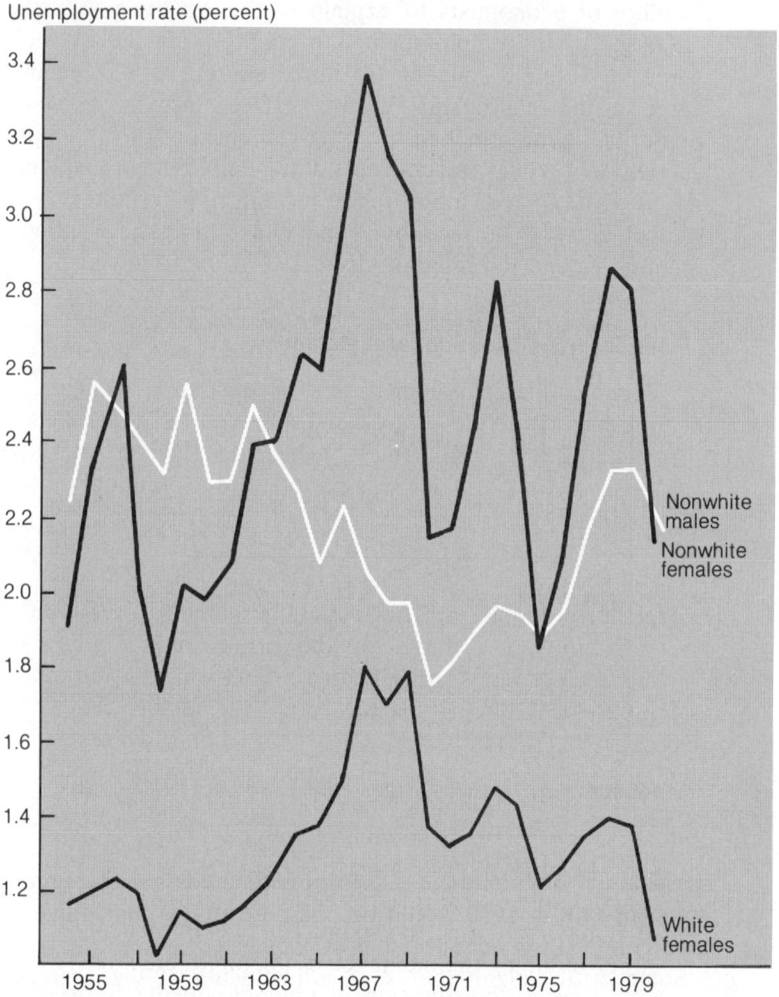

Unemployment rate (percent)

SOURCE: Bureau of Labor Statistics, *Handbook of Labor Statistics, 1981.*

*necessarily* mean that these groups are discriminated against? Is there some economic justification for the diversity of unemployment rates? To answer these questions we look at the behavior of labor markets and in the process tackle the very slippery question: What is full employment? The overwhelming proportion of the population who venture an answer state some number between 2.5 and 6.5 percent. When people are asked to justify the specific number given, few are able to do so. As a result, full employment, an economic concept, has become a political football. One's estimate of the full-employment rate is a good indicator of conservatism. The more conservative one is, the higher is the full-employment rate. The inability of economists to explain to the general public the concept or definition of full employment is partially explained by their inability to agree on a single concept. To make matters worse, economists cannot agree on the relationship, if any, between the various concepts and the numerical value attached to any given concept of full employment. This section reviews several concepts of full employment in the hope of making it less political and, more important, in order to better evaluate the past performance of the economy and understand the relationship between unemployment and inflation discussed in the following section.

### Unemployment, duration, and incidence

When the unemployment rate, u, is constant at whatever level, it equals the product of the mean duration of unemployment, DUR, times the percentage incidence INC, that is, the percentage of the labor force that becomes unemployed per time period used to compute the mean duration. Algebraically,

$$u = DUR \times INC \qquad (23-5)$$

A specific example best illustrates the validity of equation (23–5). Suppose the labor force consists of 100 people, three of whom become unemployed each month. Three people are also hired each month so that the unemployment rate is constant. Suppose further that two of the three people remain unemployed exactly one month while one person remains unemployed four months. The mean duration of unemployment is two months, and the unemployment rate is six percent. At any one time we will observe the two who will be unemployed for a month and four who will be unemployed four months, where the first of the four has already been unemployed over three months, the second has been unemployed for more than two months, and so on. The unemployment rate can be reduced by either reducing the incidence of unemployment or its mean duration.[11]

How long is the duration of unemployment? Some people get their impression of unemployment from movies and television. Particularly prior to the 1960s, the unemployed were portrayed as a surplus, the people "left over" after all the vacancies had been filled. The unemployed supposedly were people who went from office to office begging for a job, any job. After being continually rejected and financially ruined, the unemployed became "discouraged workers" who stopped actively searching for employment and dropped out of the labor force. However theatri-

---

[11] Equation (23–5) is valid irrespective of the time period used to compute the determinants of unemployment. Assuming four weeks in a month, in our example the mean duration alternatively is eight weeks, and 0.75 percent become unemployed per week, so that the equation still states the unemployment rate is 6 percent.

cally stirring such a representation may be, for many unemployed it is just that, theatrics. At any one time there are many unemployed but also many vacancies. In 1975, the postwar year with the highest unemployment rate, the median duration of unemployment was approximately nine weeks, a great hardship to be sure but not enough to financially ruin most households. In 1969, the last year unemployment was below 4 percent, the median duration of unemployment was much less, about 4 weeks. It is more accurate to think of the typical unemployed person as someone in motion through the labor market, which relatively quickly fits him or her with an existing vacancy. Of course, there are many atypical unemployed. Table 23–3 shows that the duration of unemployment is hardly the same

**TABLE 23–3   Percentage distribution of the unemployed, 1969 and 1975**

|  | 1969 | 1975 |
|---|---|---|
| Unemployment rate | 3.5 | 8.5 |
| Panel A (by duration of unemployment): | | |
| Less than 5 weeks | 57.7 | 37.0 |
| 5 to 14 weeks | 29.2 | 31.3 |
| 14 to 26 weeks | 8.5 | 16.5 |
| 27 weeks or more | 4.7 | 15.2 |
| Median duration (in weeks) | 4.3 | 8.7 |
| Mean duration (in weeks) | 7.9 | 14.1 |
| Incidence (percent per week) | 0.44 | 0.60 |
| Panel B (by reason for unemployment): | | |
| Layoffs and firings | 35.9 | 55.4 |
| Quits | 15.4 | 10.4 |
| Re-entrants | 34.1 | 23.8 |
| New entrants | 14.6 | 10.4 |

SOURCE: *Economic Report of the President, 1981.*

for everyone. The mean is substantially greater than the median duration because some remain unemployed for a long spell. A bout of unemployment does financially ruin some households.

Table 23–3 indicates that even in the best of times unemployment is not unusual. In 1969, when the unemployment rate was 3.5 percent, the incidence of unemployment was 0.44 percent each week, or approximately 23 percent of the labor force became unemployed at some point during the year, assuming unemployment struck a different person each time. Even if one recognizes that some people suffer multiple bouts of unemployment during the year, over one sixth of the labor force was unemployed for part of the most prosperous year in recent memory.

Why do people become unemployed? Panel B of Table 23–3 again presents a picture different from the movies, where virtually everyone becomes unemployed involuntarily. In 1969 only about one third of the unemployed clearly endured that state involuntarily. Persons who in some sense became unemployed through their own volition—those who quit their jobs, those who had left the labor market and were re-entering, and new entrants looking for their first jobs—made up almost two thirds of the unemployed in good times. Even in the bad times of 1975 the voluntarily unemployed equaled approximately half of the total.

### Various concepts of full employment

Armed with this brief description of labor markets, we can tackle the full-employment question. Neoclassical economics presented in Chapter 15 provides us with one concept of full employment: it simply is labor market equilibrium. What number does one attach to this concept of full employment? Neoclassical theory like all theory must simplify. It generally assumes a homogeneous product (that is, our gizmos), a homogeneous labor force, and homogeneous jobs. In such a world the full-employment rate of unemployment is zero. When all jobs are exactly alike and all workers are exactly alike, a general lack of jobs is the only reason for unemployment. What other justification could there be for the existence of people who are *willing and able* to hold *the* job but do not have one?

However convenient the assumption of homogeneity may be on occasion, it clearly is unrealistic. The problems due to heterogeneity are compounded by a lack of information and an inability to assess differences quickly and inexpensively. Neoclassical economists realize that in a heterogeneous economy it is absurd to require zero unemployment for full employment and labor market equilibrium. Go behind equilibrium to supply and demand. Neoclassicists derived the demand for labor assuming that firms maximize profits. The supply of labor assumes that households are maximizing utility in terms of leisure and consumption. When workers are heterogeneous and employers lack information so that differences among workers cannot be assessed immediately, then profit maximization does *not* require that every job be filled instantly. Although it may be profitable to hire a worker, which worker should be hired? The first person to apply for a job rarely will be the best suited. Profits typically are increased by keeping the job temporarily unfilled. Similarly, when workers lack information about jobs, then utility maximization does *not* require that every worker accept the first job. Although one may want to work in general, remaining unemployed until one finds the specific job for which one is well suited will increase earnings and utility.

What number do neoclassicists attach to full employment in a heterogeneous economy? What unemployment rate maximizes firms' profits and households' utility? In a free market economy the average unemployment rate observed over a long period of time is the full employment rate of unemployment. Why is this so? If full employment maximizes profits and utility, then firms and households attempt to get to full employment and, if unimpeded, eventually do. Therefore, the long-run average rate of unemployment is full employment.

The neoclassical view of full employment seemed pollyannaish, particularly after the Great Depression. Some wanted full employment defined so the economy does not necessarily achieve it even in the long run. A second view takes optimality and inevitability out of full employment and says that *full employment occurs when job vacancies equal the number of unemployed*. There exists an overall negative relationship between the number of vacancies and the number unemployed. Help wanted ads made slim readings during the Great Depression. The intersection of the vacancies and unemployment relationship graphed in Figure 23–4 and a 45° line

**FIGURE 23–4  Vacancies and unemployed**

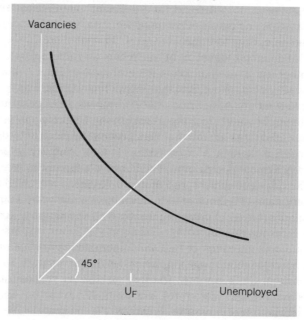

is the full-employment quantity of unemployment. According to this view, full employment is a situation of aggregate balance so that there exists a job for everyone. However, in a heterogeneous economy jobs and people need not match. Full-employment unemployment measures the necessary disaggregate imbalance when aggregate balance exists in a diverse economy.

This view emphasizes two reasons for the simultaneous existence of vacancies and unemployment: (1) lack of information and (2) a mismatch of worker skills and job requirements—the round hole and square peg problem. Corresponding to these two reasons for the simultaneous existence of vacancies and unemployment, full-employment unemployment traditionally is broken down into two types, frictional and structural. *Frictional unemployment is the unemployment which occurs due to lack of information about the qualities of the unemployed and job vacancies.* This is the unemployment stressed by neoclassicists. It is a short-run phenomenon. *Structural unemployment occurs because of a mismatch of skills and job requirements.* Structural unemployment occurs when unskilled workers are unemployed while oil companies are looking for petroleum engineers, or when West Virginians are unemployed while Wyoming coal companies have vacancies. In contrast to frictional unemployment, structural unemployment may be relatively long run. It has been used to justify numerous labor training programs. Of course, unemployment may exceed the frictional and structural amounts associated with full employment. Such unemployment is called demand-deficient unemployment, which is represented in Figure 23–4 by being on a point on the vacancy-unemployed curve below the 45° line.

Critics of the equality of vacancies and unemployed approach to full employment state that too much emphasis is placed on specific labor and job classes and their possible mismatch. An individual can fulfill many different jobs. These critics have formulated the search theory approach to unemployment. In some respects the search approach is simply a sophisticated version of the neoclassical approach to full employment. The search approach emphasizes (1) lack of information as the cause of unemployment during equilibrium and (2) the optimality and inevitability of the full-employment rate of unemployment, which to its credit is more simply called the *natural rate of unemployment.* The search approach differs from the neoclassical approach by keeping the maximization process in the forefront.

Suppose an engineer becomes unemployed for whatever reason. The engineer is not malingering when he or she refuses a job at a fast-food restaurant. It is optimal for that person to remain unemployed when employment and job search are mutually exclusive uses of one's time, as search theory assumes. While the assumption is not universally correct—professionals in particular can look for jobs while working—finding a job generally is easier and faster if one is unemployed. Evaluating jobs is difficult because jobs have many dimensions, such as current salary, potential for future advancement, location, sociability of coworkers, and so on. Suppose all the dimensions of a job can be given current dollar values so that the overall desirability of any job is measured by its "adjusted salary." The unemployed person has numerous job prospects. Lack of information implies that the adjusted salary of each feasible job is uncertain prior to spending time applying for the job. Let the solid curve in Figure 23–5 represent the unemployed's *estimate* of the probability distribution of the adjusted salaries he or she could earn. (Temporarily ignore the broken curve.) The distribution estimated by each unemployed

**FIGURE 23-5  Job search and adjusted salary distributions**

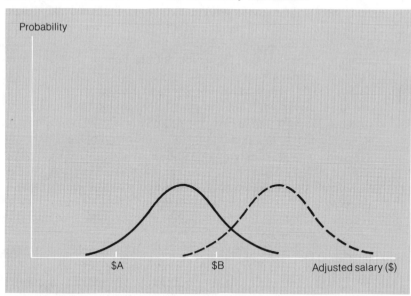

person generally will differ. The engineer's distribution is far to the right of an unskilled worker's distribution.

The engineer may be extremely lucky and find the job corresponding to the right-hand tail of his or her estimated distribution right off the bat. This typically will not be the case because the person lacks information about the particularly desirable jobs. Suppose the engineer in the first job search is offered an adjusted salary represented by point $A in Figure 23-5. Before deciding whether or not to accept the job, he or she compares the marginal cost and benefit of further search. The cost is the $A salary foregone plus any penalty costs, such as the repossession of a car due to an inability to meet the payments. The benefit is the expected additional salary from finding a better job. Suppose the cost and benefit are such that the engineer decides to make a second search. In the second round the person finds a job that pays $B. At each round the marginal benefit of further search remains constant if the last search produced an offer worse than an earlier one, or decreases if the last search produced the best offer.[12] In our example, the marginal benefit decreased since $B is greater than $A; the expected additional salary from further search is less when he or she already has an offer paying $B. At some point the additional costs of further search exceed the benefits, and the unemployed accepts the best offer.

___

[12] We are assuming that jobs remain open so that one may reject a job and subsequently accept it after further rounds of search have produced nothing better.

*The natural rate of unemployment is the rate of unemployment which occurs when the unemployed correctly estimate their probability distribution of adjusted salaries. Given some incidence of unemployment, the natural rate of unemployment occurs when the duration of unemployment is optimal.* Suppose the unemployed underestimate the distribution of salaries. In terms of Figure 23–5, the *actual* distribution is given by the broken curve, while the solid curve is the *estimated* distribution. In this case, the unemployed accept jobs too quickly. The *optimal* search and duration of unemployment, which occurs when the marginal costs of search equal the *actual* marginal benefits, is less than the *actual* search time and duration of unemployment, which depends on search costs and the *estimated* distribution of salaries. When the unemployed underestimate the distribution of salaries, unemployment will be *below* the natural rate. However, the unemployed and society in general lose because too many low-paying and, therefore, unproductive jobs are accepted. The search approach makes clear that the full-employment (natural) rate of unemployment is not a technological minimum. We shall let the reader explain why overestimates of the distribution of salaries and, therefore, prolonged durations of unemployment produce an unemployment rate which exceeds and is economically inferior to the natural rate of unemployment. *The natural rate is the optimal rate of unemployment.* The actual rate of unemployment at any moment can be less or greater than the optimal. During any short period, estimation errors are quite likely. Mistakes eventually are corrected, however. In the long run the actual and estimated salary distributions coincide, so that *in the long run the actual rate of unemployment equals the natural rate.*[13]

### Labor markets and the unemployment trend

Is an upward trend in the full-employment rate consistent with these viewpoints? Would supporters of the various viewpoints anticipate to some extent the observed diversity of unemployment rates among demographic groups? The answer to both questions is yes. Advocates of the vacancy equals unemployed approach to full employment say that teenagers and nonwhites and, to a lesser extent, young adults often are relatively unskilled while employers are hiring highly skilled people. There are not enough low-skilled jobs. Consequently, these groups have above average rates of unemployment, and their greater share of the labor force raises the national unemployment rate. The search approach says that the

---

[13] The high unemployment rates throughout the 1930s presumably exceeded the natural rate so that the long run was over a decade in that case. Since the relevance of any proposition tends to decrease with the length of the time period necessary for its occurrence, the 1930s do question the relevance of the natural rate hypothesis. However, as Chapter 15 also indicated, the 1930s can be overemphasized. As important as the 1930s may be, a theory should not be accepted (rejected) just because it does (does not) explain the events of the decade.

duration and, consequently, rate of unemployment is highest for those groups least well informed about labor markets. Little information is reflected in Figure 23–5 by a flat and widely dispersed probability distribution, in which case the benefits of additional search are great. Information is acquired by being in the labor market. Workers who were laid off or quit are better informed than new entrants and re-entrants. Since the proportion of entrants or re-entrants is larger for teenagers, young adults, and women than for other labor force groups, the three specified classes expectedly have higher unemployment rates. Of course, the economic explanation may not be the sole explanation for the diversity of unemployment rates.

Two postwar developments totally unrelated with the composition of the labor force have had the effect of raising the natural rate of unemployment. First, the proportion of the labor force covered by unemployment insurance and other social programs dependent on income has increased. Moreover, unemployment compensation and other payments, which typically are untaxed, have increased as a proportion of aftertax wage earnings. This has reduced the personal cost of search for everyone and increased search time and unemployment somewhat. Second, real income and financial assets per worker have increased markedly in the postwar period. The earnings and assets per *household* have risen even more markedly due to the increase in the number of multiple wage earner households associated with the strong upward trend in the labor force participation rates of women. Particularly when capital markets are imperfect, this has the effect of reducing the cost of search for both men and women. With a working wife, the husband can be choosier about his job. The household can withstand longer bouts of unemployment and not worry about the repossession of the car when it has more financial assets.

Unemployment insurance illustrates that government policies can influence the natural rate. Some have recommended a reduction in the amount of unemployment benefits and more stringent criteria for qualification as a means of reducing unemployment. For example, people who voluntarily quit their jobs qualify for unemployment compensation in a few states. Martin Feldstein, a leading analyst of unemployment insurance and president of the prestigious National Bureau of Economic Research, opposes payments to quitters.[14] The majority of the recommendations to reduce full-employment unemployment stress the upgrading of the lowest skill groups, either through direct government programs or through tax credits to firms which hire the unskilled. Reductions in the unemployment rate achieved in this manner clearly are costly and must be compared with the benefits.

---

[14] Martin Feldstein, "The Private and Social Cost of Unemployment," *American Economic Review*, May 1978, pp. 155–58.

## NEOCLASSICAL AND KEYNESIAN AGGREGATE SUPPLY

Armed with a knowledge of the behavior of labor markets and the meanings of full employment, we can now integrate neoclassical and Keynesian ideas about the price-output relationship into a unified theory of inflation and unemployment. Since the transformation from price-output to inflation-unemployment is relatively straightforward, this section mainly reviews the neoclassical and Keynesian price-output relationship. A brief review of the assumptions behind the alternative price-output relationships is important in its own right and facilitates subsequent construction of an intermediate case which contains elements of both neoclassical and Keynesian economics.

The price and quantity of a single commodity is determined by its demand and supply. Similar analysis may be applied to commodities in general. As previously defined in Chapter 15, *the aggregate demand curve shows the relationship between (aggregate) output and the (general) price level when the nonlabor markets are in equilibrium, given the money supply, fiscal policy, and other exogenous variables.* More is demanded at lower prices. Figure 23–6 illustrates the downward sloping aggregated demand curve. Aggregate demand increases, that is, the curve shifts from AD to AD', when the quantity of money increases or when government spending increases, assuming the demand for money does depend on the rate of interest.[15]

By definition, *the aggregate supply curve shows the relationship between (aggregate) output and the (general) price level implied by the production function and equilibrium in the labor market.* Although the last section mentioned changes in labor force composition and participation rates, which influence aggregate supply, let us assume aggregate supply remains constant. In this case, changes in price and output are due exclusively to the variability of demand, which traces out aggregate supply.[16] That is, all the observed price and output combinations are assumed to lie on a single aggregate supply curve. (We shall indicate later the modifications necessary when supply is also allowed to vary.)

The vertical line $AS_L$ in Figure 23–6 is the aggregate supply curve in the

---

[15] The aggregate demand curve was drawn in Figure 15–7, where we assumed a neoclassical, perfectly interest-inelastic money demand. In view of the "Money and the Rate of Interest at Full Employment" and "Government Spending at Full Employment" sections of Chapter 20, the reader should be able to prove for himself or herself that, in the more general case where the demand for money also depends on the rate of interest, (1) the aggregate demand curve still is downward sloping, and (2) monetary and fiscal policy shift aggregate demand.

[16] The analog in a growth economy is supply and demand curves which shift at constant and variable rates, respectively. We shall assume throughout the remainder of this chapter that the economy is initially in equilibrium but shall later drop the implicit assumption that labor is the only factor of production.

FIGURE 23-6 Aggregate demand and aggregate supply

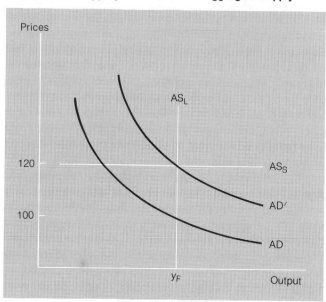

*long run.* We derived it rigorously at the end of Chapter 15. In the long run, which is the domain of neoclassical economics, firms maximize profits and households maximize utility. This produces labor demand and supply curves which depend solely on the real wage. Prices and wages eventually adjust to reach the unique equilibrium real wage and employment because disequilibrium represents a situation where all gains have not been exploited. Economic agents seeking to improve their lot eventually attain their maximum.

The long-run inflation-unemployment relationship produced by varying demand is a vertical line like the aggregate supply. The degree of heterogeneity and lack of information determine $U_F$ in Figure 23–7, that is, the unemployment rate corresponding to full-employment output. If demand remains constant at AD or AD', the price level in Figure 23–6 remains constant at 100 or 120, respectively. In Figure 23–7, the economy lands at the bliss point on the inflation-unemployment curve, that is, the zero inflation/full-employment point. Increases (decreases) in aggregate demand move the economy up (down) the inflation curve. *In the long run, increases in aggregated demand generate inflation but have no effect on unemployment.*

In the short run, which is the domain of Keynesian economics, demand creates its own supply. The aggregate supply curve in Figure 23–6 is $AS_S$, a perfectly flat curve at some "sticky" price level. In Chapter 17 we appealed to (1) labor market contracts which explicitly or implicitly give

**FIGURE 23-7  Inflation-unemployment relationship**

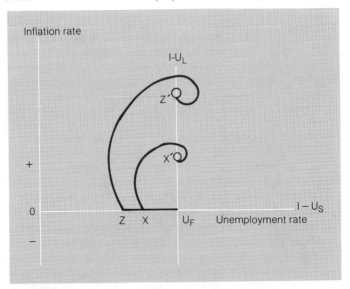

employers the option to hire any number of workers at a predetermined nominal wage and (2) firms' desire to maintain product market shares as sources of a flat short-run nonprofit-maximizing aggregate supply curve. Exhibit 2 presents a somewhat more thorough explanation for sticky short-run wages and prices. Similar reasoning to that used earlier allows us to transform the flat aggregate supply curve into a flat inflation-unemployment curve in Figure 23-7. For convenience, always start the analysis from the bliss point of short- and long-run equilibrium. The line $I\text{-}U_S$ shows the inflation-unemployment values produced in the short run by different rates of change in aggregate demand. Expanding demand moves the economy leftward along $I\text{-}U_S$ in the short run.

Assume demand increases at some given rate. Beginning from the bliss point, the economy initially moves along $I\text{-}U_S$ to, say, point X but ultimately moves to point X' on $I\text{-}U_L$. This necessarily implies that during the interim increases in aggregate demand reduce unemployment *and* are inflationary. Although the analysis does not pinpoint exact time paths, the curve linking X and X' outlines the general response of inflation and unemployment *over time* to a constant rate of increase in demand. As drawn, overshooting occurs. For a while, the rates of inflation and unemployment exceed their long-run values although initially both were below equilibrium. Suppose the curve XX' was generated by a 5 percent annual increase in the rate of monetary expansion and aggregate demand. How would the economy have responded to a 10 percent rate of increase? The greater increase in demand produces the curve ZZ'.

**EXHIBIT 23–2**

### Why prices and wages are sticky in the short run

Explicit or implicit contracts, fair pricing, and other sources of inertia are fundamental assumptions underlying the short-run supply and demand curves for labor and commodities. Continuous wage settlements would be too time consuming and economically and psychologically disruptive. As a result, labor and management execute wage contracts which last several periods. While more wage contracts are containing cost of living adjustment (COLA) clauses, they still are the exception, and the adjustment for inflation rarely is complete. Besides stipulating wages, many labor contracts explicitly give, and the remainder implicitly give, the employer the right to require overtime, albeit at a higher wage. Thus, the employer is readily able to change output in response to demand. And firms do initially respond to demand by changing production. Some firms have granted buyers options to purchase goods and must respond to demand. Although such legally mandated responses to demand are relatively rare, many firms and consumers have entered into *implicit contracts* whereby firms are expected to satisfy automatically the demand of favored customers who purchase goods frequently and ignore an occasional better deal elsewhere. Few managers will use the term *implicit contracts,* but the often expressed objective of maintaining market share is tantamount to confirming their existence.

Implicit contracts exist between labor and management as well. Labor wants management not to lay off workers at the first sign of a weakening in product demand. The firm is supposed to produce for inventories, make postponed repairs, and, at worse, just slow down the assembly line. Firms behave in this manner; productivity, the ratio of output to employment, falls during the early phase of a recession. Firms are not expected to maintain the labor force indefinitely. At some point layoffs begin. And what do firms and laid-off workers expect from each other? Firms expect workers to wait around some reasonable length of time before even looking for another job. This is illustrated by the terms used when workers are "let go." A person is fired for incompetence but laid off when demand falls. Firms prefer to rehire laid-off workers instead of new workers when demand rebounds because they avoid training costs. Workers who endure layoffs can expect them to become less frequent in the future. Layoffs are largely allocated on the basis of seniority. The low-seniority workers who are laid off first can acquire the security of senior workers only by waiting to be recalled. Most do so. About 80 percent of laid-off workers return to the same job with the same employer.

The increasing complexity of products and the growing importance of the service sector has reduced the proportion of aggregate output which can be evaluated qualitatively very easily and has strengthened the need for confidence between firms/professionals and their customers. How can a firm instill confidence about itself in its customers? One

**EXHIBIT 23-2** (*continued*)

way confidence is instilled is by adopting the medieval philosopher's "fair price" instead of the modern economist's "equilibrium price" determined by demand and supply. Economists have so highly extolled the virtues of supply and demand pricing as a rationing device that few publicly admit their belief in fair pricing. However, the very persistent and widespread attachment to the fair price has only been sublimated. It periodically surfaces with a vengeance. During calamities, pricing according to supply and demand is called profiteering and is severely punished. How does one price fairly? Ignore demand; price on the basis of cost or supply exclusively. If costs rise, it is only "fair" to pass the higher costs along in terms of a higher price. Failure to do so lowers profits. Raising price in response to demand increases profits. If a firm does this, will it also cut quality, which is not readily ascertained, in order to raise profits? The combination of fair pricing, which ties price to cost, and contracts, which fix costs, is an explanation for the legacy Keynes gave us: a flat short-run aggregate supply curve. To be sure, more work remains to be done. "After three decades, the major intellectual problem continues to be the fact that so little (short-run) response to demand shifts comes through prices and wages" (William Nordhaus, "Inflation Theory and Policy," *American Economic Review,* May 1976, p. 62).

The reader should keep firmly in mind what is held constant and is allowed to vary along these curves. Along I-$U_S$ and I-$U_L$ the time period is held constant. The curves are generated by different rates of changes of demand. The curve XX′ measures the response of the economy at different times to a constant increase in demand.

## THE INTERMEDIATE CASE

If the previous section is correct, then different changes in demand should produce a downward-sloping inflation-unemployment curve in the intermediate run characterized by a combination of the assumptions underlying the short and long run. This indeed is the case. The term of most union negotiated labor contracts is two to three years. The typical implicit contract between firms and their customers to price fairly and meet demand is considerably shorter. Define the intermediate run as a time period long enough for firms to maximize profits but short enough to prevent workers bound by contracts from maximizing their preference. The intermediate run is illustrated in Figure 23–8. Contracts which constrain workers produce the flat labor supply curve. Since the demand for labor by profit-maximizing firms depends negatively on the real wage but the

**FIGURE 23–8  Labor demand and supply in the intermediate run**

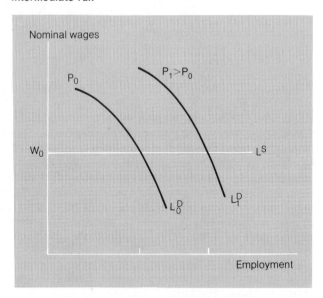

**FIGURE 23–9  Inflation-unemployment relationship by time period**

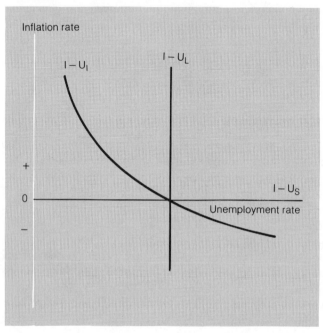

nominal wage is on the axis, there exists a demand curve for each price level. A higher price level lowers the real wage and shifts the demand curve rightward. Employment and output increase as labor is committed by contracts to work as much as employers demand. Although not illustrated, the aggregated supply curve clearly is upward sloping in the intermediate run. Higher prices induce firms to produce more.

Figure 23–9 graphs the intermediate-run inflation-unemployment relationship, I-$U_I$, implied by Figure 23–8. In the intermediate run there is a tradeoff between the goals of price stability and low unemployment. The greater is the increase in aggregate demand, the higher is the rate of inflation and employment and, consequently, the lower is unemployment. Mr. Phillips anticipated the shape of our intermediate-run curve. There is an important difference, however, between our intermediate-run curve and the traditional Phillips curve. Mr. Phillips and his supporters claim there is a *permanent* trade-off between inflation and unemployment. We claim the trade-off is only *temporary*. Precisely because we reject permanency, which is an integral part of the Phillips curve analysis, we avoided the term in the previous section and drew three curves in Figure 23–9. Henceforth we will use the term Phillips curve—it is simpler than the inflation-unemployment relationship—but qualifying time period adjectives will be attached.

## THE PHILLIPS CURVE

As this chapter's introductory section noted, belief in a stable Phillips curve thoroughly dominated professional economic analysis in the 1960s. In view of this, we should demonstrate the fallacies of the Phillips curve and not dismiss it cavalierly as contrary to our viewpoint.

Phillips initially analyzed the relationship between the rate of change of *wages* and the unemployment rate in Great Britain between 1861 and 1913. While all the wage change/unemployment points did not fall along a smooth curve like I-$U_I$, there certainly was a tight negative relationship between the variables prior to World War I. To test whether this was a true empirical regularity or a sampling fluke, Phillips also plotted the data for 1948–57. They were just as close to the curve as the original points!

Virtually immediately after publication of Phillips' study, economists feverishly rushed to test the relationship for other countries and other times. The rate of inflation, a variable much more in the public consciousness, was almost invariably substituted for the rate of change of wages without affecting the general conclusion.[17] For country after country the data suggested the existence of a trade-off between inflation and the rate of unemployment. In the euphoria of participating in the confirmation of a

---

[17] We shall see shortly that the substitution influences the height but not the shape of the trade-off curve.

veritable empirical regularity, most researchers failed to notice that the most recent study typically illustrated a weaker trade-off than earlier studies showed. Economists became more and more convinced about the trade-off as study after study showed it was becoming weaker and weaker.

Phillips and his many early imitators were more concerned about finding the curve than explaining it. This made some wag say that the Phillips curve was an empirical fact in search of a theory. Richard Lipsey took up the challenge of rationalizing the Phillips curve.[18] Lipsey observed that the rate of change of a commodity's price depends on its excess demand. The same should be true for a factor of production like labor. Lipsey reasoned that the unemployment rate was a good proxy for the excess demand for labor. The price of labor is the wage rate. Consequently, when unemployment is low, there should be a large excess demand for labor, and wage increases should be large. In order to maintain their income share, firms must pass forward any wage increase in excess of productivity gains.[19] Therefore, when unemployment is low, inflation is high. There is a negative relationship between the rates of unemployment and inflation. Although many niceties have been ignored, we captured the basic explanation for the Phillips curve.

Read the last paragraph again. Read it a third time. The explanation for the Phillips curve is straightforward and totally convincing, or at least it convinced nearly all economists for several years. Did you spot the flaw? Before explaining the flaw, we adopt the philosophy of the Phillips curve to show that a flaw does exist. Look at Figure 23–10 which graphs unemployment and inflation rates for the United States. The proof of the pudding is in the eating. There simply is no overall Phillips curve, so that the explanation for it cannot be totally accurate. Yet the explanation for the Phillips curve cannot be totally inaccurate and simultaneously so convincing. A closer look at Figure 23–10 reveals vestiges of Phillips curves. When the inflational-unemployment points are connected chronologically, as Figure 23–10 does, there appear to be numerous Phillips curves which have shifted upward over time. For several years there is a trade-off between inflation and unemployment, but after many years the trade-off vanishes.

---

[18] Richard Lipsey, "The Relation between Unemployment and the Rate of Change of Money Wage Rates in the United Kingdom, 1862–1957: A Further Analysis" *Economica,* February 1960, pp. 1–31.

[19] Labor's share of income, Py, is WL/Py, where W is the wage rate, and L is employment. For our purposes, the expression is best rearranged and written as (W/P)/(y/L), the ratio of the real wage to labor productivity, y/L. The last expression indicates that labor's share and, therefore, the share of the remaining factors are constant when real wages and productivity change by the same rate or, equivalently, when the growth of nominal wages exceeds the rate of inflation by the growth of productivity. Since shares have remained approximately constant and productivity growth is positive, the inflation-unemployment and wage change-unemployment curves have the same general shape but the former lies below the latter by the rate of productivity growth.

**FIGURE 23-10   U.S. unemployment and inflation rates, 1953-1980**

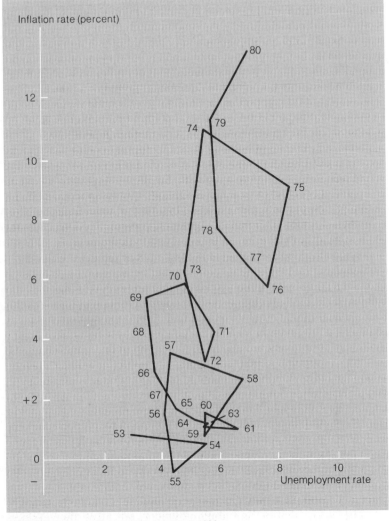

**SOURCE:** *Economic Report of the President, 1981.*

## THE FRIEDMAN-PHELPS NATURAL RATE HYPOTHESIS

Milton Friedman first pricked the Phillips balloon and Edmund Phelps totally deflated it.[20] The two main flaws in the Phillips curve argument are the implicit assumptions that (1) wages and prices are well known to everyone, and (2) contracts which create future commitments do not

[20] Milton Friedman, "The Role of Monetary Policy," and Edmund Phelps, *Inflation Policy and Unemployment Theory* (New York: W. W. Norton, 1973).

exist. Friedman and Phelps emphasize incorrect wage and price percep-
tions. The complexity of their argument has caused many to lose the
forest for the trees. Since the implications of contracts and wage and price
misperceptions are similar, we first offer a glimpse of our final destination
using the easier contracts approach, which we already have stressed, in
order to avoid the forest for the trees problem. We then travel the
Friedman-Phelps road of price misperceptions.

*When contracts exist, current wage settlements do not reflect current ex-
cess demand exclusively, but also reflect expected inflation and future demand.* In the search analysis of a single worker with many job possibilities, we defined the natural rate of unemployment as the unemployment rate which occurs when workers correctly estimate the distribution
of adjusted salaries available at one moment. Now that we want to emphasize contracts and wage and price differences over time, the analogous
definition of the natural rate is: the natural rate of unemployment occurs
when the rate of inflation is predicted correctly. The natural rate is represented in Figure 23–11 by $u_N$. The vertical line at $u_N$ illustrates that the
natural rate is consistent with any rate of inflation, provided it is anticipated.

Although both sides are ultimately interested in the real wage, assume
labor market participants strike nominal wage bargains. Continuous wage
bargains are too costly. Define the intermediate run as the average duration of labor contracts. Because of contracts, current wage settlements
reflect not only the current rate of unemployment as Phillips claimed but
also the expected rate of inflation during the intermediate run. Begin the
analysis from a position of zero anticipated inflation. On the basis of this
anticipation and other factors, a wage settlement is reached. When aggregated demand is such that the actual rate of inflation is zero, neither side is
disappointed by the outcome and feels it made a mistake. The plans of
both sides of the market are realized when the actual and expected inflation rates coincide, and the unemployment rate equals the natural rate, by
definition. The economy is at point A in Figure 23–11.

Suppose aggregate demand suddenly accelerates. The public underestimates the rate of inflation, which turns out to be 5 percent instead of
zero. In this case the unemployment rate will fall. Firms find the unanticipated inflation has reduced the real wage and respond by hiring more
workers, who have committed themselves by contracts. *The unemployment rate is below (above) the natural rate when the actual rate of inflation is
greater (less) than the anticipated rate.* The curve through points A and B
is the Phillips curve when the expected rate of inflation is zero, $\pi^e = 0$.

The expectation formation process clearly is a key element in this
theory. *An integral component of the Friedman-Phelps theory is the assumption that the expected rate of inflation depends entirely on past rates.* As a
first approximation, let the expected rate equal last period's inflation rate,
or 5 percent in our example. How does the shift to a higher expected rate

**FIGURE 23-11    Phillips curves shifted by the expected inflation rate**

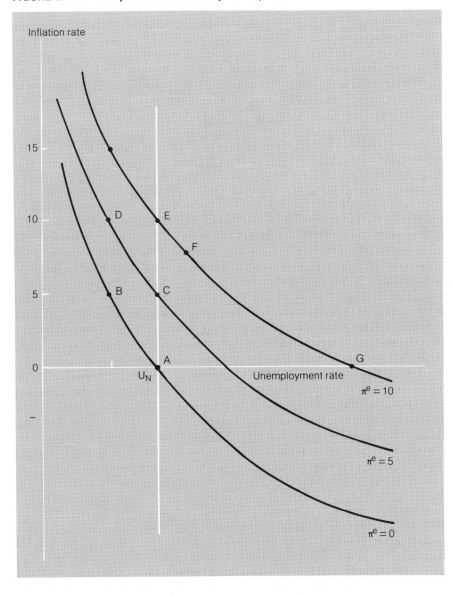

of inflation influence behavior? Wage settlements at the next bargaining round will equal the old wage settlement adjusted upward by the expected rate of inflation because firms and workers are ultimately interested in real magnitudes. For example, if the bargaining process led to a 2 percent wage increase when inflation was not expected, then the same bargaining process produces 7 percent wage increase when a 5 percent inflation rate is expected. If aggregate demand and the rate of inflation continue to rise at the same 5 percent rate, the economy moves back to the natural rate at 5 percent inflation, point C. Just as at point A, neither side is disappointed at C; plans are realized; and anticipated and actual real wages coincide. Nominal variables were correctly escalated upward at C in order to keep real variables constant. The shape of a curve formed by ABC clearly resembles our inflation-unemployment curves over time in Figure 23–7.

What inflation rate is necessary to maintain the unemployment rate at the level of point B? The inflation rate must rise to 10 percent. The movement from point A to B was caused by a real wage 5 percent less than anticipated. With the 5 percent higher inflationary expectations and wage settlement, the same 5 percent real wage reduction requires a 10 percent rate of inflation. The economy moves from point B to D. Thus, the Phillips curve is shifted upward by the expected rate of inflation.

The natural rate hypothesis says that there is a tradeoff between inflation and unemployment in the intermediate run when contracts made on the basis of a *given* expected rate of inflation are binding. However, because expectations are based on the past, movement up (down) an intermediate-run Phillips curve increases (decreases) the expected rate of inflation and future contractual wages, which shifts the curve upward (downward). What inflation rate is necessary in order to permanently maintain unemployment below the natural rate? Inflation must be *accelerating* so that the actual rate always exceeds the expected rate. What previously required a 5 percent rate of inflation now requires a 10 percent rate, then a 15 percent rate, and so on. For this reason, the Friedman-Phelps hypothesis is also called the accelerationist hypothesis. *Accelerating (decelerating), and not simply high (low), inflation rates are necessary in order to maintain the unemployment rate below (above) the natural rate.*

Friedman and Phelps emphasize temporary wage and price misperceptions and information costs as the source of shifting Phillips curves. Let the natural rate concept include correct wage and price estimates both across jobs and commodities and over time. In terms of the variables of greatest interest, the natural rate occurs when individuals correctly estimate the distribution of adjusted salaries and the rate of inflation. Begin the analysis again at point A, where constant prices and wage distributions produce the natural rate because constancy was anticipated. Now suppose aggregate demand increases by 5 percent. Because the acquisition of information is costly, some time may elapse before firms realize that aggregate demand increased. Suppose our firm then raises its prices 5 percent although it remains uncertain about the precise aggregate demand increase and the reaction of other firms. At this point the firm knows with certainty that *its* real wage has fallen. So far we ignored that *the* real wage is very different for each producer. The real wage for a firm is the ratio of *its* wage rate to the price of *its* products alone. The firm's lack of information about the prices of other products is irrelevant for its labor market decisions. A profit-maximizing firm does *not* hire more workers simply because the prices of other products rise or because other firms are paying lower wages.

Suppose firms react to the lower real wage by raising the nominal wage somewhat in the hopes of hiring more workers. Will firms be successful? Yes. Just as firms were not immediately aware of the aggregate demand increase and responded with a lag, so the unemployed will not immediately realize that the salary distribution has shifted rightward. The duration of job search declines as the unemployed think they are finding particularly good jobs. The decline in the unemployment rate moves the economy from point A to B. Provided aggregate demand, prices, and the salary distribution continue to increase at a constant rate, they all become anticipated correctly and the economy moves to C. What can keep unemployment below the natural rate? People must be fooled; the actual salary distribution must be kept on the right-hand side of the estimated. People will be fooled by accelerating inflation according to Friedman-Phelps because forecasts are based on some average of past inflation rates.

## RATIONAL EXPECTATIONS AND THE PHILLIPS CURVE

The rational expectations school, which we briefly mentioned in Chapter 15, assumes markets always clear. That is, prices and wages adjust continuously to equate supply and demand. Moreover, neither contracts nor other impediments prevent economic units from setting prices and wages that maximize profits and utility, given *their* information. If market participants had perfect foresight, then profits and utility would, in fact, be maximized. The school recognizes, however, that economic units generally will be misinformed and expectations will not be realized. The school's name is based on the assumption that economic units use information efficiently so that *expectations are not systematically wrong. Expectations are rational when any differences between realized and expected values are a random variable.* Perfect foresight is a special case of rational expectations where there are no forecasting errors, by definition.

The rational expectations approach denies that there is a Phillips curve, even in the short run. That is, this school says that there is *no* temporary, much less permanent, tradeoff between inflation and unemployment. A vertical line best measures the relationship between inflation and unemployment irrespective of the time period. Rational expectationalists are not ostriches with their heads in the sand; they do realize unemployment has not always equaled the natural rate. Rational expectations accept the Friedman-Phelps propositions that mistakes cause unemployment to diverge from the natural rate. For example, unemployment is below the natural rate whenever the actual rate of inflation exceeds the expected rate. Rational expectations say that mistakes are not systematic. That is,

individuals do *not* underestimate the actual rate of inflation for a significant period of time. An underestimate this period is just as likely to be
followed by an overestimate as by another underestimate. The distribution
of mistakes is random about zero. Consequently, the rational expectations
school says the inflation and unemployment points should be distributed
randomly about the vertical long-run Phillips curve.

Expressing the last paragraph differently, the rational expectations
school denies the natural rate/accelerationist hypothesis that you can fool
people *permanently*. Suppose the economy is at the bliss point A in Figure
23–11, and the Fed unexpectedly increases the rate of growth of money
by 5 percent. The economy moves to point B. Economic units now ask
themselves, "What is the Fed up to?" If there was any calculated reason
for the Fed's action, the public will discover it. Suppose the Fed's new
objective is the lower than natural rate of unemployment associated with
point B. When expectations are based exclusively on past rates of inflation, the Fed's objective is attained by accelerating monetary expansion
to 10 percent. The rational expectations school says that individuals look
beyond the past for their expectations of the future. Individuals discover
the Fed's strategy of accelerating inflation. A 10 percent rate of inflation
becomes expected, and the economy bypasses point D and moves directly
from B to E. Suppose the Fed learned that individuals were expecting a 10
percent rate of inflation. Could it maintain the low unemployment rate by
increasing the money supply by 15 percent? No, according to the rational
expectations school. As soon as the public realizes that the Fed is committed to maintaining the low unemployment, no inflation rate will necessarily surprise them. Ever faster rates of inflation become expected.

## WINDING DOWN INFLATION

Suppose policymakers decide to wind down inflation after reaching
point D in Figure 23–11. We look at what must be done, first according to
the natural rate/accelerationist hypothesis and then according to rational
expectations. The 10 percent rate of inflation associated with point D
becomes expected in the next bargaining round. The relevant
intermediate-run Phillips curve is labeled $\pi^e = 10$. In order to reduce the
rate of inflation, unemployment must rise above the natural rate.
Policymakers have two options. First, they could adopt a *gradualist policy*. The gradualist policy is illustrated by the stagflation point F, where
inflation has fallen and unemployment has risen moderately. However,
inflation and unemployment still remain high, at least compared to point
B. Inflation declines gradually, causing the downward shift of each period's Phillips curve to be gradual. The disadvantage of the gradualist
policy is the length of time needed to wind down inflation. The alternative
according to the natural rate hypothesis is the "bite the bullet" policy
illustrated by point G. Aggregate demand is cut so drastically that the rate

of inflation plummets, squeezing dry inflationary expectations. Next period's intermediate-run Phillips curve is $\pi^e = 0$. The disadvantage of this policy is the extremely high unemployment rate endured for a short period of time. The better policy, gradualist or bite the bullet, clearly depends on the precise shape of the intermediate run Phillips curve and on the cost of inflation and unemployment.

The rational expectations school holds out the possibility that inflation may be brought to a screeching halt without having to endure a high unemployment rate. In order to accomplish this, policymakers must convince the public that they are totally committed to ending inflation and will bear whatever cost is necessary, including massive unemployment. But the public will be convinced only if the commitment is truly genuine. Pious hosannas to the goal of price stability are not sufficient. *The credibility of policymakers is the key element*. In terms of Figure 23–11, the hope that rational expectations holds out is that although the economy may be at point E, policymakers who convince the public of their willingness to drag the economy to G can adopt policies that instead move the economy directly to A. If a 10 percent rate of inflation has existed and is expected to continue, at the next wage bargain labor asks for, say, a 12 percent wage increase. After the traditional protests about the exorbitant demands of labor, management quickly settles, since it believes that the government will rescue it by expanding the money supply and engineering an inflation which eats up the wage increase. If the government does not expand the money supply, the 12 percent wage settlement will be exorbitant, and unemployment will skyrocket.

Neither management nor labor benefits from massive unemployment. The same policy of not expanding the money supply would have entirely different effects if it had been correctly anticipated. Management never would have agreed to a 12 percent wage increase if it had known that demand was going to be curtailed so drastically that prices would remain constant. Indeed, labor never would have asked for a 12 percent wage increase. The parties would instead have settled for a 2 percent wage increase, which firms could afford without laying off workers.

While rational expectations say that the mere thought of having to take bad-tasting medicine may induce spontaneous remission, it also says that the medicine may not cure. Suppose the actual and expected rates of inflation are 10 percent. The government then timidly reduces the rate of growth of money below the expected value. Inflation moderates somewhat, but unemployment rises. The economy moves from point E to F in Figure 23–11. If the public believes that policymakers are unwilling to tolerate the higher unemployment rate and will quickly reverse themselves, then the expected rate of inflation and short-run Phillips curve will not shift down. Indeed, the short-run curve could shift up if the public believes the government will attempt to compensate for its "mistaken" policy by increasing the money supply even faster than previously.

## CREDIBILITY, EXPECTATIONS FORMATION, AND BALANCE OF PAYMENTS

The rational expectations school says that in order to gain credibility and realize the small side benefits of unemployment, policymakers should never proclaim targets which they cannot or do not intend to meet. Reconsider the issue of specifying money supply targets, which we discussed in Chapter 12 and 13. At open-market meetings the committee specifies a target range of monetary growth for the next month. We stated that no one seriously believes that monthly fluctuations in the rate of growth of money have any effect on ultimate goals such as unemployment and inflation. The effect of even quarterly monetary fluctuations is small; the goals depend on the "underlying", that is, semiannual or longer, rates of monetary growth. After saying that, we proceeded to examine the Fed's ability to control monthly growth. What was the purpose of the examination? Why worry whether the Fed can control the money supply month-by-month when monthly monetary fluctuations are irrelevant in terms of goals? The justification given in Chapter 13 was that the demonstration of monthly control guaranteed control over whatever longer period may be relevant. We now can give a second and more important justification. Monthly monetary targets should be hit simply because they are announced. The Fed's credibility would otherwise be undermined. How should the public interpret Federal Reserve statements that it failed to hit the proclaimed monetary target because the costs of interest rate variability are too high? If the costs of interest rate variability are so high, how will the Fed react to the very real costs of unemployment above the natural rate? The public might be led to believe that the Fed will not persevere in any antiinflation program.

The expectations generating mechanism of both the natural rate/accelerationist and rational expectations theories are partially confirmed and partially contradicted by the data. Look at Figure 23–10 again. There definitely are intermediate-run Phillips curves, which contradict the rational expectation hypothesis that prediction errors are random. In particular, look at the points for 1961–69. The unemployment rate continuously fell, which according to *both* theories occurs when underestimates of inflation become larger, that is, the spread between the actual and expected rates of inflation widens. A decade is long enough that such errors should be considered systematic, in contradiction to the rational expectations hypothesis.[21]

---

[21] Virtually everyone correctly states that the data for the 1930s contradict the rational expectations hypothesis. We present the 1960s data instead because of our previously stated objection to letting the 1930s be a sample of one. Moreover, we suspect that many are unaware that the 1960s contradict the rational expectations hypothesis, which was formulated in the late 1960s and early 1970s. Our suspicion is based on the almost universally accepted proposition that new theories are developed when existing theories cannot explain the recent past. Certainly, this was the Keynesian case. The rational expectations hypothesis is the exception that disproves the rule. It was formulated and gained fairly wide acceptance although it was contradicted by the recent past.

A single Phillips curve fits the British data for 1861–1913 reasonably well. This implies that for more than 50 years the expected rate of inflation was relatively constant even though the actual rate varied significantly. In contrast, the intermediate-run American Phillips curves in the approximately 30 years since 1953 are extremely unstable. For example, the 1973 boom shifted the Phillips curve up; the 1974–75 recession shifted it down; the 1976–78 expansion shifted the 1979 curve up so that it closely coincided with the 1974–75 curve. The difference in the stability of the pre-World War I and post-World War II Phillips curves is difficult to reconcile with the accelerationist hypothesis that expectations depend simply and consistently on past inflation rates. However, the stability difference is easily reconciled with the rational expectations hypothesis that past inflation rates *and* all other relevant information, including the policymaker's objectives, determine expectations.

To the extent governments had any conscious economic goals prior to World War I, they were exchange rate and price stability. Pre-World War I was the heyday of the classical gold standard, where each nation's commitment to keep the price of gold constant in terms of its currency bound them together in a fixed exchange rate system. A country's inflation rate cannot materially exceed the inflation rate of its trading partners in a fixed exchange rate system because different inflation rates change the relative price of foreign and domestic commodities and lead to balance of payments effects. For example, high inflation rates in a fixed exchange rate system cause imports (exports) to increase (decrease) as they become inexpensive (expensive) compared to domestic (foreign) commodities. This in turn leads to a balance of payments deficit, which must be corrected if the exchange rate is to remain fixed in a country with limited gold reserves.[22] The solution to the balance of payments problem is simple: stop the inflation which caused it. The discipline of the gold standard stabilized inflationary expectations. A sudden surge in the inflation rate was not interpreted as the beginning of a long-run trend.

In the early post-World War II period the United States was on a modified gold standard. Gold did not circulate, and the money supply was not directly tied to gold. Moreover, the exchange rate was an "adjustable peg," in contrast to the "pegged pegged" exchange rates under the gold standard. That is, in the postwar period it was understood that exchange rates would be adjusted, if necessary, in order to accommodate other goals, while in the pre-World War I period no other goal dominated exchange rate stability. The Full Employment Act of 1946 specified various goals, but the act's name reflects the major goal. People came to the reasonable conclusion that exchange rate depreciation and inflation would be tolerated if they reduced the unemployment rate. In 1971 the United

---

[22] Chapter 10's section on gold discusses the effect of gold purchases and sales and the evolution of the gold standard.

States formally erased any vestige of the gold standard as the dollar was no longer convertible into gold at a fixed price. Exchange rates and the price of gold became flexible. Without the discipline of fixed exchange rates, the Fed can, in principle, inflate at will. The exchange rate automatically fluctuates in accordance with inflation. Under these circumstances a sudden surge in the 1970s inflation rate could be interpreted as the beginning of a long-run trend. So long as policymakers were unaware of or did not intend to use the short-run Phillip curve, it remained stable. When the public realized in the postwar period that policymakers intended to climb up the Phillips curve, it immediately started to shift.

## THE COSTS OF INFLATION

> There is no subtler, no surer means of overturning the existing basis of Society than to debauch the currency. The process engages all the hidden forces of economic law on the side of destruction, and does it in a manner which not one man in a million is able to diagnose.
>
> John Maynard Keynes[23]

Without a credible monetary authority which squeezes dry inflationary expectations by mere threats of engineering a depression, the cost of winding down inflation is unemployment exceeding the natural rate. Are the costs of inflation sufficiently high to warrant suffering the temporary unemployment and lower output, or should we learn to live with inflation? If Keynes's estimate is correct, fewer than 250 Americans are able to answer the question, and we make no claims of belonging to that select group. Nevertheless, we cannot shy away from analyzing the costs of inflation. For our purposes we distinguish between (perfectly) anticipated and unanticipated inflation caused by the excessive growth of money and, therefore, aggregate demand. We will ignore inflations caused by reductions in aggregate supply due to droughts, higher prices for imported oil, and so on. Supply induced inflations are temporary, provided policymakers are willing to accept the lower output.

### Anticipated inflation

Economists have traditionally constructed a scenario where the costs of anticipated inflation are trivial. Suppose everyone expects a continuation of the rate of inflation, say, 10 percent, that has been occurring for a very long period of time. In such an economy all private contracts which involve the future delivery of money or goods will take the inflation into account, given no legal impediments. For example, we saw in Chapter 5 that during anticipated inflations borrowers and lenders agree that more

---

[23] *Essays in Persuasion* (New York: W. W. Norton, 1963), p. 78.

dollars should be repaid since each dollar is worth less. That is, nominal interest rates are adjusted upward for anticipated inflation in order to keep the real rate of interest constant in economies without usury laws or other legal restrictions. Long-term wage contracts and leases also would be escalated for inflation. Suppose further that the transfer and tax system is perfectly indexed so that all government receipts and payments depend on real magnitudes alone. Real aftertax income is independent of the rate of inflation in a perfectly indexed system. According to traditional economic analysis, inflation produces only two minor costs in such an economy.

First, any inflation, anticipated or not, creates "menu" costs. That is, resources must be spent marking up prices on menus and catalogues and changing vending machines' coin slots.

Second, anticipated inflation produces so-called shoe leather costs. Assume for simplicity that fiat currency is the only type of money. The mechanics of interest payments on currency are so difficult that it is invariably assumed that currency would continue to pay zero interest irrespective of the rate of inflation. Assuming that the interest rate on all other assets adjusts upward for the expected rate of inflation, the interest opportunity cost of holding money rises. Therefore, the demand for money falls, and velocity rises. Individuals economize on money, which is produced at zero cost, and use more real resources to make their transactions and better synchronize their receipts and expenditures. For example, in order to be fully invested and earn the high interest rates, individuals wear out shoe leather running to their broker's office on paydays and then running back to sell the bonds and get the cash needed to buy a can of tuna. Even if we recognize the additional opportunity cost of employing more brokers, the costs of anticipated inflation in such an economy are so trivial that they do not justify the unemployment necessary to eliminate inflation.

Before leaving that rarefied perfectly indexed world, we note two features ignored by the traditional analysis just presented. First, the monetary expansion necessary to increase aggregate demand permanently yields the government resources. If the distribution of goods between the public and government sectors is constant, "normal" taxes must be cut in order to satisfy the government budget constraint. Since some costs are always associated with the collection of any tax, the cost saving due to lower "normal" tax collections makes the net costs of monetary expansion and anticipated inflation even less than the menu and shoe leather costs.[24] When money creation is viewed as a source of government revenue, the nature of menu and shoe leather costs should be clear. They are the collection costs to the public of the inflationary tax on money. As Benjamin Franklin realized, a 10 percent inflation and a 10 percent tax on money with prices constant reduce money holders' purchasing power

---

[24] Lump sum taxes do not create an excess burden, by definition, but are costly to collect. The poll tax collector of old was a very real person who could have been producing some good or service.

equally. When money creation takes the place of income taxes, we stop running to our accountants and lawyers and instead run to our broker to avoid the tax on money.

The traditional analysis also ignores the psychological costs of inflation. Even if prices, wages, and nominal wealth all changed proportionally so that no one was hurt in real terms, most people would feel cheated by inflation. Workers attribute a large proportion of the increase in their nominal wages to their own merit or luck rather than to inflation, which, even if anticipated, is seen as being caused by the unreasonable action of others. Inflation is viewed as an unwarranted reduction in the real wage that otherwise would have been earned. "A significant real cost of inflation is thus what it does to morale, to social coherence, and to people's attitudes towards each other."[25]

### Adjustment problems and imperfect indexation

The perfectly indexed economy where, apart from psychological costs, anticipated inflation is virtually costless is a useful abstraction, but only that. First, there is the adjustment problem. Bonds and mortgages with an initial term to maturity of 30 years and more are quite common. Some real estate leases are equally long term. Therefore, even if all contracts suddenly reflect anticipated inflation perfectly, it takes at least 30 years before anticipated inflation has no effect on the economy. Those who issued 30-year bonds just prior to a rise in anticipated inflation enjoy a real gain at the expense of lenders for the full period.

Our economy hardly is perfectly indexed so that anticipated inflation redistributes income and wealth and misallocates resources beyond the adjustment period. Legal restrictions are a source of imperfect indexation. For example, resources are diverted away from borrowers when usury laws prevent them from paying the necessary inflation premium. Financial institutions prohibited by Regulation Q from paying any interest on demand deposits and competitive interest on time deposits shrank in size in the late 1970s compared to money market mutual funds which were unrestricted. While it is true that usury laws and Regulation Q are being abolished precisely because the high inflation rate of the late 1970s made them a real burden, new legal restrictions always seem to replace old ones.

The tax system produces perhaps the major distortions during anticipated inflation. Tax rates in a progressive tax system rise with income brackets. As a simple but totally adequate example, suppose the tax rate is 20 percent on incomes up to $10,000 and 30 percent on anything above $10,000. Suppose a person's income is $10,000 so that his or her aftertax

---

[25] Gardner Ackley, "The Cost of Inflation," *American Economic Review*, May 1978, p. 151. Ackley is one of the few economists who we believe correctly assigns a heavy weight to the psychological costs of inflation.

income is $8,000. What happens when this person's nominal income just keeps pace with a 100 percent inflation? He or she becomes a victim of "bracket creep" and finds real aftertax income reduced. In our example, the tax bill rises to $5,000 (20 percent of the first $10,000 and 30 percent of the next $10,000); nominal aftertax income is $15,000; and real aftertax income—the income that matters most—falls to $7,500. The government gains twice from inflation. First, the money creation which produces the inflation gives it the wherewithal to acquire commodities. Second, inflation shoves people into higher tax brackets and increases tax collections.

One obvious solution to the bracket creep problem is to tie income tax brackets to the inflation rate. Indexed brackets effectively set tax rates on real wages instead of nominal wages. However, indexed tax brackets do *not* produce a system where real tax collections are independent of inflation because other sources of income exist besides wages. In particular, consider the effect of inflation and taxes on the interest income of lenders. Suppose that the rate of interest was 5 percent when prices were stable and the tax rate was 50 percent. The real aftertax rate of interest was 2.5 percent. What happens when a 7 percent rate of inflation is anticipated, and the nominal interest rate rises to 12 percent? Nominal aftertax interest is 6 percent, and real aftertax interest is negative, −1.0 percent! The impoverishment of the lender in this example has nothing to do with bracket creep; we assumed a constant 50 percent tax rate. The lender is worse off because he or she is taxed on the 7 percent inflation premium necessary to keep real wealth constant.[26]

We have just scratched the surface of the accounting and tax problems in an inflationary economy. In principle, one could devise a tax system which avoids bracket creep, does not tax inflation premiums, allows real depreciation, taxes real but not nominal capital gains, and so on. In reality, no such tax system has ever existed, and it will exist only in one's flight of fancy.

### Unanticipated inflation

Just as an economy where all contracts and the fiscal system are perfectly indexed for inflation is a useful abstraction, so the very idea of anticipated inflation, as used in the last section and in the literature generally, is a useful abstraction, but only that. Anticipated inflation occurs when everyone correctly knows with certainty the future inflation rate. Anticipated inflation clearly is quite different from the real world situation where people construct with varying degrees of uncertainty different and possibly incorrect estimates of future inflation. In fact, *all inflations have been unanticipated.* Of course, the degree of unanticipated inflation varies.

---

[26] The 50 percent tax on the 7 percent inflation premium is 3.5 percent, which equals the reduction in the real aftertax return from 2.5 to −1.0 percent.

At one extreme, expectations are held with little confidence, vary widely among people, and are wrong on average, that is, irrational. At the other extreme, expectations are homogeneous, correct (rational), and firmly held, although not with certainty. The cost of inflation, as measured by the income and wealth redistribution and resource misallocation that occurs because the economy is imperfectly indexed, depends directly on the degree of unanticipated inflation.

There is much evidence that the variability of inflation increases with its average level.[27] Since the variability of inflation or any other factor tends to produce less accurate, less firmly held, and less homogeneous expectations, the costs of inflation are positively related to its average rate. High inflation rates are to be avoided because they are more likely to be unanticipated.

Who are the main beneficiaries of the redistribution caused by unanticipated inflation? For simplicity, assume inflation is completely unanticipated. Consider wealth redistribution first. Neither nominal interest rates nor anything else is adjusted for (totally) unanticipated inflation, by definition, so that the real wealth of holders of dollar denominated assets such as bonds falls. Conversely, bond issuers gain as the principal received exceeds the principal repaid in terms of purchasing power. What groups are net debtors whose wealth rises with unanticipated inflation? Are they the poor, professionals, farmers, and so on? Surprisingly perhaps, the wealth position of the poor is not improved by inflation. The poor simply are unable to borrow much, and they tend to hold dollar-denominated assets such as savings accounts. Households on balance are net creditors, and corporations are net debtors, so that the former lose and the latter gain from unanticipated inflation. However, because corporations are owned by households, this redistribution is robbing Peter to pay Paul. Although we sometimes talk about "our government," ownership is less immediate in this case. Given the huge national debt, unanticipated inflation transfers wealth from the private to the government sector. Within the private sector, the principal class of wealth losers are retired persons, who have a larger than normal proportion of dollar-denominated assets. The main gainers are young homeowners who have large mortgages compared to their dollar assets. Contrary to the beliefs in the 1960s, inflation does not benefit common stock holders.

Besides its wealth gain, the government gains real income from infla-

---

[27] Benjamin Klein, "The Social Cost of the Recent Inflation: The Mirage of Steady 'Anticipated' Inflation," *Journal of Monetary Economics,* supplement series, 1976, pp. 185–212; Dennis Logue and Thomas Willet, "A Note on the Relation between the Rate and Variability of Inflation," *Economica,* May 1976, pp. 151–58; Arthur Okun, "The Mirage of Steady Inflation," *Brookings Papers* 3 (1971):485–98. Note that there is no mechanical reason why inflation rates must fluctuate more when their average rate is high. For example, the inflation rate could fluctuate between 0 and 4 percent on the one hand and, between 8 and 12 on the other, so that variability is independent of the average level. What could and what does happen are different.

tion due to the bracket creep problem already analyzed. Within the private sector, what groups' relative incomes rise during inflation? There is a strong feeling in some circles that inflation has a major impact on relative income. In particular, some claim that capitalists gain at the expense of workers because prices rise before wages. Others go so far as to claim that inflation is caused by attempts of labor unions and other organized groups to raise their relative income. However, the evidence indicates that inflation has little *systematic* effect on the relative income of broad social and economic groups. Inflation does *not* systematically change the relative income of capitalists versus workers, union workers versus nonunion workers, or the rich versus the poor.[28] The retired do lose somewhat from inflation but much less so now that social security is indexed.

The misallocation of resources is the second main cost of inflation. Because long-term contracts of all kinds are riskier during inflations and because most households and firms are risk averse, long-term contracts generally, and long-term credit especially, tend to atrophy. For example, suppose the real rate of interest was 5 percent when prices were stable, and the rate of inflation now is expected to be 7 percent. The expectation is not held with certainty; it could be more or less than 7 percent. In this case, neither risk-averse borrowers nor lenders find a 12 percent nominal loan rate as attractive as a certain 5 percent real rate. Loan rates higher than 12 percent are necessary to compensate risk-averse lenders for the risk that the rate of inflation could be more than 7 percent, but loan rates lower than 12 are necessary to compensate risk-averse borrowers for the risk that the rate of inflation could be less than 7 percent. If 5 percent was the maximum (minimum) real rate the borrower (lender) would pay (accept), then a loan cannot be effected in an inflationary environment. Output falls as large-scale, long-term projects which characterize the most industrialized economies can no longer be financed because savers now purchase real estate or collectibles such as gold instead of lending.

## SUMMARY

One of the amusing facts of life is the closeness with which unemployment and price statistics are watched, yet few people know precisely what they measure. The current state of ignorance is ideal for defining the unemployment problem away. Why not reduce unemployment by reverting to the pre-1957 definition, where persons on temporary layoff or waiting to begin a new job within 30 days were *not* considered unemployed? Or should we raise unemployment by not counting as employed those who worked only one hour a week? While the first part of this chapter does not

---

[28] G. Leland Bach, "Inflation: Who Gains and Who Loses," *Challenge,* July 1974, pp. 48–55; and G. Leland Bach and Albert Ando, "The Redistributional Effects of Inflation," *Review of Economics and Statistics,* February 1957, pp. 1–13.

answer these questions, it at least shows how the statistics are constructed.

Ignorance about definitions has also contributed to our national passion for breast-beating about our high unemployment rate compared to those of western European countries. We could lower our unemployment rate simply by measuring it in the European manner. True, our unemployment rate would still exceed the average European rate. Does this mean that our economy is not as robust as European economies? Can we lower our unemployment rate by increasing aggregate demand? The Phillips curve approach optimistically says that we can permanently lower our unemployment rate by enduring a mild inflation. The more modern natural rate/accelerationist approach claims that the lower rate of unemployment can be achieved only by ever increasing rates of inflation. There is a strong presumption against such a policy. Inflation ranks very high on the national worry list. Nevertheless, economists have had little success in pinpointing the broad economic and social groups whose relative position is lowered by inflation. One beneficiary of inflation is clear: the government.

Our unemployment is consistently higher than the average European rate "simply" because our natural rate is higher. Shouldn't we worry about our high natural rate? We definitely should not be proud of it. We might try to lower it by improving the flow of information, upgrading skills, and planning more wisely so that there are no gluts in some areas and markets and shortages in others. Let us not forget, however, that these programs are costly. Moreover, our analysis of labor markets suggests that such programs may not be very successful. The quit and layoff rates and, therefore, unemployment rate will be high in any dynamic, mobile, second-chance society where occupations are not predetermined and one is allowed to return to school after dropping out. At any moment such societies appear economically stagnant. However, the very dynamism, mobility, and ambitiousness which produce a high natural rate of unemployment may simultaneously produce a high and growing level of income.

## QUESTIONS

1. Give a general definition of a price index. List the three broadly based price indexes and state the most important differences among the three.
2. Explain why the CPI may not be a good cost of living index.
3. Describe the postwar trends in the aggregate unemployment rate, the differences in unemployment rates by demographic groups, and the effects of changes in labor force composition on the aggregate unemployment rate.
4. What is the relationship between the unemployment rate, duration of unemployment, and incidence of unemployment? Describe the pattern of the dura-

tion of unemployment and the relative importance of the various reasons for the incidence of unemployment.

5. Explain and evaluate critically various concepts of full employment. Has full employment changed over time?

6. Why do job vacancies and unemployed workers exist simultaneously?

7. Define frictional unemployment, structural unemployment, and the natural rate of unemployment.

8. Discuss with the aid of graphs the inflation-unemployment relationship implied by an integration of the Keynesian and neoclassical models.

9. Define the Phillips curve. Give the theoretical justification for the Phillips curve. What are the main flaws in the theoretical justification of the Phillips curve?

10. Explain carefully the Friedman-Phelps natural rate or accelerationist hypothesis. What is the main difference between it and the Phillips curve?

11. Explain the rational expectations view about the Phillips curve.

12. The expectations generating process is crucial to any theory. Discuss (a) the expectations generating mechanism of the natural rate and rational expectations hypotheses, (b) the data which contradict each hypothesis, and (c) the importance of credibility to the rational expectations school.

13. What are the costs of anticipated inflation in an economy which is perfectly indexed?

14. Do you believe the last question is important or unimportant? Explain.

15. What are the main costs of unanticipated inflation? What demographic groups and product sectors are the main gainers and losers from inflation?

# Index

*This book has been set VIP, in 10 and 9 point
Times Roman, leaded 2 points. Part numbers
are 36 point Beton Extrabold and part titles are
18 point Helvetica bold. Chapter numbers are 36
point Beton Extrabold and chapter titles are 16
point Helvetica light. The overall type area is 30
by 47½ picas.*